INTERNATIONAL PUBLIC RELATIONS

659.2 I61c

International public
 relations

OCT 1 6 2002
APR 1 9 2007

DEMCO 38-297

LEA's COMMUNICATION SERIES
Jennings Bryant/Dolf Zillmann, General Editors

Selected titles in Public Relations (James E. Grunig/Larissa A. Grunig, Advisory Editors) include:

Cutlip • Public Relations History: From the 17th to the 20th Century. The Antecedents

Fearn-Banks • Crisis Communications: A Casebook Approach

Heath • Management of Corporate Communication: From Interpersonal Contacts to Internal Affairs

Kunczik • Images of Nations and International Public Relations

For a complete list of other titles in LEA's Communication Series, please contact Lawrence Erlbaum Associates, Publishers

INTERNATIONAL PUBLIC RELATIONS

A Comparative Analysis

Edited by

HUGH M. CULBERTSON
Ohio University

NI CHEN
University of Toledo

1996

LAWRENCE ERLBAUM ASSOCIATES, PUBLISHERS
Mahwah, New Jersey

659.2 I61c

International public
relations

Copyright © 1996, by Lawrence Erlbaum Associates, Inc.
All rights reserved. No part of the book may be reproduced in
any form, by photostat, microform, retrieval system, or any other
means, without the prior written permission of the publisher.

Lawrence Erlbaum Associates, Inc., Publishers
10 Industrial Avenue
Mahwah, New Jersey 07430

Library of Congress Cataloging-in-Publication Data

International public relations : a comparative analysis / edited by
   Hugh M. Culbertson, Ni Chen
      p.   cm.
   Includes bibliographical references and indexes.
   ISBN 0-8058-1684-4 (cloth : alk. paper). — ISBN 0-8058-1685-2
(pbk. : alk. paper)
      1. Public relations—Cross-cultural studies. I. Culbertson, Hugh
M. II. Chen, Ni.
   HM263.I65   1996
   659.2—dc20   95-53034
                                                           CIP

Books published by Lawrence Erlbaum Associates are printed on acid-free paper,
and their bindings are chosen for strength and durability.

Printed in the United States of America
10 9 8 7 6 5 4 3 2 1

Contents

Preface ix

Introduction 1
Hugh M. Culbertson

PART I: A THEORETICAL BASE

1. **Interdisciplinary Theoretical Foundations for International Public Relations** 17
   Robert I. Wakefield

2. **Global and Specific Principles of Public Relations: Evidence From Slovenia** 31
   Dejan Verčič, Larissa A. Grunig, and James E. Grunig

3. **Strategic Cooperative Communities: A Synthesis of Strategic, Issue Management, and Relationship-Building Approaches in Public Relations** 67
   Laurie J. Wilson

4. **Transnational Corporate Ethical Responsibilities** 81
   Dean Kruckeberg

5. **Public Relations' Role: Realities in Asia and in Africa South of the Sahara** 93
   James K. Van Leuven and Cornelius B. Pratt

6. Gender Issues in Public Relations Practice 107
   Doug Newsom

PART II: PUBLIC RELATIONS IN SPECIFIC COUNTRIES AND REGIONS

7. Public Relations in China: The Introduction and Development of an Occupational Field 121
   Ni Chen

8. Public Relations in Thailand: Its Functions and Practitioners' Roles 155
   Daradirek Ekachai and Rosechongporn Komolsevin

9. Power Distance and Public Relations: An Ethnographic Study of Southern Indian Organizations 171
   K. Sriramesh

10. Public Relations in the Philippines 191
    Juan F. Jamais, Mariechel J. Navarro, and Ramon R. Tuazon

11. Public Relations in South East Asia From Nation-Building Campaigns to Regional Interdependence 207
    James K. Van Leuven

12. Public Relations Practice in Japan: Beginning Again for the First Time 223
    Anne Cooper-Chen with Mizuo Kaneshige

13. Public Relations in the Middle East: The Case of Saudi Arabia 239
    Ali Alanazi

14. Elections and Earth Matters: Public Relations in Costa Rica 257
    Hernando González and Desireé Akel

15. Public Relations Performance in South and Central America 273
    Melvin L. Sharpe and Roberto P. Simoes

16. Standardization Versus Localization: Public Relations Implications of Advertising Practices in Finland 299
    Ali Kanso

17. Public Relations: An Alternative to Reality? 317
    Mauritz Sundt Mortensen

18.	**Romania: From Publicitate Past to Public Relations Future** *Judy VanSlyke Turk*	341
19.	**Public Relations in the German Democratic Republic and the New Federal German States** *Günter Bentele and Grazyna-Maria Peter*	349
20.	**European Public Relations Practice: An Evolving Paradigm** *Vincent Hazleton and Dean Kruckeberg*	367

PART III: INTERNATIONAL PUBLIC RELATIONS EDUCATION IN THE UNITED STATES

21.	**International Public Relations Education: U.S. Issues and Perspectives** *Cornelius B. Pratt and Chris W. Ogbondah*	381
22.	**Public Relations Education in the United States: Can It Broaden International Students' Horizons?** *Hugh M. Culbertson and Ni Chen*	397

About the Authors	417
Author Index	421
Subject Index	431

Preface

Relations among publics have become more complex, fragile, and often hostile in recent years due to varied factors ranging from weapons of mass destruction to regional alliances, nationalism, and the Internet. The world has become smaller thanks to many of the same factors. And the need for understanding among people of different cultures has grown.

Public relations, as a formal occupation, has spread rapidly throughout the world in the wake of such changes. However, the literature on international public relations tends to focus on how those working for western organizations—particularly multinational corporations—can best practice abroad. This volume views public relations in 14 countries and regions *from the perspective of practitioners and educators in each area covered.*

The first six chapters provide varied theoretical bases for comparing public relations from country to country. Then, 14 chapters analyze different regions and nations. A third section discusses education as a tool for professional enhancement.

The Introduction summarizes evidence for five themes which underlie the country and region chapters. We highlight three of these themes here.

First, *a nation's political system and culture do help shape its practice of public relations.* Related factors include social stratification, the nature of personal relationships, media credibility, economic development, stage of nation building, emphasis on personal loyalty and harmony, and the presence or absence of elites created in part by colonial rulers.

Second, there appears to be movement throughout the world *from one-way to two-way communication—and from emphasizing knowledge and persuasion to relationship building.* However, the latter of these changes, in particular, appears to have been slowed by authoritarian regimes and a tendency to see public relations as an adjunct to marketing and advertising.

Third, in many nations, *women practitioners are becoming both more influential and more numerous*. This is occurring despite gender-related stereotypes, male-oriented cultural beliefs, and a tendency to play the "Miss PR" role in looking after and translating for clients and other guests.

Hugh M. Culbertson
Ni Chen

Introduction

Hugh M. Culbertson
Ohio University

Obviously the world is growing smaller in many ways. Communication technology, weapons of mass destruction, joint-venture firms, transnational corporations, supersonic transports, nationalist sentiments, religious zealotry, and other phenomena insure that events anywhere in the world affect people almost everywhere else.

Such developments lead to terrifying dangers and marvelous opportunities undreamed of just a few years ago. Very often, these dangers and opportunities cross national and regional boundaries, creating an urgent need for tolerance, cooperation, and mutual understanding among people with different basic beliefs and ways of thinking. As a result, the world must build relationships that do not currently exist as well as manage and soften those that are now hostile and/or are based on misunderstanding.

Schools, churches, the media, the military, embassies, the United Nations, and countless other institutions play a part in building and destroying relationships. However, such organizations have limitations, suggesting a great need for guidance in relationship building and maintenance. Recent scholarship suggests that truly effective public relations practitioners provide exactly that guidance (Grunig, 1992).

As a formal occupation, public relations grew primarily in the United States through much of the 20th century. In recent years, however, it has spread rapidly throughout the world (Wouters, 1991). In the People's Republic of China, for example, public relations was almost unheard of until 1985. Today it employs tens of thousands in the world's most populous nation (see chap. 7). Also, in Europe, the field has developed rapidly in the face of challenges posed by the European Economic Community, the demise of the former Soviet Union, and other factors (see chaps. 17 through 20).

How does public relations as practiced differ from country to country? Only recently have the broad outlines of such differences begun taking shape in scholarly writing about the field. The existing literature on international public relations has tended to focus on how those working for western organizations, particularly multinational corporations, could best practice abroad (see, e.g., Wouters, 1991). While useful, such writings have focused on adaptation of Western approaches, not on development of new ones designed specifically for varied sociocultural settings around the world.

We pause here to offer two definitions. First, *comparative public relations* involves a search for both similarities and differences between the practice in one or more countries and that in other venues. Its primary purpose is to identify more or less universal problems that challenge many or all nations, and to search for generic principles that apply widely.

Second, *international public relations* focuses on the practice of public relations in an international or cross-cultural context. As an integral part of international or cross-cultural communication, it involves public relations practice in at least four different realms: international organizations (e.g., the United Nations, the World Bank, and the International Telecommunication Organization); intergovernmental relations (e.g., diplomatic recognition, alliance formation/disintegration, and sanctions/embargoes); transnational economic transactions (investment trading, financing of multinational corporations); and interactions among citizens of different nations (through tourism, arts, film/theater, sports).

This book focuses largely on *comparative* analysis with some attention to international public relations. Programs and problems in international and cross-cultural relations are discussed, but only in passing.

We perceived a need to pull together what is known about comparative public relations. In late 1992, we began trying to define that knowledge by querying over 30 prominent public relations educators about research by themselves, their students, and others, which might shed some light on this area. We then contacted additional scholars and practitioners in several nations as suggested by our initial respondents and others.

This informal survey revealed a great deal of interest in public relations as it is practiced around the world. Several respected leaders in the field labeled this a "hot topic." Furthermore, two presidents of the Association for Education in Journalism and Mass Communication, one past and one just elected, were among several well-known educators who showed their interest by offering to contribute, and eventually writing, chapters.

In corresponding with prospective authors, we raised seven questions which seemed to cry out for answers. Several would-be contributors endorsed these questions as "conceptual guideposts" of a type needed to structure any book of readings. Further, some have used the questions in developing measuring instruments for collecting data reported in this volume.

In abbreviated form, these questions were as follows:

1. How have political, economic, and cultural climates of various nations shaped the public relations practiced there?
2. What do public relations people around the world do? What roles do they play?
3. Have limitations on freedom of communication in some nations had discernible effects on the shaping of public relations just as they have on other communication activities? If so, what have these effects been?
4. Societies differ with regard to emphasis placed on respect among interactants and careful, slow building of trust in relationships. Also, mass media are more credible and fully developed in some places than in others. Have such differences affected the growth and character of public relations, and how?
5. How do nations differ as to how, and how far, they have progressed in the industry's evolution?
6. What sorts of people wind up teaching public relations around the world? Do they have educational backgrounds that emphasize communication? Do they have much practical experience? In other words, what are their backgrounds?
7. Some nations doubtless rely more heavily than others on educators and practitioners trained in the West. What are the implications of such reliance, and of its absence?

Section 1 of this book includes six chapters designed to provide a theoretical background. Section 2 encompasses 14 chapters, each dealing with the growth and current state of public relations in a given nation or region. And section 3 presents two chapters on education provided at universities in the United States for would-be or current practitioners from abroad.

Research reported in section 2 is varied. Several chapters provide in-depth analysis by, and observation of, small but select groups of practitioners and educators. Others (see, in particular, chapters 7 on the People's Republic of China and 8 on Thailand) combine a few in-depth interviews and historical analysis with data from large-sample surveys.

THEORETICAL BASES

In the United States, at least two theoretical formulations have been proposed to describe and account for the character of public relations. Several chapters in this book suggest that both formulations seem relevant, with some modification, to defining the field's growth and character around the world.

First, Broom, Dozier, and their colleagues have identified at least four roles practitioners tend to play:

Expert prescriber. A practitioner operating in this mode is viewed by top management of the client or organization for which she or he works as an authority on public relations problems and their solutions. Such a practitioner defines and researches problems, develops programs, and takes major responsibility for implementation.

Communication facilitator. This role involves acting as a liaison, interpreter, and mediator between an organization and its publics, with emphasis on maintaining a continuous flow of two-way communication. A major concern is with removing barriers to information exchange and keeping channels open.

Problem-solving process facilitator. The point here is to guide managers and the organization through a rational problem-solving process in planning and programming. Practitioners also strive to maintain management involvement in implementation.

Communication technician. The primary concern here is with proposing and producing public relations materials—writing, editing, designing visual messages, and working with the media. Emphasis is on communication and journalistic skills.

Research has suggested that, in the United States, the first three of these roles really collapse into one. That is, people acting as expert prescribers tend also to serve as communication and problem-solving facilitators, and so on. These individuals are often referred to as *communication managers*. And they constitute a group quite separate from *communication technicians* (Culbertson, 1986; Dozier, 1992).

In a second formulation, Grunig and Hunt (1984, chap. 2) distinguish among four stages in the evolution of public relations in the United States. These stages are:

Press-agent/publicity. Here the focus is on publicity and gaining awareness of one's client or employer. Little attention is paid to insuring either accuracy or a favorable reputation.

Public information. Practitioners in this phase seek to disseminate accurate factual information in some depth so as to gain understanding of the client organization—and why it does what it does.

Two-way asymmetric. At this stage, unlike with the first two, practitioners and their clients put forth considerable effort to learn about, and listen to, key publics. The listening is done largely to enhance *persuasive impact* so as to change publics in planned way that meets client needs.

Two-way symmetric. Here the practitioner and client listen carefully to key publics, but not primarily to enhance persuasion. Rather, the symmetric practitioner enters transactions as equal partners with publics, seeking to adjust client behavior and output so as to respect and fulfill public needs. *Relationship-building,* not persuasion, is the primary goal.

Research suggests that all four types of public relations are alive and well in various places. All play a role in specific situations. However, Grunig (1992) reported substantial evidence that truly excellent public relations emphasizes the two-way models, particularly the symmetric version. As further support, Wilson (see chap. 3, this book) provides a philosophical foundation for emphasizing two-way symmetric communication.

In chapter 1, Robert Wakefield synthesizes a variety of theories to provide a theoretical base for international and comparative public relations. This chapter focuses on global-society, management, cultural, and communication theories. Wakefield makes a strong case for studying such societal-level phenomena as acculturation, globalization, conflict, and turbulence. However, he advocates combining such analysis with research on the more micro variables which tend to prevail in American communication studies.

In chapter 2, Dejan Verčič joins with Larissa and James Grunig in identifying several *generic principles* which, they argue, help define and explain truly effective public relations around the world. Three principles stand out. First, *two-way symmetric practice, perhaps combined with other modes, generally works best* in the long run, when and where people are able to implement it. Second, *well trained and educated practitioners must be represented on, and informed fully by, management teams* if they are to be truly effective. And third, *such representation requires that some practitioners serving any organization gain sufficient stature to act as true managers,* that they become part of the formal and informal policy-setting group called the "dominant coalition."

The authors of chapter 2 acknowledge that symmetry means different things, at a concrete level, when applied in different settings. Further, their data gathered in Slovenia suggest that, in nations with both a totalitarian past and present, true partnership and relationship building require considerable patience, courage, and effort.

Chapter 4 switches the focus to philosophical discourse all too often ignored in western public relations studies. Here, Dean Kruckeberg tackles an age-old question. When in Rome, should practitioners and their clients always do as the Romans? Or can people throughout the world agree on more-or-less universal principles that do, or ought to, govern ethical decision making? For example, paying of bribes and giving jobs to close relatives are frowned on in the United States but are viewed as acceptable elsewhere. What standards should an American practitioner adhere to when working in, say, the Philippines or China?

Kruckeberg sees a strong need to search for answers to such questions and for universal principles that might aid that search. Multinational corporations, in particular, cannot avoid grappling with these problems. And, the author believes that available scholarship provides a stronger base for worldwide ethical principles than many observers have acknowledged.

In chapter 5, James Van Leuven and Cornelius Pratt report some convergence, but also basic differences, between public relations and development communication. Focusing on sub-Suharan Africa, Malaysia, and Singapore, the authors describe a widespread tendency toward information and persuasion campaigns, as opposed to symmetrical relationship building, in these varied areas. Nation building, movement toward a market economy, a growing role for multinational corporations, and problems in surmounting linguistic barriers are among many factors helping to shape communication in the developing world.

Doug Newsom analyzes issues of public relations and gender in chapter 6, focusing primarily on female practitioners in India. There, as elsewhere, women have gained in both stature and numbers recently. In India, their progress has required special determination and skill as gender issues have interacted with those of "caste, class, culture, and color." However, despite many obstacles, female role models have contributed significantly to Indian teaching and practice. Apparently these ladies are helping to challenge the asymmetric aspects of patriarchy.

PUBLIC RELATIONS IN SPECIFIC COUNTRIES AND REGIONS

Chapters 7 through 20 support at least five general conclusions, and we now discuss these. Space limitations preclude a detailed summary of results for each nation or region discussed.

Cultural Differences Matter

In chapter 2, Verčič et al. make a compelling case for several generic principles which seem to help define public relations excellence anywhere in the world. However, this book shows quite clearly that *a nation's political system and culture shape its practice of public relations*. Many and varied impacts of culture are detailed in section 2. Here we summarize only a few.

In chapter 9, K. Sriramesh focuses heavily on the fact that India has long been, and remains, a stratified society. While the rigid caste system of prior years has been "softened," the cultural dimension of power-distance (Hofstede, 1980) remains high. People of high socioeconomic status tend to assume they know best how to run things. And, by and large, those of lower status accept that assessment. Partly as a result, various groups within Indian society seldom engage in genuine dialogue. This has hampered the evolution of two-way communication and broad-based relationship building to a degree.

In China, Japan, and other Oriental societies, as well as in Latin America and Saudi Arabia, great emphasis is placed on personal interaction to establish a sense of trust, mutual understanding, and loyalty among those engaged in almost any shared undertaking. Also, the government-owned media in mainland China have lacked credibility in some quarters. As a result of these and other factors, public relations has focused heavily on interpersonal communication. Practitioners often have little media experience, though many are now gaining media-relations expertise needed to reach western audiences as well as their own citizens. (See chaps. 7, 10, 12, 13, and 15, in particular, for discussion of these issues.)

As the Philippines, Singapore, Malaysia, Thailand, and other nations have developed economically and politically, governments have sought to instill unifying ideologies and a sense of national pride. As this occurred, public relations has tended to be asymmetric—and oriented toward persuasion. However, in chapter 11, Jim Van Leuven notes that strategic planning has grown in sophistication and breadth, perhaps creating some opportunity to move toward symmetry, as these nations have moved from *nation building* to phases of *market development* and *regional cooperation*.

Loyalty, mutual respect, harmony as opposed to conflict, and graceful acceptance of blame play a prominent role in Japanese society. Thus, reporters there often do not question corporate or government leaders vigorously about new directions or alleged failings. As a consequence, felt accountability needed to insure wise policy and sound implementation of it is often lacking. Openness is also sacrificed when bad news comes up.

Also, Japanese politicians sometimes give up and resign when accused of wrongdoing. They do not defend themselves in a way that might insure a full airing of issues so as to enhance long-term public understanding (chap. 12).

In Latin America, the "viceroy" system used to establish and run Spanish colonies has contributed to widespread family ownership and control of business. Public ownership through the sale of stock, contributing to a sense of public accountability, was slow to develop. According to Mel Sharpe and Robert Simoes, this and other related factors have hampered the development of broad, open, two-way communication (chap. 15).

In Thailand, taboos against the use of words such as condom created a problem for family-planning campaigns. However, planners took note of the playful, fun-loving aspect of Thai culture. In preparing campaign material, they used the name of a government minister instead of condom. And they held vasectomy festivals in honor of the King's birthday! (see chap. 8).

Norwegian reserve may have helped set the stage for that country's military leaders to make modest claims about capturing real or imagined Soviet submarines in Norway's territorial waters during both the 1970s and 1980s. As a result, high Relative Deprivation, and associated disenchantment, were avoided when few subs were captured in the wake of some widely publicized sightings (see chap. 17).

These are but a few of the interesting social and cultural factors cited by the authors as important in understanding public relations around the world.

Managers or Technicians?

We now turn to the shape of PR practice itself. A second major conclusion is that, by and large, public relations practitioners around the world tend to operate as communication *technicians* more often than as *managers*. However, in many if not most nations studied, movement into communication management is occurring.

Conclusions in this area must be viewed as somewhat tentative because of one limitation in available evidence. Researchers generally have failed to distinguish clearly between two levels of management responsibility and activity: planning and implementation of *communication* between client or employer on the one hand and key publics on the other, as well as within client organizations; and strategic planning with respect to *overall policy and operation* of client organizations. In emphasizing the latter level, scholars have long recognized that an honest organization cannot "let people know it lives right" unless, in fact, it "lives right." Dejan Verčič along with Larissa and James Grunig (chap. 2), Laurie Wilson (chap. 3), and other authors of this book clearly suggest relationship building requires practitioner involvement in dominant coalitions that do strategic planning.

Although authors have not often taken explicit note of this ambiguity, they have reported considerable pessimism about progress toward managerial functioning in Costa Rica (chap. 14), Rumania (chap. 18), and Latin America (chap. 15). Also, a national survey in Norway suggests the citizens of that nation hold public relations in rather low regard (chap. 17).

On the plus side, however, Gee Ekachai and Rose Komolsevin report that a substantial 28% of their Thai practitioner sample enact communication-management roles frequently. An additional 21% often act as liaisons, playing what these authors and others regard as a managerial role (chap. 8). Also, a substantial majority of Chinese practitioners surveyed by Ni Chen report spending considerable time acting as managers (chap. 7).

Other authors note rather favorable conditions for an enhanced managerial focus in the years to come. Specifically:

> In Japan, most employees remain with their firms for many years, if not for a lifetime. Also, people frequently move from department to department as they advance within a corporation. Anne Cooper-Chen and Mizuo Kanishege report that this should provide public relations practitioners with varied contacts as well as opportunities to learn about all parts of a firm, including how these parts relate to each other and to the whole. Such knowledge, in turn, may pave the way for movement into higher management (chap. 12).
>
> Jim Van Leuven and Cornelius Pratt note that public relations involvement in broad strategic planning tends to increase as a nation moves from *nation-building* toward the *regional-cooperation* phase of development (chap. 5).
>
> Many Saudi practitioners surveyed by Ali Alanazi work within large public relations departments. This may suggest that a fairly high management priority as

needed to insure that such departments gain membership in dominant coalitions (chap. 13).

Two-Wayness and Symmetry

As noted earlier, the Grunig-Hunt evolutionary model specifies two developments in public relations. First, two-way communication (listening and speaking to publics) has at least begun to replace one-way (speaking only). And second, PR goals have extended beyond enhancing awareness and information level to persuasion and, ideally, to relationship building.

Taken as a whole, this book provides evidence of at least some progress along both dimensions. However, our third major conclusion is that *progress toward two-way communication has been somewhat more rapid on the whole, and more universal, than progress toward a relationship-building approach.* At least two factors help explain widespread emphasis on persuasion rather than relationship building, even among sophisticated, highly trained practitioners who seek feedback from publics carefully.

First, *somewhat authoritarian governments have often restricted true dialogue.* This has held in developing countries such as Thailand, Malaysia, China, and the Philippines, at least, during the earlier stages of development. Also, it has been reported with regimes on the political right (the Philippines during Marcos's reign, military governments of Latin America, and Singapore) as well as the left (mainland China, Rumania, and the former German Democratic Republic). Thus this book supports the proposition that authoritarianism restricts the development of public relations much as it has long been said to shackle the press (Rogers & Chaffee, 1994, p. 19).

At the same time, hopeful signs are apparent, even in threatening environments and in societies often viewed, at least until quite recently, as authoritarian.

Alanazi reports that Saudi kings have long maintained an open-door policy toward even low-status subjects through traditions such as the town meeting or *majlis* (chap. 13). Costa Rica's substantial democratic traditions have helped shape its public relations despite a rather threatening, uncertain environment (chap. 14). Günter Bentele and Grazyna-Maria Peter report considerable innovativeness and focus on service to communities in the former German Democratic Republic since German reunification (chap. 19). And Verčič et al. note that even in a nation such as Slovenia with a totalitarian heritage, persistent, courageous effort, and thoughtful planning can enhance dialogue and relationship building (chap. 2). In practice, public relations programs have often appeared to identify and meet audience needs, as viewed by audiences, in these societies.

At a theoretical level, Van Leuven's three-stage developmental model suggests increasing involvement over time in strategic planning, and hence, perhaps, in opportunities for building dialogue (chap. 11). Furthermore, while his and Pratt's nation-building and market-development stages emphasize persuasion, the third stage, regional cooperation, appears to deal significantly with relationship building which, in turn, implies some possible convergence between development communication and public relations.

Second, *public relations was introduced in many countries by large corporations. These organizations tended to view it largely as an adjunct to marketing and advertising and as a tool for "engineering consent."* (See, in particular, chaps. 8, 10, 11, 12, 13, and 18).

Within a marketing-advertising context, Ali Kanso provides hopeful evidence of sensitivity to audience needs, beliefs, and concerns. Branch managers of corporate subsidiaries in Finland reported considerable emphasis on *localized* thinking (tailoring messages to local conditions), apparently more than on *standardized* strategies (using the same basic message in different countries) (chap. 16).

Gender-Related Issues

What role are women playing in the development of public relations as a profession? The authors here provide evidence for a fourth conclusion that in many, if not most, nations, *women practitioners are becoming more and more numerous. Furthermore, they are playing an increasingly important role as leaders of the profession.*

Women's influx into the field appears to vary greatly from society to society. Ladies totaled 71% of the Thai practitioners surveyed by Ekachai and Komolsevin (chap. 8) and a substantial 34% of the Chinese respondents studied by Chen (chap. 7). However, they accounted for only a little over 1% of Alanazi's Saudi practitioners.

Newsom notes that women have worked courageously and effectively to overcome several problems (chapter 6). Three barriers seem particularly widespread.

The "Miss PR" problem is one. Chapters 7 on China, 12 on Japan, and 14 on Costa Rica address this phenomenon explicitly, while other authors touch on it. Young ladies often are hired for their beauty and charm. And they are assigned to "look after" clients and guests in addition to translating for them.

In some places, these practitioners have seemed so pervasive that political and other leaders, and perhaps society at large, have tended to equate them with the overall practice of public relations. Furthermore, a focus on good looks and charm, rather than on planning and substantive knowledge, is not always tied to gender. Mauritz Sundt Mortensen reports that American management consultant George Kenning helped shape Norway's overall practice by emphasizing these factors (chap. 17).

Second, gender roles and stereotypes often hamper women's professional advancement. Newsom provides a particularly insightful discussion here. In India, she reports, ladies are precluded from living alone near a place of work. Historically, they have had limited access to education. And they are expected to look after their young sons or daughters full time rather than seek day care. Despite these problems, Indian women have made substantial progress in public-relations practice, management, and education (chap. 6).

Third, basic cultural values extend beyond beliefs about gender behavior and status per se. Cooper-Chen and Kanishege report that Japanese beliefs have proven highly masculine in thinking about varied matters when measured on the gender dimension proposed by Hofstede (1980). And these authors note that women have found their greatest opportunities in multinational and joint-venture firms linked with the west (chap. 12).

Education and Training

Education of practitioners is important to overcoming such problems and enhancing the field's sophistication and stature. Part 3 of this book assesses implications of the fact that public relations education initially developed largely in the United States. That particular country continues to train many practitioners from abroad, and to export practitioners as well as theories.

In this regard, the book supports a fifth significant overall conclusion: *American education and theory continue to play an important role in the field's development around the world. However, "indigenous" factors, institutions, and practitioners are helping to develop public relations practice in unique ways within particular nations.*

Authors report limited development of public relations education to date in certain countries, but almost all suggest a strong desire among native practitioners for learning and advancement.

For example, in Norway, the field has never gained a strong foothold within university education (chap. 17). College-level courses in public relations also remain scarce in highly developed Japan (chap. 12) as well as in struggling, poor Rumania (chap. 18).

However, mainland China has recruited and trained a large, capable practitioner force with minimal input from abroad (chap. 7). Also, in Thailand, about 75% of the practitioners surveyed had degrees in communication, most of them apparently earned within the country (chap. 8). And in the Philippines, according to Juan Jamias, Mariechel Navarro, and Ramon Tuason, native public relations leaders have shaped the field with relatively little foreign influence (chap. 10).

In Europe as a whole, public relations education has taken on a distinctive flavor, according to Vince Hazleton and Dean Kruckeberg. Training there tends to have greater theoretical depth and cross-cultural focus, as well as less emphasis on skill training and mass communication, than in the United States (chap. 20).

In some nations, Western educators and practitioners appear to be supplementing indigenous "pioneers" and leaders in growing, useful ways. For example, a Costa Rican university has established close ties with a Florida institution of higher learning (chap. 14). And Saudi higher education in the field, born around 1971, has grown with the help of some visiting professors (chap. 13).

Two Caveats

We close this overview of the "country and region" section with two caveats.

First, this book does not provide an exhaustive comparative analysis of public relations worldwide. We have sought to cover a broad range of nations at different stages of economic-social-political development, with varied types of governments and media systems, and so forth. But space limitations preclude chapters on many important countries with growing public relations industries. Included are Taiwan, South Korea, the United Kingdom (which is discussed in an omnibus chapter on Europe), republics of the former Soviet Union, France, and the United Arab Emirates.

Second, some may wonder why we did not report on the United States. We chose not to do so partly because existing literature discusses American public relations at length. Further, our contacts suggest many, if not most practitioners, in other countries are quite familiar with that literature. And, finally, we faced severe space constraints.

American public relations education, as it relates to practice around the world, has not gotten such massive attention. We included section 3 to begin filling this vacuum.

EDUCATION FOR FOREIGN PRACTITIONERS IN THE UNITED STATES

For better or worse, hundreds of current and would-be practitioners from around the world are flocking to U.S. colleges and universities for instruction related to public relations. Are these people getting what they come for? We could find no definitive answer to this question. However, the final two chapters of this book give some basis for optimism.

In chapter 21, Cornelius Pratt and Chris Ogbandah cite a variety of sources in arguing for courses in international public relations. In a complex, interdependent world, according to the authors, practitioners cannot operate effectively as managers, even in the domestic sphere, without a basic grounding in business, marketing, and public relations practice and philosophy around the world. Equally important is the study of cultures and political/economic systems other than one's own.

Pratt and Ogbandah review many harsh criticisms regarding the superficiality, and allegedly excessive focus on journalistic skill, within American public relations education. Are these criticisms warranted? In chapter 22, Hugh Culbertson and Ni Chen answer with a qualified, partial "no" based on a survey of

33 academic units that offer at least two graduate-level courses with the phrase "public relations" in their titles.

On the down side (perhaps?), responding institutions do appear to follow a "journalism-school" model. International students enrolled there tend to take more courses in journalistic writing, editing, and production than in interpersonal-skill areas such as public speaking.

However, Culbertson and Chen question the apparent assumption of some observers that journalism versus interpersonal emphasis requires an "either–or" choice. Across universities, the number of journalistic "communication-technician" courses taken correlates positively—not negatively—with the taking of organizational communication, persuasion theory, rhetoric, technical writing, and public speaking. In short, strong programs are offering *both* depth in journalism and breadth in a variety of other areas.

Furthermore, there is no real indication that departments with the word communication in their titles are leading public relations education in substantially new and different directions.

The 33 programs studied provide fairly substantial emphasis on cross-cultural studies as a whole. However, only six institutions offer a course devoted primarily or entirely to international public relations. Furthermore, only one-half of the international students covered in the survey study at institutions which focus, as a matter of policy, both on breadth of cross-cultural study and on depth in one's own and a few other societies.

REFERENCES

Culbertson, H. M. (1986). Practitioner roles: Their meaning for educators. *Public Relations Review, 16,* 5–28.

Dozier, D. M. (1992). The organizational roles of communications and public relations practitioners. In J. E. Grunig (Ed.), *Excellence in public relations and communication management* (pp. 327–355). Hillsdale, NJ: Lawrence Erlbaum Associates.

Grunig, J. E. (1992). *Excellence in public relations and communication management.* Hillsdale, NJ: Lawrence Erlbaum Associates.

Grunig, J. E., & Hunt, T. (1984). *Managing public relations.* New York: Holt, Rinehart & Winston.

Hofstede, G. (1980). *Culture's consequences.* Beverly Hills, CA: Sage.

Rogers, E. M., & Chaffee, S. H. (1994, December). Communication and journalism from "Daddy" Bleyer to Wilbur Schramm: A palimpsest. *Journalism Monographs, 148.*

Wouters, J. (1991). *International public relations.* New York: Amacom.

I A THEORETICAL BASE

1 Interdisciplinary Theoretical Foundations for International Public Relations

Robert I. Wakefield
University of Maryland—College Park

The concept of international public relations is rapidly attracting the attention of practitioners and scholars. Since 1990, *Public Relations Journal, Communication World, Public Relations Review,* and other publications have published dozens of articles about public relations in a global context.[1] Interest is increasing in societies like the International Association of Business Communicators and the Public Relations Society of America, which recently emphasized "global public relations" in its national conference and established a section for members specializing in international practice.

This growth in international public relations is phenomenal but also haphazard (Botan, 1992). More and more countries are adapting American or European public relations principles and building a profession along their own cultural lines. But other countries relegate public relations to mere technical tasks, and business leaders in nations like Japan still view the practice as blatant hype, which is problematic in a culture that values understatement and self-effacement (Josephs, 1990).

Public relations often follows multinational organizations as they enter new markets. Many multinationals transfer their own philosophies and personnel into new territories to conduct public relations in their traditional ways. Others localize programs with little or no central coordination (Botan, 1992). Often, organizations turn their entire international communication processes over to public relations or advertising agencies.

---

[1] See, for example, Wilkinson (1990); Vogl (1990); Pinsdorf (1991); Epley (1992); Stanton (1992); Hauss (1993); and Bovet (1994).

WHAT IS INTERNATIONAL PUBLIC RELATIONS?

Ironically, this activity is taking place with little consensus on what the field constitutes. What is practiced in the name of international public relations can vary from simple hosting or promotions to diplomacy and strategic relationship building. To some, as one practitioner lamented, public relations programs "only sound international if you're on the other side of the ocean" (Anderson, 1989, p. 414). To others, the practice crosses borders but merely as a media relations role or an inexpensive way to support marketing, not public relations, objectives (L. Grunig, 1992).

To date, most articles on international public relations have been anecdotal or descriptive—what Kunczik (1990) viewed as "scientifically non-serious sources" (p. 24). They have handled topics like how a company conducted cross-cultural media relations, or how another handled a crisis in one of its host countries. Many tell how to avoid cultural blunders.

Most of the attempts at scholarly examinations have been country-specific, discussing public relations in a particular country and how it varies from other countries. If conducted well, these studies contribute to the growing body of knowledge about public relations around the world. However, they do not address the need for knowledge about *international* campaigns that deal with issues and publics across borders (Anderson, 1989; Botan, 1992).

Only a few scholars have tried to define international practice. Wilcox, Ault, and Agee (1992) called it "the planned and organized effort of a company, institution, or government to establish mutually beneficial relations with publics of other nations" (pp. 409–410). Grunig (in press) defined it as "a broad perspective that will allow [practitioners] to work in many countries—or to work collaboratively" with people in many nations (p. 7). Booth (1986) implied that the only true international practitioners are those who "understand how business is done across national borders" and perform in that context (p. 23).

Without consensus on the nature of cross-border public relations, organizations venturing into this environment do so with an unsteady road map to success. Practitioners who do not understand their own field fail to gain the trust of senior managers who desperately need their advice and performance in the complex maze of international relationship building. Worse, they become vulnerable to making, or repeating, costly and embarrassing mistakes.

There is no guarantee that those already in international public relations have adequate international expertise. Farinelli (1990) explained that "public relations has fewer people with international knowledge and experience than any of the other business sectors such as advertising, financial services, and management consulting. We all service the same clients—but public relations has the worst record of all in keeping pace with international changes" (p. 42).

THEORY BUILDING NEEDED FOR THE FIELD

What is needed is a foundation of principles and assumptions that come from scholarly research and theory building on what comprises effective practice in international public relations. Such a base would address *normative* issues, or what effectiveness *ought to* look like. These normative principles may be very different from current practices, but they would be based on mounting evidence of what effective practice looks like.

Practitioner Fred Repper (1992) explained that his peers often question whether academicians can "contribute anything of real value" to practitioners. He argued that "scholars . . . are searchers for the reason why, the foundation blocks that are needed so vitally and of such great concern to practitioners" (p. 110). This theory building occurs, as Grunig (1992) affirmed, "piece by piece. . . . It is shaped, revised, and improved to make it more useful for solving problems and directing human behavior" (p. 2).

So let us build the foundation. There are three ways to do this: assemble theories from related disciplines that have thrived internationally and test them in public relations situations; find ways to test theories on public relations in international settings; and build theories from the descriptions about public relations in various countries, using "thick description" (Geertz 1973) to investigate the real meanings behind the activity (a common practice in anthropology). The latter two activities are slowly occurring, as reflected in subsequent chapters of this book. The rest of this chapter concentrates on establishing a framework for using interdisciplinary theories in future research.

With its emphasis on building strategic relationships, public relations encompasses many forms of human behavior. Thus, to build theories for public relations, scholars have drawn from the broader social science disciplines that examine behavior (Pavlik, 1987). Because behaviors are not confined within any national boundary, using theories from other domains is equally appropriate for the study of international public relations. Some disciplines that can provide a foundation for the emerging field are sociology, psychology, political science, comparative management, cultural anthropology, speech ethnography, developmental communication, and mass communication.

MODEL FOR ORGANIZING RESEARCH IN INTERNATIONAL PUBLIC RELATIONS

The following pages outline a framework for ordering research in international public relations (see Fig. 1). Theories mentioned here represent the infinite variety that could be relevant to public relations practice across borders. The overall model presented should provide a framework for any path of study that could be pursued for future theory building in the field.

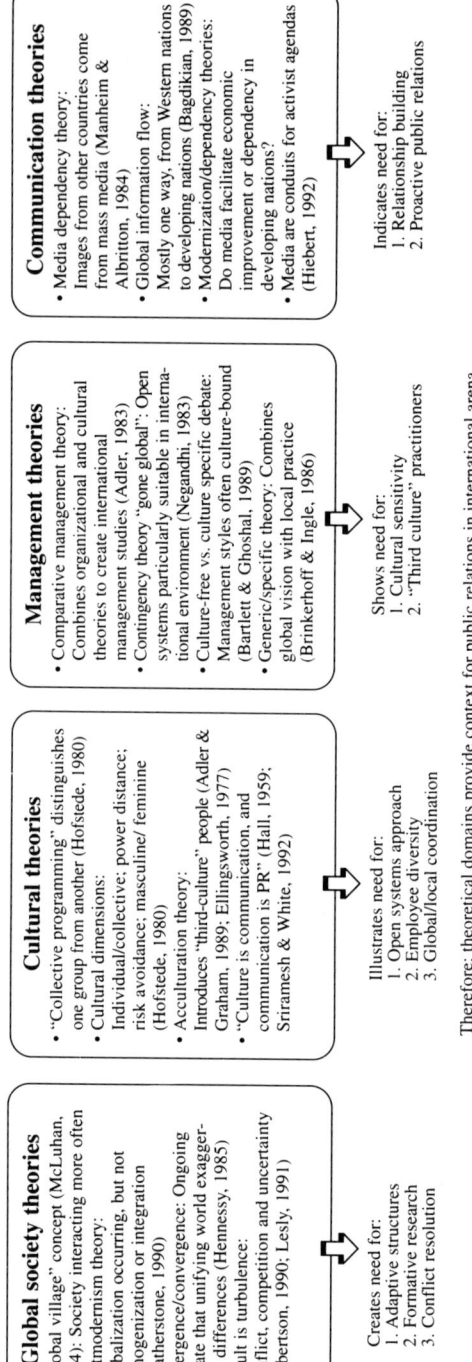

FIG. 1.1. Model for Organizing Research in International Public Relations

The model categorizes interdisciplinary theory into four main bodies: (1) theories of postmodernism and global society drawn from sociology and other disciplines; (2) cultural theories developed largely by anthropologists; (3) comparative management theories derived from international business scholars; and (4) theories on communication. Each category presents implications for international public relations. The base of the model displays representative theories in public relations that address these implications.

Global Society Theories

Scholars in many disciplines have been testing the effects of our increasingly interdependent world on individual societies. These studies often fall within the domain of sociology, but they also have come from such areas as the humanities and international relations (Robertson, 1990).

One theoretical pursuit in this vein is the global village concept espoused by McLuhan (1964). Theories of global modernity originated as early as the late 1700s, when Kant investigated the possibilities of a universal morality (Habermas, 1987). Some sociologists argue that global interdependence now is so complete that scholastic emphasis should shift from local societies to global relationships and issues (Tiryakian, 1986).

Whether or not full globalization has occurred, there is considerable debate about what it means to interacting societies. Scholars typically split into opposing positions of *convergence* or *divergence*. Convergence theorists contend that as the world integrates, its societies become increasingly similar. This is reflected in the increased omnipresence of entertainment, fast-food chains, traffic signs, and other symbols of standardization (Hennessy, 1985).

Divergence is a reaction to convergence. When external values invade a culture, they create tension between the forces for change and for maintaining the status quo (Hennessy, 1985). Divergence theory argues that the forces for the status quo will prevent a monolithic world (Featherstone, 1990). Instead, there is a powerful countertrend, a backlash against uniformity, rejection of foreign influences, and assertion of individual culture (Epley, 1992).

The effect of globalization and its resulting tug-of-war is turbulence. While societies are achieving more than ever, their citizens are more dissatisfied (Lesly, 1991). Naisbitt (1994) predicted that governments will continue to break apart, as evidenced by the upheaval of Communism and the growing political turmoil within many countries. Organizations will see an increasing need for small units that can adapt quickly to change. And they will face more hostile and better organized publics (L. Grunig, 1992).

This turbulence creates enormous pressure and opportunity for a unit within organizations that can predict change, identify its sources, and build programs to communicate with those sources to minimize potential damage to the organiza-

Cultural Theories

All international flights lead through culture; yet, many scholars have affirmed that culture is a slippery concept.[2] As Ellingsworth (1977) claimed, "the term *culture* . . . is plagued with denotative ambiguity and diversity of meaning" (p. 101). Sriramesh and White (1992) added that even "the people of the culture themselves may not be able to verbalize some of their ideologies" (p. 606). Despite this ambiguity, scholars continue to investigate culture and its influence on interactions (Tayeb, 1988).

There are more than 160 scholastic definitions of culture (Negandhi, 1983). Hofstede (1980) called it "the collective programming of the mind which distinguishes the members of one human group from another [and] that influence a human group's response to its environment" (p. 25). Adler, Doktor, and Redding (1986) identified three determinants of culture: It is shared by all or almost all members of some social group, older members of the group pass it on to younger members, and through morals, laws, or customs, it shapes the group's behaviors or views of the world.

Even though culture is a nebulous term, its influence on public relations is widely accepted (Verčič, Grunig, & Grunig, 1993). Hall (1959) said, "culture is communication and communication is culture" (p. 191). Communication and public relations also have been viewed as synonymous. Sriramesh and White (1992) explained that "linkages between culture and communication and culture and public relations are parallel because public relations is primarily a communication activity" (p. 609).

Starting with early anthropologists, scholars have identified and studied cultural dimensions. One landmark was Hofstede's (1980) study of managers in 39 nations that catalogued four different ways to differentiate societies: Self-centered vs. group-centered focus, masculine vs. feminine orientation, power distance between elites and masses in social and work structures, and the extent to which a society embraces or avoids uncertainty. Other scholars offered alternate dimensions, which Adler (1991) summarized as how cultures perceive the individual (basically good vs. basically evil) and the world (trying to dominate or harmonize with nature); activity (achieving vs. being); time (focus on tradition, on short-term results, or on future obligations); and space (whether personal space is public or private).

Sriramesh and White (1992) examined potential relationships between cultural dimensions and the practice of excellent public relations. They hypothesized

---

[2]For discussions on the difficulty of operationalizing the cultural variable, see Ellingsworth, 1977, and Adler, 1991, pp. 14–33.

that cultures displaying low power distance, authoritarianism, and individualism, but higher levels of interpersonal trust would be most likely to develop excellent public relations programs. A question for further study, however, is what influence might public relations practices have on culture?

In *Seven Cultures of Capitalism,* Hampden-Turner and Trompenaars (1993) sent ominous signals about what cultural differences imply for American organizations. They asserted that economic activity is not based on one form of capitalism, as most Americans presume, but that seven different cultural values influence decisions around the world. The aggregate of dimensions predominant in the United States values the individual and business self-interest, quantification, and short-term results. Human relations and broader societal concerns often are ignored in this worldview. By contrast, cultural values prevalent in most of Asia, Latin America, and Europe place high priority on community and social relationships. They place "all details and all particulars" into intricate patterns of connectedness (p. 109).

Hampden-Turner and Trompenaars (1993) claimed that the American value set is causing its organizations to lose ground in the emerging global marketplace. They argued that in an environment where people, technologies, and issues are constantly changing, "cultures that put the whole before its parts . . . may now have an advantage" (p. 31). To compete, American organizations must embrace what is intrinsic to holistic and communal societies—the human connectedness that increasingly drives global economic activity.

For public relations, this theory suggests a growing need for experts in relationship building, negotiation, and other communal traits. If practitioners supposedly skilled in communication cannot assume these roles, they will miss an opportunity to help guide future economic and social growth.

Perhaps a key to finding qualified international practitioners is acculturation theory from anthropology. This theory addresses what happens at the point of intercultural contact. Specifically, such contact should lead to changes in the previous patterns of individuals, cultures, or both. The nature of these changes depends on such variables as the situation (friendly vs. hostile, use of force, etc.), contact processes (order and type of cultural presentation), and the characteristics of those in contact (Adler & Graham, 1989).

One body of acculturation literature refers to *third-culture individuals* who transcend boundaries through global media, transnational education, cultural exchanges, and other means (Featherstone, 1990). These people spend considerable time outside their own culture and, while moving in and out of their native realm, become "agents of change" (Ellingsworth, 1977, p. 103.) Bovet (1994) suggested that some public relations firms are recognizing the importance of building a core of *third-culture practitioners.*

Culture certainly exerts influence, then, on international public relations. But exactly how does culture affect the practice in various countries? Cultural values may influence research methods in a particular country or the way an organization utilizes women and minority groups, for instance. And how does the acculturation process affect individual societies and lead to future public relations challenges? These and other questions await future research.

Comparative Management Theories

Just as organizational theory has guided domestic public relations research (Grunig, 1993), comparative management theory can assist with international research. The comparative management domain expands domestic knowledge by comparing the managerial decisions and behaviors from one culture with those of another culture (Adler, 1983). Ricks, Toyne, and Martinez (1990) summarized landmark research in this domain, which has evolved in a manner that public relations would do well to adopt—"away from the extreme situationalism evident in earlier years to a more theoretically grounded perspective" (p. 238).

Comparative management theories often support contingency theories. Katz and Kahn (1966) determined that effective organizations maintain an open systems perspective, meaning their external environment is as important to them as their internal processes. They know that the environment can change quickly, and they create programs to enable adaptation to those changes. This includes a continual process of identifying publics and building relationships with them (Freeman, 1984). Organizations with this philosophy increase their chances for long-term success (Grunig & Repper, 1992).

Contingency theory could be especially useful internationally. Negandhi (1983) claimed open-systems management is best for multinational organizations because it responds to the particularly dynamic environment. L. Grunig (1992) characterized international publics as increasingly hostile, better organized, and more powerful than ever. This is especially important for public relations practitioners. Because of its role in identifying and maintaining relationships with stakeholders, public relations is an ideal function to monitor and deal with these contingencies (L. Grunig, 1992).

One debate in comparative management is whether managerial behavior is *culture-free* or *culture-specific*. Many scholars assert that behavior is culture-free, meaning entities can operate the same way in any nation and be successful (Heller, 1988). Hofstede (1980), Tayeb (1988), and others postulated that culture of origin strongly influences organizational behavior.

Scholars in the culture-specific camp have identified various organizational structures in the international arena. Adler et al. (1986) discussed four: The international structure, in which the headquarters culture dominates every part of the organization; the multidomestic firm, which recognizes cultural differences and maintains highly autonomous operations in each country; the multinational firm, where cultural interaction is desirable and change comes from external forces; and the global firm, which views diversity as essential and desirable.

Bartlett and Ghoshal (1989) correlated structures with cultural variables. Organizations from Japan typically view the world as one market and centralize operations for efficiency. Their management style is group-oriented and consensual. The typical European firm provides autonomy to each unit manager because European culture has always valued "family contacts" and given its members the trust needed to thrive on their own. American organizations, by contrast, often place their own personnel and management techniques into other countries and demand standardization. This approach reflects the "America knows best" cultural worldview that Hampden-Turner and Trompenaars (1993) stated is harmful in international dealings.

Brinkerhoff and Ingle (1989) argued that neither the culture-specific nor culture-free approach is effective alone. They mediated the poles by saying that effective organizations *combine* culture-specific and culture-free values. In the process, they developed *generic* and *specific* management variables. Generic variables are overall goals and themes that can be standardized across cultures. The specifics are unique to each culture of operation, and include local communication needs, culturally derived procedures, and so forth.

The Brinkerhoff-Ingle (1989) theory offers promise for international public relations because practitioners also face decisions over what to centralize and what to conduct locally. Ovaitt (1988) and Traverse-Healy (1991) stressed that a solid combination of global and local functions is necessary for an effective international program. Wakefield (1994) and Verčič, et al. (1993) are developing and testing a global theory that combines generic and specific variables in public relations.

Communication Theories

Advancements in information technology have carried the mass media and their ideologies around the world at increasing speeds and lower costs. Never before has so much been communicated so quickly to so many people (Martin & Hiebert, 1990). Epley (1992) stated that global media have made people "more knowledgeable and opinionated than ever before" (p. 110).

These increases in media access suggest three theoretical implications for international public relations. The implications involve the nature of media messages, media imperialism and its impacts, and proliferation of global issues and activism. Because of these factors, the role of the media is important to studies of international public relations.

The first useful theory could be called "media dependency," which would show how assumptions about communication can change when placed into an international context. Since the 1960s, researchers have challenged early theories that the media influence the attitudes and behaviors of their audiences (Lowery & deFleur, 1988). However, in the global arena, there is evidence that the media become increasingly powerful as sources of information.

Manheim and Albritton (1984) theorized that most information about other countries comes from the mass media. In local confines, people can check the "reality" of coverage through their own experiences or contacts. But few people have direct experience by which to judge coverage of other countries. Therefore, these authors observed that "images of the actors and events on the international scene will be heavily . . . media dependent" (p. 643). This has at least two effects, of distortion and stereotyping. Media often create their own "reality," which can be quite different from what actually happened. This distortion gives people unrealistic images about other countries and perpetuates biases, which often are negative (Kunczik, 1990).

Another line of theory traces the global flow of information. Recent studies indicate that information and entertainment flow one way from Western nations to the developing world (Martin & Hiebert, 1990). An analysis of 29 media systems in seven regions found that news from developed countries was second only to coverage of regional issues (Sreberny-Mohammadi, 1984). American entertainment programs or their imitations are predominant in almost all countries (Varis, 1984). Bagdikian (1989) claimed that the global media are owned by a few conglomerates who form a "powerful troika" with multinational manufacturers and advertising agencies to spread cultural, political, and economic ideologies around the world.

Researchers in this domain divide into theories of *modernization* or *dependency*. Modernization theorists believe the influx of mass media into developing nations improves their economies and provides higher standards of living (Sinclair, 1990). Western technologies also are seen as "democratizing the world" (Hiebert, 1992, p. 118). In contrast, dependency theorists, comprised mostly of scholars in developing nations, view foreign media as tools for continuing imperialism and economic domination (Sinclair, 1990).

Regardless of which theory is accurate, the global media have helped to integrate publics and issues worldwide (Hiebert, 1992). Interest groups are using the media to create issues and achieve their goals (Pires, 1989). They stage events such as protests, boycotts, and even violent demonstrations (Grunig & Repper, 1992). Media cover these dramatic events, which ensures an audience for activist ideologies. As a result, interest groups are influencing the opinions of policy makers around the world (Hiebert, 1992).

These media effects should concern international public relations practitioners because the images they form create problems for multinational enterprises. Perhaps the images have helped foster the hostilities directed at multinational organizations in various countries. International practitioners must come to understand the factors underlying these resentments and respond to the affected groups before dissatisfactions arise (L. Grunig, 1992).

IMPLICATIONS FOR PUBLIC RELATIONS RESEARCH

Now we can summarize what the above research means to international public relations. Global society theories show that as cultures interact, turbulence increases. International media coverage helps perpetuate negative stereotypes, and activists use the media to vent their hostilities toward organizations. This necessitates the use of thorough scanning techniques to identify agents of change and to build relationships with them. Practitioners must become experts in conflict resolution, because conflict is inevitable.

Cultural theories show the need for public relations programs that are sensitive to diverse cultures. The management domain illustrates the value of open systems that adapt to rapid changes and balance central vision with local implementation. Both cultural and comparative studies suggest that organizations must add broader perspectives to their traditional cultural views.

Good communicators fill the needs addressed above. If they are qualified and sensitive to diverse viewpoints, they can facilitate relationships that will boost the bottom line for years. They can anticipate the challenges ahead and help organizations think and act in terms that balance their own goals with the desires of an expanding variety of international publics.

The implications address the research necessary in the future, but that research should identify even more implications and more variables of effectiveness (thus the two-way arrows in the model). There is a gap between current practice and theories that describe and explain effective practice in cross-border public relations programs. When that gap is filled, the theories can be used to determine the effectiveness of international practices. Scholars and practitioners need to close the gap.

Domestic research in public relations is reaching a state of maturity (Grunig, 1993). The body of knowledge includes data on practitioner roles, theories on publics and communication models, and assumptions about issues management, activism, and strategic public relations (Pavlik, 1987). It also contains a growing volume of critical scholarship that proposes a paradigm shift for public relations away from short-term manipulation toward the more long-term, human relations perspectives discussed above (Creedon, 1991).

Much of this research recently was compiled into a comprehensive project called *the IABC Excellence Study* (Grunig, 1992). A team of researchers examined literature in public relations and related disciplines, and identified variables that foster excellence in public relations. The group then tested these variables in more than 300 organizations in the United States, Canada, and Great Britain. Their prerequisites for effective public relations included an organizational worldview that values two-way communication and treats publics with respect; placement of the public relations manager within the "inner circle" to be able to influence decisions; and a respect for diversity within the public relations department and other employee ranks. (The IABC study is discussed more thoroughly in chapter 2.)

Now a foundation has been established for the same type of theory building to guide international practice. Some international theories are already being developed and tested (like the generic/specific theories discussed above), but others must follow. New theories could incorporate the available theories from other disciplines as well as from public relations. By developing and testing these theories, the field will obtain the model that it sorely needs for analyzing effective practice in international public relations.

REFERENCES

Adler, N. J. (1983). Cross-cultural management: Issues to be faced. *International Studies of Management and Organization, 13,* 7–45.
Adler, N. J. (1991). *International dimensions of organizational behavior* (2nd ed). Boston: PWS-Kent.
Adler, N. J., Doktor, R., & Redding, S. G. (1986). From the Atlantic to the Pacific century: Cross-cultural management reviewed. *Journal of Management, 12,* 295–318.
Adler, N. J., & Graham, J. L. (1989). Cross-cultural interaction: The international comparison fallacy? *Journal of International Business Studies, 20,* 515–537.
Anderson, G. (1989). A global look at public relations. In B. Cantor (Ed.), *Experts in action* (2d. ed. pp. 412–422). White Plains, NY: Longman.
Appadurai, A. (1990). Disjuncture and difference in the global cultural economy. In M. Featherstone (Ed.), *Global culture: Nationalism, globalization, and modernity* (pp. 295–310). London: Sage.
Bagdikian, B. (1989). The lords of the global village. *The Nation, 248* (June 12), 805–820.
Bartlett, C. A., & Ghoshal, S. (1989). *Managing across borders: The transnational solution.* Boston: Harvard Business School Press.
Booth, A. (1986). Going global. *Public Relations Journal, 42* (February), 22–26.
Botan, C. (1992). International public relations: Critique and reformulation. *Public Relations Review, 18,* 149–159.
Bovet, S. F. (1994). Building an international team. *Public Relations Review, 50,* 26–31.
Brinkerhoff, D. W., & Ingle, M. D. (1989). Integrating blueprint and process: A structured flexibility approach to development management. *Public Administration and Development, 9,* 487–503.
Creedon, P. (1991). Public relations and "women's work": Toward a feminist analysis of public relations roles. In L.A. Grunig & J.E. Grunig (Eds.), *Public Relations Research Annual:* Vol. 3. (pp. 67–84). Hillsdale, NJ: Lawrence Erlbaum.
Ellingsworth, H. W. (1977). Conceptualizing intercultural communication. In *Communication yearbook 1,* (pp. 99–106). New Brunswick, NJ: Transaction Books.
Epley, J. S. (1992). Public relations in the global village: An American perspective. *Public Relations Review, 18,* 109–116.
Farinelli, J. L. (1990). Needed: A new U.S. perspective on global public relations. *Public Relations Journal, 46* (November), 18–19, 42.
Featherstone, M. (Ed.). (1990). *Global culture: Nationalism, globalization and modernity.* London: Sage.
Freeman, R. E. (1984). *Strategic management: A stakeholder approach.* Boston: Pittman.
Geertz, C. (1973). *The interpretation of cultures.* New York: Basic Books.
Grunig, J. E. (1992). *Excellence in communication and public relations management.* Hillsdale, NJ: Lawrence Erlbaum.
Grunig, J. E. (1993). Implications of public relations for other domains of communication. *The Journal of Communication, 43,* 164–173.
Grunig, J. E. (In press) *Managing Public Relations* (2nd ed.) Fort Worth, TX: Harcourt-Brace.
Grunig, J. E., & Repper, F. (1992). Strategic management, publics, and issues. In J. E. Grunig

(Ed.), *Excellence in public relations and communication management* (pp. 117–158). Hillsdale, NJ: Lawrence Erlbaum.

Grunig, L. A. (1992). Strategic public relations constituencies on a global scale. *Public Relations Review, 18*, 127–136.

Habermas, J. (1987). *The philosophical discourse of modernity*. Cambridge, England: Polity Press.

Hall, E. T. (1959). *The silent language*. Garden City, NY: Doubleday.

Hampden-Turner, C., & Trompenaars, A. (1993). *The seven cultures of capitalism*. New York: Doubleday.

Hauss, D. (1993). Global communications comes of age: Five case histories prove power of integrated messages. *Public Relations Journal, 49* (August), 22–26.

Heller, F. (1988). Cost benefits of multinational research on organizations. *International Studies of Management and Organizations, 18*, 5–18.

Hennessy, B. (1985). *Public opinion* (5th ed.) Monterey, CA: Brooks/Cole.

Hiebert, R. E. (1992). Global public relations in a post-Communist world: A new model. *Public Relations Review, 18*, 117–126.

Hofstede, G. (1980). *Culture's consequences: International differences in work related values*. Beverly Hills, CA: Sage.

Josephs, R. (1990). Japan booms with public relations ventures. *Public Relations Journal, 46* (December), 19–20.

Katz, D., & Kahn, R. L. (1966). *The social psychology of organizations*. New York: Wiley.

Kunczik, M. (1990). *Images of nations and international public relations*. Bonn, Germany: Friedrich-Ebert-Stiftung.

Lesly, P. (1991). Public relations in the turbulent new human climate. *Public Relations Review, 17*, 1–8.

Lowery, S. A., & deFleur, M. L. (1988). *Milestones in mass communication research* (2d. ed.) New York: Longman.

Manheim, J. B., & Albritton, R. B. (1984). Changing national images: International public relations and media agenda setting. *The American Political Science Review, 78*, 641–657.

Martin, L. J., & Hiebert, R. E. (1990). *Current issues in international communication*. New York: Longman.

McLuhan, M. (1964). *Understanding media*. London: Routledge & Kegan Paul.

Merrill, J. C. (1983). *Global journalism: A survey of the world's mass media*. New York: Longman.

Naisbitt, J. (1994). *Global paradox*. New York: Morrow.

Negandhi, A. (1983). Cross-cultural management research: Trend and future directions. *Journal of International Business Studies*, 17–28.

Ovaitt, F., Jr. (1988). PR without boundaries: Is globalization an option? *Public Relations Quarterly, 33*, 5–9.

Pavlik, J. V. (1987). *Public relations: What research tells us*. (Vol. 16). Newbury Park, CA: Sage Communication Text Series.

Pinsdorf, M. K. (1991). Flying different skies: How cultures respond to airline disasters. *Public Relations Review, 17*, 37–56.

Pires, M. A. (1989). Working with activist groups. *Public Relations Journal, 45* (April), 30–32.

Repper, F. (1992). How communication managers can apply the theories of excellence and effectiveness. In J. E. Grunig (Ed.), *Excellence in public relations and communication management* (pp. 109–114). Hillsdale, NJ: Lawrence Erlbaum.

Ricks, D., Toyne, B., & Martinez, Z. (1990). Recent developments in international management research. *Journal of Management, 16*, 219–253.

Robertson, R. (1990). Mapping the global condition: Globalization as the central concept. In M. Featherstone (Ed.), *Global culture: Nationalism, globalization, and modernity* (pp. 15–30). London: Sage.

Sinclair, J. (1990). From "modernization to cultural dependence: Mass communication studies and

the Third World. In L.J. Martin & R.E. Hiebert (Eds.) *Current issues in international communication* (pp. 286–293). New York: Longman.
Sreberny-Mohammadi, A. (1984). Results of international cooperation. *Journal of Communication, 34,* 121–134.
Sriramesh, K., & White, J. (1992). Societal culture and public relations. In J. E. Grunig (Ed.), *Excellence in public relations and communication management* (pp. 597–614). Hillsdale, NJ: Lawrence Erlbaum.
Stanton, E. M. (1992). PR's future is here: Worldwide, integrated communications. *Public Relations Quarterly, 37,* 46–47.
Tayeb, M. H. (1988). *Organizations and national culture: A comparative analysis.* London: Sage.
Tiryakian, E. A. (1986). Sociology's great leap forward: The challenge of internationalization. *International Sociology, 1,* 155–171.
Traverse-Healy, T. (1991). The corporate aspect. In M. Nally (Ed.), *International public relations in practice* (pp. 29–39). London: Kogan Page.
Varis, T. (1984). The international flow of television programs. *Journal of Communication, 34,* 143–152.
Verčič, D., Grunig, L. A., & Grunig, J. (1993, November). *Global and specific principles of public relations: Evidence from Slovenia.* Paper presented to the Association for the Advancement of Policy, Research, and Development in the Third World, Cairo, Egypt.
Vogl, F. (1990). Closing the gap: New approaches to international media relations. *Public Relations Journal, 46* (July), 18–20.
Wakefield, R. I. (1994. *Excellence in international public relations: An exploratory Delphi study.* Dissertation prospectus, University of Maryland, College Park.
Wilcox, D. L., Ault, P. H., & Agee, W. K. (1992). *Public relations strategies and tactics* (3d. ed.) New York: HarperCollins.
Wilkinson, A. (1990). Globalization: Are we up to the challenges? *Public Relations Journal, 46* (January), 12–13.

2 Global and Specific Principles of Public Relations: Evidence From Slovenia

Dejan Verčič
Pristop Communication Group, Ljubljana, Slovenia

Larissa A. Grunig
James E. Grunig
University of Maryland

The world today is comprised of interpenetrating systems. Global interaction among political systems, cultures, and organizations is a fact of life. Conflict is inevitable when systems interpenetrate one another. Earlier in the history of the world, conflict was resolved through domination, fighting, and warfare. The strong won, the weak lost. Today, conflicts are numerous but limited in their scope. Still, the world is experiencing more conflict than it has for many years and in many areas: economic, ethnic, regional, cultural, class, and gender conflict. If there is such a thing as a New World Order, it is an order based on conflict.

Fighting and warfare resolve few problems today, and they are becoming obsolete. In the 1990s and in the 21st century, conflict must be resolved through communication, negotiation, and eventually collaboration. Although there are many forms of communication that can be used to resolve conflict, the profession of public relations builds a communication function into every organization or group that has a public relations person or department. Communication and collaboration are the essence of modern public relations. Thus, public relations offers the advantage of being at the strategic boundaries between organizations and publics where the small scale but intense conflicts that characterize the New World Order will be found.

Public relations, however, is influenced by the cultures and political systems within and among which it works (Sriramesh & White, 1992). A pervasive question for the public relations profession, then, is whether public relations will be different in each country or political/cultural system where it is practiced. If it is different, theorists will not be able to construct general, normative theories of what public relations does and how it should be practiced. Further, if it is different, then relations theory could not be systematically integrated into a global theory that could be taught and implemented in different parts of the world.

INTERNATIONAL AND GLOBAL PUBLIC RELATIONS

With the internationalization of business and politics, it has become almost a truism to say that public relations has become "international" or "global." Yet what do these terms mean? Does an organization hire a local public relations firm or practitioner in each country or societal culture where it works to communicate in a way that works only in the location? Or can one communication professional, firm, or department work globally—in the same way in several locations. Anderson (1989) coined the terms international and global public relations to distinguish between these two kinds of practice. In his terms:

> International public relations practitioners very often implement distinctive programs in multiple markets, with each program tailored to meet the often acute distinctions of the individual geographic market.
>
> Global public relations superimposes an overall perspective on a program executed in two or more national markets, recognizing the similarities among audiences while necessarily adapting to regional differences. It connotes a planning attitude as much as geographic reach and flexibility. (p. 413)

Anderson opted for the global model of public relations: "Global, as opposed to multinational, businesses demand that programs in distinctive markets be interrelated. While there will always be local differences and need for customization, the programs will probably share more than they differ" (p. 413).

Anderson's distinction between global and international public relations suggested the major hypothesis of this study, that public relations has generic components that will work normatively in most if not all cultures and political systems of the world. However, he also suggested that the specific applications—the strategies, techniques, and practices of public relations—will differ in each location. The purpose of our research, therefore, was to develop general principles of the profession at the theoretical level while also searching for and documenting the cultural, political, and economic conditions that require specific strategies or applications of those principles in different social systems.

Generic Principles and Specific Applications

The idea that effective public relations practices will share generic principles across cultures even though the specific applications will be different in different cultures has a theoretical basis in Brinkerhoff and Ingle's (1989) theory of "structured flexibility" in the management of development organizations. Structured flexibility is a theory of management that is similar to the symmetrical theory of symmetrical public relations (e.g., J. E. Grunig & White, 1992; J. E. Grunig, 1989). Brinkerhoff and Ingle's theory "melds a planned structuring of action . . . with a concern for creating the capacity for flexibility and iterative learning. . ." (p. 490).

Brinkerhoff and Ingle (1989) identified five management functions that they said are "generic to good performance. . . . How each one of the functions is fulfilled can vary from setting to setting" (p. 493). They explained how these generic principles and specific applications might apply to a rural development agency:

> For example, a rural development agency in country X may establish a formal goal specification and review procedure, whereas an agency in country Y may accomplish the same function with a more informal arrangement. What matters is that participants develop ways of fulfilling the functions that fit with their organizational and cultural environments. (p. 493)

To develop a global theory of public relations, therefore, we have applied Brinkerhoff and Ingle's idea to public relations in the same way that they have applied it to management. In doing so, we essentially are developing a middle-ground theory between cultural relativism and ethnocentrism. A culturally relative theory would maintain that public relations must be different in every society to fit the culture of that society. An ethnocentric theory, in contrast, would maintain that a single theory is appropriate for all societies, although the theory developed generally reflects the cultural assumptions and values of the society from which it originated.

To understand the theory that we have developed and tested in this research, it is important to recognize that the theory remains a normative one, which does not necessarily describe the way public relations actually is practiced in many countries.

Positive and Normative Theory. A normative theory describes how things *should* be done or how some activity *should* be carried out. A positive or descriptive theory explains how and why things actually *are* done. In developing a normative theory, theorists have no obligation to show that an activity actually is conducted in the way the theory describes. They must show only that if an activity were to be conducted as the theory prescribes, it would be effective. Normative theories are common in fields such as management and marketing. Most of the theories in public relations textbooks also are normative.

To say that a theory is "good in theory but not in practice" is relevant to a normative but not to a positive theory. When applied to normative theory, that statement means that the theory may be logical but it is not practical—that, realistically, it could not be implemented in an actual situation and is not a good theory. Positive theories, in contrast, describe phenomena, events, or activities as they actually occur. Positive theories can be evaluated in part by whether they correspond to reality. If public relations is not practiced as described by the theory, for example, the theory would not be a good theory.

Thus, one might react to the idea of a global theory of public relations by describing the obvious differences in public relations practice in different cultures. For example, J. E. Grunig et al. (1995) compared the models of public relations practiced in Taiwan, Greece, and India with those practiced in the United States and found two new patterns of practice that they called cultural interpretation and personal influence. We could conclude from those results, therefore, that there are national or international differences in the practice of public relations. J. E. Grunig and his colleagues did hypothesize that these new models also could be found in the United States. But suppose that a type of public relations could be found only in one country. Researchers could describe that model and use cultural and political variables to explain why it occurs. Thus, they would have a good positive theory.

On the other hand, that model, practiced in a single country, may not be effective even in that country. That model would not be a good normative theory. Nevertheless, normative and positive theories can overlap in the social and behavioral sciences in ways that they could not in the physical sciences. They overlap because humans invent normative theories and apply them in practice. Once practiced, they become positive theory because they then describe practice in the real world. At the same time, research should be able to show that a good normative theory functions in practice in the way the normative theory says it should. As Massy and Weitz (1977) explained, useful normative theory should provide solutions "under typical conditions encountered in actual practice" (p. 123).

In short, a theory of generic principles would not deny that different forms of public relations practice can be found in different locations. Instead, it would maintain that not all of these forms of practice will be effective in helping organizations resolve conflict and build relationships with their publics. Those that are effective will share underlying generic principles that explain why they are effective. If they do share those principles, then each differing practice will constitute a specific example of how that principle has been applied.

Research on the Generic/Specific Theory. The purpose of our research, therefore, was to develop a normative theory of generic principles of public relations and to identify specific contextual variables in different societies that must be taken into account when a public relations professional applies these principles. We conceptualized these generic principles and contextual conditions and then applied them to a case study of Slovenia. The development of public relations in Slovenia provides a valuable case study because it is amazingly atypical: The generic principles of public relations that we propose were introduced in what appears to be an inhospitable culture and political system. The relationship among the authors also made the research possible: Verčič is a director of the Pristop group, the first public relations firm in Slovenia; J. E. Grunig and L. A. Grunig have visited Slovenia three times and worked with Pristop.

As a former republic of Yugoslavia, Slovenia had a typical communist propaganda system of communication before liberalization of the political system began in the early 1970s. At that time, high-tech companies began to develop public relations departments. Those departments declined after only a few years, however, when the ruling Communist Party removed both the liberal government and the technocratic managers. In the late 1980s, public relations emerged again and became one of the main tools of the political opposition and subsequently of Slovenia's transition to democracy in 1990 and independence in 1991 (for more background on the development of public relations in Slovenia, see Gruban, Verčič, & Zavrl, 1994, pp. 10–13).

We used qualitative research methods in this research: participant observation and formal and informal interviews. That combination was possible because Verčič was a member of the political group that brought about the transition to democracy in Slovenia and also was one of three principal founders of the Pristop Communication Group—the object of our research.[1] J. E. Grunig and L. A. Grunig were participants when they lectured to the Slovenian Public Relations Society, to the University of Ljubljana, and to clients of Pristop in January 1992 and in June and July 1993. In addition, they conducted informal and structured interviews of the three directors of Pristop in 1992, 1993, and 1994: Brane Gruban, Franci Zavrl, and Dejan Verčič. They also interviewed informally other public relations professionals working for Pristop and observed their work with clients.

In the next section of this paper, we conceptualize the generic and specific principles of public relations. Then, we report the results of research related to three research questions. The first research question asked whether certain political, economic, and cultural conditions are necessary before the generic principles of public relations can be practiced. In particular, we asked if the generic principles of excellent public relations can be practiced in a centralized, socialist system—either in a society as a whole or in individual organizations.

Secondly, we addressed the question of whether culture alone or in combination with the structure of society or of organizations discourages the practice of excellent public relations. For this question, we interviewed the three directors of Pristop to determine where Slovenia fit on the dimensions of culture identified by

---

[1]The Pristop Communication Group is a private, limited liability company, consisting of eight profit/cost centers: a public relations center, the PR Center; a research center, prInstitut; a marketing and advertising center, Prospekt; a clipping and media analysis center, Kliping; a direct mail center, Adrema; a desktop publishing center, Prelom; and a cultural management center, Inart Center.

Hofstede (1980) and Tayeb (1988). Sriramesh and White (1992) had predicted that excellent public relations would be most likely in cultures with low power distance, high trust among workers, low individualism/high collectivism, low uncertainty avoidance, and high femininity/low masculinity.

Thirdly, we attempted to determine the extent to which the nine generic principles of excellence could be applied in Slovenia and whether the Slovenian experience might suggest additional principles. In interviews with the three directors of Pristop, we asked whether the principles have been effective in Slovenia and for examples of specific strategies used by Pristop to introduce the principles in Slovenia.

CONCEPTUALIZATION OF GENERIC AND SPECIFIC VARIABLES

From 1986 to 1995, a team of six researchers funded by the IABC Research Foundation of the International Association of Business Communicators studied the characteristics that enhance the ability of public relations departments to contribute to organizational effectiveness. The study will be completed in 1996. J. E. Grunig and L. A. Grunig were members of that team. The project was named the "excellence project" because the characteristics of the most effective public relations units are those that describe what the team called the attributes of excellent public relations departments.

The excellence project began with a thorough review of relevant theoretical and research literature from public relations, management, sociology, psychology, marketing, communication, anthropology, philosophy, and feminist studies. From that review, the team conceptualized a general theory of public relations excellence and organizational effectiveness that was reported in the book, *Excellence in Public Relations and Communication Management* (J. E. Grunig, 1992). The team also used the literature to develop a set of three questionnaires that were administered to a sample of 326 organizations in the United States, Canada, and the United Kingdom. The senior public relations person, the CEO, and an average of 14 employees completed questionnaires in each organization.

From the literature review, the team identified 14 characteristics of excellent public relations programs and three effects of such programs that were measured in the questionnaires. Initial analysis of the data provided strong support for the idea that these characteristics can be consolidated into an "excellence factor" (J. E. Grunig et al., 1991). In this chapter, we extend these characteristics to global public relations, hypothesizing that these characteristics will be generic, normative factors of excellent public relations applicable across cultures and political/economic systems. Here, we have consolidated several similar characteristics of the 14 into nine generic principles, which we now discuss.

Generic Principles

Involvement of Public Relations in Strategic Management. Effective organizations usually engage in long-term strategic planning—planning that enables them to develop a mission and set goals that are appropriate for their environment. Excellent public relations units are involved in this strategic planning process. They help the organization recognize or enact the parts of the environment that affect the organization's mission and goals. The relevant parts of the environment can be called stakeholders or strategic publics.

An organization that practices public relations strategically, therefore, develops programs to communicate with both the internal and external strategic publics that provide the greatest threats to and opportunities for the organization. Organizations strive for good relationships with the external or internal publics that limit their ability to pursue their goals. Organizations also try to cultivate relationships with publics that support their goals. Building good relationships with strategic publics maximizes the autonomy of organizations to pursue their goals, which is important because the literature shows that effective organizations are those that choose appropriate goals and then achieve them.

When public relations helps the organization build relationships, it saves the organization money by reducing the costs of litigation, regulation, legislation, pressure campaigns, or boycotts that result from bad relationships with publics—publics that become activist groups when relationships are bad. It also helps the organization make money by cultivating relationships with donors, consumers, shareholders, and legislators. With that conclusion, we arrived at an explanation of how public relations contributes to the bottom line.

Empowerment of Public Relations in the Dominant Coalition or a Direct Reporting Relationship to Senior Management. The strategic management of public relations must be an integral part of the strategic management of the overall organization. For that to happen, the public relations unit must be empowered to practice public relations according to professional principles rather than the often misguided ideas of senior managers from functional areas outside of public relations. When public relations is empowered, the senior public relations executive usually becomes part of the dominant coalition, the power-elite group of managers that makes strategic decisions for the organization. Thus, effective organizations place the public relations department in the organizational structure so that the senior public relations person is part of this powerful group of senior managers or has ready access to that group.

Integrated Public Relations Function. Many organizations develop more than one public relations unit. Organizations usually develop these units for historical rather than strategic reasons. Thus, the public relations units continue to reflect the relationship problems that were most critical to the organization when the public relations function first developed rather than those that are critical today. In contrast, excellent departments integrate all public relations functions into a single department or have a mechanism set up to coordinate the departments. Only in an integrated system of public relations is it possible for public relations to develop new communication programs for changing strategic publics—that is, to be managed strategically.

Public Relations as a Management Function Separate From Other Functions. Many organizations splinter the public relations function by making it a supporting tool for other departments such as marketing, human resources, law, or finance. When the public relations function is sublimated to other functions, it cannot be managed strategically because it cannot move communication resources from one strategic public to another as an integrated public relations function can. Public relations counsels all other management functions on their communication and relationship problems with publics, but it must be independent of any one of these functions if it is to counsel all of them.

Throughout the world public relations and marketing, in particular, often are confused to the detriment of the public relations function. Public relations practitioners communicate with *publics* that either threaten the organization's autonomy or provide opportunities to enhance that autonomy. Marketing practitioners, in contrast, create and seek out *markets* that can use or consume its products or services. If public relations becomes solely a marketing function, the organization loses its ability to build relationships with all of its strategic publics and is limited to communication with consumer publics.

The Role of the Public Relations Practitioner. Public relations practitioners fill two major roles in organizations—the manager who plans programs strategically and the technician who writes, edits, or produces publications. Without a manager to coordinate public relations activities, the public relations unit cannot be a part of strategic management. In smaller organizations, the same person may occupy both roles; and communication technicians are essential to carry out day-to-day communication activities. Yet, excellent public relations units must have at least one senior communication manager who conceptualizes and directs public relations programs or this direction will be supplied by other members of the dominant coalition who have no knowledge of communication or relationship building.

Two-Way Symmetrical Model of Public Relations. Two-way symmetrical describes a model of public relations that is based on research and uses communication to manage conflict and improve understanding with strategic publics. Excellent public relations departments model more of their communication programs on the two-way symmetrical than on the other three models, although they often combine elements of the two-way asymmetrical model with the two-way symmetrical model in a *mixed-motive* model.

In contrast, the *press agentry* model applies when a public relations program strives only for favorable publicity in the mass media, often in a deceptive way. The *public-information* model uses "journalists in residence" to disseminate relatively objective information through the mass media and controlled media such as newsletters, brochures, and direct mail. The *two-way asymmetrical* model uses research to develop messages that are likely to persuade strategic publics to behave as the organization wants. Both press agentry and public information are one-way models of public relations; they are not based on research and strategic planning. The press agentry, public-information, and two-way asymmetric models also are "asymmetrical"—that is, they try to change the behavior of publics but not of the organization.

A Symmetrical System of Internal Communication. Communication inside an organization is crucial to effective management. Excellent organizations have decentralized *management structures* that give autonomy to employees and allow them to participate in decision making. They also have participative, *symmetrical systems of internal communication*. Symmetrical communication with employees *increases job satisfaction* because employee goals are incorporated into the organizational mission.

Knowledge Potential for Managerial Role and Symmetrical Public Relations. Excellent public relations departments have practitioners who have learned a theoretical body of knowledge in public relations. Some practitioners have gained this knowledge from experience, self-study, or professional development courses. More and more practitioners are getting this knowledge from a university program in public relations, however, and most will get it that way in the future. Excellent programs also are staffed by professionals, people who not only are educated in the body of knowledge but who are active in professional associations and read professional literature.

Diversity Embodied in All Roles. The principle of requisite variety (Weick, 1969) states that effective organizations have as much diversity inside the organization as in the environment. Requisite variety is especially important in public relations because the unit is responsible for communicating with varied publics. Thus, excellent public relations includes both men and women in all roles, as well as practitioners of different racial, ethnic, and cultural backgrounds. Excellent public relations units, however, do not pigeonhole women and minority practitioners into programs to communicate only with women or other minorities. Instead, diverse practitioners interact in all public relations programs.

The feminization of the public relations profession that seems to be occurring throughout the world increases requisite variety; but it will limit the potential of a public relations department if the organization discriminates against women, who often are best educated in public relations, and keeps them out of the management role. Excellent public relations departments have mechanisms to help women gain the power they need to advance from the technician to the management role and to implement their knowledge of two-way symmetrical public relations.

Specific Variables

If these nine variables are indeed normative, generic principles of excellent public relations practice, it should be possible to practice them in diverse contexts around the world. Thus, it is important to identify contextual variables that may make it difficult or impossible to practice these generic principles or that require specific applications or strategies to implement the generic principles. We have identified five variables that seem to be most important in requiring specific strategies: the political-economic system, culture, the extent of activism, the level of development, and the media system.

In our research on Slovenia, we have concentrated on the first two variables—the political-economic system and culture. The extent of activism and the nature of the media system are heavily intertwined with these first two variables, so we also report some information on those variables as well. To test the effect of level of development, we would have to do research in Third-World countries as well as on a relatively developed country such as Slovenia.

The effect of the political-economic system can be examined effectively in Slovenia by looking at the change in communication that has taken place in the transition from socialism to democracy.

POLITICAL-ECONOMIC CONDITIONS FOR EXCELLENT PUBLIC RELATIONS

We can address the question of whether public relations can be practiced in a socialistic setting as well as in a democracy by comparing the concept of propaganda with public relations.

To do so, we must recognize that the question of whether public relations can be practiced according to global principles (principles that can be adapted to all cultures) or whether it must be practiced internationally (following different principles in different cultures) is the question not of the *comprehension* but of the *extension* of the term public relations. We are using here terms analogous to those introduced in 1662 by Antoine Arnauld and Pierre Nicole in their famous work *La Logiqiue ou l'Art de penser* (Arnauld & Nicole, 1964), often called also *Port Royal Logic,* to underline a major difference between the global and international school.

According to Kneale and Kneale (1986), comprehension of a term is "the set of attributes which could not be removed without destruction of the idea" (p. 318). For public relations, comprehension would consist of the organized use of communication between two or more social groupings. They explained: "The extension of a term, on the other hand, is the set of things to which it is applicable, or what the older logicians called its inferiors" (p. 318).

In one of the rare works that attempted to specify the conditions under which it is appropriate to talk about public relations, Ehling (1984) wrote

> . . . we can say that a public relations setting comes into existence if and only if two or more interdependently but laterally related social groupings (not individuals) are in actual or potential conflict in a social milieu where primacy is given to peaceful resolution of such conflicts and where at least one of the parties to the conflict is capable of mitigating the conflict by the peaceful means of communication. (p. 16)

For Ehling, it is possible to talk about a public relations situation, problem, management, and activities only under such a defined setting.

Ehling's extension of the term public relations is very restricted, and the majority of practitioners and scholars would not agree with his definition. But, for us, his definition of a public relations setting provides a useful starting point that shows the major difference between the global and international school to be in the extension of the term public relations: Globalists maintain that because there are some common characteristics of social behavior among all countries, the same principles of public relations are to be applied in all cultures. Internationalists are prepared to use the term public relations much more broadly, accepting certain behavior in other cultures as public relations—although they would not accept the same kind of behavior in their own country as a legitimate or even legal practice of the profession (e.g., bribery).

One such concept is "propaganda." When they first described typical ways in which public relations is practiced as four models of public relations, J. E. Grunig and Hunt (1984) used the term propaganda as synonymous with the historically first and the most primitive model—the press agentry, publicity-seeking model. In their recent work on the models, however, J. E. Grunig and L. A. Grunig (1992) followed Hellweg's (1989) suggestion and redesigned the four models in terms of two continua: one of craft and one of professional public relations (Fig. 2.1). In their words:

> Practitioners of craft public relations seem to believe that their job consists solely of the application of communication techniques as end in itself. To them, the purpose of public relations simply is to get publicity or information into the media or other channels of communication. Practitioners of professional public relations, in contrast, rely on a body of knowledge as well as technique and see public relations as having a strategic purpose for an organization: to manage conflict and build relationships with strategic publics that limit the autonomy of the organization. (p. 312)

Neither of the two models on the craft continuum employ our nine general principles of excellent public relations. Therefore, a socialist country that per-

Craft Public Relations

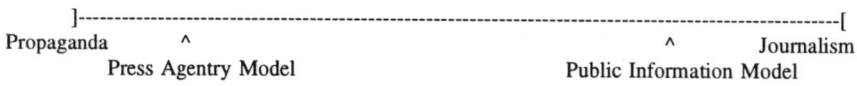

Professional Public Relations

FIG. 2.1. Four models of public relations placed on two continua. Note. From "Models of Public Relations and Communication" by J. E. Grunig and L. A. Grunig in *Excellence in Public Relations and Communication Management* (p. 312), edited by J. E. Grunig, 1992, Hillsdale, NJ: Lawrence Erlbaum Associates. Reprinted with permission.

mits only propaganda as a form of organizational communication could not practice the generic principles. The context in which the generic principles would be practiced in a communist political-economic system is even more constraining than is suggested by the idea that relations will be limited to the press agentry model in such a system.

Propaganda, like journalism, is much more than a set of communication techniques; it is a concept. It is not about communication between organizations and their publics; it is about discommunication. Its first aim is to dissolve communication between people in order to disable their ability to form publics.[2] If propaganda does not succeed in disabling publics, then it does not attempt to communicate with them but to discourage them from pursuing their cause.[3]

Propaganda, therefore, cannot be accepted as a form of public relations. First, it does not fit into a public relations setting; it does not take place between Ehling's (1985) "two or more interdependently but laterally related social groupings" (p. 16). Second, if these laterally related groups emerge in the public

---

[2]It is noteworthy that Katz et al. (1954) introduced their major book of readings on propaganda with two chapters on "The Role of Public Opinion in a Democracy" and "Definitions of Public Opinion and the Public." The second article ended with Blumer's introduction of the distinction between the mass and the public.

[3]The idea that propaganda disables publics by making people aware of constraints on their behavior has a theoretical basis in J. Grunig's situational theory of publics. In that theory, constraint recognition discourages communication behavior and fosters "constrained" and "fatalistic" behavior. See J. Grunig and Hunt (1984) for a basic overview of the theory and J. Grunig (1976) for a conceptualization of the relationship between organizational structure and constraints on individual behavior.

relations setting, the sole aim of propaganda is to destroy the setting itself; it is not about "mitigating the conflict by peaceful means of communication" (Ehling, 1984, p. 16) but about defeating the other side or at least paralyzing it.

The major tool of propaganda is not communication, which is by definition something two-sided, but information that helps to create constraints to communication or one-sided information flow described in classical communication theories as a sender-receiver model.

The concept of propaganda was described by Eugen Hadamovsky, who later became the chief of German Nazi broadcasting: "Propaganda and the graduated use of violence have to be employed together in a skillful manner. They are never absolutely opposed to each other. The use of violence can be a part of propaganda" (cited in Zeman, 1964, p. 16, and Arendt, 1973, p. 341). Or in the words of an official Nazi pamphlet, terrorist troops—the SA—were "the first and the propaganda arm" of the Nazi movement (Zeman, 1964, p. 20). Zeman added: "As a weapon of propaganda, the SA came to rank perhaps higher than Hitler's speeches" (p. 21).

Arendt (1973) went further by stating: "(It takes power, not propaganda skill, to circulate a revised history of the Russian Revolution in which no man by the name of Trotsky was ever commander-in-chief of the Red Army)" (p. 353).

The word propaganda came into the vocabulary when the Roman Church named its standing committee of cardinals in charge of missionary activities "Congregation de Propaganda Fide." What communications scholars forget when they mention this historical event is that the Roman Church introduced the concept of propaganda in the 17th century, after the Inquisition reached its peak point in the 16th century. Propaganda, in other words, essentially is little more than a symbolic expression of inquisitionist behavior.

Bernays introduced the term propaganda into the discussion of public relations by actually calling public relations "new" and "modern propaganda." In his book, *Propaganda,* Bernays (1928) wrote: "Modern propaganda is the consistent, enduring effort to create or shape events to influence the relationship of the public to an enterprise, idea or group" (p. 25). He was writing about creating or shaping events, not talking about them. To create or shape events takes power. Bernays expressed that as well when he said, "Propaganda is the executive arm of the invisible government" (p. 20). In other words, one must have government to propagandize and not vice versa.

As Arendt (1973) said in an earlier quote, it takes power to lie and to be taken seriously. Thus, the question emerges: Must the lie be believed by the liar or by anybody else to become propaganda (as persuasion theories would like us to believe)? No, on the contrary. For a lie to become propaganda, it takes power to lie and to know that no one will believe the lie. Propaganda is a lie that shows naked power behind itself. Ingrami (1992) explained that for communism, real communists exist only outside Russia. Stalin put an end to the luxuries of ideology.

Propaganda, therefore, is information about the constraints that a system places on lateral communication. As management guru Peter Drucker (1993) told us in his most recent book, the problem of making an organization effective today is that power is no longer sufficient.

> In making and moving things, **partnership with responsible workers is the *best* way** [emphasis added]. But Taylor's telling them worked too, and quite well after all. In knowledge and service work, however, partnership with the responsible worker is the *only* [emphasis added] way to improve productivity. Nothing else works at all." (p. 83)

That revelation led Drucker to a new definition. Around World War II, according to Drucker, a manager was someone responsible for the work of subordinates. A manager, in other words, was a boss, and management was rank and power. This is probably still the definition a good many people have in mind when they speak of managers and management.

By the early 1950s, however, the definition already had changed to "a manager is responsible for the performance of people." Today, we know that this also is too narrow a definition. According to Drucker (1993), the right definition today is "a manager is responsible for the application and performance of knowledge" (p. 40). But to be able to perform this role, rank and power are not enough. What is needed are lateral relationships.

The old organization was constructed according to the same design as the Prussian Army. It behaved in the same way as socialist states did—by power. The information system was propaganda. The Harvard "Human Relations" school was basically about manipulation—to increase productivity because Big Brother was watching you. But the new organization can work only through lateral communication.

The old and new organization and their communication systems are shown in Fig. 2.2. The bottom left side of Fig. 2.2 depicts a hierarchical organization based on power. It has high constraints on the behavior of members of the organization. These constraints are basically one-sided and imposed from the top of the organization on people lower in the hierarchy. These constraints discourage lateral communication. In such an organization, it is necessary to communicate propaganda in order to show constraints. Big Brother is watching by talking. The top right side of Fig. 2.2 depicts the new organization with great freedom and practically no behavioral constraints that discourage lateral communication. Excellent public relations can be achieved most easily in such a system.

In Fig. 2.2, the diagonal from bottom left to top right is a path to excellence, which shows that constraints and communication are correlated. Lateral, symmetrical communication is difficult, if not impossible, in the bottom right segment. Those who would try to introduce it would be lost in what we call the "Bermuda triangle" or even the "black hole" of public relations. Public relations

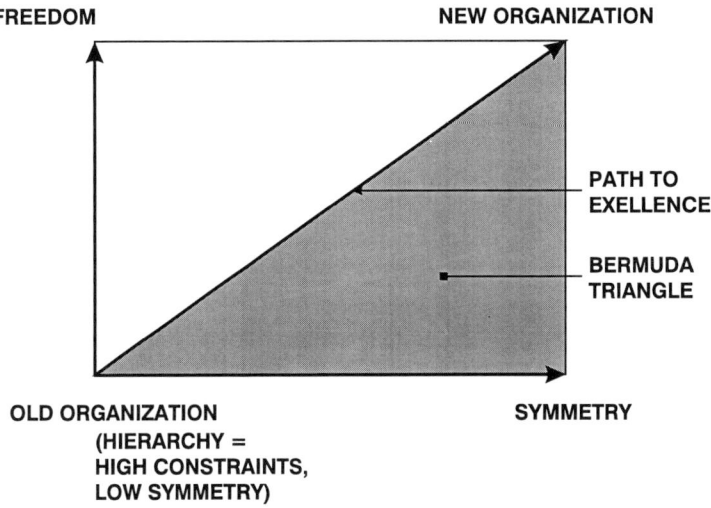

FIG. 2.2. The path to excellent public relations.

units that attempt excellent, symmetrical communication are sucked into this hole and never emerge because they try to introduce too much symmetry into communication before constraints have been removed.

The difference between hierarchically organized information systems and lateral communication systems is becoming of crucial importance. In psychology it has been advocated by de Bono (1990), in management by Drucker (1993). It is a major problem of artificial intelligence and of development of new generations of powerful computers (Kurzweil, 1990). We consider it to be a crucial contextual condition for professional public relations.

The history of organizational communication in Slovenia between World War II and the democratic elections in 1989 also shows such a change in organizational structure. Prior to 1989, public relations was not considered to be an acceptable concept for a socialist country. (According to Ivanov, 1993, the same was true for the former Soviet Union). Instead, organizations employed a different concept called "contacts with the public." The design of the department making contacts with the public was based on "the number and distribution of communists in an organization" (Dzinic, 1980, p. 187).

It is noteworthy that even the term public was not used in its plural form during socialist years. Officially, there were people's masses that formed only one public—the socialist public, which was defined as the "dictatorship of the proletariat." The plural "publics" came into the Slovenian language again only after the establishment of the Public Relations Society of Slovenia in 1990. That kind of linguistic constraint has been described in George Orwell's *1984* as "Newspeak"; and his book is, for that part, still the best analysis available of linguistic constraints in an authoritarian regime, for both authoritarian organizations and countries.

The concept of contacts with the public was developed by the information system school based at the Belgrade University, then the capital of the former Yugoslavia of which Slovenia was part until 1990, and introduced in Slovenia in 1962 by State Trade Unions, which in that year established the Worker's Information Center. In the same decade at the Ljubljana University, a group of professors, trained and influenced by Western professors, started to work on the establishment of a Communication Sciences Department. At the beginning of the 1970s, these professors were criticized by the Slovenian communist party for introducing western ideas, and communicationists lost to informationists until the end of 1980s when lateral communication was reinvented by the political opposition, which reconceptualized itself as the horizontal "civil society" against the vertical and hierarchical "political state."

Those who favor an international rather than global approach to public relations would consider contacts with publics to be a Slovenian national version of public relations. But it was not. For public relations is not about information, but communication. This conclusion suggests that the generic principles of public relations that we have defined in this paper cannot be employed or adjusted to a political system such as predemocratic Slovenia that constructs organizations in a rigid hierarchy and that uses propaganda to make people aware of the system of constraints on their behavior, especially on their communication behavior.

This conclusion, therefore, leaves our central proposition that there are generic principles of public relations that can be applied in every political-economic system subject to challenge. On the one hand, when public relations practitioners attempted to develop lateral communication in pre-democratic Slovenia, they were lost in the Bermuda Triangle of a communist state and of organizations with a similar structure and culture. The same fate no doubt would result for practitioners in many other countries with authoritarian, totalitarian, or communist political systems. On the other hand, public relations professionals who employed our generic principles have been successful in changing the political-economic system in Slovenia to a more democratic one, although they had to navigate their course carefully to avoid being lost in the Bermuda Triangle. In short, the generic principles do work in nondemocratic systems but they must be employed incrementally and slowly, and often must be couched in asymmetrical terms to avoid being swept to sea by "old" managers.

The Slovenian experience suggests that global public relations must be based on a professional culture and world view that allows practitioners to be aware of the systemic constraints on their thought and behavior. Every code of public relations ethics, national and international, incorporates certain human values that have both ethical and technical value. These values have little meaning unless lateral communication is considered to be at the core of what public relations professionals do. J. E. Grunig (1989) conceptualized this lateral communication as "symmetry," and this concept is at the center of the excellence theory we are testing in our research on Slovenian public relations. The values of lateral, symmetrical communication and their implementation seem, therefore, to be the basis of certain general principles that public relations must have to be a profession.

Political-economic systems provide strong constraints on the application of generic principles of public relations. Culture has a similar effect on thought and behavior. Next, we consider the effect of societal culture on public relations in general and on Slovenian public relations in particular.

THE CULTURAL CONTEXT OF EXCELLENT PUBLIC RELATIONS

Determining Culture

Virtually every public relations textbook alludes to the complications inherent in the process of communicating today. The increased mobility of many peoples, shifting patterns of immigration within individual societies, globalization of the economy, and increasingly sophisticated communication technologies all challenge professionals in public relations to communicate with culturally diverse publics.

Thus, we adopt a culture-specific approach to our study of global public relations. That is, we believe that culture matters in the way that organizations and their public relations departments function, even as those public relations departments employ generic principles of public relations. Hofstede (1980) equated culture with personality; he explained that culture is to society as personality is to the individual. In his study of 39 nations, he found both similarities and important differences in culture. So, we have come to reject the culture-free hypothesis, which argues that cultural effects on organizations across nations are relatively stable. As Tayeb (1988) said, scholars who look for such similarity do find it; however, they tend to ignore the critical cultural differences that may help explain organizational structure, managerial philosophy, and environmental impact.

But which elements of culture most influence the interaction between organizations and their publics? As Hall (1981) explained, the importance of the role of the cultural context is widely acknowledged yet rarely described adequately. He also believed that even when significant cultural insights emerge through adequate description, only rarely are they acted upon. In this chapter, we have focused our investigation on the cultural dimensions first identified by Hofstede (1980). Although other scholars (*e.g.*, Crozier & Thoening, 1976; Kluckhohn & Strodtbeck, 1961; Parsons & Shils, 1951; Tayeb, 1988) have emphasized different aspects of culture that may be equally meaningful, our intent was to conduct a comparative study.

Because Hofstede's cultural factors figured prominently in the conceptualization for the multicountry excellence study, we were able to juxtapose our findings in Slovenia against those of the United States, Canada, and the United Kingdom—the three countries encompassed by the excellence research. In the current study, we grouped these three together in large part because White's (1987; White, Hammonds & Kalupa, 1987; White & Trask, 1982) research on practitioners in the United States, Canada, and the United Kingdom found few differences among these groups, especially in terms of their preparation for the practice of public relations.

From his study of 39 countries, Hofstede (1980) identified four key cultural dimensions. The first, and perhaps most significant, is the continuum between *individualism and collectivism*. This dimension relates to intergroup processes; it consistently differentiates Eastern from Western cultures (Javidi & Javidi, 1991). The former are typically homogeneous and collectivistic; the latter, heterogeneous and individualistic. Yum (1994) considered East Asia's in-groupness and North America's individualism equally excessive. As early as the 1830s, de Tocqueville coined the term "individualism" to characterize American society. To Bellah, et al. (1985), individualism represents the core of American culture.

The United States, Great Britain, and Canada represent three of the four most individualistic cultures Hofstede (1980) studied. Although Hofstede also found that regions of the United States differ in their degree of individualism, Anderson (1994) argued that the extreme individualism of U.S. society on the whole makes it difficult for Americans to interact with and understand people from other cultures, especially cultures where interdependence rather than independence may determine a person's sense of self (Condon & Yousef, 1983).

Individualistic cultures stress personal goals; concern for oneself extends only to immediate members of the family. Personal achievement is supraordinate to the group. Collective cultures, on the other hand, value group goals above individual goals. They are characterized by interdependence and reciprocal obligations. For example, the community in such a culture cares for individuals in exchange for those individuals' loyalty to the group. Hui and Triandis (1986) suggested an important distinction within the collective pole: concern for a subgroup of people versus concern for the generalized collective of people.

Power distance, a second Hofstede dimension, reflects the extent to which power, prestige, and wealth are distributed disproportionately among people of different social strata or classes. The greater the concentration of power in a few elite members of the society, the greater the score on Hofstede's power-distance index (PDI).

Condon and Yousef (1983) distinguished among three cultural patterns within the context of power distance: democratic, authority-centered, and authoritarian. The PDI correlates positively and significantly with authoritarianism. Tayeb (1988) dealt with a cultural concept that also may be related to power distance—*interpersonal trust.* In studies of employees in England and in India, she found hostility and mistrust between managers and their subordinates. She attributed this distrust and antagonism to the class struggle in British society and to the Indian caste system, respectively.

Hofstede (1980) determined that the United States was slightly below the median in power distance. Yugoslavia, on the other hand, was a large power-distance country. Interestingly, Hofstede also found that latitude was a fundamental determinant of power distance. The nine countries with the lowest PDI were European democracies located at high latitudes. He hypothesized that Northern cultures may have to be more tolerant and less autocratic to ensure the cooperation necessary for survival in their harsh climates.

A third cultural dimension, *uncertainty avoidance,* refers to the extent to which a society can tolerate ambiguity. Lack of tolerance for uncertainty, which produces anxiety, often leads to formal codes of conduct in an effort to ensure uniformity among members of that culture. Risky, untested ideas are anathema. Cultures that do tolerate ambiguity, on the other hand, downplay bipolar language such as "black or white" and "right or wrong." Because the English language emphasizes bipolarity, Lieberman (1994) characterized U.S. culture as intolerant of ambiguity. Hofstede (1980), on the other hand, found American society to be relatively low (46) on his Uncertainty Avoidance Index (UAI). Thus, we have to consider several possibilities—low, moderate and high—for the United States in terms of the uncertainty avoidance.

The final Hofstede cultural dimension, *masculinity/femininity,* taps into the value society attaches to social roles based on gender. More specifically, Hofstede measured the extent to which people of both sexes in a culture endorse masculine or feminine traits. Many cultures have identified men as competitive, and assertive and women as nurturing and compassionate. As Sriramesh and White (1992) pointed out, though, this bipolar notion of masculinity and femininity is changing in Western societies.

Even in 1980, Hofstede determined that although it tended to be masculine, the United States was not among the nine most masculine countries he studied.[4] Still, he found that most countries are more feminine in terms of nurturance and caring. Further, Anderson (1994) contended that Americans of both sexes seem loud, aggressive, and competitive by global standards. We entered this research with a question mark about Slovenia, particularly on the gender factor. (The former Yugoslavia had tended toward a feminine world view.)

Hofstede's (1980) dimensions should allow us not only to enter the assumptive world of Slovenian culture but to begin to answer the question of whether effective public relations there is at all comparable to what works in cultures as different as the North American and the British cultures. However, by choosing this one approach to defining culture, we cannot make the claim of describing Slovenian culture comprehensively. Instead, we used Hofstede's attributes to

---

[4]The United Kingdom placed eighth out of 39 countries on Hofstede's scale of masculinity.

organize our insights in such a way as to render the Slovenian culture no longer incomprehensible to the majority of scholars in public relations—a group that, for the most part, has had little contact with this former Yugoslavian republic.

One further delimitation of our research is that we do not attempt to go beneath the surface description of Slovenian culture to explore the source of any differences between that culture and the cultures previously included in the excellence study. Yum (1994) made an excellent case for the need to overcome the tendency of most cross-cultural studies simply to describe "foreign" communication patterns and then compare them to North American models. In her analysis of the impact of Confucianism on interpersonal relationships in contemporary East Asia, she argued that one only can understand communication as a basic social process by studying the philosophical foundations of the culture in which it is found. Still, exploring the philosophical roots of Slovenian society is beyond the scope of this study.

Our purpose here is to overcome at least in part the limits of what can be experienced directly. Short of a direct cultural encounter with Slovenians or a deep understanding of the cultural roots of that society, scholars from other parts of the world should gain a useful understanding of the way Slovenians as a cultural group view the universe and thus develop a set of rules of behavior. Through our cultural analysis, we may be able to start overcoming the cultural parochialism that has characterized so much research in public relations to date.[5] And as Hall (1981) explained, interethnic communication also can be a source from which one discovers oneself.

In the review of literature that framed the excellence study (J. E. Grunig, 1992), we posited two propositions linking societal culture with public relations. (1) Cultures with low levels of power distance, authoritarianism, and individualism but with a high level of interpersonal trust among workers are most likely to develop excellent public relations practice. (2) Although rare, organizations operating in societal cultures without these characteristics may have excellent public relations if powerful individuals there foster participative organizational culture (Sriramesh & White, 1992, pp. 611–612). Our goal, then, was to describe Slovenian culture adequately to allow for subsequent testing of these propositions.

To generate this understanding, we probed what Barnlund (1994) called the "cultural unconscious" of three Slovenian colleagues (including one of the authors of this paper). Through lengthy personal interviews, we learned about the individual-collective continuum, power distance, uncertainty avoidance, and values attached to masculinity versus femininity there.

This kind of cultural exploration was necessary because Slovenia was not included in Hofstede's (1980) cultural analysis. As recently as 1991, Slovenia declared its independence from the former Yugoslavian Federation. Thus, al-

---

[5]For a deeper understanding of this problem, see Sriramesh and White (1992).

though we have cultural data for the three Western democracies included in the original excellence study, we needed to determine key aspects of Slovenian culture. We did so through our structured, audiotaped interviews.

In the process, we discovered just how complicated describing a given culture may be. In attempting to depict their culture in response to our questions, our Slovenian colleagues often disagreed.[6] Thus, what began as a series of predetermined questions designed to tap into the Hofstede cultural dimensions became a series of free-ranging discussions both between investigators and respondents and among the Slovenian participants themselves.

At times the discussion seemed awkward because of the divergence of opinions. When explaining the answers that were at odds with those of their colleagues, however, our participants gained what seemed to be a new and deeper understanding of their own context. Thus, we see that cultural myopia, born of inertia and habit, may be overcome both across international boundaries and within a single culture through the research process.

Also, through this process of self-reported cultural identification we could avoid the problem of *ascription,* by which outsiders enact a culture (Collier, 1994). Ascription too often results in stereotyping. Instead, we relied on *avowal,* the self-portrayal that results in a cultural representative saying "This is who I am" (Collier, 1994).

Understanding one's own culture may be as critical to effective public relations as understanding the key cultural variables that affect others' communication behavior. As Samovar and Porter (1994) put it, "Whatever the culture, you can better understand your behavior and the reactions of others if you realize that what you are hearing and seeing is a reflection of that culture" (p. 72). Thus, in this study of Slovenian culture, we discovered not only who others are but also what we are.

We must come to realize that we are influenced not only by our experience but by our culture as well. Thus, traveling to Slovenia and experiencing that culture firsthand undoubtedly would not lead to the same depiction of Slovenian culture as would result from those who are affected by what Samovar and Porter (1994) called the "cumulative deposits" of values, beliefs, and behaviors handed down from generation to generation of Slovenians. What the two U.S. authors would see there as visitors would, in turn, be influenced by our own North American cultural deposits.

Finally, we need to emphasize that within any dominant culture there exists a

---

[6]Part of the disagreement stemmed from confusion over the time frame involved. Culture is not static. Not only has Slovenian society changed dramatically over the last few years, but so have our individual participants in this research. At different ages, each participant was at a different life stage. As Pedersen and Pedersen (1994) explained, "Culture exists in people. . . . As our life space expands, our perceptions widen. We change, we become more aware, more knowledgeable, more skillful in adapting to our surroundings. The individual process of differentiation suggests change, mental diversification, and development" (p. 305).

multiplicity of cocultures. In the latest edition of their reader on intercultural communication, Samovar and Porter (1994) emphasized the need for effective communication between mainstream and cocultures. They included, as examples within U.S. society, a number of social communities that frequently conflict with the dominant culture: Hispanics, African Americans, disabled people, women, and gays and lesbians.

What we attempted to describe in this study is the *principal* culture in Slovenia. At the same time, we acknowledge that, as is true in most Western societies, there undoubtedly exist other domestic cultures. We also realize that even members of a single dominant culture may hold distinct values. This existence of competing values within a culture, in turn, necessitates what Folb (1994) called "intracultural communication."

Slovenian Culture and Public Relations

We began the process of codifying and integrating the results of structured interviews conducted in June and July 1993 by asking the principal owners of Pristop to assign a numerical score from 0 to 100 on Hofstede's indices of power distance, uncertainty avoidance, individualism, masculinity/femininity, and interpersonal trust among workers in Slovenia. The anchoring point for time was the establishment of the firm in 1990, which roughly coincided with the move toward democratization and ultimately independence in Slovenia. The numerical score served as a starting point for the discussion with the three participants in the qualitative methods used, rather than as a fixed measure of culture. Thus, the participants were free to revise their scores during the discussion or to suggest different scores for different times during the period from 1990 and 1993.

The three participants varied in their initial responses for what we determined were four main reasons. First, they agreed that change had begun to occur in all of the cultural dimensions since independence in their country; however, they did not agree on the extent of change nor on the exact point at which this transformation began. Second, we questioned whether the cultural dimensions could accommodate individual differences or only could describe the larger society. One of our three participants repeatedly reminded the group that this discussion should focus on the collective society; his colleagues, however, continued to think of individual or small-group deviations from what he considered the societal norm. Third, and as we mentioned earlier in this chapter, participants were at different life stages and thus viewed their societal culture through lenses colored at least in part by age. Fourth, and perhaps most obvious, these three men are individuals with distinct life experiences, characters, and personalities. Undoubtedly their frames of reference helped account for differences they saw even in a culture as seemingly homogeneous as Slovenia's.

Nevertheless, the participants in this research generally assigned values indicating that the Slovenian cultural characteristics are not conducive to excellent public relations, as conceptualized by Sriramesh and White (1992). And they did agree that because their society is anything but static, all of this can and will change.

We began this analysis with the dimension of *individualism*. Discussion of this property provoked the most dramatic differences in participants' responses. One rated Slovenian culture zero on individualism, reasoning that this former communist society continued to resonate with collectivist goals. Another chose the highest number possible, 100. He asserted that "Slovenian culture is extremely individualistic and competitive." He explained that today's workers think far less about the good of the organization and much more about themselves. He contended that they would be willing to work wherever the salary and benefits were best; they invest their emotions outside of the organization that employs them. And his firm, in its employee relations practice, has accommodated the fact that Slovenian individuals are trying to figure out their niche in the new society. He said: "Our experience is that when you try to explain the benefits of responsibility and things like that, you have to know how everything you say translates into individualistic terms. So, for example, you have to explain to the manager that *he* is the one who is going to gain from becoming more responsible."

Uncertainty avoidance either is increasing or decreasing in Slovenia, depending on which of our three research participants one believes. They agreed that their society falls at or slightly below the middle of the UAI—between 40 and 50. They disagreed, however, on whether that midpoint represents an increase or decrease in tolerance for ambiguity. Perhaps their difference of opinion can be explained in terms of the time frame they had in mind. As one explained, during the period immediately before independence in 1991, tolerance for ambiguity was much higher than ever before. In his words, "Everything was happening almost overnight."

Today, however, Slovenian society is increasingly uncomfortable with the uncertainty inherent in untested ideas or the lack of clear-cut rules. Our research participants explained that Slovenians avoid uncertainty because they are trying to protect their jobs, their salaries—whatever they have. People who are getting positions in the new, more unpredictable society would like to keep the *status quo*. One summed up the irony of this situation: "We are not a risk-taking society, that's for sure. We avoid it. We would like to have everything predictable, as the past was in a way—although we didn't like the past."

The *masculinity/femininity* dimension of Slovenian society produced the least discussion and the most consensus among all of the cultural characteristics we explored. Research participants agreed that before their firm was established, Slovenian culture tended toward the feminine (about 60 on the 100-point scale). As evidence to support this contention, they alluded to the high societal value placed on relationships. Now, they also agreed, Slovenian culture is becoming at least slightly more masculine as a result of the competition inherent in their new market economy.

Power distance tends to be high in Slovenian culture, as it had been in the former Yugoslavia. Our participants disagreed on just how high, but they did acknowledge that Slovenia is becoming less class oriented. Numbers cited for this dimension in 1990 ranged from 60 to 80. Today, they would assign a number closer to 30 or 40.

Before its independence, Slovenia had been characterized by very real social strata. As one participant put it, "We were very much ideologically equal but everybody understood what the hierarchy of the society was: the top political elite and the rest of society. Today [1993], there is more equality, especially in relationships between the government and trade unions." His two colleagues agreed that Slovenian culture in general is evolving toward lower social stratification.

On the other hand, for some considered elite there, stratification (at least in organizations) may be increasing. Although there was no consensus on this point, at least one of our participants contended that managers, in particular, enjoy more power than they ever had under the communist system. Another argued that the power that comes with ownership rather than managerial status is adding to his society's class consciousness. All three participants believed, though, that the level of power distance in Slovenia does not approach that of any Western democracy.

The related dimension of *interpersonal trust* among workers or between managers and workers clearly is declining in Slovenia. In 1990, we heard, the society would have been ranked at about 55 to 60 on this cultural attribute. Today, our participants agreed, they would rank it between 10 and 15. Personal trust is much lower among workers than it was; and as one person told us, "There is *no* trust between the government and trade unions."

This shift away from trust may be counterproductive for Slovenian society but it also may be good news for public relations there. One of our participants reacted to the proposition that "societal cultures that display lower levels of power distance, authoritarianism, and individualism, but have higher levels of interpersonal trust among workers, are most likely to develop . . . excellent public relations practices. . ." (Sriramesh & White, 1992, p. 611) as follows: "What you're describing is actually the difference between what Tonnies, the German sociologist, called the difference between *gemeinschaft* and *gesellschaft* societies.[7] So what you're saying is that actually you have a much better chance for excellent public relations in less-developed societies than in highly developed societies."

This research participant went on explain his reasoning in terms of the history of public relations: "When you have small communities, everybody knowing

---

[7]A *gemeinschaft* society is folk society based on small communities in which there are extensive interpersonal relationships. A *gesellschaft* society is a larger, more differentiated society with larger communities, a greater division of labor, and more specialized, impersonal relationships.

each other, there is no need for a specialized public relations function. It starts only at that time that differences are so great that you don't have all these personal relationships." In a *gemeinschaft* society, he explained, "you actually have no need for public relations because all of the differences between organizations and individuals are so low that you don't need a specialist function." He told us his colleagues and he entered the business at the time of decreasing trust among people in Slovenia—"at the time all these differences are getting bigger and the need for our business emerged at this time." He called this "our great opportunity."

"Aren't you talking about two different things," his Pristop colleague added, "the need for public relations" and the conditions that make excellent public relations easier to practice? He said that the cultural conditions identified by Sriramesh and White (1992) may make it easier to practice the generic principles of public relations but that the need for excellent public relations may be greatest when the cultural conditions are least favorable for their practice.

Predictably, this led to a discussion of ethics and professionalism. This exchange, in turn, provoked a critique of the Hofstede cultural dimensions themselves. One of the principals in the Pristop Group argued for analyzing public relations in Slovenia not from a cultural or social perspective but from an ethical, professional one. The danger of societal analysis, in his view, is that "it becomes a religion . . . a cultural wall."

Rather than analyzing what he considered "popular movements in society," this agency head suggested the criterion of ethics—what he termed "our model of excellence." One of his colleagues agreed that cultural analysis is problematic, especially in the development of general propositions that work on the level of society. He explained, "It's exactly because we're so *different* than others in the market that we're making money. We have our own ethics, our own professional standards. We are successful just because we have professional rules."

At this point, then, we interject a cautionary note about the study of culture as a basis for analyzing organizational processes. Perhaps, as our Slovenian colleagues suggested, such stark alternatives as individualism and collectivism or class consciousness and egalitarianism may reflect false choices. Sociologist James Davison Hunter (1994), writing about the reinvention of democracy to reflect the circumstances of each new generation of Americans, considered the debate over characterizing culture artificially polarized. Given the foregoing discussion in Ljubljana, we tend to agree. We have come to understand that in Slovenia the renewal of democratic life—along with its institutions, organizations, and day-to-day practices—is a transformative process that is ongoing and dynamic rather than fixed and static.

In fact, the importance of what our Slovenian colleagues called professional rules and standards suggests that the practice of excellent, professional public relations may introduce a professional culture into the interaction between societal culture and public relations. Whereas Sriramesh and White's (1992) propositions suggest that societal culture shapes public relations, our Slovenian colleagues suggested that a professional public relations culture may loosen the grip of societal culture on practitioners, freeing them to help transform that larger culture. In fact, the concept of generic principles of public relations suggests a common set of values and theories that may underlie a global culture of public relations that exists as a coculture in the specific societies in which practitioners work.

At this point, however, individualism, power distance and uncertainty avoidance tend to be high in Slovenian society. These dimensions gradually are becoming more favorable for effective communication. By contrast, interpersonal trust is diminishing among workers; and the culture, which had been relatively feminine, is becoming increasingly masculine with the advent of capitalism.

In spite of these cultural barriers, our three participants agreed that excellent public relations is possible in Slovenia. They also supported the second Sriramesh and White (1992) proposition, that organizations operating in societal cultures without these characteristics may have excellent public relations if powerful individuals there foster participative *organizational* cultures. The secret, they said, is in finding the "levels of tolerance that every society has"—the latitude of acceptance into which the generic principles can be applied. One explained, "When managers come to this limit of tolerance, they would like us to help them get back into this latitude of acceptance."

APPLICATION OF THE GENERIC PRINCIPLES IN SLOVENIA

This analysis of the political-economic and cultural conditions in which global public relations practitioners must work in different countries shows that the nine generic principles of public relations probably cannot be applied in a political system based on constraints and propaganda. However, the Slovenian case suggests that it may not be necessary to remove all political constraints—either those imposed by government at the societal level or imposed by management at the organizational level—before lateral communication (symmetrical public relations) can be introduced incrementally as a means of further reducing constraints. Culture, on the other hand, may hinder excellent public relations less than the political system, as long as public relations programs do not violate the latitude of cultural acceptance in a society.

Given these conclusions about the two specific variables, we asked our three participants to discuss whether the nine principles of excellence were indeed generic principles that could be applied in Slovenia. The participants immediately pointed out that the principles are normative rather than positive principles. They said that the principles describe how their firm practices public relations but that they do not describe how most other practitioners behave in

Slovenia. In fact, they added, it is these principles that have made their firm different from, and more successful than, other practitioners in that country. "If we didn't practice in this way, we wouldn't exist at all," one said.

In contrast to many public relations practitioners around the world, these three practitioners did not open their firm until they developed a knowledge base for their work. Two of them traveled to London where they met with the British Public Relations Institute and with "an advanced small agency" working in employee communication. They added that they also used the knowledge gained from meeting the two American authors of this chapter—in Verčič's trip to the United States in 1992 and in the Grunigs' three subsequent trips to Slovenia. In essence, then, Pristop has become a experiment in the use of the generic principles of excellence in public relations.

One of the respondents reported that three of the principles have been especially important in the success of their firm:

1. Power of the public relations function: "We have found out that the only way we can do what are doing is by having direct communication with CEOs. If we work at the highest level of the hierarchy, we are successful with our programs; otherwise we fail."
2. Professional knowledge: "The knowledge we have is a simple prerequisite for what we do. Otherwise, we could not even think about what we would like to do."
3. Separation from other functions: "We are striving not to get integrated into other functions. We couldn't discuss what we are discussing with our clients if we were integrated with marketing. We wouldn't have the special perspective of public relations."

Another of the Pristop directors emphasized the importance of a symmetrical system of employee communication:

Under the old system, management was required by law to keep employees informed so that they could make decisions. Since that system collapsed, nothing has been invented to replace the system of information, and the ties between management and the workers completely disappeared. They are two separate sectors now. They don't communicate with each other at all. Two years ago, we set up a project team to bring some new ideas to employee communication, something beside the employee newsletter. We redesigned completely the concept of the newsletter. Previously, the company newsletter was pure dissemination of information from the top down. We now have introduced upward processes as well. The newsletter was only the beginning. Now we have introduced bulletin boards, focus groups, small groups, and that sort of thing.

Another director added that strategic management of public relations is important but that few Slovenian managers understand the general concept of strategic management. His colleague added, "They cannot practice strategic management in the way we would like them to do because of their background, their expertise, their training, their education." Pristop, therefore, must often counsel clients on strategic management as well as on public relations. In essence, another said, they become management counselors as well as public relations counselors:

> In one case, we were trying to help a client think through who its most important publics were, and we started by asking where they made their profit. They couldn't give us an answer to that question. They were involved in 100 or more services. It took us nearly six months to help them actually to determine where they're making and losing money. In such cases, we are involved in some kind of intelligence or research for the company that has nothing to do with PR directly, but is a precondition for making good PR decisions.

The three respondents also were asked what if any principles they would add to the list of nine generic principles we explored with them. They added one. Ethics and integrity are especially important aspects of excellent public relations in Slovenia, they said, because of the low level of accountability and responsibility required of managers in an economic system that no longer is owned by government and still is not accountable to private stockholders. Corporate managers often seek public relations advice, they said, when accused of irresponsibility even though they have no intention of changing their behavior to make it more responsible. Taking on such a client leads only to a loss of credibility for the public relations firm, the respondents said. "We are trying to sell integrity, and for us it works very well," one director said. "If I try to bribe the media, I am out of business," another added.

Specific Applications of the Generic Principles

The three directors of Pristop, therefore, confirmed the generic character of the excellence principles. They did report nine specific adjustments they had to make to apply the principles in Slovenia.

1. Organizations generally have only technicians rather than managers working in their public relations departments. In addition, these practitioners have little visibility to top management. Practitioners "lack confidence because they question their own knowledge . . . often for legitimate reasons." Many are "happy not to be a part of the dominant coalition because they are afraid of failure." The situation is compounded, the three participants said, because management is overwhelmingly authoritarian. Therefore, Pristop begins by working on what they called the "infrastructure" and "visibility" of the public relations department. They make sure in-house practitioners attend Pristop's meetings with managers; they help the in-house practitioners develop strategic plans and produce public relations materials that will make them more visible. As the

relationship with a client matures, then, Pristop serves more of a counseling role and provides fewer technical products. "We are more profitable if we can sell our brains and strategy," one director said.

2. Knowledge of excellent public relations is, therefore, extremely important for Pristop employees and for the in-house practitioners they work to empower in client organizations. However, few knowledgeable practitioners are available in Slovenia; and public relations education did not exist before the firm was founded. To compensate, Pristop has worked closely with the University of Ljubljana to develop a public relations curriculum and has offered to provide funding for the program. Pristop also offers short courses for current practitioners to increase their knowledge base, and its directors were instrumental in founding the Slovenian Public Relations Society. Pristop employees are funded for travel to international professional conferences. Finally, Pristop has the largest public relations library in Slovenia, which is made available to other practitioners and to university students and faculty.

3. Female practitioners in Slovenia receive less respect from senior managers than their male counterparts, especially if they are young. Clients have asked Pristop "not to send a female but to send someone who is more serious." If the in-house practitioner is a woman, the problems of visibility and respect by senior management are compounded. Sometimes, it is necessary to put a man's name or the name of an older person on a proposal or to have an older man make a presentation. Experience and success—"time and results"—help to empower women, the Pristop directors said. "Although these small changes may not have much effect at the societal level," one participant added, "they can make a difference for individuals."

4. Client relationships are especially important in Slovenia. "We realize there are only a few companies in Slovenia that can afford to hire us. Unlike in the U.S. where public relations firms believe they can always get new clients, we need to develop a long-term relationship with a client if we are to remain profitable." Often Pristop has an initial contract with a client because of "some kind of crisis. We may work with a client on a short-time contract for a year or more, but then we try to move to a more long-term strategic contract."

5. Clients usually are unwilling to pay for formative and evaluative research if it is billed as a separate item in a contract. To overcome this obstacle, Pristop includes research as part of the overall program when the first contract is negotiated. Media analysis, for example, is part of every media relations program. Clients, however, often cannot "even imagine what results they can get from research. They say, 'We are buying your expertise, why do you need to do research?'" When a client is unwilling to include research as a standing cost, Pristop sometimes does the research as part of its own cost. When clients see the value of the research, many then become willing to pay for it.

6. Many Slovenian organizations have not experienced activist pressure. To incorporate the demands of activists into strategic planning, therefore, Pristop

organizes the opposition to communicate with its clients. According to one director: ". . . for maybe four or five major disputes it was not the activist group that organized themselves. Some of the major players would take advantage because the activists have no tradition of organizing themselves." His colleague explained why it has been necessary to organize the opposition:

> We have organized the activists so that management gets the other side organized to talk with. Because the basic problem at the beginning is who is representing whom? If you have several hundred people on the other side, say in some local community, you've got to talk. We help to organize the other side so that at least you can engage in negotiations. Otherwise, there is no one with whom you can negotiate.

At times, the firm has brought in environmental activists from outside to work with the group opposing the client and to do research on the problem. The outside groups "served as our consultant."

7. Organizations often request consultation from Pristop because of adverse publicity in the media or because of a crisis. Generally, the adverse publicity occurs because of poor relationships with community, employee, or governmental publics. Pristop initially helps the client counteract the adverse publicity by placing news stories in the media that present the client's position on the controversy. After the media problem is resolved, however, Pristop advises the client on how to resolve the underlying relationship problems that produced the adverse publicity. A media crisis situation, therefore, becomes a mechanism for introducing strategic management and the two-way symmetrical model to the public relations function of a client organization. In one case, for example, employees were producing anonymous newsletters that were critical of management. One participant explained:

> We first helped to open communication between the editor and the CEO, which made it easier for the editor to get information about what was going on in the company. That was actually what I consider two-way symmetrical relations between the company and the media. But then we explained to the CEO that his problem was not the anonymous newsletters, because they are only symptoms, but that he obviously has problems with his employees. At least in words, he was absolutely willing to devote resources to symmetrical communication within the company. He actually was willing to devote resources to research, to communication audits.

Another director explained that the best clients generally are those who came to them because of a crisis. "Crises are very helpful," he added.

8. The first step in working with a client must be establishing a definition of public relations—to inculcate a *world view* of public relations as a two-way symmetrical, managerial function. "Most have heard that public relations is important for their success, but they don't know what it is." The directors said

that they "were fortunate because most managers do not know what public relations is." In most countries, one added, clients might have "predefinitions" of public relations as propaganda, marketing communication, or media relations alone. If these predefinitions existed in Slovenia, he said, "I would not be able to use the knowledge I have. If the CEO believed he only had media relations problems, that would mean we would not even get the opportunity to go further." The other director added, "That is why we have been able to succeed in a relatively short period of time."

9. The two-way symmetrical model can be practiced in Slovenia, but it must be introduced incrementally—in combination with the two-way asymmetrical model as the mixed motive model:

> It is quite easy to get the CEO, at least in his words, to agree that a symmetrical strategy is the best one. It's only that the whole society around him, and his personality, are so far away from it that it's very hard to get him to understand symmetry. As a result, we have to transform him. You have to sell him symmetrical propositions in asymmetrical language.

The other director added:

> The problem is how to get the authority to start practicing [the two-way symmetrical model]. We basically are authorized to enter . . . to open a relationship between a company and somebody else. We open the channels, so to say. The problem then is to get some benefit for the company from that relationship. If they have that experience, then it's much easier to work further. Still, it's a problem because we are talking about two different things. One is how we work for them and the other is how they operate in other areas. They might actually operate very symmetrically in the very small part under our control, but all the rest is still completely asymmetrical.

The first director elaborated:

> On the one hand, they do listen to us. But on the other hand they have this split personality . . . Dr. Jekyll and Mr. Hyde in a way. They are very cooperative in many ways. But the other side of their ego says, "Why should I do this? What is in it for me?" Gradually, they will start shifting more to what we want them to do.

Effectiveness of the Generic Principles

The Pristop directors were asked, finally, for evidence that their work—and thus the generic principles—had been effective in Slovenia. They gave examples at three levels—the level of individual programs, the success of their client organizations, and the success of their own firm.

On the program level, the Pristop directors said evaluation research has supported the effectiveness of their work. For media relations, for example, Pristop has set up a sophisticated media-monitoring system to evaluate its work. One client, who contracted Pristop because of a crisis, "could not even enter the media before they approached us. We played a two-way symmetrical game with the media to allow them to enter. After 4 months, our media-monitoring system showed that they became the most quoted source in the media."

At the level of organizational effectiveness, the same director cited the case of a two-way symmetrical community relations program for a chemical company, for which the firm won an IABC/Europe award. He said the company would not have been able to begin building a plant without the symmetrical public relations program:

> We didn't need to do research . . . it's obvious we succeeded because the plant is being built. This client obviously had tremendous benefits. We can't say how much money it would have cost if the plant could had not been built because it is under construction. The fact that they're staying with us shows that they perceive that they are benefitting. We have many clients who have been with us for years.

He added that all of Pristop's clients are growing. At the time of the interviews, most were the second company in their industry. Most have entered their markets recently in competition with dominant, often previously monopolistic companies.

These benefits for clients also have made Pristop tremendously successful. After 2 1/2 years of practice, the firm had over $3 million in billings, according to one director. The other added that the growth rate from 1991 to 1992 was 800%. He said, "If we had performed PR in any other way than we did, we would not have been as successful."

CONCLUSIONS

Research on and participant observation of the introduction of normative, generic principles of public relations in Slovenia confirm that public relations can be global rather than international. The research there suggests that the principles of excellent public relations provide the basis for a global set of public relations principles that can be applied in most cultures and political systems—the basis of a professional coculture. Nevertheless, the generic principles cannot be applied without strategic research to adjust them to different cultures and political systems. And they are extremely difficult to apply in a centralized, authoritarian, or totalitarian political-economic system in which propaganda, rather than two-way, lateral, communication, is used to instill awareness of constraints that disable the communication behavior of publics. If applied carefully and incrementally, however, the generic principles can change the political system and societal culture that make the application of the principles difficult.

REFERENCES

Anderson, G. (1989). A global look at public relations. In B. Cantor (Ed.), *Experts in action: Inside public relations* (2nd ed., pp. 412–422). New York: Longman.

Anderson, P. (1994). Explaining intercultural differences in nonverbal communication. In L. A. Samovar & R. E. Porter (Eds.), *Intercultural communication: A reader* (pp. 229–239). Belmont, CA: Wadsworth.

Arendt, H. (1973). *The origins of totalitarianism.* New York: Harcourt Brace Jovanovich.

Arnauld, A., & Nicole, P. (1964). *The art of thinking; Port-Royal Logic* (translated, with an introduction by J. Dickoff & P. James). Indianapolis: Bobbs-Merrill.

Barnlund, D. C. (1994). Communication in a global world. In L. A. Samovar & R. E. Porter (Eds.), *Intercultural communication: A reader* (pp. 26–36). Belmont, CA: Wadsworth.

Bellah, R., Madsen, R., Sullivan, W., Swidler, A., & Tipton, S. (1985). *Habits of the heart: Individualism and commitment in American life.* New York: Harper & Row.

Bernays, E. L. (1928). *Propaganda.* New York: Horace Liveright.

Brinkerhoff, D. W., & Ingle, M. D. (1989). Integrating blueprint and process: A structured flexibility approach to development management. *Public Administration and Development, 9,* 487–503.

Collier, M. J. (1994). Cultural identity and intercultural communication. In L. A. Samovar & R. E. Porter (Eds.), *Intercultural communication: A reader* (pp. 36–45). Belmont, CA: Wadsworth.

Condon, J. C., & Yousef, F. (1983). *An introduction to intercultural communication.* Indianapolis: Bobbs-Merrill.

Crozier, M., & Thoening, J. C. (1976). The regulation of complex organized systems. *Administrative Science Quarterly, 21,* 547–570.

de Bono, E. (1990). *Lateral thinking: A textbook of creativity.* New York and London: Penguin.

Drucker, P. F. (1993). *Post-capitalist society.* Oxford, UK: Butterworth–Heinemann.

Dzinic, F. (1980). *Komunikologija: Sociokibernetika in psihosociologija informiranja in komuniciranja v samoupravni druzbi in zdruzenem delu (Communication science: Sociocybernetics and psychosociology of information and communication in self-managerial society and associated labor).* Ljubljana: Delavska enotnost.

Ehling, W. P. (1985). Application of decision theory in the construction of a theory of public relations management. *Public Relations Research and Education 2(1):* 4–22.

Folb, E. A. (1994). Who's got the room at the top? Issues of dominance and nondominance in intracultural communication. In L. A. Samovar & R. E. Porter (Eds.), *Intercultural communication: A reader* (pp. 131–139). Belmont, CA: Wadsworth.

Gruban, B., Verčič, D., & Zavrl, F. (1994, January). Odnosi z javnostmi v Sloveniji/Public relations in Slovenia. *Pristop,* special issue.

Grunig, J. E. (1976). Organizations and public relations: Testing a communication theory. *Journalism Monographs, 46.*

Grunig, J. E. (1989). Symmetrical presuppositions as a framework for public relations theory. In C. H. Botan and V. Hazleton, Jr. (Eds.), *Public relations theory (pp. 17–44).* Hillsdale, NJ: Lawrence Erlbaum Associates.

Grunig, J. E. (Ed.). (1992). *Excellence in public relations and communication management.* Hillsdale, NJ: Lawrence Erlbaum Associates.

Grunig, J. E., & Grunig, L. A. (1992). Models of public relations and communication. In J. E. Grunig (Ed.), *Excellence in public relations and communication management* (pp. 285–325). Hillsdale, NJ: Lawrence Erlbaum Associates.

Grunig, J. E., Grunig, L. A., Dozier, D. M., Ehling, W. P., Repper, F., & White, J. (1991, September). *Excellence in public relations and communication management: Initial Data Analysis.* San Francisco: IABC Research Foundation.

Grunig, J. E., Grunig, L. A., Sriramesh, K., Huang, Y. H., & Lyra, A. (1995). Models of public relations in an international setting. *Journal of Public Relations Research, 7,* 163–186.

Grunig, J. E., & Hunt, T. (1984). *Managing public relations.* New York: Holt, Rinehart and Winston.

Grunig, J. E., & White, J. (1992). The effect of workviews on public relations theory and practice. In J. E. Grunig (Ed.), *Excellence in public relations and communication management* (pp. 31–64). Hillsdale, NJ: Lawrence Erlbaum Associates.

Hall, E. T. (1981). *Beyond culture.* Garden City, NY: Doubleday.

Hellweg, S. A. (1989, May). *The application of Grunig's symmetry-asymmetry public relations models to internal communication systems.* Paper presented at the meeting of the International Communication Association, San Francisco.

Hofstede, G. (1980). *Culture's consequences: International differences in work-related values.* Beverly Hills, CA: Sage.

Hui, C. H., & Triandis, H. C. (1986). Individualism-collectivism: A study of cross-cultural research. *Journal of Cross-Cultural Psychology, 17,* 225–248.

Hunter, J. D. (1994). *Before the shooting begins: Searching for democracy in America's culture war.* New York: Free Press.

Ingrami, L. (1992). Knowing your partner. *Management centre Europe, global management 1992: Annual review of international management practice* (Vol. 8, pp. 275–279). London: Sterling Publications International.

Ivanov, V. (1993). From propaganda to public relations. *Newsletter of the European Association of Public Relations Education and Research, 1*(3), 8–10.

Javidi, A., & Javidi, M. (1991, Summer/Fall). Cross-cultural analysis of interpersonal bonding: A look at East and West. *Howard Journal of Communications, 3,* 129–138.

Katz, D., Cartwright, D., Eldersveld, S., & Lee, A. M. (Eds.). (1954). *Public opinion and propaganda: A book of readings.* New York: Holt, Rinehart and Winston.

Kluckhohn, F., & Strodtbeck, F. (1961). *Variations in value orientations.* Evanston, IL: Row, Peterson.

Kneale, W., & Kneale, M. (1986). *The development of logic.* London: Oxford University Press.

Kurzweil, R. (1990). *The age of intelligent machines.* Cambridge, MA: MIT Press.

Lieberman, D. A. (1994). Ethnocognitivism, problem solving, and hemisphericity. In L. A. Samovar & R. E. Porter (Eds.), *Intercultural communication: A reader* (pp. 178–193). Belmont, CA: Wadsworth.

Massy, W. F., & Weitz, B. A. (1977). A normative theory of market segmentation. In F. M. Nicosia & Y. Wind (Eds.), *Behavioral models for market analysis: Foundations for marketing action* (pp. 121–144). Hinsdale, IL: Dryden.

Orwell, G. (1949). *1984.* New York: Harcourt Brace.

Parsons, T., & Shils, E. A. (1951). *Toward a general theory of action.* Cambridge, MA: Harvard University Press.

Pedersen, A., & Pedersen, P. (1994). Counseling and culture. In L. A. Samovar & R. E. Porter (Eds.), *Intercultural communication: A reader* (pp. 305–311). Belmont, CA: Wadsworth.

Samovar, L. A., & Porter, R. E. (Eds.). (1994). *Intercultural communication: A reader.* Belmont, CA: Wadsworth.

Sriramesh, K., & White, J. (1992). Societal culture and public relations. In J. E. Grunig (Ed.), *Excellence in public relations and communication management* (pp. 597–614). Hillsdale, NJ: Lawrence Erlbaum Associates.

Tayeb, M. H. (1988). *Organizations and national culture: A comparative analysis.* London: Sage.

Weick, K. E. (1969). *The social psychology of organizing.* Reading, MA: Addison-Wesley.

White, J. (1987). *Professional development needs of UK public relations practitioners.* London: Institute of Public Relations.

White, J., Hammonds, L., & Kalupa, F. (1987, August). *Professional development needs of U.S.*

public relations practitioners. Paper presented at the meeting of the Association for Education in Journalism and Mass Communication, San Antonio, TX.

White, J., & Trask, G. (1982). *Professional development needs of Canadian public relations practitioners*. Halifax, Nova Scotia: Dalhousie University, Canadian Public Relations Society and Advanced Management Centre.

Yum, J. O. (1994). The impact of Confucianism on interpersonal relationships and communication patterns in East Asia. In L. A. Samovar & R. E. Porter (Eds.), *Intercultural communication: A reader* (pp. 75–86). Belmont, CA: Wadsworth.

Zeman, Z. A. B. (1964). *Nazi propaganda*. New York: Oxford University Press.

3
Strategic Cooperative Communities: A Synthesis of Strategic, Issue Management, and Relationship-Building Approaches in Public Relations

Laurie J. Wilson
Brigham Young University

The American business management community is in crisis and with it, all ancillary functions such as public relations and issue management, that have become strategic to the organization. The root of the crisis is a failure of the traditional rationalist and number-oriented management approach which has dominated American business for decades (Wilson, 1994a, 1994b). Business management consultants Thomas J. Peters and Robert H. Waterman (1984) commented on the prevailing model:

> Professionalism in management is regularly equated with hard-headed rationality.... The numerative, rationalist approach to management dominates the business schools. It teaches us that well-trained professional managers can manage anything. It seeks detached, analytical justification for all decisions. It is right enough to be dangerously wrong, and it has arguably led us seriously astray.
>
> It doesn't tell us what the excellent companies have apparently learned.... It doesn't show . . . that "good managers make meanings for people, as well as money." (p. 29)

As American business has expanded into the international sphere, it has become clear that the United States does not have a corner on wealth creation in a capitalist economy. The process of wealth creation, or the approach to the management of business and organizations, varies as cultures vary. Further, it has become obvious that, even within our own culture, the short-term, profit-driven method of wealth creation, which was the tonic fostering unprecedented growth, is now the prescription for failure at home and abroad.

In their book, *The Seven Cultures of Capitalism,* Charles Hampden-Turner and Alfons Trompenaars (1993) reported on extensive quantitative and qualitative research among 15,000 upper-middle managers from the major capitalist powers in the world. They identified seven "valuing processes," moral decisions originating in culture and underlying the approach to wealth creation in a society. The authors concluded that "something is out of kilter in the Anglo-American business community" (p. 1) and identified the culprit in "the prominence of the value-empty discipline of Economics" (p. 4) that is "so concerned with counting and itemizing that it has lost sight of the one component, also unmeasurable, that makes all economic activity possible: human relationships" (p. 5).

Hampden-Turner and Trompenaars (1993) discussed the circular nature of the resolution of the values of individualism (a primary value of American and British systems) and communitarianism (a value that distinguishes European and Japanese systems). They contended that Adam Smith's argument that concentrating on individual self-interest means business automatically serves customers and society better has the status of physical law in Britain and the United States. This perspective puts the individual first. European and Japanese cultures, on the other hand, believe that, if the needs of the community are considered first, Adam Smith's invisible hand will automatically take care of the individual.

While the two opposite applications of this economic theory basic to capitalism have been equally effective in developing strong wealth-creation systems in the past century in relatively discrete societies, they come into conflict as those societies enter the global business environment. Further, the self-first application becomes woefully inadequate, especially as societies, individually and as global entities, emerge as more complex and intertwined organisms requiring a communitarian approach to problem solving.

It appears that the current dominant strategic-management approach to public relations has purchased passage on a sinking ship. Yet, four trends in society should have led us to our roots in communication and relationships instead of causing us to align with rationalist business management methods. These four trends are:

1. Increasingly segmented publics requiring alternatives to traditional media channels for the dissemination of messages;

2. Business turning to communicators as relationship specialists to succeed where management techniques have failed in controlling a business environment heavily burdened with social problems;

3. A work force whose productivity is seriously affected by social problems;

4. A more knowledgeable and business-savvy public that is demanding commitment of corporate resources to solving problems that are affecting employees and their families (Wilson, 1994b).

The trends should have sparked recognition that the truly strategic role of public relations in today's organization and society is not to manipulate the environment with a bottom-line mentality, but rather to build bridges and relationships with publics to create an environment in which the organization thrives over time. The first approach suffers from the kind of short-term strategy that has rendered much of the American business community unable to compete with its foreign counterparts. The second is a visionary, long-term approach to public relations.

Inasmuch as issues management and public relations have become part of the rationalist, strategic management approach to business with its roots in economics and self-first methodology, we have abdicated our greatest potential contribution to business in the process of wealth creation; establishing and maintaining the relationships necessary for organizations to thrive over the long term.

THE EVOLUTION OF APPROACHES TO PUBLIC RELATIONS

The history of public relations in the United States is the evolution of its principal functions; press agentry, publicity, and counseling (Wilcox, Ault, & Agee, 1989). Yet, those functions have been dictated largely by the political, economic, and resultant business environments, and shaped by continually advancing technology and societal change (Cutlip, Center, & Broom, 1985). Workers in the field emerged initially as press agents and publicists. By midcentury, public relations practitioners were organizational counselors. In this era, responding to the assumptions and practices of our business employers, we engaged in manipulating the organization's environment, often in ways that might now be considered ethically questionable.

What we did not recognize then, and many still do not recognize now, is that manipulation of publics spells eventual failure for any organization. Environmental manipulation has failed to acknowledge that publics are made up of living, breathing, somewhat intelligent individuals who have concerns that may conflict with an organization's operation. As a result of conflicts over issues important to those publics, crises have inevitably occurred and organizations have turned to public relations counselors to handle them, primarily through the media.[1] Crisis communication became one of the key functions of public relations.

When crisis communication began to consume more and more of practitioners' time, and as concern for the impact of crises on the organization grew, public relations began to look ahead, to anticipate and plan for crises. We entered the crisis-management stage of public relations. Reactive crisis communication

---

[1]Examples of conflicts and crises abound, some handled well and others poorly. The Tylenol crisis is the classic example of responsible crisis communication. Exxon has been severely criticized for its handling of communication and public relations during the Valdez oil spill.

was not enough; management concepts were applied to prepare organizations for events that might occur, affecting their environments and the profitability of their operations.

Public relations had begun to look longer range, and issue management to avoid crises was naturally born.[2] Although conceived as a long-term approach to identification and resolution of problems before they become crises, the very concept of issue management has lent itself well to the adoption of traditional American business management techniques. The proactive pattern of public issue management identified by Buchholz (1985) is indicative of this phenomenon. Organizations influence change by controlling the environments in which issues emerge and are discussed. Although another of Buchholz's patterns, the interactive approach, recognizes a need to accommodate some public expectations, the focus is still on meeting organizational needs rather than on serving the community and society better.

Labeled strategic management, issue management techniques evaluate proposed action through focus on the short-term bottom line. Even though issues are identified years in advance and mediated, as depicted in Hainsworth's issue cycle (1990), the purpose is to save the organization from future difficulty, not to address the needs of organizational publics because they are intrinsically valued. This focus brought practitioners squarely into the camp of rationalist business management, and that is where many of our short-sighted colleagues thought we should be.

It is not surprising that we ended up in this position. Trends and stages in the history of public relations have consistently edged away from a "relations" orientation. In fact, the very term public relations has suffered disrepute, perhaps, because of the emptiness of the promise implied. Our recognition of the limitations of mass communication and mass media has been slow; change from the use of mass media to more targeted media has been slower still. For example, Cutlip, et al. wrote in 1985 that "the driving force in contemporary practice has been the onrush of the Information Age" (p. 51). Elsewhere, they typified the current era as the:

> Era of Information Society, 1965 to the present, with its accelerating high technology, multiplying channels of communication, and the transition from a national economy to a world economy which involves global competition and turbulence. Stresses from these profound changes place ever heavier burdens on [public relations] and its role in mediating conflicts of interest to bring about adjustment and accommodation. (p. 32)

The entire description of public relations in today's society was addressed in the context of business, economics, and competition. The dramatic changes in

---

[2]The study and practice of issue management was the subject of a special 1990 issue of *Public Relations Review* (16:1). For an overview of the literature in public relations issue management, see particularly Heath and Cousino (1990).

society and publics were ignored entirely, yet those are the very trends that are effecting shifts in business management approaches. Further, relationships are only indirectly addressed in terms of the need to "bring about adjustment and accommodation." In their 1994 edition, Cutlip, Center, and Broom change that to read "mutual adjustment and accommodation" (p. 100). However, these authors still maintain that the dominant forces of change are technology and economy, almost ignoring the changes in society, people, and audiences as shaping our field and our history.

As a reaction to the blatant bottom-line orientation of strategic management, other scholars have recently attempted to reestablish public relations as relationship building. Those in the feminist school (i.e., Creedon, 1991) demonstrate the value of relational traits of communication as a foundation for public relations. Another valuable contribution is a community relations model based on symbolic interaction and the work of the scholars in the Chicago School (Kruckeberg & Starck, 1988).

These alternative voices have returned to the roots of human communication and persuasion in devising approaches that build more personal relationships based on trust and cooperation, viewing relational communication (Anderson & Meyer, 1988) as more currently applicable than mass communication, and interpretive communities within demographic publics (Lindloff, 1988) as better determinants of message relevance than source intentionality. To reinforce the value of this approach, American business, having failed to "manage" parts of the external environment and issues upon which it is attacked by activist publics through use of its rationalist, numerative approach, has increasingly turned to those who should be the relationship specialists, the organization's communicators, to build cooperation with its key publics.

SETTING UP THE DIALECTIC: THE FAILURES OF BOTH STRATEGIC MANAGEMENT AND RELATIONSHIP BUILDING

The limitations of the strategic management approach to public relations and issue management are in its tie to the traditional, rationalist business management approach of the last several decades (Wilson, 1994a, & 1994b). Nevertheless, that approach made sense in what had been a prevailing mood, in American business, and in public relations, to control the environment and organizational influences to maintain or increase bottom-line profits (Grunig, 1993; Grunig & Hunt, 1984; Grunig and Repper, 1992). It was justified, as was the rationalist approach to business management, in the construct of "society," as defined by German sociologist Ferdinand Tonnies (1887/1957, 1971).

In the late 1800s, Tonnies developed a typology of community and society. He predicted the attributes of community sacrificed to obtain the society that enabled business to thrive and the material quality of life to soar. According to Tonnies, "community" is based on relationships and moral values. It is a consensus of wills, resting on harmony and "ennobled by folkways, mores, and religion" (Tonnies, 1971, p. 146). "Society," on the other hand, is "based upon a union of rational wills—rests on convention and agreement, is safeguarded by political legislation, and finds its ideological justification in public opinion" (Tonnies, 1971, p. 146). Society's institutionalization of processes and actions, and its legalization, are designed to remove human subjectivity and to enhance fairness.

Society was necessary for America's particular approach to growth in a capitalist economy and the accompanying technological advancement and affluence enjoyed in the United States. At the same time, Tonnies believed that the transition to society required relinquishing community—our connectedness and cooperative relationships. The result was the isolation and alienation of the individual, the root of today's social problems.

Although the business environment of the past few decades has been critical to the growth and development of our society and is responsible for the U.S. standard of living, increasingly the social problems emanating from the loss of community are affecting business in ways that prohibit it from operating as it has in the past. The accumulation of the negative effects of social issues has altered the environment that business has controlled and within which it has operated relatively unaffected, until recently, by the problems of individuals within its publics. In fact, the rapid growth and contribution of public relations practice in the last few years may be due to the organization's increasing inability to control the business environment while experiencing the latent effects of the lost attributes of community.

As a result of the trends mentioned earlier, the rationalist approach to American business management and the accompanying strategic management approach to public relations are increasingly ineffective in today's business environment, certainly in the international business environment. As several researchers (Hampden-Turner & Trompenaars, 1993; Peters & Austin, 1986; Peters & Waterman, 1984) have determined, excellence in business organizations is rooted in a value-based, people-oriented approach. As Wilson (1994b) concluded:

> Now, more than ever, the emphasis in public relations is on relationship building. The era of press agentry and publicity is past, and attempts to integrate public relations part and parcel with marketing are falling on hostile ears. What the marketers and advertisers have failed to realize is that the role of public relations has changed from "selling" in wholly profit-oriented corporate structures to creating an environment in which business can thrive, or sometimes just exist. Creating that environment has little to do with motivating consumption of products. It is focused on developing relationships with all the publics in a corporation's community. . . . In this way, public relations truly is a strategic function, not a tactical one. (p. 138)

Relationships, by their nature, are developed over time. Because they are based on trust, cooperation, and performance, they fit neither the quarterly, the annual, nor the 5-year plans typical of rationalist American business management. In fact, some international relationships are developed over lifetimes. Strategic management in one stage of corporate development may fail to identify relationships that will be critical in a later stage. Yet, unless efforts are begun early, the necessary relationships will not exist when they are needed. More simply, the rational model ignores the broader role of management that extends beyond analysis and numbers.

Stanford University's Harold Leavitt described a model of the process of management as "an interactive flow of three variables: pathfinding, decision making, and implementation" (Peters & Waterman, 1984, p. 52). Pathfinding is visionary, long-term, communitarian. Decision making is a rationalist approach. Implementation is tactical. Public relations must be capable of all three. The field has already demonstrated its strategic decision-making capability. Its use of communication tools demonstrates the tactical capability. But vision must be demonstrated by service to the community and the building of relationships which may not derive immediate benefit, but which will be invaluable over the long term.

Basically, then, the limitation of the strategic management approach to public relations in the international arena is threefold. First, it is an entirely rationalist and utilitarian approach to identifying those publics that will have an immediate impact on organizational goals, inevitably translated in terms of economics. Second, although in issue management issues are sometimes identified and targeted as much as 20 years in advance, the strategic approach to resolving those issues is almost always built on short-term thinking. It fails to recognize relationships that have no immediate benefit, but that may be critical over time. And third, it is a self-interested approach less concerned with relationships than profit, rather than a community-oriented philosophy where all actors benefit.

Criticism of the rationalist model of management and communication focuses on the "mindless systems analysis and . . . misplaced emphasis on paper rather than on people" (Peters & Austin, 1986, p. xvi). It contends that strategic management ignores our return to a cooperative community orientation and the relational communication approach typical of what Shepherd (1992) and others have termed a feminine model of communication.[3]

However, if Leavitt's model is honestly and consistently applied, relationships alone are not sufficient either. Approaches that serve only the public and do not strategically serve the organization will also ultimately result in the organization's demise. The ideal approach is a synthesis: a value-based, people-oriented approach to developing relationships that are strategic to organizational success immediately as well as over the long term.

---

[3]Characteristics identified in this model of communication are the same as those required for good relationship building, particularly cooperation and compromise.

THE SYNTHESIS: STRATEGIC COOPERATIVE COMMUNITIES

Essentially, then, we in public relations must begin to think of our publics and our organizations in the sense of community. As the American capitalist organization has developed and become more sophisticated, so has the American public. The public's knowledge of business and the creation of wealth is just sufficient to feed expectations of corporate community responsibility and contribution. The new emphasis in issue management, and especially in community relations, is on relationship building (Wilson, 1993). It is consistent with what Peters and Austin (1986) labeled a "back to basics" revolution in American business management, or a focus on people rather than profits. In the international arena, this strategic relationship approach is even more critical given the European and Japanese business management model that has for decades been based on the importance of people (Hampden-Turner & Trompenaars, 1993).

From this cooperative community model come five characteristics of public relations and issue management which parallel attributes that Peters and Waterman (1984) identified in the excellent companies. Underlying these characteristics are the fundamental "valuing processes" discussed by Hampden-Turner and Trompenaars (1993).

The first characteristic of companies operating within this framework is *long-range vision*. They see the need to identify all publics and potential issues years, and sometimes decades, in advance and to develop the relationships critical to issue resolution over time. They are also implementation oriented; believing in and respecting people, they work toward consensus for action.

Second is a *commitment to community,* not just profit. These companies are involved in their community, often leading the way in community service, with a CEO who is personally committed to both charitable work and contribution. This kind of commitment gives the company's community involvement strength and integrity because it is based on a sincere desire to serve the community, not to manipulate for the sake of profit. Firms understand that they are the beneficiaries of a community improved for all its participants and members.

Consistent with the commitment to community is a strong company value orientation emphasizing the *importance of people*. This third characteristic is evidenced in progressive initiatives that support attitudes of trust of and respect for employees. Human dignity is highly valued, and policies are designed with that value in mind.

The fourth characteristic is *cooperative approach to problem solving*. The company values a strong network of problem-solving employees. It relies on employees to work together to solve problems because they affect the entire group. Employees are given latitude to design and implement solutions within their work areas, relying on management to employ vision overall.

Fifth, such organizations are known for building *relationships with all their publics* based on mutual respect, trust, and human dignity, not on profit or personal gain. They are careful not to make decisions regarding one public that may exclude another immediately or over time. The philosophy advocates winning solutions for all members of the community. Rather than taking profit from the community, solutions are sought so that all community members profit.

Defining Strategic Cooperative Communities in Public Relations

These characteristics of public relations which are consistent with the revolution of excellence in American business lead us toward a new approach to viewing publics. In the past, we learned to segment and target publics individually, eschewing the mass. We must now realize that within each public are individuals and organizations with which we interact in relationships. The strength of those relationships largely determines the receipt and success of our messages. Further, those relationships are based on critical values that have little to do directly with financial gain.

Value-based Relationships. Values such as service, respect, and concern are at the base of the relationships we establish with people. Peters and Waterman (1984) concluded that whether those relationships are personal or business relationships does not ultimately alter the driving values. Whether our relationship is built with an individual, or with an individual representing an organization, does not change the fact that the strength of the association is determined by the salience of shared values which place high priority on people. Such a condition is wholly consistent with Tonnies' (1887/1957, 1971) definition of community, and with the Hampden-Turner and Trompenaars (1993) research on European and Japanese business models.

Over the past few years, Lukaszewski's study of the core values of publics has led him to conclude that the priority, or strength, of an organization's relationship with groups and individuals will be determined by how the organization's purpose or function affects their personal core values (Lukaszewski & Serie, 1993b). He identified the five core values; protection of property value, health and safety, peer-group pressure, quality of life (absence of conflict, peace of mind, freedom from fear, community pride), and the protection and enhancement of the environment (Lukaszewski & Serie, 1993b).

Using the rational approach, an organization attempts to get publics to do what it wants them to do, or to let it do as it wishes. Instead, modern public relations calls for a focus on cooperative relationships in which all actors work toward meeting the needs of the community as defined by the participants in that community. With this latter perspective, the core values become even more salient. Then, as Peters and Waterman (1984) found in business communities, the driving core value is that people matter.

Given the importance of people as our publics' driving core value, the values Lukaszewski identified take on a somewhat different emphasis. They become service and participation; sincerity (care and concern); safety, health and the environment; respect of family, friends, and community; and the quality of life.

The salient difference is that when we try to persuade people to do something we want them to do, we must appeal to their self-interest. Once their self-interest becomes maintenance of the community and we are working with them to meet the needs of all community actors, the focus is neighbor centered, not self-centered. It engenders a philosophical shift to the people-centered management model depicted by Hampden-Turner and Trompenaars (1993) as used in the European business arena.

Strategic Cooperative Communities. That our success in any organization is dependent upon the cooperation of key publics has been understood for some time; that those publics are composed of individuals with whom we must develop relationships is now equally clear. The strategic nature of public relationships is as evident as the traditional, rational management's inability to foster them. Durable relationships are not created out of self-serving rationality; they are created and strengthened through mutual trust, respect, cooperation, and benefit. They can be aptly termed strategic cooperative communities; relationship-based interaction to achieve actualization of all members of the community.

Essentially, strategic cooperative communities can be reduced to five descriptors. They are *relationships,* implying interaction. They are *value based,* rooted in mutual core values with the importance of people being primary. They are *cooperative,* implying joint effort to reach mutual benefits. They are *strategic,* whether in the short term or over time they are, individually and collectively, of key importance to the organizational mission. They are *dynamic,* constantly changing, readjusting, and progressing to meet changing circumstances and needs.

Cooperative communities are typically organized around one or more of the following; issues, mutual interest, proximity, and function. They are developed and strengthened by focused effort over long periods of time. They include the entire range of relationships along the spectrum of strength, from adversarial to supportive. Cooperative communities can be applied narrowly to very specific and immediate publics or broadly to relationships that need development over time and for which there is no immediate need.

That community relationships are strategic implies they are not only critical to the organization, but that their characteristics can be identified and analyzed for the purpose of creating or strengthening. *Trust* is the first and most important characteristic of cooperative relationships. Trust of an actor in a community is based on honest communication and cooperation. It is a prerequisite of cooperative relationships as well as a tangible result of them. It may be measured in terms of other community members' willingness to tolerate risk.

It follows that an actor's credibility emanates from the fundamentals of trust.

It is actually in the minds of the other community actors. Your credibility is their perception of your trustworthiness based on their perception of your words and actions (Lukaszewski & Serie, 1993a). Your credibility is their judgment, inherently emotional, of your performance on the issues of importance to the community.

Trust and credibility are not constants. They cannot be achieved and then forgotten. Rather, they must be maintained conscientiously. Developing trust in a single relationship or in a cooperative community requires time and patience to establish a track record.

A second important attribute built over time is *predictability*. The degree to which a member's actions can be predicted is a measure of the relationship's strength. Knowing and understanding someone enough to predict her or his actions and reactions in a given situation puts us in a better position to cooperate for mutual benefit.

Also characteristic of relationships is some kind of *mutual interest*. Communities generally are organized around issues or functions that typify their interest. Motivating participation and communication when there is no mutual interest is difficult, and no subsequent interaction is really meaningful or sustained.

A fourth characteristic of relationships in cooperative communities is *mutual gratification or benefit*. As coalition building for issue management teaches (Wilson, 1993), any effort to manipulate the group for anything but a win–win result will spell doom for a participant. Community relationships require cooperation, giving support because it is morally right and in turn receiving support when it is appropriate. All participants must be benefactors as well as givers.

Undoubtedly, conflicts will arise. Even in a cooperative environment, participants disagree. Nevertheless, when priority is placed on relationships, participants are much more effective in developing compromises that benefit all community members.

The fifth characteristic is *proximity*. Relationships thrive when proximity facilitates interaction, and tend to die when it is not present. Nevertheless, with today's technology, proximity is not necessarily geographical. It simply refers to easy access to each other among members for the purpose of communication and interaction.

Also evident is the sixth characteristic of *community spillover*. Although communities are focused by issues or functions, relationships are broadly applicable. A relationship developed in one cooperative community may become a critical resource in another. A relationship developed with the publisher of a local newspaper may be important in your media relations cooperative community, but it may also spill over into other communities when you discover the publisher is a member of the governor's task force on affordable health care. Many of the results of cultivating the relationship for media coverage will accrue to support for health care.

Seventh and last, the *immediacy of the collective need* to be satisfied by working with individuals within a cooperative community is a crucial characteristic. Vision and long-term thinking will identify certain short-term needs of an organization. This characteristic helps to identify the urgency of efforts to strengthen and maintain relationships so we can prioritize what we do in a strategic way.

With the characteristics of relationships identified, it is possible to evaluate relationships within a strategic cooperative community to determine where developmental effort must be focused. It must be emphasized that relationships should be built and maintained with all organizational publics. This simply means that no public is disregarded, and decisions are avoided that will enhance a relationship with one public while jeopardizing relations with another.

Obviously, there are times when publics and organizations have conflicting goals. Experience in coalition building teaches that in many such situations, solutions can be found that satisfy all publics if people work together with a willingness to compromise for the benefit of the community. In those rare cases where a compromise solution is absolutely impossible, the rules of cooperation in coalitions dictate that participants civilly agree to disagree. The ability to reach such agreement without affecting other cooperative efforts helps maintain respect for one another and strengthens relationships. But when publics are disregarded or unaddressed, the hostility from failure to recognize their positions and needs severely damages relationships, sometimes irreparably.

As focus is placed on the development of relationships strategic to the organization, the immediacy of the need for relationship development is also strategically determined by short-term as well as long-term organizational needs and issues. It is important for practitioners to devote some time to identifying and building relationships, or they will be forever caught in the reactive mode of addressing immediate problems with no long-term vision or coordination of strategic efforts. It is like being trapped in a leaky boat: If you spend all your time bailing and none of it rowing, you will never get to shore.

Given the complexity of relationships and the vast number of organizational publics (whether critical or latent), systematic tracking of relationships and publics will help public relations professionals allocate limited resources to achieve organizational goals. A periodic audit of cooperative communities, evaluating each relationship in terms of the characteristics described above, will aid public relations professionals in focusing resources and striking the optimum balance between short- and long-term efforts.

CREATING EXCELLENCE IN INTERNATIONAL ISSUE MANAGEMENT: A NEW VISION OF PUBLIC RELATIONS AS STRATEGIC COOPERATIVE COMMUNITIES

As business becomes a global arena, the public relations discipline must take the next step in its development and synthesize strategic planning and issue management approaches with relationship building. We must combine strategic management with the vision absent in the traditional rationalist approach upon which it was originally based. And we must look toward building long-term relationships that reinforce the values our publics hold dear. Only in this way can we avoid manipulative practices that are neither truly ethical nor productive in the long run.

To function well internationally, we must do more than internationalize current models of issue management. We must redesign both issue tracking and research, and issue mediation, within the context of strategic cooperative communities. Our tactical approaches to public relations and issue management will stay the same, albeit as adapted to local cultures and customs. However, the underlying philosophy which drives our purposes and action decisions will be fundamentally different. We must become cooperative community participants focused on the good of all rather than being primarily self-interested. To survive in the international sphere, our public relations, and indeed our corporate commitment, must be communitarian.

Public relations professionals are in a prime position to lead the change in philosophy and practice which synthesizes traditional strategic management with relationship building. This philosophical shift will insure that, as public relations professionals, we identify all current, latent, and potential publics of our organizations and begin to systematically build relationships that are based on critical values. This brings our organizational efforts into compliance with the expectations of international publics, and aids American business in moderating the principles that fostered economic dominance in the last century to implement practices that will maintain our position as a critical player in the next century.

REFERENCES

Anderson, J. A., & Meyer, T. P. (1988). *Mediated communication: A social action perspective.* Newbury Park, CA: Sage Publications.

Buchholz, R. A. (1985). *Essentials of public policy for management.* Englewood Cliffs, NJ: Prentice-Hall.

Creedon, P. J. (1991). Public relations and "women's work": Toward a feminist analysis of public relations roles. In L. A. Grunig & J. E. Grunig (Eds.), *Public Relations Research Annual* (Vol.3, pp. 67–84). Hillsdale, NJ: Lawrence Erlbaum Associates.

Cutlip, S., Center, A., & Broom, G. (1985). *Effective public relations* (6th ed.). Englewood Cliffs, NJ: Prentice-Hall.

Cutlip, S., Center, A., & Broom, G. (1994). *Effective public relations* (7th ed.). Englewood Cliffs, NJ: Prentice-Hall.

Grunig, J. E. (1993). Implications of public relations for other domains of communication. *Journal of Communication, 43,* 164–173.

Grunig, J. E., & Hunt, T. (1984). *Managing public relations.* Fort Worth, TX: Holt, Rinehart & Winston.

Grunig, J. E., & Repper, F. (1992). Strategic management, publics, and issues. In J. E. Grunig (Ed.), *Excellence in public relations and communication management* (pp. 117–158). Hillsdale, NJ: Lawrence Erlbaum Associates.

Hainsworth, B. E. (1990). The distribution of advantages and disadvantages. *Public Relations Review, 16,* 33–39.
Hampden-Turner, C., & Trompenaars, A. (1993). *The seven cultures of capitalism: Value systems for creating wealth in the United States, Japan, Germany, France, Britain, Sweden, and the Netherlands.* New York: Doubleday.
Heath, R. L., & Cousino, K. R. (1990). Issues management: End of first decade progress report. *Public Relations Review, 16,* 6–18.
Kruckeberg, D., & Starck, K. (1988). *Public relations and community: A reconstructed theory.* New York: Praeger.
Lindloff, T. R. (1988). Media audiences as interpretive communities. In N. J. Anderson (Ed.), *Communication Yearbook,* (Vol. 11, pp. 81–107). Newbury Park, CA: Sage Publications.
Lukaszewski, J. E., & Serie, T. L. (1993a, February). Public consent built on credibility is the goal. *Waste Age,* Vol. 23, pp. 45–54.
Lukaszewski, J. E., & Serie, T. L. (1993b, March). Relationships built on understanding core values. *Waste Age,* Vol. 24, pp. 83–94.
Peters, T. J., & Austin, N. (1986). *A passion for excellence: The leadership difference.* New York: Warner Books.
Peters, T. J., & Waterman, R. H. (1984). *In search of excellence: Lessons from America's best-run companies.* New York: Warner Books.
Shepherd, G. J. (1992). Communication as influence: Definitional exclusion. *Communication Studies, 43,* 203–219.
Tonnies, F. (1957). *Community and society: Gemeinschaft und gesellschaft* (C. P. Loomis, Trans.) East Lansing, MI: The Michigan State University Press. (Original work published 1887)
Tonnies, F. (1971). On gemeinschaft and gesellschaft. In M. Truzzi (Ed.), *Sociology: The classic statements* (pp. 145–154). New York: Random House.
Wilcox, D., Ault, P., & Agee, W. (1989). *Public relations: Strategies and tactics* (2nd ed.). New York: Harper & Row.
Wilson, L. J. (1993, May). Coalition-building among the Fortune 500: A study of an emerging approach to corporate political activity. Competitive display paper presented at the International Communication Association Conference in Washington, D.C.
Wilson, L. J. (1994a). Excellent companies and coalition-building among the Fortune 500: A value- and relationship-based theory. *Public Relations Review, 20,* 333–343.
Wilson, L. J. (1994b). The return to gemeinschaft: Toward a theory of public relations and corporate community relations as relationship building. In A. F. Alkhafaji (Ed.), *Business research yearbook: Global business perspectives* (Vol. 1, pp. 135–141). Lanham, MD: International Academy of Business Disciplines and University Press of America, Inc.

4 Transnational Corporate Ethical Responsibilities

Dean Kruckeberg
University of Northern Iowa

New Year's Day 1993, 12 European Community nation-states opened their borders to one another. Trade barriers were eliminated among Belgium, Denmark, France, Germany, Greece, Ireland, Italy, Luxembourg, the Netherlands, Portugal, Spain, and the United Kingdom. Also, the democratization of Eastern Europe shattered East-West polarization (Gordon), further unifying continental Europe.

The European Community presently has more than 320 million customers within its borders, far more than within the United States and three times as many consumers as in Japan (Bellack, 1990).

And the nation-states of the European Free Trade Association (EFTA), representing the Nordic countries of Finland, Iceland, Norway, and Sweden, as well as Austria and Switzerland, have also signed an agreement with the European Community. The creation of the resulting European Economic Area (EEA) allows individual EFTA nations to become member nation-states of the European Community if they so wish (Johannson, 1991).

THE PAN AMERICAN COMMUNITY?

A future Western Hemisphere equivalent to the European Community is not inconceivable, certainly in this post-North American Free Trade Agreement (NAFTA) era. Perhaps even worldwide agreements may be feasible.

The likelihood of increasingly close economic, cultural, and political linkages within the Pan American Community is manifestly evident, as are the potential benefits. Also, African communities of nations, closer Pacific Rim associations, and Asian Economic Communities are not inconceivable.

Such linkages within the Americas, as an example, are destined to increase, in great part, because of transnational corporations' ready use of the latest technology in communication and transportation to exponentially broaden the scope of their operations. The resultant social, political, economic impact of these transnational corporations cannot be underestimated. Elfstrom (1991) has said that the economic integration of the globe may be the single most important development of the 20th Century. He observed:

> The same advances in transportation and communication that allow a global economy, in fact mandate global competition, also foster the creation of enterprises—multinational corporations—able to scatter portions of their corporate organism across the globe. Multinational corporations are at the center of the globalization, homogenization and growing interdependence of the world economy and will continue to nurture this evolution. (p. 1)

The social, political, and economic ramifications of such transnational corporations are exceedingly complex. Elfstrom noted that countries are no longer simply home or host nations to the transnationals; neither can such nations be described as passive or as imperialistic aggressors. Although the United States is home to the majority of multinational corporations, it is also *host* to more foreign ventures than is any other nation except Canada (Elfstrom, 1991).

TRANSNATIONAL AND MULTINATIONAL FIRMS

Transnational Corporations "Live" in Many Countries

Neither should the power of such corporations go unappreciated. Although many authors (including the author of this chapter) use the "multinational" and "transnational" labels somewhat interchangeably, Shue (1983) made an interesting and important distinction. He noted that the latter live simultaneously in many countries, buying supplies and paying labor wherever they cost the least, and selling their products wherever they cost the most—an advantage not shared by even the most powerful of governments.

Shue (1983) argued that transnational corporations' greatest strength is in their unique position. While the multinationals' impact may, indeed, extend across several nations, transnational corporations are unique because they neither belong to, nor must they pledge any patriotic allegiance to, any home nation-state.

The Need for Ethics and Mutually Agreed Responsibilities

The ever-increasing social, political, and economic impact of transnational corporations, as well as their power, their assured growth in the 21st century, and their catalytic role in increasing greater linkages throughout the world, suggest a paramount need for the delineation of appropriate ethics and for mutual identification of and agreement on the responsibilities of both transnational corporations and their host nations.

This need is particularly evident and acute within the Americas because of the "First World" status of North America and the "Third World" status of many Central and South American nations. However, again, similar cases could be made for such a need throughout the Third World, including those Third World nations that are advancing economically, with massive concomitant social and political changes.

No one denies that a great many transnational corporations historically have behaved responsibly in their host nations and to everyone's benefit. However, history is also replete with ample evidence of excesses and abuses by such corporations in the Third World.

To illustrate some inherent dangers and potential negative consequences of these organizations upon host nations, it is helpful to use the model developed by Johan Galtung, and summarized and described by Kultgen (1988). Galtung argued that many injustices throughout the world are due to "structural violence," which he defines as the exploitation of one group by another through the dominant practices and institutions of a society.

Galtung maintained that the modern world is characterized by extensive structural violence over and beyond overt violence and intimidation. It is inflicted by ruling elites of developed nations on their own peripheral groups, and by elites and peripheries of these nations on the undeveloped nations, especially on the peripheral groups of these nations in collusion with their ruling elites.

Galtung argued that, because the periphery of the periphery composes a large majority of humankind, systematic structural violence is inflicted by the few on the many. Moreover, all groups, both central and peripheral, are intent upon development without regard to the ecosystem or to the future of the human species.

Are Corporations "Moral Agents"?

Can and should transnational corporations be held ethically responsible for their actions, that is, are they "moral agents" in the context usually reserved for human beings? Western European thought usually attributes moral guilt, responsibility, and merit to discrete individuals (Elfstrom, 1991).

However, Elfstrom argued that corporations have the requisite qualities for moral agency, albeit in an admittedly less elegant and more complex manner than do individual humans. Corporations are able to control their actions and to make rational decisions.

Furthermore, they usually have a spectrum of options available for their possible actions, and they have the capacity to make reasoned choices from among these options. Thus, they can be held morally accountable for the choices they select. Therefore, Elfstrom (1991) concluded that:

> In sum, corporations have the attributes of freedom and rationality required for moral agency. This agency is more complex in its nature and distribution than that of individual human beings. Nonetheless, careful analysis reveals ways in which this agency is distributed among the particular human beings holding various positions within an institution. (pp. 22–23)

He cited some of the difficulties inherent in assessing corporate moral responsibility; the absence of established and authoritative procedures to identify those breaching standards, together with little means for remedial action; lack of means to acknowledge exemplary conduct; and large participant numbers, hampering an evolving international commercial moral community.

At What Level Is Moral Accountability?

If transnational corporations are, indeed, morally accountable, at what level can this ethical responsibility be held, and must any predetermined level be maintained consistently worldwide?

The plethora of opinions often appears highly contradictory. Indeed, some international business people have questioned North Americans' assumed expectations of a globally uniform standard of values driven by U.S. administrative law rather than, say, by time-honored religious and moral codes (Dilenschneider, 1990). Indeed, this supposed national sentiment is not shared by all U.S. executives. For example, the vice president of a U.S.-based industrial equipment firm (cited in Basche, 1976) argued that:

> America cannot set itself up as the high priest of the world's business morals without serious consequences in our export trade. It would be well for us to remember that there are civilizations much older than our own in which the concepts of moral conduct are vastly different from our own ethics. I dare say that if we were extreme enough in our zealous approach to eradicate corruption from the world's business, we would damage our international trade position severely in certain countries. (p. 28).

As this example readily elucidates, confusion and disagreement often result when transnational corporate executives attempt to determine ethical policy, both their own and what they will tolerate from other individuals, institutions and organizations within host countries. This is because of varying perspectives concerning cultural universalism and cultural relativism as these perspectives relate to their subset, ethics.

For example, as long ago as in the 1970s, a slight majority of executives participating in a survey argued that U.S. companies operating abroad should adhere to one set of ethical standards as a minimum level of behavior. These standards should be U.S. standards, which the executives perceived as being generally higher than local standards. These executives said that such standards should be modified only to make them stronger where local standards may be higher (Basche, 1976).

One might speculate that such beliefs are more common among multinational corporations as distinguished by Shue (1983). Donaldson (1989) noted that, although such multinational organizations may do business internationally, they lean toward a specific nationality, both in their composition of employees and in their corporate character.

RELATIVISM VERSUS UNIVERSALISM

When in Rome, do as the Romans do?

Thus, while some executives of multinational and transnational corporations might argue for universal ethical standards, others, such as the executive for the U.S.-based industrial equipment firm cited earlier, apparently believe, "When in Rome, do as the Romans do."

These two bipolar ethical belief systems may have an infinite number of gradations between them. At one extreme, radical universalists believe that only one set of ethics must be followed by their corporations throughout the world, generally representing their own corporations' systems of ethical beliefs and values.

On the other hand, ethical relativists believe there must be variations in ethical standards depending upon individual cultures and social climates within host countries. Assorted variations fall between these extremes.

The Universalists Versus the Relativists?

So who is right, the ethical universalists or the relativists? Indeed, as many historical examples can readily attest, there are grave dangers in zealous moral imperialism of a type that may underly radical universalism.

Also, extreme universalism requires a rigid hierarchical ordering of multiple moral communities to which individuals and groups belong. To preserve complete universality in human rights, for example, the radical universalists give absolute priority to demands of the cosmopolitan moral community over other perceived lower moral communities (Donnelly, 1989).

However, a large part of the confusion between universalism and relativism, and a suspected primary reason for some people's apparent attraction to a supposed relativism, is that cultural relativism and its subset, ethical relativism, are frequently confused with cultural tolerance. In truth, cultural relativism bears little resemblance to cultural tolerance (Donaldson, 1989).

For example, people within a culture may disagree with the practice of having women wear veils. Yet, owing to their tolerance, those within this culture may believe they should refrain from forcing their views upon the Shiite Moslems who require this practice. In such a case, tolerance would count as a *moral*, not a relativistic, value.

Conversely, the true moral relativist can always answer, "Why should I be tolerant? My moral code permits me to be violent and intolerant" (Spaemann, 1989, 1982).

Vulgar Relativism Is Easily Refutable

However, even those who recognize true cultural relativism have difficulty defending their position. Williams (1982) has argued convincingly that vulgar relativism is easily refutable. He uses that term for two supposedly interrelated propositions; the term right means "right for a given society," and it is wrong for people in one society to condemn or to interfere with the values and moral behavior of another society.

Williams (1982) observed that the use of right in the first proposition is relative to a society, but the second proposition employs the term "wrong" in an obviously nonrelative way.

And Lear (1984) reasoned that, if we have to respect the rationality and autonomy of every culture, then it turns out that there is one culture whose rationality and autonomy we cannot respect—our own.

> Our moral beliefs present themselves as basic truths about how human beings should act, but we are now supposed to respect incompatible moral beliefs just so long as they are actually embodied in a culture. By the standards of rationality available in our tribe these two stances are incompatible: being forced to accept that alternative incompatible moral outlooks are equally justifiable (or equally unjustifiable) cannot help but undermine the confidence of reflective moral agents. (p. 147)

Radical Relativism Demeans Human Being

Donnelly (1989) is especially critical of radical cultural relativism because it holds the concept human being to have no moral significance. That is, it suggests that the fact that one is human is irrelevant to one's moral status.

Although many premodern societies may have defined human beings by their social status or by group membership, Donnelly (1989) has argued that this view is almost universally rejected today.

> For example, chattel slavery and caste systems, which implicitly deny the existence of a morally significant common humanity, are almost universally condemned, even in the most rigid class societies. Likewise, moral distinctions between insiders

and outsiders has [*sic*] been seriously eroded by greatly increased individual mobility and by an at least aspirational commitment to the idea of a universal human moral community. (p. 112)

In fact, cultural relativism seems to have little contemporary credence and support. Furthermore, this concept historically has had racist overtones. Hatch (1983) observed:

By the 1860s this idea about our own superiority was elaborated in a full-blown theory of anthropology, the nineteenth-century cultural evolutionary theory . . . , which took the notion of social hierarchy as a main feature. The various peoples around the world were not simply different from one another (and from us), it was thought, but the differences among us are of a hierarchical order. (p. 19)

Christians (1989) reported another dilemma the relativists cannot escape called "Mannheim's paradox":

Truth, says the cultural relativist, is culture-bound. But if it were, then he, within his own culture, ought not to see his own culture-bound truth as absolute. He cannot proclaim cultural relativism without rising above it, and he cannot rise above it without giving it up. (p. 5)

Donaldson (1989) acknowledged that cultural relativism has fared poorly as a philosophical doctrine. He emphasized that it would be difficult to name a single recognized contemporary or classical philosopher who espouses it.

However, he conceded that modified relativism recognizes that significant gray areas exist which are best called regions of moral taste, for which no rational method can give the right answer.

Donaldson (1989) said that it should be obvious such modified relativism is really a form of constrained objectivism rather than genuine relativism. Indeed, one could successfully argue, such modified relativism could just as well be called modified universalism or, better yet, tempered universalism.

An Argument for Ethical Universalism

Upon examination of this range of ethical positions, clearly an argument must be made for universalism in the determination of transnational corporate ethics, although this position may be tempered, at least minutely, according to individual cultures and the social climates of transnational corporations' host countries.

Donnelly (1989) conceded in his ethical discussion of human rights that:

It may be necessary to allow limited cultural variations in the form and interpretation of particular human rights, but we must insist on their fundamental moral universality. Human rights are, to use an appropriately paradoxical phrase, relatively universal. (p. 124)

Donnelly (1989) acknowledged that at least some variations cannot be criticized legitimately by outsiders. But, he argued, if human rights are literally the rights everyone possesses simply as a human being, such rights would seem universal by definition.

Ethical Universalism Tempered Minutely

Thus, it is argued here, ethical universalism should be the goal of transnational corporations, but this could be a universalism tempered, perhaps minutely, to take into account the moral taste of host countries.

However, while respecting host cultures' and host nations' beliefs, guest corporations must also insist upon reciprocal respect, toleration, and accommodation for their own values (Elfstrom, 1991). In addition, although corporations certainly may not be able to *reform* the nations where, for example, bribery (as it may be defined by Americans) is widespread, it may be sometimes possible for these transnational corporations to avoid participating in practices that they find morally suspect (Elfstrom, 1991).

Furthermore, it follows, other institutions such as governments and quasi-governmental organizations that interface with transnational corporations should give and demand reciprocal respect, tolerance, and accommodation for their own values.

Finally, corporations most certainly are morally obligated to maintain a level of behavior consonant with their publicly identified ethical standards (Elfstrom, 1991).

Elfstrom (1991) said that multinational corporations should have a single set of publicly announced standards to govern all of their operations; standards of moral conduct that corporations intend to uphold should be joined to whatever commercial agreements are reached with their host nations.

Elfstrom acknowledged that corporations may occasionally be obliged to compromise their ethical standards to respect the values of others. Nonetheless, transnational corporations cannot compromise their basic responsibility, shared with all moral agents, of seeking to avoid placing human life and well-being at risk (Elfstrom, 1991).

The question remains, however, of what is meant by a minutely tempered universalism. That is, how far can a host culture's moral taste deviate from the transnational corporations' norm before such attempted ethical universalism is lost.

Does minutely mean "in small ways"? Or in "unimportant ways"? It is difficult to provide a recipe for identifying parameters, especially when the parameters involve distinct cultural variations.

For example, Culbertson (1994) observed that Americans place the individual first; in contrast, Chinese historically have emphasized the group. Such different perspectives can account for considerable differences in moral taste.

As another example, an American may feel uncomfortable paying what he would consider to be bribes to facilitate services in some African nations. However, what to an American might constitute a bribe may be perceived as no more than an expected gratuity to an African minor bureaucrat.

As another example, a Moslem Arab undoubtedly would be uncomfortable in a business social environment in which alcohol was being served and consumed, and his Arab-based corporation most certainly would not sponsor such an event. However, during a business reception, should his tolerance of moral taste include an acceptance of his Western colleagues imbibing in alcohol? Elfstrom (1991) noted that:

> In some instances cultural practices will not be explicitly encapsulated within law or may be clearly outside the law, yet may effectively shape ways of doing business. Also, it is possible that national laws may require corporations to perform actions which are clearly morally impermissible according to their own standards, such as laws requiring them to inform governments of the activities of political dissidents or those requiring them to offer only menial positions to members of particular ethnic groups or social classes. (p. 48)

Ethical Universalism is not so Difficult

It seems important to note that ethical universalism in fact is not as difficult as it is often perceived. Spaemann (1989, 1982) observed that we fall victim to an "optical illusion," in which we see differences more clearly than we see similarities among different cultures.

Cooper (1989) reported a growing literature on the subject of ethical universals and on a unified theory of human nature in the disciplinary areas of sociology, anthropology, and philosophical ethics.

Indeed, there are constants in most fundamental human values. Also, there are basic concepts of good and evil that transcend cultural boundaries. These concepts are reflected, for example, in the common values and practices of the world's major religions.

Donnelly (1989) argued that the international normative consensus on human rights presents a strong prima facie case for a relatively strong universalism.

> Even if this "consensus" is largely the compliment of vice to virtue, it does reveal widely shared notions of "virtue," an underlying "universal" moral position that compels at least the appearance of assent from even the cynical and corrupt. (pp. 121–122)

In keeping with this ethical universalist perspective, Christians (1989) pointed to the need for normative standards in determining multinational corporate ethical behavior.

He questioned, "How can we legitimately appeal to the supreme value of human life, to an affirmation of universal human dignity and freedom, without accepting a network of primal norms—justice, compassion, reciprocity, stewardship—that are non-negotiable?" (Christians, 1989, p. 19).

Christians said that, without norms that are more-than-subjective, we cannot finally condemn oppression and dehumanization except on the grounds of personal prejudice or emotional makeup.

Christians' (1989) argument that the purposes of international ethics are best served when we recognize both history and culture as normed processes, is reflected in the following:

> What we seek to develop is an ethics of universal solidarity, one grounded in our being as humans and therefore not restricted to the generations now living. For those of us engaged in ethical theory beyond parochialism, we ought to aim at articulating a nonrelativistic ethics in which "human beings have certain inescapable claims on one another which cannot be renounced except at the cost of their humanity." Relativism, in my view, weakens the agenda of our universal humanness. (p. 18)

Societies are Pushed to Take Part in a Larger Community

Lear (1984) agreed with the universalist ethical position; however, he observed that this may not have been a valid position in the past. He has said that we live in a period in which societies are being drawn together by various technological, economic, and political developments. These societies are being pushed to participate in a larger world community of societies.

He argued that we have reached an historical period in which the smallest political unit that can guarantee an environment for human "flourishing" is the world community of societies. If this is so, then it may *have become true* that one's moral concern should extend to all humanity.

> It is easy to assume that if there are any moral truths, they must be timelessly true, perhaps because morality tends to present itself as universalizable. I am suggesting that such presentation may have been until recently misleading—at best an aspiration—but that it has become or is becoming true in the present historical period. (pp. 165–166)

CONCLUSIONS

A future Western Hemisphere equivalent to the European Community is not inconceivable. Neither are such economic communities elsewhere in the world nor within the world at large.

Economic, cultural, and political linkages within the Americas, as only one example, are destined to increase, in great part, because of transnational corporations' ready use of the latest technology in communication and transportation to exponentially broaden the scope of their operations. The social, political, and economic ramifications of such transnational corporations are exceedingly complex. These corporations are immensely powerful, and transnational corporations belong to no home nation-state.

It must be emphasized and ultimately accepted that transnational corporations are, indeed, morally accountable. Although there are grave dangers in zealous moral imperialism such as that which may occur through radical universalism, an argument must be made for universalism in transnational corporate ethics, particularly as we move to a larger world community of societies. However, this position must be tempered at least minutely to accommodate the moral taste of individual cultures and social climates of transnational corporations' host countries.

An American businessman may wisely forego an alcoholic drink while performing business in some parts of the world; he may have to consider whether he wants to expedite the processing of his visa in other parts of the world, perhaps with some objections to giving a gratuity to a minor bureaucrat. However, it is hoped that he has universal support from his transnational corporation in his refusal to participate in customs that degrade or endanger other humans. But, in most of his decisions, he can and must be an ethical universalist.

REFERENCES

Basche, J. R., Jr. (1976). *Unusual foreign payments: A survey of the policies and practices of U.S. companies.* New York: The Conference Board.

Bellack, D. W. (1990, January). Exploiting EEC marketing potential. *Public Relations Journal, 46*(1), p. 14–15.

Christians, C. G. (1989). Ethical theory in a global setting. In T. W. Cooper (Ed.), *Communication ethics and global change* (pp. 3–19). White Plains, NY: Longman.

Cooper, T. W. (1989). Global universals: In search of common ground. In T. W. Cooper (Ed.), *Communication ethics and global change* (pp. 20–39). White Plains, NY: Longman.

Culbertson, H. M. (1994, August). *Cultural beliefs: A focus of study in cross-cultural public relations.* Paper presented at the meeting of the Association for Education in Journalism and Mass Communication conference, Atlanta, GA.

Dilenschneider, R. L. (1990). *Power and influence: Mastering the art of persuasion.* Englewood-Cliffs, NJ: Prentice-Hall.

Donaldson, T. (1989). *The ethics of international business.* New York: Oxford University Press.

Donnelly, J. (1989). *Universal human rights in theory and practice.* Ithaca, NY: Cornell University Press.

Elfstrom, G. (1991). *Moral issues and multinational corporations.* New York: St. Martins Press.

Gordon, J. A. (1991, December). Getting a slice of the "Europie". *Public Relations Journal, 47*(12), p. 13, 20, 28.

Hatch, E. (1983). *Culture and morality: the relativity of values in anthropology.* New York: Columbia University Press.

Johannson, L. (1991, December). A new dawn arrives in the north. *Public Relations Journal, 47*(12), 16–17.

Kultgen, J. H. (1988). *Ethics and professionalism*. Philadelphia: University of Pennsylvania Press.

Lear, J. (1984). Moral objectivity. In S. C. Brown (Ed.), *Objectivity and cultural divergence* (pp. 135–170). Cambridge, England: Cambridge University Press.

Shue, H. (1983). Transnational transgressions. In T. Regan (Ed.), *Just business: New introductory essays in business ethics* (pp. 271–291). Philadelphia: Temple University Press.

Spaemann, R. (1989). *Basic moral concepts*. (T. J. Armstrong, Trans.) London: Routledge. (Original work published 1982)

Williams, B. (1982). Introduction to "an inconsistent form of relativism" and "the truth in relativism". In J. W. Meiland & M. Krausz (Eds.), *Relativism: Cognitive and moral* (pp. 167–170). Notre Dame, IN: University of Notre Dame Press.

5 Public Relations' Role: Realities in Asia and in Africa South of the Sahara

James K. Van Leuven
Colorado State University

Cornelius B. Pratt
Michigan State University

The nature and breadth of public relations work in economically advanced nations such as the United States or in Europe differ markedly from what is labeled public relations in the developing countries of Latin America, Africa, and Asia. For one thing, public relations in economically advanced nations is largely the study and practice of how organizations in the private sector relate to strategic publics in their environments. In contrast, public relations in developing countries equates to government nation building programs or countrywide public communication campaigns.

This chapter assesses these differences by first describing key elements of nation building campaigns from subSaharan Africa and from Southeast Asia. It presents three common differences in the practice of public relations in more developed countries as contrasted with that in developing and newly industrializing economies. And, finally, it assesses those differences in light of philosophical, ethical, and idealistic conceptions of what leading scholars and practitioners believe excellent public relations and excellent development communication ought to be.

According to Al-Enad (1990), public relations in most Third World nations operates as the information function in ministries and in other government agencies. Practitioners communicate with the public to achieve one or both of two goals; to educate people on subjects related to client field of work, increase knowledge about pertinent issues, and persuade the public to behave or act differently (e.g., go to school, immunize, obey traffic rules, etc.), and to publicize achievements of a client or a society as a whole so the public will feel satisfied.

It is easy to see that this description of public relations in the Third World varies greatly from that found in the United States and in western Europe. Even more striking are the differences in the underlying literatures, concepts, theories, and research findings. In other words, in order to learn more about public relations in Western societies, students would consult library bases under headings such as public relations or international public relations. However, to learn more about public relations, largely government campaigns, in developing countries, the key words would be development communication, communication for development, or diffusion of innovations. In this chapter we seek to begin merging these related literatures.

PUBLIC RELATIONS IN THREE AREAS

The African Context

One basic reason for the varying public relations practices around the world is that all nations differ in their political and economic developments, standards of living, levels of literacy, and so forth. Therefore, the nature of the issues and the range of possible solutions vary.

Development issues are particularly significant for Africans. First, poverty and economic decadence are so endemic that Davidson (1992) has argued that the dreadful 1980s have left many African countries worse off now than they were during colonialism. Ake (1991), a Nigerian political economist, wrote:

> Africa's standard of living has been falling steadily, and its share of world trade and industrial output has been declining. Poverty in both relative and absolute terms is worsening so rapidly that sub-Saharan Africa's share of the developing world's poor will have grown from 16% in 1985 to 30% by the end of the century (p. 5).

Similarly, Morrow (1992) noted that "much of the continent has turned into a battleground of contending dooms: AIDS and overpopulation, poverty, starvation, illiteracy, corruption, war, and the homelessness of wars' refugees" (p. 40). The inflation rate on the continent has increased steadily. For example, the annual rate between 1970 and 1980 was 13.9%. Between 1980 and 1991, it was 18.4%, increasing by 2.1% annually. While per-capita incomes in other Third World nations have increased in the 1990s, those in subSaharan Africa have dropped.

Second, international agencies and world governments have committed resources to stem the tide of decadence on the continent, even when a number of African countries do not have demonstrable geopolitical significance to foreign governments. Rwanda's social crisis is a case in point. The United Nations and several African countries were slow in intervening in the mayhem that gripped the country. Nonetheless, resources were committed there in hopes of creating a climate conducive to a dialogue that might foster an environment for rebuilding the nation.

In the face of such overwhelming social and political crises, there is little opportunity for practicing public relations in the Western sense of the term. Instead, governments in these countries attempt to mandate indirectly the role of the private sector in national development. Organizations in that sector, therefore, attempt to develop programs on their own to demonstrate their unwavering support of governments. For example, First Bank, one of Nigeria's premier banks, periodically uses advertisements to remind Nigerians of its commitment to national development. One such ad was titled "Spreading prosperity nationwide." As another example, St. George's Publicity, Ltd., a full service advertising and public relations firm based in Lagos, Nigeria, promotes its services with development overtones: "With the definite decreased disposable income of the average Nigerian consumer coupled with the open-door import and economy deregulation policy of the Federal Government, the business of penetrating or sustaining or actually increasing the share of your very competitive market at these times is 'akin to squeezing water out of stone'." These forms of support for national objectives are rife in African countries, even in those that are governed by the military.

One continentwide agency whose interest is development is the 20-year-old Federation of African Public Relations Associations (FAPRA). During its November, 1991 annual conference in Kampala, Uganda, it adopted a 12-point communique titled "The Kampala Declaration." This document stated, among other things, that FAPRA shall influence positively Africa's development; that it shall be involved in protecting the African environment; that it shall work toward enhancing democratic practices, the respect of human rights, and the status of women and children in Africa. Thus, "The Kampala Declaration" offers a blueprint for the role of public relations in Africa with implications for other developing regions.

Malaysia

Unlike the African context, Malaysia and Singapore represent two culturally pluralistic Southeast Asian societies where public relations came into being after World War II as the mechanism for achieving political stability and national unity. This was not an easy task, given the social devastation coupled with the loss of colonial funding from Britain, not to mention the cultural hurdles to fusing the Malay, the Chinese, the Indian, and other ethnic groups into a single nation. Thus, in a general sense, the historical rationale for developing public relations in Malaysia was not too unlike the situation in other British colonies in the years following World War II (Morais & Adnan, 1986).

When the British returned after World War II, they established a Malaysian Department of Publicity and Printing with film, broadcasting, and information units. The department's objective during the Emergency period of 1948–1960 was to wage psychological warfare against the communist guerrillas by convincing Malaysians that the British, and not the Chinese communist guerrillas (The Malayan People's AntiJapanese Army), eventually won World War II over Japan.

To boost morale and to win the hearts and minds of the people, the Department promoted the principles of *Rukunegara,* the national ideology which insures that all people are fully informed of the aims and objectives of government policies and which encourages the peoples' participation in the various measures undertaken by the government to help achieve the goals of unity, integration, and national development.

The literacy level was low at this time, and the population was dispersed throughout the rural countryside and in urban neighborhood clusters. Under these conditions, campaign materials and presentations were designed to build consensus and to defuse animosities. The people were reached via folk media and presentations at community centers by community development specialists who were often called public relations officers. Media, when used, conveyed the campaign's legitimacy to local leaders and overseas multinationals rather than serving as a primary source of campaign information for mass audiences.

These propagandistic campaigns followed the British model of psychological warfare, the only one known to Malaysians at the time. This is not surprising as Malaysia's political stability and economic viability bound the government to established ties with Britain and its allies, the United States, Australia, and New Zealand.

Even so, a subtle shift from propaganda to development themes and a diffusion-of-innovations approach began in 1960 with the ending of the Emergency and the government's launching of the Rural Development Plan. The plan was designed to enable the infrastructure to make the agrarian economy more mechanized which would, in turn, pave the way for a more industrialized, manufacturing-based economy. Thus, separate development communication campaigns began in support of road building, water supplies, community halls, and electricity for rural areas.

Next came a New Economic Policy in 1969 aimed at restructuring society so that no race would be identified with any particular vocation, and eradicating poverty among all segments of the population irrespective of race. During this period, the government information staff grew from a few hundred to approximately 2,500, or roughly 4 times the number employed in private sector public relations. Typical nation building or development communication campaigns for this period were ones to boost food production, the antidrug abuse campaign, the antihoarding campaign, the campaigns against the spread of Dengue Fever, and road safety programs.

At the same time, campaigns were launched to promote particular industries and economic interests, including the Malaysian Agricultural Research and Development Institute (MARDI), Rubber Industry Smallholders Development Authority (RISDA), Federal Land Consolidation and Rehabilitation Authority, and Fishery Development Authority of Malaysia.

MARDI, the agricultural authority, directed programs at farmers in the local community and various government agencies, whereas RISDA mounted campaigns directed at the 500,000 rubber smallholders and their household members. Overall, this group involved nearly 2.5 million people.

Although campaign implementation often involved two-way communication and feedback from the users or campaign targets, the fact is that public communication campaigns were designed basically as marketing or advertising programs. The interpersonal or two-way communication programs were carried out almost entirely through dialogue sessions, civic lessons, talks, group discussion, and house-to-house visits. The purpose of the feedback was not to establish a dialogue, but rather to improve the persuasive impact of the campaign. Moreover, principles of symmetric or two-way communication were more peripheral than central to campaign formulation.

Most recently, government communication campaigns have responded to the new "Look East" policy where Malaysians were urged to discard the models of what were deemed to be failing Western societies in favor of the Japanese and Korean societies based on a disciplined work force and strong work ethic.

And as the economy shifted from an agricultural to a manufacturing base, a new government/private sector industrial policy developed. In turn, the focus of nation building campaigns shifted from individual behavioral change to changes that motivated people to support and to participate in projects launched by the government. In the "Leadership by Example Campaign," for example, citizens were encouraged to adopt ideas and values taken from Islam as a framework for adapting to an advanced economy and urban lifestyle.

Singapore

Prime Minister Lee Kuan Yew and his People's Action Party were fully cognizant of communist infiltration activities long before Singapore became its own republic in 1965. Because the government wanted social cohesion at any cost, an initial government information policy was designed to create shared values, a common will, and a single national identity among the Chinese, Malaysian, and Indian peoples.

In recalling the beginning of public relations work in Singapore, Basskaran Nair (1986) wrote: "Planned and sustained public relations campaigns were organized to educate the public, to change negative social habits and to adopt new attitudes essential for an emerging nation" (p. 11).

Programs in the early 1960s such as the "antilitter" and "lungs for Singapore" campaigns helped create not only a clean and green environment, but also a sense of belonging to the new nation as thousands of volunteers were involved in such community projects. Overpopulation and unemployment problems led to a vigorous family planning education program. Health campaigns taught the public the dangers of malaria and Dengue Fever. By the mid 1970s, sustained campaign activities had helped create a clean and green city, thus boosting the morale and civic pride of the Singaporean. The techniques involved oral presentations and displays at community centers where programs were also organized for youth.

Perhaps people accepted these campaigns because they symbolized the establishment of a national culture, with national interests being placed above separate sectional, ethnic, or linguistic interests. Because they believed in the end, people apparently did not object to the fact that the means to that end was one-way persuasive communication. Moreover, as time passed, the citizenry recognized the economic benefits they enjoyed as a result of successful family planning and health campaigns. In short, legitimacy was fostered by a rising standard of living coupled with a stable and responsive government.

With a booming economy and the emergence of a consumer society, Singapore's public communication campaigns adopted new approaches by the early 1970s. Literacy levels rose significantly as a result of well financed public education programs. Also, by then, English had become the language spoken in schools, at businesses, and at all government functions. These factors, coupled with the widespread adoption of television, paved the way for media-based campaigns.

In fact, the media were more suited to the new types of campaigns that emphasized attitudinal rather than behavioral changes. They included "accident free/road safety," "seatbelt," "antidrug abuse," and "safety in construction and shipyard industries." Thus, as the economy changed, so did the nature and techniques of the nation building campaigns.

Typical of the new multimedia campaigns was the Speak Mandarin program launched in 1979. With support from leaders throughout Singapore's Chinese community, the Speak Mandarin campaign aimed at reducing everyday use of Chinese dialects including Cantonese, Hokkien, and Teochew in favor of Mandarin, the language version deemed by Singapore's government to be the accepted language for the Chinese community in school, at public speeches, and in other official functions.

Ironically, what began in 1979 as a campaign to unify Singaporean Chinese continues today, even though dialects are rarely spoken. Now, the new Speak Mandarin campaign objective is designed to promote business contacts with mainland China, particularly with Beijing. Similarly, the early success of the family planning campaigns has now triggered reverse, and highly controversial, campaigns to prompt university-educated women and their husbands to have 3 or more children.

This brief overview of nation building campaigns in Africa and Asia introduces this chapter's theme that core public relations practice in developing countries differs in at least three basic ways from prevailing practices in more developed societies. We now examine each.

THREE FACTORS SHAPING PUBLIC RELATIONS

Societal Level Forces

First, the nature of public relations practice is influenced and constrained by larger social forces. This is particularly true at the national level in developing societies where the design of public communication campaigns is influenced by the communication infrastructure, market economy development, and political stability, as well as by linguistic and cultural integration.

Botan (1992) was the first to develop a matrix showing the relationships between societal level indicators and the predominant form of public relations in practice. The matrix suggests the delineation of global public relations into four discriminators; the level of national development, the type of primary clients, the level of legal protection along with the political role of the practice, and the uniqueness of the history of the practice. Botan (1992) argued that these factors determine, in large measure, the amount and kind of public relations resources. These, in turn, influence both the world views and the role of the practice.

Recently, Van Leuven (1994) reported on how these societal level conditions help explain the evolution of public relations in Southeast Asia. Another group of four factors emerged, including communication and media infrastructure, market–economy development, political stability, and linguistic and cultural integration. Combining these factors, we present the following propositions.

Communication Infrastructure. The more urban the society and the more developed its communication infrastructure, the greater the use of mass media for public communication campaigns. Conversely, the more rural and dispersed the society and the less developed the communication infrastructure, the more likely it is that campaigns will be designed around interpersonal communication strategies using field agents.

Carried further, using field agents supports the political goal of maintaining high public sector employment by hiring many low-paid field staff or community development specialists and calling them public relations officers.

Market Economy Impact. At least in Singapore and Malaysia, the greater the level of market development, the more likely it is that government ministries will use private sector advertising and public relations specialists as campaign advisers. In turn, the greater the involvement of such private sector specialists in nation building campaigns, the more likely it is that campaigns will be conceptualized as persuasion programs and evaluated along those lines. It should be noted, as well, that private consultants receive an additional 15% rebate from media outlets for placement of campaign advertising messages, but no similar compensation comes from campaigns using two-way interpersonal communication channels.

Political Stability. The more stable the government, the more tolerant it is of dissent, and, therefore, the more attentive government officials are to public opinion and the more responsive they are to pressure groups and citizen involvement relating to nation building campaigns.

Linguistic and Cultural Integration. As literacy increases and the number of commonly spoken languages and dialects decreases, there is greater likelihood that public communication campaign messages will be disseminated through media channels rather than by field agents. Development communication scholars attribute this choice to the speed and consistency with which mediated messages can be disseminated.

Is Third World Public Relations a Process or a Program?

A second critical question regards whether or not public relations is considered a process or a program. In the United States and perhaps elsewhere, public relations has come to be defined as a relationship-building process, but in most developing parts of the world, the term public relations is synonymous with public communication campaigns or persuasion programs for national development.

If we define public relations as a relationship-building process, the emphasis goes to dialogue, negotiation, compromise, two-way or symmetric communication. As a result, these programs become something more than persuasion campaigns seeking short-term behavioral change. Rather, the focus shifts to long-term attitudinal and cognitive change and adjustment.

Moreover, U.S.-based practitioners and scholars believe that public relations should be a two-way symmetrical process where the interests of the development agency are balanced in favor of both the agency and the receivers of the agency's messages. In such a process, message dissemination is not the driving force. Rather, the agency and its receiver publics establish mutually beneficial relationships that enhance information delivery, acceptance, and understanding. This notion is consistent with Hiebert's (1992) argument that a new public relations theory should "depict levels of effectiveness—the extent of impact of a message on a receiver, and the impact of feedback on a sender. Only if both these impacts are powerful will the communication be truly interactive" (p. 119).

Third World governments have been eager to establish information offices staffed with officers likely to provide the much needed government publicity. Publicity, in its narrow sense, not public relations, is the emphasis of communication programs.

Publicity has often been the benchmark for evaluating the effectiveness of Third World public relations. Public relations efforts geared toward communicating the wishes of the powers-that-be reflect the asymmetrical, two-way communication model. That is, goals are established largely to achieve the self-interest of government development agencies, which are usually subservient to the government and not necessarily to their strategic publics.

A few development programs in the Third World are guided by a symmetrical, two-way public relations model. These programs strive for a symmetry of interests reflecting those of both the agency and its publics. Such symmetry should encourage Third World businesses and development agencies to innovate as a first step toward changing their environments. Grunig and Grunig (1990) argue that organizational innovation in the developing countries is predicated on changes in management and communication techniques, changes crucial to the overall development. These steps are important first steps toward development in the Third World.

What Types of Relationships are Being Established?

A third consideration has to do with the types of relationships established. In developed societies, the emphasis tends to be on relationships between an organization and its strategic publics.

In developing countries, relationships are being established at the interface between a national development goal and the culture or values of particular subgroups. Al-Enad (1990) calls this the interface between the material and nonmaterial aspects of culture.

Viewed in another way, the relationships being established in Western societies generally involve private interests about which there is little agreement. In contrast, development communication or nation building campaigns typically relate to issues of public good which command considerable agreement but little popular appeal.

Also, Third World public relations tends to adhere to the press agentry, publicity, and public information models (Bhimani, 1986; Pratt, 1985: Pratt & Ugboajah, 1985; Sriramesh, 1992). In essence, practitioners in the developing nations are "less inclined to seek information from their publics because they do not intend to shape organizational activities to the needs of their environment" (Sriramesh, 1992, p. 204). Beyond that, even if they demonstrate an interest in shaping an organization's culture, such practitioners usually cannot do so because they tend not to be a part of an organization's dominant coalition. Thus, they have little influence in charting an organization's response to its strategic publics and to the threats of its environment.

The role(s) that public relations practitioners play on a day-to-day basis must be understood to fully grasp the scope of their contributions to the relationship-building process. Carried further, are the relationships being established strategic and functional, or are they routine and functionary?

Practitioners can also contribute to decision making in relation to the development process, using communication strategies to translate government programs to the poor or the needy. That is, practitioners can contribute to the development process by building interest in alternative paradigms of development. It behooves Third World practitioners, most of whom are government staffers, to contribute to development by using strategies that are sensitive to the public interest. In doing this, practitioners will necessarily be applying the ideals of social responsibility within the public relations process.

Third World public relations, as noted earlier, is largely a communications, information generating function, not a management function (e.g., Mohamed, 1984; Pratt, 1985; Sriramesh, 1992). Some "shades of gray" do exist. In China, for example, two-way symmetrical practice in local government and some private-sector operations coexists with the persuasive marketing approach of the central government (Chen & Culbertson, 1992).

Because it focuses on giving information, public relations in the Third World plays a largely functionary role—informing and persuading people. This focus makes communication more of a conduit for communicating "programmed" development news than for nurturing development-oriented norms among audiences. Practitioner responsibility is largely to the limited interests of the government, a point iterated by French philosopher Jean-François Revel (1991):

> The claim of Third World countries to their own "cultural identity" enables the ruling minorities in many of them to justify, among other things, the censorship of information and the exercise of dictatorship. Under the pretext of protecting their peoples' "culture purity," these leaders do their utmost to keep them ignorant of what is going on in the world and what the rest of the world thinks of them. They might let a trickle of news seep through, inventing, when necessary, scraps of information that permit them to mask their own failures and to perpetuate their impostures. (p. 12)

Because of these limitations in Third World public relations, there has been a continuing search for ways to achieve national development and to demonstrate practitioners' social responsibility. Oftentimes, the practitioner's responsibility is defined in terms suggestive of mandated, unified national development roles. Thus, practitioners are considered socially responsible only when they contribute directly to national development. Governments usually assume responsibility for national development plans, and expect loyalty and compliance from communication practitioners. However, as Hiebert (1992) observed, many Third World practitioners now question the development policies by which Third World leaders legitimize their control.

Taken together, these three issues—societal level forces, a focus on program versus process, and types of relationships sought—suggest considerable differences in public relations practice between developed and developing worlds. All too often, scholarly works do not reflect differing underlying philosophical and ethical assumptions about what excellent public relations and excellent development communication should be.

Further, public relations should reflect the sociopolitical environment in which it is practiced. Because practitioners develop programs that can influence their publics in a variety of ways, they are expected to do so in order to demonstrate an organization's responsibility to its publics. Practitioners should be responsible primarily to their strategic publics, and not just to their organization's managers.

Consider, for example, the idealized social role for public relations as set forth by James Grunig and colleagues in *Excellence in Public Relations and Communi-*

cation Management. These authors wrote that, in a normative sense, public relations should serve the public interest, develop mutual understanding between organizations and their publics, contribute to informed debate about issues in society, and facilitate dialogue between organizations and their publics.

Not surprisingly, development communication scholars have taken the same tack in arguing against the top-down, persuasive nature of nation building campaigns. Typical is Melkote's (1991) critique that nation building campaigns are propersuasion, pro-one-way communication, pro-mass media, and proliteracy. In short, nation building campaigns are not relationship-building processes as much as they are one-way, top-down, linear programs.

Generally, he said, government publicity programs involve one-way, persuasive messages from the government to the people, using whatever media are available, but mostly a large network of field staff including agricultural extension agents, community development specialists, public health workers, and public relations officers.

In this context, messages tend to be transmitted interpersonally and in small group contexts. Sometimes audience feedback is noted. Yet Melkote (1991) did not believe that delivery of campaign messages through interpersonal channels proceeds in accordance with two-way, symmetric or dialogic communication.

Moreover, Melkote (1991) contended that one-way asymmetric communication, while interpersonal, often produces a vicious cycle. Early adopters gain information first and know how to use it, thereby creating an even bigger income disparity between themselves and late adopters. Also, emphasis on media exposure favors the literate and educated.

Carried further, Melkote (1991) noted that such programs tend to break down local cultural traditions and to support existing ruling groups, especially as the poor have little access to the media.

As a result, Melkote (1991) has suggested shifting the posture of development support communication programs from a one-way asymmetrical stance to two-way symmetrical communication. That shift would lead to more equity in the distribution of information and other benefits of development, active participation of people at the grassroots, independence of local communities to tailor development projects to their own objectives, problem-solving approaches based on user suggestions, tailored messages, assessment of audience needs, use of folk media and entertainment formats on television, help in developing a country's cultural identity, acting as a vehicle for citizen self-expression, facilitating problem articulation, and serving as tools for diagnosis of community problems.

In short, Melkote's (1991) suggestions line up with the sense of the idealized social role as set forth by Grunig and colleagues. That is, public relations and development-communication scholars both appear to believe that public relations operates best in pluralist or progressive societies where conflicting views are reconciled through compromise and peaceful resolution.

Beyond this very general consensus, however, the idealized social role concept is appropriate only in a limited sense as a normative public relations model for developing societies. It is not at all clear, for instance, that the public interest, and not private political interests—are served just because those in power claim to be speaking in the public interest. Furthermore, political leaders do not disagree in the abstract that dialogue and two-way communication contribute to mutual understanding between governments and their citizens just as they do between organizations and their publics.

Moreover, the gaps between the idealized social role and the realities of nation building campaigns imply new questions for practitioners and scholars. Public debate has not led automatically to peaceful resolution of competing interests because governments have made concerted efforts to limit public exposure of groups who are at odds with government policy. Governments measure social progress in terms of how fast they achieve target development goals. Thus, the process mitigates against time consuming, bottom-up communication or relationship building between various local interests and those of the national campaigns.

By now, it should be clear that there is no natural strain or tendency toward increased use of two-way over one-way communication as societies develop and economies expand. On the other hand, the more stable the government, the greater the opportunity exists for dialogic communication. Ironically, too, the more developed the market economy and the higher the literacy level, the heavier the use of one-way mass media channels to convey consistent messages rapidly across all subgroups.

CONCLUSIONS

In this chapter, we have tried to show how larger social, economic, political, cultural, and information infrastructure conditions influence the nature and extent of public relations practice in the Third World and among the newly industrializing economies. Further, we suggest that formulations of public relations concepts, even normative and idealized ones, cannot be transferred automatically across cultures without first accounting for levels of societal development, whether public relations is regarded as a relationship-building process or a communication campaign or program, and assumptions about the nature of the relationships being established.

We conclude with the very modest assessment that what constitutes ethical and socially responsible public relations is more culturally defined than heretofore generally acknowledged.

REFERENCES

Ake, C. (1991). Rethinking African democracy. *Journal of Democracy, 2*(1), 32–44.
Al-Enad, A. H. (1990, Summer). Public Relations Role in Developing Countries. *Public Relations Quarterly, 35*(2), 24–26.

Bhimani, R. (1986). Status of PR in India: The image of a peacock and the status of an ostrich. *International Public Relations Review, 10*(2), 19–23.

Botan, C. (1992). International public relations: Critique and reformulations. *Public Relations Review, 18*(2), 149–159.

Chen, N., & Culbertson H. M. (1992, Fall). Two contrasting approaches of government public relations in Mainland China. *Public Relations Quarterly, 37*(3), 36–41.

Davidson, B. (1992). *The black man's burden: Africa and the curse of the nation-state.* New York: Times Books.

Grunig, L. A., & Grunig, J. E. (1990). Strategies for communication on innovative management with receptive individuals in development organizations. In M. Mtewa (Ed.), *International science and technology: Philosophy, theory and policy* (pp. 118–131). New York: St. Martin's Press.

Grunig, J. E., & White J. (1992). The effect of world views on public relations. In J. E. Grunig (Ed.), *Excellence in public relations and communication management* (p. 53). Hillsdale NJ: Lawrence Erlbaum Associates.

Hiebert, R. E. (1992). Global public relations in a post-Communist world: A new model. *Public Relations Review, 18*(2), 117–126.

Lowe, V. (1986). *Asian p. r.* Singapore: Times Books International.

Melkote, S. R. (1991). *Communication for development in the Third World: Theory and practice.* New Delhi, India: Sage.

Mohamed, R., II (1984, January). Public relations in Lebanon: No task for the timid. *Communication World*, 35–38.

Morais, B., & Adnan, J. (Eds.). (1986). *Public relations: The Malaysian experience.* Kuala Lumpur, Malaysia: Federal Publications Sdn. BhD. for Institute of Public Relations Malaysia.

Morrow, L. (1992, September 7). Afrida: The scramble for existence. *Time*, pp. 40–46.

Nair, B. (1986). *A primer on public relations in Singapore.* Singapore: Asian Mass Communication Research and Education Centre.

Pratt, C. (1985, February). Public relations in the Third World: The African context. *Public Relations Journal, 41*(2), 11–12, 15–16.

Pratt, C., & Ugboajah, F. O. (1985). Social responsibility: A comparison of Nigerian public relations with Canadian and U.S. public relations. *International Public Relations Association Review, 9*, 22–29.

Revel, J-F. (1991). *The flight from truth: The reign of deceit in the age of information.* New York: Random House.

Sriramish, K. (1992). Societal culture and public relations: Ethnographic evidence from India. *Public Relations Review, 18*(2), 201–211.

Van Leuven, J. K. (1994, July). Developing criteria for explaining public relations practices in internations contexts: Advances in Singapore and Malaysia. Paper presented to International Communication Association annual conference, Sydney, Australia.

6 Gender Issues in Public Relations Practice

Doug Newsom
Texas Christian University

India is attracting attention as one of the world's largest democracies, and as a country where the dramatic growth of a middle class is changing the nature of society. Both of these elements have generated a growing demand for public relations practice.

Joining the ranks of some leading women public relations practitioners are new entrants to the field who are now able to get public relations degrees. They do face some hardships. Educational critics say their degrees are not as strong as they should be. In the workplace, they often have a difficult time combatting age-old traditions reinforced by their culture. Their cultural environment also makes it difficult for them to live alone if they are young and unmarried. Also, if they are married and have children, care for preschoolers must be provided by family members.

These women do have some strong role models, though, women practitioners who are nationally and internationally known. For women just entering the field, the best opportunities for jobs with pay and responsibility at levels which males achieve seem to be in agencies and the corporate sector. Both of these domains also represent areas of greatest growth in India's changing economy.

The more recent contributing factors to what has been called a "boom" in public relations include increased foreign investment as a result of liberalized economic policies, expanded privatization and deregulation, and more public offerings by domestic companies, according to Michael Neri, chief executive of Profile, a GCI Group affiliate based in Bombay (Bovet, 1994, p. 9). The nation has also received a great deal of financial attention from nonresident Indians (NRIs) who, although living abroad, have maintained an interest in their country's development.

Burson-Marsteller Roger Pereira Communications Pvt. Ltd. in Bombay notes that the opening up of capital markets in the 1970s helped improve the climate for public relations. Efforts to reach financial publics gave public relations communicators enhanced status. The agency also sees consumerism's growth as another major factor. The consumer era, they say, was introduced by the transformation of India from an agro-based economy to an industrial one. Although this transformation is far from complete, it is well along in its development.

The maturing of public relations has come from a time in the 80s when ". . . the managing directors of companies were more satisfied seeing their photograph in print (to now when) . . . they are more interested in putting across their point of view" (Burson-Marsteller Roger Pereira Communications Pvt. Ltd., 1994). Corporate communication managers now also work more closely with personnel managers to improve internal communication.

Increasing economic and political power for a growing middle class in a democracy that was one of the first developing nations to embrace technology has meant steadily increasing communications with various definable publics.

BACKGROUND

India became independent in 1947, reorganized in 1956, and then made more changes in 1960 and 1966, all along linguistic lines. India lists 14 languages in its constitution and still recognizes 16 different official languages but uses English as the language of business. Efforts to unify the country with Hindi continue to meet resistance in the South. The complexity of the situation is exacerbated by the fact that these languages belong to four different families; the Indo-European, the Dravidian, the Austro-Asiatic, and Sino-Tibetan.

In addition to 12 major or dominate regional languages, there are at least 200 other languages. A literate Indian, then, must be able to read and speak Hindi which is the official language of the Union, and English, the international language which is common to the country from the British colonial days, as well as a regional language of the state and perhaps another language or dialect of one's birthplace.

This linguistic diversity carries with it cultural implications and is of such significance that public relations and advertising communicators have their hands full preparing messages in a multiplicity of languages and styles to accommodate regional preferences in a vast nation that celebrates diversity.

Media are diverse too, with members of a particular tribe putting out their own newspaper through desktop publishing. However, more traditional print media include a well-established English language press and strong regional newspapers in the language of a particular area. The home of Sanskrit (dating back to the 3rd century B.C.), one of the oldest languages in the world, India still has a strong print orientation. The 1990–1992 figures show 2,538 newspapers.

Magazines have become increasingly popular, although their content is still better than their production qualities.

India has television delivery through both cable and satellite. The Cable News Network is available, as is Sky TV from Rudolph Murdoch's communication conglomerate. The state-owned television has recently gone from two channels to 10, and viewers have about 16 channels to choose from (Bovet, 1994). VCRs are very popular, and small stores carry cassettes for both sale and rent. Radio receivers are everywhere. Ear plugs attached to a radio receiver and boomboxes are common sights. Broadcasts are in many different languages.

The complexity of the nation and the natural tensions created by diversity increase the need to communicate and to generate consensus for the democracy to function. In this socioeconomic-political climate, some public relations practitioners have been working for a long time, and they are experts, able to hold their own against any practitioners the world has to offer. However, these people constitute a thin layer at the very top of the field.

The 1980s saw an explosion of growth in the middle class. Symptoms and causes included more demands for education, more clamoring for consumer goods, more voices joining in the creation of public opinion, and the communication technology to connect these voices, although the latter is still racing to catch up, especially in rural areas. The country is changing so quickly, and the need for public relations talent is growing so exponentially, that the supply cannot begin to meet the demand.

Many of India's top public relations professionals are in their late 40s and early 50s, were educated abroad, and have international business experience. Most are employed by transnational companies (Newsom & Carrell, 1994). Their predecessors, India's public relations pioneers, were mostly publicists and press agents whose jobs grew out of the need to disseminate information about World War I (Reddi, 1988).

World War II heightened the significance of the Central Bureau of Public Information set up by the British colonial government in 1923. The same function is carried out today by the Press Information Bureau (Reddi, 1988). The British also promoted passenger travel on the Indian Railways through The Publicity Bureau of the Railways in London. The Bureau used newspaper and magazine stories as well as film and exhibits. In 1945, the House of Tata established a public relations division in its Bombay office (Reddi, 1988).

After independence, the new government put the Press Information Bureau in its new Ministry of Information and Broadcast which also has several other divisions such as publications, drama, and song (Reddi, 1988). Corporate offices also changed under the new government, and companies like Dunlop India and Phillips put in public relations units. By 1958, the Public Relations Society of India had formed.

In this period, public relations is said to have emerged in India as a definable discipline. The field's visibility was enhanced by a very public battle. In the early

1950s, two major oil companies, Shell and Stanvac, competed to win public opinion for setting up refineries (Burson-Marsteller Roger Pereira Communications Pvt. Ltd., 1994). Twenty years later, some companies with large advertising budgets added public relations as an "add-on," and the advertising agencies followed suit, providing public relations services at little or no cost. By the mid 1970s this pattern changed and corporations hired more public relations professionals.

In the mid 1980s, public relations consultancies began to emerge. Now India has three major consultancies which are joint ventures with international public relations firms, six major consultancies that have international affiliations, and eight other national consultancies without such affiliations. In a parallel development, companies redesigned their in-house units to form corporate communications departments.

THE ROLE OF WOMEN

Women have participated in this development. They have worked as practitioners in India since the early days of independence, but the society is still paternalistic. However, with the recent growth of the middle class the demand for public relations practitioners has grown. Also, more women have been looking to careers apart from and in addition to their family roles. In seeking those jobs, they have often received pay equal to that of male practitioners with comparable jobs and comparable credentials.

Women often hold positions with status equal to that of men with comparable skills, but the environment for women is more favorable in some areas of public relations practice than in others. Public relations agencies or firms have the largest number of women employees, with corporations ranking second. Fewer women work in government practice, in their own public relations firms, and in nongovernment organizations (NGOs).

The annual growth in public relations firms has been called "massive," especially for firms with strong western ties (Bovet, 1994). Part of this growth seems to stem from the growth in marketing communication, although marketing and public relations have experienced some of the same tension in India that they have in the United States (Bahl, 1993). Sushil Bahl, general manager of publicity and public relations for Greaves Cotton, said, "Communications experts today believe that it is time for rethinking the standard segregationist approach to communications in marketing and public relations."

Reconceptualization of the public relations function has also affected corporations in that they have begun to pay more attention to employee relations and are giving greater attention to internal communication (Bahl, 1993). Increasing competition in the Indian economic environment has made management aware of the need to alert employees to changes in the economy that affect their businesses. There also has been growth in professionally managed newsletters and house publications as well as in the trade press. These outlets serve as primary sources of information for many industries.

Growth in both number of firms and corporate public relations positions is good news for women, as these are the two environments most receptive to hiring female practitioners.

Outstanding Women Role Models

Many women are among the new players in the public relations field. Although just now emerging as owners and managers, they have some impressive role models.

The Public Relations Society of India (PRSI) had a woman president when it began its Foundation, an important impetus for research and education. Adity Syam is the corporate public relations manager for ITC Limited and has been with the company since 1969. She is known far beyond her Calcutta base. She says she learned public relations "on the job" and was fortunate enough to have a good male mentor. She pushed for organization of the Foundation for Research and Education largely to raise the level of professionalism of practice in India and to provide assistance to those who now must learn on the job.

Another successful practitioner, Rita Bhimani, has her own business in Calcutta. The owner of Ritam Communications, a corporate public relations consulting firm, she has written a new book about the field, *The Corporate Peacock*, published in India. In a chapter on education, she writes that, although public relations is taught as a management tool in communication, it seldom is offered in business schools.

Bhimani also has been teaching at Bhavan's College of Communication and Management, and says that experience has been "a highly stimulating learning process." She comments that, "I do believe that practitioners owe it to the profession to take time off to teach because it also gives us a chance to update ourselves, read, do some research, and come in touch with what students and prospective entrants into the profession are looking for" (R. Bhimani, personal communication, 1994).

Prema Sagar of Genesis Public Relations, public relations consultants based in New Delhi, says that more and more women are turning to public relations as a career option. "Today," she says, "around 10% of the public relations practitioners are women. In the next five years, women will form 25% of the public relations force" (personal communication, 1994).

PUBLIC RELATIONS MOVES TOWARD PROFESSIONALISM

Sagar (1994) noted that the professionalism of public relations practice is increasing. The PRSI is now 28 years old with 20 regional chapters and 2,500 members. Approximately 10% of the nation's practitioners are members of that organization.

The effort to move public relations toward professionalism also means educating clients as to what public relations is, particularly that it is much more than publicity. Sagar is quoted as having refused to sign on a client who was organizing a conference because the people involved "wanted me to put in writing how many articles newspapers and magazines would publish about them" (cited in Vaidyanathan, 1993, p. 69).

Sagar has said the big boost to a broader use of public relations in India came from the multinationals that moved into the country. "It was natural for the MNCs to look for legal consultants, financial consultants and public relations consultants. Once that happened, the Indian industrial houses, too, started looking for people who could give them a high-profile image" (cited in Thakur, 1994, p. 1).

Bombay Standard Chartered Bank's director of public relations, Bina Thakore, has said that ". . . the whole concept of and approach to public relations has changed, especially with the management" (cited in Barbhaya, 1994). It has changed from being a host or an expendable nicety to something important. The reason, according to Pragnya Ram, public relations manager of Hindustan Ciba-Geigy, is that ". . . increasingly, companies are concerned about their corporate image and are interested in building a distinct corporate identity." Ram has changed her designation from corporate public relations to corporate communications because so much of her work is directed internally. "This is because managements are beginning to realize that it helps corporate performance if employees are satisfied with their jobs and with management."

Moving beyond publicity and image building to the role of issues and problem solving has been difficult, according to Sabina Mehta Sood, accounts director of Good Relations (India) which began as a subsidiary of Cox & Kings from the Tata Group. "We are still trying to figure out how to go about doing issue-based public relations," she said. The 6-year-old agency has as its clients the two Taj hotels in Delhi and one in Bombay, and handles public relations for Tata Steel and the Tata Press Yellow Pages as well as AT & T and Airbus.

Problems for All Public Relations Practitioners

Credibility and acceptance, especially by the new media, continue to be problems for public relations people. Some practitioners blame the difficulty on the lack of training for people who move into public relations from all sorts of fields such as banking and teaching. The lack of training prevents these people from knowing how to work successfully with journalists, some of whom say they cannot trust the accuracy of news releases from certain sources. Also, editors accuse some practitioners of flooding newsrooms with useless press releases.

The more critical problem is that some corporate public-relations people are still seen as stonewallers, convivial hosts, and even "bag carriers," supplying corporate bribes. Sagar agrees that public relations is still looked down on as unworthy of being a profession. She sees this as a simple explanation of why very few men work in the field.

Material from Burson-Marsteller Roger Pereira Communications Pvt. Ltd. says that

> [F]or a profession that has really been in existence for four decades in the country, public relations has not yet been able to carve a distinct niche for itself as an independent discipline. Misconceptions still prevail with public relations often being perceived as a wining and dining show which involves receiving high-level corporate guests or arranging a few conferences. The need (for public relations) is felt only at the time of a crisis—a reactive "fire-fighting" style which primarily involves press relations (Burson-Marsteller Roger Pereira Communications Pvt. Ltd. , 1994).

Some Other Obstacles: Caste, Class, Culture, and Color

Women's ability to advance is often predetermined to some extent by birth. Caste and class still make a difference, as does religion, not only in contacts that provide opportunities but also in access to education.

India has outlawed the caste system, but caste remains a shadow over all relationships. Women are especially affected because birth status provides or denies power, and hence leverage, critical to women in a patriarchal society.

Caste also affects the working relationships, especially in public relations, because those in power often foster top-down communication structures. To some extent, caste also affects working relationships, although men find it easier to work across such lines than women do.

An unspoken factor affecting women's opportunities is color. Lighter skins are favored in India, even in the southern states where darker skin is the norm. This is apparent in all kinds of advertising and television programming, especially where women are concerned. It seems more permissible for men to have dark skin. As a result, some women with very dark skin have fewer business opportunities in general, except, perhaps, in institutions of higher learning.

Caste and class, as well as religion, carry with them some expectations for the role of women. In some situations these are more restrictive than in others. Some women, both Muslim and Hindu, find working outside the home difficult because of family expectations and the lack of available child care. If no immediate family members are available to care for young children, working outside the home is problematic even though domestic staff may be available.

The culture also does not support a single woman's living alone. Thus, women must work where they can live with some family member, however extended, or they must marry. Women do not have apartments or live alone in a home unless they have inherited the family home or are widows. Even then, a member of the family generally lives with them. Some working women who are married but have no immediate family in the cities where they work leave their children with grandparents in other locations such as nearby towns or villages and only see them on weekends, at least until the children are of school-age.

Access to education also depends in many ways on caste, class, religion, and culture. Although education is very important in India and has been historically, it has been and continues to be limited. A court ruling in 1993 decreed that education is a right only up to age 14, and that professional colleges could reserve 50% of their seats for people prepared to pay substantial fees. The court also decided that there could be no quota for families, castes, or communities that might have set up colleges. The universities have been under a mandate to set aside a certain number of admissions for scheduled castes and tribes, and this has created some tension among the higher castes who have encountered growing competition among their peers. This is all part of India's ongoing battle to provide equal educational opportunities. Struggles have become even more difficult with increased demand for education in all fields, including public relations.

Curricular Development in India

Responsible critics in India have cited four major concerns about higher education in general. These include the unplanned growth of colleges and universities, the loose structure of Indian academic life which they call "proverbially soft" with a "lot of liberty taken with norms" resulting in a lack of rigor, outdated examination formats, and lack of adequate financing (Bahl, 1993, p. 3).

Some feel that public relations education "has a long way to go when compared with education in other professions like finance, personnel or even legal and medical" (Bahl, 1993, p. 7). The situation for women is especially critical because, according to 1990–1991 statistics, only one third of the women in India have an opportunity for higher education.

While these observations seem accurate, education for public relations is exploding in India. Fortunately, most of this explosion is occurring under the watchful eye of the Public Relations Society of India's Foundation for Public Relations Education and Research, founded in 1989. Although the organization has no actual control over academic content, it does exert considerable influence. The Foundation offers a course in public relations taught by professionals for professionals, but this is outside of the academy. In 1990 and 1991, the Foundation offered professional diploma examinations in three cities for students from all over India who wanted to qualify as public relations practitioners.

Most of the new public relations courses are being offered as diploma programs in the so-called "open universities" which many adults without undergraduate degrees attend, generally on a part-time basis. Some students also are seeking advanced degrees in these professionally oriented institutions.

India's first open university, established in 1982 in Hyderabad by the Andhra Pradesh state legislature, first offered a postgraduate diploma in public relations. The diploma has now been upgraded to a bachelor's degree. Diploma programs are also now being offered at such places as the Indian Institute of Mass Communication in New Delhi, the Delhi University, and Osmania University, as well as at XLRI in Jamshedpur. This listing includes some distance learning classes.

Outside the government recognized programs are some institutes such as Bhavan's Colleges. Bhavan's program generally gets high marks from professionals. Another quality institute is the Mudra Institute of Communications at Ahmedabad. This is an autonomous, nonprofit academic institution founded in 1991 by the Mudra Foundation for Communications Research and Education. It offers certificate and diploma courses designed to implement integrated communication. The problem for these academic programs is recognition of "outside" credentials by many corporations.

Vice Chancellor Syed Bashirrudin at Dr. B. R. Ambedkar Open University in Hyderabed said when he was chair of the journalism department at Osmania University that India must ". . . rise above diplomas and unstructured correspondence courses and mature toward excellence in seeking the frontiers of expanding awareness of communication and the behavioral sciences that would truly make the science of public relations a profession" (Bashiruddin, 1988).

Rita Bhimani (1994) agrees,

> We will be making a serious mistake if we feel that our one-year and two-year diploma courses, our master's degrees, and our crash courses in public relations will be doing the job of getting people on the practical road faster. These are useful courses, but we also need to have full-fledged recognized undergraduate public relations programs which will confer the degree of bachelor of arts or bachelor of science in public relations and will equip both degree holder and company alike with a newly qualified professional to be given a specific PR job in a well-defined PR department.

Bhimani was chair of the International Public Relations Association's Research and Education Committee which published a Gold Paper on Public Relations Education, Recommendations, and Standards in 1973.

Bhimani and Bashirruddin both recommend that public relations be taught in programs leading to the master's degree in business administration. Bhimani thinks it is the role of public relations practitioners and educators to develop MBA curricula. Some areas, she thinks, that should be included are issues monitoring, mergers and acquisitions, liaison with special groups (including government relations), media monitoring, financial public relations, industrial relations, and global communication.

To supplement traditional teaching in these areas, Bhimani views case studies a good teaching tool. When teaching at Bhavan's College of Communication and Management, she had students complete a study paper structured like a thesis.

She used this paper to insure that students think about an issue, complete a special project, or deal with some aspect of public relations in a way that has some basis in reality.

"My suggestion would be to try and see if companies could actually sponsor some of these studies, which would be in their interest and would be of some use to them ultimately," Bhimani said (1994, personal correspondence). In the United States, this approach flowered in the well-known case studies of the Harvard University Business School.

In India, one problem for all academic programs in public relations is finding qualified, experienced faculty. There are not enough now, and there is no "pipeline." Furthermore, the lack of academic tradition in public relations means that preparation at the doctoral level is unlikely in the near future. Also, there remains some concern among professionals about what is happening at the master's and undergraduate levels.

A second problem is unavailability of literature. Imported books are costly and often not as useful as ones by national authors could be. In sum, the discipline is so new in Indian higher education that the scholarship is somewhat thin. As a result, some practitioners and educators have called for closer ties with professionals not only in India, but also in other nations, through organizations such as the International Public Relations Association (Bahl, 1993, p. 11).

CONCLUSIONS

More public relations practitioners are needed in India and other countries with a growing number of middle-class consumers. There is also an expanding need for practitioners in the newly democratized countries whose governments now must influence public opinion to gain support for proposed policies. Many of these nations must explain economic changes stemming from restructuring and privatization.

The demand far exceeds the supply, and most new practitioners are coming from the news media without any formal training in their new field. In some other countries, as in India, seminars organized by seasoned practitioners are helping to bridge the gap. However, in the newly democratized countries where public relations is a totally foreign concept, the only practitioners available come from abroad. That is not ideal.

Some international organizations can help. For example, the International Public Relations Association has fostered agreement on general concepts and standards of practice that seem valid across national borders.

Women are drawn to the field in emerging and developing nations just as they are in many developed nations. Yet, they often find the path to professionalism very difficult. Many try to practice in patriarchal cultures that do not favor the basic concept of female practitioners as counselors to top management. Furthermore, in some countries, even literate women have been denied access to higher education and an opportunity to gain other credentials.

In some emerging nations, young women, usually in their 20s, and who have learned another language, are gaining appointment to positions of international relations for various government bodies such as municipalities. These people often serve as "hostesses" and informal translators for visiting dignitaries. They have no formal skills, nor are they likely to receive any. Because their jobs are new, they lack role models, male or female, to emulate. The whole concept of public relations is new. Furthermore, problems are worsened by that fact that, in emerging nations, older universities are strongly traditional.

In India the government held its first public sector public relations conference in 1979. However, there, as in many countries, the public sector has grown without corresponding growth in public relations (Reddi, 1992). The greatest need in India today is for government public relations people because the government is trying to mount major development programs as well as deal peacefully and affirmatively with the diversity of a large country. But, the government is not hiring women for its jobs. Furthermore, the greatest demand for professional skills is coming from the private sector, which is also willing to pay top salaries. The private sector is hiring women, and that is positive. However, the government is not. Unfortunately, many women lack the necessary skills and education to meet the required performance levels.

The world public relations community must find a way to identify and reach inexperienced practitioners, to help them do their jobs better, and to give them a vision of the field's vast potential.

REFERENCES

Bahl, S. (1993). *Public relations education: Industry's expectation.* New Delhi, India: India Foundation for Public Relations Education and Research.

Barbhaya, M. (1994, March 2). The changing face of corporate PR. *The Indian Express.*

Bashirruddin, S. (1988, February). *A strategy for higher education and research in public relations and communication in India.* Presentation at the Eleventh All-India Public Relations Conference, Hyderabad, India.

Bhimani, R. (1994). Personal correspondence.

Bovet, S. F. (1994, June). Public relations in India growing exponentially. *Public Relations Journal, 50*(6), 9, 14.

Newsom, D., & Carrell, B. (1994). Professional public relations in India: Need outstrips supply. *Public Relations Review, 20,* 183–188.

Reddi, C. V. N. (1988, February). *Indian public relations today.* Paper presented to the Eleventh All-India Public Relations Conference, Hyderabad, India. [Republished as a pamphlet]

Reddi, C. V. N. (1992). *Public relations in public transports.* Hyderabad, India: Sharada Publications.

Thakur, Punam. (1994, May 14). In their own image. *Sunday Times of India,* p. 1.

Vaidyanathan, S. (1993, December 22). Prodded into professionalism. *Business Today (India),* 68–71.

II PUBLIC RELATIONS IN SPECIFIC COUNTRIES AND REGIONS

7 Public Relations in China: The Introduction and Development of an Occupational Field

Ni Chen
University of Toledo

These days, new professions and fields of studies are spreading to societies where they seem alien. Mainland China offers many useful examples. Since the early 1980s, Western public relations, advertising, business administration, management, marketing, and related fields have entered the world's most populous nation in the wake of dramatic political and economic changes.

This research examines the process by which an occupation with Western roots—public relations—has diffused and evolved within the People's Republic of China. Primary research questions were: What is the nature of Chinese public relations practice in terms of roles practitioners play and models they adhere to most closely? and What factors appear to correlate with their behavior, beliefs about, and approaches to public relations? The author then concludes by discussing differences between public relations in China and in the West.

AN OVERVIEW

Western public relations has taken hold in China since the early 1980s. Now, Chinese officials claim that about 100,000 practitioners work in almost all sectors of society (Jia, 1992). Also, universities are offering public relations curricula, and many public relations firms and agencies have opened.

We begin by examining the broad context in China as it has developed since the late 1970s.

Political, Economic, Social, and Cultural Contexts

Although often attributed to changes in the economic system, the introduction and development of public relations in China actually have much deeper roots, an earlier change in political ideology (Chen & Culbertson, 1992). The death of Party Chairman Mao Zedong, the end of the Great Cultural Revolution, and the new Chinese leadership headed by Deng Xiaoping in the late 1970s brought substantial changes. These were first reflected in political thinking; the decision to open doors to the West, the goal of achieving Four Modernizations (in agriculture, industry, national defense, and science and technology), and reduced state control. Meanwhile, the political changes set the stage for reforms in the economic system. A mixture of state-planned and market-oriented economic systems was introduced.

All of this created a climate receptive to new ideas and prepared the groundwork for public relations, a Western concept, to take hold in the Chinese context. The new field helped facilitate transactions, maintain smooth relations, and further establish mutually beneficial relations between organizations and their various publics in a society undergoing lots of changes.

In China, the ruling ethic of Confucianism of emphasis on personal relationships, honesty, high moral standards, and loyalty to one's groups, was highly valued. However, a corrupted form of this set of practices, *gao Guanxi,* had become part of everyday life, especially with leniency and openness accompanying the reforms. Dissatisfaction with bribery and other aspects of this corrupted version of Confucian, relationship-based ethics pushed many to seek a system truly in harmony with traditional values. In addition, as Chinese life became increasingly complex and contacts with outsiders gained in importance, public relations came to be viewed by some as an effective substitute for certain elements of organizational behavior that had been weakened or had proved unworkable in modern times.

The Development and Practice of Public Relations

Public relations' development must be seen as a multidimensional process. First, the field underwent a vertical development, gaining acceptance and growth. And second, after being introduced in some key industries, it spread horizontally to other areas. Vertical development, as with any newly introduced field, was limited by misunderstandings about its meaning, concepts, uses, and potentials. And horizontal diffusion was confined at first to Western joint ventures.

Regarding its vertical development, public relations in China has undergone three stages (Men, 1990); introduction, upsurge, and rethinking. And the field has now entered a fourth stage.

The introductory stage lasted from 1980 to 1985, paralleling China's move toward a partial commercial economy. Awareness of the concept was followed by study and popularization of the new field. At this stage, misunderstandings stemmed in part from traditional prejudices. Confused, unqualified practitioners misused existing practices.

The second stage, public relations' upsurge or explosion, lasted from 1986 to June 1989. During this period, many people became aware of and interested in the field. Public relations associations at different levels, public relations departments in various organizations, and public relations books as well as articles mushroomed. Though confusion about the goal, roles, and practice remained, more and more people learned the basics and began trying to use them. Misunderstood principles slowly became better understood. And, as this happened, public relations usage also expanded into new areas.

Stage 3 was a rethinking stage. This began after June 4, 1989. The shock to the power elite resulting from the 1989 student prodemocracy movement and the government's crackdown on that day caused the leadership to call for reconsideration of all ideas imported from the West. A new policy stressed the definition of socialist public relations with Chinese features. The policy emphasized that Western public relations could not be copied without change. Public relations with Chinese features, then, must develop in accordance with unique Chinese characteristics (An, 1990). China is a socialist country, governed by the Communist Party. It follows that both the Party and the government must supervise practice in the field.

In Spring 1992, Deng Xiaoping visited several coastal cities in the South. His posttour speech set the tone for continuation of an open door policy, emphasizing that, whatever it takes (capitalism or socialism), as long as it enhances productivity, a practice should be encouraged (Yuan & Han, 1992). That ended the debate over public relations with socialist features and under Party leadership. Since then, public relations development has entered a more stable phase with movement toward professional status.

In the horizontal development, public relations practice spread from its initial niche in joint-venture manufacturing corporations to service firms, government institutions (Chen & Culbertson, 1992), and even peasant-owned enterprises.

Obviously, the basic philosophies, principles, roles, and functions of public relations in China would be expected to differ from those in the United States and other Western countries. We now explore these differences in some detail.

LITERATURE REVIEW AND HYPOTHESES

The research tests the assumption that modern public relations, like other concepts and fields with Western roots and influence, diffused from the southern coastal regions around Guangzhou (often viewed as the country's innovation center) to the commercial and government capitals (Shanghai and Beijing, respectively), and then to more conservative inland cities such as Nanjing (a typical medium-sized inland city without a preponderance of Western influence). This assumption is based on clear differences among the regions as to a presumed level of influence by Western concepts and practice.

Moreover, the differences among the four cities may apply to the study of early adopters, assumed to predominate in the Guangzhou region and, to a lesser degree, Beijing and Shanghai, and later adopters, perhaps seen quite heavily in Nanjing. Literature on the diffusion of innovation (Rogers, 1983) shows that innovators and early adopters in a variety of fields differ systematically from the later adopters and "laggards" regarding their communication behavior, thinking patterns, and so forth.

These arguments suggest three testable hypotheses on the evolution, over time, of Chinese public relations:

Hypothesis 1. Public relations has become widespread with public relations departments or agencies earlier in Guangzhou region than in Shanghai and Beijing, and it was found earlier in the latter two cities than in Nanjing;

Hypothesis 2. The dates by which public relations majors and sequences became established at major universities were, in general, in the following order: Guangzhou region, then Shanghai and Beijing, and finally Nanjing.

Hypothesis 3. Senior practitioners working in Guangzhou region, Shanghai, and Beijing, in general, have studied public relations (or studied from professors trained) in their own cities and regions. Practitioners in Nanjing tend to have studied in or studied from professors trained in locations other than their own.

Regarding hypothesis 3, diffusion of public relations thought and practice from Shenzhen in particular, and the Guangzhou region in general, to the rest of China might be hampered by the need for citizens throughout the country to gain special permission before entering a special autonomous zone. This may have reduced the opportunity for even Beijing and Shanghai practitioners to study and work in or learn from those teaching and practicing there. The restriction now is relatively relaxed.

The next three hypotheses deal with the current state of public relations practice as viewed in light of diffusion theory (Rogers, 1983), role theory (Broom & Dozier, 1986), and the evolutionary model of Grunig and Hunt (1984).

Broom and Dozier defined four major public relations roles; expert prescriber, communication facilitator, problem-solving process facilitator, and communication technician. They, along with several colleagues, have also demonstrated a gradual shift from the role of communication technician, framing and disseminating messages, toward the manager role. Although apparently still not dominant numerically among American practitioners, communication managers have gradually become the ideal as portrayed in texts, and academic conferences

(Cutlip, Center, & Broom, 1985; Grunig & Hunt, 1984). Definitions of subroles within communication-management and technician positions are often debated (Culbertson, 1985). However, a great deal of research has helped refine the role instrument proposed more than a decade ago by Broom and Dozier.

Grunig and Hunt (1984) proposed a four-stage evolutionary model (press agent/publicity, public information, two-way asymmetric, and two-way symmetric) as a basis for examining the history of American public relations. The authors suggested that the press agent/publicity model was predominant early in the field's evolution, but that there has since been a move from emphasis on one-way to two-way communication, and from persuasion to relationship building as a primary goal.

Some research suggests that public relations has progressed from a "craft" practiced by people trained in such varied areas as law, engineering, and counseling to a self-contained occupation (some would argue, a profession) with its own specialized system of training, apprenticeship, accreditation, and recognition. However, in reality, some who have worked and studied in other fields still invade American public relations departments and agencies. Such invasion is said to detract from the autonomy, hence quality, of public relations (Grunig, 1992).

Assuming some parallels between China and the United States, we propose three hypotheses:

Hypothesis 4. The proportion of practitioners playing the communication-manager roles are in the following rank order: Guangzhou region > Shanghai and Beijing > Nanjing. Conversely, the proportion of practitioners focusing largely or entirely on the communication-technician role or roles are ranked in the reverse order of that just given.

Hypothesis 5. The proportion of practitioners who practice and define public relations largely or primarily as two-way communication would be in the following rank order: Guangzhou > Shanghai/Beijing > Nanjing. Conversely, the proportion who focus on one-way communication would be ranked in the reverse order of that just given.

Hypothesis 6. The proportion of practitioners with academic training which includes an academic major or minor in public relations would be in the following rank order: Guangzhou region > Beijing/Shanghai > Nanjing. Conversely, the proportion of invaders without academic work in the field would be ranked in the reverse order of that just given.

Although the above hypotheses were derived in part from the literature on diffusion of innovations, this research investigated other and varied areas as well.

First, social conditions seem likely to influence the philosophy and practice of public relations in every society. One such condition is the dominant theory of the press in that society (Al-Enad, 1990).

The Chinese communication system is structured on Marxist-Leninist philosophy of communications (Cheng, 1989). The main function of the media is defined as promoting the policies of leadership and helping to control society. News is information that serves the interests of the government and the ruling party, advancing its goals and policies. The Communist Party maintains a monopoly over channels and content of communication (Schramm, 1956). Thus, media in China serve as the official, authoritative mouthpiece of both the Communist Party and the government (Howkins, 1982).

Communication generally in this setting is presumed to be of a one-way, persuasive form with an asymmetrical, imbalanced purpose to serve source rather than audience goals. If a certain theory dominates press conditions, press relations must develop accordingly.

Second, freedom of choice (Janis & Mann, 1977) refers to the degree to which decision makers are free to choose among viable alternative courses of action that might serve their purposes. A society or organization that values individualism and independence will allow greater freedom of choice than will a restrictive, centralized one. Also, the range of choices available to the decision maker will affect an individual's decision making by indicating which routes, policies, practices, and outcomes are permissible under the rules of the society or of an organization.

When there is a wide range of choice, the decision maker is able to search various approaches. Each approach is then evaluated on its merits. However, where the range of choices is restricted, creativity is limited. Decision makers find that new approaches or different avenues are discouraged. Thus, new sources or types of information are not sought, nor are new or different ways of evaluating, processing and using information easily accepted. Accordingly, the nature of the organization influences the roles their public relations practitioners play.

Based on the previous discussion, one can make the following observations:

1. Public relations in governmental institutions operates in light of certain defined communication modes; in China, this is a one-way, persuasive mode. Both freedom of choice and range of choice are limited. Practitioners within such a system are thus tightly constrained to serve as communication technicians. Public relations, then, is used as an information control agent in governmental institutions.

2. In governmental institutions, where powerful socializing forces, peer pressures, and orders from above tend to enforce centrally selected doctrines and approaches, public relations practitioners traditionally act according to officially stated policy lines. If these lines are sufficiently implanted in a person, the person and the policy should act as one, and the person may feel reduced stress.

3. Joint-venture manufacturing industries would no doubt be under much

looser government control. The participating Western corporations especially would insist on retaining a substantial role in managing such firms so as to insure profitability. This Western role should, in some measure, encourage a focus on openness to new ideas and audience needs.

4. Service industries should be somewhat more open and innovative in public relations practice than are the manufacturing firms. That is partly because service industries seek to reach and serve Western tourists and other guests, and because service industries may require relatively little infrastructure and long-term investment, making them less relevant to the government's centralized planning than the manufacturing sector.

5. Public relations practitioners in governmental institutions will be less interested than those of the private sector in new developments within the field. Such a practitioner serves a limited, one-way function to begin with, thus his or her intentions are totally directed toward passing a message along a downward path without investigating or fulfilling the information needs of the recipient. All of which suggests little investigation of new or previously unused channels, approaches, or information.

In sum, a typical governmental institution in China is, or at least used to be, structured so that those at the top undertake all decision making and enforcement. Other personnel, including most public relations practitioners, help carry out instructions from above, passing messages downward and, in the process, seeking attainment of organizational objectives. Such a structure and process produce asymmetric and imbalanced effects, serving the client organization only. Therefore, one would assume that the dominant mode of public relations practice in government would be one-way and persuasive. Also, being excluded from the decision-making team, the practitioners would basically act as communication technicians with little power and autonomy.

Based on these assumptions, the following hypotheses are proposed:

Hypothesis 7. Public relations practitioners in government do less research than public relations practitioners outside of government;

Hypothesis 8a. Public relations practitioners working in the government are more likely to define and practice public relations as one-way communication than those working in manufacturing and service sectors. The rank should be in the following order; government > manufacturing > service industries;

Hypothesis 8b. Public relations practitioners working in the government are more likely to play the role of communication technician than those working in other sectors.

The roles of practitioners in government institutions seem apt to be tightly defined, whereas the roles of those working in the service sector are, comparatively speaking, loosely defined. That is, service sector people are more likely to be given a large number of options. Thus, there is a logical progression of restriction, ranging from a low restricted joint-venture service-type corporation to a joint-venture type manufacturing corporation to a state-owned corporation and, finally, to the highly restrictive government agency. Hypotheses 8a and 8b test the effect of that progression on public relations practice.

> Hypothesis 9. A practitioner's power and autonomy in decision making, derived from the freedom of choice available, are in the following rank order: service sector > manufacturing > government.

Grunig (1972), in his information systems theory, argued that information processing denotes a passive mode in which attention is given to information that happens to come along. Information seeking, on the other hand, denotes an active mode involving information seeking, purposive selection, integration, and interpretation. His theory suggests that a high recognition problem correlates with active information seeking. Public relations practitioners in service industries can hardly insure a competitive success victory without inventions and innovations. Thus, they are not likely to feel secure in the amount of available information and always feel pressed to seek and process more. In addition, a perception of constraints as opposed to a message often leads to the passive information-processing mode. Finally, involvement in a situation may bear on information seeking and use behavior, and involvement is generally regarded as a stimulant to active information seeking. For those working in government, involvement will be low, as orders from above limit participation in decision making.

Obviously, this is closely related to the adoption of new ideas or concepts such as public relations. If practitioners are constrained by orders from above and are low involved technicians with little uncertainty about goals, strategies, and tactics, they would tend toward passive, information processing not apt to develop a profession. It follows that:

> Hypothesis 10. Public relations practitioners' intensity and breadth of information seeking are in the following rank order: service > manufacturing > government.

In further support of Hypotheses 7, 8a, 8b, 9 and 10, Janis and Mann (1977) pointed out that, in order to maintain cognitive consistency and to avoid or end cognitive dissonance, people tend to seek information with which they are already predisposed to feel comfortable, that is, they avoid or reinterpret new information they are uncomfortable with. And the methods used to enhance consistency at the expense of dissonance are certainly affected by one's cultural environment.

In connection with public relations practice, government practitioners in China have generally been presumed to obey officially stated policies. To avoid cognitive dissonance, practitioners seem likely to internalize the party line. Service and manufacturing industries seem apt to provide much more acceptance of varied approaches or ideas. Thus, the practitioners in these sectors, more often than in government, should have high flexibility in avoiding dissonance by reinterpreting new data, rejecting it, or changing behavior.

One final hypothesis remains. Although there is little direct support for this last hypothesis in public relations literature, mass communications scholars (Cobbey & McCombs, 1979; Meyer, 1978) report that careful audience study (i.e., viewing communication with one's audience as a two-way process) does and should lead to careful definition of rather narrow audience segments. This suggests:

Hypothesis 11. Practitioners who adhere to a two-way model of public relations define audiences more narrowly and specifically than do one-way model practitioners.

The above hypotheses set the stage for exploratory investigation of two broad research questions. The first question is what factors most influence the models public relations practitioners adhere to most closely and the roles they play in practice? Does age have an effect? Or gender? Or practitioners' education level? Or position and administrative status? How important are the ways in which they define their publics? And what is the role of perceptions of public relations? Second, what factors influence practitioners' perceptions of public relations? Does age have an effect? Sex? Type of organization? Education level and type? The way they view their audiences? How about other factors such as years of working experience, one's status and position within organization?

RESEARCH METHODS

Participants

A survey was conducted in 1991 among registered practitioner members of public relations associations in Beijing, Shanghai, Nanjing and Guangzhou. A total of 475 practitioners were selected from the membership lists. Of theses, 281 responded, yielding a 59% response rate.

Pretest

To insure that questions were clear conceptually and linguistically, a pretest was conducted in Beijing, Nanjing, and Shanghai. Twelve respondents, 5 females, 7 males, four from each city, were given copies of the partial questionnaire. Responses were evaluated carefully in a search for possible conceptual or definitional misunderstandings, language-based errors, and other difficulties. The questionnaire was first developed in English and translated into Chinese. Then the author back-translated into English for comparison with the original English language version so as to gauge accuracy and ease of understanding. A few appropriate changes were then made.

Sampling

The public relations associations of three cities, Beijing, Shanghai, and Nanjing, and one region, Guangzhou, were selected based on clear differences among the cities as to presumed level of influence by Western concepts and practices. Also each city seemed to epitomize a particular segment of society.

Each public relations association was assigned a target figure of 100 responses. This sample size would yield a limit of error of no more than approximately plus or minus 10% when describing practitioners in any one city, five per cent with the total sample. Most analyses focus on the entire sample or compare the cities. To allow for nonresponse, sample sizes were increased by 25% except in the case of Nanjing. The Nanjing Public Relations Association is smaller than with the other selected cities and region. Thus, it seemed reasonable to exclude Nanjing from the 25% increase used in other locations without unduly lowering precision.

Regular interval sampling from a randomly chosen starting point was used. Questionnaires went out with self-addressed, stamped envelops in early August 1991. Three consecutive attempts were made before those who failed to respond were dropped. In such cases, the next person on the list was then sent a questionnaire. Data collection ended in late December 1991.

Of the sample of 475 selected practitioners, 281 responded (90 from Beijing, 55 from Nanjing, 71 from Shanghai, and 65 from Guangzhou).

Operational Definitions

One-way Versus Two-way Public Relations. In measuring one's primary approach here, each individual was given a brief description of the four Grunig–Hunt models and asked to indicate his or her primary adherence to a particular model by putting a "2" before that model along with a "1" in front of each secondary option and a "0" before the model(s) he or she did not follow at all. Those who practiced and defined public relations largely or primarily as press-agent/publicity or public information were said to practice in a one-way mode. Those who selected two-way asymmetric or two-way symmetric were lumped together as two-way.

Communication Manager Versus Technician. In gauging role orientation, respondents estimated what percentage of time they devoted to each of the four roles defined by Broom and Dozier (1986) expert prescriber, communication facilitator, problem-solving process facilitator, and communication technicians, yielding a total of 100%.

Then, in a second operational definition, each person rated the philosophical emphasis they placed on 25 public relations activities. Twenty Broom–Dozier items were used, and five others were added based on observation of meaningful behaviors among Chinese practitioners. Factor analysis of these 25 items yielded two summed indices labeled *communication manager* and *communication technician*.

Power. Respondents were asked to rate their level of power on a scale from 1 (very low) to 7 (very high) within two realms: power to influence overall organizational policy, and power in communication-related activities.

Autonomy. A 7-point scale was used to tap how much autonomy each respondent had in making decisions concerning public relations planning and execution without others limiting their range of choice. Scale values ranged from 1 (extremely low) to 7 (extremely high).

Statistical Analyses

Both the processing and the statistical analysis were done with SPSS-PC+ (the Statistical Package of Social Analysis). Chi-squares, t tests, university analyses of variance, Pearson product-moment correlation, and Scheffe's tests were used, along with stepwise multiple regression.

Factor analysis, with principal-axis solutions followed by varimax rotation, yielded two summed indices of communication management and communication technician, which were then used to measure respondents' emphasis on various public relations roles. Also, alpha coefficients were computed as measures of internal consistency reliability.

FINDINGS AND DISCUSSION

The Diffusion Pattern, Public Relations Education, and Training

The diffusion model discussed earlier describes quite well the spread of public relations in mainland China. In general, the data confirmed that public relations entered China in the Guangzhou region, often viewed as an innovation center. It then spread in sequential order to the cosmopolitan centers of Shanghai and Beijing and, finally, to the inland city of Nanjing. Rogers (1983) reported similar geographic diffusion of many innovations.

Hypothesis 1 stated that public relations began earlier in the Guangzhou region than in Shanghai and Beijing, and earlier in the latter two cities than in Nanjing. Data clearly supported the hypothesis based the following measures; years that respondents had been aware of the concept of public relations; years that respondents had practiced it; and years of public relations departments' existence in respondents' organizations (see Table 7.1).

This sequence also held with years of availability of public relations majors and sequences. Thus, Hypothesis 2 gained support, specifying that the dates at which public relations majors and sequences became established at major universities were in the order of Guangzhou (1985), then Shanghai and Beijing (1987), and finally Nanjing (1990).

Furthermore, with respect to training patterns, Hypothesis 3 was fully supported. Specifically, the data showed that senior practitioners working in the Guangzhou region, and in Beijing had studied public relations in their own cities and region, whereas practitioners in Shanghai, and especially, in Nanjing tended to have studied in locations other than their own. About 44% of all Nanjing practitioners ($n = 24$), 26% of those in Shanghai ($n = 18$), and 3.4% of personnel in Beijing ($n = 3$), received their training "upstream" in the flow from Guangzhou to Beijing and Shanghai, to Nanjing, $\chi^2(3, N = 273) = 49.892, p <$

TABLE 7.1
Mean Years Organization has had Public Relations (PR) Department, has Practiced PR, and has had Personal Awareness of PR in Four Locations

	Nanjing	Shamghai	Beijing	Guangzhou	F
Years of PR Dept's Existence	1.78 [ab]	2.62 [c]	3.13 [a]	3.74 [bc]	8.91 ($df = 3, 100$ $p < .0001$)
	($n = 18$)	($n = 21$)	($n = 30$)	($n = 35$)	
Years of PR Practice	1.98 [a]	2.89 [a]	4.05 [a]	4.87 [a]	87.25 ($df = 3, 260$ $p < .0001$)
	($n = 52$)	($n = 65$)	($n = 87$)	($n = 62$)	
Years of PR Awareness	3.33 [a]	5.37 [a]	6.81 [a]	8.22 [a]	180.4 ($df = 3, 268$ $p < .0001$)
	($n = 54$)	($n = 67$)	($n = 87$)	($n = 64$)	

Note. Means with the same superscript differ significantly based on Scheffe's test of selected comparisons.

.001. These people apparently acted as "opinion leaders" in diffusion within their own areas. Not a single person received training "downstream" from his or her current place of work.

The same upstream pattern was obvious regarding the where respondents' instructors received their public relations training. Respondents from Nanjing confirmed that 86% of their instructors ($n = 43$) were trained somewhere else. This figure was 47% in Shanghai ($n = 28$) and 38% in Beijing ($n = 31$). No one had studied under a professor trained downstream $\chi^2(3, N = 252) = 60.72, p <$ .001. Thus, professors appeared to play a key role in diffusion.

In looking at the proportion of practitioners with academic majors or minors in public relations, or journalism or mass communications, the same rank order appeared, though this order could have occurred by chance. Around 28% of respondents from Guangzhou, 24% from Beijing and Shanghai, and 19% from Nanjing had majored or minored in one of these subjects.

Such a clear downstream diffusion has been evident not only in the evolution and development of public relations, but also in other areas from stock markets to horse race gambling. Generally speaking, China is divided between new and old in this fashion, though perhaps, as diffusion of various things progresses, even the inland areas will eventually modernize for better or worse.

Sam Black (1992), former president of the International Public Relations Association, reported, after three visits to China, that "the concept of public relations first developed in China in 1981 in the Shenzhen Special Economic Zone through contact with foreign joint venture partners. This led to the introduction in September 1981 of a full-time public relations degree course at Shenzhen University" (p. 41), which has later become a prominent center of practice and education in the field. His comments square well with results of this study.

As the diffusion process and professionalization have continued, public relations education in China, born in the Guangzhou region in the early 1980s (Committee on PR Education, 1989), has developed into a well-established multifaceted system offering innovative multilevel programs with short-term sessions sponsored by local public relations associations, distance learning through the Chinese Central Television station and local television outlets, correspondence courses offered by some major universities, 2-year degree programs through specialized vocational schools, and formal 4-year B.A. degree programs at colleges and universities (Chen, 1994).

About two-thirds of the respondents (64.8%) had at least bachelor's degrees. Most had a major in mass communications, the social sciences, or the humanities. And all the respondents claimed they had taken at least two public relations courses. These findings bode well for the field's future in light of recent literature (Culbertson, 1991; Grunig, 1985) asserting that public relations is interdisciplinary, with a need for breadth in applied social sciences and the liberal arts.

Roles & Models

Broom and Dozier's (1986) role theory and Grunig and Hunt's (1984) 4-stage evolutionary model proved useful in studying Chinese public relations practice. Chinese practitioners at least found American concepts meaningful in describing their own goals and work.

According to Broom and Dozier (1986), an expert prescriber works as an authority on public relations problems and their solutions, defines and researches problems, develops programs, and takes major responsibility for implementation. A communication technician operates as technician, proposing and producing public relations materials; writing, editing, and working with media.

Hypothesis 4 stated that the proportion of practitioners playing the communication-manager roles would be in the following rank order: Guangzhou region > Shanghai and Beijing > Nanjing. Conversely, the proportion of practitioners focusing largely or entirely on communication-technician activity would be ranked in the reverse order of that just given.

Based on overall rank orders, Hypothesis 4 was not supported fully. There was little apparent variation among locations in proportion of time each respondent reported having spent on playing the roles of a problem-solving process facilitator and communication facilitator from city to city. However, there was a significant difference between Beijing respondents and all others as to the proportion of time spent on playing the roles of an expert prescriber and communication technician. Compared with the respondents from the three other locations, Beijing people spent significantly less time acting as expert prescribers ($M = 14.71\%$, $SD = 18.36$; $M = 23.95\%$; $F(\text{df} = 3) = 6.08$, $p < .05$), but more time on playing the role of communication technician ($M = 35.28$, $SD = 24.63$ in Beijing vs. $M = 26.53\%$ in other locations; $F(\text{df} = 3) = 4.17$, $p < .05$).

In measuring respondents' model orientation, Hypothesis 5 was not supported. This hypothesis specified greatest emphasis on two-way communication in Guangzhou, followed by Beijing and Shanghai, with Nanjing ranking last. Although this was not confirmed, Beijing practitioners (44%) tended more toward one-way communication more often than practitioners in other cities (33%), but this difference was not significant. This is consistent with the idea that technicians tend to be one-way oriented (Grunig & Grunig, 1989).

In sum, although locations did not predict role or model orientation clearly, the data indicated that the practitioners in Beijing lean toward technician behavior, and perhaps slightly toward one-way practice. Public relations diffusion throughout the country did not necessarily carry particular concepts with it. However, Beijing, as China's capital city, may have relatively tight government control. New ideas arriving there may result in a tug of war between East and West, and between communism and capitalism. This may shape the profession to a degree.

Another measurement of the respondents' role and model orientations was to compare sectors of society—types of organizations and clients the practitioners worked for. The underlying expectation was that the organizational culture, structure, and objectives would relate to the roles practitioners play and models they adhere to.

The data showed that many public relations practitioners worked in joint-venture corporations (15.8%) though service industries were well represented (15%), suggesting a thriving practice there. This fits into the development pattern of public relations in China. Public relations practice began in joint-venture corporations, then spread to other industries and finally, to government institutions.

Hypothesis 8 specified that government practitioners should tend more than others to practice in the one-way and technician modes. With regard to model orientation, the hypothesis was partially confirmed. Government practitioners ($n = 10$, 48%) leaned toward the one-way mode more heavily, $\chi^2(3, N = 253) = 11.04$, $p < .05$ than did people in manufacturing industries ($n = 14$, 26%) and other fields.

Surprisingly, those in service industries ($n = 61$, 49%) were also quite one-way oriented. Partly as a result of this, government and nongovernment people, as a whole, did not differ significantly as to percentage of time devoted to playing the technician role and overall emphasis placed on technician roles (summed index).

In studying the practitioners' role and model orientations, correlational analyses yielded some interesting findings in two areas.

First, we note the centrality of the expert-prescriber role within the communication-management function. This point hinged on several specific findings. Time spent playing the expert-prescriber role, but not the other roles, based on global ratings, correlated very highly and substantially with the summed index of communication-management emphasis (philosophic orientation toward role items, $r = .64$). Communication-management emphasis also correlated positively and significantly with adherence to the two-way symmetric model ($r = .24$).

In other words, when practitioners emphasized management roles, they tended to devote much time and thought to working as an expert prescriber. And their primary orientation toward practice was most often two-way symmetric. Thus, this study suggests a link between roles and models as reported in the United States (Grunig & Grunig, 1989). Communication managers tended to emphasize the two-way symmetric model ($r = .24$) whereas communication technicians downgraded the same model, but upgraded the press agent/publicity model slightly ($r = .19$). All of this supports the contention of Broom and Dozier (1986), Culbertson (1991), and Grunig and Hunt (1984) that communication management should emphasize listening as much as speaking to the publics—a symmetrical approach.

People with an expert-prescriber focus had considerable autonomy and power in defining problems, as well as proposing and implementing programs. Thus, time spent on the expert-prescriber role correlated highly and positively with power ($r = .52$) and autonomy ($r = .53$), and mildly with primary adherence to two-way symmetric public relations ($r = .20$). As suggested in American research, an expert prescriber is a member of the management team with autonomy. Also, in China, he or she often has claims to have power in making overall organizational decisions. Such power is not always apparent in U.S. analyses.

In sum, by virtue of playing the expert-prescriber role, the practitioners claimed to focus on management roles, concerning themselves with defining public relations problems, devising strategies to solve the problems, and implementing the strategies. In addition, playing management roles did not correlate with liaison or problem-solving facilitator activities. All these factors validate the central nature of the expert-prescriber role in management as viewed by Chinese practitioners.

Second, the data suggested considerable progress among practitioners in moving into management roles. When people say they move into the management function, they operate at two levels in public relations; managing a public relations department, making decisions about hiring, job assignment, and so forth; and being part of the management team of the organization as a whole, bringing public relations perspectives into broad, policy-oriented decision making. In this study, many Chinese practitioners appeared to operate at the second level, holding some administrative titles within their organizations. In fact, about two-thirds described themselves as functioning at managerial levels, and 40% reported they worked at the top- or middle-management level.

The idea that practitioners are often part of management and decision-making teams was confirmed by analyses based on two measures. First, the practitioners spent more than two-thirds of their time in management roles, with only about one-third of their time as technicians. And second, management emphasis correlated with adherence to the two-way symmetric model ($r = .24$).

More than 70% of the respondents reported involvement in some kind of research, although they appeared to define research very broadly to encompass reading journal articles, writing for trade magazines, and so forth. In addition, among those who claimed to do research rather routinely, 90% said they placed moderate to extremely high emphasis on learning new public relations concepts and practices. Thus, in China, as in the U.S., public relations managers appeared to emphasize scholarship, environmental scanning, and definition of clients' political, social, and economic contexts. These factors are important in defining public needs as the two-way symmetric model requires.

These findings seem to indicate possible progress among Chinese practitioners in moving into genuine management roles, suggesting that Chinese public relations people think a great deal about and participate in setting of organizational policy. Obviously, further research is needed to gauge their actual behavior clearly for mainly two reasons. The evidence in this regard rests largely on the centrality of expert-prescriber behavior. However, Broom and Dozier, as well as others, pointed out that expert prescribers sometimes do not have much clout at top-management levels. High-ranking managers may give public relations directors responsibility for defining and solving public relations problems, but without much authority or many resources. Furthermore, the Broom–Dozier items and the ratings of time spent on various activities are open to a social desirability response set.

The majority of the respondents were young, as is the profession. And, as the regression results confirm, Chinese societies revere age in public relations as in most other things. Thus, one might question the reality of Chinese public relations people's heavy involvement in policy making at the overall organizational level as claimed by the respondents.

Finally, the data in this study seemed to indicate that, rather than four roles, there were really only two—communication manager and communication technician—in Chinese public relations. Recent U.S. research gave comparable findings (Culbertson, 1985; Stone, 1990).

Practitioner Differences by Sector

The remaining hypotheses, except Hypothesis 11, all zeroed in on possible differences between practitioners in government institutions and those in service and manufacturing industries.

Hypothesis 7, which specified that government public relations people do less research than other practitioners, was not confirmed. Nevertheless, the data hinted at a possible tendency of government people to study both the audience and the message whereas nongovernment practitioners focused on one or the other, $\chi^2(1, N = 273) = 8.91, p < .001$.

Regarding level of autonomy in decision making Table 7.2 supported hypothesis 9: Service people scored higher than government personnel. Also as hypothesized, the manufacturing people's score fell in between. However, the analysis of variance and accompanying Scheffe's test revealed a significant difference only between service and government practitioners.

As to the practitioners' perceived power in decision making, service people exceeded manufacturing personnel; and the latter scored higher then government people (see Table 7.2). Although means were in the predicted direction, they did not differ significantly. Thus, Hypothesis 9 received only tentative, partial support.

Furthermore, the data revealed that the level of autonomy and power in decision making related closely to both one's role and one's model orientations. Autonomy and power correlated highly with emphasis on communication management ($r = .68, r = .74$, respectively). This is understandable given that management roles theoretically require considerable autonomy and power in defining problems as well as in proposing and implementing programs.

TABLE 7.2
Mean Autonomy and Power Scores of Practitioners by Sector

	Sectors			
	Service (n = 125)	Manufacturing (n = 53)	Government (n = 21)	F
Autonomy	4.7120 [a]	4.2453	3.5714 [a]	7.1659 ($df = 2, 196$, $p < .001$)
Power	30.7200	28.9811	25.0476	4.4738 ($df = 2, 248$, $p < .05$)

[a] Means differed significantly based on Scheffe's test.

Hypothesis 10 specified that practitioners in service industries should be more active in information seeking than manufacturing people, and that the latter should be more active than government employees. This hypothesis gained no support. Practitioners working in different sectors of society did not differ in terms of their intensity and breadth of information seeking.

Hypothesis 11 asserted that practitioners who adhere to a two-way model will define audiences more narrowly and specifically than will one-way model practitioners. The data provided no support.

In sum, the hypotheses comparing different types of organizations were largely rejected. Of course, lack of precision in measures and small subsamples may help explain these negative results. Nevertheless, the quantitative analyses did lead to a clear-cut conclusion: Government practitioners, especially in Beijing, lean toward the communication-technician roles, and in some measure toward one-way models, although the data comparing sectors and cities with respect to model adherence did not yield clear and generally significant differences. This squares with current literature. Chen and Culbertson (1992) recognized the existence of two varied approaches in Chinese government public relations: One resembles two-way symmetric (prevailing in such local government as Tianjin), and the other, asymmetric, or press-agentry (in the national government).

Unfortunately, the questionnaire failed to distinguish the practitioners in local government from those in central government. Also, a very small number of people—only 21 of 281—worked in government institutions. This small subgroup may have precluded significant differences. Future research can help remedy these problems.

Research Questions

We approached the general research questions in two ways; through two-variable analysis and multiple regression, examining relationships among as many variables as possible.

Bivariate Analyses. First, we report on bivariate analyses of the first research question: What factors most influenced the practitioners' role and model orientations?

First, age correlated positively and highly with emphasis on the expert-prescriber role (a managerial role) at .49, but negatively with communication-technician ($r = -.39$) and communication-facilitator ($r = -.16$) roles. And these correlations were statistically significant ($p < .002$).

Age also correlated fairly strongly ($r = .48$) with the summed index gauging emphasis on playing communication-management roles; but negatively ($r = -.41$) with emphasis placed on playing communication-technician roles ($p < .001$). The tendency of managers to be older is to be expected in a society that has great respect for age and experience.

Although age seemed to exert considerable influence on roles played, it did not relate closely to emphasis on stages in the evolutionary model.

The analysis provided some intriguing answers to the impact of gender on role and model. Males ($n = 180$, $M = 43.87$, $SD = 12.25$) exceeded females ($n = 93$, $M = 39.77$, $SD = 12.18$) significantly on emphasis devoted to playing managerial roles, $t(187.03) = 2.63$, $p < .01$. Conversely, females ($M = 35.96$, $SD = 8.61$) exceeded males ($M = 31.52$, $SD = 7.94$) in playing technician roles, $t(173.36) = -4.15$, $p < .001$. This result parallels American findings (Broom & Dozier, 1986).

Furthermore, the literature suggests that some young women got into the field because they were physically attractive, and these people usually worked as high-level receptionists whose main job was to entertain guests (Wang, 1989). Thus, it seemed reasonable to focus on the specific technician activity of entertaining guests per se.

In line with this view, females placed more emphasis ($M = 4.90$, $SD = 1.79$) than did males ($M = 3.83$, $SD = 1.65$) on the role of entertaining guests $t(173.25) = 4.79$, $p < .001$. Also, a young female practitioner at the staff level without a college degree was most likely to work as a high-level receptionist entertaining guests.

Chinese culture emphasizes education, assuming that a college degree symbolizes knowledge and potential for success. Those with a higher education are often rewarded with prestige and self-esteem. That is why one may find that those who hold administrative positions and who function at managerial levels usually have college degrees. On the other hand, those without a college degree often work as hosts or hostesses, sort of glorified valets.

Gender also seemed to make a difference as to model orientation. Males ($n = 124$, 69%) tended somewhat more often than females ($n = 48$, 52%), $\chi^2(1, N = 172) = 7.12$, $p < .01$, to report practicing primarily according to two-way models. A contributing factor is that women were positioned to play technical roles. This may suggest that, if women were placed in a managerial position, they would practice in the two-way symmetric mode.

Third, did practitioners' education level have an impact? The data showed that degree holders tended more than nondegree holders to emphasize management activities, but this difference was not significant.

Fourth, were positions and administrative titles related? One-way analysis produced highly significant differences showing that, the higher one's position and title, the less likely she or he would be to emphasize communication-technician activity, but the more likely to focus on communication-management orientations. The analysis yielded a clear stair-step relationship (See Table 7.3).

Thus, as in American research (Broom & Dozier, 1986), the real leaders in an organization engaged in managerial activities, whereas the lower-level people did mostly the communication-technician work.

Furthermore, age correlated with administrative position (see Table 7.3). In addition, 37% percent of all males, but only 17% of the females, were directors or managers, indicating a strong tendency for male domination at the top organizational level.

In all, people engaged in management-type activity tended to be the directors or managers at top organizational levels and older males. These results square with the Chinese culture's respect for elders and male dominance in society. In contrast, those American practitioners who have administrative titles take part in managerial discussions, but also do a fair amount of technical work such as writing, editing and producing. And American communication managers often are relatively young (Broom & Dozier, 1986). This apparent difference may stem from the different cultural values in the two nations.

However, the positions and titles practitioners held did not make a significant difference as to the models they primarily adhered to.

Fifth, what influence did the way in which practitioners define their publics have on roles and models, or vice versa? In theory, two-way symmetric people should tend to study their publics very carefully so as to understand needs and contexts fully. Culbertson (1989) argued that, as one studies the audience carefully, he or she is inevitably driven to look at the different segments of it separately.

Although not relating closely to roles played, the approach one takes in defining his or her audience appeared to relate to adherence to the two-way symmetric model. The data showed a rather clear tendency for two-way symmetric practitioners (31% of them did so vs. 18% with non-two-way people) to think in terms of the audience as specialized and homogeneous. On the other hand, non-two-way symmetric individuals (44.4% vs. 26.7% with two-way

TABLE 7.3
Mean of Summed Indices of Communication-Management and Communication-Technician Activities, and Age on Practitioners' Position Levels and Administrative Titles

		Position Levels				
	1.	Top (n = 25)	Middle (n = 86)	Low (n = 60)	Staff (n = 103)	F (df = 3,270; p < .0001)
		Administrative Titles				
	2.	Manager (n = 22)	Director (n = 63)	Ass. Dir. (n = 75)	Staff (n = 120)	F (df = 3,276; p < .0001)
Emphasis on Comm.-Management	1.	59.200 [a]	49.733 [a]	38.833 [a]	34.806 [a]	75.6649
	2.	55.136 [a]	52.571 [b]	43.400 [abc]	34.033 [abc]	55.7494
Emphasis on Comm.-Technician	1.	24.560 [a]	31.500 [a]	32.883 [b]	36.204 [a]	16.9282
	2.	26.273 [ab]	28.841 [ab]	33.773 [b]	35.875 [a]	13.0682
Age	1.	48.708 [a] (n = 24)	38.060 [a] (n = 84)	35.298 [a] (n = 57)	29.577 [a] (n = 97)	46.2262
	2.	46.619 [a] (n = 21)	42.771 [b] (n = 61)	34.457 [abc] (n = 70)	29.757 [abc] (n = 115)	45.6694

Note. Means with the same superscript differ significantly on Scheffe's tests.

people) tended to define their audiences in broad, general terms, $\chi^2(4, N = 272) = 10.19, p < .05$.

Finally, how did practitioners' perceptions of public relations shape their role and model conceptions? Much as expected, those who defined public relations as a management function scored higher ($M = 46.42$, $SD = 12.71$) in emphasizing communication management than did those who perceived public relation as an image-building effort ($M = 40.39$, $SD = 9.61$). The difference was significant, $t(79.45) = 2.72$, $p < .01$. Also, practitioners who said they defined public relations in terms of image building tended to place higher emphasis on playing technician roles ($M = 35.27$, $SD = 6.19$) than did the people who defined public relations in terms of the management function ($M = 30.67$, $SD = 7.89$), $t(76.67) = 3.27$, $p < .01$.

In a related analysis, about 72.4% of these people emphasized two-way public relations, but only 50% of those defining public relations mainly as an image-building effort placed primary emphasis on management activity $\chi^2(1, N = 272) = 9.09, p < .01$.

We now discuss the bivariate results of the second research question: What factors influenced practitioners' perceptions of public relations other than their model orientations?

First, one-way analysis of variance showed significant variation by age in practitioners' perceptions of public relations. The older practitioners tended to define public relations as a management ($M = 38.25, SD = 10.05$) rather than image-building function ($M = 34.13, SD = 9.37$), $F(1, 2) = 5.77, p < .01$. This is in line with the other findings of this study: Older people were more likely to be at top management within organizations, holding some administrative titles, and placing emphasis on management roles. Thus, one would expect them to define public relations in terms of management.

Second, 44% of male practitioners, but only 33% of females, viewed public relations in terms of management. Conversely, 66.5% percent of females but only 56% of males thought of the field as image building. This difference is not marked, but it is significant, $\chi^2(1, N = 181) = 6.30, p < .05$. Again, these data agreed with other findings in this study. Males were overly represented at the top management level and in management roles, whereas females worked mostly at lower management and staff levels, emphasizing and playing technician roles. Thus, it was not surprising that men and women thought of public relations in different terms.

Third, there was a marked tendency for those working in joint-venture corporations (74.2%) to perceive public relations as a management function compared to those working in the manufacturing (46.3%) and service (42.2%) sectors. The latter two, especially the service people (57.8%), tended to think of public relations in terms of image building. This overall relationship was highly significant, $\chi^2(2, N = 163) = 30.92, p < .01$, and expected. Underlying this expectation is the belief that joint-venture people are under less government control, and are exposed to many Western ideas. The service and manufacturing practitioners, on the other hand, deal mainly with the nuts and bolts of attracting clients and selling their products.

Fourth, 61% of highly educated practitioners, compared with 22% of those without degrees, tended to think of public relations quite heavily in terms of management. This difference was statistically significant, $\chi^2(1, N = 154) = 17.66, p < .01$. Obviously, education goes along with a move from communication-technician to management orientation. As discussed earlier, nondegree holders tended to emphasize and play more communication-technician roles and to practice more one-way public relations than did degree holders.

Fifth, the ways in which the respondents defined goals so as to persuade or meet the publics' needs correlated with how they viewed public relations. Approximately 68% of those stressing persuasion as a goal defined public relations primarily in terms of image building. On the other hand, 70% of those who sought mainly to meet audience needs stressed management aspects. The difference was statistically significant, $\chi^2(1, N = 187) = 28.08, p = .0001.$ Also, those focusing largely on audience needs basically practiced two-way symmetric public relations, whereas asymmetric, public-information and press-agent approaches emphasized image as an aspect of public relations, and persuasion as the main vehicle to enhancing it. This indicates that Chinese practitioners divide into two camps: Some are two-way oriented, focusing on meeting audience needs whereas others are one-way oriented, emphasizing persuasion.

Finally, practitioners' years of experience, administrative titles, and positions did not appear to correlate with perceptions of public relations. Thus, they are not discussed in detail.

In sum, the study found that key correlates of role definitions were; age, gender, administrative title, position within organizations, and public relations perception. Further, significant factors with models were; age, gender, way of defining publics, and perception. These variables seem worthy of considerable emphasis in future research.

Results related to Research Question 2 documented that age, gender, type of organization one works for, educational level, and ways of treating audiences appear to help shape practitioners' perception of public relations.

Also, roles, models and perceptions should not be viewed exclusively as dependent variables. They may influence some of the independent variables discussed above. Clarification of causal direction awaits further research.

We now present exploratory multiple regression analyses which examined the independent impact of variables just discussed and others.

Multiple Regression. Multiple regression allows one to examine several independent variables at one time and see which one is the strongest predictor or makes the most significant differences on dependent measures with other independent variables controlled or held constant.

We selected five dependent variables that proved useful in earlier analyses in characterizing the status and approaches of public relations practitioners, and 10 independent variables that in earlier analyses correlated with at least some of the selected dependent measures.

The five dependent variables were the summed indices of communication management, communication technician, power, level of autonomy, and time spent on communication-technician role. These variables seemed of considerable interest in the study of public relations practice in China.

From a theoretical standpoint, the 10 independent variables were divided into three blocks or categories; demographics (gender, education level, and age) describing practitioners, more or less, independently of their work; level of practitioners within organizations (top, middle, lower, and staff) and in organizational sectors of society, joint ventures or government institutions; and three variables describing a practitioner's beliefs about and approaches to public relations—his or her primary adherence to the idea of two-way versus one-way communication, goal definition as persuasion or meeting audience needs, and audience definition as general and broad or specific and homogeneous.

Furthermore, the product-moment correlations of the 10 independent variables pitted against one another showed that these variables were intercorrelated to a degree, but not sufficiently to create problems of multicollinearity.

Turning to the order of entry of independent variables into regression, it seemed important to control for fundamental demographic characteristics of the respondents prior to assessing the independent contribution over and above these factors of variables describing practitioners' jobs in public relations. And, within that latter set of variables, it seemed wise to control for structural variables having to do with geographic location of one's job, the type of organization one worked for, and one's location or status within the organization before inquiring as to the significance of one's beliefs about and approaches to public relations.

Moreover, in Chinese society where a lot of attention is paid to education, where people respect their elders greatly, and where authority is attached to one's status within social and organizational settings, it is expected that the structural and demographic characteristics would count for much of the variance in power and autonomy and in the tendency to play communication-management rather than technician roles. Also, one would expect that the variables in the third block, having to do with beliefs about and approaches to public relations, would count for relatively little variance compared with structural and demographic factors.

Therefore, the independent variables were entered in the following order; demographics, locations of job in the nation and within organizations and sectors of society, and finally, beliefs about and approaches to public relations.

Three regression analyses were conducted for each of the dependent variables. As seen in Table 7.4, demographics accounted for substantial amounts of variance in all five dependent measures. As expected, gender, education, and age had much to do with the way the practitioners viewed public relations even with other factors controlled.

When structural and locational variables were added to demographics, we saw that those variables in Block 2 accounted for a substantial amount of variance, almost as much as did the variables in Block 1, as revealed by adjusted multiple r^2 increments.

When the variables in Block 3 were added into the regression equation, there was little enhancement in variance accounted for beyond that already explained by Blocks 1 and 2.

Now, we discuss the key independent variables. Age clearly was the most potent predictor for level of autonomy, and emphasis on management activities. Education correlated moderately with power and autonomy. Gender correlated

TABLE 7.4
Standardized Regression Coefficients With Emphasis on Five Orientations Toward Public Relations as Dependent Variable

	Dependent Variables				
Independent Variables	Power	Autonomy	Emphasis on Comm.-Mgt. Activity	Emphasis on Comm.-Tech. Activity	Percent of Time of Comm. Tech. Role
Block 1 -- Demographics					
Gender [a]	.04	.01	.02	.14*	.11
Education	.14**	.14**	.07	.08	.11
Age	.15	.23**	.15*	-.13	-.05
Block 2 -- Location of Job in Nation, Org'n and Section					
J. Ventures [b]	-.04	.15**	.08	-.05	-.12
Government [c]	-.17**	-.24**	-.03	.03	.03
Location	.04	.10	.02	.04	-.03
Level of Org'n	.56**	.44**	.58**	-.33**	-.46**
Block 3 -- Beliefs about and Approaches to Public Relations					
2- or 1-way [d]	.03	.03	.03	-.08	.02
Goal	.01	.01	.09	-.05	-.14
Audience [e]	-.23**	-.12**	-.22**	.02	.07
	$F = 28.00$	$F = 25.04$	$F = 29.04$	$F = 11.11$	$F = 7.59$
Adjusted Multiple R^2s					
(Block 1)	.28	.26	.30	.18	.17
(Blocks 1 & 2)	.53	.53	.53	.24	.32
(All 3 Blocks)	.56	.54	.57	.24	.33
Adjusted Multiple R^2 Increment with					
Addition of Block 1	.25	.27	.23	.06	.15
Addition of Block 3	.03	.01	.04	.00	.01

[a] Gender is entered as a dummy variable with 1 = male, and 2 = female.
[b] This dummy variable is entered with 1 = not working for joint ventures, and 2 = working for joint venture.
[c] This dummy variable is entered with 1 = not working for government, and 2 = working for government.
[d] It is entered as a dummy variable with 1 = non-two-way PR, and 2 = two-way PR.
[e] This variable is entered with 1 = audience definition as specific and homogeneous, 2 = broad and general, 3 = both.
*$p < .01$, **$p < .001$.

only with emphasis on communication-technician activities, indicating that women tended to emphasize that aspect of work more than men did. One's status or level within the organization correlated highly and positively with all five dependent variables. Obviously, high-level managers tended to outdo middle- or lower-level managers, who in turn, outdid staff personnel with respect to emphasis on management activities, power, and autonomy. On the contrary, status correlated substantially and negatively with both communication-technician measures, indicating clearly that type of communication activities carried out by Chinese public relations practitioners depends more heavily on their status or levels within organizations than on other independent variables utilized. People who worked for government tended to have lower power and autonomy than did people outside of government. Work for joint ventures correlated very mildly but significantly with autonomy, indicating that those who worked for joint-venture firms tended to have greater autonomy than did other practitioners in the sample. Definition of audience: The more a practitioner emphasized specific, homogeneous audiences in his or her thinking, the greater that person's focus on communication-management activities, and the more he or she had power and autonomy.

In sum, a practitioner's position, or level within an organization was the strongest and most important single predictor of all five dependent measures. The higher the position, the more he or she emphasized communication-management activity, and had power and autonomy. Also, the less he or she was involved in communication-technician work.

Age also correlated significantly with only three of the five dependent variables. The older practitioners tended to emphasize the management aspect of the work, and reported having higher power and autonomy. But the regression coefficients on age are low when all other variables are entered into the equation. Thus, age apparently led to power, autonomy, and managerial emphasis primarily (although not entirely) through its translating into high status and responsibility within the organization.

The importance of seniority and position as shown by correlation and regression analyses squared with the qualitative data. In Chinese society, respect for authority is emphasized and is based in substantial measure on seniority and age.

The tendency to think about specialized rather than general, broad audiences made modest but significant differences. Apparently, a carefully segmented definition of the audience, enhancing precision in defining one's audience, paid off careerwise. The more a practitioner emphasized study of specific, homogeneous audiences, the more management responsibilities, power, and autonomy he or she gained. Careful study of audience reflects a practitioner's maturity and sophistication in thinking. Perhaps this is an area in which teaching of public relations should focus.

Also, coming from the right sector of society, getting the right job, and good education influenced what a practitioner did.

CHINESE VERSUS WESTERN PUBLIC RELATIONS: SOME DIFFERENCES

Clearly, Chinese public relations differs from Western practice. Differences lie in the social, political, and economic systems; cultural traditions, values, and morals; and ultimate goals of public relations. Although some basic Western public relations tenets carry over into the Chinese environment, many others are politically, socially, and culturally bound and do not transfer well.

Unique goals and features of Chinese public relations stem in part from Confucius. That great sage's emphasis on personal relationships, honesty, high moral standards, and loyalty to one's group affects every aspect of individual and organizational life in China. (For a discussion of this and the following points, see Chen & Culbertson, 1992).

Key ideas of Confucius include the following. He defined specific behaviors as appropriate for specific people in specific relationships defined largely on the basis of the participants' level of intimacy with each other, status, and situational context (Yum, 1991). Chinese culture distinguishes strongly between in-group and out-group members. Confucian emphasis on *li*—adherence to propriety and respect for social order—requires all people to follow accepted rituals in relating to others. This, in turn, makes it very difficult to form new relationships with outsiders quickly. Chinese culture tends to mix personal and public relations. Because of the Confucian concept of *i*, Chinese find it difficult to accept purely business dealings. They prefer that transactions be carried out on a personal, warm, human level. This point is obviously reflected in the definition of "public relations with Chinese features" by the *Zhongguo Gonggong Guanxi Da Cidian* [Encyclopedia of Chinese Public Relations] (1993, pp.45–46). The definition emphasizes "human touch" as the essence of Chinese public relations. Human touch places personal and human approaches far above businesslike attitudes in dealing with people. Thus, interpersonal relationships serve as the main basis for strong public relationships, all of which leads to the saliency of relationship building, also called *guanxi,* in Chinese culture in general, and public relations practice in particular.

More specifically, guanxi is a network of personal relationships that has become so important that people often could not get anything done without connections. Of course, obligations and favors are created through guanxi. Thus, the higher one's position, and the more power one has, the more easily he or she builds such a personal network.

Guanxi seems asymmetrical at first glance with its emphasis on status and preordained relationships, but it embodies principles implied in symmetry when viewed in its depth (Chen & Culbertson, 1992). The saliency of relationship building gained support from the data described earlier.

In the present sample, almost all practitioners in the sample reported emphasis on relationship building regardless of their age, education, status, and position.

In particular, young female practitioners without a college degree holding staff position worked as high-level receptionists whose job was to entertain guests so as to build relationships on behalf of the organization.

Also related to the importance of guest relations is the media system and its function in China. As discussed earlier, Chinese media are tightly controlled by the central government and the ruling party, functioning as mouthpieces. Resulting limitations of credibility and performance among government-owned media have made them less desirable and accessible to many organizations as means of communicating with key publics. Thus, other channels such as guanxi are stressed as means of communication, giving much weight to building guest relations. In contrast, Western literature has not emphasized this area.

In line with this, 80% of all respondents here had never worked in the media prior to entering public relations. In the U.S., until quite recently, it was considered almost a must for a public relations practitioner to have some media experience. Such background is still regarded as highly desirable, although the number of public relations people without media experience presumably has increased as the field's definition has broadened in recent years. Apparently, then, the two nations' public relations professions grew from different roots.

In sum, the importance of guest relations among Chinese practitioners, especially lower level ones, seems to represent a major point of contrast between Chinese and Western public relations.

All of this illustrates the complexity and subtlety of interpersonal and societal relationships in China, which, in turn, requires a much more sensitive role-taking approach (Culbertson, 1991) when practicing public relations or doing business in China. Clearly, Western officials and business people may fail when dealing with the Chinese unless they develop the patience and wisdom to understand such subtleties and the importance of personal relationships.

CONCLUSIONS AND IMPLICATIONS

This study is a pioneering attempt and lays a foundation for future research to build upon.

Public relations was introduced in China in the late 1970s after political and economic changes paved way. The Rogers (1983) diffusion model described quite well the spread of public relations in China. Public relations, like other things with some Western influence, diffused from the southern coastal regions around Guangzhou to the commercial and government capitals (Shanghai and Beijing, respectively) to more conservative inland cities such as Nanjing. In fact, China is dividing between "new" and "old" in this fashion. However, as diffusion of various things progresses, even the inland areas will eventually modernize for better or worse.

After about 15 years of study and practice, people have argued that public relations is becoming a profession in China (W. Wang, personal communication, November 15, 1994; Z. Zhu, personal communication, October 17, 1994). Confusion about the meaning and functions of public relations continues. Some think of practitioners as high-level receptionists whose main job is to entertain guests. Some equate the field largely with the use of attractive young women for service and product promotion as well as relationship building with clients (Liu, 1994). Others view public relations as an adjunct to advertising and marketing, and thus call for an integration of public relations (E. Z. Guo, personal communication, June 30, 1994). Focusing almost entirely on short-term profit, some marketing-oriented CEOs are blind to the value of public relations and devote few resources to it (Zhang, 1994).

Public relations education, like the practice itself, began in Shenzhen (within Guangzhou region) in the early 1980s and spread inland. Now, the nation has a well-established, multifaceted system including short-term training sessions sponsored by public relations associations, distance learning through the Chinese Central Television station and local TV outlets, specialized vocational schools offering 2-year degree programs, and formal 4-year B.A. degree programs at colleges and universities.

Broom and Dozier's role theory (1986) and Grunig and Hunt's 4-stage evolutionary model (1984) proved useful in studying Chinese public relations practice. However, the four locations studied, reflecting different points in the diffusion process, differed little as to role and model orientations.

Age, gender (male), education, status within one's organization, and focus on specific definition of homogeneous publics all correlated positively with the tendency to emphasize managerial behavior and to think in two-way asymmetric terms.

What was the primary determiner or influencing factor among all these? Multiple regression analyses provided a clear-cut answer. It was a practitioner's status, or position within organizations. The higher the position, the more one emphasized communication-management activity, had power and autonomy, and the less he or she was involved in communication-technician work. Age apparently led to power, autonomy, and managerial emphasis primarily, although not entirely, through its translation into high status and responsibility within the organization. This spelled out the importance of seniority and position in Chinese society, where respect for authority is emphasized, and is based in substantial measure on seniority and age.

The data also indicated that government practitioners, especially in Beijing, leaned toward the communication-technician roles and one-way practice. This supports the literature that has documented the Chinese central government's tendency to focus on promotion and image-building, in contrast with the more modern approaches evident in municipal governments such as the one in Tianjin, the service industries, and joint-venture firms.

Beijing is China's capital city with relatively tight government control. Thus,

Western ideas arriving there often result in a tug of war involving East versus West and Communism versus Capitalism.

In studying the practitioners' role and model orientations, correlational analyses yielded some other interesting findings. In particular, the expert-prescriber role seemed central within the communication-management function. Also, Chinese practitioners appear to have made considerable progress in moving into management roles.

The data also indicated that, rather than four roles or specialties, there were really only two distinct roles—communication manager and communication technician—in Chinese public relations. Recent U.S. research gave comparable findings (Culbertson, 1985; Stone, 1990).

As to whether Chinese public relations differs from Western public relations, the data suggests a resounding yes. Differences apparently lay in the social, political, and economic systems; cultural traditions, values, and morals; and also the ultimate purposes or goals of practicing public relations.

Interestingly, respondents placed high emphasis on guest relations among Chinese practitioners, especially lower level ones. Given that Chinese culture tends to mix personal and public relations, and personal relations are central to the culture, the saliency of relationship building—guanxi—seems inevitable. Moreover, the limitations of credibility and accessibility in government-controlled media push many to seek other means of communication. Thus, guest relations becomes quite important in the practice, perhaps a bit more so than in western public relations.

Audience definition made modest but significant differences. Apparently, carefully segmented definition of the audience, enhancing conceptual precision, pays off careerwise. The more a practitioner emphasized study of specific, homogeneous audiences, the more management responsibilities, power, and autonomy he or she gained. Also, coming from the right sector of society, getting the right job, and a good education influenced what a practitioner did.

Also, very much in line with the previous findings, age, gender, and education correlate with one's perception of public relations. Older male practitioners with college degrees tended to perceive public relations in terms of management. In addition, those who worked for joint ventures, and those who defined their primary goal as meeting the audience needs, appeared to stress the management function of public relations.

Practitioners who emphasized management roles, practiced two-way symmetric public relations, and had power and autonomy showed greater intensity and interest in seeking information relating to their practice.

With regard to research orientations, one's status and education made a difference. Directors or managers, and degree holders were most involved in doing research. Also, they showed a relatively strong tendency to do both audience and message research.

Finally, the data showed that a typical Chinese public relations practitioner is a 37-year-old male (two-thirds of the respondents were male) who has a college degree, holds some kind of administrative position, and has been working in the field for about 2 years. This indicates that public relations people are relatively young. Given the profession's youth and the often noted openness of young people to new ideas, this is not surprising.

The findings provide several implications and areas for future research.

Practical Implications

First, the data showed that the more a practitioner emphasized study of specific, homogeneous audiences, the more management responsibilities, power, and autonomy he or she possessed. Apparently, careful segmentation, enhancing precision in defining audiences, pays off careerwise. In addition, careful study of one's audience reflects a practitioner's overall maturity and sophistication in thinking. Moreover, research ability and interest seem to help practitioners join the management team. Unfortunately, as far as the author knows, research methodology is not yet included in the public relations curriculum of any major Chinese university. Obviously, this is a gap worthy of careful attention by educators.

Second, leading public relations educators in China need to establish contacts with influential government officials such as the former mayor of Tianjin. These people endorse and advocate public relations, especially two-way symmetric practice, and attend to public needs carefully. Named professorships, visiting lecturers, nominations to university advisory boards, and other vehicles can involve these people actively in public relations education so as to gain their input and support. This seems especially important because little can be done in China without government and Communist Party backing. And, given that it is young and still evolving, public relations in China hinges on understanding and support from these people. Furthermore, it is just possible that thoughtful study of the field might, in some small way, point toward political as well as economic reforms.

Third, one interesting descriptive finding was that relatively few Chinese practitioners had worked in the media prior to entering public relations. Media relations are certainly important in public relations. Thus, internships and course offerings in mass communication may warrant increased emphasis in Chinese public relations education at a time when such emphasis is being challenged in the West.

Fourth, the data also indicate the centrality of managerial activity in Chinese public relations practice. Practitioners, despite their youth and inexperience in the field, perceive themselves as managers, placing heavy emphasis on this area both in terms of beliefs and of actual time spent playing managerial roles. This seems to validate management and organizational communication as important components in public relations curricula. Also, varied social science emphasis seems called for, encompassing management, speech communication, and other social sciences.

Fifth, this study revealed the great emphasis placed on persuasion as a public relations goal in China. This is not surprising as, traditionally, public relations throughout the world has tended to focus on persuasion and gaining support. Indeed, most observers surely agree that persuasion is an important element. However, persuasion literature developed in the U. S. has tended to be heavily experimental, focusing largely on college students and other elite audiences. Thus, there is little reason to believe that U. S. persuasion theory is applicable in China. This suggests a strong need for Chinese scholars to develop their own literature and skills relating to persuasion.

In sum, this has been a highly exploratory study of Chinese public relations. It illustrates the role of both qualitative and quantitative methods as scholars seek to understand the field in its broad social, political, economic, and cultural contexts.

REFERENCES

Al-Enad, A. (1990, Spring). Public relations' roles in developing countries. *Public Relations Quarterly, 35*(1), 24–26.

An, Gang 1990. (*Chuangban you Zhongguo tese de gongguan* [Establish public relations with Chinese Features]. Gonggong Guanxi [Public Relations Journal]. Vol. 2.

Black, S. (1992). Chinese update. *Public Relations Quarterly, 37*(3), 41.

Broom, G. M. & Dozier, D. M. (1986). Advancement for public relations role models. *Public Relations Review, 12*(1), 37–56.

Chen, N. (1994, Spring). Public relations education in the People's Republic of China. *Journalism Educator, 49*(1), 14–22.

Chen, N., & Culbertson, H. M. (1992, Fall). Two contrasting approaches of government public relations in mainland China. *Public Relations Quarterly, 37*(3), 36–41.

Cheng, J. Y. S. (Ed.). (1989). Introduction: China's modernization programme in the 1980s. In J. Cheng (Ed.), *China: Modernization in the 1980s.* Hong Kong: The Chinese University Press.

Cobbey, R. E., & McCombs, M. E. (1979). Using a decision model to evaluate newspaper features systematically. *Journalism Quarterly, 56,* 469–476.

Committee on PR Education. (1989, May). *Ganggang qibu de Zhongguo gongguang jiaoyu.* [Public relations education in China at its initial stage.] Unpublished report at the second annual national convention of Public Relations Associations, Beijing, China.

Culbertson, H. M. (1985). Practitioner roles: Their meaning for educators. *Public Relations Review, 11*(4), 65–72.

Culbertson, H. M. (1989). Breadth of perspective: An important concept for public relations. In J. E. Grunig & L. A. Grunig (Eds.), *Public relations research annual* (Vol. 1, pp. 3–25). Hillsdale, NJ: Lawrence Erlbaum Associates.

Culbertson, H. M. (1991). Role taking and sensitivity: Keys to playing and making public relations roles. In L. A. Grunig & J. E. Grunig (Eds.), *Public relations research annual* (Vol. 3, pp. 37–65). Hillsdale, NJ: Lawrence Erlbaum Associates.

Cutlip, S. M., Center, A. H., & Broom, G. M. (1985). *Effective public relations* (6th ed.). Englewood Cliffs, NJ: Prentice-Hall.

Grunig, J. E. (1972). Communication and the economic decision-making process of Columbian peasants. Madison: University of Wisconsin Land Tenure Center.
Grunig, J. E. (1985, April). Hard thinking on education. *Public Relations Journal, 41*(4), 30.
Grunig, J. E., & Hunt, T. (1984). *Managing public relations.* New York: Holt, Rinehart & Winston.
Grunig J. E. & Grunig L. A. (1989). Toward a theory of the public relations behavior of organizations: Review of a program of research. In J. E. Grunig & L. A. Grunig (Eds.), *Public Relations Research Annual* (Vol. 1, pp. 27–63). Hillsdale, NJ: Lawrence Erlbaum Associates.
Grunig, L. A. (1991). Court-ordered relief from sex discrimination in the Foreign Service: Implications for women working in development communication. In L. A. Grunig & J. E. Grunig (Eds.), *Public relations research annual* (Vol. 3, pp. 85–113). Hillsdale, NJ: Lawrence Erlbaum Associates.
Grunig, L. A. (1992). Power in the public relations department. In J. E. Grunig (Ed.), *Excellence in public relations and communication management* (pp. 483–501). Hillsdale, NJ: Lawrence Erlbaum Associates.
Howkins, J. (1982). *Mass communication in China.* New York: Longman.
Janis, I. L., & Mann, L. (1977). *Decision making: A psychological analysis of conflict, choice, and commitment.* New York: Free Press.
Jia, G. (1992, November). *China's public relations frontier.* Paper presented at national conference, Public Relations Society of America, Kansas City, MO.
Liu, Z. (1994, August 11). Gongguan Wuqi. [Areas of misunderstanding in public relations]. *Gonggong Guanxi Bao* [PR News], p. 3.
Men, X. (1990). *Zhongguo guongguan de xianzhuang yu weilai.* [The present state and the future of Chinese public relations: A discussion of Chinese PR with socialist features]. Presented at the third annual national convention of Public Relations Associations, Guangzhou, China.
Meyer, P. (1978, January-February). In defense of the marketing approach. *Columbia Journalism Review, 16*(5), 60–62.
Rogers, E. (1983). *Diffusion of innovation.* New York: Free Press of Glencoe.
Schramm, W. (1956). The Soviet Communist theory of the press. In F. S. Siebert, T. Peterson, & W Schramm (Eds.), *Four Theories of the Press* (pp. 105–146). Urbana: University of Illinois Press.
Stone, D. B. (1991). *The value of veracity in public relations.* Unpublished doctoral dissertation, Ohio University, Athens, Ohio.
Wang, X. (1989, November 15). Zhongguo wenhua yu zhongguo gonguan de youlian zuantong [Chinese culture and Chinese public relations]. *Gongguan Yanjiu* [Public Relations Studies], *5,* 11–14.
Yuan, S., & Han, Z. (1992). *Deng Xiaoping Nanxun hou de Zhongguo* [China after Deng Xiaoping's visit to southern regions]. Beijing: Gaige Press.
Yum, J. O. (1991). International cultures: Understanding diversity. In L. Samovar & R. Porter (Eds.), *Intercultural Communication* (6th ed., pp. 68–71). Belmont, CA: Wadsworth.
Zhang, X. (1994, February 10). Gongguan pu jingli de fannao [A PR detractor and his vexation]. *Gonggong Guanxi Bao* [PR News], p. 2.

8 Public Relations in Thailand: Its Functions and Practitioners' Roles

Daradirek Ekachai
Southern Illinois University at Carbondale

Rosechongporn Komolsevin
Bangkok University

Public relations in Thailand has come a long way since its inception more than 60 years ago. It has developed from a primarily one-way asymmetrical toward a two-way symmetrical communication, with practitioners making increased use of management and research skills.

Public relations is now practiced widely in various types of organizations. In 1993, it was reported that 1,810 governmental units, state enterprises, corporations, and nonprofit organizations (317 in Bangkok metropolitan and 1,493 in other 71 provinces) carried out at least some public relations activities (National Public Relations Committee, 1993).

Furthermore, the public relations major is offered at both undergraduate and graduate levels by almost all universities. As more practitioners have received specialized training, their practice has gradually become more professional, moving from product orientation toward a focus on the consumer and society as a whole. However, public relations scholars and experts still see room for improvement, reporting that most organizations have not used public relations to its fullest potential (Worakitpokatorn, 1993).

This chapter discusses the development of public relations practices and functions in Thailand. Part 1 gives an overview of the field and Part 2 reports empirical data on Thai practitioners' roles.

BACKGROUND

Former Minister for the Prime Minister's Office Lt. Charn Manuthum once said in a speech to provincial public relations directors and broadcasting station directors that public relations is a planned and continuous activities to establish mutual understanding for the purpose of generating cooperation among all concerned parties. He defined the field's major goal as furtherance of Thai national development in many, if not all, of its social, economic, and political aspects (Tananchaibutra, 1986). His statement illustrates quite vividly how much significance the Thai government has attached to public relations. Indeed, political change really gave birth to the nation's public relations industry.

When Thailand changed her political system from an absolute monarchy to a constitutional monarchy in 1932, the new government felt it necessary to inform and educate Thai people about the new political system and about the government's policies to gain public understanding and cooperation. Thus, the military-led government founded the Publicity Office, which was upgraded in 1940 to the Publicity Department. The unit was renamed the Public Relations Department in 1952.

Public relations activities in the earlier years could be characterized as primarily press agentry/publicity (Grunig & Hunt, 1984). The government attempted to inform and educate the people, mostly through broadcast media, about the democratic system, which seemed quite innovative political concept at that time. In addition, the government used the Public Relations Department as a propaganda mouthpiece to disseminate information about its activities. This approach involved little effort to seek feedback from the people or to encourage their participation in government-related communication.

Some labeled government efforts as deceptive to the public and destructive to the nation's political stability. Such problems appeared to stem from the government's lack of a coherent policy, its lack of planning and trained personnel, and a wide gap between the large amount of information provided to people in urban areas and the small amount to rural folk (Tananchaibutra, 1986).

Toward Two-Way Communication

Recognizing such shortcomings in previous administrations, Prime Minister Kriangsak Chamanand made a historical move in 1980 by announcing five principles to govern national public relations policy. He urged both public and private practitioners to use these as guidelines in their professional practice.

The principles highlighted the importance of the two-way communication and public relations practice at the grassroots level. Also emphasized were coordination between the Public Relations Department and the Association of Public Relations Practitioners of Thailand, the use of systematic planning and strategies based on research, and enhanced recognition or acceptance of public relations practitioners.

Although Chamanand's administration was short lived, his modern public relations policy served as a building block for the national public relations plan and policy officially instituted in 1988. At that time, a 24-member National

Public Relations Committee was formed to set guidelines for short- and long-term public relations planning. Also, the committee was to monitor and evaluate ongoing public relations activities.

The evolution of public relations practice from one-way to two-way communication was made apparent in an analysis of public relations policies and plans in Thailand's National Economic and Social Development Plans from 1961 to 1988 (Kunpongsa, 1989). The analysis revealed that the earlier plans involved basically one-way communication designed specifically to sell the public on the government's provision of fundamental services and infrastructure such as transportation and communication. Not until Thailand's political ideology shifted to democracy did communication policy and practices become more two-way oriented, emphasizing information exchange and cooperation between the government and the people.

Functions

In addition to information dissemination and the establishment of understanding and cooperation between the government and its internal and external publics, the Public Relations Department has emphasized national and rural development (Srichanachaichok, 1989). Also with guidance from the department, six regional public relations centers implement public relations activities specially designed for each region in collaboration with the national public relations plan. The Public Relations Department also uses its Radio Thailand, the Educational Radio Broadcasting Network and Television of Thailand (Channel 11) to broadcast governmental news and programs daily nationwide.

In the private sector, a public relations department typically operates within units such as marketing, advertising, or personnel, or under direct supervision of an organization's top executives (Poobuapuan, 1989). Growth in business promotion and marketing surely has contributed to the increase in public relations activities.

Bangkok Bank, for example, has used public relations extensively, especially to increase awareness of new projects (Prajammuang, 1988). Further, other service sectors such as the hotel, airline, and entertainment industries have used public relations expertise in image building, impression management, and marketing support (Chaiwatanarat, 1988; Maneechoti, 1988; Satitamorntham, 1988; Thanabunlertluck, 1988; Wongsarot, 1988).

Public relations deals extensively with both employees and external publics (Satitamorntham, 1988). Practitioners seek to establish mutual understanding among employees, and to discern their needs, habits, attitudes, and preferences so that management can respond to those needs effectively.

Key public relations objectives in the business arena focus largely on the creation of positive images and marketing support. Unlike the government realm, private businesses usually have well-researched public relations plans, both short- and long-term, initiated by top management. Evaluation of a plan usually follows implementation. Factors considered in planning include the organization's goals and policy, needs of target market, and competitive forces in the marketplace (Poobuapuan, 1989).

Problems

Common problems encountered in implementing public relations programs included shortages of knowledgeable personnel as well as inadequate budget and equipment, limited freedom of operation, lack of understanding of public relations work and its significance from administrators, and lack of cooperation from the media (Thammasat University, 1987).

On the other hand, success appears to hinge largely on managerial support, adequate public relations budgets and cooperation by all parties concerned (Poobuapuan, 1989)

Limited scope of activities also was seen as an obstacle of the profession's development. A study of trends over 10 years at the Royal Thai Police Department found heavy emphasis on press releases and publicity, clearly one-way asymmetric role behavior (Tantivetchakul, 1988). Major obstacles, according to the researcher, stemmed from ignorance and indifference within the department relating to public relations.

Problems encountered in national development public relations include practitioners' lack of training, inadequate budgets and tools for implementation, lack of systematic planning, and public indifference to the significance of government projects (Srichanachaichok, 1989).

However, some signs point to an optimistic future for public relations practice in Thailand in general, and for practitioners, in particular. Organizations have been increasing their public relations staffs, expanding their scope of activities, and augmenting budgets as well as equipment. Some administrators, in addition, have started to require that their personnel departments recruit only the practitioners trained in the public relations or communication discipline (Dechacheep, 1988).

PRACTITIONERS: SOME BASIC INFORMATION

Number

It is difficult, if not impossible, to count the public relations practitioners in Thailand. The Association of Public Relations Practitioners in Thailand had about 1,200 members in 1993 but most practitioners were not affiliated with the association. (In our survey reported later in the chapter, only 10 of 127 practitioners held membership in the professional organization.)

The National Directory of Public Relations Practitioners compiled by the government's Public Relations Department listed some 1,800 people "responsible for" the public relations functions. But the directory only included the head officers' names and many of these people did not have public relations titles. Encouragingly, however, many people listed were top-level executives such as vice-presidents, managers, and administrators.

Educational Background

Most practitioners in the public sector lack formal training and education in the communication discipline (Srichanachaichok, 1989), although many have received some professional workshop training. However, previous studies have documented a gradual change practitioners holding communication degrees from 16% in 1981 to 33% in 1986 (Satawedin, Apiratanakul, Asawadorndecha, & Suthiworaset, 1981; Satawedin, Ekachai, Kansuwan, & Lerk-Klang, 1986). Further, in both studies, a strong majority (96% in 1981 study and 70% in 1986 study) of all practitioners held at least bachelor's degrees.

Roles

The dominant role behavior of Thai public relations practitioners in both the public and private sectors appears to be governed by the press-agentry and public-information models. Heavy emphasis is placed on technical aspects of message production and distribution.

Three prominent practitioners in the Public Relations Department, Thai Airways International, and the Hyatt-Rama Hotel reported in an interview that they and their subordinates focused primarily on press-agent/publicity tasks (i.e., fashion shows, international food festivals, free coupons, giveaways). Their main purpose was to enhance public awareness of and interest in their organizations ("Public Relations Practitioners' Views," 1978).

Emphasis on the communication-technician role was also prevalent in organizations that reported quantitative measurement of communication performance. In such cases, management measured success or failure largely on the basis of the number of newspaper articles documented with clips. Thus, practitioners felt compelled to send out as many news releases and set up as many press conferences as possible.

In governmental organizations, practitioners devoted most of their time to technical chores of disseminating information to target audiences. Heavy emphasis was placed on implementing rural development (Photisuvan, 1988). In particular, knowledge was provided on forest resource conservation, land reform, reforestation (Chancharatwatana, 1989, Malasri, 1989 & Papui, 1989). Development-related public relations involved primarily one-way asymmetric communication with transmission of one-sided messages (Chancharatwattana,

1989; Chantarasiri, 1989; Malasri, 1989; Papui, 1989 & Srichanachaichok, 1989).

Specifically, innovations and their beneficial impacts were described so as to enhance awareness and adoption of development projects introduced by the government. Primary channels used included interpersonal communication, print and electronic media, videotapes, bulletin boards, and newsletters. In such a setting, public relations persons sought primarily to disseminate development information so as to help change attitudes and behavior. In doing this, it was essential to enhance awareness, knowledge, and interest.

Evaluation after implementation of a project was rare because of lack of funds and personnel. Without proper follow-up, government public relations often amounted to little more than a "have-to-do" activity to complete policy proposed in the National Development Plan (Srichanachaichok, 1989).

Nonetheless, administrators within the government have increasingly recognized a need for systematic, planned public relations. Perhaps this understanding stemmed in part from developments in the corporate sphere. One study found a widespread belief among corporate managers that public relations department, typically housed in such units as marketing or advertising, was very significant for the organization and should be separate and independent from other units (Dechacheep, 1988). Prachuab In-Odd (personal communication, November 2, 1993), former director of public relations for Bangkok Bank and a recognized guru of Thai public relations, agrees. However, he did not envision such autonomy in the near future because most public relations offices still operate within other departments tied more clearly to short-term organizational profits.

According to In-Odd, the stature of public relations activities will depend largely on the administrators' experiences leading to genuine recognition of public relations' significance. That, inturn, will require the development of thorough, clearly-written public relations policies, as well as systematic, effective implementation of related plans.

Social, Political, and Economic Contexts

The social or cultural, political, and economic climates have shaped the Thai public relations industry in unique ways.

For one thing, the practice has become more stable in the past decade partly because of the nations's political and economic stability. Government and corporations have begun to recognize the importance of public relations as a vital tool for promotion, image building, and public corporation—goals that require long-term thinking.

Thailand's democratic system is still young and lacking when compared with some Western nations. However, the concepts of people's political participation and rights are sufficiently well established that politicians cannot ignore the need for public support. Thus, more efforts have been geared toward establishing "relations with the public."

To date, however, this rising recognition of public relations' importance has not really facilitated a full application of Grunig and Hunt's (1984) two-way asymmetric ans symmetric communication models. In-Odd (personal communication, November 2, 1993) explained that, in such "bottom heavy" political, social, and economic structures as Thailand, organizations have found it convenient to rely on one-way approaches in which practitioners publicize activities and programs. Little effort has been devoted to studying publics' needs or the degree to which government information helps meet those needs.

Culture also helps shape public relations practice and roles. In Thai society, seniority and social status are of great importance. Practitioners must be aware of these cultural norms and behave accordingly. Public relations professor Jitraporn Suthiworatset (personal communication, August 29, 1994) commented that personal relationships and cooperation require patient, sensitive effort. Aggressiveness or assertiveness, valuable characteristics in other cultures, may not lead to favorable outcomes in Thailand.

Social norms and values also affect public relations strategies in some information campaigns. Family-planning campaigns conducted by the Population and Community Development Association (PDA) illustrated successful use of tactics adapted to Thai culture.

According to PDA Public Relations Director Praween Payapwipapong (personal communication, August 19, 1994), sexual matters are seldom discussed even by Thai husbands and wives, let alone by people outside the family circle. Thus, family-planning campaigners, led by the former Ministry of Interior Deputy Minister Mechai Viravaidya, found it hard to introduce birth control concepts to Thai couples without creating any embarrassment.

Because people were embarased to say condom, the minister's first name, "Mechai," was used in place of that word to make conversation easier and more comfortable. Further, the campaigners realized that a main characteristic of Thai people is "Ruck Sanuck" (fun-loving). Thus, they appealed to the Thai sense of humor and fun by handing out condom key chains at official dinners, selling T-shirts with lighthearted family-planning slogans, and holding vasectomy festivals in honor of the King's birthday. The campaign helped greatly in reducing Thailand's overall rate of annual population growth from 3.2% in 1970 to 1.3% in 1991.

In the economic realm, Thailand's booming economy in recent years played a major role in increasing the status and the development of public relations, especially in business sector. In a highly competitive environment, businesses have been driven to rely more and more on publicity and advertising. Most executives agreed some time ago that public relations has contributed enormously to the prosperity of Thai businesses.

However, many organizations still have not used their public relations to its full potentials. Rather, they have treated it as a "must-be-there" element in the business practice. Also, the field has often been used to fulfill organizations' interests instead of the public needs (In-Odd, personal communication, November 2, 1993).

Organizational size and culture often greatly influence the scope of public relations activities. Large organizations such as banks and consumer goods industries have long acknowledged the significance of public support and understanding. These firms have used public relations quite extensively and involved practitioners in decision-making at the policy level. In such settings, practitioners seem destined to play an increasing role within management.

PRACTITIONER ROLES: EMPIRICAL DATA

A series of studies on practitioner roles, orginally conceptualized by Broom and Smith (1979), and carried out in the United States, consistently found that practitioners play two distinct roles—*communication manager* and *communication technician* (Anderson, Reagan, Sumner, & Hill, 1989; Broom, 1982; Dozier, 1984, 1992). Also, Grunig and Hunt (1984) proposed a 4-stage evolutionary model of public relations behaviors; press agentry/publicity (one-way asymmetrical), public information (one-way symmetrical), two-way asymmetric, and two-way symmetric. This model stated that a public relations practitioner might practice all behaviors, but one usually will be dominant.

The *press agentry* stage is characterized by activities designed both to promote the organization and to seek to change public attitudes and behaviors. Practitioners who engage in these activities devote most of their effort to disseminating information beneficial to the organization without necessarily considering the needs or interests of various publics. The *public-information* practitioner provides accurate information about her or his organization to the public but does not volunteer negative information.

Turning to the two-way behaviors, the *two-way asymmetric* approach involves the study of public opinion so as to enhance support without having to change the client organization's policies. *Two-way symmetric* communication, on the other hand, implements strategies of bargaining and negotiation to bring about changes designed to benefit both the organization and its publics.

To explore the role behaviors the Thai practitioners and to determine whether their roles could be described or categorized similarly to their American counterparts, the authors surveyed public relations people in Bangkok in February of 1994. Questions adapted from those used in Broom's (1982) role research were asked of a purposive sample of 200 public relations practitioners working in various public and private organizations. A total of 127 completed questionnaires were returned.

Most respondents (52 out of 127 or 41%) worked for organizations that provided consumer goods or services (banks, travel, insurance). Fifteen respondents (12%) worked at public relations agencies, 13% worked at advertising agencies, and 11% with educational institutions. Others served hotels, hospitals, and entertainment companies. Only one governmental public relations officer responded to the survey, so findings may not apply to the governmental sector.

Demographics

In line with the conventional wisdom that public relations is a "women's job," 71% (90 of 127) of all respondents were female.

The average age was 28 years old. The majority of the practitioners surveyed (73%) held college degrees and one fourth of the degrees was in public relations. Another one third of degree holders had majored in journalism, mass communication, or advertising. The remaining respondents had an educational background in business or marketing (14%), languages (15%), economics (10%), or political science (2%).

Respondents had worked an average of 3.4 years in public relations (ranging from less than 1 year-17 years) and 2.5 years in journalism (from 0–11 years). All but nine individualss had worked as full-time practitioners in at least one organization. The median of their annual salary was 156,000 bath (about $US 6,300) but this figure might not be representative because 77% of all respondents did not report their income. Of all participants, only 10 were member of the Association of Public Relations Practitioners in Thailand, a professional organization that includes practitioners mostly in the corporate sphere but also targets other practitioners.

Public Relations Practitioner Roles

The authors used a battery of 24 role items developed by Broom (Broom, 1982; Broom and Smith, 1979) to measure emphasis placed on various public relations roles. One goal here was to see whether Broom's role concepts apply to practitioners in another culture.

Broom (1982) developed six itmes designed to tap each of four public relations roles; expert prescriber, communication technician, communication process facilitator, and problem solving facilitator. Each role represents a distinct behavior pattern, but a practitioner may perform more than one role or develop a certain pattern as a dominant role behavior.

Expert prescribers are responsible for designing a public relations program as well as for diagnosing public relations problems and prescribing solutions to them. These individuals are regardd as the best informed persons in their organizations regarding public relations.

Communication facilitators operate as "go-betweens" or information mediators between an organization and its audiences. Their primary function is "to facilitate the exchange of information so the parties involved have adequate information for dealing with each other and for making decisions of mutual interest" (Broom & Smith, 1979, p. 50).

The *problem-solving process facilitators* help an organization identify and solve its problems through a systematic problem-solving process.

The *communication technicians* designs and arrange for dissemination of messages as needed to help carry out public relations programs. Enactors of this role use such technical skills as writing, graphic production, photography, and organization of evebts designed to gain publicity.

Since the 24-item set of role questions was proposed in set in 1979, several studies have used factor analysis to identify underlying roles or dimensions. Researchers have concluded that the three conceptual roles of expert prescriber, communication facilitator, and problem-solving process facilitator are highly intercorrelated and actually constitute one single role dimension, the *public relations manager,* as distinct from the *communication technician* role (Anderson et al., 1989; Broom and Dozier, 1993; Dozier, 1984, 1992).

To examine whether Thai public relations practitioners perform the roles exhibited in the U.S. studies, the 24-role items were subjected to an exploratory principal component factor analysis and rotated to a varimax solution. Four clearly defined factors and one isolated item emerged from the factor analysis, accounting for 72.9% of all variance in the set.

As in previous studies, the *manager* role emerged as the first factor in the Thai sample, accounting for 49.5% of the variance (see Table 8.1). The second factor, labeled the *communication liaison,* accounted for 9.1% of the variance.

TABLE 8.1
Factor Loadings and Alpha Reliability Coefficients for Four Public Relations Practitioners Roles
(N = 127)

Manager (alpha = .94)	Factor Loadings
I encourage management participation when making important public relations decisions (PF)	.82
I keep management activity involved in every phase of the public relations program (PF)	.77
I take responsibility for the success or failure of my organization's public relations program (EP)	.74
I plan and recommend courses of action for solving and/or avoiding public relations problems (EP)	.74
When working with managers on public relations, I outline alternative approaches for solving problems (PF)	.70
I make the communication policy decisions (EP)	.67
I represent the organization at events and meetings (CF)	.67
I operate as a catalyst in management's decision making (PF)	.65
I work with managers to increase their skills in solving and/or avoiding public relations problems (PF)	.56
I observe that others in the organizations hold me accountable for the success or failure of public relations programs (EP)	.51

(Continued)

TABLE 8.1 (*Continued*)

Communication Liaison (alpha = .93)	Factor Loadings
I report public opinion survey results to keep managaement informed of the opinion of various publics (CF)	.82
I keep management informed of public reaction to organizational policies, procedures and/or actions (CF)	.80
I diagnose public relations problems and explain them to others in the organization (EP)	.68
I conduct communication audits to identify communication problems between the organization and various publics (CF)	.63
I create opportunities for management to hear the views of various internal and external publics (CF)	.62
In meeting with management, I point out the need to follow a systematic public relations planning process (PF)	.57
Because of my experience and training, others consider me to be the organization's expert in solving public relations problems (EP)	.57

Media Relations Specialist (alpha = .70)	
I am the person who writes the public relations materials presenting on information on issues important to the organization (TECH)	.77
I maintain media contacts and place press releases (TECH)	.72
I keep others in the organization informed of what the media report about our organization and important issues (CF)	.56

Graphic Technician (alpha = .78)	
I produce brochures, pamphlets, and other publications (TECH)	.83
I do photography and graphics for public relations materials (TECH)	.82
I handle the technical aspects of producing public relations materials (TECH)	.78

Note. Identifications of Broom's (1982) conceptual roles; EP = Expert Prescriber; PF = Problem-Solving Process Facilitator; CF = Communication Facilitator; TECH = Communication Technician.

Interestingly, the Thai practitioners split the communication technician role into two factors—the *media relations* specialist and the *graphic technician*. The fifth factor was defined entirely with by one communication-technician item which loaded at .89. That item was "I edit and/or rewrite for grammar and spelling the material written by others in the organization."

Cronbach's alpha reliability coefficient were .94 for the manager factor, .93

for the communication liaison factor, .70 for the media relations specialist factor, and .78 for the graphic technician concept. These coefficients indicate acceptable levels of internal consistency reliability.

The manager role was tapped by five items designed to measure the problem-solving process-facilitator role, four expert-prescriber items, and one question viewed by Broom and colleagues as measuring communication-facilitator behavior. Activities that defined the *manager* role in the Thai sample include encouraging management participation in public relation decision making, keeping management involved in public relations programs, recommending actions to solve public relations problems, making communication policy decisions, and being held accountable for the success or failure of the public relations programs.

Items loading primarily on the *communication-liaison* factor were similar, if not identical, to those of forming Broom and Dozier's (1993) "senior adviser" role scale. Questions here included four on communication facilitation, two measures of expert prescription, and one item dealing with problem-solving process facilitation. Specifically, the liaison activities include keeping management informed of the public opinion survey results as well as of public reactions to organizational policies or actions, diagnosing public relations problems, and creating opportunities for management to hear the views of its various publics. Dozier (1992) characterized enactors of this role as informal managers without policy-making power. Further, this role appears to correspond to components described in Grunig and Hunt's (1984) two-way asymmetric model of the public relations role.

The six measures of communication-technician behavior, as defined by Broom and colleagues, were split into two factors and one isolate, accounting for 14.2% of variance. The *media- relations specialist* writes materials presenting information on issues important to the organization, maintains media contacts and places press releases, and inform others of what the media report about the organization and related important issues. The *graphic technician* handles the technical aspects of producing public relations materials such as brochures and pamphlets in addition to doing photography and graphic arts work. Unlike in American samples, Thai practitioners appeared to enact two distinct roles they performed. The one-item *editor* factor could be interpreted as suggesting that Thai public relations practitioners also saw the editing for language mechanics as separate from other technical aspects.

Overall, however, Broom's role scales appear to have a cross-cultural application, at least with the Thai sample. The *manager* and *communication-liaison* factors found in this study were consistent with the a series of role studies conducted by Broom and Dozier (Broom, 1982, Broom & Dozier, 1993; Dozier, 1984, 1992). However, items describing technical aspects of public relations work did not emerge on a single factor as in previous studies. We hypothesize that, in practice, Thai practitioners view media relations and graphic arts as two distinctly different areas of technical skill and expertise.

Based on the factor analysis result, items loading most strongly on each factor

TABLE 8.2
Precentages of Thai Public Relations Practitioners' Four Roles

	Frequency of Roles Performed [a]			
	Infrequent	Moderate	Frequent	
Role Types	(1 -2.99)	(3 - 4.99)	(5 - 7)	N
Manager	38%	34%	28%	120
Liaison	49%	30%	21%	123
Media Specialist	19%	33%	48%	124
Graphic Technician	34%	34%	32%	127

[a] From 7-point scales, measuring frequency of different aspects of public relations behavior, where 1 = never and 7 = always.

were combined to form an index, and raw scores were calculated to get frequencies for each role (see Table 8.2). More than one fourth (28%) of the sample performed the manager role frequently. Also, almost half (48%) said they almost always or always performed tasks related to media relations. One third (32%) stated that their work involved technical aspects frequently, whereas 21% of the respondents acted often as liaisons promoting two-way communication between the organization and its publics.

The above findings illustrate a substantial shift from a predominantly press-agent mode some 60 years ago toward two-way communication and playing a management role today, especially in the private sector. The dominance of *communication-manager* in the present factor analysis shows that Thai practitioners perceived a clear, coherent managerial role in their public relations work. The *communication-liaison* role, although not widely practiced, entails two-way, asymmetric elements. Taken as a whole, these data suggest encouraging, progressive steps toward management emphasis in Thai public relations. This held even though only 28% of practitioners reportedly enacted the manager role frequently whereas only 21% did likewise with the liaison role.

Grunig and Grunig (1989) explained that the majority of practitioners in any organization appears to be in technician roles, although they may also perform managerial tasks.

CONCLUSION

To summarize, public relations activities in Thailand have been publicity-oriented and have aimed quite strongly at promoting the interests of client organization. Information disseminated by the government via any mass-media channels is directed primarily toward educating the public while simultaneously promoting favorable images of the government. Also, many businesses adhere to a similar philosophy of one-way public relations.

However, this study suggests a progressive move toward two-way, asymmetric communication in public relation practice. Scientific methods are being used increasingly to measure public opinion and to gain feedback.

An increasing number of university-trained practitioners, growing emphasis on management functions within public relations, and a promise of better understanding and cooperation from management bode well for the future. It is hoped that, in the near future, Thailand's public relations can focus heavily on the change and negotiation focused, two-way symmetric model. Then, both organizations and their publics can benefit greatly from public relations.

ACKNOWLEDGMENT

The authors gratefully thanks Dr. Glen M. Broom for allowing them to use his role questionnaire in this study.

REFERENCES

Anderson, R., Reagan, J., Sumner, J., & Hill, S. (1989). A factor analysis of Broom and Smith's public relations roles scales. *Public Relations Review, 15*(3), 54.

Broom, G. M. (1982). A comparison of sex roles in public relations. *Public Relations Review, 8*(3), 17–22.

Broom, G. M., & Dozier, D. M. (1986). Advancement for public relations role models. *Public Relations Review, 8*(3), 37–56.

Broom, G. M., & Dozier, D. M. (1993, August). *Evolution of the managerial role in public relations practice.* Paper presented at the meeting of the Public Relations Division, Association for Education in Journalism and Mass Communication, Kansas City, MO.

Broom, G. M., & Smith, G. D. (1979). Testing the practitioner's impact on clients. *Public Relations Review, 5*(3), 47–59.

Chaiwatanarat, C. (1988). *Karn rabrong lookkha radab VIP khong phai prachasamphan rongram Oriental* [Reception of VIP guests of the Oriental Hotel], Project Abstracts, 65, Thammasat University, Bangkok.

Chancharatwatana, W. (1989). *Prasithiphol khong sue videtat nai karn puaiprae krongkarn E-sarn keaw* [The effectiveness of video tape for Green E-sarn Project Publicity], Master's Thesis Abstracts, 329, Chulalongkorn University, Bangkok.

Chantarasiri, S. (1989). *Karn damnoen ngan rabob kruakhai karn prachasamphan radab rongrean khong krom saman suksa: Suksa chapaw nai Krungthep Mahanakorn* [The implementation of public relations network system in schools under the Department of General Education: A case study in Bangkok Metropolis], Master's Thesis Abstracts, 333, Chulalongkorn University, Bangkok.

Dechacheep, S. (1988). *Khunsombat lae nahtee khong nak prachasamphan nai ongkarn* [Qualifications and responsibilities of public relations practitioners in organization], Master's Thesis Abstracts, 318, Chulalongkorn University, Bangkok.

Dozier, D. M. (1984). Program evaluation and roles of practitioners. *Public Relations Review, 10*(2), 13–21.
Dozier, D. M. (1992). Organizational roles of practitioners. In J. E. Grunig (Ed.), *Excellence in public relations and communication management* (pp. 327–357). Hillsdale, NJ: Lawrence Erlbaum Associates.
Grunig, J. E., & Grunig, L. A. (1989). Toward a theory of the public relations behavior of organizations: Review of a program of research. In J. E. Grunig & L. A. Grunig (Eds.), *Public relations research annual* (Vol.1, pp. 27–66). Hillsdale, NJ: Lawrence Erlbaum Associates.
Grunig, J. E., & Hunt, T. (1984). *Managing public relations*. New York: Holt, Rinehart & Winston.
Klinpongsa, P. (1989). *Vikrah phaen karn suesarn khong prathet Thai nai phaen pattana settakit lae sangkom haeng chart 2504–2531 B.E.* [An analysis of communication planning in Thailand's National Economic and Social Development Plans 1961–1988], Master's Thesis Abstracts, 77–79, Thammasat University, Bangkok.
Malasri, W. (1989). *Prasithipaab lae prasithiphol khong sue singpim tee chai puaiprae nai krongkarn pattanan din kem phak tawanork chiang nua* [The efficiency and effectiveness of printed media used in the Northeast Thailand], Master's Thesis Abstracts, 327, Chulalongkorn University, Bangkok.
Maneechoti, J. (1988). *Karn damnoen ngan prachasamphan rongram Hyatt-Central Plaza: Suksa chapaw koranee sue singpim pua karn prachasamphan* [Implementation of public relations of Hyatt-Central Plaza Hotel: Selected study of print media], Project Abstracts, 65, Thammasat University, Bangkok.
National Public Relations Committee (1993). *Tumniab chaonaati prachasampan lae sue muanchon nai Prathet Thai 2536* [Directory of public relations and mass media personnel in Thailand]. Bangkok: Public Relations Department.
Papui, S. (1989). *Prasithiphol khong nuai ngan prachasamphan kluantee nai karn hai kwamroo lae tasanakati dan karn anurak sappayakorn pamai kae prachachon nai mooban changwat Chiang Mai* [Effectiveness of the public relations mobile units in providing knowledge and views on forest resource conservation in Chiang Mai], Master's Thesis Abstracts, 337, Chulalongkorn University, Bangkok.
Photisuvan, T. (1988). *Suksa krabuan karn kamnot nayobai lae phaen karn prachasamphan pua karn pattana nai prathet Thai* [A study of public relations policy and planning process for development in Thailand], Master's Thesis Abstracts, 26, Thammasat University, Bangkok.
Poobuapuan, O. (1989). *Karn suksa karn wang phaen karn prachasamphan lae satanaphab karn damnoen ngan prachasamphan khong nuai ngan thurakit nai Krungthep Mahanakorn* [Planning and implementation of public relations in business firms in Bangkok Metropolis], Master's Thesis Abstracts, 339–340, Chulalongkorn University, Bangkok.
Prajammuang, K. (1988). *Karn prachasamphan pua songserm thurakit* [Public relations for business promotion], Project Abstracts, 64, Thammasat University, Bangkok.
Satawedin, P., Apiratanakul, W., Asawadorndecha, K., & Suthiworaset, C. (1981). *Raingarn karn wijai ruang satanapab khong bookalakorn lae nuayngarn prachasamphan nai Prathet Thai* [Research report on status of public relations departments and practitioners in Thailand]. Faculty of Communication Arts, Chulalongkorn University, Bangkok.
Satawedin, L., Ekachai, D., Kansuwan, S. & Lerk-Klang, P. (1986). *Tassanakati khong sue muanchon lae nak prachasamphan nai karn tamngarn ruamkan dan khawsarn* [Attitudes of mass media and public relations practitioners in information service cooperation]. Bangkok: Bangkok University.
Satitamorntham, P. (1988). *Withee karn khian lae roob bab khong warasarn pai nai "Rak Koon Tau Pha" tee panakngan karn bin Thai tong karn aan mak teesud* [Writing styles and patterns of "Rak Koon Tau Pha" internal publication preferred by employees of Thai Airways International], Project Abstracts, 66, Thammasat University, Bangkok.
Srichanachaichok, R. (1989). *Karn damnoen ngan prachasamphan pua pattana chonnabot nai*

prathet Thai kab naew nayobai lae phaen karn prachasamphan haeng chart [The practice of public relations of rural development in Thailand and the national public relations policies and plan], Master's Thesis Abstracts, 326–327, Chulalongkorn University, Bangkok.

Tananchaibutra, B. (1986). *Patanakarn khong nayobai karn suksa nai prathet Thai: Karn suksa vikrah naew nayobai lae mae bot karn prachasamphan haeng chart* [Development of communication policies in Thailand: Analysis of the national public relations policies and the related master plans]. Unpublished master's thesis, Thammasat University, Bangkok, Thailand.

Tantivetchakul, T. (1988). *Naewnom ngan prachasamphan khong krom tamruat pai nai chuang pee 2532–2542 B.E.* [Trends of the public relations activity of the Police Department during 1989–1999], Master' Thesis Abstracts, 306, Chulalongkorn University, Bangkok.

Thammasat University (1987). *Loom loom don don karn prachasamphan* [Public relations' peaks and valleys]. Bangkok: Thammasat University.

Thanabunlertluck, J. (1988). *Karn damnoen ngan prachasamphan khong rongram Oriental* [Implementation of public relations activities of the Oriental Hotel], Project Abstracts, 65, Thammasat University, Bangkok.

Wongsarot, R. (1988). *Krabuan karn prachasamphan khong rongram Asia* [Public relations process of the Asia Hotel], Project Abstracts, 66, Thammasat University, Bangkok.

Worakitpokatorn, P. (1993). Paappot: Kwammai soongsud khong karn prachasamphan [Image: The utmost meaning of public relations]. The Public Relations Department's Annual Report, pp. 49–52, Bangkok.

9 Power Distance and Public Relations: An Ethnographic Study of Southern Indian Organizations

K. Sriramesh
Purdue University

Public relations practice has been regarded widely as a U.S. phenomenon. Among others, Pimlott (1951), after studying public relations practice in the United States, wrote that public relations is first and foremost a U.S. practice. He saw a social and political role for public relations in American Society.

After 40 years, Pimlott's assertion still seems valid. Scholars continue to echo similar sentiments, contending that public relations originated in the U.S., and that organizations in other parts of the world have only replicated the public relations practiced in the United States (Sriramesh & White, 1992). Existing public relations theory also has an American bias. Most theorizing in the field has taken place only in the United States. All elements of this still-evolving theory have been identified by scholars in the United States, and the theorizing has been based largely on empirical evidence gathered by analyzing U.S. organizations.

However, the relevance and practice of public relations is not restricted to the United States. Organizations around the globe use public relations for publicity and other communication purposes. The political, economic, and industrial changes that began in the late 1980's have shrunk the world and increased interdependence among nations. The 1990's have heralded further changes such as the unification of Western Europe as a common market and a crystallization of the shift in economic and industrial focus away from the Western hemisphere to the Pacific Rim countries and Asia. Organizations that operate in this multinational environment are forced to cross national borders to stay competitive. In doing so, they are forced to communicate with peoples of different cultures. They certainly use public relations to perform some of this communication. Therefore, it is critical that efforts be made to increase our awareness of the environment for, and the practice of, public relations in other countries.

Based on this rationale, the author conducted a systematic investigation of public relations in Bangalore, a southern Indian city. Although the organizations were located in one city, the major findings are generalizable to Indian public relations as a whole because of the range of organizations studied. The study began with a search of the literature which showed that very little information is published on public relations in India.

LITERATURE ON PUBLIC RELATIONS IN INDIA

Only three books that focus on Indian public relations are currently available (Kaul, 1988; Narain, 1975; Reddi, 1978). Kaul's volume was the first comprehensive description of public relations in India. In his preface to the first (1976) edition, Kaul alluded to the lack of literature on Indian public relations. The author began his second edition (Kaul, 1988) by charting the history of the practice of public relations in India to 300 B.C. Kaul referred to the rock and pillar edicts that the Indian Emperor Asoka [pronounced Ashoka] used for communicating to his subjects:

> The inscriptions were meant to inform the people about the policies of his [Asoka's] government, to persuade them to carry out certain tasks and to create goodwill amongst them for the establishment. Interestingly enough, the Asokan inscriptions were in the local script. Thus, those found in the north-west are in the Kharoshthi script derived from the Aramaic script used in Iran. At the extreme west of the empire, near modern Kandahar, the inscriptions are in Greek and Aramaic; elsewhere in India they are in the Brahmi script. Clearly this is not only an example of public relations but a fairly developed form of it which takes into account the need to approach various sections of the people in their own languages. (p. 1)

Kaul listed some "popular notions" prevalent in India about public relations practitioners. One was that in India public relations practitioners are generally viewed as "fixers, a breed of people who will wangle things for you by the most questionable methods . . . [such as] 'wining and dining' . . ." (p. 2). Noting that public relations should not be equated with publicity as is normally done, Kaul accepted the definition of public relations proposed by the Institute of Public Relations in the UK which sees public relations as "the deliberate, planned and sustained effort to establish and maintain mutual understanding between an organisation and its public" (p. 3). However, Kaul (1988) also emphasized the importance of building corporate image:

> The positive effects of goodwill and a favourable public image can hardly be overrated. Such goodwill cannot only ensure the survival and growth of an organisation but also create a climate in which it will be able to carry on its business operations with much greater ease than would otherwise be possible. Other things

being equal, there is little doubt that between two competing firms it is the one with better PR that will steal an edge over the other in the long run. (p. 5)

Noting that a historical account of public relations in India has yet to be written, Kaul (1988) listed four stages that, according to him, characterize the development of public relations in India. The first stage extended up to World War II during which public relations was used primarily to disseminate information "out of a liberal and philanthropic approach" (p. 22). The Tata Iron and Steel Company, established in 1912, is heralded as the harbinger of the need to focus on community relations. Employees of this private corporation were provided basic necessities such as housing, water, electricity, and healthcare at subsidized costs. Primary education (elementary school education) was provided free to the children of employees.

The second "conscious" stage of public relations that Kaul identified started during World War II. According to the author, three factors contributed to the development of this second stage: "the emergence of a vocal public opinion . . . mass circulated newspapers and an influential press . . . and the outbreak of the Second World War and the need for mobilising public opinion in favour [sic] of the war effort" (p. 24). It was also during this stage that an Indian organization first set up a public relations department. In 1943, the industrial house of Tatas formed a public relations department at its corporate head office in Bombay which started publishing monthly newsletters in 1944.

India's independence from British rule in 1947 was the harbinger of what Kaul identified as the third stage in the development of public relations in India. The multinational corporations already operating when India gained independence found it necessary to liaise with the new legislators and the government. The third stage, then, saw organizations responding to the changes brought about by the growth of democratic institutions in India such as the federal parliament and the state legislatures.

According to Kaul, the fourth stage of the development of public relations in India was the stage of professionalism during which practitioners began to organize themselves as a professional group. The Public Relations Society of India (PRSI) was formed in 1958 and became active in promoting improvements in the standards of public relations in India. Around this time, the first course on public relations was offered in Calcutta by the public relations officer of Tata Steel. The first conference of public relations professionals was organized by PRSI in New Delhi in April, 1968. At that conference, members decided that a code of professional ethics was very essential because of the wide spectrum of people who were "masquerading as public relations practitioners [but] . . . were . . . nothing better than fixers and lobbyists of various kinds operating with the most dubious of methods" (Kaul, 1988, p. 26). The data for this study were collected from organizations in Bangalore just after the city had hosted the 1990 conference of the PRSI.

Reddi (1978) analyzed the multimedia information campaign conducted by the municipal government of Hyderabad, a metropolitan city in southcentral India. The objective of this campaign was "to create civic consciousness among the citizens towards a cleaner city" (Part 2, p. 7). In particular, people were asked to clear slums or improve them, get the slum dwellers involved in this clean up, and educate the uneducated slum dwellers on the need to adopt family welfare (family planning) measures. The municipal government focused on publicity to attain these objectives by using the print and broadcast media, billboards, exhibitions, publication of leaflets and pamphlets, and a personal campaign in the slums. Folk forms of entertainment such as dance dramas and songs were also used to draw the attention of the public.

Like Reddi's work, Narain's (1975) book on Indian public relations is thorough in description but limited in scope. Whereas Reddi studied only one municipality, Narain focused only on the annual reports of a sample of 66 public sector companies. Of the 66 organizations in Narain's sample, only 30 had public relations departments leading the author to lament that "in India, the P. R. work is in its infancy . . . Not all public enterprises in India have recognised the need of public relations, and where this function has received recognition, the scope of its work . . . differs widely" (Narain, 1975, p. 5). Of the remaining organizations, 10 entrusted the publicity work to another executive such as the development manager, executive officer or the marketing manager. Five organizations reported that public relations was not considered as a distinct organizational activity.

Significantly, Narain (1975) found that the importance the chief executive officer of an organization attached to public relations was critical to the status and functioning of the public relations department. He quoted the chief executive of a large public sector enterprise to support this view: "Howsoever good and able a Public Relations Officer may be, he cannot do much unless the chief executive appreciates the value of the public relations . . ." (p. 38). Narain also found most annual reports to be less forthcoming in narrating the activities of the organization—an example of press agentry as expounded by J. Grunig and Hunt (1984). Narain suggested that organizations should take an open system approach when he remarked that "the annual report should . . . aim at providing a correct, comprehensive and coherent picture of the enterprise" (p. 79).

Although it is a thorough document and makes significant contributions to one's understanding of public relations in India, the scope of Narain's book is limited only to annual reports. Only the first chapter is completely devoted to the public relations departments of public sector enterprises based on data gathered from the public relations managers of the sample of organizations through a self-administered questionnaire. The remainder of the book focuses on the inadequacy of annual reports in making explicit financial disclosures to the parliament and the public. Further, the author himself admits that the book lacks a theoretical underpinning by remarking: "this study is purely factual. The theoretical discussion, as far as possible, has been avoided" (p. 5).

A review of these three books revealed that a theoretically based analysis of the public relations practices of a range of Indian organizations was long overdue. Therefore, this study was envisaged. Based on the rationale of the *Excellence project* funded by the IABC (J. Grunig, 1992), each organization selected for this study was a corporation (including public sector enterprises), non-profit organization, government agency, or association. One objective was to look for the presence of public relations variables such as the models of public relations (J. Grunig & Hunt, 1984) and the public relations roles (Broom & Dozier 1986) in the sample organizations. More significantly, the study sought to evaluate the impact of power distance, a dimension of culture, on public relations.

Sriramesh and White (1992) argued that culture affects the world views and communication practices of managers and practitioners. Because public relations, a communication activity, is driven by the world views of practitioners and decision makers, culture affects public relations. Culture also has a bearing on the nature of activism present in an organization's environment. Only when challenged by activists, organizations turn to public relations. However, not all scholars agree that a linkage exists between culture and organizational activities.

PERSPECTIVES ON CULTURE

The Culture-free Approach

Hickson, Hinings, McMillan, and Schwitter (1974) were among those who urged the culture-free approach to organizations, arguing that the characteristics of organizations would be stable across societies and cultures. They theorized that regardless of the "social structure" (an aspect of societal culture) prevalent in a society, the causal linkage between the stakeholders of an organization and the organization's operating technology and structure would remain the same:

> [Our] hypothesis rests on the theory that there are imperatives, or "causal" relationships, from the resources of "customers," of employees, of materials and finance, etc., and of operating technology of an organization to its structure which take effect whatever the surrounding social differences . . . Whether the culture is Asian or European or North American, a large organisation with many employees improves efficiency by specialising their activities but also by increasing controlling and coordinating specialities. (p. 64)

Haire, Ghiselli, and Porter (1966) also advocated the culture-free thesis, although they did not totally disregard the effect of culture on work-related attitudes of organizational employees. The primary goal of their study was to identify whether managers in different countries think alike. Haire et al. selected 3,641 managers of corporations (they excluded nationalized and quasi-nationalized industries as far as possible) from 14 countries and administered similar questionnaires in English for those who understood the language, and in local languages for nonEnglish speaking respondents. Based on the responses, the authors concluded that "national differences make a consistent and substantial contribution to the differences in managers' attitudes" (p. 9). In arriving at this conclusion, they attributed about 25%–30% of the variation they observed among managers of different countries to national differences. However, they seemed to advocate the culture-free thesis when they stated:

> One might take the position that being a manager is a way of life and that, as such, a French manager might be expected to be more similar to an Indian manager, say, than to a French non-manager. The considerable similarity among managers' responses throughout the instrument lends some real support to this belief in the universality of managerial philosophy. (p. 9)

Tayeb (1988) found conceptual and methodological flaws in studies taking the culture-free approach. She contended that Haire et al. (1966) made inferences that completely ignored the fact that most of their respondents had been undergoing management training courses during the time they participated in the study and therefore they were being exposed to similar management philosophies. These ideologies were still fresh in their memory when they responded to the questions posed by the researchers. Tayeb contended that these imposed management philosophies undoubtedly may have influenced the responses of these managers.

Tayeb also pointed out that Haire et al did not study the structure of the organizations supervised by these managers. Furthermore, information was not gathered on the perceptions of the subordinates of these managers on how the organization was being run.

The Culture-specific Approach

The culture concept is no longer restricted to anthropological literature. The impact of culture on the mass media has been studied for several decades but only since the 1970's has the concept also become pervasive in literature on organizational theory. "Culture is an idea whose time has come," wrote Smircich (1983, p. 339), heralding the assimilation of the concept into organizational theory. Jelinek, Smircich, and Hirsch (1983) echoed the same sentiments when they stated that the concept of culture helps academicians and practitioners to address the "interactive, ongoing, recreative aspects of organizations, beyond the merely logical or economic" (p. 331).

Culture is generally viewed by cultural anthropologists as a construct that reduces ambiguity and facilitates interaction in social settings. Organizations also are social settings, argue advocates of corporate culture, and therefore the impact of culture on organizations cannot be overstated. Jamieson (1982, p. 73) referred to culture as "a key variable in accounting for differences in economic and organizational behavior in different countries." The author elaborated:

> The major problem in looking at another society's arrangements for ordering economic life is that they are not isolated; those arrangements are woven into the very fabric of the whole society. Thus, in order to understand the working of a large Japanese business enterprise, it is necessary to place it in the context of Japanese society as a whole. (p. 72)

Tayeb (1988) echoed the sentiments of many scholars (e.g., Hofstede, 1980; Negandhi, 1985; Shenoy, 1981) who advocate viewing organizational members and activities through a cultural approach in understanding organizational processes:

> The major strength of the cultural perspective as a whole is its recognition of (a) the important role that culture plays in shaping work-related values, attitudes and behaviours of individual members of various societies; (b) the fact that cultural values and attitudes are different in degree from one society to another, and (c) the fact that different cultural groups behave differently under similar circumstances because of the differences in their underlying values and attitudes. (p. 40)

This study approaches the problem at hand—understanding the public relations practices of selected Indian organizations—through the strategies advocated by the first school of thought that Smircich (1983) identified. Smircich posited that proponents of this point of view see culture as an independent variable almost synonymous with country, which is imported into the organization through the employees (e.g., Hofstede, 1980; Tayeb, 1988). These scholars typically chart the similarities and differences among nations and cultures and try to compare management practices cross-nationally and cross-culturally. Smircich (1983) noted that such studies would be especially helpful to multinational organizations as evidenced by the popularity of *Theory Z* (Ouchi, 1981) and *The Art of Japanese Management* (Pascale & Athos, 1981). This study argues that studying the linkage between societal culture and public relations should precede the investigation of the influence of corporate culture (culture internal to organizations) on public relations.

It is possible for an organization's corporate culture to be dissimilar to the societal culture prevailing in its environment. In particular, this may hold if the organization is relatively young and under the control of an overbearing CEO whose personality is quite different from the mainstream societal culture (Sriramesh & White, 1992; Sriramesh, J. Grunig, and Buffington, 1992). Although such deviations do occur, societal culture has a significant impact in shaping an organization's corporate culture. Scholars who have identified the determinants of culture have pointed out that it is not uncommon for the personality of individuals to vary with the culture of the predominant percentage of members of their society.

Origins of the Culture Concept

Having thus established that organizations are cultural entities and that cultural idiosyncracies make themselves apparent in various organizational processes, it is important to trace the origins of the culture concept.

Culture, the basic concept of anthropology, ironically lacks a universally accepted definition. Edward Tylor is credited with providing the first comprehensive definition of the term in 1871. According to Tylor, culture is "that complex whole which includes knowledge, belief, art, morals, custom, and any other capabilities and habits acquired by man as a member of society" (p. 1). Kroeber and Kluckhohn (1952) listed 164 definitions attempted by various scholars for the term. They estimated that they had identified close to 300 different notions that anthropologists had in mind when they used the term *culture*. The culture concept, according to the authors, encompasses a "set of attributes and products of human societies, and therewith of mankind, which are extrasomatic and transmissible by mechanisms other than biological heredity" (p. 145).

Garbarino (1977) separated the many definitions of culture into two major categories; *realist* and *idealist*. Sathe (1983) referred to these categories as the "adaptationist" and "ideational" schools of thought. The realist or adaptationist approach focuses on what can be observed directly about the members of a community such as patterns of behavior, speech, rituals, and cultural artifacts. The ideational approach, on the contrary, attempts to understand a culture through the researcher's interpretations of the culture bearer's ideas of societal values and norms. Simply put, the former point of view believes culture is observable whereas the latter position holds that culture is inferred. Sathe argued that both perspectives are important for organizational managers and theorists.

The Determinants of Societal Culture

Because societal culture is the underpinning of this study, it is important to identify what factors determine the cultural idiosyncracies of a society. Kaplan and Manners (1972) attempted this task by identifying what they called the four *subsystems* of culture; ideology, social structure, technoeconomic structure of a society and personality of members of a society. The authors stated that these "subsystems are a set of variables or aspects of institutionalized behavior that can be analytically isolated for purposes of explaining, at least in part, how a society both maintains itself and undergoes change" (p. 89).

The first cultural determinant that Kaplan and Manners identified is *techno-*

economics. Advocates of cultural materialism have often tried to explain a society's culture from a technoeconomic perspective. The first part of the term *techno* refers to the technical material, equipment, and knowledge available to a society. The second part, *economics,* is indicative of the arrangements employed by a given society in applying its technical equipment and knowledge to the "production, distribution, and consumption of goods and services" (Kaplan & Manners, 1972, p. 93). *Technology* also can be viewed as the opportunities available to a society and *economics* as the way in which that opportunity is exploited to the benefit of the society. Kaplan and Manners speculated that Karl Marx may have had these two phenomena in mind when he distinguished between "means of production" and "mode of production."

To explain the second cultural determinant, *social structure,* Kaplan and Manners (1972, p. 101) quoted the noted British anthropologist Radcliffe-Brown who defined social structure as "the continuing arrangement of persons in relationships defined or controlled by institutions." Social structural theorists attempt to study the distinctions between the various elements of a society such as the stipulation of societal roles (based on caste, class or gender distinctions), or differences between egalitarian lineage and ranked lineage.

Kaplan and Manners said that the third cultural determinant, *ideology,* is representative of values, norms, knowledge, themes, philosophies, and religious principles, world views, and ethos held by members of a society. Human beings are basically conceptualizing and symbolizing animals. This implies that the same ideologies and symbols that humans use to order their social and natural environments will be utilized to set up, maintain, and change social and cultural structures. Anthropologists generally disagree on how much of a determinative role ideological factors play in the maintenance and change of culture. The debate on this issue is mainly based on the fact that the elements of a society's ideology are subjective in nature, and hence involve a great deal of interpretation on the part of an ethnographer studying a culture.

Personality is the fourth cultural determinant that Kaplan and Manners identified. The study of mental processes is not new to the field of anthropology. Anthropologists of the 18th and 19th centuries provided racial, biological, and genetic explanations of cultural determination. The popularity of Freudian psychology in the 1920s and 1930s gave an enormous impetus to theorizing about personality and culture in anthropology. American anthropologists began systematic studies of child rearing practices in various cultures in accordance with the Freudian theory that human personality was molded by childhood experiences. They believed that a society's institutions are either primary or secondary. The family unit is the primary institution. The child rearing practices of a society, give rise to personality traits (basic personality structure) which are shared by members of a society. This basic personality structure determines a society's secondary institutions like art, religion, mythology or folklore.

The Dimensions of Societal Culture

Having reviewed literature on the definition and determinants of culture, it is important to determine the dimensions of culture that helps one to distinguish between two societies. Hofstede's (1980) extensive study of the influence of culture on organizational processes provides insights into a culture's dimensions. He investigated the work-related values and attitudes of managers in 39 countries working for a multinational corporation (the author used the acronym HERMES to refer to this anonymous corporation) and identified four cultural dimensions that can be used to distinguish between countries; power distance, uncertainty avoidance, masculinity/femininity, and individualism/collectivism. The author contended that these four basic cultural factors determine how organizations are structured and managed. The impact that each of these four dimensions has on organizational processes is very extensive. Therefore, each dimension needs to be analyzed separately for its impact on public relations.

The current study focused on the impact of power distance on public relations. Drawing from Kakar (1971) and Tayeb (1988), two cultural dimensions related to power distance, authoritarianism and deference to authority, were also linked with the public relations practices of the sample organizations.

Power Distance

Hofstede (1980, p. 92) contended that human inequality is universal. It manifests itself in a given society in areas such as social status and prestige, wealth, power, laws, rights and rules. The author also contended that inequality in organizations is often inevitable and functional. Such inequality is usually visible in what Hofstede called "boss-subordinate relationships." Generally, bosses tend to exercise authority over their subordinates. Mulder (1976), in his Power Distance Reduction theory, stated that subordinates will try to reduce the power distance between themselves and their superiors whereas most bosses will try to retain the status quo or enlarge the distance. Hofstede's (1980) study, however, suggested that the level of equilibrium attained in this boss-subordinate power struggle is determined by a society's culture. This equilibrium is depicted in the Power Distance Index scores (PDI) that Hofstede's study derived from the mean scores for each country in the HERMES survey. To arrive at this index score, the study elicited responses from employees on three principal aspects; their perceptions of the superior's style of decision making, their fear to disagree with superiors, and the type of decision making they preferred in their boss.

Rank inequalities in societies manifest in different ways. Bohannan (1969) identified three distinctions in social inequality; caste, estate, and class. The caste system, an Indian phenomenon, has traditionally placed members of different castes in different levels of the social hierarchy. Estates, as they existed in feudal Europe, were categories of people with specific rights and obligations although there was no effort in organizations to unite members of the same category. Modern sociology sees the class system as a categorization of people who share characteristics such as prestige, wealth, and power, which are used to rank them in the societal hierarchy. Members of a social class typically are identified by their economic activity or educational background or both and in most cases share the same values, thus forming subcultures.

These distinctions are relevant in the Indian case because although India has traditionally practiced the caste system, it is the class system that is more visible in organizations. Political and financial might, no more the exclusive domain of the upper castes, determines who wields power in the society and in organizations. Both Hofstede (1980) and Tayeb (1988) found greater power distance among superiors and subordinates in Indian organizations. Tayeb concluded that this distance in power relationships caused Indian organizations to have centralized structures.

Authoritarian Nature of Indian Culture

Kakar (1971) conducted a content analysis of 31 stories in the textbooks prescribed in three Indian states and concluded that the superior character in all stories was portrayed as an autocrat. These authoritarian figures were either assertive or nurturant and enforced their authority either by providing emotional rewards or by arousing guilt in their subordinates. Further, the author found that it was typical for the subordinate characters to readily accept the authority of their superiors. Such acceptance was "so complete," Kakar (1971) observed, "that it takes the form of active submission" (p. 100).

Tayeb (1988) studied the same concept, calling it *tolerance*. Her data from employees of Indian organizations showed a high tolerance rate among Indians. However, she found only moderate support for this concept of tolerance based on the response of her subjects to a related characteristic; accepting other points of view. A much smaller percentage of her respondents perceived themselves to be less receptive to others' points of view. A significant percentage (34%) of her Indian respondents thought that Indians have a tendency to impose their own opinions on others. These scores indicate the extent of authoritarianism present in Indian society.

Deference to Authority

Tayeb (1988) found that deference to authority overrides the Indian cultural trait of intolerance of others' points of view. Almost 91 percent of her Indian respondents agreed that Indians have the cultural trait of being deferential to people in authority. Authority may arise out of social or class status, age, or seniority in organizations. A large percentage of her respondents thought that Indians like to be told what to do. The high level of tolerance seems to complement this trait.

Seniors are intolerant of others' viewpoints and therefore tend to be authoritarian, whereas their subordinates are tolerant and deferential to authority.

However, once employees rise to positions of some power, they lose their tolerance in interactions with those below them in the official hierarchy, another example of the elitist nature of Indian culture dictated by high power distance. Indian managers are also known to defend their authoritarian style by arguing that their subordinates do not have the qualifications or the faculty to make work-related decisions.

By combining the above two dimensions, this study surmised that the intolerance among Indians to others' viewpoints is predominantly present among supervisors and managers in organizations. Individuals seem to impose their views only on their subordinates but they remain deferential to their superiors.

The Ethnographic Method

This study primarily used the ethnographic method for data collection and analysis. Ethnographers visit and stay amidst the people they are studying as participant observers and make every effort to understand the *natives'* perspective.

Ethnographers integrate with the natives by participating in their daily routines and take meticulous field notes. This fieldwork methodology is indicative of an important precept of anthropology: *One cannot truly understand others by observation alone.* One also interacts with the natives, learning both by observation *and* interaction. Further, the ethnographer is interested not only in the interactions between researcher and respondent but also in the interactions *among* respondents. Spradley (1980) succinctly described ethnography:

> The essential core of ethnography is this concern with the meaning of actions and events to the people we seek to understand. Some of these meanings are directly expressed in language; many are taken for granted and communicated only indirectly through word and action. But in every society people make constant use of these complex meaning systems to organize their behavior, to understand themselves and others, and to make sense of the world in which they live. (p. 5)

In keeping with this ideology, the researcher spent a period ranging from 4–8 days in each sample organization (duration based on the size of the public relations department) observing the activities of the public relations department. In addition, extended dialogues were held with most public relations professionals and with as many CEO's as possible. An analysis of public relations tools such as newsletters, annual reports, and house journals was also conducted.

Sample

A sample of 18 organizations was selected based on ownership, size and nature of operation. The organizations were based in Bangalore, a city located in

Southern India, which is also known as the "silicon valley of India" because of the many hi-tech industries located there. Bangalore is also home to organizations in such diverse industries as aeronautics, automobiles, electronics, machine tools, telephones, and textiles. Some of these organizations are privately owned while others (public sector enterprises) are owned by either the state or the federal government.

The private sector organizations in the sample varied in size from an entrepreneurial firm employing eight individuals to a large service organization employing about 5,000. Studying small businesses is critical to understanding India's economic scene and so they were included in the sample. All the public sector organizations in the sample were large. The smallest employed just under 8,000 individuals and the largest, over 35,000. They were engaged in power generation (hydroelectric and nuclear), manufacturing precision instruments and tools, mining, marketing, production of heavy electrical equipment, and the production of sophisticated electronic and radar equipments for the defense industry.

In 1991, the current federal administration reversed the socialistic policy in force since India's independence, and began an ambitious program of economic liberalization aimed at dismantling the stranglehold that public sector enterprises have had on the Indian economic system. Until then, the federal government had invested taxpayer monies in these monopolies to generate employment as well as to make the accruing profits accessible to the society at large. As a result, despite their sub-par performance, public sector enterprises had been a central to India's industrial and economic development.

A government agency and a non profit organization were also included in the sample. Attempts to include multinationals in the study were not fruitful. When contacted, the regional offices of two multinational corporations explained that they did not have a public relations department as all publicity functions were conducted by their head offices in Bombay.

THE FINDINGS

Definition and Scope of Public Relations

One of the primary purposes of this study was to learn how Indian public relations practitioners as well as organizational decision makers defined public relations. By understanding the definition of public relations, one can better understand the activities practitioners perform as well as the status of the profession. A successful practitioner defined public relations as "a bit of everything which promotes and helps a smooth functioning [of the organization]." When probed, he explained that he paid special attention to details such as scheduling and arranging a place for the meeting, and making sure that snacks, food, and beverages were available, and so forth. It was obvious that he did not participate in the communication process itself but his efforts were limited to making the meeting a pleasant and comfortable experience for the executives who performed the substantive communication.

A good public relations practitioner "works behind the screen," another practitioner noted. A senior manager had a similar response saying that one of the purposes of public relations is to do the "spade work" for the activities of the organization or senior managers. Not unlike Dozier's (1984) findings, most practitioners in the sample of organizations for this study seemed to possess the managerial title without the power to make policy decisions. In their communication liaison role, they did not engage in substantive communication but focused on administrative chores that facilitated the communication activities of senior executives.

Public relations was equated with marketing (often as a subsidiary to marketing) by most practitioners. One practitioner said that the role of public relations was to help build "identification of the product with the company." Another defined public relations as the effort "to promote the awareness of the product" marketed by his organization. The comments of a company secretary (the senior executive who supervised the public relations manager) typify the perception among senior managers that public relations is a subsidiary of marketing. When asked why his organization had a very small public relations unit, he replied:

> Consumer industries need public relations more than us. I am [my organization is] 100% export-oriented. My selling is restricted to international clients. Then, so far as public relations is concerned, it is a minor need for us. To the extent that we have to inform people about what we are doing, we do public relations.

This senior executive, it was obvious, equated public relations with product promotion. Most practitioners and senior executives also perceived public relations as an effort to build and maintain the positive image of the organization. A senior public relations manager (head of the public relations department of a large public sector enterprise) who defined public relations as the effort aimed at "creating a positive, permanent image in the minds of relevant publics," lamented that public relations has yet to gain acceptance as a profession in India.

The public relations practitioner of a large public sector enterprise (who holds a postgraduate diploma in public relations), linked public relations with advertising. "Public relations and advertising are complementary," she said. Advertising was found to be an integral part of all the public relations departments in the sample organizations.

Other senior executives also saw image-building as the primary role for public relations. The chief executive officer of a service organization listed "projecting the real image" of his organization as the fundamental task for his public relations department. He emphasized that every member of his organization should be a public relations officer and help propagate the corporate image of the organization. This executive did not see a strategic function for public relations. Consequently, his organization did not have a public relations department. These findings are similar to Narain's (1975), which concluded that 9 of the 10 large public sector enterprises he studied listed building corporate image as the primary objective of their public relations departments.

Typical Public Relations Activities

Media relations was one of the main activities performed by the public relations departments of the sample organizations. Some practitioners possessed formal journalism education whereas others had worked as journalists before entering the PR profession. These practitioners used their journalistic skills to write press releases and manage media relations. Stating that journalists were among their most vital publics, most practitioners said that they tried to meet journalists outside office hours to socialize with them in order to enhance their personal influence. An internal memorandum circulated to the public relations personnel of a large public sector enterprise stated that press relations was the primary goal of the public relations department.

Practitioners predominantly used three techniques to establish and maintain their personal influence with journalists. *Press conferences* were arranged not only to disseminate publicity information aimed at enhancing the image of the organization, but also to increase the public relations professional's personal influence with the members of the media. In addition to supplying a press kit with relevant information about the organization, special efforts are made to humor media persons by serving good food, snacks, and beverages. *Press junkets* were another tool used by the affluent organizations to influence journalists. The public relations officer of a power generation company explained that his organization takes journalists four or five times a year to its power generation plants. The professed purpose of these "information gathering media tours" is to help journalists write reports on the operation of these projects. However, on most occasions, the emphasis is on humoring the journalists by proffering them with comforts so that they will write positive news stories about the organization.

As with press junkets, almost every media relations activity was aimed at establishing and maintaining *interpersonal communication* with representatives of the media. The public relations manager of one public sector enterprise said that she frequently carried press releases to newspaper offices in order to meet with reporters and urge them to publish the release. The public relations officer of another public sector enterprise said that he visited the press club at least once a week with the sole purpose of socializing with members of the press and maintaining friendships with them. The public relations officer of a non-profit organization said that she considered keeping journalists in good humor to be one of her most important duties. She went personally to every media office to deliver her press releases because she believed that "What gets published depends on whom you know; it is very subjective." This leads us to one of the primary findings of this study the use of personal influence as a public relations tool.

Personal Influence and Public Relations

As theorized by J. Grunig and Hunt (1984), most organizations in the sample favored press agentry over the two-way models whereas the government agency followed the public information model. However, the sample organizations also practiced personal influence, a typology of public relations activity that was not included in J. Grunig's models. Practitioners used various techniques such as hospitality, giving gifts, and brokering of influence, to build lasting friendships with strategically placed individuals with the aim of seeking favors in return. Almost all practitioners stated that providing hospitality to visiting dignitaries was one of their responsibilities. Most linked hospitality with corporate image stating that being hospitable to visiting dignitaries and guests helped build a positive image for the organization. Typical of this mindset was the response of the chief public relations manager of a large public sector enterprise who had more than 20 years of experience: "Although [guest] hospitality is not a public relations function, it is a management function and cannot be alienated . . . The image of a company is not only product-based; hospitality is also important for corporate image."

Dilenschneider (1990) borrowed the term "favor bank" from Tom Wolfe to refer to such personal influence activities. Using the metaphor of a bank, the author advised public relations practitioners to build a good "credit rating" with strategically placed individuals in society by doing favors. When in need, the public relations practitioner expects favors in return. The statement of a senior executive typifies the use of "favor banks" in India. When asked to define public relations, this executive described public relations as a "quid pro quo" activity. Organizations use their personal influence to prevent government regulation, to circumvent existing regulation, or to cut through bureaucratic red tape.

Although much of the public relations theorizing is silent about this issue, the use of personal influence as a public relations technique is not unique to India. Unscientific observation seems to indicate that lobbyists and public relations consultants in the U.S. often use personal influence to conduct their public relations activities. The "revolving door" practice where government officials become lobbyists and consultants after they leave government service is a good example. These former officials rely on the contacts they made during their tenure in government service to help their clients.

A future study might examine the use of personal influence as a public relations tool in different cultures. Such a study might also study the impact of culture on the use of personal influence, a pervasive public relations technique. Although personal influence as public relations activity seems to be pervasive in many countries, certain aspects of personal influence may be culture-specific. For example, one may find greater interaction between individuals belonging to different strata in societal cultures with lesser power distance. Class-oriented cultures, on the contrary, may emphasize interactions only between people of similar status. But, this has to be determined by conducting systematic research.

The discovery of personal influence as a primary feature of public relations in India may well be an outcome of using the ethnographic method, which is most suited to exploring new phenomena. Because most studies that have contributed to building existing public relations theory have relied on traditional survey instruments designed only to evaluate the presence of specific elements, they have ignored the use of personal influence practices in the U.S. organizations they studied.

Culture and Public Relations

Power Distance seemed to have a profound impact on the public relations activities conducted by the sample organizations. Most public relations practitioners were relatively younger than senior executives and operated at either the middle managerial level or at a lower, supervisory level. They reported that they routinely followed the directions of senior managers (who were generally older or had been in the organization longer) and executed their communication policies. Many practitioners lamented that they did not have any autonomy. Most were reluctant to express this to their superiors because they thought it would not make any difference. One practitioner said: "The PRO is given little importance. He is only there to be used. He is often given no recognition. . . ." When asked where he thought the public relations manager must be placed in the organizational hierarchy, a senior executive stated that the PRO should be placed at least at the middle-management level. The same executive, when asked what he thought were the most fundamental duties of the public relations practitioner, said: "A PRO represents the institution. Therefore, the PRO should project the image that the CEO wants . . ."

Whereas most practitioners indicated that they perceived greater power distance between their superiors and themselves, there were interesting contradictions between practitioners of the same level within an organization. For example, of the three practitioners from a large public sector enterprise, two agreed that there was greater power distance between the different strata in their organization whereas the third indicated that she did not perceive any power distance between herself and her superiors. Despite such inconsistencies in responses, it was clear from the ethnographic interview and observation that power distance does exist in all organizations in the sample.

It was also apparent that subordinates generally accepted the wide power distance between themselves and their superiors, a sign of deference to authority. Those in power need not demand compliance or obedience from subordinates.

Even though some did not agree that they were fearful of such reprisals, ethnographic evidence suggested that these practitioners consciously attempted to appease their supervisors, or at least attempted not to dispute their supervisor's views. Therefore, although the research questions were framed in such a way that it was the managers who tried to maintain the status quo of greater power distance, it is also true that often subordinates defer to authority and tend to be subservient to their superiors. This may also be a result of the hierarchical structure that has the power to penalize subordinates.

The presence of power distance in Indian organizations is not surprising. India has been, and continues to be, a class-oriented society. Until a few decades ago, social status was determined by birth under the caste system. With the dawn of independence and the adoption of a new constitution that has instituted and enforced affirmative action programs (including quotas), the focus has shifted from caste to class. Especially in urban areas, people are able to garner wealth and political power regardless of their caste. Wealth and power in turn have brought social status to them. This shift has not wiped out social distinctions. It has only shifted the focus of power and wealth to a different group of people. Consequently, the society continues to make class distinctions.

In Vyakarnam's (1987) study of the social responsiveness of Indian management graduates, the author found that most management graduates came from families that had economic capital. In India, the working class continues to remain in economic poverty. The managerial class, by being wealthier and more elitist, wields more influence in the society as well as in the organization. Wealth, elitism, and authority breed power distance, which was very evident in the sample organizations. The distinction began with the most basic artifacts of objective culture (Schein, 1985) such as office space, furniture, and perquisites such as cars and chauffeurs. Most of the senior managers (chief executive officers, general managers, and deputy general managers) worked in comfortably furnished, spacious offices. Many offices were also equipped with room air conditioners, which are a sign of luxury in India. They also had a closed door policy requiring one to go through a secretary to gain access to the CEO or a senior executive.

In contrast, the offices of public relations managers were much smaller, had fewer fancy furnishings, and no air conditioners. Only a few public relations managers had relatively larger offices and adequate furniture, but without air conditioning. The decline in physical comforts was even more drastic in the case of lower level employees (supervisors and clerical staff) who were crammed into small office spaces (between 3 and 10 to a room) or given a desk space in a large office area with about 30 other clerks. This was one of the most obvious signs of power distance between the managerial and clerical staff.

There was evidence of an effort to introduce a more egalitarian culture in one organization. The chief executive officer of this private organization holds a management diploma from a foreign university. He had attempted to break the hierarchical mentality of his firm. He had asked all his senior managers to regularly visit far-away regional branches and interact with employees in those branches.

Despite these efforts, the CEO found it difficult to reduce the power distance between the two strata, attributing the failure to the insecurity among Indian managers. According to him, managers generally feel threatened when trying to appear friendly with their subordinates. Many public relations managers expressed similar sentiments. More than half of them agreed that employees (subordinates) lose respect for a boss who consults them before making a decision. This indicated that managers felt more powerful only when they were "distant" from their subordinates.

In conclusion, this study found that decision makers in Indian organizations viewed promoting the positive image of the organization as a primary public relations objective. To achieve this goal, organizations predominantly used press agentry. The study also found that public relations practitioners used personal influence, so far unmentioned in most of the public relations theorizing, to conduct public relations activities including interacting with journalists. Evidence was also found on the impact of power distance, a cultural dimension, on the practice of public relations in India.

This research suggests useful directions for future studies that attempt to use culture in explaining public relations practices. The success of the ethnographic method in this study is a sign that this could be the method of choice for many future public relations research endeavors, particularly those with a multinational sample.

REFERENCES

Bohannan, P. (1969). *Social anthropology.* London: Holt, Rinehart & Winston.
Broom, G. M., & Dozier, D. M. (1986). Advancement for public relations role models. *Public Relations Review, 7*(1), 37–56.
Dilenschneider, R. L. (1990). *Power and influence: Mastering the art of persuasion.* Englewood, Cliffs, NJ: Prentice-Hall.
Dozier, D. M. (1984). Program evaluation and roles of practitioners. *Public Relations Review, 10*(2), 13–21.
Garbarino, M. S. (1977). *Sociocultural theory in anthropology: A short history.* Prospect Heights, IL: Waveland Press.
Grunig, J. E. (1984). Organizations, environments, and models of public relations. *Public Relations Research & Education, 1,* 6–29.
Grunig, J. E. (1992). *Excellence in public relations and communication management: Contributions to effective organizations.* Hillsdale, NJ: Lawrence Erlbaum Associates.
Grunig, J. E., & Hunt, T. (1984). *Managing public relations.* New York: Holt, Rinehart & Winston.
Haire, M., Ghiselli, E. E., & Porter, R. W. (1966). *Managerial thinking: An international study.* New York: Wiley.
Hickson, D. J., Hinings, C. R., McMillan, C. J., & Schwitter, J. P. (1974). The culture-free context of organization structure: A tri-national comparison. *Sociology, 8,* 59–80.

Hofstede, G. (1980). *Culture's consequences.* Beverly Hills: Sage.
Jamieson, I. M. (1982). The concept of culture and its relevance for an analysis of business enterprise in different societies. *International Studies of Management & Organization, 12*(4), 71–105.
Jelinek, M., Smircich, L., & Hirsch, P. (1983). Introduction: A code of many colors. *Administratice Science Quarterly, 28,* 331–338.
Kakar, S. (1971). The theme of authority in social relations in India. *Journal of Social Psychology, 84,* 93–101.
Kaplan, D., & Manners, R. A. (1972). *Culture theory.* Englewood Cliffs, N.J: Prentice-Hall.
Kaul, J. M. (1976). *Public relations in India, (2nd ed).* Calcutta: Naya Prokash.
Kaul, J. M. (1988). *Public relations in India, (2nd ed).* Calcutta: Naya Prokash.
Kroeber, A. L., & Kluckhohn, C. (1952). *Culture: A critical review of concepts and definitions.* Cambridge, MA: Harvard University Press.
Mulder, M. (1976). Reduction of power differences in practice: The power distance reduction theory and its applications. In G. Hofstede & M. S. Kassem (Eds.), *European contributions to organization theory* (pp. 79–94). Assen, Netherlands: Van Gorcum.
Narain, Laxmi. (1975). *Public enterprise in India.* New Delhi: S. Chand & Co. (Pvt) Ltd.
Negandhi, A. R. (1985). Management in the Third World. In P. Joynt and M. Warner (Eds.), *Managing in different cultures* (pp. 69–97). Oslo: Universitetsforlaget.
Ouchi, W. G. (1981). *Theory Z: How American business can meet the Japanese challenge.* Reading, MA: Addison-Wesley.
Pascale, R. T., & Athos, A. G. (1981). *The art of Japanese management.* New York: Simon & Schuster.
Pimlott, J. A. R. (1951). *Public Relations and American Democracy.* Princeton, NJ: Princeton University Press.
Reddi, C. V. N. (1978). *Public relations in municipal government.* Hyderabad: Sharada Publications.
Sathe, V. (1983). Implications of corporate culture: A manager's guide to action. *Organizational Dynamics,* Autumn, 5–23.
Schein, E. H. (1985). *Organizational culture and leadership.* San Francisco: Jossey-Bass.
Shenoy, S. (1981). Organization structure and context: A replication of the Aston study in India. In D. J. Hickson & C. J. McMillan (Eds.), *Organization and Nation* (pp. 133–154). Farnborough: Gower.
Smircich, L. (1983). Concepts of culture and organizational analysis. *Administrative Science Quarterly, 28,* 339–358.
Spradley, J. P. (1980). *Participant observation.* New York: Holt, Rinehart & Winston.
Sriramesh, K., & White, J. (1992). Societal culture and public relations. In J. E. Grunig (Ed.), *Excellence in public relations and communication management: Contributions to effective organizations* (pp. 597–614). Hillsdale, NJ: Lawrence Erlbaum Associates.
Sriramesh, K., Grunig, J. E., & Buffington, J. (1992). Corporate culture and public relations. In J. E. Grunig (Ed.), *Excellence in public relations and communication management: Contributions to effective organizations* (pp. 577–595). Hillsdale, NJ: Lawrence Earlbaum Associates.
Tayeb, M. H. (1988). *Organizations and national culture: A comparative analysis.* London: Sage.
Tylor, E. (1871). *Primitive culture.* London: John Murray.
Vyakarnam, S. (1987). *The social relevance of postgraduate management education: A case study of India.* Unpublished doctoral dissertation submitted to the Cranfield Institute of Technology, Cranfield, England.

10   Public Relations in the Philippines

Juan F. Jamias
Mariechel J. Navarro
University of Philippines at Los Banos

Ramon R. Tuazon
Asian Institute of Journalism

Names now etched in the pantheon of national heroes waged a spirited campaign in the 1880s seeking colonial reforms from Spain. The Filipino expatriate writers and activists included the foremost national hero, Jose Rizal, along with Marcelo H. del Pilar, Graciano Lopez Jaena, and Apolinario Mabini. From 1880 to 1895, they wielded their pens and personal contacts in what came to be known as the Propaganda Movement. The movement's products, notably the two novels of Dr. Rizal, triggered the Philippine Revolution. Schumacher (1973) described the revolution as the first successful challenge by an Asian people against their Western colonial masters.

Some current Filipino practitioners trace their roots to those revered patriots. Somehow this emotional and intellectual connection rings true given both the socioeconomic and political circumstances in Philippine society since the end of the Second World War and today's festering problems. Appropriately, then, participants in the National Congress of Public Relations of 1993 committed themselves anew to the cause of economic advancement, national unity, and, in particular, the Philippines 2000 vision of becoming a Newly Industrializing Country.

The modern public relations industry's accomplishments since its beginnings in the 1950s underscore corporate social responsibility, a focus of work with the business community. Students learn this from Philippine case books (Corteza-Tinsay, 1987; De la Cruz, 1992), in conference proceedings, and in the yearly publications for the Anvil Awards competition, dubbed the "Oscar of Public Relations." Leading public relations executives interviewed for this chapter likewise stressed this ideological orientation.

The annual Anvil Awards, which began in 1962, recognize outstanding programs and projects. In 1993, the jury selected for the Grand Award a campaign to save the Philippine eagle. Among the winners in the outstanding public relations category were an endeavor to electrify depressed urban and rural areas and a campaign for voter education and information. Outstanding use of public relations techniques was also recognized.

The Philippine Business for Social Progress (PBSP), a nationwide program for countryside and other social-development projects, towers in its impact and funding. Since its inception in 1970, this private nonprofit foundation has made concrete the Philippine business's growing sense of social responsibility. Conceived essentially as a public relations initiative, the PBSP helped create prosperous communities by expanding the people's economic opportunities. No less than 162 member corporations joined by 1993. Each contributes annually a percentage of net profits from the previous year. The PBSP also works with over 700 nongovernment organizations (Luz & Montelibano, 1993).

Both major categories of public relations in the Philippines, namely corporate and governmental, have been responding to large-scale challenges in society. The Public Relations Society of the Philippines (PRSP) includes mostly practitioners in the private sector. The Public Relations Organization of the Philippines (PROP) has been organized for public-information officers in the government departments, agencies, corporate bodies, and the armed forces.

THE FIELD'S EVOLUTION

Beginnings of Public Relations

Public relations began gaining prominence in the islands soon after the liberation of Manila from Japanese occupation in 1945. The United States Army had its press-information officers. The returning commonwealth government also initiated the role of press secretary. And with the return of the free Philippine press, particularly the daily newspapers, business pages and sections thrived. Business coverage by the Manila dailies prompted several firms to assign people to handle press relations and later, full-fledged public relations.

In 1947, the Business Writers' Association of the Philippines inaugurated its award to businessmen who excelled in their fields or who engaged in social-action projects. This project further stimulated interest in corporate public relations.

However, the focus was still largely on the practical or operational activities of public relations as shown in an overwhelming preference for the press release as vehicle for communication. Then Jose A. Carpio expounded on the theory of the profession. He spoke and wrote about a right or proper approach encompassing far more than just publicity.

Carpio, the acknowledged Father of Philippine public relations, viewed the function as a planned program of policies and conduct designed to build public confidence in and understanding of an individual or organization (Carpio, as cited in De la Cruz, 1992, p. 49).

Colleagues soon shortened his definition to its essentials. One document defined public relations as the sum total of good performance plus good reporting (Army Troop Information, as cited in De la Cruz, 1992, p. 83). Villanueva (1994) interpreted this to mean Performance Recognition.

In the 1950s, Carpio became managing director of the Philippine Association. At this point, some say, formal planning and strategic thinking began to take hold (Edralin, 1993).

Professionally carried out, foreign programs successfully attracted foreign investments to the fledgling republic. (The Philippines became politically independent in 1946.) As promoted by the Philippine Association, the concept of overall public relations permeated corporate communication.

Actually, Carpio's generation, and even the present one, had hailed from educational backgrounds in fields other than public relations. Carpio had a business-administration degree while others came from journalism, law, engineering, liberal arts, and other disciplines.

In 1975, the Public Relations Society of the Philippines proposed a 4-year public relations curriculum, and it was approved by the Ministry of Education and Culture. Today, several universities offer just one or more courses embedded in various undergraduate programs such as the A.B. in Communication Arts. Among these are the Ateneo de Manila University in Quezon City and the Lyceum of the Philippines in Manila.

PRSP was founded by Carpio and other stalwarts of corporate public relations in 1957. The association would spur professional growth through seminars, workshops, training programs, awards, publications, interpersonal contacts, and networking.

Membership in the PRSP stood at 105 in 1993. Two thirds of those named in the membership directory were public relations managers and allied company executives. At least 31% hailed from public relations agencies. The few others came from the government sector or the public mass media.

The general objectives in the by-laws of the Society express the group's commitments. These objectives continue to be reflected in the industry's programs, projects, and activities. The objectives are as follows:

1. To continually cultivate in the membership the practice of public relations as a planned program of policies and conduct that seeks to build public confidence in what their organizations are doing and to create a better understanding and acceptance of what they are trying to do.
2. To encourage the continuing study of and improvements in the theory, practice, and techniques of public relations.
3. To promote public confidence in the profession of public relations through the prevention or correction of abuses which tend to undermine that trust.

4. To serve as a center of information by making available to members the latest data or information on the practice of effective public relations.
5. To generate public support of public relations projects aimed at promoting the general welfare.
6. To assist the government in its development efforts through the adoption of projects that possess socioeconomic impact.
7. To pursue a continuous dialogue and coordinate with the government in the upgrading of guidelines for the promotion of public relations as an effective tool in unifying the Filipino people through positive goals and projects (Corteza-Tinsay, 1987, pp. 253–254).

The Components and Functional Areas of PR

Public relations managers and agencies made up the bulk of the PRSP's membership as of 1993. Other parts of the industry include public relations departments of advertising agencies, individual public relations counselors, information officers, publicity and assorted promotions practitioners, and government public relations or information officers (Virtusio, 1981).

Following the end of the Marcos administration, public-affairs and political-election consultants have gained in importance. Also vying to be accepted as legitimate practitioners are the numerous entertainment publicity agents who work mostly in the movie industry.

In spite of problems, public relations in the Philippines continued to expand. By the 1980s, its professional networking had spread to member countries of the Association of South East Asian Nations (ASEAN). The scope of public relations now embraces public-opinion formation, public affairs, government relations, industrial relations, community relations, financial affairs, international relations, consumer relations, research, and media relations (Pantaleon, 1980).

A milestone in the field's growth was the setting up of a public relations office by the San Miguel Corporation in 1967. This was quite a belated development. The company, one of the country's biggest corporations, had been in existence since 1890.

Maximino J. Edralin, Jr., who had earlier served the San Miguel Corporation as public relations coordinator, commented, "The old Spanish executives of San Miguel objected to the establishment of the PR office because this was going to add to the overhead (cost) "(Edralin, 1993). This initial resistance melted thanks to persuasive efforts by Joe Carpio and colleagues. As senior vice president and public relations manager of the San Miguel Corporation, Carpio headed the largest public relations department in the Philippines.

Younger than Edralin, who was younger than Carpio, Danilo A. Gozo represents what might be called the third generation of local public relations leaders. Gozo holds the title of vice president for public affairs of the giant Ayala Land.

This company has successfully developed the modern business and financial center of the Philippines in the Manila suburb of Makati.

Before joining Ayala Land, Gozo served in the Philippine Information Agency during the administration of former President Corazon C. Aquino. This was immediately after the February 1986 People Power Revolution. Quick, nearly bloodless, and loved, the uprising restored freedom and democracy to the nation after 14 years of authoritarianism.

Gozo is an alumnus of the University of the Philippines Institute of Mass Communication established in 1965 in the UP Diliman campus, Quezon City. (The Institute is now called the College of Communication.) Thus, he and other recent entrants to the field possess an education more closely related to public relations than that of their predecessors. Gozo's background allows him to identify changes in the profession and to interpret them in light of the total environment.

Gozo highlights the fact that corporate public relations interprets for management public opinion about certain ideas and products. Contemporary scholars describe this as symmetrical public relations in contrast to the asymmetric or one-way communication that still characterizes most corporate communication. As a management function, public relations is designed to create a positive response to a corporation so people will invest in it and support it.

Gozo also characterizes shifts in orientation that have occurred through the years. Most corporations initially were family owned, so their relationships with other sectors were limited. Public relations as a function then was informal and less structured. Expertise was limited to media relations and to reaching the broad, general public.

Eventually, corporations expanded and required an infusion of outside capital. This trend democratized ownership. It also led to deliberate efforts to attract outside investors. Corporations had to project the image that they were well-managed and that they possessed good fundamental values. Thus, people could entrust funds to them.

Furthermore, the electronic media and new communication technologies have changed the communication scene. Communication functions vied for more and more sophisticated hardware and software.

More shifts in public relations practice have been noted by CEO Antonio Zorilla, head of one of the largest and first Filipino-owned public-affairs agencies. He avers that, until the late 1970s, public relations and public-affairs practitioners had diverse training as well as diverse job assignments. Lawyers were sometimes charged with public-affairs activities while public relations assignments went to former newsmen and publicists.

Gozo notes that the influence of business schools has resulted in public relations persons assuming greater management roles, particularly in strategic planning and policy formulation. The public relations practitioner's position in corporations has been elevated so that he or she becomes part of the decision-making team rather than a mere support staffer.

In many locally owned corporations, either a director or a vice president for public relations is assisted by a core staff. Other corporations retain counsel.

Increasingly, public relations has been viewed as a corporate communication function. Marketing and public relations activities highlight a product's image, and strategies have become more scientific. Some firms like Purefoods Corporation sponsor sports teams and events to help project their institutional images. Many corporations maintain professional basketball teams. Players are required to be well-behaved and worthy of respect for the sake of the company's image of quality.

A new but critical function of Public Affairs is to establish cordial relations with government. Zorilla (1983) has urged practitioners to take public policy into account when setting corporate agendas. This is necessary because of the increasing and often very skeptical scrutiny of business by the government, activists, and the media.

The martial-law years of the Marcoses (1972–1981) stifled democratic processes. Government interventions then shaped to a considerable extent public opinion as well as the fates of business establishments. Zorilla (1983) revealed that a tendency to expect such external influence remains. For this reason, business institutions are turning to public relations and public affairs to turn the tide of flawed public opinion and government policies.

The distinction between public relations and public affairs has also become blurred due to the changing national climate and the strong presence of "third-party" advocates. Ideological concerns of consumerists, environmentalists and religious groups have changed the rules, according to Zorilla (1983). Media influence on public policy has become rather strong as newspaper columnists and television talk-show hosts have gained greater power much to the chagrin of some. "It is already very difficult to draw the line between traditional objective news reporting and opinionated writing," Gozo (1994) commented.

The recent shift of political power from Manila to the local governments has reduced the central government's involvement in business. Such decentralized power has resulted in less uniform policies nationally.

Other effects of third-party advocates abound. For example, a plan to set up a liquid petroleum gas-terminal plant in a town south of Manila was scrapped, despite national-government endorsement, due to pressure from activists and environmentalists. Obviously, public issues must be managed well to prevent damage to product and corporate reputations.

CEOs see the need to have a greater grip on public policy to counteract so-called third-party voices who get substantial media mileage and therefore may swing public opinion. These voices are perceived to be well-financed, powerful, expert communication strategists.

Lobbying and advocacy involve coalition building, constituency mobilization, balanced media coverage, and even advertising. These require that relevant audiences be educated on the logic of a corporation's point of view. Thus, public relations practitioners in the Philippines have had to develop techniques to promote better understanding of public issues and concerns.

Recently, innovative institutional public relations projects were waged. The Del Monte Corporation set out to save the endangered Philippine eagle. The California Food Corporation supported a program for physically handicapped children. Although not directly promoting product sales, these projects associated companies with positive values in the public mind. For instance, IBM's "Bukas Palad" (Open Palm) project sought to help the physically handicapped become productive members of society. This created an image of "bigness, humanity, and concern for the less fortunate."

CX Manila, local subsidiary for Cathay Pacific, saw the need to incorporate environment-friendly systems into its business. Among other activities, it initiated an artificial reef project to help fishermen rehabilitate their deteriorating environment. Also, the Ayala Foundation is committed to preserving the culture of the Mangyans, an ethnic group in Mindoro. Such varied projects highlight social responsibility and community relations.

On the other hand, shady public relations operators do exist. Such sleazy practitioners sow intrigues with regulatory bodies, spread false stories, and feed on the media penchant for sensationalism. Military psychological-warfare techniques are also used.

PUBLIC RELATIONS IN GOVERNMENT

Public relations has become a critical part of governance. Public-information work seeks to create awareness and to generate acceptance of public policies and programs. It mobilizes public participation in development undertakings and projects an image of good, legitimate government.

Never in Philippine history has the role of public relations (with focus on image building) been highlighted more than during the Marcos years. From the time martial law was declared in 1972 until Marcos's rule was forcibly ended in 1986, the government put on a massive and sustained propaganda campaign, both locally and worldwide, especially in the United States. Emphasis was on insuring sustained U.S. government and military support, and on technical assistance to the Philippine government.

Another Marcos Legacy

The Marcos government set up an elaborate, well-funded nationwide media infrastructure. This well-oiled information machinery may have been largely responsible for the continuous 20-year rule of the Marcoses (including wife Imelda) despite human-rights abuses, graft, and corruption.

The Marcos government illustrated convincingly the power of public relations in government. Henceforth, the propaganda apparatus was recognized as "too important" to dismantle. Indeed the two succeeding governments of Presidents Aquino and Fidel V. Ramos have maintained the monolithic government media and information system. After the 1986 revolution, the government acquired former Marcos-controlled media organizations and those of his cronies. But the privatization of such media has been held in abeyance since then, and these continue to be under government control. Included are at least three broadcast networks and a newspaper chain.

Re-Imaging Government Information and Public Relations

Immediately upon taking office in 1986, the Aquino government assessed the existing government information system carefully. One finding was that "little distinction was made between political and development-oriented information, hence resources for public information were often used for political purposes. In most instances, political information and/or political propaganda crowded out development-oriented public information" (Philippine Information Agency, Republic of the Philippines, 1986).

The same study pointed out that basic programs "focused more on the moulding of public opinion toward unquestioning acceptance of government thinking" and that the flow of information was predominantly one-way, that is, from government to the people.

To distinguish between these two basic functions, then, President Aquino issued several executive orders decreeing that the Office of the Press Secretary shall handle political media relations while the Philippine Information Agency (PIA) shall take care of development information.

Created in December 1986, the PIA aimed to provide for the free flow of accurate, timely, and relevant information to assist people in decision making and in identifying opportunities to improve the quality of life. This would enable citizens to participate meaningfully in democratic processes.

In February 1989, President Aquino also created the Foreign Information Council (FIC) "to provide an effective overseas information and communication strategy crucial in enhancing Philippine foreign relations and image abroad." Other government agencies involved in communication-related activities include the National Economic Development Authority (NEDA), APO Printing Office, and the Government Printing Office.

The PIA has a mandate to either initiate development information programs or provide technical support to various government line agencies in their own information activities. The PIA can do communication training, infrastructure development, creative services, and communication research. In short, the Agency's functions resemble those of both an advertising and a public relations agency in the business world.

Government Information: Assets and Liabilities

Government officials commonly blame "lack of information," "miscommunication" and "dis-information" for breakdowns in the delivery of government services or for public outcries against unpopular policies such as the value added tax law (VAT) and oil-price increases. The government's standard operating procedure in these instances is to launch an "information campaign."

Despite a recognized need to do so, efforts to rationalize and strengthen government information have been slow.

Almost all government line agencies (departments) have information units with names ranging from Public Information and Liaison, to Public Affairs, Press Relations, and so forth. In a survey, the Public Relations Organization of the Philippines (PROP) found no standard information structure in government.

Some public relations personnel occupy high positions in the bureaucracy whereas others simply serve in sections under the administrative division. In most agencies, information officers have also been deployed down to the regional level.

Earlier, there were no regular (plantilla) positions for government information officers. Where such positions existed, people with a given job description varied as to title and salary.

The lack of financial resources is a perennial problem in government information offices. A study conducted by the Media Studies Division, Philippine Information Agency, revealed that in 1993, only 0.35% of the national budget (i.e., P1,081,691,000 or US$40,062,630) was allotted for information and communication activities. The exchange rate in 1993 was 27 pesos to US$1.

The same study reported that, for information, the government spends only 16.48 pesos (US$0.6l) per Filipino. For comparison, the per capita expense is P515 for education, P320 for national security, P309 for infrastructure development, P185 for local government, P125 for agriculture, and P110 for health.

In addition, foreign grants have also been received and used specifically for information dissemination in family planning, health care, environment, agriculture, and education along with other such areas. Among the biggest donors are United Nations agencies and bilateral institutions.

Another inadequacy of the existing government information system was the duplication of mandate, duties, and responsibilities among government information offices. This may lead to a waste of scarce resources, duplication of efforts, and possible dissemination of conflicting information (Braid, 1990).

Interdepartment and interagency coordination on information policy has generally occurred ad hoc, or upon identification of particular needs, rather than on a formal and sustained basis (Tolentino, 1989). A 1989 attempt to institutionalize coordination eventually lost steam.

The Public Relations Organization of the Philippines (PROP)

To improve coordination among government information officers, the Public Relations Organization of the Philippines (PROP) was founded in 1972. It seeks to foster cooperation among its members, to develop dedication, discipline, and professionalism in government information work, and to raise the status of public relations practitioners in government.

PROP conducts training courses to upgrade members' communication skills. It is also involved in policy advocacy. In addition, the organization has battled to upgrade the working conditions of government information officers and to create public-information offices in all government agencies (Public Relations Organization of the Philippines, 1992).

In 1992, PROP initiated the Gawad Oscar M. Florendo Award. The annual awarding rites give recognition to outstanding public information programs, projects, and tools initiated by government agencies (Public Relations Organization of the Philippines, 1993).

In 1994, PROP had 600 members nationwide. Regional chapters also exist.

An Outstanding Government Information Program

The Department of Health's *Oplan Alis Disis* (Banish Disease) is perhaps the most popular and successful information program initiated by the Philippine government in recent years. This national campaign was initiated by the Department of Health (DOH) to mobilize all sectors of society in support of National Immunization Days (NID) scheduled twice a year from 1993–1995.

In its initial year, at least two million children, age 6 years old and under, or 95.7% of targeted children, were immunized. UNICEF, the World Health Organization, and various nations throughout Asia and Latin America have viewed the project as a model for public health-care programs worldwide.

As one important indicator of success for *Oplan Alis Disis*, all sectors of society were mobilized to support the campaign. These included the national and local political leaders, international development agencies, businessmen, top people in the fields of religion, academe, and labor, and even Communist and Muslim insurgents. Adding to the 73,000 DOH personnel, some 40,000 volunteer public-school teachers, social-welfare officers, soldiers, agriculturists, and foresters provided support in 1993.

National and provincial mass media—print, radio and television—gave all-out support. The DOH estimated about P15 million (US$555,555) worth of air time allotted to NID announcements that were either provided free by the broadcast stations or paid for by business sponsors. The secretary of health appeared almost daily in prime-time TV programs, especially in entertainment shows. All over the islands, radio stations and movie houses aired the NID plug free of charge, courtesy of the Philippine Information Agency. Volunteer popular movie and TV personalities helped promote the campaign.

Thousands of educational materials from stickers to pocket calendars and comics leaflets were produced and distributed. For what seemed like a multimillion dollar campaign, the DOH spent only P8.9 million (US$329,630) to produce the IEC materials and P2 million (US$74,074) to distribute them. Businesses and civic groups also volunteered to help foot the bill.

The most crucial change agents in the community were the public-health workers, midwives, health-center nurses, and doctors. These health workers and other community volunteers used traditional or folk, as well as mass, media to reach out to the various clientele. The Post-NID Coverage Survey revealed that the health workers were the primary source of NID information (acting as sources 65% of the time). Radio was second.

Oplan Alis Disis was followed by other equally successful campaigns of the DOH—*Oplan Sagip Mata,* (for the eyes) *Araw ng Sangkap Pinoy* (for micronutrients), and *Yosi Kadiri* (for antismoking).

At the center of all these campaigns was Health Secretary Juan Flavier, the most popular cabinet secretary in the Ramos government, according to surveys. His wit and other winning personal traits endeared him to journalists as well as television and movie personalities. Although only 4 feet 11 inches tall, Flavier consistently topped popularity and performance rating surveys done in various opinion surveys. In truth, he was DOH's No. 1 public relations officer.

PUBLIC RELATIONS IN A POST-COLONIAL CONTEXT

Keeping the U.S. Connection

U.S.-based public relations firms have been hired to represent the interests of Third World countries in the U.S. Congress and on Capitol Hill. Autocratic countries, in particular, need "image engineering" to positively influence U.S. public opinion toward national leaders.

Public relations is also needed to promote or protect a country's economic as well as political interests. Sustained lobbying in the U.S. Congress is necessary for continued U.S. aid, preferential status in trade, and to counter growing protectionist attitudes. For example, since the late 1980s, American soybean interests and sympathizers have been waging a "war" in Congress to label coconut oil as "saturated fat" and therefore hazardous to health. This move threatened the Philippines' export of coconut oil to the U.S. market. To protect the interests of over 17 million Filipinos dependent on the coconut industry, the Philippine Coconut Authority in 1988 contracted the Sawyer Miller group, a public relations agency in Washington D.C., to help counter the disinformation drive.

American public relations firms are still being employed. In March 1993, the

Philippine government hired the New York-based GCI Group for $360,000 to "provide public relations counseling and services, establish appropriate media contacts and produce necessary communications materials . . ." After the contract ended in May 1994, the Philippine government contracted with separate organizations for public relations work, consultation on international trade and investment, and lobbying (Lopez-Wendling, 1994).

Some reservations have been expressed about hiring American public relations firms. A common criticism is that a poor country like the Philippines cannot afford to retain the services of such firms on a long-term basis. Another is the difficulty in quantifying potential benefits.

However, other government officials believe the practice not only is important but is inevitable. The Philippines has to exert extra effort to establish a strategic (economic) relationship with the United States. Moreover, the Philippines has to compete with other countries for better trade relations, foreign aid, and the like with the United States as well as with other new and traditional trading partners.

Public Relations in a Developing-Country Context

During the 1993 National Public Relations Congress, Dr. Florangel R. Braid, president and executive dean of the Asian Institute of Journalism, and Ramon R. Tuazon of the Institute described the role of public relations (and advertising) in the current task of nation building.

The Philippines has launched an ambitious public relations and advertising campaign designed to ensure the nation's effort to achieve Newly Industrializing Country (NIC) status by the year 2000. Thus, the slogan *Philippines 2000*. Malaysia has embarked on a similar campaign. Called *Wawasan* (Vision) *2020*, that effort seeks to ensure the country's full industrialization by sustaining the economic growth already achieved.

Countries in the region with a clear national vision or ideology based on indigenous culture have gained a head start in achieving economic progress. This ideology has served as a unifying and mobilizing force for the people. Along this line, Indonesia has its *Pancasila*, Malaysia its *Rugun Negara*. Also, Japan, South Korea, and China derive national unity and strength from *Confucianism*, which emphasizes social harmony and a strong work ethic.

Public relations and advertising, as professions, can help popularize and crystallize such an ideology so that all the people can share it as a common value. Specifically, in the Philippines, there is a strong need for hope. Dominant media images tend to destroy the Filipino's belief in his or her ability to overcome current crises. The mass media are in dire need of images and messages—success stories—that can inspire, energize, and mobilize people toward authentic development.

Public relations can also seek to improve the Filipino work ethic so as to increase productivity and profitability. Such Filipino values as entrepreneurship, industriousness, frugality, quality consciousness, and passion for excellence need to be rekindled.

When lobbying for economic policies and programs, public relations practitioners must consider the common good rather than be used for vested interests. In a Third World country, only the elite can afford public relations services. Who can lobby for the rights and interests of the poor and marginalized?

In a developing country, the media are usually owned and controlled by a political and business elite. Those at the margins often are ignored. In that connection, the close relationship between journalists and public relations practitioners has sometimes led to unethical practices such as "envelopmental" journalism where money is given in envelopes to journalists in exchange for favors. Even more insidious is the ability of some advertising and public relations practitioners to define or influence media content on behalf of vested interests.

On the other hand, public relations practitioners have been devoting much effort to developmental programs, to wit, health, nutrition, environment, education, livelihood, and other areas that enhance the quality of life. But they should also help give marginalized groups access to mass media so they can express themselves on important issues. When these things are done, we can expect a massive renewal of the good performance and image that have often eluded the advertising and public relations worlds.

SUMMARY

Public relations is a concept from the West that has been transplanted to Asia—and transformed in the process. It has been growing in the Philippines for nearly half a century. As shown here, however, Philippine public relations has been drawing most of its sustenance from its own country's soil.

And the practitioners themselves have been making it so. Importantly, they have been faithful to their own culture and environment, making the field strong and relevant. For this, Philippine public relations deserves much credit, particularly for the leading lights or personae in the profession. The Father of Philippine public relations, the late Jose A. Carpio, has reason to be proud of this feat, as of course do those who have come after him.

On the whole, the craft may be characterized as having been self-propelled, relevant, dynamic (i.e., adaptable to changes), and increasingly professional in deeds and in thought. Nevertheless, there have been negatives as noted earlier.

Unlike Manila journalism, which has been dominated by Western precepts, public relations in the Philippines has been virtually autonomous from external direction. Perhaps that's partly because the field has had to depend on recruits educated in other fields. This has allowed the discipline's intellectual leaders to accommodate the local culture in general and the local corporate setting in particular.

Much of the knowledge diffusing to the early practitioners came from interpersonal exchanges such as meetings and conventions where the field's guiding lights held forth. National and local meetings continue to this day for private-sector as well as government practitioners. The focus on the Philippine setting and needs is reflected by the general objectives stated in the by-laws of the Public Relations Society of the Philippines. The by-laws, as amended, were adopted in Manila on April 8, 1975. Beyond the profession-building provisos embodied in objectives 1 to 4, (see pp. 193–194, this chapter), the declarations of purpose underscore projects promoting the general welfare, assisting the government in its pursuit of development, and unifying the Filipino people by using public relations effectively.

Later, this thrust of social orientedness would echo in the reports and articles written by practitioners. For instance, Virtusio (1981, p. 15) noted that "the skills of PR have been utilized in a wide range of undertakings," both government and private, designed to improve public welfare or to enhance the quality of life in food production, nutrition, reforestation, control of drug abuse, energy conservation, cultural reawakening, sports development, and tourism.

Public relations' emphasis on relevance is shown by the winners of the annual Anvil Awards, documentation of the nationwide program of the Philippine Business for Social Progress, and other approaches focusing on social responsibility.

Along with relevance, dynamism, and openness allowing adaptation to rapid changes have proceeded well. Space limitations preclude further exploration of these characteristics of Philippine public relations. Declares the paper of Braid and Tuazon (1993):

> In an emerging global economy characterized by global alliances, ASEAN PR practitioners should work closely to craft distinctly ASEAN PR strategies which can be based on common culture. This could perhaps be strengthened through regional PR alliances which will speak with a unified vision of ASEAN similar to that of the European community's One Europe. PR practitioners should help ASEAN businessmen flex their muscles rather than take a back seat as . . . has (been) done in the past (p. 6).

More directly concerned with trends shaping the field, Villanueva (1982) noted the changing complexion of PR practice.

> For one, the PR person is evolving into some sort of "a man for all seasons"—conceptualizer, visualizer, communicator, philosopher, and manager. As the issue of business humanism begins to permeate corporate corridors and conference rooms, the PR person will become truly integrative. He will see the relationship between substance and form, message and gesture. He will think less of posture or image and speak more of character. He will stop pretending that he can engineer consent. Instead, he will consider it a moral duty to listen and to make himself understood."

Ultimately, the measure of effectiveness will take into account the degree of professionalism nurtured in the local setting. This point brings back to mind the very first sentence of this article. Is one's name the same as the person? Is the sign or word the same as the thing or idea referred to? To think about the answer is to get to know the essential truth of public relations in the Philippines or elsewhere.

REFERENCES

Braid, F. R. (1990). *Communication for the common good: Towards a framework for a National Communication Policy.* Manila: Asian Institute of Journalism.

Braid, F. R., & Tuazon, R. R. (1993, September 23–25). *Public relations in the Philippines: Creating the dragon image.* Paper presented at the National Public Relations Congress of the Philippines, Cebu City, Philippines.

Comments on Senate Bill 1666. (1992). Public Relations Organization of the Philippines, Manila.

Corteza-Tinsay, E. (1987). *Public relations case studies in Philippine setting.* Makati, Philippines: Special Promotion Services.

De la Cruz, R. R. (1992). *Public relations: Theory and practice.* Manila: R. R. De la Cruz & Co.

Edralin, M. J., Jr. (1993, September). *Relevance of public relations in a developing country environment.* Remarks delivered at the National Public Relations Congress in the Philippines, Cebu City, Philippines.

Gozo, D. A. (1994, February 12). Personal communication.

Information outlay in the 1993 General Appropriations Act. (1993). Manila: Media Studies Division.

Lopez-Wendling, M. (1994, June 27). Government hires new PR firm in U.S. *Philippine Daily Inquirer*, p. 6.

Luz, J. M., & Montelibano, T. Y. (1993). *Corporations and communities in a developing country: Case studies, Philippines.* Manila: Center for Corporate Citizenship, Philippine Business for Social Progress.

National Public Relations Congress of the Philippines. (1993, September 23–25). *One Image, One Nation.* [Souvenir Program]. Cebu City, Philippines.

Pantaleon, V. (1980, October 20). *Public relations in ASEAN.* Paper delivered at a training seminar, Asian Institute of Journalism, Sta. Mesa, Manila.

Philippine Information Agency. (1987). [Brochure]. Quezon City: Philippines: Media Center.

Public Relations Organization of the Philippines. (1992). *Commitment and unity through information.* Manila: Philippine Information Agency.

Public Relations Organization of the Philippines. (1993). *Second Annual Gawad Award Oscar M. Florendo.* [Souvenir program]. Manila. (This annual award recognizes the outstanding public-information programs, projects, and tools of this government information agency.)

Republic of the Philippines, Philippine Information Agency. (1986, May). *Toward a new government information system.* Information staff working paper. Manila: Ministry of Public Information.

Schumacher, J. N. (1973). *The propaganda movement: 1880–1895.* Manila: Solidaridad Publishing House.

Tolentino, G. N. (1989, May 27). *Towards formulation of a national communication policy framework: Reorganization of government communication information agencies.* Paper presented to fourth Multi-Sectoral Consultative Conference. Pasig, Philippines: Development Academy of the Philippines.

Villanueva, A. L., Jr. (1980). *What is public relations?* Lecture delivered at a training seminar, Asian Institute of Journalism, Sta. Mesa, Manila.

Villanueva, A. L., Jr. (1982). Whither public relations in RP? Twenty-fifth year directory of the Public Relations Society of the Philippines, Manila.

Villanueva, A. L., Jr. (1985). PR in a changing environment. *Business Eye,* 2(4), 32-33.

Virtusio, R. P. (1981, February 12). Public relations in the 1980s: The social role. *Public Relations Journal,* pp. 11-16.

Zorilla, T. (1983). *Public policy and the public's opinion.* A paper distributed by the author. Makati, Philippines: ZPA/PR Consulting, Inc.

11
Public Relations in South East Asia From Nation-Building Campaigns To Regional Interdependence

James K. Van Leuven
Colorado State University

Public relations practices in the newly industrializing economies of Singapore and Malaysia are noteworthy on at least two counts. First, they illustrate how professional practices change in response to economic growth, integration of language groups, shifting societal norms, and expansion of the media along with other communication outlets.

Second, public relations' development over the course of these two countries' short histories demonstrates the transition from a practice dominated by government nation building campaigns to one that is privately owned, yet continues to give concerted attention to nation building or development communication programs.

In this sense, the study of public relations in Singapore and Malaysia represents a fusing of two very different international communication literatures. The first, and the more developed, literature addresses public relations in terms of nation building public communication campaigns (often called development communication) in Third World cultures. The second includes an academic literature as well as professional writing regarding cultural barriers and strategic challenges facing multinational corporations operating in various international settings and diverse cultural contexts.

This chapter reports on a 4-month exploratory study undertaken in late 1993 to record, assess, classify, and then make tentative generalizations regarding evolving public relations practices in two of the world's fastest growing economies. The study involved literature reviews, in-depth interviews with 20 public relations leaders in Singapore and Malaysia, and two presentations to practitioner groups designed to induce feedback regarding past and current practices. Interview and feedback session reports were then summarized by issue and grouped under one of three phases or time frames as a preliminary framework for describing changes in the practice over time. The phases are labelled *nation building, market development,* and *regional interdependence.*

Practitioners were questioned on the following four general topics whose selection was guided by issues posed in the public relations literature over the past few years:

1. Where is the practice of public relations located? Is it with the government, in the consultancies, or the corporations?

This question responds to the concern of academics and practitioners located outside the United States who regard the U.S. literature on public relations as giving primary emphasis to the corporate, departmental, or organizational context. Elsewhere in the world, public relations work centers in consultancies, firms, or agencies. The practice of nonprofit public relations is quite diminished outside the U.S. As well, public sector public relations work is housed almost exclusively within governmental bureaucracies headed by political appointees rather than by trained public relations practitioners.

2. How does the relationship between the government and the press influence the practice of public relations?

This question responds to Al-Enad's (1990) argument that the dominant theory of the press in a society influences public relations philosophies, goals, and practices. He reports that "Where the authoritarian theory of the press dominates, for example, communication is one-way, its purpose is unbalanced, and the tools are the mass media which not only publish and transmit whatever comes from government public relations, but have no power to edit or change any part in most cases" (p. 25).

Such a rationale assumes that change in the practice of public relations is contingent on changes in the nature and style of government, for example, from an authoritative style to a participative one.

3. What is the relative importance of various public relations activities and planning practices, and how do they account for language, cultural, and educational differences among population subgroups?

At present, the authors of public relations texts, at least in the United States, describe the steps in planning public relations campaigns and communication programs with no real regard for cultural, linguistic, and social differences, let alone differences in the development of a society's information or media infrastructure.

4. What specific dimensions of public relations management appear in Singaporean and Malaysian practice?

Answers to this question would respond to Botan's (1992, p. 153) argument that defining public relations as a management function assumes the largely private sector orientation to the field found in the United States and certain other Western societies.

THE SHORT HISTORY OF PUBLIC RELATIONS IN SINGAPORE AND MALAYSIA

Public relations is said to have begun in Malaysia immediately after World War II when the British returned. Singapore's start is pegged to 1965 when it became its own nation after separating from the Federation of Malaya.

In both countries, the early years of public relations were characterized by government-run, nation building campaigns not unlike those found in other Third World nations where, as Pratt (1986, p. 15) put it, public relations serves "as a conduit for communicating development news, and for nurturing a development-oriented norm among audiences."

According to Morais and Adnan (1986), public relations started in Malaysia in 1945 when the British established a Malaysian Department of Publicity and Printing with film, broadcasting, and information units. The department's objective was to put down Communism by convincing Malaysians that the British, not the Chinese Communist guerrillas (the Malayan People's AntiJapanese Army), eventually won World War II over Japan. Two dominant campaign themes were "help to end the war sooner so that the money used to buy bullets can be used for the benefit of the people instead" and "blame the Communist terrorists for the misery suffered."

The next great expansion of nation building efforts came in 1960 when the Malaysian government established the Rural Development Plan and the beginning of a massive development support communication program aimed at providing roads, a water supply, community halls, and electricity. Although similar campaigns were mounted in Singapore, the task was much more difficult in Malaysia owing to its larger land base and rural population.

When Singapore became its own republic in 1965, a government information policy similar to Malaysia's was instituted, That is, the job was to create shared values, a common will, and a single national identity among the Chinese, Malaysian, and Indian peoples. Prime Minister Lee Kuan Yew and his People's Action Party (PAP) wanted social cohesion at any cost to preclude the build-up of Communism in Singapore.

In recalling the beginnings of public relations work in Singapore, Basskaran Nair (1986) wrote:

> Planned and sustained public relations campaigns were organized to educate the public to change negative social habits and to adopt new attitudes essential for an

emerging nation. Campaigns in the early 1960's such as the "Anti-Litter" and "Lungs for Singapore" campaigns helped to create not only a clean and green environment but also a sense of belonging to the new nation as thousands of volunteers were involved in such community projects.

Overpopulation and unemployment problems led to a vigorous family-planning education programme [sic]. Health campaigns taught the public the dangers of malaria and Dengue fever. By the mid-1970's, sustained campaign activities had helped create a clean and green city, boosting the morale and civic pride of the Singaporean. (pp. 4–5)

Thus, the initial campaigns in both countries conformed to Al-Enad's prototype of Third World public relations where the government ministry "communicates with the public to achieve one or both of two goals: to educate the public on subjects related to the client's field of work and to increase its knowledge about pertinent issues and persuade it to behave or act differently, and/or to publicize achievement of client and/or society as a whole, and to make the public feel satisfied" (1990, p. 26).

We now examine the nation building phase in more detail.

NATION BUILDING PHASE

Locus of Public Relations Work

Because virtually all public relations work emanated from government information ministries, those calling themselves public information workers numbered in the hundreds. For many, the more appropriate title would have been extension worker or community development specialist (Ministry of Information, Malaysia, 1993). That is, these information workers were really general aides or paraprofessionals at best. Their conversational skills were thought to be more effective than the media in reaching campaign audiences given the low literacy rates, numerous Chinese dialects, and the absence of mass media to serve neighborhood and rural audiences.

Not until the early 1970s did private sector public relations take hold in both countries despite the fact that Eric White and Associates of Australia established offices in Singapore and Kuala Lumpur some years earlier to service oil multinationals and a few other accounts. And, even then, private sector public relations activity was directed at winning government favor by lending financial support to the government's nation building campaigns, according to M. Arun, who directed Mobil Oil's public relations office and later administered the Singapore Hill & Knowlton office (Arun, 1993). Jefkins and Lowe (1991) added that corporate public relations was often used to narrow the cultural distance between themselves and the local environment by creating special events to detract from the foreign status and profit making activities of the corporation.

Media and Communication System

By today's standards, the media systems of the two emerging nations were rudimentary. Although privately owned, newspapers could hardly be viewed as anything but adjuncts to the government information system in part because reporters were seldom trained in journalistic news values. Another limitation was the existence of such cultural practices as withholding potentially embarrassing questions at press conferences or elsewhere for fear that the interviewee would somehow lose face.

As a result, newspapers tended to accept, if not embellish, news releases pertaining to government campaigns. Editors understood, at least implicitly, that they were to provide news space and editorial endorsement for government campaigns. They also served another function for their largely literate and urban readers. That is, they legitimized the importance of various campaigns in the eyes of community opinion leaders and for the benefit of their overseas readers at the multinational corporate headquarters.

Communication Planning and Public Relations Practices

Planning at the nation building phase generally referred to synchronizing dissemination of media materials with oral community presentations by field workers and extension specialists, along with local religious and language group leaders who were recruited to bolster campaign credibility. Campaign topics emphasized antilitter, antismoking (Lungs for Singapore), family planning, malaria, and dengue fever.

Thus, typical campaign activities included open-air concerts featuring Malay martial arts, Chinese opera, and Indian dances. In Singapore, for example, campaign workers also organized "Citizens Consultative Committees" and worked with local leaders at newly formed neighborhood centers. These community activities prompted thousands of Singaporeans to work together on common national tasks rather than on special tasks that appealed to the needs of the separate Chinese, Malay, and Tamil language groups.

Despite the newspaper and radio coverage, Singapore's early nation building campaigns were not designed around media messages. Instead, selection of communication channels for campaigns reflected the needs of neighborhood oral cultures that relied primarily on traditional folk media, interpersonal communication, and staged community events. Large-scale media campaigns came later once television sets saturated the island.

Campaign messages and government news releases were printed in four languages—Malay, Chinese, Tamil, and English—in order not to alienate any segment of the ethnic press. Moreover, Lowe (1986) reported that image and emotion-provoking communication campaigns often fared better than more rational sounding appeals.

Public relations activities in the private sector began with the few oil multinationals informing their shareholders in Western countries about their activities in the region. Soon, however, they began courting government and public favor by underwriting sports, arts, and educational programs. In fact, governments tended to define corporate social responsibility in terms of financial support for the various nation building efforts (Arun, 1993).

Esso, for example, began major sponsorship of Singapore arts in the late 1960s. At the same time, Esso began a program of supporting public education in Malaysia. Even today those programs consume 60% of Esso's public relations budget for Malaysia. Shell initiated educational campaigns that taught kids about road signs. Mobil underwrote the Singapore Arts Festival beginning in 1977.

Because economic survival was all that mattered to the government between 1965 and 1975, Singapore's government ministries appreciated all that business did to underwrite and sponsor programs which the government could neither fund nor coordinate.

Management Dimensions

Although many were employed in the government information ministries, the literature provides no evidence that those who administered these programs possessed any special insight regarding public relations and communication management. They were either political appointees or long-time government officials with no specific training in public relations. This finding lends support to Sriramesh's (1992) discussion of public relations management in class-oriented and bureaucratic societies.

MARKET DEVELOPMENT PHASE

Trade expansion, a growing manufacturing base, and government housing programs combined to produce a rising middle class in Malaysia relatively recently just as those same factors did in Singapore more than a decade ago. New markets for consumer goods also signalled more opportunities for practicing public relations.

Locus of Public Relations Work

Multinationals brought big public relations budgets to Singapore and Malaysia, and these monies attracted multinational public relations and advertising agencies. At the same time, local consultancies sprung up to serve local industries that either could not afford the big consultancies or believed their business plans were better entrusted to well-established native speakers. In point of fact, many of these smaller agencies actually specialized in graphic design, brochures, or video production although they billed themselves as public relations or marketing firms.

Although government information ministries still employed the greatest numbers of public relations workers, the big change came with consultancies being hired for the first time to take on both the planning and strategy development segments of the government campaigns. The ministries turned to private consultancies for help with campaign design, media contacts, and special events management. Today, almost every major consultancy in Singapore or Kuala Lumpur derives 20–30% of its income from one of the various government ministries.

Private consultants who had good media contacts were also brought in by the Malaysian government to handle crisis communication when, for example, a toothpaste manufacturer found its products being boycotted by Muslims who heard it rumored that the toothpaste was made with lard. Sometime later, private consultants were hired by a cigarette distributor who faced a boycott from Chinese retailers and consumers after they learned that the company replaced its Chinese employees with Malays.

The public relations staffs of Singapore's government-linked statutory boards and industries grew noticeably as market conditions improved. This was particularly true with Singapore Telecom, Singapore Airlines, the Economic Development Board, the Tourist Promotion Board, the Port of Singapore Authority, and Singapore Broadcasting Corporation.

Media and Communication System

In Singapore at least, the growth of consumer markets coincided with television's widespread diffusion and adoption. For the government-linked Singapore Broadcasting Corporation, the task was to establish broadcast services serving Chinese, Malay, Indian, and English speaking viewers. Television advertising expenditures grew quickly because businesses desiring to reach Chinese as well as English speakers were required to advertise on at least two channels.

In short order, television, or at least videotapes, became the medium of choice for the public communication campaigns, too. Television reached more people faster with a consistent message than did extension field workers and communication-development specialists. Furthermore, the campaign topics or issues were being increasingly directed at literate urban audiences who were less attracted to government-run neighborhood community centers or to the Chinese street dramas, two principal venues for disseminating government messages.

Interviewees here agreed that television and new media channels lessened practitioners' dependence on any single element of the press, however, they did not indicate that the new media environment changed the government's relationship to the press. Moreover, they did not agree that market forces in Southeast

Asia altered journalists' conceptions of social responsibility as Hiebert (1992) has suggested may be the case in Eastern Europe.

Communication Planning and Public Relations Practices

One of the hallmarks of the market-development phase is that campaign planning became more comprehensive, oftentimes involving outside consultants whose approach to planning generally followed the 4-step planning process (Research, Action, Communication, and Evaluation). Surprisingly, however, it was the advertising and not the public relations consultancies in Singapore, Kuala Lumpur, and Penang that benefitted most from market development. Ad agencies were the experts in campaign design, according to those interviewed here (Yap, 1993). Interviewees explained that advertising agency staffs were seen as working with production of commercials and high-quality brochure layouts. On the other hand, public relations practitioners were former journalists whose tools were news releases and media contacts (Tan, Jo Chin, 1993). In fact, the public relations staffs of many government ministries believed that paid advertising and strong graphic identity programs were the new ingredients for campaigns to be successful in reaching literate, urban audiences.

Bolstering that rationale was the changing focus of public communication campaign topics. Whereas communication campaigns of an earlier phase concerned cultural assimilation and issues related to national development, a whole different set of issues faced the consumer society as seen by such campaignsas "accident-free/road safety", "seatbelt", "antidrug abuse", and "safety in construction and shipyard industries" (Nair, 1986). And today, campaigns concern such attitudinal and motivational topics as courtesy and worker productivity.

Typical of the new multimedia campaigns was the "Speak Mandarin" program. Launched in 1979 with support from leaders throughout Singapore's Chinese community, this campaign aimed at reducing the everyday use of Chinese dialects including Cantonese, Hokkien, and Teochew in favor of Mandarin, the dialect chosen by Singapore's government to represent the Chinese community in school, in public speeches, and in other official functions.

According to Professor Eddie Kuo (1984), the campaign represented a concerted government effort in defining and modifying language use in various domains to promote the use of a "proper" language, at the expense of local dialects. Ironically, though, what started out in 1979 as a campaign to unify Singaporean Chinese continues today even though dialects are spoken rarely. The new "Speak Mandarin" campaign objective is to promote business contacts with mainland China.

As with most nation building campaigns, the newspapers and broadcast media were brought into the planning process weeks or even months before the campaign launch so they would begin using their news columns and air time to prompt a need for the campaign. Then, extensive media coverage went to the campaign launch. Public pronouncements by government leaders appeared every day in the paper and on television. Specially labeled feature pages in the newspapers detailed campaign progress and personal success stories.

Moreover, the media conducted and reported their own benchmark surveys of campaign success. In turn, government officials used these reports as independent indicators of campaign success. For example, the *Straits Times* interviewed 746 Chinese Singaporeans in 1981 and reported that 81% between the ages of 12 and 19 were now speaking Mandarin. A Chinese daily, the *Nanyang Siang Pao,* conducted a similar survey at coffee shops, hawker stalls, and restaurants whereas *Sin Chew Jit Po,* another Chinese daily, gathered person-on-the-street interviews at hawker stalls and supermarkets.

Perhaps the hallmark of private sector public relations during the early phases of market development was the shift from publicity in the news media to emphasis on controlled media (brochures, slide presentations, etc.) and special events for promoting grand openings, groundbreakings, product launches, and hotel as well as tourism promotion (Tan, Jo Chin, 1993).

Management Dimensions

Interviewees were quick to observe that public relations had become a more sophisticated decision-making function during this phase. However, they were referring to the fact that consultants and some corporate practitioners were making more decisions regarding campaign design and project administration. Clearly, they were not describing public relations as a core management function in organizations.

Absentee ownership and the heavy use of advertising agencies explain some of the dynamics, but the impression from this study is that the functions associated with managing communication appear only selectively among the banks and airlines, and with the statutory boards including Singapore Telecom and Singapore Broadcasting Corporation. Perhaps the notable exceptions are the government-linked Development Bank of Singapore and Singapore Airlines.

Although DBS's 13-person corporate public relations staff may be considered lean by some counts, the staff is headed by a nationally recognized leader who, as vice president, reports directly to the bank's CEO. Moreover, the practitioners not only perform all of the principal public relations functions, but they are organized in a quasimatrix arrangement with key consultants being assigned to the various marketing and bank service divisions (Nair, 1993).

The corporate affairs staff at Singapore Airlines is several times bigger, as it also includes environmental scanning, issues management, and other governmental relations activities related to negotiating landing rights and gate assignments at international airports around the globe. As well, SIA is Singapore's only major corporation employing a myriad of public relations consultancies in major world capitals.

REGIONAL-INTERDEPENDENCE PHASE

A third phase of public relations development is emerging in Singapore. Its defining parameters much resemble Joseph's (1991) recent description of public relations activities in Hong Kong:

> The establishment and development of stock markets throughout Asia, the privatization of government-run companies, the increasing number of Asian firms seeking business and capital in international markets, for example, have driven the need for corporate positioning, financial communication, and investor relations programs. Restrictive government legislation and pressure from special interest groups has increased the demand for crisis communication and issues management as well as high-level public affairs programs." (p. 21)

Jasmine Tan (1993), writing for Singapore's *PEAK* magazine, said, "Today's PR reveals a new face that's been shaped by the changing business environment in Asia—an influx of multinational corporations into Asia, the regionalization of Asian firms, and a burgeoning level of sophistication in the region—all of which pound and sculpt a new profile for the [PR] industry" (p. 53).

Others refer to more specific attributes of growing regional interdependence. Wilcox, Ault, and Agee (1992) saw this phase being driven by satellite, computer, and cable television technologies, whereas Mai Lin Tan (1993) of Singapore's Burson-Marsteller office spoke and wrote of Singapore's wanting to be seen internationally as a bridge for communication and technology transfer between well-developed and developing nations. Gavin Anderson (1989) focused on the need for more accountability to consumers, public opinion, and regulators.

Moreover, the new phase is reflected in a shift from mass audiences and large consumer markets to niche markets and strategic constituencies. As Grunig (1992) noted, these new parameters require practitioners to develop corporations' positions on international issues and articulate these to a host of constituencies.

In many respects, the dynamics of public relations practice in the regional interdependence phase can be observed through the corporate trend of decentralizing into regional subsidiaries with accompanying foreign stock exchange listings distinct from those of the parent company. Such arrangements foster regional public relations decision making and supersede the commonly held assumption that private sector public relations is two-tiered, where planning and strategy were coordinated centrally while implementation is done locally to adapt to commercial communication, lifestyle, and political-system differences, according to Harold Burson (cited in Epley, 1992, p. 112).

Locus of Public Relations Work

Increasingly, Singapore's big private and government accounts go to consultancies with regional capabilities. This process, in turn, leads to a rush toward specialization on the part of smaller consultancies. In fact, several agencies are awash in financial and investor relations work from the Asian subsidiaries of multinationals which are conducting initial public stock offerings (IPO's) in preparation for listing on the Kuala Lumpur and Singapore stock exchanges.

Now, much of the communication work supporting high technology products is coming to public relations consultancies in preference to advertising agencies. At least three such specialized information technology (IT) consultancies are situated in Singapore. They administer not only the full scope of public relations programs, but also marketing communication activities including trade and consumer advertising along with production of sales materials.

As well, the scope of in-house corporate public relations work broadens at the regional interdependence phase following privatization of government-linked banks, public utilities, and telecommunication organizations. Privatization means that noticeably more attention must go to consumer relations, marketing communication, and media contact.

Media and Communication Systems

Regional interdependence is further defined by privatization of government-linked broadcasting systems, an onslaught of regional satellite and cable services, and constant use of such interactive media technologies as E-mail, fax, BITNET, and databases to provide clients with regional information. In fact, some regional public relations networks are linked electronically to research institutes.

Communication Planning and Public Relations Practices

Practitioners are utilizing planning processes in at least three more comprehensive and demanding ways than had been the case. First, public communication campaigns are now targeted to reach specific audience sectors based on lifestyle and demographic indicators, reports Dr. K. Ismail Sudderuddin (1993), director of publicity for Singapore's Ministry of Information and the Arts. Moreover, campaigns such as "Speak Mandarin," "Courtesy Month," and "Sing Singapore" utilize targeting to contain costs and still achieve annual objectives and quotas because government campaign appropriations have not kept pace with jumps in media advertising rates, and so forth.

Second, the changing nature of financial and investor relations work illustrates the growing importance of regional public relations. The Singapore regional offices of multinational public relations agencies report that 20–30% of their income comes from regional clients they have cultivated in contrast to those coming from corporate headquarters. These locally developed clients with South East Asian businesses expect that all of the business strategy and not just the communication support functions, will be planned and conducted from Singapore or Kuala Lumpur. For example, a client wishing to raise capital in one or several of the regional stock markets would ask the consultancy to determine market feasibility, develop a positioning strategy, and cultivate underwriters as well as business partners. All of these planning tasks are performed before the more customary media relations and communication support functions.

Third, a broader range of media and interpersonal communication techniques are now utilized as illustrated by Singapore's social development campaign. Social development is the name of the government sponsored matchmaking and Love Boat cruise-type campaign directed at pairing well-educated single men with well-educated professional women while the women are still of child bearing age. Because the campaign planners believe that the target audience members must be shy, they have attempted to locate these "targets," using well-established networking techniques drawn from the small group and organizational communication literatures. That is, coworkers are encouraged to identify their unmarried colleagues and to invoke group pressure techniques along with downward communication from management to prompt the targets into attending ice-breaking group barbecues or mixers. A series of government sponsored and increasingly intimate social events follows over the next few weeks and months.

Management Dimensions

As already noted, several specialized aspects of public relations work are becoming more prevalent across the region. These include financial and investor relations, issues management, and environmental scanning. Because working with each of these specialities requires knowledge of general business strategy, and not just public relations programming strategy, there is reason to feel that the consultancy business will take on more counselling roles and management responsibilities in the years ahead (Lines, 1993).

No similar trend was found among corporate public relations staffs or government agencies, although there is evidence from each group that more management-level status is being sought by the offering of more comprehensive programs and by the utilization of a wider range of evaluation techniques. The situation may change in coming years, however, once Singapore's first university-trained public relations graduates enter the job market in mid-1996.

GENERALIZATIONS AND CONCLUSIONS

Public and private sector public relations work is undergoing rapid change in Singapore and Malaysia as economic and educational accomplishments multi

In some cases, though, the new practices appear as reflections of those already at work in Western Europe, the United States, and Hong Kong. Yet, for the most part, the phases in the development of Malaysian and Singaporean public relations are marked by unique responses to policy initiatives and market development opportunities. The evidence comes from studying the complexities of public communication campaigns, the locally developed resolutions to intercultural communication crises, and the outcomes of community relations programs and corporate sponsorships.

Thus, certain generalizations emerge from viewing public relations practices across the phases constructed here.

Generalization 1

The locus of public relations practice shifts from governmental settings in the nation building phase to a combination of government and consultancy public relations during the market development phase. Consultancy public relations dominates the regional interdependence phase, although the scope of in-house corporate public relations increases following privatization of government-linked banks, public utilities, and telecommunication organizations.

Generalization 2

The practice of public relations generally, and media relations in particular, hinges on government control and prevailing press theory during the nation building phase. Practitioners become somewhat less concerned with press regulations during the market development phase as interest shifts from the news columns to the advertising ones and as practitioners spend more time reaching their audiences with controlled media and special events. In the regional interdependence phase, practitioners extend their geographic reach by relying less on mass media dissemination and more on interactive communication technologies and specialized media for maintaining constant contact with strategic constituencies.

Generalization 3

The nature of public relations planning differs by phase. At the nation building phase, planning often refers to synchronizing dissemination of media materials with oral community presentations by field workers and extension specialists. Planning in the market development phase generally means using the 4-step planning process (Research, Action, Communication, and Evaluation) for programs and campaigns. At the regional interdependence phase the context for planning shifts to overall strategic business plans.

Generalization 4

Many attributes of public relations management as defined by U.S. theory are barely discernible in newly industrializing economies until the regional interdependence phase. Not until this point—at least in Singapore and Malaysia—is there a pool of university graduates well trained in public relations. As well, only at this advanced stage is there likely to be a civil service system that promotes public relations practitioners to director or management-level positions. And only late in the day do corporate public relations departments become broad enough in scope to emphasize management functions over production ones.

Taken together, these generalizations and the 3-phase approach suggest an initial framework for studying public relations practices in international contexts and diverse cultural settings. Necessary follow-up requires applying the approach to other cultures, recasting the generalizations into a network of theoretical and operational variables, and then testing relevant hypotheses over time.

At this juncture, it is somewhat unclear which changes came about because of increased professionalism and knowledge of public relations practices, and which ones were the natural spinoffs of economic development and social progress. Even so, the indications from this study are that the functions performed by practitioners, if not the effects of their work, do change over time.

The interviews and feedback sessions conducted in Singapore and Malaysia suggest that time spent doing media relations work, for example, shifts in focus from writing to media contact. The total time commitment in media relations may decrease, too.

Time spent monitoring environmental change and public opinion increases perhaps as clients, and the societies of which they are a part, become more cognizant of public opinion. As well, the nature of marketing communication work appears to shift over time from grand openings, promotions, and product launches to more complex backgrounding, consulting, and liaison with business journalists and the trade press.

In any event, the scope and quality of public relations practice differs noticeably across cultures, and even within cultures, as regards competing language groups. And, although the experiences from such fast-growing economies as Singapore and Malaysia may not resemble conditions elsewhere, these two societies serve as ideal study venues because so much change in the practice of public relations has been compacted into a relatively short, 28-year time span in Singapore and fewer than 40 years in Malaysia.

That said, the 3-phase study design utilized here prompts additional implications and cautions. First, there is more convergence than generally acknowledged between government public communication campaign design and public relations practiced in the private sector. In fact, the well-regarded and highly pervasive public communication campaigns in Singapore suggest that campaign practices as well as the study of development support communication in Singapore and Malaysia represent comprehensive public relations at a fairly high level.

Second, the 3-phase construction used here is for descriptive purposes only and is not intended to portend some sort of stage-like development model with discrete stop and start points. Rather, the reality is that practices attendant to the market development phase became superimposed on those of the nation building phase, and those of the regional interdependence phase are superimposed on both the nation building and market development phases.

All three phases are now in full bloom across Singapore. Also, the conditions supporting the nation building and market development phases are well established in Malaysia.

In summary, the exploratory study undertaken here indicates that as the practice of public relations becomes more intercultural and international in scope, scholars will need to extend the repertoire of descriptive and predictive theory to demonstrate if and how public relations practice enhances political, social, linguistic, and economic change.

REFERENCES

Al-Enad, A. H. (1990, Summer). Public relations roles in developing countries. *Public Relations Quarterly, 35* (2), 24–26.

Al-Enad, A. H. (1992). Values of public relations conduct in Saudi Arabia. *Public Relations Review, 18*(2), 213–221.

Anderson, G. (1989). A global look at public relations. In B. Cantor (Ed.), *Experts in action* (pp. 412–422). New York: Longman.

Arun, M. (1993, August 12). [Interview]. Institute for Policy Studies, Singapore.

Botan, C. (1992). International public relations: Critique and reformulation. *Public Relations Review, 18*(2), 149–159.

Epley, J. (1992). Public relations in the global village: An American perspective. *Public Relations Review, 18*(2), 109–116.

Gregory, D. (1993). *The primary client: Serving different interests for different cultures*. Unpublished manuscript, Department of Technical Journalism, Colorado State University, Ft. Collins, CO.

Grunig, L. (1992). Strategic public relations constituencies on a global scale. *Public Relations Review, 18*(2), 127–136.

Heng, W. (1993, September 9). [Interview]. Singapore Air Lines, Singapore.

Hiebert, R. E. (1992). Global public relations in a post-Communist world: A new model. *Public Relations Review, 18*(2), 117–126.

Hill & Knowlton (1993). *Hill & Knowlton in the Asia-Pacific region*. Singapore: Hill & Knowlton.

Institute of Public Relations (1993, September 28). *Current Trends in U.S. Public Relations Practices*. Presentation, Singapore.

Jefkins, F., & Lowe, V. (1991). *Public relations in action: Case studies from the third world*. London, UK: Macmillan.

Jefkins, F., & Ugboajah, F. (1986). *Communication in industrializing countries*. London, UK: Macmillan.

Josephs, R. (1991, September). Hong Kong: Public relations capital of Asia? *Public Relations Journal*, pp. 21–25.

Kuo, E. C. Y. (1984). Mass media and language planning: Singapore's "Speak Mandarin" campaign. *Journal of Communication, 34*(2), 24–35.

Lines, V. (1993, September 27). [Interview]. Hill & Knowlton, Singapore.

Lowe, V. (1986). *Asian p. r.* Singapore: Times Books International.

Lowe, V. (1993, October 8). [Interview]. Universiti Sains Malaysia, Malaysia.

Ministry of Information. (1993, October 23–24). *Crisis Communication and Media Relations Principles*. Presentation to public relations officers and ministerial liaisons, Langkawi Island, Malaysia.

Morais, B., & Adnan, H. (Eds.). (1986). *Public relations: The Malaysian experience*. Kuala Lumpur, Malaysia: Federal Publications Sdn. BhD. for Institute of Public Relations Malaysia.

Nair, B. (1986). *A primer on public relations in Singapore*. Singapore: Asian Mass Communication Research and Education Centre.

Nair, B. (1993, November 26). [Interview]. Corporate Headquarters, Development Bank of Singapore.

Pratt, C. (1985, February). The African context. *Public Relations Journal*, pp. 11–16.

Sriramesh, K. (1992). Societal culture and public relations: Ethnographic evidence from India. *Public Relations Review, 18*(2), 201–211.

Sudderuddin, K. I. (1993, November). [Interview]. Singapore Ministry of Information and the Arts, Singapore.

Tan, Jasmine (1993). Knockin' on Asia's doors. *The Peak, 9*(9), 53–56.

Tan, Jo Chin (1993, July 20). [Interview]. Image Public Relations, Singapore.

Tan, Mai Lin (1993, October 6). [Interview]. Burson-Marsteller, Singapore.

Van Leuven, J. K. (1992). *Public relations and development communication: Merging two perspectives*. Presented to the Institute for the Advancement of Policy Studies in the Third World, Orlando, FL.

Wilcox, D., & Ault, P., & Agee, W. (1992). International Public Relations. *Public relations: Strategies and tactics*. New York: HarperCollins.

Yap, B. T. (1993, September 20). [Interview]. Macro Communications, Singapore.

12 Public Relations Practice in Japan: Beginning Again for the First Time

Anne Cooper-Chen*
Ohio University

"The Cold War is over," declared Paul Tsongas during the 1992 U.S. presidential primaries, "and Japan won." From the ashes of World War II, defeated Japan has built an economy second only to that of the United States. Today, the Japanese $3 trillion economy and the U.S. $5 trillion economy together make up 42% of the world's GNP.

Yet Japan, with more than half the U.S. population, has only about 10 major public relations agencies. Even Japan's Ministry of International Trade and Industry deemed the situation critical enough to state that 10 "is far too few for an economic superpower" (*Nikkei*, 1994, p.17). But changes are brewing.

One practitioner (*Nikkei*, 1993, p.22) contends that "in Japan we are at the beginning of PR." Another (*Nikkei*, 1993, p.18) sees business and consequently business communications as now "undergoing revolutionary changes." Still another (A. Kuse, personal communication, June 18, 1993) foresees a dramatic shift from publicity to political counseling and research. The president of the Public Relations Society of Japan (PRSJ), Tsuneo Kuromizu (*Nikkei*, 1991, p.17), sees investor relations, risk management and environmental efforts as future counseling areas.

To date, however, the technician rather than the manager role has dominated public relations practice. Indeed "PR" in Japan has tended to mean "*P*ress *R*elations" for two reasons; the pervasiveness of the mass media and the nature of the press club (*kisha*) system. With newspaper saturation the highest in the world (587 copies/1,000 people) and high TV viewing (3.5 hours per day per person), a

---

*With the assistance of Mizuo Kaneshige, *Chubu University Junior College*

message in the media will assuredly reach a large audience, and be believed, due to mass media's high credibility.

For those who have access to individual journalists and the *kanji* (club captains), Japan's 400-plus kisha clubs (involving about 12,000 journalists) provide a ready-made publicity system. "We don't do news releases," explains Sakae Ohashi, president and founder of the Kyodo PR agency (personal communicaton, July 15, 1994). "We build opinion by approaching opinion leaders."

Both government entities and industry associations create clubs for the beat reporters who cover them, providing physical facilities and exclusive press conferences. All reporters covering, say, the electronics industry belong to the club attached to that industry's trade association. Through this "institutionalized symbiosis between journalists and the System's organization" (Van Wolferen, 1993, p. 124), practitioners from electronics manufacturers can convey messages about new products.

Westerners might see a need for "them" to catch up with "us." However, public relations Japanese style will never "go West" because the "homogeneity of Japanese society leaves little room for incorporating outside elements, its fabric so intricately and finely woven to a negative extreme" (Nakane, 1988, p. 6). This negative extreme has serious implications for organizations that need to adapt to changing environments. Ouchi (1981), for example, emphasizes the importance to Japanese firms of adaptability and innovativeness.

Despite some similarities, cultural differences between Japan and the West (Gudykunst & Nishida, 1994) mean that the Japanese public relations community marches to its own drummer. According to the *Nikkei Weekly* (1994, p. 17), "Japanese society as a whole, and thus corporations, do not have the same sort of PR needs as do Western companies." Certain Western matters of concern never become issues in Japan.

For example, good public relations in a firm requires public relations representation in the dominant coalition (White & Dozier, 1992). In the Japanese lifetime employment system, whereby employees move in and out of public relations functions as they rise in a company, the representation happens naturally.

In Japan, values, especially the overarching value of *wa* (harmony or concord), affect public relations practice. Where the Westerner may see inefficiency, the Japanese sees avoidance of conflict:

> In Japan patience is not so much a virtue as a way of life. . . . This is important in PR, where the question of when to make a press release can be more important than the content, and where the amount of time spent in preparing for a special event can appear out of all proportion to the significance of the event itself. Preparation is everything: surprises and sudden decisions are to be avoided, as they can run the risk of causing embarrassment or trouble. (Dentsu PR Center, 1988, pp. 13–14)

Harmony means that consumers do not engineer boycotts very often, that the media do not investigate business practices, that trust exists between employers and employees, and that group welfare prevails over individual desires.

However, the dark side of harmony means that executives prefer either cover-ups or doing nothing to going public with bad news. Furthermore, the trait of *ishin denshin* (taciturnity or nonverbal communication) is viewed positively and nontalkativeness is a mark of maturity (Mizutani, 1981; Tsujimura, 1987). In tandem with the desire for consensus and *ittaikan* (feeling oneness), these aspects of Japan's "collectivism" (Lebra, 1976) make for slow reactions to crisis situations, such as the one that Minolta experienced (discussed later).

In collectivistic cultures, "the boundary between an ingroup and an outgroup is very important" (Gudykunst & Nishida, 1994, p. 22). In exchange for loyalty, the group looks after its members. Thus, in Japan, clients (members) remain loyal to the agency (group) unless monumental problems occur; on the agency side, not doing one's utmost for a client would be unthinkable.

The following pages explore these unique traits of public relations Japanese style. These traits include longevity of client-agency relations; mixing the roles of advertising and public relations, with an emphasis on public relations as publicity; compliant media that make publicity tasks somewhat easy; domination of both public relations and advertising by a few powerful agencies that handle competing clients; no system of professional accreditation; identity as a company employee rather than with public relations as a profession; little cross-firm sharing and networking by corporate public relations divisions; no strong, well-publicized ethical codes of conduct; a vertical career path within the company with movement in and out of public relatioms; emphasis on where one studied rather than on what is crucial in entry-level hiring; almost no public relations majors or practicum courses at universities; little academic research on public relations with surveys carried out by ad agencies; arrogant attitude towards consumer protesters; and centralization in Tokyo, the site of the national media's head offices, corporate headquarters and major public relations agencies.

This chapter draws on many interviews with Tokyo agencies and corporate headquarters. But an effort has been made to include non-Tokyo practitioners as well.

POSTWAR PUBLIC RELATIONS IN JAPAN

Although public relations practice has developed a nonwestern ethos, it started from Western sources. Allied Occupation forces created central and regional public relations offices to disseminate information, which established the linkage of public relations with publicity. By the time the Occupation ended in 1952 (see Table 12.1), Japanese government offices had set up similar *koho-bu* (public relations offices) to communicate with the public.

David Finn, cofounder of Ruder and Finn Inc., (Messerly, 1966), commented on early "instinctual" corporate PR efforts:

You might say that public relations began here . . . In one aspect, employee relations, America is just beginning to catch up to Japan . . . Japanese newspapers and other companies have been sponsoring public service events . . . for years. (p.3)

By the 1960s, some large (e.g., the Mitsubishi group) and some medium-sized firms had created public relations departments that focused mainly on publicity (*Nikkei,* 1993, pp. 18–22). These corporate public relations managers established a voluntary association in 1964; in that same year, the Tokyo Olympics showcased Japan's postwar reconstruction. Another watershed international event for Japan, EXPO '70 in Osaka—the first world's fair in Asia—gave industries a chance to carry their message of pride and accomplishment to a global audience.

But in the 1970s, this flexing of industrial muscle also brought corruption, scandals, pollution and product deficiencies, prompting protests by normally docile citizens. Instead of just instinctual public relations efforts, corporations beefed up their public relations staffs and began to seek out help from agencies (PRSJ, 1991).

As Table 12.1 shows, a burst of activity occurred in the 1980s. Japan's

TABLE 12.1
Timeline for Japanese Public Relations

Year	Event
1945	August 14--Emperor broadcasts news of Japan's surrender (radio).
1946	Allied Occupation sets up offices to disseminate information.
1952	April 29--Peace Treaty takes effect; Occupation ends.
1955	Sakae Ohashi establishes first PR firm, renamed Kyodo in 1964.
1961	Dentsu PR Center established.
1964	Japan PR Association (JPRA) established in Tokyo. Mitsubishi Public Affairs committee created to restore trust.
1973	Burson Marstellar opens Tokyo office.
1975	Japan PR Industry Association (JPRIA) established.
1980	JPRA and JPRIA merge to form PR Society of Japan (PRSJ).
1982	First issue of *PRSJ Newsletter.*
1984	Osaka branch of PRSJ established (only group outside Tokyo).
1985	20 million visit Tsukuba EXPO's 29 corporate exhibits. Keizai Koho center sponsors first Outstanding PR Awards.
1986	IPRA Board of Directors, from 16 countries, meets in Tokyo.
1988	Approved by MITI, PRSJ is incorporated; I. Tanaka, president of Dentsu PR Center, becomes president.
1990	First PR Summit of municipal governments held at Kuse, Okayama; T. Kuromizu, president of Dentsu PR Center, named PRSJ president. Association for Corporate Support of the Arts established; First Mecenat Grand Prix for arts support awarded.
1991	Hakuhodo ad agency establishes Corporate Communication unit. *Nikkei Weekly* publishes first annual PR supplement.
1992	Brazil Earth Summit increases corporate/municipal campaigns. PRSJ adopts an ethics charter. Dentsu ad agency establishes a Corporate Communication unit.
1993	Japan Investor Relations Association established.
1994	Academics work to establish Japan Society for Public Relations.

pioneer agency man, Sakae Ohashi, had gathered other firms together in 1975 to form an association. In 1980, Ohashi's group joined with the previously established corporate association to form the Public Relations Society of Japan.

In the 1980s, two trends marked the field: corporate identity and the growth of the borderless economy. The new (especially the young) Japanese consumer began to consider the company's level of corporate citizenship when buying products, in addition to the price and quality of a product.

The borderless economy had both domestic and overseas public relations implications. To help foreign companies trying to break into the domestic Japanese market, about 15 foreign public relations firms set up branches or entered into joint ventures; they offered management services that domestic clients did not need. Furthermore, Japanese firms began adding non-Japanese or bilingual staff members. To counteract Japan's geographical and psychological insularity, internationalization became "a sincere goal of governmental, cultural and educational leaders" (Wray, 1990, p. 17).

Overseas, the many Japanese companies buying property or setting up production overseas needed "to conduct ambitious PR activities to nurture feelings of friendship in local communities" (PRSJ, 1991, p. 8). Corporate Japan faced in the 1980s "almost a classic marketing problem," stated New York public relations expert John Scanlon. High-visibility acquisitions, such as Mitsubishi's investment in Rockefeller Center and Sony's purchase of CBS Records and Columbia Pictures, had "touched off a deeper layer of American suspicion about Japan," says Scanlon (as cited in Conant, 1990, p. 60).

In New York, the Nippon Club and the Japan Chamber of Commerce International (JCCI) have published an 85-page guide in both English and Japanese entitled "'Joining In,' A Handbook for Better Corporate Citizenship in the United States." This publication includes a wide variety of information as well as a list of charities and nonprofit organizations that Japanese corporations could contribute to, from the Red Cross and the Children's Defense Fund to the YMCA.

Yet, according to Conant (1990), Japanese corporations find themselves in a public relations Catch 22:

> They have been advised to reach out and contribute to the community, but on more than one occasion their public relations ploys have been thrown back in their faces by critics. A paranoid culture sees the pariah everywhere: the underwriting of public television news programs was interpreted in an article in the *Columbia Journal Review* as a way to subtly influence programming, grants to universities have been criticized in the *New Republic* as a devious way to turn American academia into a pro-Japan lobby. (p. 62)

The xenophobia seems to be easing in the 1990s, probably partly because Japan is beginning to open up its domestic markets to U.S. products like rice and apples.

PUBLIC RELATIONS IN THE 1990s

When the Occupation introduced public relations into Japan, the Japanese translated the term as *koho,* which literally means "wide reporting" or disseminating messages. The first character of the two-character word "advertising," which means "wide," was combined with the second character of information, which means "report."

To this day, Japanese people confuse public relations with advertising because of the shared character and also because of the nature of advertising itself. A successful ad campaign "frequently has a corporate image aspect, thus fulfilling what is often a basic PR function"; rather than pitching a particular product, ads often aim to create a mood of reassurance about the corporation (Dentsu PR Center, 1988, p. 18).

As for clients, they are willing to pay for advertising, but they think public relations "should come free as an attached service," explains Yoshiaki Ishikura of the Nambokusha ad and public relations firm. "Advertising is information. You can calculate the cost for reaching X number of readers. But you can't calculate the cost per person of PR" (personal communication, July 15, 1994).

According to Kuromizu, "We never charge on a time basis; clients don't understand this. We charge retainers plus actual expenses." He adds that "we need PR for PR. *Koho* has the meaning of propaganda; we need a new word" (personal communication, July 15, 1994). One answer to the dilemma involves doing away with Japanese words entirely and adapting the English term "corporate communications," or more simply "CC."

The change, a major trend in the field, represents more than simply hanging out a new shingle. Corporations such as Zexel, Omron, and TOTO have created new offices to handle all communications "that are directly related to managerial policies," including crisis management and training executives in how to address the press (Dentsu, 1994, p. 226). The two dominant Japanese ad agencies, Dentsu and Hakuhodo, have created CC bureaus by combining public relations and corporate identity divisions. (See Table 12.1.)

In addition to broadening the field beyond publicity, a second public relations trend of the 1990s relates to retrenchment. Although the 1993 handbook of the Public Relations Society of Japan lists 458 individual members in Tokyo and Osaka, the 1994 figure at this writing stands at only about 430. The drop occurred due to the bursting of Japan's "economic bubble," which devastated the advertising field and wounded the public relations field. In fall 1992, one third of companies had reduced their public relations budgets, whereas 60 % stayed at 1991 levels. Dentsu PR Center will take on a few new employees in 1995, its first new hires for about four years, according to Kuromizu.

Looking ahead, the class of 1997 should be the last to experience severe job competition. The number of 18-year-olds peaked in 1993, after which numbers will decline steadily. Resulting competition for students has fostered a boom in university identity (UI) communications; name changes, new logos, songs, and high-profile forums (Rissho University, for example, invited Margaret Thatcher to its 120th anniversary in fall 1992).

A third trend involves crisis management. Missteps are changing the way many companies react to unexpected, negative events. In 1991, Nomura Securities executives opted to sit out a scandal involving the brokerage house. In 1992, a U.S. District Court ordred Minolta to pay Honeywell $96.35 million for patent infringement. Minolta reacted too slowly to gain any sympathy.

Politicians, too, "don't understand or care about PR," states PRSJ president Kuromizu of Dentsu PR Center. "They don't take the offensive and explain a crisis. They just give up and resign" (personal communication, July 15, 1994).

But if disaster strikes, one cannot just walk away. When a China Airlines airplane crashed at Nagoya in 1994, a Dentsu PR Center staff member saw it on TV and rushed to Nagoya. Dentsu "handled all the crisis communication with a team of 15 people," related Kuromizu. "For Virgin Atlantic Airlines [a Dentsu client], we have contingency plans already in place."

The media should get the whole story quickly and avoid endless followups, believes Atsushi Kuse of Dentsu Burson Marstellar (personal communication, June 18, 1993). "Consumers who bought a certain whiskey selling at duty free shops found foreign objects in the bottles. In 3 months we did a recall and relaunch. We offered a new product with a purity guarantee (80% chose this) or refund in cash. We, a crisis team of eight, also set up a consumer hotline."

AGENCIES

As of July 1993, PRSJ had 84 agency members, most of them one- or two-person operations. In terms of employees, Japan's top five agencies are (Dentsu PR Center, 1988): Dentsu PR Center, International Public Relations, Kyodo PR, Ozma PR and PRAP Japan. Other large firms (with more than 50 employees) are Cosmo, Dentsu Burson Marstellar, IR Japan and Omnicom PR Network.

This small number of major agencies is subdivided into four types due to Japan's unusual mass communication history. In general, the Japanese firms excel at publicity, whereas the western firms emphasize nonpublicity functions, according to Atsushi Kuse, vice president of Dentsu Burson Marstellar (personal communication, June 18, 1993).

Agencies with Western Connections

If a foreign company wants to enter Japan, it may want to "start with PR: it's cheaper," notes PRSJ president Kuromizu. (A full-page black and white ad in the national *Yomiuri Shimbun* newspaper costs about $450,000.) In general, women professionals fare better at these Western-linked firms than at Japanese firms.

Joint Ventures. Dentsu Burson Marsteller Co., Ltd. of Tokyo, with about 50 employees, was formed in January 1989 when Burson Marstellar (51% owner), which had operated in Tokyo for 15 years, joined with Dentsu (49% owner). The joint venture also has offices in New York and Brussels. Its Tokyo staff of Americans and Japanese are almost all U.S.-trained.

Other firms in partnerships with large Western agencies include PRAP, associated with Ketchum, and International PR and Universal PR, both with the Shandwick group. Although the recession hurt some firms, PRAP did well in the early 1990s, says executive vice president Satoshi Sugita. With "international business our fastest growing segment," PRAP helped with the Toys "Я" Us store opening that featured George Bush and organized concerts for McDonald's (personal communication, July 11, 1994).

Branch Offices. Firms with Tokyo offices are Edelman Public Relations Worldwide, Gavin Anderson & Co. (Japan) Inc., Hill and Knowlton, Manning, Selvage and Lee, and the Rowland Co. The "bilingual and bicultural" Cosmo Public Relations Corp. of Tokyo, with 50 employees, has another office in New York. Clients include Hyatt Hotels, Hitachi and Sumitomo 3M.

Japanese Agencies

Ad Agency-Related. Dentsu PR Center, the largest public relations firm in Japan, is affiliated with Dentsu, one of the largest advertising and communications agencies in the world. Established in 1961, the center had total revenues of ¥11,000 million (more than $110 million) by 1993. With offices in Tokyo, Osaka, Nagoya, and New York, it has 130 full-time domestic clients, including Canon, Fuji Film, Yamaha, NTT (Nippon Telegraph and Telephone), and Tokyo Electric. The firm's 20 foreign clients include Amway, Coca-Cola, IBM, Microsoft, and Volvo.

About one third of its nearly 300 employees "maintain almost daily contact with the media people they know personally and professionally," according to an ad for the center. The president of Dentsu traditionally serves as president of PRSJ (see Table 12.1).

Dentsu's reach and clout, which may please its clients, worries some critics. Calling the Dentsu group "the hidden media boss," Van Wolferen (1993) states:

> Dentsu is in a position to intimidate large firms, since it can make corporate scandals known and hush them up again. Moreover, companies hardly dare switch agencies because of rumours that Dentsu will report irregularities in their business to the authorities. (p. 234)

In addition to the independent public relations Center, Dentsu itself has a public relations division, as does Hakuhodo, Japan's No. 2 ad agency. The divisions number 200–300 people. Similarly, smaller ad agencies have sections that do some public relations; for example, Nambokusha, 51% owned by Toyota, works specifically in the auto industry, with activities about 90% in advertising and 10% in public relations.

Independent. Newer and smaller firms can sometimes survive by carving out a special niche. IBI Inc., for example, established in 1972, specializes in investor relations and financial reports.

Japan's first independent firm, Kyodo, can boast some clients (such as Kobe Steel) whose relationships with the agency date back 30 years. In addition to clients, the firm's president and founder, Sakae Ohashi, has long personal acquaintances with journalists. Presently employing 103 people, Kyodo has seen many former employees start their own companies. Clients include Japan Air Lines, Orient Watch, Chubu Electric Power, and UNICEF Japan.

"Even corporations with large PR staffs need agencies," states Ohashi (personal communication, July 15, 1994). "They can't arrange the one-on-one media connections. We don't do corporate ID; we communicate it."

CORPORATIONS

Indeed, the corporate public relations staffs are quite large. Shiseido, the largest cosmetics firm (and top magazine advertiser) in Japan, has 32 people in public relations. In addition, each of 105 domestic branch offices has a public relations program. And the firm has 25 people in its new Corporate Culture Division, started in 1990. The division evolved naturally from the firm's history of sponsoring events that linked Shiseido with France and art.

That same year saw creation of a corporate arts association and an awards program (see Table 12.1). By 1993, according to a survey, more than 50 corporations had created community or cultural affairs departments. Some such divisions, for example, that of the Mitsubishi group, have operated for 30 years, but have recently changed direction.

"For 16 years we brought one Asian journalist to Japan annually," stated Shigetsugu Tateyama, secretariat director of the Mitsubishi Public Affairs Committee (personal communication, June 23, 1993). "Now we find grassroots programs to be more important. We want to target one or two Asian nations." Beginning in 1990, its Asian Children's Art Festival annually awards prizes and has travelled to Brunei, Hongkong, and Vietnam.

Although only a few corporations can afford community or culture divisions, corporate identity is "established as a business strategy, involving companies in nearly all sectors" (Dentsu, 1994, p. 213). In 1990, *Weekly Diamond Magazine* even conducted a Corporate Image Survey; Honda Motor Co. won.

Some firms have used anniversaries, mergers, or restructurings as occasions to change corporate symbols and promulgate new corporate doctrines. In commemoration of its 70th anniversary, Nikko Securities Co. established the Nikko Shoken Dream Ladies, a women's soccer team, in 1991—the first women's soccer team in a Japanese enterprise.

Most seem satisfied that earlier investments in "CI" (coorporate identity)—the Japanese have adopted the English acronym—paid off in helping them weather the early 1990s recession (Dentsu, 1994). In some cases, the chief executive himself established the firm's identity; for example, Sony's Akio Morita, Honda Motor Co.'s Nobuhiko Kawamoto and Shiseido Co.'s Yoshiharu Fukuhara "often appear in the mass media, acting as public relations officers for their firms" (Dentsu, 1992, p. 264).

External communication has benefitted from Japan's technological prowess. Tokyo Gas, Meidensha Electric, and other firms send out video newsletters. Appropriately, Japan Data General sends its newsletter out by personal computer. Internal communication routinely uses satellites to convey the president's New Year's speech, changes in executives' postings, and presentations at stockholders' meetings.

Companies are paying attention to publics in more traditional ways as well. The Japanese obsession with narrative comic books (*manga*) prompted Otsuka Pharmaceuticals to publish a manga about the human body by commissioning 10 famous cartoonists to draw educational strips.

The recession focused corporate attention on a neglected public-private investors. As institutional investors pulled out of the market, firms turned to individuals to fill the gap. The Tokyo Stock Exchange has "established a system for officially honoring companies which have taken steps to increase the number of private stockholders" (Dentsu, 1994, p. 219). In 1993, a new association (see Table 12.1) aimed to "strengthen communications between enterprises and their shareholders" (Dentsu, 1994, p. 219).

Nomura Securities Co., the largest brokerage house in Japan, set up Nomura Investor Relations in 1991 after the firm was involved in a major scandal. Daiwa and Yamaichi securities firms likewise set up investor relations (IR) sections. The trading house C. Itoh established an IR team within its public relations department. The Sumitomo Corp. published a first-ever public relations booklet for individual shareholders.

In the industrial field, Rohm, a semiconductor producer, was the first manufacturer to set up an IR office. Nippon Steel held a meeting attended by 400 institutional investors and securities analysts. A continuing public relations problem remains with the disruptive appearance at stockholders' meetings of *yakuza* (underworld gang members).

MUNICIPALITIES

Politically, Japan is divided into 47 prefectures, within which even the smallest village units perform public relations functions. Large-scale nationwide health campaigns are run by the national government rather than nonprofit groups like the Cancer Society. These include AIDS, antidrug, and antismoking campaigns (cigaratte ads still run on late-night television).

Almost all municipalities conduct public relations efforts related to garbage (*gomi*), including attention to recylcing. (In Japan, citizens must separate burnable and nonburnable items. Recycling is usually optional.) The Tokyo Metropolitan Government in 1989 created *Gomira,* an animated character symbolizing garbage, to help educate citizens about its garbage crisis.

Like corporations, municipalites employ CI (or MI - municipal identity) to promote themselves. In 1990, the Public Relations Society of Japan presented the top award in its pamphlet contest to Kuse Town, Okayama prefecture, west of Kobe, at a seminar on the topic "PR: a must for local governments" (Dentsu, 1992, p. 264).

Regional public relations efforts also exist. For example, the five cities and towns around the Koise River in Ibaraki Prefecture, northeast of Tokyo, held a campaign to purify Lake Kasumigaura, the second largest lake in Japan (Dentsu, 1992).

The recession has been a blessing in disguise for various rural districts. For example, Yamaguchi Prefecture created a "graduated from Tokyo" campaign to entice residents who had left home for urban universities to come back. The campaign was called in Japan "the U-turn phenomenon" (Dentsu, 1994).

Aside from campaigns, what day-to-day activities engage a typical public relations staff? The city of Ogaki near Nagoya has a staff of two who do the following (Michio Tsuchiya, personal communication, October 27, 1992). They pursue arrangements for Ogaki's five "friendly city" relations, including a brochure printed in various languages and exchange programs; they produce a newsletter twice a month to be delivered to each house (other cities insert newsletters into newspapers); they publish the booklet *Ogaki City* (2,000 copies a year); they produce a 20-minute show for TV Gifu twice every month; they create both 10-minute radio anouncements once a week and Videotex messages for 1,000 terminals (NTT); they update Ogaki Station's moving electrified sign announcing events and information; they supply information to the press (several items a day); they arrange a monthly mayoral press conference; and they give city building tours for housewives and kids.

Staff members are more likely to have backgrounds working for the municipality, often in varied jobs, than to have come from outside public relations positions. The exam taken by prospective employees asks, What kind of job do you want? One joins the city staff and may not get one's first choice. Every April, staffs rotate. The senior public relations staff members teach new people in an apprenticeship system.

THE FUTURE OF JAPANESE PUBLIC RELATIONS

As the year 2000 approaches, six major factors are affecting segments of Japanese society, which in turn have implications for public relations in Japan. First, the "bubble" economy of the 1980s burst in the early 1990s, probably putting an end to the system of lifetime employment, consumer complacency, and quiet stockholders. Second, the upheaval in politics, which came to a head July 18, 1993, meant the end of Liberal-Democratic Party (LDP) rule and the beginning of true multiparty politics. Third, the United States continues its pressure on Japan to open domestic markets. Fourth, the falling birthrate and other indices indicate female dissatisfaction with male-dominated Japanese society. Fifth, environmental awareness is increasing. Sixth, the disillusionment of the public with scandals and corruption, notably the Recruit scandal of 1989 and the Kanemaru scandal of 1992, has forced attention on ethics in all walks of life.

Because we have not discussed them elsewhere, let us elaborate on the last three points; environmental citizenship, women's roles and ethics.

Beginning about 1990, the public relations efforts of grassroots ecology groups affected the public relations activities of governments and corporations. One group of citizens, to publicize the dangers of tropical deforestation, even bought an ad in *The New York Times* directing readers to write to, among others, the president of Mitsubishi Corp. Eventually Mitsubishi Corp. set up a special environmental unit; Mitsubishi Motors published a "Green Book" in English, French, and Spanish; and Mitsubishi Electric Corp. sponsored a "green" concert for John Lennon's 50th birthday, at which Yoko Ono Lennon appeared (Dentsu, 1992).

Aside from nature-friendly activities, environmentalism will put more emphasis on the overall quality of life:

> The disadvantages to local residents of traffic jams, water pollution, and noise will undercut cconomic benefits by corporate operations. Increased tension between the two sides will make PR activities more important in community relations. (Dentsu, 1992, p. 266)

Although lacking a satisfying physical environment, Japanese have plenty of money (an average salary of $30,020 in 1988). However, in 1988 women working full time made only 50.7% of men's monthly cash earnings. Wages for new graduates were more equal.

In their senior year, college students take various corporate entry tests. At large corporations, management will place some of the new hires in the public relations section, but in later years may move them to entirely different sections. They will probably never be fired. The recession severely affected women's initial job offers, but even in good times, lifetime employment never applied to them.

"I never hire women graduates," said the president of one major agency. "They leave and get married" (personal communication, July 15, 1994). Indeed the common term for public relations practitioner is the Japanese-English phrase "PR man."

In 1990, a special section in the popular young women's magazine *Hanako* did much to publicize public relations as a career, but little to emphasize its professional management function. Headlined "Fashionable Female PR Staff," the articles described "Fantastic Announcement Meetings, Exhibitions, and Press Conferences."

Statistics from PRSJ as of July 1993 in various employment categories showed a gender ratio markedly different from that of the U.S.: women are only 12 % of corporate members; 19 % of public relations firm members; 7% of ad firm members; 10% of production firm members; and 14% of 458 government association members. In all professions, Japanese women represent only 1.0% of managers, compared to 11.1% in the United States.

Japan has laws against employment discriminaton, but they carry no penalties. The "velvet ghetto" issue discussed in relation to U.S. public relations has no meaning in the highly masculine Japanese culture—which scored 95 of 100 on Hofstede's (1980) masculinity scale, compared to 62 for the United States. In the absence of sanctions, an ethical sense of fair play has not sufficed to bring equality to the workplace for women.

The ethics on both sides of the press-public relations relationship takes on special nuances in Japan, where people in business assume that a *honne* (true intention) lies behind the *tatemae* (surface expression). One agency president called mass media ethics codes tatemae and journalists' actual behavior honne.

"Japanese media violate their own ethics codes," he related (personal communication, July 15, 1994). "They ask PR people for tickets. When an agricultual association invites media people to tour the countryside, they routinely accept these free trips." Some 'black journalists' even write incriminating stories and then demand bribes not to release them. Others ask for interviews, write flattering stories and then take payment to run them." But such extreme behavior is not common.

"Most media people won't take money," states Toshiaki Ishikura of the Namboku agency (personal communication, July 15, 1994). "But golf, drinking or parties paid for by special interests are OK." According to Prof. Takeshi Maezawa, who decries the custom, "In most newspapers, free tickekts or invitations for trips, theaters or restaurants offered by news sources are not only acceptable but welcomed" (as cited in Vanden Heuvel & Dennis, 1993, p. 76).

Providing opportunities for journalists to write differs in degree from mass media's direct acceptance of public relations material. Prestige newspapers generally do not trust news releases, stated an agency employee, but "you CAN be sure of placing material in small magazines. They willingly accept your news about new products. They like barter: a paid ad in exchange for running editorial copy. But such magazines have little credibility" (T. Ishikura, personal communication, July 15, 1994).

Conversely, what kind of pressure do ad or public relations people exert on mass media to change or soften content? Extremely intense and effective pressure, according to Van Wolferen (1993):

A Dentsu executive once boasted in a speech that the daily *Yomiuri* newspaper, after having invited consumer activist Ralph Nader to Japan, heeded a warning from Dentsu by breaking up a planned two-page special report and toning down the segment. Around the same time, the *Mainichi* newspaper, also under instructions from Dentsu, ran a "moderate" story on the consumer movement. (p. 234)

However, according to an agency employee (personal communication, July 15, 1994): "The agency people may try to talk with the ad men at the newspaper, who then approach editors, but usually they won't change stories. They say the facts are the facts. The best we can expect is to take the product name out of the headline or omit the president's name."

Regarding political public relations in the now defunct one-party system, a cozy relation existed between Dentsu and the Liberal Democratic Party (Van Wolferen, 1993):

> The ninth bureau [of the LDP] absorbs over one-third of the PR budget of the prime minister's office and some 40% of that of the other ministries. Dentsu also has a near monopoly on disposal of the LDP's PR budget. . . . The role of the major "advertising agencies" as servants of the system illustrates admirably the impossibility of drawing a line between the private and public sectors in Japan.(pp. 236–7)

But precisely this kind of corruption and collusion, as well as the other forces noted above, set in motion changes that have probably altered "business as usual" in Japan forever. These social forces will likely shape the public relations field in the following ways. There will likely be a full development of political public relations and media strategy counseling. In addition, these forces may lead to a full development of crisis public relations (contingency stategy, media plans).

Public relations education will be included in university curricula and a PRSSA-like organization will be established enabling students to meet professionals. There will be more vertical job switching with employees doing similar jobs at varied firms. With these changes there will be more foreign firms entering Japan and needing public relations consultants. As public relations becomes more established, there will be a stronger role for professional organizations, an emphasis on continuing education and accreditation, and need for an industrywide publication of news and research. (At present *Dentsu PR News* is Japan's only professional newsletter).

Further changes may include better recognition of quality efforts in the field through a prestigious, competitive awards process; more discussion of and attention to ethics; the movement of women into public relations top management positions; and a desire for businesses to communicate their cultural or social role.

REFERENCES

Conant, J. (1990, April). Secrets of the Nippon Club. *Manhattan, Inc., 7*(4), 57–63.
Dentsu PR Center (1988). Communicating: *A guide to PR in Japan.* Tokyo: author.

Dentsu (1991). *Marketing and advertising yearbook, Japan 1991*. Tokyo: author.
Dentsu (1992). *Marketing and advertising yearbook, Japan 1992*. Tokyo: author.
Dentsu (1993). *Marketing and advertising yearbook, Japan 1993*. Tokyo: author.
Gudykunst, W., & Nishida, T. (1994). *Bridging Japanese/North American differences*. Newbury Park, CA: Sage.
Hofstede, G. (1980). *Culture's consequences*. Beverly Hills, CA: Sage.
Lebra, T. (1976). *Japanese patterns of behavior*. Honolulu: University of Hawaii Press.
Messerly, A. (1966, November 14). Japanese pr praised by David Finn of U.S. *Asahi Evening News*, p. 3.
Mizutani, O. (1981). *Japanese: The spoken language in Japanese life*. Tokyo: Japan Times.
Nakane, C. (1988). Japan in the context of Asia. *Japan Foundation Newsletter, 15*(4), 2–6.
Nikkei Weekly (1991, June 29). Special supplement on public relations, pp. 17–18.
Nikkei Weekly (1993, March 1). Special supplement on public relations, pp. 18–22.
Nikkei Weekly (1994, March 7). Special supplement on public relations, pp. 17–24.
Ouchi, W. (1981). *Theory Z: How American business can meet the Japanese challenge*. New York: Avon.
PRSJ. (1991). *Japan pr directory*. Tokyo: Public Relations Society of Japan.
Tsujimura, A. (1987). Some characteristics of the Japanese way of communication. In D. L. Kincaid (Ed.). *Communication theory from eastern and western perspectives*. New York: Academic Press.
Vanden Heuvel, J., & Dennis, E. (1993). *The unfolding lotus: East Asia's changing media*. New York: Freedom Forum Media Studies Center.
Van Wolferen, K. (1993). *The enigma of Japanese power*. Tokyo: Tuttle.
White, J., & Dozier, D. M. (1992). Public relations and management decision making. In J. E. Grunig, (Ed.), *Excellence in public relations and communication management* (pp. 91–108). Hillsdale, NJ: Lawrence Erlbaum Associates.
Wray, H. (1990, March). Creating a more international Japan. *Intersect*, pp. 17–20.

13 Public Relations in the Middle East: The Case of Saudi Arabia

Ali Alanazi
King Saud University, Riyadh, Saudi Arabia

Public relations has entered a new era in the Arab world. In the minds of many, Arab nations use public relations as a "weapon" to achieve political goals. The 1991 Gulf War, pitting the United States and its allies against Iraq, provided many examples. Hiebert (1991) noted that without "smart public relations" techniques on the part of Arab allies, America's "smart bombs" would not have achieved their objectives.

The Western model of public relations has a short history in the Middle East. Systematic public relations was introduced in Saudi Arabia only in the late 1930s, when international oil companies started to explore the Saudi desert. Over the last 30 years, Saudi Arabia's economy developed tremendously, and the Kingdom became a modern state. Further, the story of Saudi Arabia's economic, social, and political development has been presented to the Saudi people and to the outside world with increasing vigor by the Saudi government through available communications tools.

To establish baseline information, in 1992 I conducted one of the first Western studies of public relations practices in Saudi Arabia. Much of this study's background is summarized in the pages that follow. Utilizing Broom and Dozier's (1986) role-models theory, I found Saudi public relations fit descriptive models developed in the West. Such sharing of ideas and practices across cultures can be of profound significance as the West and the Third World are drawn together inexorably.

In the only other published investigation of Saudi Arabian public relations practitioners, Araby (1984) assessed the applicability of Broom and Smith's 1979 role-model theory to public relations practices of Saudi governmental organizations in Riyadh.

ARAB PUBLIC RELATIONS: A LONG TRADITION

Communication in general, and unsystematized public relations in particular, have existed in the Arab region since the beginning of Arabian and Middle Eastern cultures. Leaders of ancient empires such as the Babylonians, Egyptians, Greeks, Persians, and Romans presented messages to their people, using communication tools available to them.

Hammurabi of Babylonia used the sheep-shearing season to gather his employees and give them his guidelines. Ancient Egyptian pharaohs used the irrigation season to celebrate the Nile River and disseminate their news and information (Al-Tohami & Al-Dakoki, 1980). Historical evidence also indicates that public relations was practiced many centuries ago in the present nation of Iraq. In what today would pass as a "press release," a circular handwritten on a crude type of paper told Babylonian farmers, around the year 2000 B.C., how to increase their crop yields. This bulletin resembled press releases put out by the U.S. Department of Agriculture almost 4,000 years later (Nolte, 1979, p. 33).

The Assyrians were the first to use pictorial bulletins to document their victories. These bulletins, designed to whip up public enthusiasm on the "home front," drew attention to conquests on far-off battlefields by portraying captured enemy prisoners. Such pictures gave credibility to the bulletins and helped Assyrian military leaders persuade citizens about battlefield successes. Often, the portraits were displayed in public squares, demonstrating in ancient times the power of both pictures and words (Fakhri, Alsheekly, & Zalzala, 1980, p. 35).

Egyptian pharaohs also used communication to rally support on the home front and strengthen their soldiers' morale during wars. The ancient Egyptians often wrote messages on stones or leaves of special kinds of trees (Fakhri et al., 1980, p. 36).

In some of the more mature areas of the Arab world, leaders emulated the public relations practices of the ancient Greeks and Romans by encouraging public forums to assess and measure the intensity of public sentiment and opinion. Special occasions in which people gathered and communicated publicly were popular throughout the Arabian Peninsula 2,000 to 3,000 years ago. Attendants engaged in debate, recited poetry, or made public speeches. One Arab tribe would attempt to reach out to another; tribes from one part of the region often traveled to maintain these intertribal relations. Okaz Souk, an open market in the Arab Peninsula before Islam, served as an a example. At this market, Arabian tribes' poets and speakers competed for glory in demonstrations and competitions with other tribes.

According to Mansfield (1981, p. 13), poetry was the most popular art in the Arabian culture and a model for much of the public communication that appeared. Poetry was particularly important to the roving, nonpermanent tribes of the region. Bedouins congratulated each other in verse for three achievements; "the birth of a boy, the emergence of the poet and the foaling of a mare." Besides reflecting the importance of communication in Arab culture, poetry illustrated the importance of public speech there. According to Glubb (1987, p. 291), Arabs were innovators in poetry and romance writing. Despite their high illiteracy rate, the Arab people have always been committed adherents of poetry.

Poets and their poetry played a major role in the Arab culture beyond entertainment. The poet was considered to be the press secretary of his tribe, attacking the tribe's enemies, praising its accomplishments, and strengthening the fighters' morale (Fakhri et al., 1980, p. 34). Effective Arabic rhetoric is conveyed better through verse than through prose. Its structure makes it well suited to the art of poetic disputation, which has traditionally been used in dueling for power (Al-Odadi, 1992).

Poetry still plays a very important role in the Arab culture. Al-Odadi (1992) examined the use of poetry and rhetoric by both sides in the Gulf War. Saddam Hussein used "vast arsenals of poetic imagery, rhetorical devices and religious references which cannot help but move the captive listener." The Saudi government used poetry extensively in "the media to combat the propaganda of the Iraqi leadership," publishing poetry in the printed media and broadcasting "an endless supply of poems on Saudi Arabia's radio and television which reached all neighboring countries" (Al-Odadi, 1992).

Using a public gathering to communicate with others was a sort of public relations technique now popularly known as a special event. This indicates the ancient roots of public relations in the region.

Saudi Arabia's Unique Role

The Kingdom of Saudi Arabia is not only a political and economic power, it is also a religious center for the Islamic world because of the presence of Mecca and Medina. It has been difficult for Saudi leaders to adopt innovations from the West without considering their impact on the country's Islamic roles.

The Kingdom of Saudi Arabia also has gained recognition around the world primarily for its huge oil production. This rather narrow, incomplete perception has been due to the lack of communication between Saudi Arabia and the outside world in the past and, to a lesser degree, in the present.

The role of communication gained attention before World War I during the reign of King Abdulaziz Ibn Saud, who first realized its importance and used its methods effectively in consolidating the country. After the liberation of Riyadh, King Abdulaziz unified the Saudi state under his rule and began the development of a modern nation. To unite the country, he employed methods to communicate with all of its parts.

Interpersonal communication was the King's dominant approach from the 1920s through the 1950s largely because of a lack of equipment and experience in mass communication. At that time, Saudi society was small and uncomplicated by Western standards. The government was simple and very small. The

King was the head of state, directly carrying his orders and messages to his people.

The Saudi state remained essentially unchanged after unification. "Its organization was still entirely personal, a traditional desert principality writ large" (Holden & Johns, 1981, p. 99). Abdulaziz continued to use his *majlis* (an open meeting in a tent, house, or council) as a forum to conduct the business of the new state and to talk with ordinary people. He made himself accessible to everyone, in his palace, during his travels in the country by caravan, or in his open *majlis*.

The open *majlis* which Abdulaziz used in governing Saudi Arabia was derived from Arab culture and customs. In Arab tradition, one need not make an appointment to meet with a person or official. This symbolized the hospitality of the Arabs and was a forum where dialogue and speeches could take place among people and their leaders.

Ibn Saud received guests, ministers, and foreign representatives in an open *majlis*, usually every evening or sometimes in the morning, in the King's house or tent. Ibn Saud might receive a bedouin and talk to him while at the same time hosting a foreign ambassador (Howarth, 1964, p. 199). While he tried to listen to everyone in his kingdom, this technique had to be changed or modified, but not eliminated, after the expansion of the kingdom and the resulting complexity and diversity of Saudi society.

The introduction of the telegram, radio, and posts helped introduce these modifications, making Ibn Saud more accessible to the people. Complainants could send their messages and receive replies through these instruments (Howarth, 1964, p. 200).

The purpose of the *majlis* in Arab society is to permit idea exchange and public interaction. Local sheiks used the *majlis* to enhance their credibility and prestige among the people. According to Holden and Johns (1981, p. 13), the Sheikh of the tribe either listened to his people in his *majlis*, or counseled them regarding tribal or family issues. This tradition has continued with King Fahd, the current ruler of Saudi Arabia, who holds an open court for his subjects to enhance his credibility among the tribes folk (Holden, 1981, p. 13).

Ibn Saud followed the two-way symmetric model of communication in dealing with the people of Saudi Arabia and with political, economic, and social situations. He combined persuasive communication with a willingness to change his position if it benefited the two sides, and if it helped to avoid misunderstandings and confrontation. The two-way symmetric communication model defines an organization or agent as "changeable" or willing to listen to external and internal publics. His willingness to receive people in his tent or palace strengthened and improved the two-way symmetric approach established in the Abdulaziz era.

While communication in Saudi Arabia during the early period of King Abdulaziz' reign was limited to interpersonal communication, government policy implementation was also limited by very primitive communication techniques. When Abdulaziz united the country, he tried to overcome these limitations by using mediated as well as strictly interpersonal channels. The country's large geographic spread made it necessary to establish local governments for every province of the Kingdom. This action forced people to communicate with the national government by going through provincial governments.

The restrictions and strict adherence to Arab culture, especially in the Arabian Peninsula, are due to bedouin customs. Most of the people of Saudi Arabia are bedouin, and the King belongs to one of the largest Arabian tribes. Thus, bedouin and Arabian culture affected communication techniques used by the government of King Abdulaziz.

Radio, television, and even newspapers were unknown in the Arabian Peninsula when King Abdulaziz began to govern Najid province and first addressed the people of Saudi Arabia. Abdulaziz often spoke to people in a general meeting in his *majlis* and let these people diffuse his messages around the country. He discussed his country's domestic affairs, foreign affairs, world events, and most other issues during speeches to his people.

Abdulaziz's speaking ability was one of his most important assets. When he faced a problem that required a difficult decision, he used his public-speaking skills to convince his opponents or those suspicious of his stand. He learned public speaking through intuition, not through formal education.

Communication innovations, among Ibn Saud's major interests, were adopted throughout the country despite strong opposition from both traditionalists and some religious leaders. During this period of change, Saudi society was closed and unwilling to adopt new ideas from the outside world, especially from the West. The nation's culture played a major role in shaping this kind of behavior toward outsiders.

After the conquest of Hejaz province, King Abdulaziz found that the Hejazi people were familiar with the press. This new instrument of communication sparked his interest in the media. Use of the media became a necessity for several reasons, including the country's size and the diversity of its population.

Only after World War I did the people of Saudi Arabia witness such innovations as the automobile, the airplane, and wireless technology. The first car arrived in Riyadh in 1924. Interest in these new innovations awakened Abdulaziz to the benefits and advantages of their use in peace and war. To pave the way for their use, Abdulaziz had to convince conservative theologians and some religious people. Appeals of expediency proved effective (Armstrong, 1966, p. 103).

The year 1932 was a turning point both for Saudi Arabia and its nascent public relations field. That year, the many disparate tribes that lived on the Arab Peninsula officially formed the Kingdom of Saudi Arabia. Almost immediately, the founder of the new nation faced and began to tackle several problems, including communication with leaders in the widely separated cities of this sparsely populated country (Boyd, 1973). To dialogue with these leaders, Abdulaziz purchased a package of wireless radio-telephone equipment from Marconi representatives.

Although radio was by then several years old, it was seen as a radical innovation. In fact, radio was unacceptable to large numbers of Saudis, especially traditionalists and some religious leaders who perceived it as a work of the devil. This illustrated a feature of Arabian society that would dog many communication ventures through the 20th century: society revered the status quo and did not easily accept ideas from the outside.

According to Holden and Johns (1981, p. 103), some Saudi religious leaders sent emissaries to the radio stations immediately after they signed on in order to "trap" Satan on one of his visits. These leaders were motivated by a strong adherence to traditional religious practices, and a lack of experience with sophisticated new communication technologies.

One Saudi religious sect was particularly active in rejecting modern innovations such as cars, telegraph, telephone, and radio. This sect was comprised of the *ulama*, or "religious people," who fought newer means of communication (Abir, 1988, p. 21).

Some religious leaders threatened to revolt against Abdulaziz if he continued to follow the road to modernization. One of their demands was the destruction of all foreign inventions. Also, they accused him of abandoning the faith for which they fought. Armstrong wrote that they considered "telegraphs, telephones, wireless and such-like things were witchcraft and of the devil. They demanded that he enforce all the Wahabi rules in Hejaz, and that he abolish the taxes and destroy the foreign inventions" (Armstrong, 1966, p. 204).

Abdulaziz asked the religious leaders to establish a religious committee to reach decisions on the issues concerning them. The committee asked him to lift taxes and suggested that the wireless and telephones not be used. Ibn Saud obeyed their decision and dismantled the wireless station outside Medina city (Armstrong, 1966, p. 206). That was the first setback for the diffusion of innovations into Saudi Arabia. However, despite the traditionalists, the country continued to modernize.

Through persuasion and determination, Abdulaziz convinced religious leaders that the wireless, the telephone, and the motor car could be used to serve both religious purposes and the citizens of the country (*Arab News*, 1992). In doing so, he had to show that the Prophet had not necessarily forbidden such inventions. He persuaded the religious leaders to accept radio by broadcasting readings from the Koran. Hearing this, opponents concluded that no machine could be evil if it repeated the word of God (Howarth, 1964, p. 157). This persuasion technique was very effective. Abdulaziz then used other techniques, such as work with opinion leaders, to persuade some religious leaders and traditionalists to accept various innovations.

Later, King Abulaziz used logic to show opposition religious leaders that the new devices could serve Islam rather than harm it. He convinced them that radio could carry their messages effectively and quickly to teach people around the world about Islam and connect all Muslims to their leaders, especially in the country that hosts the two Holy places. According to Rogers' diffusion-of-innovation concept, traditionalists normally resist innovations. These people fear uncertainty and resist change (Rogers, 1983, p. 22).

The Arrival of Western Influence

Everything changed with the formation in 1935 of "Aramco," formally known as the Arabian-American Oil Company. The presence of foreigners in general, and Americans in particular, finally created a climate that fostered the acceptance of Western communication innovations. The story of Aramco has been told repeatedly. Americans entered Saudi Arabia in their search for oil. And when oil was discovered, Standard Oil of New Jersey, Standard Oil of California, and several other American oil companies formed a joint operating agreement with the Saudis. To secure this agreement, a corporate consortium, Aramco, was formed.

When Aramco started its work in Saudi Arabia, communication problems between Saudi Arabians and Americans began to materialize. They were not seen at first, when Aramco had used Western labor under the supervision of Americans. However, when Aramco began to expand dramatically in the late 1930s and was forced to hire local laborers to fill unskilled jobs, major difficulties were encountered. Aramco based many of the solutions on Western concepts and models. To a substantial degree, contact between Saudi and American employees motivated Aramco to end the isolation of the Saudi people from foreigners who worked in their country (Van der Muelin, 1957, p. 191).

The advent of Aramco marked the beginning of professional public relations in Saudi Arabia—and the increased embracing of Western techniques and innovations. Aramco established a Research Department to study the Saudi people, their language, their history, and the nation's social conditions. This information-gathering step was necessary to understand how to best communicate with the Saudi people. The department contacted specialists and created a library which included manuscripts and other necessary sources (Van der Meulin, 1957, p. 193).

The presence of Americans in Aramco promoted change in the Saudi society in the Eastern part of the country. The company, today controlled by Saudis, played a major role in introducing new communication ideas and still contributes such concepts. Its public relations department is one of the biggest within Saudi Arabian governmental agencies. It is considered to be a window for Saudi Arabia to the outside world.

Traveling outside Saudi Arabia helped Ibn Saud to explore new innovations in different settings. Through travel, one can observe others' new ideas or innovations and learn to modify them according to the needs of the society to which he or she belongs. In this way, culture and science are transferred from place to place. The concept of communication was of great concern to Abdulaziz when he traveled outside Saudi Arabia, partly because of the country's size.

The setbacks and resistance to modernization did not prevent the country from obtaining necessary instruments of technology. Modernization does not equal Westernization. This notion should be stressed in undermining objections to the use of new technology, especially objections to new communication technology. Saudi Arabia today is an important example of large-scale, rapid adoption and of the use of most new technologies as soon as they become available.

Both public relations and advertising agencies have also been established rapidly in Saudi Arabia. A few years ago, there were few such agencies. However, they grew to take advantage of the advanced technology used in modern communication.

ROLE MODELS IN PUBLIC RELATIONS

Practitioners define their jobs and standards in various ways described in part by various researchers such as Grunig and Hunt (1984), and Broom and Dozier (1986). These scholars' models have been used widely in attempts to define the field.

Beginning in the 1990s, scholars began examining the applicability of Western models to countries and backgrounds alien to those in which the models were developed (Chen, 1992). This researcher extended that analysis to Saudi practitioners.

Broom and Smith (1979) were among the first to recognize the need for a research-based model of public relations roles. Beginning in the 1970s, Broom and his colleagues developed a role typology (Piekos, 1990).

Broom's early research focused on four primary roles: expert prescriber, communication facilitator, problem solving process facilitator, and communication technician (Broom & Dozier, 1986, pp. 37–59). Defined more fully elsewhere in this volume, these roles have been discussed widely. Research has shown that the first three listed above were really aspects of one role called communication manager (Reagan, Anderson, Sumner, & Hill, 1990).

Public Relations and the Saudi Government

Public relations is an important element in implementing government policy. As relations between the different sectors of the government and the various publics become more complex, it is necessary to create a good climate for communication. Publics are affected by government decisions and vice versa, and those who support government or grant it legitimacy must grasp these relationships.

Good information is a critical input factor. According to Bennis, "In a world of growing complexity, leaders are increasingly dependent on their subordinates for good information, whether the leader wants to hear it or not. Followers who tell the truth and leaders who listen to it are an unbeatable combination" (as cited in Wilcox, Ault, & Agee, 1992, p. 372).

Governments must win public support by influencing public opinion. Hiebert (1991) pointed out that political leaders today use public communication and public relations to do just that—inform, influence, change, or at least neutralize public opinion. He added that in Operation Desert Storm, "the American government and its military fought the war for public support at home by using all the classic practices of public relations, including political strategies, media relations, community relations, employee relations and crisis management" (p. 108).

With the development of communication technology and a "world information order," developing nations find it impossible to keep a low profile regarding certain issues around the world. The spread of television and radio stations, combined with a vast number of inexpensive receivers, permit people everywhere on earth to obtain news regarding their country. Developing nations and their information ministries must counter many problems.

Public relations practitioners who communicate with a government are divided into two groups. One works for a corporation in presenting its point of view to the government. In some big corporations, sectors dealing with the government are called "public-affairs departments." The second group helps government agencies present their policies to internal and external publics.

Corporate lobbyists have become critical in influencing governments. A lobbyist is "a person acting for a special interest group who tries to influence the voting on legislation or the government administrators" (Wilcox et al., 1992, p. 375).

Lobbying techniques are used not only by Western governments, but by other nations as well. Some governments in the Middle East lobby influential opinion leaders, offering them certain privileges or giving them gifts to win their support. One important technique provides these opinion leaders access to decision making by building connections within the government to give them special treatment and prestige.

Targeting the outside world, embassies serve a public relations function in addition to their diplomatic tasks. Saudi Arabia has established a strong relationship with the United States hinging in part on issues such as oil, weapons procurement, and the Arab–Israeli conflict.

Saudi Arabia faces strong resistance every time it wants to buy weapons from the United States. This resistance is led by the pro-Israeli lobby in Congress and in the government. Saudi Arabia decided to use lobbying techniques to improve its relationship with Congress and influential leaders, and to present itself to the American public.

The need for lobbying in the United States became apparent as understanding of the American political system matured. In the past, most Arab leaders thought the U.S. president had the power to do everything. But they found that, despite the vital U.S. interest in the Arab world, American administrations could not resist the influence of Congress and were especially susceptible to lobbying on certain issues.

In 1984, Saudi Arabia appointed Prince Bandar Bin Sultan as its ambassador to the United States. His most important job has been to promote the Saudi point of view in the United States on every issue concerning his country. He helped create a favorable climate between the two nations and has become very influential with both Congress and the administration. Bandar also has spoken directly to the American people through the media to promote understanding between the two countries.

Public relations must be used in development projects in developing countries. In the last two decades, Saudi Arabia utilized its oil income and strategic positioning to develop. Derks (1979, pp. 26–28) described the importance of communication in this growth by saying, "As we learn about the Middle East—we will be staying in touch with all developments—we can be of assistance to many firms that do work in that part of the world."

Public relations in the Arab world became a field of research at the end of the 1970s. Several studies were conducted in Egypt from 1975 to 1980, Iraq in 1978, Sudan in 1979, and in the United Arab Emirates in 1984 (Hussein, Mohammed, & Harron, 1991). These studies found several common problems facing public relations in these societies. These problems include the lack of a public relations role at the top in organizations; a different definition of the duties of public relations than that used in the West; limited vision of public relations among organizations' employees, and a view of public relations activities as being secondary in importance; small budgets devoted to public relations; lack of public relations professionals and the undesignated choice of the employees; lack of research and a scientific plan to carry out public relations duties; interference between the public relations department and other departments, and an absence of coordination among departments; and lack of recognition of the public relations role by the top management of organizations (Hussein, 1991, p. 30).

A seminar on public relations held in 1981 at Yarmuk University in Jordan emphasized these conclusions about the practice of public relations in Arab countries (Hussein, et al., 1991, p. 32). To understand public relations, one must grasp its purpose, function, and roles. Such understanding apparently is lacking throughout the Middle East, including Saudi Arabia (Hussein et al., 1991, pp. 161–169).

Egypt is the biggest and most influential country in the Arab world. Its connection with Western concepts of communication is very deep. Because of the long foreign presence in Egypt, mass communication, and especially the printed press, developed earlier and more completely there than elsewhere in the region.

Despite growth of the private sector in Egypt, the perception of public relations there is still vague. There is a failure to distinguish between public relations and advertising, or to believe in the former at all. Local business people do not understand that a public image should coincide with reality. Also, Egyptian culture differs from the American and European approach to customers. Rada Research (Spiers, 1992), an Egyptian public relations agency, offers four types of public relations services to its clients. These include media relations, special events, clipping, and monitoring of Egyptian and Middle East media on matters concerning clients, and marketing support of public relations programs.

Nevertheless, new technology is not used effectively within public relations in Egypt (Spiers, 1992, p. 42). To contact the media in Egypt, one must meet journalists personally. Using a fax or telephone is useless in media relations. A practitioner must explain to reporters personally one's message and carry out a follow-up.

Al-Enad (1990) found that public relations is perceived as "general information" instead of public relations in the Arab world. He used this label due to political sensitivity about the word "public." In developing nations, public relations employees work largely as receptionists and/or communication agents. Al-Enad concluded that the function of public relations serves two goals: "to educate the public on the subject related to the client, and to publicize achievements of the client"(p. 24).

Ministries of information work to tell the people about government policies and educate them on subjects related to the government. They use publicity to strengthen the government's image and showcase its achievements. Opening ceremonies, visiting new projects, and attending social activities are examples of publicity used by information ministries.

Public Relations in Saudi Arabia

Saudi Arabia realizes the importance of public relations in disseminating information regarding its development and government activities to the outside world by using the media. Saudi Arabians recognize that, despite their development efforts, their country is viewed stereotypically in the West as an empty desert with oil, camels, and lazy millionaires.

According to Derks, the Saudi government spends huge sums on solar research, trying to diversify resources by building many petrochemical projects and dozens of water desalinization plants. Pointing to such activity, officials use public relations to reach both the American media and the Americans to build an impression of the Saudi people as friendly and their government as progressive. Derks (1979) added that they seem to have a friendly relationship with the American people.

Saudi Arabia contracted with former United Press International correspondent Crawford Cook and his firm in order to conduct a public relations campaign in the United States. The purpose of the campaign was "to sell the Saudis to the Americans." Cook pointed out that the Saudis were willing to make available all information regarding their development. The biggest challenge facing Cook was lifting the image of the Saudis in the eyes of the nation (Derks, 1979). He conducted a campaign to mobilize public and congressional opinion in favor of selling F-15 planes and other advanced weapons to the Saudis.

In a study of public relations practiced in Saudi organizations, Al-Hazmi (1990) found strong agreement among the public relations personnel that a professional public relations unit should be part of every government ministry. The role of public relations increased from 1977 to 1989 in Saudi organizations, Al-Hazmi reported, indicating that improving the image of the Saudi Kingdom is now a concern of ministries (Al-Hazmi, 1990, p. 153).

Al-Hazmi concluded that the definition of public relations is vague and depends on several factors. The size of its budget determines the nature of operations. Education contributes to the importance of public relations. And the top management of an agency decides what role public relations can play (Al-Hazmi, 1990, p. 157).

In a study of the use of research in public relations in Saudi governmental agencies, Hussein, Mohammed, and Harron (1991) found that most research (53%) concerned particular crises and not public relations as an ongoing profession. Thirty percent of related research was done by personnel within the organization, and 22% by outsiders. Face-to-face communication was the most common approach used within organizations, whereas the print media were used most often in commnicating with external publics.

Top managers of Saudi governmental agencies and people who work in public relations departments in the same agencies perceive public relations in almost the same way—as a propaganda function rather than as one that focuses on decision making and consultation. Regarding the role of public relations, Osman Al-Araby (1984, pp. 32, 99–100) found that there were three role perceptions among Saudi managers and three roles among practitioners. These roles were communication expert, which was dominant among the managers; problem solver, which was stressed by most practitioners; and program manager, perhaps created in response to cultural differences between Saudi Arabia and the West.

In a study of public relations values in Saudi Arabia, Al-Enad (1990) divided models of public relations into three categories: organizational public relations (OPR), responsible public relations (RPR), and balanced public relations (BPR). The three categories were defined according to the priority of interest that public relations serves. The OPR considers the interest of the organization first, RPR regards the public interest as its top priority, and the BPR tries to serve the interests of both the public and the organization. Al-Enad (1992) found that the BPR approach was used most frequently, with 79.6% of respondents reporting a primary focus on both public and organizational interest in their performance of public relations.

In his study, Sieny (1979) reported that all 24 ministries analyzed practiced some public relations. The ministries reported a mix of local and international targets for their efforts, with targets depending on the nature of the ministry. For example, the Ministry of Pilgrimages has an international target.

The several studies of public relations in Saudi Arabia support several conclusions. Misunderstanding of the meaning of public relations is widespread, expertise and training are lacking, and limited financial resources are devoted to public relations departments. However, recent studies have suggested that the field is growing.

Broom and Smith's (1979) classic study of public relations roles found four models. Later, Culbertson (1985), Reagan and his colleagues (1990), and Stone (1990) found only two roles, technician and manager. They argued that managers sometimes play all three managerial subroles mentioned by Broom and Dozier (1986); expert prescriber, communication facilitator, and problem solving process facilitator. Reagan, et al. (1990) went on to stress that difficulty in distinguishing among the three managerial subroles might come in part from a lack of rigorous definition in the original research.

The four roles played by public relations practitioners are not clearly defined specialties. Broom and Dozier (1986) found that many, if not most, practitioners play all four roles in varying degrees.

Whether these conditions prevail in Saudi Arabia has remained uncertain because of the shortage of literature devoted to the field in that country. This researcher's study, described later, helps remove much of this uncertainty.

Saudi Arabian Public Relations Today

My 1992 study explored the following research questions: (1) Is there a dominant public relations role model among Saudi Arabian public relations employees in government ministries, general organizations, or companies? (2) Are there major differences in the practice of public relations among government ministries, general government organizations, and government companies? (3) What are the primary targets of public relations efforts in Saudi Arabia? and (4) What general procedural and theoretical differences are apparent when targeting Saudi as compared with non-Saudi audiences?

Respondents were asked to complete Broom's self-administered questionnaire, acquired through personal contact with Broom. Some changes were made for appropriateness to the Saudi setting.

The sample of 319 practitioners was drawn from government public relations employees working in all 21 government ministries, 34 government public agencies and 6 government companies. Of these, 228 responded, for a 71% return rate. These ministries and agencies are located in the nation's three major cities—Riyadh, Jeddah, and Dammam. The list of public relations employees was compiled through a "snow-ball" technique, with initial respondents identifying later ones because there was no available list of government public relations employees in Saudi Arabia.

Findings and Conclusions

The findings from this exploratory study of public relations in Saudi Arabia supported several important conclusions discussed in the following paragraphs.

There seems to be no single dominant public relations role in Saudi public organizations, although communication technicians are somewhat more common than are practitioners of other roles.

Differences were found in the practice of public relations among government organization types, but these differences were not necessarily large or important.

Saudi Ministries, internal departments, and other organizations commanded the greatest public relations resources, whereas Saudi nongovernment organizations ranked lower, and non-Saudi targets remained minor in use of resources despite the importance of the country in the Islamic and resource-producing world. This importance is derived from the presence of the two Holy places (Mecca and Medina) and the huge production and reserves of oil.

Saudi and non-Saudi targets were approached differently. Organizations relied primarily on Saudi staff with domestic experience and on internal public relations departments when investigating and developing strategies to communicate with Saudi targets. However, when targeting non-Saudi audiences, hiring non-Saudi practitioners and relying on non-Saudi staff with international experience were the preferred paths. Such tendencies were not universal, however.

Education level, crucial in public relations, showed encouraging results. Appropriate education allows practitioners to perform their jobs effectively. Although some respondents reported having earned less than a college degree, this was not necessarily a bad sign for two reasons. First, mass higher education is a relatively recent phenomenon in Saudi Arabia, so it is not surprising that most of the older employees have not attended college. Second, most respondents with lower educational attainment have solid experience in the field.

Around 10.5% of public relations employees reported having graduate-level education, an encouraging finding in this relatively new profession. Further, education level correlated positively and significantly with emphasis on all four roles proposed by Broom.

Public relations was the most often-reported college major among respondents, followed by general communication. Decision makers and organizational leaders have determined that an educational background in public relations or communication is essential to efficient practice of the profession. Public relations and communication majors were first offered at Saudi universities in the early 1970s. That the professional practice developed so rapidly after its academic introduction indicates that public relations has good prospects in Saudi Arabia.

Most respondents reported that their organizations offer in-service training, indicating that they recognize the need for it and are willing to address it. One fourth reported that training is offered constantly, and three fourths said it is available sometimes. Over 90% stated that more training is needed. In declining order of importance, areas requiring further training are campaign management, research, media relations, and crisis management. Special events and speech writing were also mentioned as areas in which practitioners needed more training than they were typically receiving. The prominence of campaign management and crisis management may be due in part to the 1990 Gulf Crisis, which awakened practitioners to their importance.

A plurality of respondents were in Civil Service ranks 6 to 8, followed by the Civil Service rank 9 and above (on a scale where a Civil Service rank of 15 is of deputy-minister level). This indicates the relatively high professional recognition accorded to practitioners in government institutions.

The number of employees gives an indication to the organization's recognition of public relations. The more employees there are in an organization, the more recognition public relations appears to be given. Among respondents, 22.4% reported that their employing organizations have one to five public relations employees whereas 52.7% report having from 6 to 15, and 20.4% more than 16. Organizations reporting the greatest number of public relations employees were most closely tied to international business enterprises such as the oil giant Aramco.

In the West, media experience can influence the efficiency or success of a public relations effort. In contrast, two thirds of the Saudi public relations respondents reported that they had never worked with the media. However, because the government agencies and the media are government-controlled, they share the same underlying mission. Thus, there is little or no conflict between them, and media experience is not necessarily needed to avoid dissension.

Seventy-nine percent of the respondents reported having worked in public relations from 1 to 10 years, and 20% for 11 or more years. Thus, only 20% of respondents reported long experience in the field. This indicates a lack of experience among many practitioners, but it also suggests that the field is growing rapidly. A large majority (88%) reported that they had worked with only one organization, their current one. This indicates that few public relations practitioners have experienced much diversity in their careers, perhaps limiting their flexibility in facing new situations.

Most respondents reported working in organizations that were either less centralized or not centralized at all. Most also worked in small public relations departments with 5 or fewer employees. This later finding might indicate a relatively small role for public relations in decision making. However, almost half of all respondents reported being consulted at least some of the time when decisions were being made. Significantly, more than half reported their advice was followed more often than not. Practitioners, then, were not always brought into the decision making process. But when they were, their advice tended to be taken seriously.

Public relations departments hire domestic Saudi employees in seeking information when their primary target is a Saudi Arabian audience. The organization's public relations department is the second most important information source when Saudi audiences are targeted. This is a good sign for public relations in Saudi Arabia as it indicates recognition of the field by government organizations.

When organizations seek information about non-Saudi audiences, they most often hire a public relations firm in the targeted country, indicating the importance given to public relations outside the country. The second most common approach is to hire non-Saudi public relations personnel, followed by hiring non-Saudi staff with international expertise, holding information and training seminars, and seeking cooperation from outside organizations.

No single role was clearly dominant in Saudi public relations, but all four roles were practiced to some degree. Exploratory factor analysis revealed five factors, but limiting the solution to two factors revealed two roles—managerial and technical—similar to those found in American research. These roles had not previously been examined.

Finally, public relations in Saudi Arabia remains a male-dominated field. Only three of the 228 respondents were females, with only 26 female employees being reported in all of the respondents' organizations.

CONCLUSION

Public relations, developed in the West, is based upon certain assumptions about behavior and cultural understanding. Saudi Arabia is not a Western country; it is different from the West in many ways. It is not surprising, then, that such concepts as Broom's role-models theory, developed in the West, do not perfectly explain the profession as it is practiced in Saudi Arabia. Still, Broom's models provide a useful general analytical tool applicable across cultures.

The applicability of theories and descriptive models across cultures is not in dispute. The tendency is to develop a general model with wide applicability, yet one that is also specific enough to have meaning. The major question in this research, then, is not whether Broom's model can be applied to the Saudi case, but whether the Saudi case fits the general model. For if it fits the model, then the model is strengthened.

This research found that public relations in Saudi Arabia is now practiced in varied roles and with some sophistication. Araby's 1984 study found that public relations was regarded as a weak profession that did little but generate publicity. The present research indicates that the field is now considered to be a powerful and useful management tool, often with a permanent place in organizational decision making processes. In addition, the advice of public relations departments and employees is often sought and, when sought, it is almost always listened to. Often, in some areas around the world, organizations ask for information and then turn a deaf ear.

Araby (1984, p. 99) reported that the primary roles practiced were publicist–

journalist and media specialist, whereas the current study found that all four of Broom's major role models—expert prescriber, communication technician, communication facilitator, and problem solving process facilitator—are now important and widespread in their application, despite overlaps. Overlaps may suggest another role that has not yet been identified. However, the four models tend to fit Saudi public relations to a degree.

Why were there such differences between the 1992 findings reported here, and the study conducted by Araby? The passage of time may help explain these differences. In 1984, public relations was a younger, less mature, and less advanced field than in 1993. In addition, the larger sample size in the present research may permit more finely tuned analysis. Accuracy, validity, and reliability were improved, and recency of completion adds relevance to the study.

This illustrates the need to update scholarly knowledge regularly on growing fields such as public relations. This is particularly true in Saudi Arabia, where little still is known about the field. Providing more accurate information and adding to the existing knowledge base, as limited as it might be, were goals of the 1992 study.

More work needs to be done. Yet, the study of public relations in the Middle East is important. Such research can have immense practical implications as the Western world and the Arab nations move toward a closer partnership in the years ahead.

REFERENCES

Abir, M. (1988). *Saudi Arabia in the oil era: Regime and elites: Conflict and collaboration.* Boulder, CO: Westview.

Al-Enad, A. (1990, Spring). Public relations roles in developing countries. *Public Relations Quarterly, 35,* 24–26.

Al-Hazmi, W. (1990). *The development of public relations in Saudi Arabia.* Unpublished doctoral dissertation, Wayne State University, Detroit, MI.

Al-Odadi, M. (1992, September). Poetry as a weapon: Saudi poems in the Gulf War. *Al-Mubtaath, 138,* 33–35.

Al-Tohami, M., & Al-Dakoki, I. (1980). *Principles of public relations in the developing nations.* Beruit: Da Alama'arefa.

Arab News, September 23, 1992. p. 9.

Araby, O. (1984). *Perception of the public relations profession among top managers of Saudi Arabian governmental organizations and its effects on the role of public relations.* Unpublished master's thesis, University of Colorado, Boulder.

Armstrong, H. C. (1966). *Lord of Arabia, Ibn Saud: An intimate study of a king.* Beirut: Khayat.

Boyd, D. (1973). The story of radio in Saudia Arabia. *Public Telecommunication Review, 1,* 53–60.

Broom, G. M., & Dozier, D. M. (1986). Advancement for public relations role models. *Public Relations Review, 12,* 37–59.

Broom, G., & Smith, G. (1979). Testing the pratitioner's impact on clients. *Public Relations Review, 5,* 47–59.

Chen, N. (1992). *Public relations in China: The introduction and development of an occupational field.* Unpublished doctoral dissertation, Ohio University, Athens, Ohio.

Culbertson, H. (1985). Practitioner roles: Their meaning for educators. *Public Relations Review, 11,* 5–21.
Derks, S. (1979, March). Selling the Saudis from South Carolina. *The South Magazine,* pp. 26–28.
Fakhri, S. J., Alsheekley, A. A., & Zalzala, F. S. (1980). *Public relations.* Baghdad: N.P.
Glubb, J. B. (1987). *A short history of the Arab people.* London: Quartet Books.
Grunig, J., & Hunt, T. (1984). *Managing public relations.* New York: Holt, Rinehart & Winston.
Hiebert, E. R. (1991). Public relations as a weapon of modern warfare. *Public Relations Review, 17,* 107–116.
Holden, D., & Johns, R. (1981). *The house of Ibn Saud: The rise of the most powerful dynasty in the Arab world.* New York: Holt, Rinehart & Winston.
Howarth, D. (1964). *The desert king: Ibn Saud and his Arabia.* New York: McGraw-Hill.
Hussein, S., Mohammed, K., & Harron, R. (1991). *The public relations departments in the governmental organizations in the Kingdom of Saudi Arabia.* Riyadh: Public Administration Institute, pp. 186–191.
Mansfield, P. (1981). *The new Arabians.* New York: J. G. Ferguson.
Nolte, L. (1979). *Fundamentals of public relations, professional guidelines, concepts and integrations.* New York: Pergamon Press.
Piekos, J. M. (1990). Roles and program evaluation techniques among Canadian public relations practitioners. *Public Relations Research Annual, 2,* 97.
Reagan, J., Anderson, R., Sumner, J., & Hill, S. (1990). A factor analysis of Broom and Smith's public relations roles scale. *Journalism Quarterly, 67,* 177–183.
Rogers, E. M. (1983). *Diffusion of innovations.* New York: The Free Press.
Sieny, S. (1979). *Public relations activities carried out by the government of Saudi Arabia.* Unpublished master's thesis, California State University, Chico.
Spiers, P. (1992, February). Public relations in Egypt and the Middle East. *Communication World,* p. 42.
Stone, D. (1990). *The value of veracity in public relations.* Unpublished doctoral dissertation. Ohio University, Athens.
Van der Meulin, D. (1957). *The wells of Ibn Saud.* New York: Praeger.
Wilcox, D., Ault, P., & Agee, W. (Eds.). (1992). *Public relations: Strategies and tactics.* New York: Harper-Collins.

14 Elections and Earth Matters: Public Relations in Costa Rica

Hernando González
Desireé Akel
Florida International University

ECO-TOURISM AND PUBLIC RELATIONS

The green iguana scurrying at the river's edge may not know it, along with the morpho butterfly gliding lazily on its foot-wide blue wings, or the keel-billed toucan calling noisily to its mate, but keeping their habitat in the rain forest may be due, in part, to public relations inside and outside Costa Rica.

The effort to save the environment is not over yet, as deforestation continues, but for the moment, some of the rain forest may have won a reprieve. In recent years, government and private organizations have teamed up in saving the wilderness and its creatures for generations to come. The key to this effort is called eco-tourism, and Costa Rica is showing its neighbors how to make the rain forest pay without destroying it in the process (Boza, 1992; Perez, 1994).

Outside Costa Rica, international environmental organizations, such as Nature Conservancy, the World Fund for Flora and Fauna, and the World Wildlife Fund, have purchased some of the country's external debt from foreign banks at about one fifth their face value, using funds these organizations have raised from public information campaigns in the United States and elsewhere.

In turn, the Costa Rican government buys this debt with short-term bonds, with the stipulation that the money be used for conservation. More than $40 million has been raised in this innovative "debt for nature" arrangement (Barry, 1991, p. 123).

Inside Costa Rica, government agencies have launched educational campaigns on sustainable growth, and instituted what many consider "the most progressive park system" in the Americas. Also, the government has trained residents living near these forests as park rangers and tour guides, providing them with an alternative means of livelihood while conserving nature (Instituto Costarricense de Acueductos y Alcantrillados, 1994; Instituto Costarricense de Turismo, 1993c; Keller, Brosnahan, & Rachowiecki, 1992).

The results appear to be encouraging. Eco-tourism has risen dramatically over the last few years. There is a chance that Costa Rica, unlike most of Latin America, may keep its rain forest and make a living from it, too.

In 1993, tourism finally became the top dollar earner for Costa Rica with $577 million in revenues, overtaking bananas, its former export leader, by $46 million (Moncreiff, Clark, & Henriquez, 1994). As the government had predicted, it was only a matter of time before tourism earned more than any of Costa Rica's traditional agricultural exports (Comisión de la Comunidad Europea y el Instituto Costarricense de Turismo, 1993).

A RICH, PROUD HISTORY

Quiet, Effective Public Service

Costa Rica has always done things a bit differently, often in a quiet way. During the 1970s and the 1980s, it came very close to the edge, with war and revolution in Central America. Among others, Sandinistas and Contras in Nicaragua ventured into its territory at different points in time, threatening to sweep the oldest democracy in Latin America into the conflict (LaFeber, 1993). The weight of Costa Rica's international debt in the early 1980s also made it vulnerable to outside pressure.

Having abolished its army as a matter of national policy in 1949, Costa Rica apppeared to have little protection against the violence that pervaded its neighbors (Melendez, 1991; Rojas, et al., 1989). At least, this held until the country decided to use reason and diplomacy, consistent with its reputation as "the Switzerland of Latin America." Oscar Arias, who was president at the time, proposed a bold peace plan calling for the withdrawal of all foreign military advisers, a ceasefire and negotiations among the warring parties, and free elections, over the objections of some countries outside the region who had a stake in the outcome. The peace plan eventually became a reality, leading to electoral transition in Nicaragua and to ceasefire and peace talks elsewhere. In 1987, Arias won the Nobel peace prize for his efforts (Black, 1988; Krauss, 1991).

Democracy and a market economy have made Costa Rica a model of development in Central America. Its equitable social policies have contributed to internal stability, which has encouraged, in turn, business and investment from both local and foreign sources. Without an army to support, Costa Rica has invested in its people instead. It spends about 23% of its national budget on education, a record for Latin America. As a result, it has 93% literacy, one of the highest rates in the world

The availability of safe drinking water in Costa Rica ranks third to the U.S. and Canada, and infant malnutrition is the lowest in the whole continent (Comisión de la Comunidad Europea y el Instituto Costarricense de Turismo, 1993; Mata, 1994). Costa Rica has national health insurance and virtually free medical care. It has one of the lowest infant mortality rates in the world. The government finances or subsidizes various universities, and recently invested in computers in public schools.

In 1993, the economy grew by more than 6%, exports by 17%, while single-digit inflation maintained the standard of living as the highest in the region for its population of about 3 million (McPhaul, 1994). All this Costa Rica has achieved without giving up on democracy or human rights. Other countries in the region looking for alternative models of development may not have noticed Costa Rica in the past, with its self-effacing ways, but it provides stark contrast to Cuba, with its failed socialist experiment (Soto, 1987; Zeledon, 1987).

The end of the Cold War has opened new space for democracy and economic development in Latin America. The fall of the Soviet Union and its Eastern European allies has made politics and ideology less central and confrontational (Castañeda, 1993; Smith, DeGeorge, & Pearson, 1992).

A PANEL OF PRACTITIONERS AND JOURNALISTS

In Costa Rica, we asked a panel of 14 public relations practitioners in government, private industry, and education how they expected public relations to contribute to future economic growth and what was needed to improve the profession. Nearly half of these respondents were women. All had management positions and had worked an average of about 10 years in public relations, with experience ranging between 3 and 24 years.

Also interviewed were all the the public relations sequence chairs in the four universities offering public relations at the bachelor's level. Respondents were selected based on a listing of media industries in Costa Rica compiled by the Latin American Journalism Program (LAJP) in the School of Journalism and Mass Communication at Florida International University. With an outreach office in San José, Costa Rica, LAJP has the most extensive training program anywhere for professional journalists in Central America (Programa Centroamericano de Periodismo, 1993; Programa Latinoamericano de Periodismo, 1994).

We also asked eight print and broadcast journalists in Costa Rica to comment on media relations with public relations practitioners. Their views are presented later in this chapter. Both groups responded to a standardized questionnaire, based in part on suggestions and previous work by Professors Hugh M. Culbertson (Culbertson, Jeffers, Stone, & Terrell, 1993) and Ni Chen on culture and the social structure. All respondents were assured of anonymity to enable them to speak freely about the government and the practice of journalism and public relations without compromising their present work. They were interviewed between 1993 and 1994.

The public relations panel perceived that the end of the Cold War has helped in the rapid recovery of the economy in Costa Rica over the last few years by providing, in part, a measure of government stability and business certainty in the region. Warring parties in neighboring countries have laid down their arms and are now competing for elective office. On the other hand, panelists felt that the effect of those factors on the practice of public relations in Costa Rica was indirect and may require some lead time.

POLITICS AND PUBLIC RELATIONS

The Role of Electoral Politics

More than any other event, according to the public relations panel, the presidential elections every 4 years dramatize the use of public relations in Costa Rica. In 1994, the two leading parties used U.S.-style campaigning, combining public relations and marketing communication tools in presenting their candidates and contrasting them with the opposition.

The National Liberation Party candidate was Jose María Figueres, former agricultural minister and son of the president who abolished Costa Rica's army. Figueres is a West Point graduate and has a master's degree from Harvard's Kennedy School of Government. The Social Christian Unity Party's candidate was Miguel Angel Rodriguez, former congressman and successful businessman, with a doctorate in economics from the University of California at Berkeley.

As in previous years, this campaign was punctuated by media events such as effusive rallies, colorful motorcades, and party flagwaving, as well as advertising and mudslinging. Charges ranged from cattle rustling to exporting tainted beef and even murder. As in U.S. elections, the negative campaigning tended to shift public attention from the real differences between the candidates from time to time, with Rodriguez supporting a more open economy, including the privatization of the national banking system, and Figueres running on a more cautious platform of state-guided development (Darenblum, 1994; McPhaul, 1994).

Figueres won by a slight margin, receiving about 52% of the vote. He said he viewed the state not as an obstacle, but "an instrument to modernization and social development" (Servicios Cablegráficos Combinados, 1994, p. 4A). Rodriguez readily conceded the vote after the results were announced, and unlike with many other countries in the hemisphere, Costa Rica went back to work the following day. There was no fear of violence or even a hint of reprisal among the losers. After all, at least one presidential candidate in the past had to run twice before finally taking office, so there was always another chance.

According to the general manager of a public relations firm:

In Costa Rica, public relations is dramatized in very real terms every 4 years. Political parties identify their objectives, and try to achieve them by using a variety of means with a single-mindedness that is somewhat surprising because it is so out of the ordinary. Once the political line has been determined, all campaign workers try to work toward the same enterprise.

Similarly, the public relations chair of a national association observed that political parties seem to use public relations mainly during elections, when they have to create and maintain a certain image for their candidates. But after the votes are counted, all parties, including the winners, seem to lose interest in public relations.

"Unlike in the U.S., political parties in Costa Rica seem to hibernate after the presidential elections," the public relations director of a government agency observed. "The parties that lost the elections are rarely heard from, except through their representatives in the legislature." She added that "This is not necessarily bad, as it lessens politicking in the conduct of government."

"During the campaign, the party in power sometimes calls on the public information offices of all government agencies to help elect its official candidate, raising questions of impropriety," according to the president of a public relations company. He also expressed "doubts about the legality of this practice, which may put the opposition at considerable disadvantage."

The use of public relations during election campaigns appears to have intensified in recent years, a government public relations manager said. He added that the campaigns provide a good number of professionals with work, but they also bring in foreign consultants, who apparently are more familiar with the newest techniques in political campaigns. But this strategy has negative consequences as well. Sometimes, foreign consultants are not as familiar with local conditions or how the mass media work and could make serious mistakes. Political parties still have to find the right balance between local know-how and foreign expertise.

Another government public relations manager said that foreign consultants seem to have contributed to hotter political campaigns in recent years. They use the newest persuasion techniques in the U.S., including negative campaigning. The other parties have no recourse but to call in foreign consultants of their own.

Freedom of Expression

The panel agreed that freedom of expression in Costa Rica has a positive influence on public relations. It enables practitioners to practice the profession openly, and to participate meaningfully in the sharing of opinion and information. Commitment to the truth also lends professionals some prestige and credibility. However, as in other Western democracies, free expression is not absolute. Practitioners need to know the limits, such as good taste, fair play, and decency.

Certain regulations are necessary to prevent abuse, the director of a government press office said. "Some people and organizations may misinterpret freedom of expression with disrespect for the law, as happens from time to time with suggestive sexual advertising."

The ownership of the mass media may also limit free expression to some extent, according to the general manager of a public relations firm. She said that, at the interpersonal level, one can say whatever one wants to. "But at the mass communication level, the media function as gatekeepers. For example, if the content of your message does not coincide with the interests of the owners, you may be denied access to that medium."

Some panelists pointed out that shareholders of some leading newspapers are identified with one or another political party. To some extent, this partisanship applies to the other media as well. As a result, each medium takes on a different "political color."

A government public relations manager said that this type of partisanship "has affected public relations efforts in terms of news coverage and opinion, since these media may want to create and maintain the desired image of the political parties and the candidates that they support."

Similarly, a manager of a public relations firm noted that the press is independent of the government and may be considered the fourth estate. However, the partisanship of media owners with one or the other political party "sometimes blurs the separation between these institutions."

Government Control

The panel agreed that government control is absent for the most part, allowing the practice of public relations with minimal constraint. The one exception is Law 4420 (later revised by Law 5050) which established a "College of Journalists" in 1969. Unlike the U.S., only journalists who are members of this professional association can work in the media. Public relations practitioners also qualify for membership, *not* as journalists, but as public relations professionals.

A blurring of the boundaries between the two professions occurs in Article 24, which says that *only journalists* who are members of the college "can assume the office of the director or chief of public relations in government institutions." In other words, unless public relations practitioners have previously worked as journalists, they cannot head offices with public relations functions in government agencies. This restriction does not apply to private companies, however.

Panelists want this restriction lifted for a number of reasons. They said that it unfairly discriminates against those who have worked only in the public relations field. "If one is a good journalist, it does not necessarily mean that she or he will be a good public relations professional," according to the public relations manager of a government agency. "While public relations involves certain journalistic functions, the profession requires more than a sense of what's news, or editing and writing ability. The planning, implementation, and evaluation of campaigns are normally considered outside of journalism."

A public relations manager at a private company observed that journalism usually involves one-way communication, while public relations is primarily interested in two-way communication. The response to the message or the campaign is as important to the practitioner as the process of information dissemination. Journalists are not necessarily trained in two-way communication.

According to a public relations manager of a government agency: It appears that no administration in Costa Rica has ever understood what public relations is all about. Consequently, the government has no plans for its development outside of the College of Journalists. Naming their journalist friends to public relations offices in government agencies does not necessarily solve the problems of communication. This policy is not only unwise but it has wide-ranging negative implications—even strategic ones. For example, a good journalist could be a bad manager of public information campaigns.

A university public relations professor said that "Politicians often use government public relations positions to reward journalists who helped them during the political campaign. As a result, their careers as public relations managers are coterminous with any change of administration."

Other panelists working for the government appeared to be more optimistic about the prospect of change. They see some improvement in qualifications among recent appointments in government public relations positions.

Interestingly, practitioners look toward the government to help develop the profession. Over the last few years, some panelists have been lobbying for new legislation to create a "College of Communicators" where journalists, public relations practitioners, advertising professionals, and others working in the field of communication would have their place. A group of public relations practitioners have submitted a formal proposal to the legislature, where interest in creating a new professional association appears to be low at the moment. In addition, the existence in Costa Rica of an independent association of advertising agencies, which regulates its members through its own code of ethics, may have watered down the demand for a more encompassing professional college.

In May 1995, the Costa Rican Supreme Court ruled that licensing by the College of Journalists was unconstitutional. It declared that Article 22 of the 1969 law, which required all journalists to join the guild, violated Article 13 of the American Convention on Human Rights. The court said that the international accord, which defines a broad right to "seek, receive and impart information and ideas," takes precedence over local law.

The mandatory licensing rule was originally adopted to help improve the quality of journalism by limiting the professional gathering and reporting of news only to university journalism school graduates licensed by the guild. In a country with an exemplary human rights record, the College of Journalists has used its authority sparingly to seek the prosecution of unlicensed journalists over the years. The present ruling was handed down when the government asked the Surpreme Court to rule on the conviction of U.S. journalist Stephen Schmidt, a reporter in the English-language *Tico Times,* who received a one-year suspended sentence in 1985 for practicing journalism without a license. The Inter-American Court of Human Rights, an agency of the Organization of American States based in San José, Costa Rica, found unanimously that the licensing law under which Schmidt was convicted violated the American Convention on Human Rights. Until now, successive governments in Costa Rica have ignored the ruling.

Eduardo Ulibarri, editor in chief of *La Nación,* said that competition for jobs will improve the quality of journalism. On the other hand, supporters of the mandatory licensing law predicted an erosion of journalism standards by opening the field to people other than journalism school graduates licensed by the College of Journalists (McPhaul, 1995, p. 14A).

The Supreme Court ruling, which enables anyone to practice journalism, has implications for public relations as well. By making membership in the College of Journalists optional, public relations practitioners may no longer have to lobby for an expanded College of Communicators, which includes journalists, public relations practitioners and advertising professionals. What the ruling means to the communication industry will have to be sorted out within the next few years.

PUBLIC RELATIONS: ITS EVOLUTION AND POSTURE

Manager or Technician?

Although panelists conceded that practitioners could assume both management and technician roles, they regarded the majority of public relations professionals in the country as technicians. Strategic decisionmaking is still a management prerogative, although a few public relations managers are allowed a certain measure of autonomy.

An executive at a public relations firm observed that, although many practitioners maintain good communication with upper management, she did not know of anyone at this level with a public relations portfolio. "At present, practitioners are not part of the dominant coalition, either in government or private industry. They usually follow the overall plans laid down by management but do not take part at this level of decision making."

A university professor in public relations said practitioners with management roles are extremely uncommon. "On the other hand, the very few professionals with management functions prove that practitioners can assume these positions," he added.

Some government public relations managers interviewed in this study appeared to be involved in strategic planning and decision making within their agencies. An example is the Defenders of Water Youth Club (Club Infantil Defensores del Agua), an ecology-oriented association for young school children with chapters around the country. The project began in 1993 at the initiative of the water authority and the support of private industry, as part of a public relations campaign on the conservation ethic. Activities of the club include contests, field trips and lessons on the value of the environment (Instituto Costarricense de Acueductos y Alcantrillados, 1994).

Foreign Influence

Foreign consultants are brought in mainly by political parties from time to time, however, direct foreign influence on the public relations industry appears to be minimal. "These consultants have more credibility with political parties than local know-how, but the limited amount of time that they spend in Costa Rica during election campaigns does not usually allow for a professional exchange of ideas," a public relations manager at a government agency said.

Instead, public relations is *indirectly* affected by textbooks from abroad and by multinationals in Costa Rica, such as Coca-Cola and McDonald's. Most textbooks used for reference by university public relations faculty come from the U.S., but also from other Spanish-speaking countries, including Argentina, Mexico, Spain, and Venezuela. This has led to industry practices modeled mainly after those in the U.S. Panel members said that U.S. influence on public relations could have been greater in Costa Rica, but language remains a barrier. Most students and faculty would prefer Spanish translations of current U.S. texts because public relations in the U.S. is widely perceived as being on the cutting edge. However, translations are few and far between.

The public relations manager of a national association said that nearly all source materials used at the college level, including reprints of articles, are foreign and do not necessarily reflect local conditions. Educators and practitioners have to make an effort to adapt these materials to their needs.

A government agency public relations manager said that she takes imported models and adapts them to the requirements of her institution. "The result is not always an exact fit," she noted, "but it's better than in the past, when some practitioners used these models without taking specific variables in a company or a situation into account."

A manager at a public relations firm said that "Some educators do not have sufficient preparation to localize foreign course materials. As a result, they produce students who know all about foreign social conditions and structures. However, these factors differ greatly from those shaping the conduct of business in Costa Rica."

A university professor in public relations said that "There are no local textbooks on public relations because practitioners lack sufficient credibility and cannot obtain financing for such a venture." He said that an international exchange program with public relations associations and universities could help professionalize the industry and lead to the development of learning materials. In collaboration with local practitioners, they could exert a positive influence in Costa Rica. At present, no practitioners appear to have trained or practiced professionally in the United States.

Formal Education

Four universities offer public relations degrees at the licienciatura level, which is equivalent to a bachelor's degree in the United States. They are the Universidad de Costa Rica, Universidad Autónoma de Centro América, Universidad Latina, and Universidad Panamericana.

Qualifications for teaching public relations differ from one university to the next, but educators are usually expected to have a licienciatura, preferably in public relations, in order to teach at that level, as well as membership in the professional College of Journalists and several years of experience in the field.

The porous boundaries between journalism and public relations as defined in the law that established the College of Journalists means that journalists can also teach public relations. In addition, a number of journalists practice both professions at the same time and do not necessarily see a conflict of interest.

Inadequate textbooks and insufficient academic preparation of educators appear to be among the major obstacles to the practice of public relations. A government-agency public relations manager noted that "universities are now revising their curriculum requirements based on the perceived needs of the industry, which they failed to respond to in the past." A university professor in public relations said that educators need additional training, and this can only come from abroad.

In an attempt to enhance the profession, two public relations associations have recently been established along university lines. Faculty and graduates of the public relations program at the state university (Universidad de Costa Rica) comprise one group, and graduates of the other universities make up the other public relations association. Both associations are actively recruiting members and in the process of organizing training seminars.

Although local universities offer advertising and marketing at the master's level, public relations is taught only at the licienciatura level, indicating a need to improve expertise in the field. The professor mentioned previously noted that his school is now exploring the possibility of an exchange program for students and faculty with a Florida university.

At least 70% of the students in public relations across all four universities are women. The industry is also dominated by women, although a sea change appears to have occurred recently as more male students choose public relations as a career. The manager of a public relations firm said that men are beginning to understand that public relations is not exclusively for women, and that "it is more than just looking good, smiling sweetly, and organizing fiestas." She added that "The taboo, that all male students in public relations are gay, is dead. After all, the public relations managers of government agencies are predominantly men." She explained that part of the misperception may have been rooted in machismo, an exaggerated view of manliness often found in Latin societies.

A university professor said that as the field changes, there is a need to train and hire practitioners on the basis not of gender, but of jobs available now and in the future. A government agency public relations director said that "As we leave the stereotyping of careers aside, it is important to remember that it is possible to have excellent public relations practice regardless of gender, based on the ability of each individual."

Panelists predicted that, in the near future, more corporations will include public relations functions among their activities, thus opening new job opportunities. But for now, employment is still limited and starting salaries are low. This slow development of public relations is part of the reason why a number of panelists expected a "lag time" between economic recovery and the return to peace in Central America as well as the end of the Cold War. "Public relations in private industry is still in diapers compared to that in government agencies," according to a public relations manager in a government agency. "But as the field becomes more professional in public institutions, particularly at the national level, private industry will certainly follow."

Multinationals in Costa Rica are also providing a good example. A number of companies have established corporate relations departments to carry out public relations functions. "In the past, some multinationals were confined to manufacturing in Costa Rica or had nearly complete control of the market, making public relations less of a priority," a manager at a public relations firm observed. "But as the economy opens up to more competition, these multinationals will find public relations a necessity," she added.

The growth of eco-tourism, including nature hikes, birdwatching, and white-water rafting, is also contributing to the growth of public relations as a profession.

Although Costa Rica is just about the size of West Virginia, it has more than 850 species of birds, a higher number than that found in the continents of North America, Europe, or Australia. It also has over 200 species of reptiles and another 200 species of mammals, drawing nature lovers from all over the world (Keller et al., 1992).

A government agency public relations manager said that "Hotels and related tourist services have to move beyond the present stage of naming friends and relatives to public relations jobs as the boom in tourism grows. The tourist industry requires more than dinners or social gatherings for public relations."

At the same time, public information campaigns on the sustainable use of natural resources, including the rain forest, will require competent professionals. New graduates in public relations require skills in planning, implementing, and evaluating public relations campaigns.

Four Models

Among the four models of public relations that Grunig and Hunt (1984) identified, panelists agreed that the two-way symmetric model was the ideal. However, feedback and interactivity as a regular part of the process are often considered unattainable, given the level of available resources (cf. González, 1989). Not surprisingly, the one-way press agent and public information models were the most common.

Feedback and interactivity are present quite rarely, and then only to a limited degree. Thus, even the best planned public relations campaigns often use the two-way asymmetric model as a compromise.

A public relations manager of a national association said that while the two-way symmetric model is fundamental in public relations, it is not a realistic option for many companies. Instead, they settle for at least one type of feedback in order to make the necessary changes in their campaigns. Informal measures, such as "convenience" sampling, represent a common type of feedback. However, they are subject to different threats to validity and reliability.

According to a manager in a public relations firm: "The four models may be ranked in the order of frequency as well as importance. The press agent model is used most commonly, particularly in private enterprise, while the public information model is often used by government agencies, along with press agentry. The two-way asymmetric model is rarely found, even with its shortcomings, and the two-way symmetric model is even rarer still."

"Most of my experience with private industry involves the dissemination of information," a director of a public relations firm said. "Only a minor level of feedback, if any, is received."

There appear to be certain exceptions. The public relations manager of a public utility said that "Feedback is an essential part of our work, enabling us to make good progress on our ongoing programs. Any government agency which does not receive feedback is finished."

Hierarchy and Society

Most panelists agreed that government public relations in Costa Rica reflected a hierarchical society, where information flowed mainly one way, from top to bottom, with little or no feedback. The general manager of a public relations firm said that most of the time, "the government is simply interested in disseminating information. This type of information flow is also more consistent with the traditional pattern of authority."

However, a director of another public relations company said that "The structure seems to vary from one agency to another. Some are better at receiving feedback than others. In those agencies, the flow of information is more horizontal, rather than vertical." He explained that "The manager of a government public relations office should also serve as its eyes and ears in the information sector. He should facilitate two-way communication with the public, expecially through the press, instead of only providing information."

In contrast, most panelists said that private companies in Costa Rica appear to be more open to feedback and interactivity by their very nature. "Private companies try harder at two-way communication perhaps because their efforts are related to marketing goods and services," the general manager of a public relations firm said. "Their success in the marketplace depends on how well they judge its needs and preferences."

The manager of a national association pointed out that "Public relations managers may have a better chance of influencing management decision making in private industry. They could present their findings on how certain products or services are being received, along with the response to the ongoing marketing communication campaign."

Similarly, the manager of a public relations firm said that "In private industry, public relations managers do not have to contend with government politics unlike their peers in public institutions. They do not have to worry about the political color of the administration or the patronage of the president. If only for these reasons, the hierarchical pyramid is less evident in private companies than in government agencies."

Other panelists pointed out, however, that there are also more traditional companies that have not fully accepted the concept of symmetrical communication, and where the flow of information is predominantly one-way.

Media Relations

For a view of media relations in Costa Rica, we asked eight journalists from different print and broadcast media how well they worked with practitioners. Although relations are for the most part cooperative and friendly, some expressed doubt as to whether most practitioners could be considered "serious partners in disseminating information" or "necessary to the production of news" as they knew it. As found in other countries, most press releases received had "questionable news value" and limited public interest.

These journalists agreed that they needed additional help in obtaining accurate, complete, and timely news about different organizations and government agencies. They said practitioners needed to understand everyday media problems such as "meeting deadlines, attracting reader interest, and making the best use of media time and space."

"While practitioners have no problems with disseminating good news, some tend to obstruct journalists or play favorites when the news is less favorable," a newspaperman from the leading daily said.

"In general, practitioner relations with the media are good but tend to be concerned with trivial matters," a journalist from the largest TV network observed. "Oftentimes, releases talk about management personalities or activities with little or no news value. Some practitioners also try to hide bad news from the media so as to minimize its impact."

The panel was somewhat divided on the question of how much news releases should be revised. About half said they used most releases with little or no editing, whereas others made substantial revisions. However, most journalists agreed that these releases were often of little help to journalists who were trying to develop their own stories.

On the other hand, these journalists gave practitioners a backhanded compliment by keeping an open mind about their trustworthiness and by withholding judgment on whether public relations is a profession equal in status to journalism.

A radio journalist said, "It is not uncommon for journalists to work in public relations when a new administration assumes power in the government." She added that "they have no problems with their peers when they return to journalism after that administration leaves office. For some, their background in journalism makes them good collaborators in public relations."

"Because the status of public relations as a profession in Costa Rica is somewhat ambiguous, practitioners could make an impact by providing leadership in ethics and professionalism," a reporter said. "They could shift their focus from political patronage or from corporate personalities. This could help build more credibility and a more desirable image for public relations," he added.

CONCLUSION

With economic recovery, the public relations industry in Costa Rica appears to be ready to play a larger role in its economic development. The peace process seems to be holding in the region, shifting its priorities from politics to a market economy. The growth of nontraditional exports, along with trade in what economists call "invisibles," exemplified by the tourism boom, seems to define Costa Rica's new relationship with the world market.

Practitioners have identified a number of factors that could hold back more rapid growth in the industry. Included are limited education of both students and faculty, lack of adaptation of current knowledge to local conditions, limited continuous education for professionals, and perhaps, need for redefinition of how public relations should be perceived in relation to journalism, advertising, and other fields of communication.

Even Costa Rica itself may owe part of its history to an early form of public relations. Not long after its discovery by Christopher Columbus, Spain decided to call this new land "the rich coast," in part to encourage people from the colonizing country to settle there. Compared to other colonies in the New World, Costa Rica turned out to have poorer mineral resources than most. But this relative poverty turned out to be a blessing, because settlers had to work their own land and generate new wealth from agriculture. This process eventually produced a society with fewer extremes of poverty and wealth and a sensitivity to hard work, fair play and conserving nature (LaFeber, 1993; Melendez, 1991; Rodriguez Vega, 1992).

About 20% of Costa Rica remains as rain forest, and the struggle continues to maintain it as a renewable resource. A director at one of Costa Rica's largest ecological foundations, Fundación Neotropica, warned that some damage due to the destruction of the rain forest, including the loss of certain species, may be irreversible. Part of the new danger arises from "too much success" in promoting eco-tourism. Some national parks are inundated with tourists, but can accomodate only a few hundred at a time. In addition, the construction boom in tourist hotels and related facilities near the protected areas may also impact on the survival of wildlife. The Fundación Neotropica is helping to expand buffer zones around these parks (Boza, 1992; Fundación Neotropica, 1988; Tasker, 1994).

In trying to solve this new problem, public relations is again playing a part. A number of private companies have incorporated environmental messages in their marketing campaigns. If these governmental and private sector efforts succeed, they may prove that Costa Rica was appropriately named after all, because as nature renews itself, "the rich coast" could be there forever.

REFERENCES

Barry, T. (1991). *Central America inside out*. New York: Grove Weidenfeld.
Black, G. (1988). *The good neighbor: How the United States wrote the history of Central America and the Caribbean*. New York: Pantheon.
Boza, M. A. (1992). *Parques nacionales de Costa Rica* [National parks of Costa Rica]. San José, Costa Rica: Ministerio de Recursos Naturales, Energía y Minas.
Castañeda, J. G. (1993). *Utopia unarmed: The Latin American left after the Cold War*. New York: Knopf.
Comisión de la Comunidad Europea y el Instituto Costarricense de Turismo. (1993). *Plan estratégico de desarrollo turistico sustenable de Costa Rica, 1993–1998* [Costa Rica's strategic plan of sustainable tourism development, 1993–1998]. San José, Costa Rica: Author.
Culbertson, H. M., Jeffers, D. W., Stoner, D. B., & Terrell M. (1993). *Social, political and economic concepts and contexts in public relations: Theory and cases*. Hillsdale, NJ: Lawrence Erlbaum Associates.
Darenblum, J. (1994, January 24). Un inusual panorama electoral en Costa Rica [An unusual electoral panorama in Costa Rica]. *El Nuevo Herald* [The New Herald], p. 9A.
Fundación Neotropica. (1988). *Desarrollo socioeconómico y el ambiente natural de Costa Rica: Situación actual y perspectivas* [Socioeconomic development and the natural environment of Costa Rica: Present situation and perspectives]. San José, Costa Rica: Author.
González, H. (1989). Interactivity and feedback in Third World development campaigns. *Critical Studies in Mass Communication 6*, 295–314.
Grunig, J. E., & Hunt, T. (1984). *Managing public relations*. New York: Holt, Rinehart & Winston.
Instituto Costarricense de Acueductos y Alcantrillados. (1994). *Memoria, 1993–1994* [Annual report, 1993–1994]. San José, Costa Rica: Author.
Instituto Costarricense de Turismo. (1993a). *Encuesta aerea de extranjeros, julio-agosto 1993* [Survey of foreigners arriving by air, July-August 1993]. San José, Costa Rica: Author.
Instituto Costarricense de Turismo. (1993b). *Encuesta aerea de extranjeros, octubre 1993* [Survey of foreigners arriving by air, October 1993]. San José, Costa Rica: Author.
Instituto Costarricense de Turismo. (1993c). *Anuario estadistico de turismo, 1992* [Statistical yearbook of tourism, 1992]. San José, Costa Rica: Author.

Instituto Costarricense de Turismo. (1994). *Plan anual operativo 1994* [Annual plan of operations, 1994]. San José, Costa Rica: Author.
Keller, N., Brosnahan, T., & Rachowiecki, R. (1992). *Central America*. Hawthorn, Australia: Lonely Planet.
Krauss, C. (1991). *Inside Central America: Its people, politics and history.* New York: Simon & Schuster.
LaFeber, W. (1993). *Inevitable revolutions: The United States in Central America* (2nd ed.). New York: Norton.
Mata Jimenez, L. (1994, February 22). Costa Rica: Jaque a la pobreza [Costa Rica: Keeping poverty at bay]. *El Nuevo Herald* [The New Herald], p. 6A.
McPhaul, J. (1994, February 4). Ataques personales marcan reñida campaña política en Costa Rica [Personal attacks typify a quarrelsome political campaign in Costa Rica]. *El Nuevo Herald* [The New Herald], p. 4A.
McPhaul, J. (1995, May 19). Law on licensing journalists struck down. *The Miami Herald*, p. 14A.
Melendez Chaverri, C. (1991). *Historia de Costa Rica* [History of Costa Rica]. San José, Costa Rica: Editorial Universidad Estatal a Distancia.
Moncreiff Arrarte, A., Clark, P., & Henriquez, H. (1994, October 24). America Central: Las naciones del puente [Central America: Nations on the land bridge]. *El Nuevo Herald* [The New Herald], p. 10A.
Perez, G. (1994, May 22). Costa Rica: Celebrar la ecología [Costa Rica: Celebrating ecology]. *El Nuevo Herald* [The New Herald], pp. 1F-3F.
Programa Centroamericano de Periodismo. (1993). *Guía de medios centroamericanos de comunicación, 1993* [Guide to mass media in Central America, 1993]. Miami: Escuela de Periodismo y Medios de Comunicación, Universidad Internacional de la Florida.
Programa Latinoamericano de Periodismo. (1994). *Guía de medios centroamericanos de comunicación, 1994* [Guide to mass media in Central America, 1994]. Miami: Escuela de Periodismo y Medios de Comunicación, Universidad Internacional de la Florida.
Rodriguez Vega, E. (1992). *Biografía de Costa Rica* [Biography of Costa Rica]. San José, Costa Rica: Editorial Costa Rica.
Rojas Bolaños, M., Morales, F., Valverde, J. M., Rivera Araya, R., Donato, E., Guendell, L., Rivera, R., & Perez Iglesia, M. (1989). *Costa Rica: La democracia inconclusa* [Costa Rica: The inconclusive democracy]. San José, Costa Rica: Editorial Departamento Ecuménico de Investigaciones.
Servicios Cablegráficos Combinados (1994, February 7). Figueres gana elecciones en Costa Rica [Figueres wins Costa Rican elections]. *El Nuevo Herald* [The New Herald], pp. 1A-4A.
Smith, G., DeGeorge, G., & Pearson, J. (1992, June 15). Multinationals step lively to the free-trade bossa nova. *Business Week*, pp. 56-60.
Soto Acosta, W. (1987). *Ideología y medios de comunicación en Costa Rica* [Ideology and mass media in Costa Rica]. San José, Costa Rica: Editorial Alma Mater.
Tasker, G. (1994, August 1). Too much of a good thing? Eco-tourism boom changes the face of Costa Rica. *The Miami Herald*, pp. 1A-12A.
Zeledón Cambronero, M. (1987). *La desinformación de la prensa en Costa Rica: Un grave peligro para la paz* [Press disinformation in Costa Rica: A grave threat to peace]. San José, Costa Rica: Instituto Costarricense de Estudios Sociales.

15 Public Relations Performance in South and Central America

Melvin L. Sharpe
Ball State University

Roberto P. Simoes
Pontifical Catholic University of Rio Grande do Sul, Brazil

Public relations is emerging as a socially mandated profession in South and Central America just as it is in other parts of the world. Advancements in democracy and communication technology, along with growing economic and environmental interdependence, are the primary globally shared reasons for the profession's growth and development.

THE HISTORICAL PERSPECTIVE

Aside from the global pressures, however, the cultural influences of the Old World on the New World, combined with geographical isolation, have helped shape the ways in which public relations has developed and is progressing within South and Central America. The student or practitioner interested in working in organizations with South and Central American customers, or in multinational corporations with locations in the Hispanic countries south of the U.S. border, will find it helpful to understand key factors that have influenced government and media functioning in Latin America. An examination of such cultural influences helps one understand how to practice public relations in South and Central America. Also, such study helps North American students and professionals discern with enhanced objectivity how cultural conditioning has shaped public relations performance in the United States.

A look at the early historical influence of Spanish and Portuguese settlement, in particular, increases understanding of the influences that have shaped and continue to affect the performance of government and private enterprise as well as the professions of journalism and public relations in Latin American countries.

It should be noted that, although countries in South and Central America share certain characteristics due to common historical influences, public relations performance differs from culture to culture within the region. Just as cultures differ widely throughout North America due to variations in historical development, the same holds from country to country within Latin America, and from region to region within countries.

For example, southern Brazil has a culture shaped by the large numbers of German and Italian immigrants who settled the area. In sharp contrast to that, the culture of northeastern Brazil has been formed in part by the settlement of Portuguese sugar cane plantation owners and their African slaves.

In the United States, a similar contrast exists between the cultures found in the South, settled by wealthy Anglican Royalists from the south and west of England along with their indentured servants and slaves, and the austere New England culture shaped by ancestors of the Puritan faith (Fischer, 1989).

North and South American Commonalities

The intent of this chapter, however, is to look beyond regional and national cultural variations so as to enhance a general understanding of reasons why different kinds of public relations performance are needed on the two American continents. Before examining such differences, however, this chapter offers some insight as to the commonalities in background and self-interest that are continually drawing the peoples of the two continents closer together. The shared self-interests, expanding communications technology, and social interdependence are also increasing the degree to which people on both continents demand common things of their governments and institutions. Therefore, public relations performance differences found today can be expected to decrease as people demand a greater voice in government and institutional decisions along with greater responsiveness.

Settlement by Competing Countries. During periods of exploration and colonization, Spain, Portugal, England, France, and the Netherlands competed to claim and occupy territories throughout South, Central, and North America. All have influenced the existing cultures found within South America today, just as all except Portugal have helped shape North American cultures through their occupation at some point in time of North America. (Portuguese culture has influenced North American culture, of course, through immigration.)

Similar Immigration Patterns. During periods of major immigration from European countries into the United States around the turn of the century, the same immigration movements from Europe into South American countries were occurring as well, particularly from Italy, Germany, and Poland.

Orientals also were bringing their cultures to seaport cities in South America, just as in California. These folks came on ships as sailors, and as imported laborers for major construction projects. Japanese immigrants have come in substantial numbers to both continents during the past decade. Thus, it is not unusual to find South Americans with oriental physical characteristics in South America as well as in North America.

British Isle surname immigration occurred in Chile as early as the coastal city visitations of Sir Francis Drake. After the U.S. Civil War, many Southerners migrated to Chile. Immigrants from Germany and Italy, as well as from many other countries, helped make Chile a melting pot. Also, the natural barrier provided by the Andes, preventing contact with other South American countries, has helped create a uniquely Chilean culture. Chile today is "no more Spanish than the United States today is English," a fact noted by Johnson in 1965 (p. 120).

During the period when slave trading was at its peak, native people from many regions of Africa were transported forcibly to work on thriving sugar cane plantations in South America as well as on cotton plantations in the United States. African cultures, therefore, have had a significant impact on South American cultures as they exist today.

Also influencing Latin American culture, particularly in countries such as Mexico, Colombia, Bolivia, Paraguay, and Peru, are the descendants of the indigenous people who occupied all of the American continents before the landing of European settlers. And, just as in North America, the conquest and treatment of the indigenous cultures in South and Central America serves as a black period in the advancement of the dominating cultures which saw their conquests as morally right and sanctioned by Divine Providence.

In such countries as Chile and Uruguay, settlers exterminated nearly all of the native peoples. In part, this was done unknowingly through the introduction of diseases to which American Indian populations had no immunity. However, near extermination also resulted from slavery, relocation, and in some cases, just as in the United States, from a drive to free lands for resettlement by European immigrants and to make them safe for the new owners.

Trade Relationships

For many years, trade between North and South American countries was prevented by Spanish and Portuguese restrictions on their colonies that allowed trade only with the mother colonizing countries. According to Crow (1985), colonies were even "prohibited from trading among themselves. Goods had to go to Spain first and them come back to another colony" (p. 177). The "exorbitant prices collected by Spanish merchants kept colonies in poverty for two centuries" (p. 181), a condition similar to the one that sparked the American Revolution in 1775.

With South American independence, however, north and south trade routes opened with many products of exchange continuing to the present day. Vanilla, Brazil nuts, bananas, cocoa, rubber, coffee, sugar, rum, nitrates, copper, and tin are some of the products of South and Central America enjoyed by North Americans. Latin American countries, in turn, have looked north for the machinery needed in industry, for home appliances, and more recently for computer equipment.

Today, the trade relationships are complex and inter-related. Corporations in the United States have production divisions in South and Central America. International franchises such as Radio Shack, McDonalds, and Pizza King can be found all over South America. Latin American financial institutions have full operations in New York City and Miami. Japanese investment exists on both continents. Obviously international marketing and advertising is contributing to many economies, and north and south tourism has become a major contributor to the economies of countries on both continents.

Little thought is given today to a product's origin by consumers in the United States. In fact, North American consumers often may be unaware that they are wearing shoes made in Brazil or eating beef products from Mexico or Argentina, or that the house plants, fish, or birds in their homes may have had their origins in Central and South America.

The same internationalization is rapidly occurring in Latin American countries. Changes over the past 5 years are evident to regular north and south hemisphere travelers. Clothing styles, particularly of young people, have become indistinguishable from one continent to the other. Computer products, home appliances, and convenience products common in U.S. homes are increasingly available in South and Central American stores, particularly in the now universal shopping malls and supermarkets.

Geographic and Language Isolation

Because Spain was the dominant colonizer in South America, and because of the early Spanish trade restrictions, Spanish is the dominant language of the continent. The exception is Brazil where Portuguese is the major language, due to an historical division arbitrated by Pope Alexander VI in 1493 and proclaimed in the treaty of Tordesillas signed on June 7, 1494. That agreement was reached to maintain peace between Spain and Portugal in their drive to claim the right of conquest of South American territories (Crow, 1985).

The division established Portugal's territory as reaching 370 leagues west of the Azore islands. In relation to today's maps, the Tordesillas Treaty boundary would have been close to the 51st meridian. The invasion, however, of what is now Brazil's west by "Bandeirantes," organized groups seeking gold and precious stones, extended Brazil's boundaries far beyond the Treaty of Tordesillas frontier to create what is now South America's largest country, a nation larger in geographical area than the continental United States.

15. PUBLIC RELATIONS IN SOUTH AND CENTRAL AMERICA   277

The geographic isolation of both North and South America from Europe and other parts of the world resulted in the emergence of populations without language knowledge beyond their official national languages. This becomes particularly evident to an English-speaking visitor accustomed to travel in Europe where today nearly everyone has some knowledge of English. North American visitors to South America generally do not know Spanish so they often experience real communication isolation because many South Americans have not mastered English.

However, a growing number of young people in Latin America are learning English because it has become the language of the financial community in South America just as it has in other parts of the world. The increasing knowledge of English is allowing communication with the business communities of the Japanese, Chinese, Middle Eastern, European, and former Soviet block countries.

The teaching of Spanish has also increased in Brazil. And Portuguese is being taught increasingly in Spanish-speaking countries, facilitating the development of continental communication systems.

Yet, many South American citizens share an attitude similar to that held by North Americans in relation to the learning of a new language. These people recognize no real need to learn another language because of the changes they see occurring in global society. Many North Americans are being lulled into believing that learning a foreign language is not essential because of worldwide growth in use of the English language. In a parallel development, South Americans read and hear news reports citing the growth of Hispanic cultures in the United States and of bilingual developments in locations such as Miami, southern California, and Texas. Such reports apparently contribute to a belief that Spanish will in time become the dominant language of the Western Hemisphere. Weight is given to this perspective by the fact that the population of all countries with Spanish and Portuguese as their primary language equals the populations of countries where citizens speak primarily in English.

However, the fact that worldwide communication has moved from French and German to English in the areas of global trade, diplomacy, and scientific communication exchange has required, and will require, continued bilingual development in English in South and Central America. Although North America undoubtedly will continue in its own bilingual development of a knowledge of Spanish as well as English, English has become a language of international communication for people from every part of the world in travel and at international conferences.

The growth and development of the Cable News Network may be a new contributing factor, but sociologists credit the present day use of English on a global basis to the expansion of the British Empire in the last century and to the cultural influence of military personnel from the United States, Great Britain, Canada, and Australia throughout the world during and following World War II. Latin American countries remained largely uninvolved in the global conflicts of that period which provided what can now be recognized as language and culture interaction opportunities.

The need for access to information in the "global information superhighway" should motivate Latin American public relations professionals to seek new employees with English-speaking ability who can help provide instantaneous access to information. A preponderance of information on public relations originates in the United States and Great Britain. Thus, knowledge of English seems important for access by the public relations professional, educator, and student to the extensive information available in professional associations and university libraries, textbooks, dissertations and theses, and in professional and research journals published in the United States and by the International Public Relations Association.

At present, the public relations and textbook library resources available in Brazil and the Hispanic countries are extremely limited. Problems of access relate to the cost and time required in translation and to the lack of international copyright and distribution agreements. Internet and fax machines are making all published resources available throughout the world. However, access to such materials often hinges on the user's knowledge of English.

MAJOR HISTORICAL DEVELOPMENTS THAT HAVE INFLUENCED PUBLIC RELATIONS IN SOUTH AMERICA

Although there is some danger in singling out events in history as having major influence when in reality all types of factors influence cultural development, one can identify a number of historical actions that clearly have shaped the development of Latin American cultures and organizations. Similar influential factors, some positive and some negative, can be identified in all cultures. Such factors are discussed here to explain development in Central and South America, not to pass judgment on these developments or show advantages of one culture over another. The facts of history cannot be altered retroactively. Also, it cannot be assumed that, if men and women today had been a part of previous historical cultures, their actions would have been any different in light of the cultures and belief systems of the time periods analyzed. However, historical analysis allows understanding of reasons for the existence of institutions, attitudes, and behaviors.

Government

When Columbus sailed to the New World in search of a shorter route to India, Spain was not yet the great nation it was to become. Instead, New-World wealth was to enable Spain to become a world power. The first discoveries in the New World were disappointing at a time in history when Spain's financial needs were great. King Ferdinand and Queen Isabella of Spain, therefore, focused much of their attention on the unification of Spain, rather than on the development of the New-World territories claimed by Columbus and later explorers.

Several cultural conditions evolved in the New World, resulting in part from the influence of the Spanish culture as well as from the conditions created by Spanish inattention to long-range colonial-development needs.

One of these factors relates to the way many Latin American governments have functioned from that day to the present. When territories were claimed for Spain in the New World, a *viceroy* or representative of the crown was named to oversee the territory. This individual was responsible for accumulating the wealth of the area for the monarchy. Gold, silver, emeralds, raw materials, and various products were claimed for use in Spain.

The compensation and official rewards for this government service, and for those in the employ of the viceroy, can be described as "miserly" in comparison to the wealth continually transported to Spain. Dozer (1962) related that "discoverers and colonizers received from their sovereigns little but paper authorizations and high-sounding titles. They were compensated for their expenses and hardships by the prospect of finding riches and by the enlarged opportunities open to them" (p. 99).

Clearly the feudal system philosophy dominant in Europe at that time was fully in operation in Spain. In that system, the ruler collected most of the wealth for himself, leaving what remained to be shared in a disproportionate ratio down the hierarchy to the lowest level. Those at the top enjoyed great luxury while people at the bottom lived in poverty and dependency.

The result was predictable. Because viceroys and lower-level officials were compensated poorly in light of the riches they were collecting and returning to Spain, a government culture evolved in which each level of government hierarchy attempted to compensate for low salaries by profiting from government service. The bureaucracy surrounding the Spanish monarchy tolerated and expected leaders to profit some from their positions. Crow (1985) reported that "graft was accepted as a matter of course even by the king" (p. 168). But when a viceroy was seen as too bold in self- or family compensation, routine replacement could be expected following a number of years in office.

The leadership attitude that developed from this condition of insecurity among officials was that when you have power, it is wise to take advantage of the situation as rapidly as possible to gain economic protection against possible later disfavor. Dozer (1962) described the process as one in which the "royal official had to accumulate from his office enough money, first to recoup the original cost of the office" (the sale of offices, even for life, was done to raise money for the crown), and "second, to sustain himself and his family in Spain for the rest of their lives, and to buy off the judges" sent by the monarchy to observe and report back to the monarch the performance of the official (p. 109). The behavior of graft and corruption on the part of government officials over time became ingrained in the culture, causing officials to see compensation as a privilege of government service rather than as an unethical behavior.

Another factor that contributed to concepts of government service as an opportunity for personal and family reward was the fact that those sent to the New World for service frequently were second sons and individuals from noble but impoverished families. The Laws of Toro in 1505 extended the right to leave family estates to the eldest child, safeguarding the stability of noble property. In 1520, Charles I established a fixed hierarchy of rank naming 25 grandees of Spain.

The New World, therefore, was a place where those without opportunity in Spain had a chance to establish themselves and, even more importantly to the Spaniards and Portuguese of that time period, to build status for their family names in Spain and Portugal. In order to build family status, however, appointees had to empower other family members as rapidly as they could following their own elevation in Spanish New-World governments. This could be accomplished through nepotism, a practice already common in Spain and feudal Europe. As soon as an official was appointed to a position of stature, he sought lesser government positions for all of the extended family members possible. Another avenue was to assure that government contracts were awarded to family members whenever possible. "By the beginning of the 17th Century, most local offices had become both proprietary and hereditary and municipal administration had passed into a narrow circle of wealthy and influential families" (Bailey & Nasatir, 1973, p. 184).

Families, as social groups, became dependent upon government bureaucracies for jobs and economic security. And government bureaucracies grew to service the patronage needs of the government power structure. Historians Bailey and Nasatir (1973) related that:

> Government jobs brought such honor and prestige and were closed to so many classes of society born in the New World, job "mania" and nepotism became the order of the day. A job with government meant the open door to quick wealth and social standing. As the centuries advanced, there was an excessive number of officials in Spanish America and jobs were created for relatives of those in power. (pp. 185–186)

The system of government levels that profited from the financial reward received for performing services for wealthy families was a system patterned after what existed in Spain as a part of the monarchy. In fact, the term "red tape" derives from the bureaucratic system that bottlenecked as decisions slowly moved up through the many levels of government review required before final approval could be obtained from the monarch or his representative. Philip II, for example, is referred to as the king of endless files (Crow, 1985). According to Bailey and Nasatir (1973), the Spanish monarchy was absolute in Spain and monarchs intended to maintain the same exclusive control. Petitions in need of attention were tied with red ribbons and stored in chambers awaiting a final authoritative decision and frequently remained there for years before receiving action. Thus, an indication that the decision process was still tied up in red tape meant that the petition had not yet been brought to the attention of the final decision maker. With South American officials this usually was the king or his Council of the Indies.

Dozer (1962) provided a 1784 example in which

> the bishop of Oazaca in New Spain submitted to the Council of the Indies certain recommendations for the improvement of relations with the Indians; 14 years later he was informed the Council had not yet had the opportunity to examine his proposals. (pp. 104–105)

In Brazil, the pattern of control under the Portuguese was much the same. The Portuguese monarch ruled Brazil directly from Portugal until a Council for the Indies was created in 1604 to handle much of the decision making. Commercial policies were chiefly directed toward "increasing the Government's (Portugal's) revenues, preventing competition, providing benefits for privileged interests" (Bailey & Nasatir, 1973, p. 142).

Three other factors have had a major impact on the development of private businesses in Latin American countries.

One was the Spanish culture which viewed family ownership and control as all important in the area of business investment. Family ownership, however, failed to create the recognition of serving the community as a facet of public relations performance that public shareholder ownership generates. Therefore, the recognition of a need for improved communication with employees and external audiences has evolved slowly, particularly in countries with strong Spanish influence where the formality of communication between managers and employees has long been an historical tradition. Brazil and Chile are the exceptions.

A second factor related to the way in which Spanish colonies sought to protect their own interests when the acceptance of laws from Spain was viewed as not being in the best interest of the colonists. Crow (1985) stated that such views helped establish a local sentiment that the law "shall be respected but not enforced" (p. 175). For example, because trade was prohibited with countries other than Spain or Portugal, the smuggling of items needed by the colonists into a country and their sale in the black market became an accepted practice, with officials simply looking the other way and not enforcing the edicts. Crow (1985) points out that "The psychological significance of all this [the ignoring of higher administrative edicts] struck roots that ran deep into the character of Latin American political practice" (p. 175).

A third influential factor was the refusal of the Catholic Church hierarchy to redefine the Church's values related to usury. Major investment from Spain was needed and would have accelerated development in South America. However, the Biblical prohibition against allowing investors to make a profit from loaning money was upheld by the Church, discouraging potential Spanish investment in the high-risk ventures of colonization.

The slowness of the Catholic Church in redefining the ethics of loaning money for profit gave England just the edge it needed to surpass Spain in New-World development. Henry VIII allowed a 10% profit from the loaning of money for investment as early as the year 1545 (Nelson, 1969). However, a new Code of Canon Law allowing profit from the loaning of money was not established by the Catholic Church until 1917 (Langholm, 1984). Thus, Spain and Portugal failed to provide the private investment that would have prevented much of the legacy of public dependency upon government and much of the poverty that led to the revolutions within their colonies in the New World.

The Move Toward Democracy and Public Relations

The move toward democracy in the 1800s in South America began with revolutions freeing countries from their domination by European powers. Two liberators, in particular, Simon Bolivar in the north and Jose de San Martin in the south, are honored today in South American countries much as North American's revere George Washington. Other Latin American countries in the Caribbean, as well as Mexico, Chile, and Uruguay, honor liberators for freeing their countries from European rule. Further, the American and the French revolutions were influential in spreading the concepts of self-rule among those who would become recognized as the liberators.

Following liberation, constitutions were developed, most of them being patterned after the U.S. Constitution. The newly formed governments made little progress, however, in instituting democratic reforms. The new leadership feared empowering of the uneducated masses. Also, those who controlled the wealth resisted land redistribution. Resistance by wealthy land owners, and by the power structure that had been in control during European domination, simply proved too great for the achievement of real democracy.

Military governments capable of employing even larger numbers of the population became the solution for increasing the size of a middle class, and for controlling unrest among the "have-nots." The control, however, could not be achieved without tight constraints against freedom of the media, the lack of which delayed any real development of public relations as a profession.

As stated at the beginning of this chapter, one factor that has propelled South America toward democracy relates to advancements in global communication. These advances are allowing South American audiences to follow developments in the United States and other parts of the world on a daily basis. Interest in what happens in the United States relating to government and politics, trade negotiations, Hollywood, the war on drugs, and so forth, is so high that both Latin American newspapers and television cover the events daily.

Presidential elections in the United States are covered extensively, as are steps taken to assure the ethical performance of elected politicians and organizational managements. Obviously, therefore, educated young people in South and Central America know far more about activities and events in the United States than educated young people in the United States know about activities and events in Latin America.

South Americans have not yet demanded open-record laws at the state and federal levels, nor have consumer protection movements emerged as they did in the United States in the 1970s.

Brazil does have a law to protect consumers which went into effect in 1991. The Consumer Defense Code has received much media attention, but it appears to have had little effect on the public relations profession. Ombudsman positions have been created as a result of the code. However, because the public relations community did little to support the code, which was supported by members of the legal profession, lawyers have been the professionals appointed to such positions. The code came about not through public action, but rather through official action which has also defined the government organizations responsible for defending consumer interests. This undoubtedly helps explain the code's ineffectiveness in stimulating improved public relations performance.

There is considerable questioning of the role of lobbyists in society, particularly by young people who challenge the ethics of lobbying by public relations professionals. The highly bureaucratic governments require the action of lobbyists on behalf of organizations within the system to achieve movement when government approval is required. Even the professions that are basically unionized within government must continually lobby to protect their professional turf. The concept of equalizing the power of organizations within the social system by limiting the power of lobbying influence and increasing the power of public opinion has not yet been championed by people within the emerging democratic systems. Environmental pressure groups are beginning to emerge, but the influence of environmentalists has largely come from pressure groups outside the countries affected.

A reason given by Brazilian intellectual leaders for the lack of movement in these areas is that South Americans, again due to historical Spanish and Portuguese influence, think in terms of elevating family, placing the support of family needs above "outsider-" or community-support needs. In contrast, North Americans often place high priority on the community social environment and play activist roles in accomplishing social reform which can be viewed as contributing more to the welfare of the greater social system than to the needs of their immediate and extended family members. Because of this attitude, nonprofit social service organizations have played a limited role in South American social systems. Also, the concept of fundraising from the public to serve community needs through nonprofit agencies is missing. Meeting the needs of the poor is viewed primarily as a responsibility of the Church and the government rather than of private corporations and businesses or of individual citizens.

In a 1987 visit to a General Motors Brazil plant in Sao Paulo, co-author Sharpe noticed protesters with placards at the entrance to the large, very modern Detroit quality facility. A company official explained that the demonstrators had been organized by an area priest who felt the company should help meet the needs of the citizens living near the plant.

When asked what community-relations support programs General Motors Brazil had in place for the local community, the official explained that the firm paid its employees well above area salaries. Also, it provided all employees and their families with their own private company recreation club. Other community-relations outreach had been viewed as unnecessary until the picketing began. The demonstrators were asking that General Motors Brazil provide financial support for construction of a playground to be used by poor area children from non-employee families.

The public demonstration caused managers at General Motors Brazil to recognize a need for the type of community support that General Motors plants in the United States would routinely provide. The concept of community service, however, was a new one to the Brazilian managers who had recognized the employee or family needs of the organization through the construction of a beautiful recreation facility, but who saw the larger community social needs as some other institution's concern. No social responsibility was recognized to give something back to the community supporting the plant. Factors contributing to this included dependency upon government lobbying rather than public approval; the self-sufficiency of General Motors Brazil in supplying its own security, electricity, and other needs rather than depending on the community for these services; and, until the picket line, a failure by the community public to express the right to a return for what might be defined as social system support and tolerance of the plant in their neighborhood. Outsider-support needs simply were not seen, in this case, as "institutional family" concerns.

Advancement of Communication Along With Journalism

The relationships among literacy, economic development, and democracy are clearly evident in South America. Advertising is a crucial support base for the development of good newspapers as well as for radio and television stations. Thus, an economy's health is directly related to organizations' ability to spend money on paid communication.

In countries where, until recently, an educated middle class was very small compared to the number with extreme wealth and those in poverty, neither the economic base nor the literacy development existed for a thriving mass-media industry.

This condition has changed rapidly, however, in the past 25 years. Although much progress is still needed, literacy levels are increasing. As the middle class has grown and literacy has improved, newspapers, radio, and television stations have increased correspondingly. Major cities now support many newspapers, more than are found in U.S. cities of equal size. Many newspapers are directed to specialized audiences such as readers interested in finance or sports.

Also, communication managers are adopting North American promotional methods to attract new readers, listeners, and viewers for several reasons. First, competition for audience members has increased. Second, as literacy levels have gone up, so has the number of potential readers. And third, technological advances are expanding the capabilities of the media.

Radio has become the best medium for reaching remote rural audiences and, particularly, for reaching those in rural areas without the ability to read. Because of the distribution difficulties with other media in reaching remote audiences, radio is playing an increasing role in political campaigning and for educational purposes, as well as for entertainment and news. Brazilian radio now provides information about the weather, highways, fairs, health campaigns, and so forth, 24 hours each day. Improved news coverage has increased the credibility of broadcast content, making radio more attractive to sponsors who seek to build goodwill or to gain more customers.

Television has developed more slowly due partly to the greater economic advertising base required for the financial stability of a private television station. Another factor has been the much higher cost of transmitting equipment and production compared with that of radio transmission and of printing. Still, TV has advanced in major and very apparent ways, even over a short 5-year period. CNN is definitely having an impact and is available to viewers in many hotels and businesses, contributing to instantaneous global communication.

The most apparent improvements in South American television have been the enhanced quality of advertising and increased choice of programming during just the past 5 years. Competing stations now exist in what were one-station cities. Hours of station operation have also increased so that television viewing is possible earlier and later in the day. Communication groups are establishing agreements for joint ventures in radio and television. A Chilean based group, Diarios da America, has proposed a cable television network with 20 or more channels for countries in South America.

American-produced television programs and movies, all with Spanish language sound tracks, fill much of the viewing time. Thus, Latin American perceptions of the United States have been influenced by the lifestyles shown in U.S.-produced programming. The result is an image of the United States derived from old movies, and from movies depicting intercity life that South American viewers may assume reflects widespread conditions.

Chicago, for example, may be identified with the problems of gangster-era movies, whereas New York City may be associated with the drugs, crime, and the 49th Street environment shown in an action thriller. California is often portrayed with decadence dramatized in films depicting Hollywood lifestyles. And Texas is probably seen as the wild west conveyed in old Grade B movies. Thus, modern communication technology may lead mothers who are preparing to send sons and daughters to live in U.S. homes as exchange students, to fear for their children's safety and possible moral corruption.

Obviously, then, the growth of television both facilitates and distorts the understanding by people in South America. What viewers in the United States do not take seriously on American television and view only as escape, South American viewers may see as portraying reality. Image is reality to viewers everywhere. For Americans with an abundance of new and old televisions programs and movies ready for distribution, the consequences are not all positive.

The increase in television viewership in Latin America is creating a new industry in many South American countries; that of television program production. Brazilian television is now producing "telenovelas," similar to soap operas and of excellent quality, which are exported to more than 60 countries. All types of marketing messages, as well as ideological and educational messages, are now transmitted in telenovelas. Some sociological critics have questioned the ethics of telenovela writers and producers on the grounds that they have promoted conformity among the people.

Two other communication avenues used frequently by public relations professionals in the United States have only limited use in South American countries at present. Although telephone and postal services have improved continually throughout Latin America, both channels remain inadequate in allowing public relations professionals to reach South American target publics.

Although the number of people with telephones is continually increasing in metropolitan areas, many urban residents do not yet have phones in their homes for economic reasons. Also, remote regions often have no telephone service. And the lack of dependable mailing lists often makes it impossible to reach people with direct-mail informational and promotional items.

In 1994, co-author Sharpe discussed the need for a research project with government officials in Uruguay. When inquiry was made as to how voters could be reached for a scientific survey, the officials concluded that neither telephone nor direct-mail surveys could be used because neither avenue would reach needed audiences. Defining a population in order to obtain a statistically valid sample for a mail or telephone survey appeared to be virtually impossible.

South American solutions to these limitations involve the use of loudspeakers on automobiles or minibuses to transmit messages while driving slowly through neighborhoods, on-the-street distribution of pamphlets, and saturation of frequently traveled areas with posters and billboards. However, the next decade should bring continual, even dramatic, change in the methods of communication delivery available to South American public relations practitioners as they seek to reach audiences.

Advancements in computer technology have reached into all areas of the communications industries in South America. As the technology improves and becomes more accessible, communication products are improving in quality. Advancements in the use of computer technology are also occurring within the communication divisions of organizations. Although the use of such advancements has not yet approached levels of usage in the United States, the adoption of such advancements can be expected to be much more rapid than it was in the United States due to improvements in equipment and cost reduction resulting from the development of the technology in American markets.

Today, television and newspaper newsrooms in South America look about the same as those in the United States. Computers are the rule, not the exception. Although the educational programs, do not have all of the computer equipment enjoyed in U.S. universities and colleges, they do provide an increasingly sophisticated level of education taught by competent professors, many with doctoral degrees from universities in the United States and Europe. Technological developments clearly are contributing to major advances in all of the communication professions, and the gap between the United States and Latin America in sophistication of equipment and facilties is narrowing.

Today, Brazil has 52 undergraduate public relations programs. Regulated by the Ministry of Education, these are mostly 4-year degree programs. Most classes are taught in the evening, drawing students with work experience and a knowledge of the organizational workplace (Thomazi, 1991). About 40% of all enrollees eventually find employment in public relations. In addition to the educational programs, social communication programs feature public relations courses offered under the title of organizational communication or enterprise communication.

Since 1968, Brazil has had both master's and doctoral programs specifically designed for public relations. In general, graduate programs in the country are designed to train educators rather than public relations managers.

There are serious problems with the development of journalism in South American countries, however. One problem relates to the common practice of government agencies in buying advertising space to convey information to the public. Due to the practice, newspapers have become dependent on the government for financial support. Thus, the little investigative reporting needed to enhance the government occurs because publishers fear it might alienate a vital financial sponsor. Also, the lack of open-records laws facilitating access to government information blocks investigative opportunities that might allow the development of competing newspapers without economic dependence on the government.

Another problem relates to the licensing of journalists. Government interference and control in the licensing process is no longer viewed as a problem by professionals, whereas journalism's relationship to public relations is. In an effort to protect their employment, journalists have been successful in requiring their employment in organizational positions responsible for what would be identified as media relations, within the public relations field, in the United States, Great Britain, and many other countries. Public relations professionals without journalistic credentials are prohibited by law from holding the media relations positions.

In the United States, of course, employment of journalists in public relations positions is not prohibited. Upon employment in a public relations capacity, however, the journalist loses his or her identity as a journalist and gains identity as a public relations professional or as a communication specialist. In South America, licensed journalists working within government and private industry produce material that is submitted to journalists employed by the media. These individuals generally accept that material without change or question because to offer such a challenge would be an affront to another licensed journalist who, in practice, is a member of the same trade group.

As with the separation of Church and State in achieving real democracy, the importance of the separation of journalism and public relations in achieving and protecting real democracy is evident. The checks and balances that each profession needs to provide and to demand from the other, are missing without such separation. The procedures in South America just described have led to the common practice of payments to corporations by the media for the opportunity to interview and acquire information on a corporation's business operations, to a lack of in-depth investigative reporting of an organization's operations, and to a far too cozy relationship between public relations and journalism. None of these factors contribute to a healthy democracy where the need is for journalists to serve as the watchdog for the public interest, and where public relations professionals have the clout to counsel corporate managements as to the importance of upholding the public relations principles of honesty and openness in the exercise of responsibility to the public.

Some of the cost to the social systems can be observed in the lethargy of the public. The Brazilian people seldom fight for their interests. Instead, they wait for someone else to fight for them, leading to the emergence of demagogic and populist leaders.

Social Interdependence Factors Affecting Governments and Corporations

The most obvious area of global social interdependence apparent in South America relates to economic dependencies. Banker Carlos Penny with Citibank in New York City reports that, in 1990, the total flow of capital into Latin America was around $14 billion. In 1991, it was $40 billion. A restructuring of the economies in Latin American countries is identified by Jose Manuel Campa at the New York University Stern School of Business as the reason for the change. Governments are increasingly allowing private companies to assume responsibility for previously controlled government activities.

Nationalism and protectionism are decreasing, according to Campa. He blames both for distorted price structures in South and Central American countries. The move is to stabilize prices rather than use a barter system which has been a common means of selling goods in Latin America. These changes are resulting in increased consumer confidence. Governments are working to control spending and, as a result, stock markets have dramatically increased their volume in dollar terms (Strauss, 1993).

Barbara Burns, who has lived in Brazil and is now managing director for Consultants in Public Relations SA in New York City, sees public relations becoming more broadly understood by the public in Latin America in relation to protecting the environment and in promoting improved agricultural practices (Strauss, 1993, pp. 15–16). At present in Brazil, however, the culture of corporativism dominates; that is, a system through which organizational and professional groups seek to protect their self-interests by lobbying the government to pass laws which provide corporate, organizational, or professional protection.

In recent years, the need for protection of rain forests and native populations, and for the preservation of endangered species in South America, have all received extensive media attention throughout the world. To be sure, governments and citizens of South America express resentment of outside interference and question the right of Americans, in particular, to criticize abuses that occurred during the industrial revolution era of development in the United States. However, media attention is increasing awareness of the influence of global public opinion and of the need for a new responsiveness by governments and private businesses to global-village concerns.

THE STATUS AND STATURE OF PUBLIC RELATIONS

Public relations in South American countries truly began to develop with the fall of military governments in Brazil, Argentina, Paraguay, Chile, Uruguay, Peru, and Panama. Abolition of military control resulted in new freedom for the media. Also, the creation of unions, the nonprohibition of strikes, and the development of satellite television are viewed as important contributors to the profession's growth.

The development can be related directly to the status of the government in controlling the news media, however, and repressive setbacks have occurred as reported by Humberto Lopez y Lopez at the XIV Interamerican Conference in Sao Paulo (as cited in Thomazi, 1991). Lopez cited the persecution of public relations in "Colombia, Mexico, Ecuador, Peru, Chile, and Venezuela" and noted that "in some universities the teaching of public relations had been suspended." For example, such teaching reportedly was suspended in "1975 at the International Center for Higher Studies in Journalism for Latin America in Quito, Ecuador" (p. 201). The academic program had been in place since 1959.

In Chile, Barbara Delano (1990) relates that the profession began in 1950 with the creation of a department of public relations at the Braden Copper Company under the direction of Mario Illanes Penafiel. At the same time, Ramon Cortes Ponce opened a consultancy targeting private industry clients. And a modern School of Journalism was established at the University of Chile in the same time period. Ponce would become director of the school and a teacher of public relations (Delano, 1990).

In Colombia, the airlines AVIANCA and LANSA and the Tropical Oil Company established departments of public relations as early as 1948. However, not until 1966 would the profession develop sufficiently for the creation of the Colombian Society of Public Relations (Serra e Gurgel, 1985).

In Brazil, the beginning of public relations can be traced to 1914 with the creation of a department of public relations at the Sao Paulo Tramway Light and Power Company Ltd. The creation of this department was registered as follows:

> Sao Paulo, January 30th, 1914. General Notice: Beginning with February 1st, there will be established in this Company a new department known as Relacoes Publicas, which will have immediate charge of the company's business with the State and Municipal authorities, school tickets and such other business as may be hereafter assigned to it. Dr. Eduardo Pinheiro Lobo [an engineer] is hereby appointed chief of this Department.
> Yours truly, W. G. McConnel, Asst. General Manager. (Serra e Gurgel, 1985, p. 15)

The teaching of public relations in Brazil began in 1949, after World War II, by Mario Wagner Vieira da Cunha at the Institute of Administration of the University of Sao Paulo. Other courses followed at the Rio de Janeiro Institute for the Rational Organization of Work (1949) and at the Sao Paulo Getulio Vargas Foundation Brazilian School of Public Administration (1950).

By 1954, the Brazilian Association of Public Relations (ABRP) was founded in Sao Paulo by 27 professionals, most of whom were associated with either the Institute for the Rational Organization of Work or the University of Sao Paulo's Institute of Administration. Today, ABRP has a central governing board and 14 state sections.

In 1967, the practice of public relations was regulated by law by the Brazilian military government, and a School of Communication and Arts was created at the University of Sao Paulo. Prior to this time (for 53 years), public relations in Brazil had been recognized by the government only as an administrative function. Following this action, public relations began to be associated with academic programs in communication. In 1968, the government issued guidelines for the performance of public relations within all communications units of government (Serra e Gurgel, 1985).

Brazil is particularly important in the development of the public relations profession in South America because of its geographical size and economic potential. Geographically, Brazil occupies half of the South American continent and, according to 1992 census, has a population of 146,917,459 people, equivalent to half the population of South America. Brazil's economy presently ranks 10th in the world.

Maria Elvira Salies Ferreira of Brazil traces the real advancement in the public relations profession in South America to the year 1960, the date of the first Inter-American Conference on Public Relations held in Mexico City. On that occasion, the Inter-American Federation of Public Relations Associations (FIARP) was founded with member countries including Mexico, Panama, Dutch Antilles, Costa Rica, Venezuela, Colombia, Ecuador, Peru, Bolivia, Paraguay, Chile, Argentina, Uruguay, Brazil, and Canada (Ferreira, 1993). FIARP was founded with the goal of promoting unity and reciprocal collaboration among public and private public relations professional organizations. It also has the goals of facilitating the professional exchange of ideas and experiences related to public relations, promotion of the profession's reputation on the continent, and elevation of the quality of public relations education in member countries.

In 1985, FIARP was reorganized as the Confederacion Interamericana de Relaciones Publica (CONFIARP). It now has 13 national public relations associations in membership: Argentina, Brazil, Columbia, Costa Rica, Chile, Ecuador, Mexico, the Netherlands Antilles, Panama, Paraguay, Peru, Uruguay, and Venezuela (Senac, 1993). FIARP was and still is an association of associations, not of individuals. Thus, the Board of Directors consists of the presidents of national associations. One of the founders, and the first president, was Venezuelan Frederico Sanchez Fogarty. Biannual conferences are sponsored by the organization, and recommendations for strengthening the profession are made to the national associations.

Another professional association, the Ibero American Confederation of Public Relations (CIRP) has become an organization for the exchange of information with the public relations professional community in Spain and, potentially, in Portugal.

In addition, national chapters of the International Public Relations Association (IPRA) have resulted in the hosting of a number of IPRA conferences in Latin American countries, drawing international attendance. The exchange of information in these international forums has contributed to an understanding among Latin Americans as to how the function is viewed and performed in other parts of the world.

According to Ferreira, CONFIARP has identified 56 college-level public relations courses taught throughout Latin America. One of the first such courses offered was in Lima, Peru at the Journalism School in the Pontifical Catholic University of Peru. Generally, public relations in Latin America is being organized by working professionals who also teach a course in a nearby university which has recognized the need for a curriculum in the new professional area (Ferreira, 1993).

In some countries such as Argentina, that course is emerging in programs related to diplomacy and protocol, but most such offerings are associated with communications programs. The need for interdisciplinary knowledge of public relations is recognized in many cases, however, resulting in public relations educators with academic training in the social sciences and management as well as communication.

Research completed within academic institutions is still limited due to the part-time teaching responsibilities of most educator or professionals. However, Brazilian authors have published a total of 30 public relations books, more than in any other Latin American country (Ferreira, 1993). Only about half of the books remain in print, however. [Brazil is the only country in Latin America with a doctoral program in public relations. The degree program was established in 1986 at the University of Sao Paulo. Nearly 80% of all the college-level public relations courses in South America are taught in universities in Brazil.]

Research conducted in the Communication School at the University of Sao Paulo in Brazil has identified 8,000 practicing public relations professionals in that country alone (Ferreira, 1993). These are professionals registered in the Professional Council of Public Relations. Because many practitioners identify themselves with titles in social communication, endomarketing, political marketing, or social marketing, and so forth, the actual number in Brazil is believed to be much higher.

Research has not been done to estimate the number of working professionals in either South American or Latin American countries as a whole. However, growing interest in public relations, as shown by the growing attendance of practitioners at conferences for educators and professionals, makes it clear that the numbers are increasing in countries with growing economies. Large groups of professionals can now be identified in Argentina, Peru, and even Cuba.

In addition, those who teach public relations are improving in their exchange of information. And the number of professionals involved in teaching, as well as the number of full-time educators in the field, is increasing. Just within the past few years, groups in Uruguay, Chile, Argentina, and Bolivia have begun contributing to the exchange of information among educators, students, and professionals. In Argentina, public relations educational programs are being developed as a part of the existing academic programs for the study of diplomacy and protocol, an academic association also common in universities in Spain and Portugal.

The visiting American speaker to South America is frequently confronted with professional organizations that compete and downgrade each other's abilities and performance to the detriment of the public relations profession's advancement. This appears to be a carryover from Spain where there is a real effort to control competition by keeping competitors out of professional organizations where membership carries status. Faced with such exclusion, practitioners create new competing public relations organizations.

Development of the field requires expansion of professional development so that it is available to all practitioners for the purpose of enhancing the overall image of the profession. Also, unified professional support is needed for educational programs in public relations, and to facilitate communication among all practitioners and educators. The divisions interfere with progress.

Brazil, as was stated earlier, was the first country in the world to regulate the profession of public relations (Law 5377, December 11, 1967). The regulation established degree requirements for entry into the profession and a professionally controlled licensing process. Panama regulated the profession in 1980, and Peru in 1990. Currently, professionals in Argentina, Colombia, Venezuela, and Chile are working to establish similar legal requirements for the performance of public relations (Ferreira, 1993). Although the licensing process can be seen accurately as a means of government control, quality control is enhanced because the process requires graduation from a qualified educational program followed by peer evaluation.

The Effect of Social Conditions on Concepts of Public Relations

The differences required for public relations performance in the United States and in Latin American countries are revealed by the differences in the concepts of public relations as defined by co-authors Sharpe and Simoes. An examination of this variation in perception enables the student to recognize how performance needs in public relations in the United States differ from those in Latin American countries, at least at this point in time.

Co-author Simoes sees public relations as the administration of the political function of organizations within social systems (Simoes 1983, 1992). He sees organizational decisions achieving legitimacy through public relations activity. Simoes views the planned and continuous effort of an organization to achieve legitimacy as the way organizational credibility and trust are generated.

The challenge for the public relations profession, Simoes believes, is the creation of a common code for the community of public relations which will facilitate the teaching and learning process and give new "status" to the professional practice of this activity.

Simoes (1992) provides a paradigm shown in Table 15.1 for public relations based on his concept.

Co-author Sharpe sees public relations as resulting from the increasing empowerment of public opinion in society and of the organizational need to maintain stability in a changing social environment comprised of many competing self-interests. He views public relations as recognition of what Edward L. Bernays has identified as Thomas Jefferson's principle that, in a democratic society, everything depends on the consent of the public.

The global social system's movement toward increased democracy, Sharpe believes, is the result of shared communication. He sees the movement as a public-opinion force factor that has forced organizations to treat audiences eth-

TABLE 15.1
The Outline of the Paradigm for Public Relations

(A)	Conceptual definition (What is public relations?)	As an activity, public relations is the administration of the political function (subsystem) or organizations.
(B)	Objects of the science in question (Scientifically, what does public relations work with?)	Material; organization and publics. Formal; conflict in the organization-public social system.
(C)	Operational definition (How is this activity performed?)	To analyze tendencies; to predict consequences; to advise the decision-making power; and to implement planned programs of information.
(D)	Cause for the existence of the activity	Conflict is imminent in the organization-public social system.
(E)	Levels of the problem (What is the symptomatology?)	From integrated interests all the way to social convulsion.
(F)	The raw material (What is the matter that avoids and solves conflict?)	Information
(G)	The political aspect (Why political and not communication only?)	The relationship is political. The instrument is communication--Two sides of the same coin.
(H)	A parenthesis (What is the role of myth?)	Myth is intrinsically to organizational discourse.
(I)	The instruments (How does one search and send information?)	Any and every means, existing or to be created that carries messages from the organization to the publics and vice versa.
(J)	The objective (At what does public relations aim?)	To legitimize, give credibility, organizational decisions.
(K)	The ends (What for legitimacy?)	To facilitate the transactions of the organization with its various publics, besides the clients, keeping them faithful.
(L)	Ethics (Is it moral to do public relations?)	To persuade others to accept one's own ideas as ethical.
(M)	Esthetics (What is the benefit to society?)	Searches for harmony in behavior.

ically, a requirement for public relations performance as he demonstrates through a model designed to show behavioral relationships.

Sharpe, therefore, identifies public relations as the behavior that is required to harmonize individuals and organizations in social systems and to maintain harmonious relationships. He views public relations performance as the application of behavioral principles and recognizes that the behaviors will not be in place without management commitment. He also recognizes that, if such achievement were easy, public relations problems would not exist. The difficulty of achievement in a modern, globally interdependent, ever-changing world society, he believes, is mandating the professional management of communication and of relationship building of all organizations in a global society (Sharpe, 1992).

Sharpe has developed a model (Table 15.2) describing the behavior required for the achievement of harmonious relationships, identifying the reasons for the difficulty of achievement of the behaviors, and indicating what the cost to organizations is and will be if the behaviors as a management function are not accomplished by organizations or individuals.

Sharpe sees the challenge facing the profession as that of identifying standards on the part of public relations professional organizations for organizational performance (Sharpe, 1986, 1987). Sharpe believes that the lack of management guidance and of public understanding as to what should be in place in organizations before ethical public relations performance can take place, prevents social systems from being able to evaluate whether an organization has a commitment to ethical public relations performance or not. The empowerment of public assessment, not organizational or professional assessment, he believes, will elevate the responsibility public relations professionals have in society, to the organizations they counsel, and to the social system in which these organizations function. Sharpe (1986) recommends that public relations professional organizations identify and communicate the following as evidence of its commitment to ethical public relations performance; the organization's ethics policies, the organization's two-way communications policies, and the criteria defined for the employment of internal and external counsel.

The two concepts offered by Simoes (1992) and Sharpe (1994) agree in relation to the importance of the achievement of organizational credibility, of the relationship of ethical performance to public relations, and of the need for achievement of harmony. Both concepts have been developed independently within social systems with very different cultural conditions. The cultural conditions have shaped the variation in views of organizational application and of professional needs, but even the variation in cultures has not interfered with the understanding as to what public relations requires.

If any conclusion can be drawn from observing public relations performance in the Americas, it is that the same principles that apply to performance in the United States will apply throughout the world as well. The culture, particularly the level of social system democracy, will affect the way in which progress can

TABLE 15.2
Behavioral Requirements for Achievement and Maintenance of Effective Public Relations—A Behavioral Theory Model for Public Relations

Behavior	Reason	Difficulty	Means of Achievement	Cost to Public Relations Performance if Not Achieved	Cost to Organization if Not Achieved
Honesty	Credibility	New knowledge/ Social value change	Environmental Research/Continual self-analysis	Message rejection/ Ineffective communication	Loss of internal & external support
Openness/ Consistency	Confidence	Openness need is situational	Public opinion analysis/Management commitment & control	Message rejection/Mistrust	High cost of ineffective communication/Loss of internal & external support
Fairness	Reciprocity	Concepts differ/ Basis must be communicated	Public opinion analysis/Continuous self-evaluation of basis/ Willingness to adjust	Damaged relationships/ Communication rejection	Loss of repeat sales/ Govt. regulation/Punitive regulation/ Loss of support/ Increased taxation/ Loss of employee loyalty
Continuous communication	Prevent alienation/ Build relationships	Overcoming communication roadblocks/ Maintenance of two-way communication	Continuous evaluation of communication effectiveness/ Strategic public relations planning	Communications rejection/ Misinformation/ Uneducated audiences/ Lack of change adjustment	Increased cost of repairing relationships/Time required in rebuilding relationships/Loss of support for mnaagement goals/ Target audience self-interpretation of organizational messages
Accurate image analysis	Corrective adjustments	Achievement of accurate self-analysis/ Management reluctance to change existing behavior	Continuous target public opinion analysis/Corrective communications strategies/Behavioral change	Ineffective public relations programs/Dependence on one-way communication strategies/Misinformation without awareness/Image damage without knowledge	Expense of using ineffective communication and public relations strategies/Inadequate information upon which to base sound management decisions/ Lack of achievement of full productivity potential/Unionization

Reprinted by permission of Dr. Melvin L. Sharpe, Ball State University, developed May 5, 1994.

be made in the application of public relations principles. This recognition allows the professional to understand the value of learning as much as possible about the culture in which public relations performance is to take place. But it also emphasizes the value of using localized public relations counsel in the process, whether the performance is needed in South, Central, or North America.

REFERENCES

Bailey, H. M. & Nasatir, A. P. (1973). *Latin America: The development of its civilization.* Englewood Cliffs, NJ: Prentice-Hall.
Crow, J. A. (1985). *Spain, the root and the flower: An interpretation of Spain and the Spanish people* (3rd ed.). Berkeley, CA: University of California Press.
Delano, B. (1990). *Las relaciones publicas en Chile* [Public relations in Chile]. Santiago: Editorial Universitaria.
Dozier, D. M. (1962). *Latin America.* Tempe, AZ: Center for Latin American Studies, Arizona State University.
Ferreira, M. E. S. (1993). Public relations in Latin America, *International Public Relations Review, 16*(3), 4–5.
Fischer, D. H. (1989). *Albion's seed.* New York: Oxford University Press.
Johnson, W. W. (1965). *The Andean republics.* New York: Time, Inc.
Langholm, O. (1984). *The Aristotellian analysis of usury.* Bergen, Norway: Universitetsforlaget.
Nelson, B. (1969). *The idea of usury.* Chicago: University of Chicago Press.
Senac, R. P. (1993). CONFIARP—The Interamerican Confederation of Public Relations. *International Public Relations Review, 16*(1), 9–10.
Serra e Gurgel, J. B. (1984, July). Congresso Brasileiro de Relacoes Publicas [Brazilian Congress of Public Relations]. Belo Horizonte, Brazil.] *Journal of the Department of Communication,* University of Brasilia, p. 45.
Serra e Gurgel, J. B. (1985). *Cronologia da evolucao historica das relacoes publicas* [A chronology of the historical evolution of public relations]. Brasilia: Linhu Grafica.
Simoes, R. P. (1983). *Relacoes publicas: Funcao politica* [Public relations: A political function] (2nd ed.). Porto Alegre, Brazil: Sagra.
Simoes, R. P. (1992). Public relations as a political function: A Latin American view. *Public Relations Review, 18*(2), 189–200.
Sharpe, M. L. (1986). The professional need: Standards for the performance of public relations. *International Public Relations Review, 10* (4), 17–25.
Sharpe, M. L. (1987). Standards for organizations in the performance of public relations. In Public Relations Society of America Task Force on Demonstrating Professionalism (Ed.). *Demonstrating public relations professionalism* (pp. 19–20). New York: PRSA.
Sharpe, M. L. (1992). The impact of social and cultural conditioning on global public relations. *Public Relations Review, 18*(2), 103–107.
Strauss, G. H. (1993). The boom in Latin America—Is it real? *International Public Relations Review, 16*(1), 14–15.
Thomazi, M. S. (1991). *The teaching and research in public relations in Brazil and its repercussion in the profession.* Unpublished doctoral thesis, University of Sao Paulo, Brazil.

16 Standardization Versus Localization: Public Relations Implications of Advertising Practices in Finland

Ali Kanso
Kansas State University

Many foreign markets now offer more opportunities for business expansion by Western firms than does the home market. Consumers all over the world are constantly exposed to higher quality products and services in a more and more competitive environment. And, for most firms, the primary stimulus to enter nondomestic markets is competition. More than ever before, competitors operate on a worldwide level. Thus, to grow and survive, many companies must develop markets abroad.

In fact, American marketers have been thinking and acting internationally. In 1993, the aggregate foreign sales of the 100 largest U.S.-based multinationals totaled $703 billion. Of these firms, 23 had larger sales volumes in foreign markets than in the United States itself. Also, 33 of the 100 companies made more profits from sales abroad than from those at home (Zajac, 1994).

As companies grow and flourish, they become true multinationals with direct investment in several nations. Upon doing this, they must make business decisions based on choices available anywhere in the world (McCarthy & Perreault, 1993). As the multinational firm strives for growing participation in world markets, it faces tough choices that influence the marketing mix. One such choice is whether to use standardized (unified) or localized (customized) advertising campaigns to reach foreign markets.

Proponents of the standardized approach claim that consumers anywhere in the world have the same basic needs and desires, and can therefore be persuaded by universal appeals. On the other hand, adherents of the localized approach assert that consumers differ across countries and must, accordingly, be persuaded by advertising tailored to their respective nations.

The debate over the use of standardized versus localized advertising campaigns has intensified in recent years. Much research has centered on international advertising decisions made by U.S. corporate headquarters. However, very few studies have examined the roles of American and non-American subsidiaries in designing and implementing advertising campaigns for nondomestic markets.

OBJECTIVES

This study focuses on international advertising practices in Finland. Such a focus should provide a framework of factors that influence public relations as well as advertising strategies. Many worldwide advertising agencies have blended operations involving public relations, creative advertising campaigns, direct mail, and other efforts. Advertising and public relations basically serve two different functions—commercial and noncommercial. However, the two fields work together within the promotional element of the marketing mix.

The objectives of this study are as follows;

1. to investigate whether American and non-American subsidiaries use localized or standardized advertising approaches in the Finnish market;
2. to scrutinize the impact of culture on international advertising as perceived by advertisers in Finland;
3. to pinpoint major problems that American and non-American firms may encounter in planning advertising campaigns for the Finnish market; and
4. to construct a framework for international advertising and public relations practices that considers market conditions in Finland.

Why Finland?

Finland was studied for four major reasons. First, it is an advanced industrial country with a cultural blend attractive to international marketers. The country is Western, but under heavy Russian influence. Second, Finland is part of Scandinavia and is a new member of the European Union (EU). Thus, study of this nation supplements other research on Scandinavian and EU countries. Third, the country is a part of northern Europe that has attracted relatively few international communication scholars. And fourth, Finland has been a leading country in advertising expenditures as a proportion of its gross national product.

Although the study addresses international advertising practices in Finland, the implications of such practices for public relations are clear. A public relations practitioner, wishing to target a certain public, designs specific messages to reach that public and selects media that deliver these messages most effectively and efficiently. He or she can benefit from the advertiser's experience and learn more about market conditions, creative strategies, legal constraints, and cultural attributes. For example, if culture impacts on advertising, a public relations practitioner should be fully aware of cultural differences and avoid pitfalls that hamper the effectiveness of creative strategies.

Knowledge of various market conditions will, undoubtedly, help practitioners coordinate with advertising people in providing guidance for future campaigns. In this study, a review of international business and marketing decisions helps put current international advertising in perspective.

BASIC BACKGROUND

International Business Practices

The growing trend toward international operation has led American multinational corporations to reconsider their organizational strategies and planning procedures. Certainly, marketing is no exception to this rule. International marketing managers have argued whether they should apply their domestic strategies to international markets or give subsidiaries great autonomy in devising and implementing their own programs.

Early in the evolution of multinational corporations, Perlmutter (1969) identified three orientations of international business operations; *ethnocentrism, polycentrism, and geocentrism*. A few years later, Wind, Douglas, and Perlmutter (1973) added *regiocentrism* as a fourth type of orientation, and the profile became known as EPRG.

In the ethnocentric orientation, plans for overseas markets are developed in the home office, using policies and procedures identical to those employed domestically. Top executives within some multinational corporations view domestic techniques and personnel as superior to foreign, and therefore as most effective in overseas markets. Thus, promotional overseas strategies are as similar as possible to those used in the home country.

In the polycentric approach, each overseas subsidiary operates independently of the others, establishing its own marketing objectives and plans. Local personnel and techniques are viewed as best equipped to deal with local market conditions.

In the regiocentric and geocentric orientations, the company views the region or the entire world as a potential market, overlooking national boundaries. The company also develops policies and organizes activities on a regional or worldwide basis. Marketing personnel include people from throughout a region or from any country in the world. Promotional policies are developed regionally or worldwide to project a uniform image of the company and its products.

Wind et al. (1973) interviewed senior international marketing executives from 10 U.S. corporations in order to determine the conditions under which different EPRG marketing strategies are appropriate. The ethnocentric position seemed most appropriate where the absolute or relative volume of overseas sales was almost insignificant. In such cases, separate advertising appeals and messages were developed for an individual market only if sales in that market were sufficiently large to justify the additional cost involved.

However, most executives tended to regard the polycentric position as most desirable because market conditions differed significantly across countries.

At the same time, respondents felt that the regiocentric and geocentric approaches might improve coordination and control over regional or global market segments which cut across national boundaries. Because geocentrism entails high cost in collecting data and administering policies worldwide, the regiocentric appeal was generally viewed as more economical and manageable.

Wind et al. (1973) concluded that there was no single superior or dominant international orientation. In general, the advantages and disadvantages of each orientation varied considerably with the company's financial situation, product line, and size of potential overseas markets. These findings help shape an ongoing debate over the appropriate use of standardized versus localized advertising approaches in international markets.

Standardization and Localization of Advertising

Early advocates of *standardization* (Elinder, 1965; Fatt, 1967) argued that the availability of international media and the increasing similarity in consumer tastes across countries make uniform advertising approaches possible.

Levitt (1983), a catalyst for the renewed debate on standardization versus localization, saw *globalization* (another term for standardization) as a necessity for the successful global corporation. His claim was based on the assumption that consumer needs, interests, and buying habits are becoming increasingly homogeneous throughout the world. He also argued that a firm can achieve substantial economies of scale in production and marketing by supplying global markets.

Proponents of *localization* (Amine & Cavusgil, 1983; Helming, 1982; Kanso, 1992; Kotler, 1986; Ricks, Arpan, & Fu, 1974) counterargued that to assume a high similarity in buying motive across national boundaries may be simplistic at best and dangerous at worst. These authors contended that cultural, social, economic, legal, and other differences among nations may be insurmountable. Thus, they argued, promotional strategies must be tailored for local conditions.

On a more theoretical level, Wind (1986) and Porter (1986) criticized Levitt for failing to note that increased homogenization of needs across international boundaries has gone hand-in-hand with greater segmentation of needs within countries, making standardization an untenable strategy. Douglas and Wind (1987) added that standardization not only is fraught with problems, but it is rarely feasible in relation to all elements of the marketing mix.

Two major reviews of the debate have summarized the literature and reported a few cases of standardization.

The first review suggested that empirical evidence for standardization is thin. Furthermore, the support that does exist is based exclusively on surveys of marketing managers (Walters, 1986). The second review concluded that a decision on whether and how much to standardize is situation-specific. Cost–benefit issues involved in each particular situation make it very difficult to offer a single, universally valid prescription (Onkvisit & Shaw, 1987).

A compromise solution such as *pattern standardization* has been proposed (Peebles, Ryans, & Vernon, 1978). Here a global promotional theme or positioning is developed. However, execution is adapted to the local market. Proponents of this approach feel that the faults of both standardized and localized strategies lie in implementation, not in basic validity of the concepts.

A similar middle-of-the-road approach has been recommended by Sriram and Gopalakrishna (1991). These authors viewed standardization as not requiring implementation of an entire campaign across countries. Rather, they suggested the development of uniform themes, images, and even brand names whereas messages and overall strategies are tailored to local conditions.

Studies relating to standardization versus localization include many content analyses of advertisements. These have tended to focus on execution differences, themes, appeals, and embedded cultural values (Dowling, 1980; Frith & Wesson, 1991; Graham, Kamins, & Oetomo, 1993; Hitchon & Zong, 1994; Hong, Muderrisoglu, & Zinkhan, 1987; Marquez, 1979; Rice & Lu, 1988; Tansey, Hyman & Zinkhan, 1990).

Other studies have examined levels and types of standardization and localization (Donnelly & Ryans, 1969; Dunn, 1976; Kanso, 1991; Whitelock & Chung, 1989). Still, other researchers have distinguished between strategy and execution of standardized advertising campaigns (Moriarty & Duncan, 1990; Peebles et al., 1978; Plummer, 1986; Ramaprasad & Hasegawa, 1992).

More recently, scholars have investigated structural dimensions of standardization (Szymanski, Bharadwaj, & Varadarajan, 1993). In particular, one study suggested that standardization of advertising decisions depends more on the client's need for efficiency than on the need for effective message creation and distribution (Moriarty & Duncan, 1994).

Missing Link

A missing link in the literature is the study of subsidiaries' views on standardization and localization. If an international advertising campaign is to be judged on the basis of implementation, the opinions of those in charge of actual campaigns seem important. Unfortunately, many studies have examined attitudes of executives at corporate headquarters only. The author could find only two studies on related opinions of advertising executives at subsidiaries. And these studies must be viewed with some reservation.

One of the studies (Sorenson & Wiechmann, 1975) reported on personal interviews with 100 executives from 27 major American and European multinational corporations. The researchers tried to assess similarities and differences in marketing decisions across countries. However, respondents were defined simply as managers with marketing or management responsibility for Europe and the United States at corporate headquarters, regional offices, and local subsidiaries. Managers of local subsidiaries were not analyzed separately. And the three types of executives were not compared.

The other study (Keown, Synodinos, & Jacobs, 1989) compared advertising practices in five European countries, but it did not specifically address the execution of creative strategies. Rather, the researchers defined creative approaches simply as either *informative* or *emotional*. Such a definition can be applied to either domestic or international advertising, and the authors did not distinguish between these two realms. In addition, Keown et al. (1989) did not report whether they studied only, or primarily, representatives of multinational corporations. Rather, the authors defined respondents simply as individuals responsible for the advertising of leading brands of four durable and eight nondurable products in five countries.

RESEARCH QUESTIONS AND HYPOTHESES

The controversy over the use of standardized and localized advertising approaches is far from settled. Roles and orientations of subsidiaries have been overlooked. Furthermore, no single study has compared the attitudes of advertising executives within American and non-American subsidiaries. Thus, this study addresses the following research questions and hypotheses:

Research question 1: Do American and non-American subsidiaries tend to use standardized or localized advertising approaches in Finland?

Research question 2: What are the most serious problems that subsidiaries face in planning advertising campaigns for the Finnish market?

Research question 3: What are the most important obstacles that impede standardization of advertising campaigns as perceived by Finnish executives?

Hypothesis 1: Attitudes of advertising executives toward controversial cultural issues pertaining to standardization versus localization are significantly related to the advertising approach (i.e., standardized or localized) they use in the Finnish market.

Hypothesis 2: Advertising managers of American and non-American subsidiaries differ significantly in attitudes toward controversial cultural issues.

Hypothesis 1 basically specifies a positive correlation between general beliefs regarding standardization (or localization) and respondents' actual planning and implementing of campaigns. Hypothesis 2 is nondirectional, as the literature provides little basis for predicting the nature of differences between American and non-American firms.

METHODS

Participants

The study dealt with advertising executives of American and non-American subsidiaries in Finland. The firms covered sell products and services ranging from business-to-business products (industrial equipments, machinery, etc.), business-to-business services (management consulting, corporate investment, advising, etc.), consumer durable goods, and consumer nondurable goods to consumer services. The sample consisted of 31 American subsidiaries and 36 non-American subsidiaries or a total of 67 firms. The number was carefully selected after two exhaustive attempts to insure that all firms were engaged in business activities and advertising in Finland.

The first attempt was an exploratory effort to identify and locate foreign subsidiaries in Finland. The author screened three lists of international business firms operating in Finland. The lists were obtained from the Finnish Advertising Association, the Finnish Chamber of Commerce, and the Directory of American Firms Operating in Foreign Countries. After comparing all three lists to eliminate overlap, a tentative roster of 112 firms was developed.

The second attempt was confirmatory and aimed at getting a precise list of advertising executives within those subsidiaries. Here the author, while in Finland, placed telephone calls to the selected firms. These calls led to the elimination of 35 companies from the tentative list because the subsidiaries neither produced nor placed advertising in Finland.

Materials

Questions dealt with types of advertising approaches, degrees of standardized messages, serious problems that managers face in planning advertising campaigns for the Finnish market, obstacles that impede the standardization of advertising campaigns, and controversial cultural issues.

In the first section, each executive was asked to indicate the percentage of advertising messages for which his or her firm used a standardized approach (i.e., use of identical messages in both the home country of the corporate headquarters and for the Finnish market). The percentage of standardized messages was presented in seven brackets; never use, 1–19%, 20–39%, 40–59%, 60–79%, 80–99%, and always use. A subsidiary that reported use of standardized messages less than 40% of the time was defined as localized. A response of 40% or more was categorized as standardized. In a previous study, standardized usage was defined as at least 50% (Kanso, 1992). However, this study used 40% as the cutting point because responses were skewed toward the localized end. Substantial numbers of both localized and standardized firms were required for analysis.

Controversial cultural issues that subsidiaries might face in their advertising campaigns dealt with unique traditions and values, impact of satellite television broadcasting on advertising, government regulations, language diversity, choice of illustrations, advertising appeals, themes, and symbols.

To examine relationships between executives' attitudes toward such issues and types of advertising approaches (i.e., localized and standardized) used by their firms, executives responded to 13 attitudinal statements. Responses were on a 6-point forced-choice scale ranging from strongly agree (+6) to strongly disagree (+1). In testing hypothesis 2, responses to the 13 statements were compared for American and non-American subsidiaries.

Executives also were given a list of 15 obstacles that might impede standardization of international advertising campaigns. They were asked to select the five obstacles they considered to be of greatest importance, and to rank these from 5 = most important to 1 = least important. The list included: heterogeneity of national populations, cultural differences, government regulations of advertising media, legal constraints on message content, differences in consumers' lifestyles, variations in market infrastructure, language diversity, lack of reliable media research, political instability, preservation of national identity, unavailability of accurate marketing research data, trade restrictions, variations in reaching certain target publics, and differences in media availability. The last obstacle was labeled "other" so respondents could specify any factor not included in the list.

Prior to data collection, five Finnish executives not in the sample reviewed a draft questionnaire to determine the readability of the 13 questions presented. As a result, one open-ended question was rephrased to eliminate potential double meaning.

The questionnaire was written in English as all participants were fluent in that language. This was not surprising because most Finns speak four languages; Finnish, Swedish, German, and English. The author had established the understandability and apparent face validity of most questions in a previous study of U.S.-based advertising executives (Kanso, 1992).

Procedure

Data were collected through a mail survey from February 10 to March 30, 1992. Two waves of the same questionnaire included cover letters and self-addressed return envelopes. Due to limited funds, Finnish stamps on return envelopes went with the first mailing but not with the second. The recipients were assured that the study was conducted for a scholarly purpose and that their replies would be confidential and used only in combination with other answers for analysis. Also, respondents had an opportunity to request a summary of the study findings. In the second wave, a month after the first mailing, recipients were asked not to fill out the questionnaire if they had already responded.

Of the 67 advertising executives, 40 completed and returned the questionnaire, making the response rate 60%. Twenty-two respondents were executives of American subsidiaries whereas 18 worked for non-American firms.

FINDINGS

Research question 1 dealt with advertising approaches used by subsidiaries in Finland. In all, 30 subsidiaries (i.e., 75% of the respondents) followed the localized approach whereas only 10 firms (25%) were classified as standardized. None of the advertising managers reported that they always use standardized messages (see Table 16.1). About three fourths of the firms use the localized approach predominantly, but with occasional standardization. Thus, classification was based on the extent of standardization rather than simply on use or nonuse of it.

Of the 35 subsidiaries that use standardized messages sometimes, 17 said they modify copy and illustrations to fit the Finnish market. Thirteen respondents indicated that they translate messages and make idiomatic changes. Five reported changing all materials except the central theme to suit local conditions. None of the subsidiaries reported presenting standardized messages in the original language of the country where corporate headquarters were located.

Research question 2 dealt with serious problems that subsidiaries face in planning advertising campaigns for the Finnish market. Answers to an open-ended question identified problems in the three major areas of economics, message considerations, and data and research.

Economic concerns include high media costs for reaching fragmented target

TABLE 16.1
Percentage of Standardized Messages Used by International Subsidiaries in Finland

Percentage of Messages Used	Number of Firms	Percent of Total	Cumulative Percentage
Never use	5	12.5	12.5
1 - 19%	22	55.0	67.5
20 - 39%	3	7.5	75.0
40 - 59%	5	12.5	87.5
60 - 79%	3	7.5	95.0
80 - 90%	2	5.0	100.0
Always use	0	0.0	100.0
		100.0%	

publics, budget constraints, high production costs in reaching a small population, and an unstable economy that makes long-range planning difficult.

Message considerations consist of difficulties in adapting international or Pan European campaigns to local ones, focusing a campaign on the right people, integrating local and international messages, finding the right copy strategy, and tailoring one's message for target groups.

Research-related problems involve lack of database marketing, insufficient statistics describing the Finish population, and difficulties in measuring results.

In addition to the three major areas, subsidiaries claimed that headquarters do not listen closely enough when they recommend modification of advertising messages to reach the Finnish market effectively. Overall, subsidiaries' concerns were similar to ones reported by Terpstra and Sarathy (1994).

Research question 3 addressed obstacles that impede standardization of advertising campaigns. Executives were provided with a list of 15 potential obstacles and were asked to select and rank the five most important ones. Weighted mean rankings of these obstacles (with 0 assigned where a respondent failed to place a given problem among the top five, 5=most important, and 1=least important among his or her chosen five) were as follows; cultural differences ($M = 3.52$), differences in consumers' lifestyles ($M = 1.97$), variations in worldwide market infrastructure ($M = 1.92$), language diversity ($M = 1.77$) and government regulation of advertising media ($M = 1.17$).

Hypothesis 1 stated that attitudes of advertising executives toward controversial cultural issues were significantly related to their use of standardized and localized advertising approaches. The hypothesis was partially supported. Student's t tests revealed significant differences on only two of 13 issues (see Table 16.2). Managers who follow the standardized approach tended to agree more often than their localized counterparts that advertising campaigns can be standardized in all markets ($t = -2.86, p < .05$) and that government softening of broadcast media regulation would encourage advertisers to place greater emphasis on standardized campaigns ($t = -2.95, p < .02$).

On the other hand, managers with a standardized approach and those who adopt localized strategies seemed to agree that an advertiser should design messages that fit unique traditions and values in each country; the time has not come to devise a universal campaign; the expansion of satellite television broadcasting creates a greater demand for standardized campaigns; the maze of government regulations makes it difficult to create universal campaigns; the choice of illustrations and colors must be related to the consumers' aesthetic sense; advertising for different markets should make use of the same brand name; layout of advertising can be universally understood; advertisers must use symbols that are uniquely recognizable and meaningful to each market; and advertising appeals must be entirely compatible with consumers' lifestyles.

Also, both groups of managers generally did not report strong beliefs that,

TABLE 16.2
Managers' Responses to Controversial Cultural Issues Regarding Approaches to Advertising Campaigns

Statements	Mean Ratings		T	p
	Standard-ized	Local-ized		
To guarantee effective advertising, an advertiser should design messages that fit the unique traditions, values, and beliefs in each country.	4.30	4.53	.59	N.S.D
Although need satisfaction is based on cultural considerations, advertising campaigns can be standardized in all markets.	3.80	2.94	*-2.86	< .05
Consumer differences in various countries are diminishing, but the time to devise a universal compaign has not come yet.	4.10	4.30	.40	N.S.D
The worldwide expansion of satellite TV broadcasting creates greater demand for standardized global advertising.	4.50	4.46	.09	N.S.D
The maze of government regulations in various countries makes it difficult to create a universal advertising campaign.	3.90	3.46	.09	N.S.D
Government softening of broadcast media regulations would encourage advertisers to place a greater emphasis on standardized campaigns.	4.70	3.86	**-2.95	< .02
The language diversity in world markets necessitates the use of local communication expertise in each market.	4.80	5.13	1.04	N.S.D
In designing advertising messages for various countries, the choice of illustrations and colors must be related to the consumers' aesthetic sense.	4.90	4.43	-1.06	N.S.D
Advertising for different countries should be identical in content and make use of the same brand names.	4.50	3.90	-1.14	N.S.D
No matter how we perceive cultural differences, layout of advertisements can be universally understood.	4.10	3.66	-1.00	N.S.D
Due to differences in traditions and customs, an advertiser must use symbols that are uniquely recognizable and meaningful to each market.	4.50	4.30	-.52	N.S.D
In presenting advertisements for foreign use, an advertiser must make sure that appeals are entirely compatible with consumers' lifestyles.	4.80	4.76	-.11	N.S.D
Despite cultural differences, consumers' perceptions of advertising theme should be the same for all markets.	3.40	2.86	-1.30	N.S.D

*$p < .05$; ** $p < .02$.

despite cultural differences, consumer perceptions of an advertising theme should be the same for all markets. However, both groups appeared to believe that the language diversity in world markets necessitates the use of local communication expertise in each one.

Hypothesis 2 specified that advertising managers of American and non-American subsidiaries differ significantly in attitudes toward controversial issues. The hypothesis was not confirmed. In fact, American and non-American subsidiaries differed on only one issue—the choice of illustrations ($t = 2.03, p < .05$). Managers of American subsidiaries tended to believe more than those affiliated with non-American firms that, in designing messages for various countries, the choice of illustration and colors must be related to the consumers' aesthetic sense.

ADVERTISING AND PUBLIC RELATIONS TRENDS

It appears that the majority of subsidiaries in Finland seek to practice *polycentric localization* of advertising. Executives seem to recognize that culture plays a significant role in designing and implementing advertising campaigns. Even subsidiaries that follow the standardized approach appear to admit that cultural differences should no longer be ignored.

Compared with studies conducted several years ago, this research suggests that the polycentric orientation is gaining ground in the international marketplace. In a related literature review on management of multinational corporations, Kinzer and Bohn (1985) identified the ethnocentric and polycentric orientations of public relations management as the two most common.

Allthough the data focused on international advertising in Finland, they are comparable to findings from studies on international public relations. Several scholars in the latter area have stressed understanding of other cultures to effectively negotiate and compete in world markets (Botan, 1992; Fitzpatrick & Whillock, 1993; Sharpe, 1992; Snowdon, 1986; Walters & Walters, 1994). To some critics, public relations should be more culture-bound than advertising. M-L. Rosberg (personal communication, October 25, 1994) president of Oy AC-tiedotus Ab, a major public relations agency in Helsinki, Finland, articulated the reasons as follows:

> Public relations is a more diversified discipline than advertising. It tackles more problems, addresses more issues and targets smaller but different groups of publics. Public relations is two-way communication while advertising is mainly one-way. A public relations practitioner has to adapt his/her approach to the local environment to survive.

Lack of recognition of local foreign cultures can only lead to undesirable, often painful, consequences. In a national survey of Public Relations Society of

America members, respondents with international experience attributed the ineffectiveness of public relations campaigns implemented in foreign markets to two main factors; the failure to observe local cultures, and the failure to adhere to local business practices (Fitzpatrick & Whillock, 1993).

In the same study, about 77% of all participants perceived significant differences between national and international public relations. Also, 76% claimed they did not possess the knowledge and skills needed to practice international public relations. And 64% of the respondents with international experience saw it as very important to secure local public relations counsel before entering a foreign market (Fitzpatrick & Whillock, 1993).

Social, economic, and cultural complexities inherent in worldwide business expansion have given rise to a greater need for public relations. The emergence of more than 60 national and regional public relations associations is just one indication of this (Kruckeberg, 1989).

For many companies, substantial opportunities in public relations have developed in overseas markets (Wouters, 1991). Support for that conclusion came from an International Public Relations Association study of chief executive officers for large companies in 17 nations. In total, 83% of the respondents rated public relations as either "very valuable" or "valuable" to their companies (Fry, 1992).

PRACTICAL LESSONS

Although this study focused on international advertising in just one country, the findings strongly suggest opposition among subsidiary executives to the concept of a unified advertising campaign for all locations. Further, public relations practitioners can learn several lessons from advertising practice in Finland.

First, barriers to standardized public relations programs are very high. Cultural considerations, differences in consumer lifestyles, variations in market infrastructure, and government regulations are primary impediments. In a previous study, senior public relations practitioners with heavy international experience identified similar barriers (Ovaitt, 1988). In fact, odds against successful standardization of public relations campaigns seem stronger now than ever before.

Second, use of diverse languages should be considered seriously even where national foreign publics speak an international language such as English. As Rosberg (in press) said:

> It is almost mandatory to have somebody in Finland to help you in communication and public relations, in spite of the fact that English is taught in all elementary and high schools. You can communicate in English, German and French without mentioning Swedish, but sooner or later you will notice that the Finnish civil servant or journalist prefers to have your facts confirmed in Finnish.

Third, use of similar appeals, symbols, and even themes in campaigns targeting foreign markets is ill-advised. Thus, the multinational company should weigh its desire to maintain the same image everywhere against its endeavor to achieve a competitive edge in various markets. The latter goal requires a strong commitment to local vision.

Fourth, the key to successful international public relations is adaptation to environmental differences in each country. Adaptation requires conscious effort to anticipate the influence of uncontrollable factors (i.e., market infrastructure, cultural, economic, and legal forces, etc.) on the public-relations plan. In adapting a program to foreign markets, practitioners must fully comprehend the impact of uncontrollable environmental elements on their plan for each market. The process of evaluating these elements, as Cateora (1993) described it, often entails substantial doses of cultural, political, and economic shock.

Fifth, although strategists have traditionally defined "environments" as outside factors that cannot be controlled by the business firm, one may argue that an environmental factor such as government constraints can be changed through negotiation, lobbying, and issue advertising. Thus, public relations practitioners must use their contacts and skills to deal with constituent publics so as to support clients and minimize the harmful effects of legal constraints.

Interactions with foreign government officials may occur at various levels and may address a host of issues ranging from lobbying for more favorable access to national media to presenting a case for easing restrictions in national technology policies. The practitioner's credibility and cultural sensitivity frequently decide the success or failure of corporate requests (Crespy, 1986).

Sixth, the main task of the international public relations practitioner is to become familiar with various publics in each market. Such familiarity requires viewing publics as the publics view themselves. That insight, in turn, requires considerable intelligence about one's market. By being informed, the firm often can proactively prevent serious damage to a firm's reputation. In contrast, a reactive approach often brings only disaster. Intelligence gathering works best when a firm avoids stereotypic thinking.

Seventh, foreign subsidiaries must have substantial autonomy and representation in the dominant coalition of parent firms. Also, their emphasis on intelligence gathering involves listening carefully, as well as speaking, to their audiences. These points square with generic principles of excellent public relations stated earlier by Veric, Grunig, and Grunig (see chap. 2).

In conclusion, a multinational corporation's very survival depends in large part on how it presents itself in both the commercial (marketing and advertising) and noncommercial (public relations) realms. Marketing, advertising, and public relations work well when they square with overall business strategy, and thus, with each other.

This study is only one of a series on the practices of international advertising as viewed by foreign subsidiaries. In analyzing the standardization or localization of international public relations activities, future research should examine the following major elements: process and development of the program; goals, objectives, and strategies; the use of public relations techniques, messages, and visual approaches; and procedures for measuring campaign results.

ACKNOWLEDGMENTS

This research project was funded partly by a grant from Kansas State University. The author thanks the following faculty colleagues: Dr. Carol Oukrop, director of the A. Q. Miller School of Journalism and Mass Communications, for her encouragement to pursue the project; Dr. William J. Adams for his computer assistance in analyzing the data; and Dr. Carol Pardun for her insightful comments. The author also thanks Dr. Richard Alan Nelson, now on the faculty of Louisiana State University, for inspiring the project.

REFERENCES

Amine, L., & Cavusgil, T. (1983). Mass media advertising in a developing country. *International Journal of Advertising, 2,* 317–330.

Botan, C. (1992). International public relations: Critique and reformulation. *Public Relations Review, 18,* 149–159.

Cateora, P. R. (1993). *International marketing* (8th ed.). Homewood, IL: Irwin, Inc.

Crespy, C. (1986, Summer). Global marketing is the new public relations challenge. *Public Relations Quarterly, 31,* 5–8.

Donnelly, J., Jr., & Ryans, J., Jr. (1969, April). Standardized global advertising, a call as yet unanswered. *Journal of Marketing, 33,* 57–60.

Douglas, S., & Wind, Y. (1987, Winter). The myth of globalization. *Columbia Journal of World Business, 22,* 19–29.

Dowling, G. (1980, Fall). Information content in U.S. and Australian television advertising. *Journal of Marketing, 44,* 34–37.

Dunn, S. (1976, October). Effect of national identity on multinational promotional strategy in Europe. *Journal of Marketing, 40,* 50–57.

Elinder, E. (1965, April). How international can European advertising be? *Journal of Marketing, 29,* 7–11.

Fatt, A. C. (1967, January). The danger of 'local' international advertising. *Journal of Marketing, 31,* 60–62.

Fitzpatrick, K., & Whillock, R. (1993, November). *Assessing the impact of globalization on U.S. public relations.* Paper presented at the Public Relations Society of America convention, Orlando, FL.

Frith, K., & Wesson, D. (1991). A comparison of cultural values in British and American print advertising: A study of magazines. *Journalism Quarterly, 68,* 216–224.

Fry, S. (1992, March). '92 IPRA president tracks global public relations. *Public Relations Journal, 48,* 25–26.

Graham, J., Kamins, M., & Oetomo, D. (1993, June). Content analysis of German and Japanese advertising in print media from Indonesia, Spain, and the United States. *Journal of Advertising, 22,* 5–15.

Helming, A. (1982, May 17). Pitfalls lie waiting for unwary marketers. *Advertising Age*, p. M-8.

Hitchon, J., & Zhong, H. (1994, August). *A comparative study of television commercials in the People's Republic of China and the United States*. Paper presented to the Advertising Division, Association for Education in Journalism and Mass Communication conference, Atlanta, GA.

Hong, J., Muderrisoglu, A., & Zinkhan, G. (1987). Cultural differences in advertising expression: A comparative content analysis of Japanese and U.S. magazine advertising. *Journal of Advertising, 16,* 55–62, 68.

Kanso, A. (1991). The use of advertising agencies for foreign markets: Decentralized decisions and localized approaches. *International Journal of Advertising, 10,* 129–136.

Kanso, A. (1992, January-February). International advertising strategies: Global commitment to local vision. *Journal of Advertising Research, 32,* 10–14.

Keown, C., Synodinos, N., & Jacobs, L. (1989). Advertising practices in Northern Europe. *European Journal of Marketing, 23,* 17–28.

Kinzer, H., & Bohn, E. (1985, May). *Public relations challenges of multinational corporations*. Paper presented at the International Communication Association conference, Honolulu.

Kotler, P. (1986, Spring). Global standardization—Courting danger. *The Journal of Consumer Marketing, 3,* 13–15.

Kruckeberg, D. (1989). The need for an international code of ethics. *Public Relations Review, 15,* 6–18.

Levitt, T. (1983, May-June). The globalization of markets. *Harvard Business Review, 61,* 92–102.

Marquez, F. (1979, Spring). Cross-cultural research: A decision factor in standardized versus nonstandardized global advertising. *Gazette, 25,* 150–162.

McCarthy, J. E., & Perrault, D. W., Jr. (1993). *Basic marketing* (11th ed.). Burr Ridge, IL: Irwin.

Moriarty, S., & Duncan, T. (1990). Global advertising: Issues and practices. *Current Issues and Research in Advertising, 13,* 313–341.

Moriarty, S., & Duncan, T. (1994, August). *Organizational dimensions of standardization*. Paper presented to the Advertising Division, Association for Education in Journalism and Mass Communication conference, Atlanta, GA.

Onkvisit, S., & Shaw, J. (1987, Fall). Standardized international advertising: A review and critical evaluation of the theoretical and empirical evidence. *Columbia Journal of World Business, 22,* 43–55.

Ovaitt, F., Jr. (1988, Spring). PR without boundaries: Is globalization an option? *Public Relations Quarterly, 33,* 5–9.

Peebles, D., Ryans, J., Jr., & Vernon, I. (1978, January). Coordinating international advertising. *Journal of Marketing, 42,* 28–34.

Perlmutter, H. (1969, January-February). The tortuous evolution of the multinational corporation. *Columbia Journal of World Business, 4,* 9–18.

Plummer, J. (1986, October-November). The role of copy research in multinational advertising. *Journal of Advertising Research, 26,* 11–15.

Porter, M. (1986, Spring). The strategic role of international marketing. *Journal of Consumer Marketing, 3,* 17–21.

Ramaprasad, J., & Hasegawa, K. (1992, January-February). Creative strategies in American and Japanese TV commercials: A comparison. *Journal of Advertising Research, 32,* 59–67.

Rice, M., & Lu, Z. (1988). A content analysis of Chinese magazine advertisements. *Journal of Advertising, 17,* 43–48.

Ricks, D., Arpan, J., & Fu, M. (1974, December). Pitfalls in advertising. *Journal of Advertising Research, 14,* 47–51.

Rosberg, M-L. (in press). Finland. In J. Epley (Ed.), *Handbook of global public relations: Cross cultural perspectives*.

Sharpe, M. (1992). The impact of social and cultural conditioning on global public relations. *Public Relations Review, 18,* 103–107.

Snowdon, S. (1986, August). How to gain the global edge. *IABC Communication World,* pp. 29–30.

Sorenson, R., & Wiechmann, U. (1975, May-June). How multinationals view marketing standardization. *Harvard Business Review, 53,* 38–42, 48–49, 54, 166.

Sriram, V., & Gopalakrishna, P. (1991). Can advertising be standardized among similar countries? A cluster-based analysis. *International Journal of Advertising, 10,* 137–149.

Szymanski, D., Bharadwaj, S., & Varadarajan, R. (1993, October). Standardization versus adaptation of international marketing strategy: An empirical investigation. *Journal of Marketing, 57,* 1–17.

Tansey, R., Hyman, M., & Zinhkan, G. (1990). Cultural themes in Brazilian and U.S. auto ads: A cross-cultural comparison. *Journal of Advertising, 19,* 30–39.

Terpstra, V., & Sarathy, R. (1994). *International marketing* (6th ed.). Orlando, FL: The Dryden Press.

Walters, P. (1986, Summer). International marketing policy: A discussion of the standardization construct and its relevance for corporate policy. *Journal of International Business Strategies, 17,* 55–65.

Walters, L., & Walters, T. (1994, April). *Implications of the "new global" order for public relations and advertising practitioners.* Paper presented at the International Academy of Business Disciplines conference, Pittsburgh, PA.

Whitelock, J., & Chung, D. (1989). Cross-cultural advertising: An empirical study. *International Journal of Advertising, 8,* 291–310.

Wind, Y. (1986, Spring). The myth of globalization. *Journal of Consumer Marketing, 3,* 23–26.

Wind, Y., Douglas, S., & Perlmutter, H. (1973, April). Guidelines for developing international marketing strategies. *Journal of Marketing, 37,* 14–23.

Wouters, J. (1991). *International public relations.* New York: AMACOM.

Zajac, B. (1994, July 18). Getting the welcome carpet. *Forbes,* pp. 276–279.

17 Public Relations: An Alternative to Reality?

Mauritz Sundt Mortensen
Division of Disaster Psychiatry,
Norwegian Defense Headquarters

When he set foot in North America in 992 A.D., almost to the day 500 years before Italian-born Christoforo Colombo (Christopher Columbus) believed that he had discovered India, Norseman Leif Erikson hardly speculated about any possible public relations effects of his own travels (see Fig. 17.1).

Most of what the world got to know about the Norse discovery of America was reported 250 years later by Snorre Sturlason and other Icelanders. Knowledge of Leif's north Atlantic crossings and the tiny Norse settlements in Newfoundland, perhaps picked up during a visit to Reykjavik, may have helped Columbus get his ship under way. However, the Italian pursued a PR strategy markedly different from Leif's.

Long before setting out on his voyage, Columbus announced that he was bound for India. Upon reaching his destination, shipwrecking on Christmas Day, he believed he was in India. And, back in Spain, he told his sponsors that he had been to India. For the rest of his life, Columbus believed he had discovered India.

Later, it was established that he had actually re-discovered America. One significant long-term effect of Christoforo's large-scale PR campaign was, however, that natives on two American continents came to be called "Indians." And the same name is applied, of course, to Indians living in India, which may be rather confusing!

More than 1,000 years after Leif's arrival in Newfoundland, recently documented by archaeological excavations and discovery of original artifacts, the event is celebrated by many Americans. Columbus's self-declared discovery of India is celebrated, too, on October 10, especially by the U.S. Postal Service! Thus, two separate historical events and their ensuing celebrations may serve to

FIG. 17.1. Leif Erikson discovers America, painting by Chr. Krogh (courtesy National Gallery of Norway). A true duplicate hangs in the U.S. Senate.

illustrate some significant aspects of the process and effects of public relations, specifically with regard to the problem of truth.

Even in today's wired world, as the 20th Century draws to a close, much public relations work undoubtedly is being carried out in accordance with the methods laid down by Leif Erikson and Christopher Columbus, respectively. One approach is low-key or "laissez-faire," with hardly any planning at all and no anticipation of tangible effects. The other is a hard-hitting fund-raising strategy, sometimes based on dubious facts, that may lead to long-term results.

Although these approaches are still the most applied methods all over the world, both have their deficiencies in establishing public relations as a truly international profession. Only time will tell whether, and how, practitioners will move toward that end. At present, many loose ends must be tied up for a clear path of professional development to become apparent.

Information and Public Relations

Information as a concept is, of course, as old as history itself. News and tales of people and events were always welcome as entertainment, but they also served as useful intelligence for planning future actions in peace and war. Modern news services, created with the invention of the telegraph in the mid-19th century, demonstrate this clearly.

Public relations, on the other hand, is not a clearly defined concept. Rather, it is a construct formulated to market a special kind of expertise and service to potential buyers or users. Having evolved in this way, public relations seems to be what each practitioner decides, more or less consciously, to make out of it.

This was quickly realized in 1949 by a few men who founded the Norwegian Public Relations Association (NPRA) just one year after the Public Relations Society of America (PRSA) was born. Hans Olav, who had lived in Brooklyn since 1924 while editing the *Nordisk Tidende,* a Norwegian-language weekly, was perhaps the most experienced of the NPRA founders.

Soon after the attack on Norway by Nazi Germany on April 9, 1940, Olav had been appointed head of the Norwegian Information Service in the United States. In that capacity, he explained to the American public Norway's freedom struggle under Nazi occupation, and the valuable contribution made to the allied war effort by a thousand Norwegian fuel tankers and other merchant ships. Thus, Olav played an important role in the fight against the Nazis.

After the war, he returned to Norway as head of the Public Information Division in the Ministry of Foreign Affairs. He was later promoted to ambassador, first to neighboring Finland and then to India, Burma, and Ceylon.

Attractive Service

In founding NPRA, Olav was joined by Odd Medboe, an enthusiastic journalist who had just been appointed head of public information for the newly established

Scandinavian Airlines System (SAS). A specialist in airplanes and flying, Medboe was elected president of the NPRA. Three years later, he was a founding member of the International Public Relations Association of which he served as president from 1955–57.

Although Olav attended Columbia University from 1925–27, neither he nor Medboe had any academic credentials relating explicitly to the processes and effects of public relations. Their competence was rooted in their knowledge of message content, not of public opinion or the psychological processes involved in influencing it. Their methods consisted largely of keeping in close contact with newspaper journalists. Their tactics included offering free trips, providing information at press conferences and in news releases, distributing pool pictures, and so forth. In short, they focused primarily on press relations and obviously practiced it with great skill.

Public relations soon became a useful catch phrase. Several journalists, tired of plain news work, turned themselves into public relations chiefs, consultants, advisers, and so forth, offering their services to companies and public institutions. Public relations soon became a flourishing business, although only for a few people. In 1959, 10 years after its founding, the NPRA still had only 43 members, which included a few women. Education in public relations skills and methods was acquired through a series of "how-to" evening courses and three-day seminars. These offerings remain important to this day as a strong tradition within Norway, thereby creating the impression that proficiency in public relations can be achieved in less than a week.

Chiefs and Experts

By 1974, NPRA membership had increased to 154, 15 of whom (10%) were women. Titles varied from marketing director in a large bank, director of the Norwegian Marketing Association, and secretary general of the National Association for Coffee Information to chief of information services, PR representative and editor of trade publications. Members were employed mostly by banks and insurance and oil companies, as well as by travel, tourism, and PR agencies. Many, but not all, practitioners came from journalism. Others entered the field with educational backgrounds ranging from business to engineering. No advanced education in public relations or mass communication was listed at that time.

News clippings from those years show that public relations practitioners were quite active at times, particularly in promoting their own skills. This led company managers to conclude that public relations experts ought to be placed in marketing divisions where their press services could contribute to short-term profits. When appointing managers of marketing and public relations, however, the companies often picked "good-looking" engineers, economists, lawyers, and even theologians, with former journalists hired as staff to do the work.

This development, noted in several large companies from around 1970 on, seems to have had detrimental effects. Traditionally, commercial marketing had low credibility in the public eye, and this tended to contaminate the information services provided by practitioners with backgrounds in journalism, presumably a field dedicated to revealing "truth." In a nation often dominated by others (notably Denmark, Sweden, Nazi Germany, and possibly soon the European Union), most people are extremely suspicious of anything that seems like mental manipulation. The very phrase public relations reminded Norwegians of "PRopaganda."

Back to the Basics

In 1982, the credibility problem led to reorganization of NPRA so as to include editors of company publications. A name change to Association for Information and Public Affairs clearly signalled less emphasis on hard-hitting, one-sided propaganda. The focus shifted to responsible public information.

A classic conflict, accompanied by much debate, continues between public relations as a contributor to quick profits in marketing and open information designed to strengthen long-term institutional credibility (Grunig, 1993). The latter "open" approach even seeks to help attain such grand goals as promotion of democratic processes and world peace.

Interestingly enough, many advertising educators (in the United States) are in favor of integrated marketing communications (IMC), whereas public relations educators tend to oppose it (Rose & Miller, 1994). One rationale for completely separating marketing from public relations is that the latter may preserve a company's reputation and very survival, even when an over marketed product proves to be dangerous or unpopular.

EDUCATION, RESEARCH AND PROFESSIONALISM

In the Ivory Tower

At the University of Oslo, founded in 1811, things started to happen after World War II with the establishment of a Social Science Faculty. Although sociology had been pioneered there 100 years earlier by clergyman Eilert Sundt (1817–1875), the Institute of Sociology was not formally established until 1952.

At first, the department was dominated by scholars with law degrees. Teaching focused largely on role theory and such related concepts as conformity and deviation. The university had very little to offer students on the processes and effects of human communication or, more specifically, on public relations.

The Oslo University Institute of Press Research, established in the early 1960s, was an offspring of, and was always closely related to, the Institute of

Political Science. With backgrounds in Political Science, History of Economics, and Philosophy, the professors picked up some catch-words from pioneering North American studies. Included were notions such as "the two-step flow" in election campaigns, and, of course, McLuhan's hard-to-test statement that "the medium is the message." The latter concept implied technological determinism, which soon became and still is gospel at the University of Oslo.

Research there tended to analyze such mundane topics as fluctuations in the use of newsprint from 1860 to 1960. Studies in social psychology related human communication processes were never allowed to develop. Notably the government-sponsored "Who have Power in Society" Study (NOU, 1983) was characterized by pre-Klapper, maximum-effects perspectives. Courses relevant to public relations were not offered. Mainly due to lack of active social-science research, the Institute eventually was taken over by the School of Languages and re-named The Institute of Media and Communication.

Limited Research

Problems relating to public relations or public opinion do not seem attractive to researchers in this corner of the world. Recent (1993 and 1994) project catalogues covering ongoing media and communication research in three of the four Nordic countries (excluding Iceland) reveal heavy emphasis on studies of "media institutions," considerably less interest in "human communication processes," and no reference to information service or public relations.

Mutual Contempt

From the very beginning, there was overt mutual contempt between newspeople and public relations practitioners on one side and the academic nobility on the other. Lacking practical experience and professional perspectives, the latter group tended to isolate itself from daily life in the real world. This continued for more than 40 years.

Recently, business schools and scattered district colleges have introduced brief courses in information services, mostly in combination with profit-oriented marketing attached to their basic curricula of accounting and administration. In an ad (*Aftenposten,* Aug. 23, 1994) announcing an evening course in marketing, the Business Academy combined "PR/Information Service work" with 14 other subjects including practical law, business finance, budgeting, and marketing activities. All of this was to be covered in just 1 year of study! Such programs may provide some statistical skills useful in measuring public opinion. However, they are too superficial to convey a deeper understanding based on socio-psychological theory concerning attitudes, mass communication, interpersonal communication, and so forth.

During the last few years, lobbying services have turned up as kind of a new fad, often performed by retired politicians with inside information and personal connections, or by young aspiring politicians with inflated self-esteem. In this area, a variety of catch words such as "issues management" and "corporate profiling" have shown up over the years. However, these seem to be empty slogans with little foundation in research-based knowledge about processes and effects, and short-cutting democratic processes.

Battlefield With Five "Armies"

Against this backdrop, public relations in Norway consists of a virtual battlefield involving the 5 groups now discussed.

The first group includes public relations (or Information-service) directors, division heads, managers, and so forth, who have been educated in a variety of disciplines generally considered irrelevant for public relations. Fields covered include theology, social economics, civil engineering, linguistics, law, and business. In the defense system, management positions in information-services units are occupied by career officers trained in artillery or as fighter pilots, for example. These individuals have little inclination to enhance PR professionalism.

The second group includes practitioners with extensive experience in producing press releases, press conferences, annual reports, press tours, and so on. Most of these individuals are former journalists on daily newspapers or in the electronic media.

The third group is comprised of secretarial personnel with extroverted personalities and some training in writing press releases, answering routine phone calls, and other similar activities.

The fourth group encompasses public-service practitioners, titled as information secretaries, who serve in government ministries and agencies. These people often have low- to medium-level political or teaching backgrounds and are hired to help political leaders handle the press on a routine basis. According to government regulations, such practitioners are permitted to distribute some factual news and information as needed in order to implement and understand policies and regulations. Only politically appointed secretaries can present "politicized" information and arguments for or against such measures in public statements and interviews with the media.

Finally, the fifth group includes a varied horde of amateurs, with a mixed background in TV news-reading, politics, theology, and so forth. These folks market themselves as world champions in the art of persuasion and influencing others.

Thus, at least five groups work in public relations. These "clusters" of people have little in common as to professional perspectives or theoretical knowledge, and methods relating to their presumed focus—the process and effects of human communication.

Similarly deplorable situations seem to exist in other societies (Ehling, 1992).

A handful of people with graduate training from leading universities in the United States are effectively pushed aside with the sweeping argument that they were trained in a "positivistic" tradition and thus are implicitly uncritical of that position's weaknesses. Some "experts," often working with subsidiaries of large public relations agencies, have managed to gain a foothold in the private sector, based on what some colleagues see as "banal slogans" and "simplified methods." Any possible theoretical foundation for the advice given by these gurus is often hard to detect.

Organizations

Personnel employed in public relations, information services, and corporate trade journalism are organized into various professional associations. Most prominent is the Norwegian Association of Journalists, founded in 1894 and now including 3,700 of the nation's 5,000 journalists employed by 150 newspapers, a handful of TV stations, and some radio channels as well as by institutional and company publications. Strongly committed to freedom of both the press and speech, the Association acts as a strong bulwark against owners who see profit making as their only goal, and politicians who want to impose limitations.

Personnel in private companies also often hold membership in the Norwegian Association for Information and Public Affairs. Information-service personnel in state administration and national agencies, as well as in counties and communities, tend to join the Association for Public Information. Each of these organizations has nearly 1,000 members with the proportion of women climbing rapidly toward 50%.

Public relations managers with educational and career backgrounds generally unrelated to human communication rarely are members of any of these professional organizations. They seem to be hired on the basis of different types of qualifications known only by the CEOs who hire them.

Due to weak professionalization, the field obviously is vulnerable to ruthless abuse by opportunists who use PR jobs as stepping stones and short cuts to higher-status positions, thereby reducing the credibility of public relations as an operational concept and effectively blocking a natural development toward professionalization.

Craft or Profession?

A professional is understood to be an expert who is generating, transmitting, or utilizing research-based knowledge in his or her work (Rivers & Schramm, 1969, p. 240).

This implies that a professional must have extensive, advanced education that covers theoretical knowledge and must show how that knowledge is produced and applied. That, in turn, means that a professional must be trained in research.

Conversion of theoretical knowledge into applicable procedures may be learned through additional work experience. Only universities concentrate on providing such research knowledge. Thus, it would seem, a professional must hold an academic degree in his or her specified field.

Skills mastered by a craftsman or a clerk can be learned through lower-level schooling, apprenticeships, and job experience. However, the professional possesses systematic, theoretical knowledge which must be updated continually through papers presented at scientific conferences and articles in refereed journals. The craftsman practices clearly defined skills, whereas the professional tries to solve problems through the application of new knowledge derived from research.

In Norway, journalists and public relations practitioners often call themselves craftsmen. To some extent, this may explain the near absence of academic perspectives and internationally accepted standards of professionalism. A study of PR professionalization in Austria, Norway, and the United States (Coombs, Halladay, Hasenauer, & Signitzer, 1994, p. 32) stated that "the American and Austrian practitioners were more likely to be managers, whereas the Norwegian practitioners were more likely to be technicians." One explanation of this reasonable conclusion may be found in the groupings mentioned above and in the fact that the Norwegian sample analyzed ($N = 300$) was drawn from the Association for Information and Public Affairs (with a response rate of 50%). Members are recruited from secretarial and teaching backgrounds and from news journalism (35%–40%) and included very few academics or executives.

Measuring Effects

One of the most difficult problems in professional public relations relates to defining goals and measuring effects. Short-term effects of fluffy advertising often seem to impress management more than possible long-term public relations cultivation effects on public opinion.

Only when their companies are on the brink of bankruptcy do some CEOs call for a PR crisis plan, usually too late.

Thus an important problem for professional public relations practice is to develop methods for measuring the effects of projects and multiproject campaigns. The sophistication of methods used may reveal the level of professionalism in an organization's public relations division.

Some methods include *counting the PR division's activities,* such as number of press conferences held, press releases sent, and phone calls answered by press spokesman, as proof of their efficiency; *counting clippings* of press releases printed, news slots on radio or TV, and number of times the name of the company or its CEO has been mentioned by various media; *public-opinion polls* based on representative samples, with data presented in simple frequency distributions indicating widespread attitudes toward and knowledge of a given problem, company, agency, or person; and *full-scale research*, testing hypotheses derived from viable theories of human communication and attitude formation, applying complex cause-and-effects models, and presenting the results in reports containing thorough explanations of the findings.

Most companies and agencies seem to use the first two methods in evaluating and presenting their own activities. The third method is mentioned on occasion. It is extremely rare, however, to find any reference to method 4 in applied public relations research.

Priorities

A 1992 survey of members of the Association for Information and Public Affairs showed that media contact, production of printed publications, and membership information had top priority. Crisis management was defined as "avoiding bad press." Planning was mentioned sometimes, but analysis based on mass-communication theory and methods, often considered a major activity in a public relations division, generally was nonexistent.

Perhaps respondents failed to mention analytical activity partly through neglect or because they lacked awareness of what was going on. However, another obvious reason was a lack of functional connection between academic institutions for human-communication research on the one hand and practitioners, their companies, and their career systems on the other.

Professional Public Relations

Professional public relations is often believed to thrive in a symbiotic relationship with public opinion. Thus, one functional approach may be to study theories of public opinion—its nature and composition, its flexibility and fluctuations, its processes and effects—along with pertinent research methods. Such analysis would relate closely to the process and effects of human communication. In building bridges between theoretical research and practical application of related knowledge, some conceptual models may be useful.

Lasswell's still valid paradigm of 1948: "Who (source) says what (message) to whom (goal group) in which channel (medium) under what conditions (local situation: introduced later) with which effects (attitudes)?" is tailor-made to serve certain public relations purposes. Although the question is old, many possible applications are new.

In laying out an operational PR plan and explaining it in detail to a potentially suspicious management, however, the model should be reversed. Generating confidence in an institution requires strategies quite different from those designed to market more crackers. This can be shown by rewriting Lasswell's question so it reads somewhat like: "Which effects do we want to produce? Which conditions (including small-group, interpersonal communication) favor the process? Which media could be useful? Who are our target publics? What is our message (ideally content based on true reality, with its form tailored to fit each medium)? Who ought to be our sources?"

If the communication-process model is to function optimally, each element in it must meet certain criteria specified through research. High credibility has been shown by research to be crucial.

Also helpful is Triandis's (1971) model of human attitudes. This formulation identifies three measurable components: (a) knowledge (the cognitive component), (b) emotions (the affective component), and (c) experience (the conative component). These, in turn, yield an attitude which appears to be expressed in a fourth component (d) the attitude statement communicated in writing or verbally in an exchange of opinions, or in reply to a pollster's question.

The summed average of attitudes in a representative sample gives public opinion, presumably, in the population. It is accepted that an attitude, as an individual statement of commitment, may translate into action only under favorable conditions. Although an attitude statement (d above) is extremely difficult to influence directly, it may be possible to do so through a combination of one or more components.

A third useful concept is "Relative Deprivation" (RD), derived from the discrepancy between expectations and achievements in an individual or a sample, independent of a zero-point (Davies, 1962; Gurr, 1970; Lerner, 1974). Low RD is said to correlate with general satisfaction and mental equilibrium. On the other hand, high RD may result from high expectations in a situation of declining achievements. This is presumed to yield a lack of satisfaction, perhaps leading to individual, social, or political breakdown. Such disastrous results as suicide, divorce, mutiny, and revolution may ensue.

In a medium-RD situation, individual attitudes and summed public opinion might be characterized by frustration, resulting in reduced believability or credulity attributed to one's self, spouse, group, company, or government. These entities, in turn, may be viewed as sources in Lasswell's model. Low credulity may entail unwillingness to participate in common projects, pay taxes, vote for one's political party, or fight for one's country. Mass media have been found to stimulate fluctuations in expectation.

A procedure (Lazarsfeld and Reitz, 1975) for a functional public relations project and/or campaign would consist of four steps: analysis of public opinion relevant to one's project, a strategic Plan (including goal definition and operational methods) with a detailed description of various tactical steps, implementation with room for readjustments, and evaluation of results in light of one's goal.

Recently developed perspectives designed to involve sender and receiver in a series of mutually dependent changes (Grunig, 1992; Grunig & Grunig, 1990) are lifting public relations to higher levels and creating a path for new and hitherto unknown applications.

Credibility: A Key Factor

Realizing that credibility is a key factor in effective news communication and public relations, a series of research projects was started in the early 1980s (Mortensen, 1987). Television was repeatedly shown to earn higher credibility than newspapers. The newspaper, as the most important channel for news and information, seemed to convey more knowledge than television and radio, even with controls introduced for sex, education, and interest. Television was confirmed to be basically an entertainment medium.

Taking the research one step further (Mortensen, 1994b), the credibility of various occupations, sometimes used as sources for news and information, was investigated.

In two studies, random samples representative of the Norwegian population over 15 were asked about their perceptions of the credibility of various occupations. Data were collected by Nielsen-Norway in April 1991 and April 1994.

The question asked was; "People from various occupations sometimes give information in newspapers, on radio or TV. Such persons may be said to have

TABLE 17.1
Mean Credibility Rathings Assigned to Various Occupations

	1991			1994		
	Women	Men	All	Women	Men	All
	N = 634	N = 610	N = 1244	N = 567	N = 545	N = 1112
Occupation						
Clergyman	4.22	4.04	4.14	4.21	4.20	4.21
Police officer	4.16	4.03	4.10	4.22	4.26	4.24
Doctor	4.09	4.06	4.07	4.13	4.10	4.12
Teacher	3.93	3.84	3.88	3.98	3.91	3.94
Scientist	3.89	3.74	3.81	3.97	3.90	3.94
Radio/TV rep.	3.74	3.62	3.68	3.67	3.64	3.66
Mayor	3.71	3.59	3.65	3.77	3.80	3.78
Spokesman	3.63	3.40	3.52	3.64	3.50	3.57
Army officer	3.58	3.36	3.47	3.46	3.49	3.48
NP editor	3.28	3.19	3.23	3.29	3.31	3.30
Bank manager	3.04	2.83	2.93	3.30	3.19	3.25
Rep. Soc. P.	2.87	2.85	2.86	2.93	2.97	2.95
Rep. Cons. P.	2.90	2.80	2.85	2.77	2.92	2.84
Rep. Cent. P.	–	–	–	2.80	2.75	2.78
PR director	3.01	2.65	2.83	2.80	2.73	2.76
NP journalist	2.78	2.76	2.77	2.85	2.94	2.89
Marketing mgr.	2.50	2.34	2.42	2.42	2.47	2.44

more or less credibility, depending on whether you believe that they speak the truth or not, for example keeping important information to themselves, etc. I shall now read some occupations to you, and please tell me how credible you think each of them is."

Reply categories were 5 = "very credible"; 4 = "somewhat credible"; 3 = "just a little credible"; 2 = "somewhat incredible"; 1 = "not at all credible"; a = "do not know."

Source persons generally regarded as professionals (clergymen, police officers with law degree, and medical doctors) received higher credibility ratings than did personnel with trade-school education and elected representatives. Public relations directors, newspapers journalists, and marketing managers for car companies occupied the lowest positions. Data did not seem to be affected by the crises in banking and insurance experienced from 1991–92. Further research is underway to study the relationship between professionalism and perceived source credibility.

SOME CASES

Attitudes Toward Defense

Questions related to national security and defense tend to affect citizens in smaller countries more than in larger, continental nations. In Norway, most people have tended to favor a strong national defense after World War II and close ties to NATO ever since that organization was formed in 1949 (Mortensen, 1981, 1982b). Occasional fluctuations occurred, however, and some of these created conditions favorable for research.

In the early 1980s, both the Warsaw Pact and NATO deployed long-range missiles, threatening each other's territories and populations. Self-appointed task groups organized campaigns for or against such deployment, with varying effects upon public opinion.

In West Germany, large-scale demonstrations occurred on October 22, 1983 against NATO deployment of Pershing II missiles as counter measures to the setting up of SS missiles by the Warsaw-Pact countries. Instant coverage by American television of a reported 600,000 demonstrators created an overwhelming impression that an entire nation's population had turned against NATO, their own defense organization (Mortensen, 1983b). However, this enormous number amounted to barely 1% of West Germany's 60 million people. Polls made public later ("A peace movement," 1983) confirmed that the demonstrators were supported by another 7%, totalling 8% of the entire population. At the same time, 67% supported the NATO deployment decision whereas, as in most such cases, about 25% were undecided. The case illustrated clearly the unreliability of "blind" television reporting based solely on visual impressions.

In Norway, two campaigns were staged. One, called "No to nuclear weapons," was anti-NATO. The other was "For Norway, with NATO." The pro-NATO group combined a media campaign with colorful stickers. The anti-NATO movement conducted a media offensive along with a door-to-door campaign to collect personal signatures protesting the deployment of the NATO Pershings.

Research (Mortensen, 1984) conceptualized in light of the Triandis model showed that, although the pro-NATO campaign affected the *knowledge* component of attitude, the opposing effort had a stronger impact on the *emotional* component. Overall, the emotional anti-NATO campaign, inducing fear of nuclear war and collecting signatures, affected public opinion about defense and nuclear weapons more strongly than did the pro campaign which increased knowledge.

Earlier studies of the fear syndrome (Mortensen, 1982a) showed a curvilinear effect of the emotional component upon attitude. That is, a medium level of fear correlated with pro-defense attitudes whereas high fear went along with less positive assessments. Knowledge of defense and NATO seemed to immunize against fear to some extent, and high fear tended to block reception of new information.

Monsters and Submarines: In the Sea, and in the Head

People in the Nordic countries have always had close relations with nature and the creatures believed to live there, including trolls in the forests and monsters in the sea. In the deceptive Arctic light, a school of porpoise could easily be taken for a sea dragon, and a patch of fog in the early morning might look like a frightening monster. For centuries, there was nothing unnatural about such reports.

In the 1970s and 1980s, however, sightings of sea monsters tended to become increasingly rare. At the same time, news about "foreign" submarines violating national waters became almost daily fare in the Swedish and Norwegian media.

The Swedes got their proof in October 1981 when they found a Soviet submarine of the Whisky class firmly grounded on a skerry near the Karlskrona naval base. A modern, highly efficient press center was quickly established under the leadership of a navy captain. Soon the Swedish Navy was inundated by national and international media. The climax apparently was reached when hundreds of media people from around the world attended the presentation in Stockholm on April 26, 1983 of the Swedish Submarine Report. This report stated with absolute certainty that there had been a dramatic increase in clandestine operations by Soviet submarines in Swedish territorial waters and fiords.

The next morning, two divers operating from a dingy in a narrow fiord in neighboring Norway spotted something interesting about 500 yards away. Only 20 years earlier, they might have told about a sea monster. Now, they reported having observed "a foreign submarine."

17. PUBLIC RELATIONS: AN ALTERNATIVE TO REALITY? 331

First, they alerted the largest newspaper, the tabloid *VG*, which sent 15 reporters to the area within a few hours. Second, they called the Navy, which deployed its units shortly after. Soon international-media personnel, just about to leave Stockholm, became aware of the situation. They crossed the border into Norway and soon stormed the little village of Leirvik on the island of Stord, while numerous naval units within sight combed the fiords day and night for more than a week without finding any tangible traces of "one or more" foreign submarines allegedly hiding below. The media excitement level rose considerably, yielding headlines of a size usually reserved for wartime. Also, alarm may have become common in the population as a whole.

A Crisis Model. With Norway's commanding admiral and his tiny staff virtually overrun by national and international media, a crisis-management model was urgently needed.

There were three absolute prerequisites. First, the primary PR goal was to maintain positive public attitudes toward the Navy and a strong defense in general. Second, there should be no fiddling with the truth. Every word said to the public via the media should be the truth and nothing but the truth. And third, because a major routine of the Navy was to check unidentified objects along the coast, naval operations should be presented as routine.

One hypothesis, derived from Davies (1962), was that high public expectations of catching a foreign submarine, presumably resulting from sensationalist journalism, combined with a no-sub result, could create medium to high relative deprivation (RD) with correspondingly negative public opinion. In a situation with modest chances to deliver a real, freshly caught foreign submarine, three measures designed to maintain a low level of public expectations were implemented in order to keep RD low and stable by maintaining public expectations at a low level.

First, a policy of "maximum disclosure at minimum delay" was implemented. Thus, whenever there was a development of potential news value, the Navy immediately sent a sober press release with all necessary detail to discourage sensational coverage.

Second, by appointing a low-ranking (lieutenant commander) press spokesman to handle the follow-up, the Navy signalled to the mass media and the public that most of the news was non-dramatic and routine.

Third, by introducing the nondramatic term "unidentified submerged object" (USO) and avoiding reference to "foreign submarine," the Navy signalled its perception that any possible incident was routine. Interviewed about the "submarine chase," the Navy spokesman would confirm that "a USO has been reported by a civilian observer, and the Navy has deployed units to investigate and identify it." In radio interviews, he tended to begin with, "Thanks to alert observers along the coast, the Navy has received information . . ." thus stimulating further alertness. "But aren't you chasing a foreign submarine?" the follow-up question might be. "We don't know," the spokesman would respond, "because the object has not yet been identified." All of which was the plain truth. This procedure was applied for the rest of the 1980s. As expected, the media storm slowly calmed, although some flashes of unrealistic sensationalism showed up on occasion.

So, although the Swedish Navy was publicly chasing "Soviet submarines" in shallow fiords, harvesting public ridicule for not getting any visible results, the Norwegian Navy was "investigating reports of unidentified submerged objects," thereby avoiding public scorn when the object turned out to be a rotten log, an old kitchen sink, or a flock of ducklings.

Nothing Promised, Nothing Found. There were some significant real-life incidents, however. The Swedish Navy actually had its "Whisky on the Rocks," as mentioned. And some Norwegian fishermen got a Soviet submarine in their trawl off Haugesund on the southwestern coast, although in international waters. Foreign submarines were real enough, in enormous numbers, but obviously not present to the extent reported by the media. A simple public relations procedure, in this case, helped to present a more realistic news picture than the media alone were able to give.

After a long period (1969–1982) with frequent reports of "foreign submarines" all along the rugged 2,000-mile coast (including. 150,000 islands), official figures from the Royal Norwegian Navy showed that only 3 of 175 reports of possible foreign submarines had been identified as "sure" violations of territorial waters by such vessels. The pattern throughout the 1980s was similar. Furthermore, some of the incidents might have been caused by sea monsters in the head, well known for centuries by coastal people.

In a report made public recently (*Svenska Dagbladet,* August 30, 1994), the Swedish Navy admitted that sounds picked up with extremely sensitive instruments, and believed for years to originate in Soviet submarines, may have come from sea mammals such as the mink, otter, or seal.

It appears that the strategic decision to apply careful terminology was well justified. But the case also serves to demonstrate that public opinion, as well as media coverage, can vary considerably from one situation to another, depending on the terminology used in the agenda-setting process.

Public Opinion. Research showed that public opinion was affected substantially by "submarine" coverage in the media. In Sweden, the percentage who wanted to strengthen defense forces rose from 22% in September 1981, before the Whisky incident, to 42%, in November just afterwards (Tornquist, 1983). However, the percentage fell slowly to 29% in fall 1982 but rose sharply to 46% in May 1983, just after the Submarine Report had been published.

In Norway, this author found that those who believed that foreign submarines "for sure" had been violating national waters most strongly favored increased investment in modern naval equipment for submarine search. Later, the politicians voted to equip the Navy with VDS (Variable Depth Sonar), which increased efficiency considerably. Unfortunately, an attempt to test discrepancy hypotheses derived from the Davies-Gurr model could not be carried out due to a lack of suitable data.

Management Versus Public Relations

The relationship between management and PR expertise seems to be a crucial factor in all development of professionalism. American leadership guru George Kenning has done immense harm to the shaky development of public relations as a profession in Norway.

A car-factory worker from Janesville, Wisconsin, Kenning managed to bluff his way to the top management levels in five large U.S. corporations, and five Norwegian companies, with disastrous results. Holding that "a leader is a leader is a leader," regardless of education and professional socialization, the Kenning philosophy was eagerly embraced in the 1980s by ambitious youngsters, the so-called YAPs (YUPPIES), with almost religious fervor.

Kenning's alluring 31-slogan program created options for nonprofessionals to capture leading positions in public as well as private organizations without having to learn the trade and climb the cumbersome professional ladder. Some of these young leaders surrounded themselves with well-paid supporting groups that shared their beliefs in quick success without commitment, particularly in administering public relations. Nils Schjander, a business publisher in Oslo, wrote a book in Norwegian based on Kenning's philosophy (Schjander, 1987).

Against this backdrop and largely on the basis of visual appearance, news readers were randomly picked from the TV news desks and made PR directors overnight. Seemingly, public relations was considered a road to instant fame based on looks and charm. There was no room for research-based knowledge and a deeper understanding of human communication processes.

Whatever the boss decided was praised and cheered by public relations personnel whose most prevalent qualifications were blind faith in the Kenning religion and total loyalty to the CEO. Cheerleaders were amply awarded. In the course of a few years, the country's largest bank, then being run by managers, some of whom had minimal professional training in the banking system, increased the number of nominal "directors" from 3 to 327. For the nation as a whole, the number of bank directors tripled from 500 to 1,500, including the newly created public relations managers.

The results turned out to be disastrous.

Banking and Insurance. From 1991–1992, Norway's two largest banks and its largest insurance company experienced virtual breakdowns, with thousands of private investors losing their savings. Total losses ran into billions of dollars, leading to a government takeover for rescue purposes. Although the crisis situations were somewhat different, they produced data yielding valuable insight into corporate public relations.

In the insurance company, the CEO was a 37-year-old, self-admittedly devoted Kenning follower, surrounding himself with a crowd of young, cheering directors. Later, studies showed that the Kenning religion fostered a company culture according to which it was in bad taste to question the ideas and the decisions of the CEO. Only supportive comments were welcomed. This applied, in particular, to the hand-picked PR Director, a former clergyman who had been a TV news reader while studying theology.

In an attempt to buy up an insurance business beyond the national borders, company assets were overextended at great risk. Upon losing the takeover bid, the company was declared broke, with stocks written down to zero and the government throwing out a life line.

The CEO and his gang of cheerleaders, including the public relations director, had to go in August 1992. This raised some pertinent questions with regard to the role of the director. Should he have stuck loyally to a CEO who wanted to minimize publicity about potentially high risks, thus endangering the savings of thousands of stockholders? Or should he have felt committed to higher principles of open, truthful information, thereby informing mass media about the imminent crisis and giving stockholders an opportunity to withdraw their savings while there was still time? What could be expected of a public relations expert committed to professionalism? Should he resign if forced to lie, or withhold the truth? In this case, the theologian was richly rewarded for staying to the bitter end.

In one of the large banks, the public relations director was a former TV newscaster with a degree in history. Based on his TV fame, he was hand-picked by the CEO with the declared purpose of creating "good press" for the bank. In this capacity, he served as media spokesman, quite often praising various products and services to customers and thereby trespassing into the dangerous mine field of marketing.

When the crisis came in the fall of 1991 and the stockholders lost their savings, he was caught in his own methods, and had to abandon ship with the CEO, equipped with a generous parachute.

Furious Investors. Investors and savers were publicly furious. After the government takeover, a newspaper headline stated that the bank was "begging for credibility," indicating that the public relations director had put its credibility at risk.

Referring to the Davies-Gurr model, it might be hypothesized that public frustration became so serious partly because expectations had been stimulated by the praising—even bragging—of the spokesman. When the crisis came, relative deprivation turned out to be more severe than if public expectations had been lower. The case again raises the question of whether the director should oversell management decisions at any price or help prepare the public for possible crises by lowering the expectation curve to a realistic level. Such lowering might have minimized RD, the resulting frustration, and finally the loss of credibility for an entire industry.

In the aftermath of these disasters, business people concluded that newscasting was not the very best training ground for public relations directors after all. Now they seem to feel that a business education is much better. In this way, the same system, still based on the Kenning religion, is being carried on, with yet another type of nonprofessional filling the role of public relations director. Business bosses hire business people for public relations jobs. "Loyalty" to the boss is often listed in newspaper ads as the most important qualification for the PR staff. This system of awarding nonprofessionals is virtually strangling any attempt to introduce professional perspectives.

Formulations about the field such as Grunig's 4-stage evolutionary model mean little to people who lack basic understanding of human-communication processes. Business executives obviously tend to master accounting and finance. Engineers know a great deal about technology. However, neither group cares much about separating administration from leadership (i.e., applied human communication).

Professionalization in public relations requires the use of modern methods in analyzing public opinion and equally important approaches for defining and carrying out ethical public relations. These developments clearly require managers with much more than just an intuitive understanding of human communication as a prerequisite for good leadership and effective public relations.

Small-Scale Whaling

Due to geographical location, it was only natural that Norway should become a leading whaling nation. Small-scale whaling has been carried out for centuries along the nation's long coast, especially in North Norway which borders on vast, Arctic bodies of water.

In 1904, Norwegian expeditions started to harvest the huge resource of large whales in the Antarctic for the production of oils and bone meal. In the peak season of 1930–31, more than 10,000 Norwegian whalers participated in 41 expeditions with 232 corvette-size whale catchers. These vessels bagged 40,000 large 75-foot whales, producing 2.3 million barrels of whale oil (almost two thirds of the world's total output in that period), with a value amounting to approximately 10% of the country's exports.

Having had a commission to regulate whaling since 1924, Norway took the initiative in 1936 to save the large species, specifically blue and fin whales, by limiting the catch through quotas. Other nations, notably Japan and Nazi Germany, refused to comply. Norwegian companies then unilaterally reduced their activities to 14 expeditions per year. However, when 17 nations finally gathered in 1946 for the signing of The International Whaling Agreement, it was too late to save the giants of the sea. Large-scale whaling in the Antarctic ended in 1963.

In North Norway, however, a totally different form of hunting for small (12–15-foot) whales had been going on for hundreds of years, harvesting meat for human consumption. Around 1990, after years of preservation, the population of mink whales had grown to an estimated 90,000 animals. Researchers advised the government to allow small-scale whaling. A few Norwegian whalers in North Norway, traditionally involved in this activity, were permitted to catch approximately 300 small whales each year. (See Fig. 17.2.)

This caused an outcry from scattered groups of idealists, mainly in the United States and Germany, who threatened to stage boycotts of Norwegian fish and other products. For some time, there was a danger that the U.S. government might be pressured to impose sanctions unless the Norwegian authorities banned all whaling completely.

To counter the arguments from various protest groups and explain the actual situation in Norway, an American public relations firm was hired to carry out a campaign, so far with unknown results.

International Public Relations

The actual example just discussed shows how difficult it is to explain a complex situation in one country to inhabitants of another (Mortensen, 1980). Thus, perhaps there is a real need for international public relations as a specialized field of study, closely related to research in international news communication.

When receiving new information from elsewhere, people inevitably try to

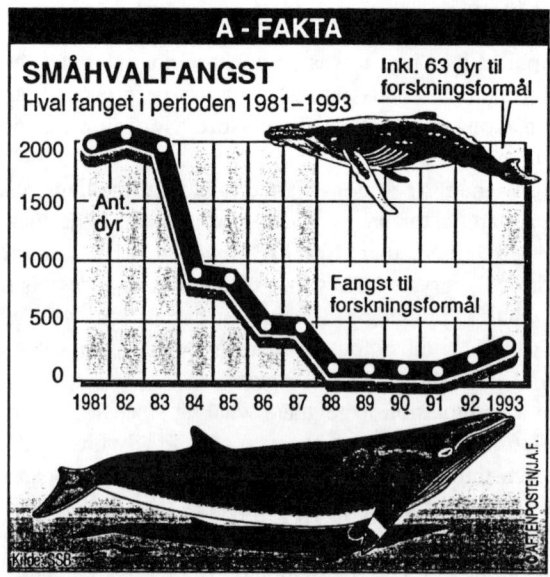

FIG. 17.2. Catch of small whaltes in north Norway, 1980–1993 (courtesy *Aftenposten,* Oslo).

interpret it in light of meaningful patterns (mental schemata) present in their own familiar environments.

Addressing a target group in the midwestern state of Wisconsin, for example, one might compare small-scale whaling to deer hunting. In Wisconsin, deer hunters are permitted to harvest just over 200,000 animals annually. That amounts to 20% of the estimated 1 million deer in that state. Such a proportion seems appropriate to maintain a stable deer population. And the need to strive for such stability is a principle generally accepted in most societies. By comparison, Norwegian whalers harvest only 0.3% of the estimated whale population which is reproducing at a much slower rate.

Furthermore, another important difference seems apparent. Whereas most deer hunters in Wisconsin are amateurs, the whalers in North Norway are experts with extensive experience from many years of fishing and hunting in Arctic waters, supported by biological scientists. Given Norway's documented record as a nation with great concern for environmental protection and responsible harvesting of natural resources, there may be good reason to accept small-scale whaling within strict quota limits enforced by legal authorities.

Unpredictability?

Speaking of public opinion, some turbulence in one sector may produce unpredictable results in another. Recent research (Kolstad, Rundmo, & Svarva, 1995) has shown that the successful Winter Olympics at Lillehammer in February 1994, led to enhanced self-confidence in certain segments of the Norwegian population (pride in being Norwegian was up from 79% before the games to 88% after) accompanied by a somewhat increased (skepticism toward foreigners). These sentiments may have spilled over into the national referendum in October the same year, on whether Norway were to join the European Union as a full member, when the result turned out to be a meager majority of 51.8% opposing such membership. But how could the connection and its outcome have been predicted? Obviously, sophisticated research is the only answer.

Public Relations for Peace?

In the course of just a few years, the number of United Nations peacekeeping and peacemaking soldiers has increased from 12,000 to 80,000 as the United Nations has taken more active steps to curb budding wars. Originally intended to stop wars between nations, peacemaking and peace-maintaining operations have recently been used to prevent civil wars from spreading and escalating into larger international conflicts.

The U.N. apparatus for negotiating peace between warring parties is still geared toward conflicts between governments, however. Negotiations in Geneva and other diplomatic centers often fail to solve problems on the micro level. Military peace forces tend to curb overt hostilities by keeping warring groups apart and freezing the front lines, but the underlying local conflicts continue to smolder, seemingly forever, in places such as Kashmir, Cyprus, Lebanon, and Somalia.

Military peacekeeping operations clearly follow a pattern of confrontation with threats, sanctions, and punishment (Mortensen, 1994a). Other systems, introduced by people such as Mahatma Gandhi, Pater Dominique Pire, Nobel Peace Prize winner in 1959, and Willy Brandt of Germany, recently joined by former U.S. President Jimmy Carter, are less aggressive. Within a framework suggested by these men, a sophisticated public relations approach might aim at bringing people together so as to enhance dialogue, information sharing, exploring of common values, creation of mutual human understanding, and cooperation before hostilities break out. All parties might benefit.

There seems to be an urgent need for such new methods directed at the ethnic or tribal level in local societies. Although research at these levels traditionally has proceeded under the banner of social anthropology, methods for solving such problems might just as well be a hot topic for public relations experts.

According to the two-way symmetric model (Grunig & Grunig, 1990), two or more parties in a conflict move through a series of changes leading toward equilibrium and possible peace. At the initial stages of an escalating conflict, this system might be suitable for use by specially trained U.N. peacekeepers or peacemakers in their field operations. It ought to be refined and developed for application on the micro level in pre-civil war situations, possibly in cooperation with social anthropologists and other social scientists.

CONCLUSION

In operation for thousands of years without a proper name, public relations is a fascinating construct with a potentially important role to play in the future. Through most of this century, ambitious public relations professionals have had to defend themselves on two sides. Attacks came from the ruthless power of marketing, seeking short-term profits at the expense of truth and credibility, and from sensationalist journalism with little concern for truth and reality.

Squeezed between two such mighty forces, what space can possibly be left for a public relations profession committed to ideals of interpersonal understanding, with the potential to create goodwill among individuals and groups, and even, perhaps, to further peace among tribes and nations?

The answer may lie in the development of new international perspectives, more sophisticated, research-based operational models, and intensified drives toward universally accepted professionalism.

REFERENCES

A peace movement peacefully masses against missiles. (1983, October 31). *Time*, pp. 48–49.
Coombs, T. W., Halladay, S., Hasenauer G., & Signitzer, B. (1994). A comparative analysis of

17. PUBLIC RELATIONS: AN ALTERNATIVE TO REALITY? 339

international public relations: Identification and interpretation of similarities and differences between professionalization in Austria, Norway, and the United States. *Journal of Public Relations Research, 6,* 23–39.

Davies, J. C. (1962). Toward a theory of revolution. *American Sociological Review, 27,* 5–19.

Ehling, W. P. (1992). Public relations education and professionalism. In J. E. Grunig (Ed.), *Excellence in public relations and communication management* (pp. 439–464). Hillsdale, NJ: Lawrence Erlbaum Associates.

Grunig, J. (Ed.). (1992). *Excellence in public relations and communication management.* Hillsdale, NJ: Lawrence Erlbaum Associates.

Grunig, J. (1993). The relationship between public relations and marketing as a management function. In T. Duncan, C. Caywood, & D. Newsom (Eds.), *Preparing advertising and public relations students for the communications industry in the 21st Century* (Task Force Report). Columbia, SC: Association for Education in Journalism and Mass Communication.

Grunig, J. E., & Grunig, L. A. (1990, August). *Models of public relations: Review and reconceptualization.* Paper presented to the Public Relations Division, Association for Education in Journalism & Mass Communication, Minneapolis, MN.

Gurr, T. (1970). *Why men rebel.* Princeton, NJ: Princeton University Press.

Kolstand, A., Rundmo, T., & Svarva, K. (1995). *The XVII Olympic Winter Games: Ethnocentrism and the Olymic Ideals.* Paper, Department of Psychology, University of Trondheim.

Lasswell, H. D. (1960). The structure and function of communication in society. In W. Schramm (Ed.), *Mass Communication* (pp. 117–130).

Lazarsfeld, P. F., & Reitz, J. G. (1975). *An introduction to applied sociology.* New York: Elsevier.

Lerner, D. (1974). Toward a communication theory of modernization: A set of considerations. In W. Schramm & D. Roberts (Eds.), *The process and effects of mass communication* (pp. 861–889). Urbana, ILL: Illinois University Press.

Mortensen, M. S. (1980). *Beyond the horizon: International news communication and the increasing danger of war.* Unpublished paper.

Mortensen, M. S. (1981). Psychological defense preparedness: Concept and reality. *Norwegian Journal of Military Science, 3,* 113–126.

Mortensen, M. S. (1982a). Fear of war and attitudes toward defense: Is there a causal relationship? *Norwegian Journal of Military Science, 6,* 239–250.

Mortensen, M. S. (1982b). Attitudes to military defense in Norway. *Armed Forces and Society, 9,* 49–62.

Mortensen, M. S. (1983a, October). *Crisis in NATO: Perceptions and reality.* Paper presented to the Inter-University Seminar on the Military and Society, Chicago, IL.

Mortensen, M. S. (1983b, October). *Does modern news reporting contribute to international misunderstanding?* Speech delivered at Sigma Delta Chi conference, St. Louis, MO.

Mortensen, M. S. (1984). Attitudes to NATO: Toward an analytical model, *Forum International* (SOWI), *4,* 97–134.

Mortensen, M. S. (1987). *Troverdigheten teller: Fernsyn og avis under lupen* [Credibility counts: Focus upon newspaper and television]. Fredrikstad, Norway: Institute for Journalism.

Mortensen, M. S. (1990, August). *The U.N. peace-keeper: A new type of soldier?* Paper presented to American Sociological Association, Washington DC.

Mortensen, M. S. (1994a, July). *Peace-keeping/making: Soldiers alone cannot do it.* Invited paper presented to the International Sociological Association Convention, Bielefeld, Norway.

Mortensen, M. S. (1994b). Roles and role-playing in journalism, information services and propaganda. Unpublished manuscript.

NOU no. 3 (1982). *Massemedier og mediepolitikk* [Mass media and media policy]. Oslo: State of Norway.

Rivers, W. L., & Schramm, W. (1969). *Responsibility in mass communication.* New York: Harper & Row.

Rose, P. B., & Miller, D. A. (1994, Summer). Merging advertising and PR: Integrated marketing communication. *Journalism Educator, 49*(2), 52–63.

Schjander, Nils (1987). *Hvis is jeg bare hadde en bedre sjef* [If I only had a better boss]. Oslo: Hjemmets Bokforlag.

Tornquist, K. (1983). *Ubotshotet och svensk opinion* [The Threat of Submarines and Swedish Public Opinion]. Stockholm: Beredskapsnamnden for psykologisk forsvar [The Administration for Psychological Defense].

Triandis, Harry C. (1971). *Attitudes and attitude change*. New York: Wiley.

18   Romania: From Publicitate Past to Public Relations Future

Judy VanSlyke Turk
University of South Carolina

It was the fall of 1992, and Romania had been free for almost 3 years. Life was bleak, bleaker than most Romanians had expected. A revolution and the execution of a hated Communist dictator should have made life better for most Romanians, but instead there was grinding poverty where there should have been plenty. Despair and frustration prevailed where there should have been jubilation.

Few Romanians had money—the average family of four subsisted on a weekly wage equivalent to $50 U.S.—and even those who tried could find little to buy. Shop windows were dusty, mostly empty. Inventory was unpredictable: there might be laundry detergent and some canned fruit today but none tomorrow, and lines at bakeries and markets that stocked milk formed before dawn because the supply certainly would not last until midday.

Going about one's daily routines, getting children dressed for school and adults off to work, was difficult. There might or might not be hot water for bathing; in fact, there might not even be any water coming out of the tap at all. Electricity came and went capriciously. Long lines formed at the handful of petrol stations that served the entire Bucharest metropolitan area of several million people.

The country's newspapers and radio and television stations, once tightly controlled, censored and subsidized by the central Communist government, now seemed tightly controlled by greed.

The owners and publishers of these media seemed to know little and to care less about journalism and the role it might play in Romania's transition from oppression to freedom. Front page stories focused not on the economic, political, and social conditions in Romania but on tabloid sensationalism and fiction, which certainly sold newspapers in 1992 Romania. One day's top story was headlined, "Hillary Clinton Gives Birth To Alien Baby."

Many Romanians, especially the younger ones, wore on their faces looks of resignation, as if to say, "These conditions were inevitable. We were foolish to expect more from freedom. We have everything to learn. We have no democratic traditions. We don't understand democracy. It's nobody's fault that we don't, but this is the way things will be until we do."

It was into this environment that Veronica Savanciuc launched her new public relations, advertising, and marketing company. A former operations manager in Bucharest for DHL Worldwide, a courier service, with a college degree in economics, Savanciuc was among the first of a new breed of communications entrepreneurs in Romania who responded to the new marketing opportunities created by the entry of multinational giants like Coca-Cola, Colgate-Palmolive, and Philip Morris into the Romanian and Eastern European markets.

Savanciuc's revenue in those early days consisted almost entirely of fees her firm collected for media placement: placing in local media advertising developed elsewhere, generally Western Europe, by large multinational advertising and public relations firms, or by a manufacturing company's advertising and public relations staff. That is really not surprising considering the relative immaturity of Romania's media, not to mention the lack of a market in Romania for many of these big-name brands largely because few Romanians had the money to purchase any of the advertised goods.

There also was some trade show business for Savanciuc's firm, organizing exhibits for foreign and Romanian companies, and some "above the line" activity primarily in the area of event sponsorship.

But that was then, and this is now. A more robust Romanian economy, a political system that is beginning to open itself to outside view and popular input, and a climate of guarded optimism about individual and collective futures in the country have changed the Romanian landscape. Shop windows and shelves are full again, and there are even new shops that stock imported delicacies and luxuries.

There are no more bread lines, although shoppers still line up for milk before daylight to insure they can purchase that necessity. Romanians, especially the young, and 35% of the country's population is under the age of 25, seem to have more money to spend, despite an annual inflation rate that approaches 1000 %, and they are buying cassette tapes and CDs, tickets to concerts and the opera, and Lee and Levi jeans as well as necessities.

There seems to be more gaiety and less despair although those who hunger for accurate, factual, objective reports of major political and economic news in their newspapers or on radio or television are terribly frustrated to find that alien babies and other sensationalist "trash" still get the most prominent play.

And new public relations firms seem to be springing up like mushrooms after several consecutive days of rain. Compared with the handful of firms in business when Savanciuc started her firm, there are now more than 50, most of them either local affiliates of major Western European or U.S. firms or small, specialized "boutique" firms that do only event sponsorship or trade association work.[1]

In this increasingly upbeat environment, Savanciuc's firm, Plus Advertising, has thrived, growing in 18 months from a staff of fewer than 20 to more than 40, and from just one major client, DHL, to annual billings of more than $1.5 million U.S. and a client list that includes major European, Japanese, and U.S. companies such as Gauloises cigarettes, Hewlett-Packard, Levi Strauss, Toyota, and Johnson & Johnson.

Romania seems to have "discovered" public relations. But it is a different public relations, a less mature public relations, than what is practiced in the United States, in the rest of Europe, or even in the rest of Eastern Europe. Eva Hoffman, in her *Exit Into History: A Journey Through the New Eastern Europe* (1993), noted that one of the myths imposed on Eastern Europe over the last 40 years was the myth of uniformity, which suggests that shared Communist ideology and politics made one Eastern European nation pretty much like its neighbors.

With freedom, however, has come the recognition that the countries of Eastern Europe are a melange of different ethnic groups, classes, and subcultures. Romania, more frequently an arena for imperial struggles and expansion throughout its history than the other countries of Eastern Europe, has responded in unique ways to the challenges and opportunities of this new freedom.

As Hoffman (1993) observed:

> Among all the shortages in Romania, perhaps the most serious is the shortage of a usable past. The recent past represents a kind of negative capital, an almost pure deficit. And, if the new goal is something like a pluralist democracy, the longer past has few precedents for it, few points of reference around which new ideas might coalesce. Romania's history is marked by discontinuities more than by continuities, by oppression more than by independence, by various forms of authoritarianism more than by liberalism . . . Even economic recovery is very much dependent on certain social legacies. Nobody knows how to do the transition in Romania because there's no social base, no tradition from which to start. (p. 293)

GENERIC PRINCIPLES: GUIDEPOSTS FOR THE FUTURE

It is no wonder, then, that public relations in Romania would fail to share the generic principles of effective public relations that Grunig (1992) and his col-

---

[1] Major international firms with affiliates in Romania include Gray, Young & Rubicam, McCann-Erickson, Saatchi & Saatchi, Leo Burnett, and BBDO. Most emphasize advertising over public relations but, nevertheless, embrace the concept of integrated communication, offering advertising, marketing, and public relations support for a client's communications objectives. These large international firms generally delegate only media placement and plan implementation to their Romanian affiliates, maintaining creative and strategic planning control in their European headquarters.

leagues identified in their seminal research. Grunig did not deny that different forms of public relations practice can, and perhaps even should exist in different cultures and locations; rather, he proposed that effective public relations will share generic principles across cultures.

Among those principles or characteristics are an emphasis on strategic management, separation of the public relations and marketing functions, a direct reporting relationship to top management for the senior public relations practitioner within an organization, use of the two-way symmetric model of public relations, and management of the public relations function by senior practitioners who have learned the theoretical body of knowledge in public relations and who oversee a staff that includes both managers and technicians.

Anecdotal evidence and data collected through administration of a questionnaire indicated that public relations as practiced in Romania is largely nonstrategic, is closely linked with marketing, is rarely located near the top of the organizational hierarchy, almost never follows the two-way symmetric model, and is practiced by would-be technicians with virtually no public relations training.

An organization that practices strategic public relations, according to Grunig (1992), develops programs "to communicate with the publics, both external and internal, that provide the greatest threats to and opportunities for the organization (p. 6)." This presumes that public relations practitioners have identified organizational publics, categorized them as external or internal, identified the positive and negative linkages between each public and the organization, and prioritized those publics on the basis of the magnitude of those positive and negative linkages.

Public relations practitioners in Romania do differentiate between external and internal publics. However, they tend to view the external public as one large, homogeneous mass public reached through the mass media. One Romanian practitioner who works for a federal agency put it this way: "We choose a nice person to do public relations, not necessarily someone who has skills. And these people don't have an understanding of targeting media channels or audiences."[2]

In Romania, public relations is practiced almost exclusively as propaganda and promotion, two techniques that were very much a part of the tradition under Communist rule.

Indeed, in the Romanian language, the word "publicitate" is used to describe both propaganda and publicity, as if the two were one and the same.[3] And, given the nature of the economic development in Romania, it also is not surprising that,

---

[2]Focus group interview July 6, 1993 in Bucharest, Romania.

[3]Both public relations practitioners and journalists in Romania agree that taking the propaganda out of publicity, the information public relations practitioners provide to the mass media, is proving a difficult lesson to learn. Stefan Niculescu-Maier, an editor at *Romania Libera,* one of the country's largest national newspapers published in Bucharest, said in an interview on July 6, 1993 that public relations practitioners "are not viewed as legitimate sources of information" by the news media. "I

rather than being a separate function from marketing, public relations is closely tied to marketing objectives. When asked to identify those activities they performed most often for their employers or clients, Romanian practitioners listed product-promotion news releases, trade show expositions, product launches, and sponsorship of community, cultural, and sporting events.[4]

Most of these practitioners said they rarely have contact with the chief executive or operating officer of their organization or of their client organizations.[5] In some cases, they had not even met this individual, and in all cases, access to her or him to gather information or discuss strategy was almost unheard of. "Our companies do not understand the value of public relations," said one practitioner. "They see image as something that just is, that exists regardless. We must convince executives that what we do is important and necessary before they will treat us like they treat the accountants or other managers in the company."[6]

Persuasion and Press Agentry: Focal Points

Responses to a questionnaire used to identify which model or models of public relations an organization practices[7] indicated that the press agentry/publicity and two-way asymmetric models of public relations prevail in Romania. Given the heavy emphasis on product promotion and publicity-as-propaganda in Romanian public relations practice, these tendencies came as no surprise. Romanian practi-

---

don't use much PR pre-made information because it is publicity, not news," Niculescu-Maier said. "What I want is news, and I have to get that from the general manager or company executive, not from a spokesperson who often doesn't really know what is happening." The problem with the Romanian view of publicity, Maier and public relations practitioners agreed, is that in Romania, publicity is not news but is "exaggerated benefits of products, comparisons with competitors' products that cannot be verified, and sometimes false images instead of truth." Western-style publicity and media relations thus have limited value for public relations practitioners in Romania: The news media generally ignore this information because it lacks credibility and is not trustworthy. So public-relations practitioners instead rely heavily on press-agentry "hype" and on promotional communication and events where propagandistic tendencies are more expected and acceptable.

[4]Focusgroup interview July 6, 1993 in Bucharest, Romania. Six practitioners (three working for central government agencies, two for public relations or advertising/public relations agencies, and one for a corporation) participated in the focus group conducted by the author. Participants were selected as a purposeful sample of representative practitioners by the Faculty of Journalism and Mass Communication Studies at the University of Bucharest.

[5]*Ibid.*

[6]*Ibid.*

[7]The questionnaire administered by the author to Romanian practitioners was adapted from instruments used by Grunig to ascertain which organizations practiced which models of public relations. It consisted of 16 statements, four per public relations model, to which respondents were asked to indicate agreement or disagreement on a 5-point scale. The 14 respondents were practitioners selected by the author from a larger pool of applicants to be the recipients of a week-long training program conducted in Bucharest by the College of Journalism and Mass Communications of the University of South Carolina under a grant from the United States Information Agency.

tioners tended to agree most often, and most strongly, with the following statements that point to the use of the press-agentry/publicity (PA) or two-way asymmetric (2A) models: "The purpose of our public relations is, quite simply, to get publicity for this organization" (PA); "We determine how successful our PR programs are from the number of people who attend an event or who use our products or services" (PA); "In our PR programs, we mostly attempt to get favorable publicity into the media and to keep unfavorable publicity out" (PA); "Before starting a PR program, we look at attitude surveys to make sure we describe the organization and its policies in ways our publics would be most likely to accept" (2A); and "Our broad goal is to persuade publics to behave as the organization wants them to behave" (2A).

What was somewhat surprising was that despite their tendency to favor public relations approaches and tactics whose goal is persuasion, even when the communication involved is two-way, most Romanian practitioners also said their purpose frequently was to develop mutual understanding between the management of the organization and the publics the organization affects. This clearly suggests a two-way symmetric approach.

Most practitioners in Romania have no training, formal or informal, in public relations. Their college degrees are in engineering or economics or philology (a discipline not found in Western higher education but one that seems to combine philosophy, rhetoric, and mythology).

They could not have studied public relations in college even if they had wanted to, for the first recognized college-level course in public relations was not taught in Romania until 1993 at the University of Bucharest.[8] And that course was taught by a member of the faculty with no training or experience in public relations, so what formal education exists may be of questionable professional value.

Romanian practitioners are acutely aware of their lack of training and experience. As one put it, "The neglect of training in the theoretical and conceptual foundations of public relations, like persuasion and opinion formation, is responsible for the poor public relations performance in our country."[9]

Plus Advertising's Savanciuc said she had even considered selling an interest in her agency to an international public- relations firm, or affiliating with such a firm, just to get training for herself and her staff. "There's very little training available except through the big firms like Saatchi & Saatchi," she said. "We have to go to Europe or the United States, and we cannot afford that unless we work for companies who pay for us to come for training."[10]

---

[8] A noncredit course in public relations also has been offered sporadically by AZR, an association formed by the country's newspaper publishers. But it is not recognized by the country's higher education establishment, nor is it accredited by the federal agency that monitors quality of educational offerings.

[9] Focus group interview July 6, 1993 in Bucharest, Romania.

[10] *Ibid.*

CONCLUSION

Although public relations in Romania may not yet be effective based on Grunig's generic principles, it seems reasonable to expect that effectiveness and excellence in public relations may lie ahead for Romania if current trends within Romania's economy, within its social order, and within the public relations practitioner community continue.

Industries formerly owned and controlled by the national government are slowly being privatized. Foreign investment in Romania's manufacturing and service industries continues to grow, albeit slowly. Romanians are beginning to experiment with their newfound personal freedoms, and are beginning to demand and expect more openness and truth telling in communication between government and the governed, between media and media consumers. All of these developments point toward an environment that will be supportive of an expanded role for public relations.

Even more promising for the future than these developments, however, is the hunger of Romanian public relations practitioners, and young professionals from other fields who want to be practitioners, for formal education and training in the field's theories, concepts, and techniques.

Although not all U.S. or Western European perspectives and practices can be compatible with Romanian culture, it is, nevertheless, to Europe and most especially to the United States that Romanian practitioners look for education, training, and examples of effective practice.

REFERENCES

Hoffman, E. (1993). *Exit into history: A journey through the new eastern Europe.* New York: Penguin Books USA.

Grunig, J. E. (1992). *Generic and specific concepts of multi-cultural public relations.* Paper presented to the Association for the Advancement of Policy, Research and Development in the Third World, Orlando, FL.

19 Public Relations in the German Democratic Republic and the New Federal German States

Günter Bentele
Grazyna-Maria Peter
University of Leipzig

After the opening of the borders of the German Democratic Republic (the former East Germany, GDR), due to the pressure of an enormous wave of would-be emigres on November 9, 1989, and after the reunification of the two German states, which hardly anyone would have deemed possible, even in Germany, only 1 year earlier, a completely new economic development along the lines of the market economy began in the east German states, massively supported with financial aid from the Western states.

This development included the speedy establishment of a free press based on private ownership, which provided relevant economic reporting, and an extension of a "dual broadcasting system," that is, the coexistence of private and public broadcasting (radio and TV) to the "new" federal states of Brandenburg, Mecklenburg-Vorpommern, Saxony, Saxony-Anhalt, and Thuringia.

Along with these developments came the rise of a public relations field largely patterned after that in the West. Components of the field included public relations departments in newly created companies and those reconstructed from GDR industrial enterprises, departments in the eastern branches of Western firms (e.g., banks, the car industry), and new advertising and public relations agencies. Also, the last few years have brought expansion and a new self-concept among institutions engaged in municipal and state public relations.

In order to understand this development and the present state of the public relations sector in the eastern federal states, we first describe in broad outline the public-communication section that existed in the German Democratic Republic. Then, we deal with the newly developing public relations sector in the new federal states.

PUBLIC RELATIONS IN THE GERMAN DEMOCRATIC REPUBLIC: CONCEPTS AND STRUCTURE

In the east of Germany, where a second German state, the German Democratic Republic, existed within the Soviet domain from 1949 to 1990, the term public relations was well known. However, the phrase carried negative connotations and was not used very often.

Officially, in line with the ruling Marxist–Leninist party and state ideology, public relations was regarded as an instrument of the manipulative practices of capitalist society. Therefore, the German term *Oeffentlichkeitsarbeit* (working for the public) was used. That word had been used as a synonym for public relations in the Federal Republic of Germany since the early 1950s. At present, the terms Oeffentlichkeitsarbeit and public relations are viewed as equivalent in Germany. The phrase public relations is preferred by industry and public relations agencies, as well as by individual consultants. On the other hand, Oeffentlichkeitsarbeit often refers to comparable activity on the state and community levels, by associations, and in the nonprofit sector.

In the GDR, the genesis of Oeffentlicheitsarbeit was closely related with economic development, and it came about primarily because of intensified economic contacts with markets in western Europe in the early 1960s. The situation in the other communist states of eastern Europe was similar. An important event here was the Second Conference of the Foreign Trade Promoting Organizations of COMECON, the Soviet-led economic system of the eastern bloc, held in Prague in March 1964. On the one hand, participants warned against uncritical adoption of Western public relations concepts. On the other hand, they recommended derivation of certain ideas from these concepts for use in public relations relating to trade among socialist states (Tamme, 1964).

Public Relations und unsere Aussenhandelskontakte auf kapitalistischen Maerkten (Public relations and our activities in foreign trade with capitalist markets), written by Alfred Klein and published in the journal *Neue Werbung* (New Advertising) in East Berlin in 1964, was the first article that publicly advocated the introduction of the term Oeffentlichkeitsarbeit in the GDR. After this publication, a sometimes controversial discussion began about the meaning, tasks, and methods of Oeffentlichkeitsarbeit and how these differed from advertising (cf. Klein, 1964).

During this discussion, two polarized groups emerged. On the one hand, advertising experts regarded Oeffentlichkeitsarbeit as the economically oriented promotion of products and firms. Some of these people wanted to draw a clear line of separation between Oeffentlichkeitsarbeit and the political agitation and propaganda undertaken by the parties and the state organs. On the other hand, representatives of press offices and social scientists understood Oeffentlichkeitsarbeit in its real, comprehensive sense, but postulated a monopoly of ideology and information by the Socialist Unity Party (SUP; i.e., SED) and its state power. This view, although phrased in several different ways, did not change until the end of the GDR. The concept was expressed well in the definition taken from the *Woerterbuch der Journalistik* (Dictionary of Journalism, Karl Marx University, 1971):

> *Oeffentlichkeitsarbeit* is the continuous or ad-hoc information about the goals, achievements and problems of an organization or institution disseminated by political parties, social organizations and state institutions—especially by institutions in the economic field—through various journalistic and non-journalistic channels. By Oeffentlichkeitsarbeit it is intended to create or intensify, in the general public or in a specific target group addressed both at home and abroad, a specific attitude toward the projects, views and achievements of the organization or institution concerned or a willingness to cooperate in solving their tasks, respectively. Oeffentlichkeitsarbeit fulfills an important function in the development of the citizen's socialist consciousness. In accordance with the congruence of the basic interests of all social forces in the socialist state, Oeffentlichkeitsarbeit as practiced by a socialist organization or institution—in contrast to public relations determined by class antagonisms and competition in an imperialist society—always also serves to solve the general tasks of the socialist society. (p. 266)

Thus, Oeffentlichkeitsarbeit was regarded as an important sphere of ideology formation and ideological struggle (Karl Marx University, 1971). This definition also incorporated the views held by the foreign-trade functionary, Fred Merkwitschka, who wrote the GDR's first doctoral dissertation about the subject of Oeffentlichkeitsarbeit (Merkwitschka, 1968). The author explicitly referred to important West German and Austrian publications with regard to both the theoretical premises and the methodological tools of Oeffentlichkeitsarbeit. Merkwitschka made two statements that were remarkable for the GDR at that time. First, he perceived an objective interest of the socialist society in "that all its members, enterprises, and institutions—as well as state, social and municipal agencies—should mutually inform each other about their activities in a truthful manner" (Merkwitschka, 1968, p. 40). Second, he presumed that Oeffentlichkeitsarbeit enhanced the transparency of the socialist social order for the individual citizen (Merkwitschka, 1968, p. 45).

Such views may have been held honestly. However, neither at that time nor later were they in agreement with the practices of the SUP and its state power, that is, with the reality of the GDR's information policy. A great number of security regulations, such as the "Decision of the Council of Ministers of the G. D. R. concerning the principles of guaranteeing security and order in the state and economic organs, the associations of nationally owned enterprises, nationally owned collective combines and firms" of September 25, 1968, regulated the dissemination of information to the public. As a consequence, the individual ministries and the state press office of the GDR issued internal lists advising their subordinate units of taboo issues excluded from public information. In particular, economic issues, questions of import/export, information about electronic hardware and software, and information about the development of certain combines were placed on taboo-lists (cf. Holzweissig, 1991, p. 16).

All of this caused state and economic functionaries responsible for releasing information to exercise much restraint. These people often acted with great caution based on anxiety. At party congresses of the SUP and in meetings with the media, however, the thesis decreeing comprehensive, prompt release of information to citizens was repeated constantly. The decision adopted by the Politburo of the SUP, the GDR's most important political leadership body, on "The Further Tasks of the Party's Political Educational Work among the Masses" of May 18, 1977, contains the following sentence in a section titled "Approaching All, Reaching Everybody":

> It is to be guaranteed that the state functionaries and economic managers unreservedly fulfill their obligation to the working people of providing information and rendering account and practice active Oeffentlichkeitsarbeit (Politbuero, 1977, p. 81).

In contrast to this, some utterances by leading party and state functionaries must be viewed as pure demagoguery. For example, the chairman of the GDR Council of Ministers, Stoph, asserted in a press interview that good Oeffentlichkeitsarbeit was important "for guaranteeing a close relationship of trust between the state organs and the editorial offices of the press, radio, and television" (as cited in "Interview with Willie Stoph," 1966, p. 4).

In fact, these high-sounding words about the obligation of providing information and practicing Oeffentlichkeitsarbeit in maintaining a close relationship with citizens remained a *fata morgana* (mirage) throughout the life of the GDR. There was a discrepancy between the goals and claims associated with the concept of Oeffentlichkeitsarbeit in programmatic papers, on the one hand, and the reality of information processes directed from above, on the other. However, editors and journalism scholars frequently made explicit reference to those idealistic formulations. Journalists did so when gathering and disseminating information, and journalism scholars when writing in specialized publications, in order to make optimal use of the normatively defined margins of freedom.

However, in the long run, the enduring contradictions between the objectively growing communication needs of society and the one-sided political propaganda provided could not be resolved in the GDR. The goals of disseminating comprehensive, objective, clear information and narrow-minded partisanship in favor of the ideology of Marxism–Leninism were always in conflict. For this reason, those journalists, journalism scholars, press-office staffers, and even some state and economic functionaries who were committed as individuals to performing effective Oeffentlichkeitsarbeit failed to make a major impact.

Which fields of activity really made up the professional field of Oeffentlichkeitsarbeit in the GDR—beyond the rhetoric in official statements?

As the SUP and the social sciences it dominated viewed things, all information activities performed by state and economic institutions fell within the sphere of Oeffentlichkeitsarbeit. That concept, as defined in regulatory norms and in the literature, truly applied only to these institutions. Special departments responsible for Oeffentlichkeitsarbeit existed in the economic field in the 175 collective combines (trusts) directly subordinated to the industrial ministries, in several big regional enterprises, in the state trading organizations (domestic and foreign trade), and in the state transportation services.

Departments of Oeffentlichkeitsarbeit also existed in the spheres of culture, science, and national education; in the universities and professional colleges, big theaters and museums; and, within state organs, at the Council of Ministers and its individual ministries as well as in central agencies. On the regional level, the concept applied within councils of the districts and big cities. All managers of enterprises, mayors, or department heads were also required to undertake Oeffentlichkeitsarbeit within the framework of their responsibilities. Tasks there included primarily the provision of written, pictorial, or oral information to the mass media, the publication of brochures, and the organization of exhibitions, open-house days, and public events.

It is important to note that, according to common opinion and practice, only information activities targeted to outsiders by the performing institution were regarded as Oeffentlichkeitsarbeit. An organization's own staff was not viewed as a public within this context. As a consequence, the publication of the 667 house journals having a total circulation of 2.21 million copies (as of January 1, 1988) and appearing weekly or fortnightly did not become labelled as Oeffentlichkeitsarbeit for the employees of a given institution or its branches (Halbach, 1988, p. 33).

However, this did not mean that this field of information was regarded as irrelevant and was overlooked. On the contrary, responsibility for such publications rested directly with the SUP and not with government-appointed managers. The official party handbook *Journalistische Arbeit im Betrieb* (Journalistic Work in an Enterprise) stated:

> Thus, the position of the enterprise newspapers of our party in the working collective is characterized by the fact that they are leadership instruments of the leaders of the party organizations in the enterprise. They serve the party to implement the ideological leadership in the working collective. (as cited in Zwanzig, Ruhr, & Schreier, 1984, p. 29)

Editors of the enterprise newspapers were employed by the party apparatus of the SUP and were exclusively responsible to it. Even the press offices of the same collective combine that worked under the label of Oeffentlichkeitsarbeit or Presse-und Oeffentlichkeitsarbeit did not have any power here. Overall direction of all enterprise newspapers rested with the department of agitation of the central committee of the SUP in Berlin. Enterprise newspapers often dealt with internal matters of an institution and with other topics that the SUP defined as internal and wanted to conceal from the public. Thus, these periodicals were barred from public circulation and were not offered through the postal service's public distribution network. Export of such periodicals, even to other countries of the Eastern bloc, was not permitted either. To give an example, even the numbers of workers, employees, or products (e.g., cars) were secret.

Within the GDR media system, which had been built on Marxist–Leninist structures, the editors of the press, radio, and television were all, directly or indirectly, subject to the influence of the party leardership of the SUP and used information received primarily from the staffs of the departments of Oeffentlichkeitsarbeit as raw material. No government-appointed manager had the right to issue directives to the party's editors. The SUP was at the top of the social hierarchy, and the state ranked only second.

The information activities performed by parties and social organizations, as well as by associations for the benefit of the general public or specific target groups, were termed "political educational work for the masses." This held even with programs implemented via journalistic institutions.

Oeffentlichkeitsarbeit was regarded as part of the system of ideological and political education. Most of this indoctrination was carried out through the mass media. And Lenin's maxims were the yardstick for both media theory and practice in the GDR. Lenin (1959, p. 88) had characterized the press as an "organ of the dictatorship of the proletariat" and as a "collective propagandist, agitator, and organizer" (Lenin, 1959, p. 11). He declared that the whole propaganda of communism must be geared to the practical direction of building the state (Lenin, 1959, p. 366).

Thus, it is only logical that the university textbook on journalism (Poerschke, 1980) said:

> What socialist journalism accomplishes for the social process of cognition, for the dissemination of the socialist ideology and for the social exchange of information, draws its specific features only from the character of journalism as an instrument of political leadership. (p. 12)

On the whole, Oeffentlichkeitsarbeit in the GDR was unambiguously motivated and targeted politically. Depending on changing social circumstances, it was defined more precisely or accentuated differently in specific times and places. However, its political character remained unchanged at all times.

Decisions by the ruling party concerning political and ideological education always served as general and binding guidelines for Oeffentlichkeitsarbeit in the GDR. On these bases, a number of state regulations for the Oeffentlichkeitsarbeit of state and economic institutions, universities, academies, and so forth, were drawn up. These regulations all proceeded from the party's principles just mentioned, but they also listed a great number of practical methods which, in the final analysis, had frequently been borrowed from western literature and adapted to conditions in the GDR, or were derived from home-grown empirical studies.[1]

Oeffentlichkeitsarbeit in the GDR, viewed as a whole, was was never investigated extensively or given a theoretical foundation. This was because no central body dealing with Oeffentlichkeitsarbeit existed in the centralistically directed spheres of policy, ideology, and the economy of the GDR. Because Oeffentlichkeitsarbeit was an element of managerial work, the relevant structural units were, in principle, directly subordinate to the minister or general manager. Thus, responsibility rested in each case with the head of the institution in question. Scientific and scholarly institutions dealt only with specific aspects of Oeffentlickeitsarbeit, seldom if ever bringing these to the attention of the community of relevant public relations experts.

Some theoretical foundations for Oeffentlichkeitsarbeit in the GDR were spelled out primarily at the Department of Journalism of the Karl Marx University in Leipzig, the GDR's only institution devoted to studying and teaching journalism. Almost all relevant dissertations and diploma theses about Oeffentlichkeitsarbeit originated there. Four doctoral dissertations and nearly three dozen diploma theses were written, mostly by staffers of various press offices of state institutions and economic enterprises of industry and foreign trade of the GDR, when these people participated in extension courses.[2]

In the 1970s and 1980s, aspects of Oeffentlichkeitsarbeit were treated marginally in courses dealing with the system of the mass media and its position in the political system of the GDR. These courses were taught at the Department of Journalism in Leipzig.

Clearly, Leipzig was the center of journalism training and journalism research in the GDR. However, other universities also devoted occasional attention to the topic of Oeffentlichkeitsarbeit. At the Academy of Political and Social Sciences in Potsdam, the central institution for the education and further training of GDR state functionaries, partial aspects of the Oeffentlichkeitsarbeit performed by the state authorities were taught and published. And at Berlin's Humboldt University, a relevant doctoral dissertation was written in 1972 (Schmelter, 1972).

---

[1]Examples of state regulations concerning Oeffentlichkeitsarbeit in the GDR: (a) Aufgaben und Verantwortung der Leiter der Staats- und Wirtschaftsorgane und ihrer Presseinstitutionen fur die Oeffentlichkeitsarbeit im Zusammenwirken mit der staatlichen Nachrichtenagentur ADN, Presse, Rundfunk und Fernsehen. Beschluss des Ministerrates vom 6.12.1967. In Mitteilungen des Ministerrates der DDR, Vertrauliche Dienstsache, Berlin; Ausgabe Nr. 13 vom 8.12.1967, (b) Ordnung ueber die Oeffentlichkeitsarbeit des Ministeriums fuer Volksbildung vom 20.5.1965. Berlin, (c) Ordnung ueber die Oeffentlichkeitsarbeit der Deutschen Akademie fuer Landwirtschaftswissenschaften vom 1.4.1970, Berlin.

[2]The following doctoral dissertations about Oeffentlichkeitsarbeit were written in the GDR at the Department of Journalism of the University of Leipzig: Merkwitschka (1968), Poerschke (1972), Woeltge (1973), Liebold (1974).

In summary, the following characteristics of Oeffentlichkeitsarbeit in the GDR are pointed out.

The largest sphere in which public information was disseminated via "one-way communication" was political propaganda. Political activities of information and guidance directed by the SUP and its state authorities were, in essence, carried out with the aid of the mass media, which had to fulfill a clear political mission and thus, were directed accordingly. This gives rise to the question of whether political propaganda, disseminated via the mass media, may generally be regarded as Oeffentlichkeitsarbeit in a more precise sense. In spite of functional similarities to the type of publicity described by Grunig and Hunt (1984), the answer can only be no. Neither the political propaganda practiced by the regime of the National Socialists nor that of present-day socialists can, or should be, understood as a type of public relations. Political propaganda practiced in the GDR constitutes a peculiar type of public communication that was, or still is, characteristic of countries having a Marxist–Leninist state and social order. The characteristics of this type of communication include the following.

First, a predominance of one-way information was based on the organized and institutionalized guidelines issued by the organs of the political leadership.

Second, media messages focused on structuring reality and evaluating it, with a major element being the definition of boundaries within which the Federal Republic of Germany (West Germany) and capitalist countries as a whole would be portrayed as foes.

Third, GDR political communication had a rather superficial concern with truthfulness. The primary criterion for quality of reporting was partisanship in favor of the interests of the working class; in fact, of the SUP. Objectivity in reporting was defined in partisan terms. That is, only that viewed as useful for the working class, or more precisely for the party, was seen as objectively accurate. This led to consistent emphasis on the supposedly positive aspects of socialism and accentuation of the negative aspects of capitalism. Taken together, these standards resulted in a distorted world view.

Finally, there was a lack of the critical function of the mass media which is viewed as central in democratic parliamentarian societies. The mass media were a primary instrument of the party and, thus, the mouthpiece of the party leadership. This functional similarity to many rather low-ranking press offices in private or public enterprises does not, however, justify subsuming this type of political propaganda under the label of "public relations."

In addition, Oeffentlichkeitsarbeit in the form of information not completely dependent on the party leadership and its official reporting existed in the economic field (175 collective combines, or trusts), in large regional enterprises, and in the spheres of culture, science, and national education. Also, with Oeffentlichkeitsarbeit performed at the Leipzig Fair, public relations as defined in the Western one-way *publicity/press-agent* and *public-information* models was possible. Here, as in other spheres, constant emphasis was placed on achievements of the socialist GDR.

Internal communication in the economic field was not subsumed under the concept of Oeffentlichkeitsarbeit. Seen from today's perspective, this work must be regarded as a portion of the public relations sector in the GDR. In this sphere (enterprise journals), ideological ties were particularly strong because of organizational subordination to party bodies. Even trivial internal information (such as the number of blue- and white-collar workers) was largely kept secret.

A constantly widening gap existed between the political and ideological programs laid out by the rulers, on the one hand, and the experience of reality by citizens, on the other. Unlike citizens elsewhere within the Soviet sphere of control, most East Germans were able to use Western electronic media as alternative sources of information. That contributed decisively to weakening the GDR's political system and reducing the trustworthiness of "semiofficial" information. Such problems could not be solved by either the theory or the practice of topical media reporting and public relations as long as the GDR existed.

PUBLIC RELATIONS TODAY IN THE NEW FEDERAL STATES

The Practice in Germany and Its Development in East Germany

The development of public relations in the five new federal states, where one fifth of the 80 million citizens of the Federal Republic of Germany live, is taking place against the backdrop of profound sociopolitical and economic changes that must be coped with during the transition from an unsuccessful socialist planned economy to a market economy.

Some figures illustrate the dimensions of the problem. In 1992, the new federal states generated only 6.9% of the German gross national product. Per capita income is less than one third of that in the old (West German) federal states. Nursing the economy back to health and overcoming the comparatively high unemployment rate of more than 15% requires a radical economic restructuring in eastern Germany on the one hand, and long-term financial aid from the western region on the other. Both of these processes lead to problems of communication in both the east and the west. These challenges, in turn, create an urgent need for dialogue-oriented communication in politics and the economic realm.

In the western part of Germany, the professional field of public relations is very well developed. The roots of German public relations practice can be traced back to the 1870s in both private business (e.g., Krupp) and in communication of ministries and the state. However, modern public relations in the business realm began after World War II.

For the entire Federal Republic of Germany, a total of about 30,000 to 35,000 journalists work in permanent positions and as interns (cf. Schneider, Schoenbach, Stuerzebecher, 1993). Moreover, about 15,000 to 20,000 people now work as full-time free-lancers. And roughly 10,000 to 15,000 full-time public relations practitioners appear to function in the country as a whole, though this is only an estimate.

In the eastern part of Germany, the quantitative ratio between journalists and public relations practitioners (which is three to one for the entire Federal Republic) has not yet been reached. The work force in journalism has not grown very much, but public relations has expanded greatly during the last 10 years and is still growing. Public relations practitioners are active in all big and medium-sized companies, in business and other associations, in state and community departments, in cultural and scientific institutions, and so forth.

The Deutsche Public Relations Gesellschaft (DPRG, German Public Relations Association), founded in 1958, has over 2,300 members. Also, the larger public relations agencies (ranging from about 15 to 150 employees each) have their own association (Gesellschaft Public Relations Agenturen, GPRA, Association of Public Relations Agencies). And many practitioners work alone as consultants.

Just as in the United States, public relations practitioners still do not have the best reputation. However, professionalism is increasing, and public relations jobs are proving very attractive for many students. Although free access to journalism and public relations jobs has been an important rule in Germany since 1945, a representative survey of DPRG members in 1990 showed that more than 60% of all German practitioners have at least one academic degree (diploma, masters degree, or doctorate). This level of educational attainment is very similar to that of German journalists.

Discussions about models, curricula, and content of public relations education at the universities, academies, and private institutes, began in 1980 and have intensified within the last 5 years. The modern understanding of public relations in Germany is dialogue-oriented as reflected in official, normative papers of the public relations associations and in some public campaigns (e.g., environmental and anti-AIDS programs).

Professionalization in the field is developing quickly. A number of practical handbooks on public relations for Germany and a growing theoretically oriented literature have developed (cf. Bentele, 1994; Ronneberger & Ruehl, 1992; Signitzer, 1992). Also, some empirical studies provide information about the means and tools used in public relations practice as well as the structure of practitioner motivations, value concepts, and professional ethics. Practitioner views of professional morality also have been studied (e.g., Becher, 1993; Boeckelmann 1988, 1991).

At present, no empirically supported inventory of professional public relations people similar to that for media personnel (e.g,. Meyn, 1994; Puerer & Raabe, 1994) has been compiled for the entire Federal Republic. However, the same may also hold in other countries.

Public Relations in the East: The Business Sector

Only a few surveys, mostly of a nonrepresentative kind, exist for the new federal states in the Federal Republic of Germany. However, these studies give some important clues as to the professional landscape of public relations in the eastern part of Germany. Drawing on these studies, we seek to describe the area's public relations landscape by reconstructing the most important trends and problems in development. Taken as a whole, this should provide a rather realistic picture of the situation at present.

At a fundamental level, a first observation can be made. *Public relations does not play as important a role in the eastern part of Germany as it does in the West.* Certainly that is true based on practitioner numbers. One indicator of the obviously smaller number of practitioners in the east is membership in the professional association, the Deutsche Public Relations Gesellschaft (DPRG). Members clearly account for a lower proportion of the population in the new federal states than in the old ones. However, there is a trend toward equalization. Observable communication activities in the East are distinctly on the rise.

In a survey conducted in late 1992 by the Hamburg communication service, PR-Report, and the Berlin branch of the Burson-Marsteller agency, 88% of all 1,000 enterprises questioned in the new federal states were engaged in active public relations. Two thirds of these organizations had been involved in public relations since 1990. However, only 20% had their own public relations personnel on the premises by 1992, and only 4% of the enterprises surveyed were working with public relations agencies. Fifty-six percent of the enterprises sampled were satisfied with their success in the east, but one fourth said they were more successful in the West.

In all, 92% of the enterprises surveyed reported being active in the field of press relations. Nearly two thirds engaged in public relations at trade fairs whereas 57% held press conferences, 26% organized symposia, and 15% sent out invitations to seminars for journalists (see Gross, in press).

Wolf-Dietrich Gross, a PR-agency owner who works primarily in the eastern part of Germany, comments on the increase in public relations activities as follows:

> Compared with 1990, journalists in the east are now clearly more approachable and knowledgeable. If there was obvious distrust toward the PR activities of western senders after the initial bad experience in 1990 . . . the eastern media have long since translated their early experience into western-style professionalism. As a rule, only clean messages and facts . . . can now be placed. (Gross, in press, cited in Haller, 1995)

Concerning the general state of public relations in the business sector, the recently published state-of-the-art report of Boeckelmann, Mast, & Schneider (1994, p. 384) stated that the field directly mirrors the general business situation.

Most firms have only a few employees in public relations, and most of these people are not very well educated. For that reason, there is a strong need for advanced training in the field.

Public Relations Agencies and the Municipal and State Sectors

Several small studies of public relations agencies have been carried out. A survey of 58 well-known agencies in early 1994 by the Berlin agency, *cmi,* yielded a response rate of only 25%.

According to this survey, 80% of the public relations agencies serve business enterprises, and four-fifths also have West German clients. Seventy-four percent of those questioned were also engaged in public relations work for ministries and municipalities, two thirds for associations. Most common agency activities included press relations (by 93% of all firms), cooperation with the media (by 73%), the design of brochures and other print products (by 93%) and advertising (by 80%).

Only about one third of the agencies saw themselves as competent in the field of crisis communication, and less than half offered services in trade-fair communication. Most agencies (87%) specialized in a specific field or niche such as the building trades, culture, the environment, trade, tourism, energy management, urban rehabilitation or municipal location marketing, video presentations, or layout and design or corporate design.

Sixty percent of the responding agencies confirmed the need for development of the field. Forty percent regarded the agency scene as still underdeveloped and saw a need for enhanced qualifications. An obvious rise in quality was noted by only 13% (Gross, in press).

A 1992 study at the University of Leipzig, investigating the public relations market in Leipzig, concluded that the bad economic situation in the new federal states was the biggest obstacle to the development of a demand for public relations. Also, the research showed that orders were rarely placed with public relations agencies (Schulze, 1992).

A 1994 inventory, also at the University of Leipzig, showed that only 3 of 23 Leipzig communication agencies carried the term public relations in their titles. Interviews showed that all 23 agencies were active in the public relations sector (Peter, 1994). Exclusion of the term public relations might be due only in part to the economically weaker situation of the east which still makes investment in the field often seem inopportune. Also involved may be an understanding of public relations, primarily among clients, which does not yet distinguish clearly between advertising and public relations.

In the field of municipal and regional public relations, an obvious improvement, compared with the situation in the GDR, presumably has materialized. Current press relations of city administrations, as well as tourism-related regional and city marketing and both regional and city public relations connected with such marketing, have received a strong impetus from the market economy. A city such as Leipzig (with 500,000 inhabitants) has a well-appointed municipal press office, with 12 employees in permanent positions. The range of products offered by this press office equals that of a comparable normal big city in the West.

However, most municipal public relations practitioners are not educated in journalism or public relations. Rather, they come from other occupational areas and received "on-the-job training" in public relations. And many still equate public relations with the one-way information flow characteristic of the GDR.

Due to decentralization of the government apparatus and the political administration (i.e., the establishment of the five federal states of Brandenburg, Mecklenburg-Vorpommern, Saxony, Saxony-Anhalt, and Thuringia), a number of press offices and departments of public relations have been established in the political field. These offices are responsible for communication between legislative and executive branches and the people.

One week after the opening of the borders in 1989, a lot of political campaigning, undertaken by the press and information office of the West German government, began in West Berlin and at the border with the GDR. Sixteen "info-buses" were activated, and more than 7 million copies of a brochure entitled "Welcome to us: Information for visitors from the GDR" became available to GDR citizens coming to the West. Within a few weeks, many more specialized informational brochures were offered to visitors from the east. These activities were intensified between 1990 and 1993 and were viewed as very successful (Oblaender, 1993).

In summary, we make a second key observation. *West German standards have not been reached in the sphere of public relations agencies. However, public relations in the municipal and political sectors has developed in accordance with Western standards.*

The Self-Concept and Orientation of Public Relations in the New Federal States

A third important conclusion became apparent in conversations with public relations agencies and in the available studies. *Public relations is frequently thought to be identical with advertising,* and the distinction between the two within marketing activities is made with insufficient clarity. In fact, many economic enterprises and public officials regard public relations merely as the placement of advertisements (Gross, in press). For this reason, many east German public relations firms call themselves full-service agencies.

Beyond that, the phrase "integrated entrepreneurial communication" is very often and quickly used to denote all communication activities by business enterprises (public relations, advertising, marketing). This unclear distinction stems in part from the still underdeveloped economic situation in east Germany, on the one hand, and deficiencies in the self-conception of public relations, on the other.

A current image campaign initiated in 1993 by the city of Leipzig, using a central slogan ("Leipzig is coming"), seeks to combine the marketing and public relations functions. Much of this campaign is paid for by enterprises investing in Leipzig. The basic goal is to make Leipzig stand out as a new economic location and service center in the east. This campaign is entrusted to a western advertising agency. An important goal, in addition to strengthening the economic status of Leipzig, is to enhance awareness that the economy is on the upswing.

In the spring of 1993, the *Wochenpost,* the largest weekly paper circulating in the eastern federal states, in cooperation with the professional association of advertising experts, BDW, held a competition among east German agencies to find innovative concepts that might encourage investment in Germany. Viewed as to content, the concepts proposed early were in the realm of public relations. However, because proposals came from advertising agencies, the tools suggested were severely limited to advertisements.

Overall, then, the boundaries between public relations and advertising are fluid in the minds not only of both customers and clients, but also of agencies, in the east. Frequently no distinction is made between these communication channels which clearly are viewed in the west as separate.

If, on the other hand, the focus is on pure public relations work, some symptomatic differences between the east and the west may be observed. These differences are indicated by a 1993 survey of 71 graduates of nonacademic courses which offered continuous training in public relations (Voigt, 1993). All those questioned held that different ways of thinking exist in the east and in the west. Nearly half of those surveyed stated that public relations work would also necessarily differ, permanently or temporarily, between the two areas.

Ninety percent of those interviewed saw credibility as an important goal of public relations. Also, 87% thought it essential to show understanding for audience members' life experience. However, none of the respondents regarded the topic of lifestyles as important. Only one-fifth viewed wit or humor as an element of text writing. And 90% regarded the job market and wages as the most important topic for public relations communication.

A fourth and final overall conclusion is that *some differences in ways of shaping public relations communication and addressing particular publics exist and will remain—at least for the time being.* Such differences appear to stem from variations in people's mentalities and the two regions' economies. Some folks gained a great deal of experience with false promises in GDR times and also became victims of dubious sales strategies of salesmen from the west soon after the border between east and west opened. These people are now focusing on a search for credibility, on trustworthy and factual communication, not on lifestyles. This suggests that there will be differences between public relations work in the east and that in the west, at least over the medium term.

Advantages exist for the east. Money invested there is being channeled into state-of-the-art technology. Openness and a readiness to innovate have been viewed as necessities and have almost become the rule in the east. This is obvious, also, in training and education. At the former institution for training journalists in the GDR (the University of Leipzig), new structures have been and still can be created which also are innovative for the west. An important development for university training in public relations throughout Germany was the establishment and filling of the nation's first Chair in Public Relations at the University of Leipzig in 1993.

REFERENCES

Becher, M. (1993). *Public relations und Ethik: Eine empirische Studie zu ethisch relevanten Bereichen im Berufsfeld PR* [Public relations and ethics: An empirical study of ethically relevant areas in the field of PR]. Diplomarbeit, University of Bamberg.

Bentele, G. (1994). Public relations und Wirklichkeit: Beitrag zu einer Theorie der Offentlichkeitsarbeit [Public relations and reality: Contribution to a theory of public relations]. In G. Bentele & K. R. Hesse (Eds.), *Publizistik in der gesellschaft* [Public communication in society]. Konstanz: Universitatverlag.

Beschluss des Ministerrates der DDR ueber die Grundsdtze zur Gewaehrleistung von Sicherheit und Ordnung [Resolution of the council of ministers about the principles to guarantee safety and order]. (1968, October 29). In *Mitteilungen des Ministerrates der GDR* [Announcements of the Council of Ministers of the GDR], No. 18. Berlin: Vertrauliche Dienstsache.

Boeckelmann, F. (1988). *Pressestellen in der Wirtschaft* [PR departments in business]. Berlin: Spiess.

Boeckelmann, F. (1991). *Pressearbeit der organisationen* [Media relations of associatons]. Munchen: Olschlager.

Boeckelmann, F., Mast C., & Schneider, B. C. (Eds.). (1994). *Journalimus in den neuen Lndern: Ein Berufsstand zwischen Aufbruch und Abwicklung.* [Journalim in the new federal states: A profession between new beginning and abwicklung (officially decided and legitimized liquidation of different social institutions)]. Konstanz: Universitatsverlag.

Gross, B. W. (in press). Menschen, Markte, Moglichkeiten: Zur Situation der PR in den neuen Bundeslaendern. [Men, markets and possibilities: The situation of public relations within the new federal states]. In Haller, M. (ed.), *Presse Ost-Presse West: Journalismus im vereinten Deutschland* [Press east, press west: Journalism in the reunified Germany]. Berlin: Vistas.

Grunig, J. E., & Hunt, T. (1994). *Managing public relations*. New York: Holt, Rinehart & Winston.

Halbach, H. (1988). *Das journalistische System der DDR im Uberblick* [The system of journalism in the GDR]. Leipzig: Karl-Marx-Universitaet, Sektion Journalistik.

Haller, M. (Ed.) (1995). *Presse Ost-Presse West: Journalismus im vereinten Deutschland* [Press east, Press west: Journalism in the reunified Germany]. Berlin: Vistas.

Holzweissig, G. (1991). *DDR-Presse unter Parteikontrolle*. [GDR-press under party control]. Bonn: Gesamtdeutsches Institut.

Interview with Willie Stoph. (1966, January 13). *Neues Deutschland*, p. 4.

Karl Marx University (1971). *Woerterbuch der Journalistik* [Dictionary of journalism]. (1st ed., pp. 266–267). Leipzig: Author, Department of Journalism.

Klein, A. (1964). Public Relations und unsere Aussenhandelstatigkeit auf kapitalistischen Markten [Public relations and our foreign-trade contacts with capitalist markets]. *Neue Werbung, 3*, 4–5.

Lenin, W. I. (1959). *Werke* [Works] (vol. 28, p. 88). Berlin: Dietz Verlag.

Lenin, W. I. (1959). *Werke* [Works] (vol. 31, p. 366). Berlin: Dietz Verlag.

Lenin, W. I. (1959). *Werke* [Works] (vol. 5, p. 11). Berlin: Dietz Verlag.

Liebold, R. (1974). *Die Oeffentlichkeitsarbeit im sozialistischen Industriebetrieb—vorwiegend dargestellt an den Beziehungen der Pressestelle des VEB PCK Schwedt zu den journalistischen Massenmedien der DDR* [Public relations in a socialist industrial concern described as to the relationship between the PR department of the state-owned company PCK Schwedt and the mass media in the GDR]. Unpublished doctoral dissertation, Sektion Journalistik, Karl-Marx-Universitaet, Leipzig.

Merkwitschka, F. (1968). *Die auslandsinformatorische Pressearbeit als wichtiger Bestandteil der Oeffentlichkeitsarbeit eines sozialistischen Unternehmens—dargestellt am Beispiel des Leipziger Messeamtes* [The public relations work, particularly to provide information abroad, as an important part within the PR of a socialist company—described through the example of the Leipzig fair office]. Unpublished doctoral dissertation, Fakultat fur Journalistik, Karl-Marx-Universitaet, Leipzig.

Meyn, H. (1994). *Massenmedien in der BRD* [Mass media in the FRG] (Rev. ed.). Berlin: Colloquium.

Oblaender, M. H. (1993). *Informationskampagne in den neuen Bundeslandern* [Public campaigns in the new federal states]. In Arendt, G. (1993). *PR der Spitzenklasse* [Excellence in PR] (pp. 159–174). Muenchen: Verlag moderne industrie.

Peter, G. M. (1994). *Kleiner PR-Wegweiser durch Leipzig* [Small PR guide through Leipzig]. Liepzig: Universitaet Leipzig.

Poerschke, K. (1972). *Zu Aufgaben und Problemen der sozialistischen Offentlichkeitsarbeit, besonders dargestellt an der Oeffentlichkeitsarbeit im Hochschulwesen der DDR* [Duties and problems of socialist PR as illustrated through the PR of the universities of the GDR]. Unpublished doctoral dissertation, Sektion Journalistik, Karl-Marx-Universitaet, Leipzig.

Poerschke, H. (1980). *Theoretische Grundlagen des sozialistischen Journalismus* [Theoretical foundations of socialist journalism]. Leipzig: Sektion Journalistic, Karl-Marx-Universitaet.

Politbuero des ZK der SED [Politburo of the Central Committee of the Socialist Unity Party]. (1977). *Die weiteren Aufgaben der politischen Massenarbeit der Partei* [Duties (or assignments) of the political mass work of the Party]. Berlin: Dietz Verlag.

Puerer, H., & Raabe, J. (1994). *Medien in Deutschland: Presse* [Media in Germany: The press]. Muenchen: Oelschaeger.

Ronneberger, F., & Ruehl, M. (1992). *Theorie der Public Relations: Ein entwurf* [Theory of public relations: A prospect]. Opladen: Westdeutscher Verlag.

Schmelter, R. (1972). *Die Funktion der sozialistischen Oeffentlichkeitsarbeit bei der Herausbildung des sozialistischen Bewusstseins und der Leitung des weiteren sozialistischen Aufbaus in der Deutschen Demokratischen Republik* [The function of socialist public relations in terms of developing a socialist consciousness and of leading the continuing socialist structure of the German Democratic Republic]. Unpublished doctoral dissertation, Sektion Marxistisch-Leninistische Philosophie der Humboldt Universitat, Berlin.

Schneider, B., Schoenbach, R., & Stuerzebecher, D. (1993). Journalisten im vereinigten Deutschland: Strukturen, Arbeitsweise und Einstellungen im Ost-West-Vergleich [Journalism in the reunited Germany: Structure, working methods, and attitudes in an East-West comparison.] *Publizistik, 38*(3), 353–382.

Schulze, K. (1992). *Stand und Aussichten des PR-Marktes Leipzig—Eine vergleichende Untersuchung mit dem PR-Markt Frankfurt/Main unter besonderer Beruecksichtigung der kommunalpolitischen Entwicklungskonzeption "Medienstadt Leipzig"* [The situation and outlook of the PR market in Leipzig—A comparative study with the PR market in Frankfurt, with special consideration to the local political development strategies of "Media City Leipzig"]. Diplomarbeit, Universitat Leipzig.

Signitzer, B. (1992). *Theorie der Public Relations* [Theory of public relations]. R. Burkart & W. Hoemberg (Eds.), Kommunikationstheorien: Ein Textbuch zur Einfuehrung [Communication theories: An introductory textbook] (pp.). Wien: Braun Muellor.

Tamme, F. (1964). Kluge Oeffentlichkeitsarbeit im Ausland [Intelligent public relations abroad]. *Neue Werbung, 6,* 4.

Voigt, B. (1993). *Public relations in den neuen Bundeslaendern: Historische Entwicklung, Themen und eine empirische Fallstudie* [Public relations in the new federal states: Historical developments, topics, and an empirical study]. Diplomarbeit, Universitat Bamberg.

Woeltge, H. (1973). *Wissenschaftliche Grundlagen sozialistischer Oeffentlichkeitsarbeit: Zu einigen allgemeinen theoretischen Fragen der Oeffentlichkeitsarbeit in der DDR unter besonderer Beachtung ihres Bezuges zum Wirken der sozialistischen Massenmedien* [Scientific basics of socialistic public relations: Some general theoretical questions of public relations in the GDR with special consideration to its effects on socialist mass media]. Unpublished doctoral dissertation, Sektion Journalistik, Karl-Marx-Universitaet, Leipzig.

Woeltge, H. (1979). *Theoretische Probleme der Offentlichkeitsarbeit in der DDR* [Theoretical problems of public relations in the GDR]. Lehrheft [Working material], Sektion Journalistik, Karl-Marx-Universitat.

Zwanzig, K., Ruhr, K. H., & Schreier, H. (1984). *Journalistische Arbeit im Betrieb* [Journalistic work in an enterprise]. Berlin: Dietz Verlag.

20   European Public Relations Practice: An Evolving Paradigm

Vincent Hazleton
Radford University

Dean Kruckeberg
University of Northern Iowa

Consider the words of Eberhard Von Kuenheim (as cited in Gross, 1992), former chair of BMW AG, who compared the automobiles made by his European company to vehicles manufactured by the Japanese.

> (W)e have a huge advantage, and we are very proud of it. You see, we have our background, two to three thousand years of history coming from the Greeks and the Romans, and the tie of the Renaissance. All that styling—look, for example, at a Greek temple, what you call the golden mean—was invented in Europe. Look at the relation of dimensions, of styling—for example, French fashions, or a good men's suit from Italy—that is the value. And I think we can keep that value, because for that you need heritage, and education for centuries. (p. 74)

Although the Japanese might resent this unfavorable comparative assessment of their heritage and education, Kuenheim's point has some validity. Respect is due to the Europeans for who they are as well as for their traditions.

However, Europe is a large and heterogeneous collection of countries encompassing a diverse area with different economies, languages, religions, and cultures. In this chapter, we consider three groups of European nation-states.

First are the original members of the European Economic Community, which has evolved into the European Union, what most people think of as Europe. Second is a group of smaller countries, such as Austria, Finland, and Switzerland, that have only recently sought to join this European community. Finally are the countries of Eastern Europe that present unique challenges for public relations.

Most of our attention in this chapter of *International Public Relations: A*

Comparative Analysis focuses on the first two groups. Consider first the original members of the European Union. Although Kuenheim leaves it unsaid, perhaps particular tribute must be paid to the Germans, if not for their heritage, most certainly for their post-World War II economic recovery (Jackson, 1992).

In public relations theory and practice, little international recognition has been given to the Germans, or, for that matter, to those in other non-English-speaking European countries. The most sophisticated European public relations is supposedly practiced by the British.

While this popular assessment may seem unfair, the impression is readily understandable as we examine the history of European public relations. A German organization had one of the first, if not the first, public relations departments. By 1890, Alfred Krupp's company had a "news-bureau" composed of as many as 20 staff members ("The German public relations business has yet not declared itself essential for industry and it still has to prove itself," Author, 1987).

Yet, it is the British who are lauded for their pioneering leadership in European public relations. Even the first European use of the label has been attributed primarily to the British; only later was the term "public relations" widely adopted on the Continent (Mallinson, 1991).

Granted, the United Kingdom today remains greatest among the European nation-states, both in the numbers of its public relations firms and of its practitioners. It also allegedly is the European leader in its technical advancement in public relations. Indeed, Pierre Hervo, who heads Paris-based Relations Publiques Internationales, has recommended that U.S. public relations practitioners who want to form European alliances should go first to the United Kingdom; only afterwards should they approach professionals in Germany, France, Italy, and Spain (Gordon, 1991).

BRITAIN'S ADVANTAGE IS ITS U.S. RELATIONSHIP

How did British public relations practitioners achieve this global recognition, this supposed European dominance, and this alleged professional supremacy over their counterparts on the Continent and elsewhere throughout Europe? The United Kingdom's advantage came through its close relationship with the United States. Mallinson (1991) said the U.S. term public relations and its "concomitant jargon" was exported to Europe primarily through Great Britain. Because of historical and linguistic ties, and the military alliance between the United Kingdom and the United States during World War II, Britain was the beneficiary of a large share of U.S. postwar overseas investment. Also, public relations was used, particularly during the Cold War, by both the U.S. and British governments.

Thus, the increasing use of public relations in European business occurred mainly (albeit not exclusively) in the United Kingdom. Also, throughout Europe, Britain's practice has been popularly considered to be most similar to that of the United States (Mallinson, 1991).

The "linguistic ties" Mallinson cited have been particularly significant in the diffusion of U.S. public relations practice to Great Britain. Yukio (1992) maintained that English-speaking peoples and countries enjoy control of the media, that is, the channels and content of communication. He observed that the English language dominates the world, not only on the external and material levels, but also on the internal and psychological levels. The advantage of a nation-state's use of the English language cannot be overstated. English is the most commonly used second language throughout Europe. In European schools, English is usually taught beginning in the fourth grade. And, even though many Europeans may not feel comfortable speaking English, the language is widely understood throughout Europe. Furthermore, English is the common language of international business in all European countries—as well as worldwide. Throughout Europe, all business-to-business public relations practice depends on the English language for communication.

Third, in such European geographic areas as Scandinavia, the broadcast electronic media use English as their common language. Whereas cable and satellite technologies may lead to the development of native-language electronic media in such areas, economic factors make any rapid development of native-language electronic media unlikely.

Therefore, because of such contributing factors, it can be easily appreciated that contemporary public relations practice, born in the English-speaking United States, would be most readily and closely adopted in Europe by an English-speaking nation-state.

However, this British supremacy in public relations may soon be challenged—and on several fronts! Even though Great Britain's European leadership in public relations practice may not be in immediate jeopardy, its position is not as secure as it once was. A challenge might come, not only from the German nation-state alluded to earlier, but also from other individual European interlopers.

THE EUROPEAN UNION COULD IMPACT ON PUBLIC RELATIONS PRACTICE

Furthermore, a *collective* challenge to the British supremacy of European public relations is a distinct possibility. The formalization and continuing dynamics of the European Union will strongly influence, if not dictate, how Pan-European public relations will evolve.

The European Union is essentially the product of a political process by which individual nation-states have agreed to construct or to accept a common body of laws. The European Union has its own judicial, administrative, and legislative bodies which have substantively changed member states.

With the formalization of the European Economic Community in 1992, it has become clear that public relations as a profession and as an academic discipline will experience phenomenal growth in Europe, and that the European Union may well assume a leadership position in the continuing development of public relations as a profession and as a disciplinary area of study.

For example, issues that cut across Europe's national boundaries, such as environmentalism, have created the potential for new and powerful political and social groups whose existence has been facilitated by the European Union and who most assuredly possess keen interest in public relations.

Also, the need for public relations practice has increased with the flow of workers from Southern Europe to the more prosperous North. Likened to the Depression-era U.S. migration of rural Southern whites and blacks to the North, this migration has accentuated the differences in language and the associated ethnic and cultural dissimilarities that create barriers to understanding. Business, education, and the political infrastructure of the European Union undoubtedly will attempt to overcome these barriers through professional public relations practice. In a related area, the significance of national and ethnic identities appears to be increasingly important to Europeans, particularly among the smaller countries whose peoples fear the potential of economic and cultural assimilation because of the European Union. Resolution of such issues will require the increasing use of public relations.

Brussels, the political center of the European Union, has become a major center for the public affairs activities of member states, as well as those of public and private organizations. Many, if not most, major public relations counseling firms having international ambitions either have located or plan to locate offices in Brussels. Indeed, most components of the infrastructure of the European Union certainly will benefit from professional public relations practice.

The European unification places more than 320 million customers within the European Union borders, far more than in the United States and three times as many consumers as in Japan (Bellack, 1990). Removal of trade barriers through the adoption of 300 directives establishing common business standards means that European companies will have to position themselves for national, Pan-European, and global markets (Europe 1992: A threat to mid-sized firms?, Author, 1989).

Complexity and Turbulence Will Be Increased

As these examples readily illustrate, the overall consequences of the European Union will be to increase the complexity and turbulence of the environment for public relations practice. This complexity and turbulence is reflected in an increasing demand for public relations in Europe and a corresponding growth in the number of public relations practitioners there.

The European Union will place greater economic strain on existing European public relations firms, especially mid-sized ones that do not have the resources to invest in the new Pan-European marketplace. The president of Hill and Knowlton International predicts that European public relations firms will have to improve the quality and range of their services. The traditional European emphasis on consumer publicity and crisis communications will no longer be enough (Europe 1992: A threat to mid-sized firms?, Author, 1989).

One fundamental thrust of the laws and rules enacted by the European Union has been to reduce barriers to economic competition across national boundaries. Joint ventures and acquisitions are being recognized as means to lessen competitive pressures.

These joint ventures will create a need for public relations in the areas of institutional identity, employee relations and community relations.

Furthermore, as goods, services, and the organizations that produce them cross national boundaries, communication goals related to marketing and community acceptance can only increase in importance. Organizations that previously had not used public relations are now faced with increased competition and undoubtedly will seek public relations counsel. In a highly competitive environment, European companies undoubtedly will attempt to equal, if not supersede, their competitors' public relations activities.

The European Community's new "Euro-brands" will require that public relations contracts be awarded centrally; European companies will want global public relations strategies that can provide substrategies tailored to national markets (Stoltz, 1991).

Increased business competition and the opening of previously inaccessible markets have significantly increased European organizations' capital needs. Capital is needed to expand and to modernize production capabilities, as well as to accommodate the increasing marketing costs associated with growth and competition. Because capital may now flow freely across national boundaries within the European Union, international ownership and investment will increase the need for "professional" investor and financial-relations specialists.

Facilitation of technology transfer throughout Europe is another factor impacting the development of public relations; the European Union has encouraged a technology transfer between member states that will affect the present-day European practice of public relations in many ways. For example, applications of cable television and satellite technology have already begun to affect the communication consumption behaviors of European publics. One European sportswriter has observed that, with the arrival of cable television, his newspaper has increased its sports reporting. The newspaper no longer must incur the costs of sending reporters to events that can be viewed locally.

The European Union May Further Define Public Relations

Establishment of the European Union may help define and unify European public relations into a "Pan- European" practice—at least at the strategic macrolevel.

However, any evolving unification of practice might result in a model and a theory of public relations that is considerably different from those closely related models exemplified in present-day Great Britain and the United States. Indeed, reflection upon the changes brought about by the European Union might suggest that contemporary British and U.S. practice may prove inadequate for future Pan-European public relations needs.

White (1991) acknowledged that public relations practice in the United Kingdom is often ranked second only to U.S. practice. However, he warns that senior U. K. practitioners believe that public relations practice in Great Britain is at the same stage in its development that British marketing was in the 1960s.

Furthermore, British public relations practice might also be inappropriate in Continental Europe. Mallinson (1991) questioned: "Is British Public Relations European, or is European Public Relations British?" He observed two opposing tendencies between British and Continental Public Relations.

> (F)irst the Anglo-Saxon one, where the state limits itself to allowing the various professional categories to set their own regulations and norms; second, the European one, where states establish the laws that discipline the requirements for obtaining professional status. This means that when, and if, economic and political convergence does lead to a legally regulated European Public Relations professional practice (CERP already has a self-regulated one), the British could have problems. (p. 28)

Do Not Assume That Public Relations Will Be Diffused "As Is"

Thus, no assumptions should be made that either British or U.S. public relations practice and accompanying theory will be diffused into and adopted "as is" by other European Union nations.

A coalition of European Union countries might well determine that British public relations is either inadequate or is largely inappropriate as a unified practice within the European Union. Or, conversely, other nation-states throughout Europe might individually determine that a unified public relations practice, perhaps desirable at a supranational abstract level, cannot satisfy the indigenous national and local needs that must take precedence in European public relations practice.

Cultural Distinctions Will Fade Gradually

It must be remembered that cultural distinctions will fade only gradually within the Pan-European community, and assuredly some distinctions will always remain. "European" public relations, therefore, may not be able to exist, at least not until and to the extent that a common European culture concurrently develops. The recent failure of the European Union to adopt a common currency reflects this tendency to resist cultural homogenization.

Mallinson (1991, p. 27) questioned whether European public relations presently *does* exist "as a closely definable business discipline." He argued that it cannot exist constitutionally as a definable discipline until it is recognized at a supranational level as a profession. He observed that there is no legally enforceable mechanism to ensure one common standard, although unified professional practice to which practitioners voluntarily subscribe exists through the European Public Relations Confederation (CERP) and its voluntary Code of Conduct.

Many Conclude That Public Relations Is Culturally Specific

There is support for Mallinson's contention! Many public relations scholars and practitioners conclude that public relations practice is socially, as well as culturally and geopolitically, specific.

Thus, public relations practice and theory can be pan-European (or pan-global) only in so far as a concomitant social, cultural, and geopolitical commonality evolves throughout Europe (or worldwide).

If Kruckeberg and Starck (1988) are correct that articulation of public relations depends upon an explanation growing from historical and social forces, it would seem reasonable that distinctions among different social, cultural, and geopolitical systems would result in different public relations problems thus requiring different "public relations solutions" from indigenous practitioners.

Ovaitt (1988) concurred, arguing that public relations may be even more culture-bound than is either marketing or advertising. Thus, he said, it will be even harder to conduct public relations programs based on concepts that extend across international boundaries. Furthermore, Al-Enad's (1990) observation about public relations practice in Third-World nations may apply to Europe's lesser developed former Eastern Block countries. Al-Enad observed that Western public relations literature places public relations between an institution and its publics or environment.

However, Al-Enad maintained that:

> in developing nations it is located between the material and the nonmaterial aspects of the culture. It functions in the same manner; it tries to adapt each side to the needs and expectations of the other. In both cases, its role may not meet the standards as stated by public relations theoreticians. But playing it does help in maintaining the equilibrium of the system. (p. 26)

Sriramesh and White (1992) contended that, because a society's culture affects the pattern of communication among the members of that society, this culture would have a direct impact on the public relations practice of that society's organizations. This is because public relations is first and foremost a communication activity.

Networks Have Been Formed Throughout Europe

In recognition of the exceedingly diverse European climate as well as in appreciation for the ramifications of such an environment for public relations, networks of national agencies have been formed throughout Europe that include individual firms usually managed and staffed by practitioners indigenous to each country.

A public relations agency may form a grand strategy for an internationally ambitious client, but local offices would adapt and interpret that strategy to local practices and knowledge (Dossier frontier posts, Author, 1988). Already, several networks and international firms have substantial operations in Europe, and many European agencies have alliances with more than one such network (Gordon, 1991).

SUMMARY AND CONCLUSIONS

Thus far, it has been argued that British public relations practice historically has reigned supreme in Europe because of Great Britain's close relationship with the United States and because of the linguistic advantages of its native English language. However, this supremacy could be challenged collectively by other European nation-states, and British practice may, indeed, prove inadequate or largely inappropriate as a unified practice develops within the European Union.

Conversely, and in dynamic tension with the preceding scenario, nation-states throughout Europe could determine that a unified public relations practice, save at a highly abstract supranational level, cannot satisfy indigenous needs and attempts to unify public relations practice would be futile.

In light of these factors, what is going to happen to public relations practice in Europe? To a considerable extent, European public relations will be influenced by the professional education of its practitioners. And, because of the value placed on education among Europeans, the professionalization of public relations in some form may proceed relatively quickly now that the need for public relations is being increasingly recognized.

However, one must remember that significant differences exist between the predominant, familiar, and homogeneous U.S. public relations education model and those of most European nation-states. Such programs may differ widely throughout Europe, but virtually all of these European programs differ significantly from the U.S. model. An evolution of public relations in Europe would not necessarily resemble or follow the evolution in the United States.

European public relations education programs are by-and-large exclusively oriented toward preparing students for management positions. Not emphasized in these programs is training for technical skills; rather, European public relations education programs devote relatively more time to reflective learning and theory.

There are no journalism schools. Rather, it is assumed that European public relations students have learned basic skills before they enter a professional education program or that they will quickly acquire these skills through on-the-job experience.

A European public relations education curriculum is most likely to be located in a theory-oriented mass communication program. Thus, it is obvious that European practitioners tend to value education for managerial roles more so than for technical ones.

However, despite such a theoretical orientation, European students receive far less breadth in their higher education than do Americans students. In Europe, general education is entrusted to the Europeans' equivalent to U.S. secondary education schools.

European college students typically do not attend large, multidisciplinary universities. Rather, they enroll in "institutes" that are roughly equivalent to American academic "departments." During the 4 to 5 years spent in higher education, a student takes most of the classes at her or his institute.

Thus, European students receive degrees in public relations that are far more specific and in-depth than are most counterpart public relations education programs in the United States. A European institute provides its students with not only the equivalent of their junior and senior years of undergraduate education in American universities, but with master's-level instruction as well.

As Europeans share what promises to be a rapidly growing body of scholarship in response to the increasing European demands for public relations, their contributions to the professional literature undoubtedly will be significant. In all likelihood, their contributions will further the development of public relations theory in much the same ways that European philosophers in the past have influenced rhetorical studies and critical studies in mass communication.

The Germans could become interesting players in this European drama, not only because of their economic vitality (including their already powerful role in the communication industry), but also because of their intellectual tradition in communication that lends itself well to theory-building in public relations. The Germans have demonstrated an aggressive interest in public relations, including the considerable attention they are paying to the development of public relations practice within the former East Germany.

Starck and Kruckeberg (1991), in their discussion of mass communication and mass-communication education, asked: "Will there be a 'Europeanization' of such education and scholarship?" (p. 25)." Or, for that matter, a renewed Europeanization of communication theory. Again, the Germans in particular have the potential to contribute greatly to public relations because of their intellectual tradition. Hardt (1979) observed that the history of mass communication as a field of scholarly study is much older in Germany than in the United States. Carey (1979) reminded us that many of the originating impulses behind research in mass communication were German.

Also, many of the greatest American scholars of the late 19th Century were trained in Germany. Because the German tradition of scholarship is grounded in philosophy, these Americans learned to examine society and its institutions in a synoptic, rather than in a disciplinary, frame. They viewed mass media not in the narrowed context of psychology and the small group, but rather in the larger framework of politics, economics, and culture (Carey, 1979).

It is difficult to predict with certainty what will happen to European public relations. However, public relations scholars and practitioners throughout the world can watch this drama unfold with great fascination! For better or for worse, existing paradigms of public relations may be changing in Europe; British and, by extension, U.S. dominance may be challenged by the other Europeans.

REFERENCES

Al-Enad, A. H. (1990, Spring). Public relations' roles in developing countries. *Public relations quarterly, 35*(1), 24–26.

Author. (1988, August 11). Dossier frontier posts. *Marketing,* p. 29.

Author. (1989, June). Europe 1992: A threat to mid-sized firms? *Public relations journal, 45*(6), pp. 8, 10.

Author. (1987, April). The German public relations business has yet not declared itself essential for industry and it still has to prove itself. *PR world,* p. 8.

Bellack, D. W. (1990, January). Exploiting EEC marketing potential. *Public relations journal, 46*(1), pp. 14–15.

Carey, J. W. (1979). Foreword. In H. Hardt (Ed.), *Social theories of the press* (pp. 9–14). Beverly Hills, CA: Sage.

Gordon, J. A. (1991, December). Getting a slice of the "Europie". *Public relations journal, 47*(12), pp. 13, 20, 28.

Gross, K. (1992, November). Eberhard Von Kuenheim. *Automobile, 7*(8), pp. 71, 74.

Hardt, H. (1979). *Social theories of the press.* Beverly Hills, CA: Sage.

Jackson, J. O. (1992, Oct. 19). A bold peacemaker: Willy Brandt: 1913–1992. *Time, 140*(16), p. 55.

Kruckeberg, D., & Starck, K. (1988). *Public relations and community: A reconstructed theory.* New York: Praeger.

Mallinson, B. (1991). A clash of culture: Anglo-Saxon and European public relations. New versus old, or just dynamic interaction? *International public relations review, 14*(3), p. 24–29.

Ovaitt, F., Jr. (1988, Spring). PR without boundaries: Is globalization an option? *Public relations quarterly, 33*(1), pp. 5–9.

Sriramesh, K., & White, J. (1992). Societal culture and public relations. In J. E. Grunig (Ed.), *Excellence in public relations and communication management* (pp. 597–614). Hillsdale, NJ: Lawrence Erlbaum Associates.

Starck, K., & Kruckeberg, D. (1991, Fall). Mass communication education and the international challenge, *Phi Beta Delta international review, 2,* pp. 21–31.

Stoltz, V. (1991). New challenges for public relations in the new Germany. *International public relations review, 14*(1), pp. 15–18.

White, J. (1991). Education, training and qualifications around the world. In M. Nally (Ed.), *International public relations in practice: First hand experience of 14 professionals* (pp. 183–201). London: Kogan Page.

Yukio, T. (1992). The dominance of English and linguistic discrimination. *Media Development, 15*(1), 34.

III INTERNATIONAL PUBLIC RELATIONS EDUCATION IN THE UNITED STATES

21 International Public Relations Education: U.S. Issues and Perspectives

Cornelius B. Pratt
Michigan State University

Chris W. Ogbondah
The University of Northern Iowa

> . . . *[T]he professional worldwide public relations executive must understand global cultures if he or she is going to play a significant role in future business and government decisions.*
> *If . . . students get some global knowledge and experience, they will set themselves apart, and it will give them a much more effective résumé when they go job hunting.*
> —Donald G. Dowd (as cited in Fowler, 1983, p. D20), president of the then-Dan Dowd Communications, Chicago, in an address to students at Michigan State University.

The views in the preceding paragraphs, even though expressed more than a decade ago, stand the test of time because they highlight the significance of global perspectives to U.S. public relations education, and of the typical "stateless" corporation to the competitive marketplace, both then and now. The purpose of this chapter, therefore, is to establish a rationale for international public relations courses in the curricula of university public relations education in the United States and to outline the content of such courses.

The rest of the 20th century will indeed pose continuing economic and social challenges to public relations practitioners worldwide. These challenges will be dictated by many reasons, including the liberalization movements in Europe and the demise of the cold war; the political and economic reforms that indicate the supplanting of geopolitics by gaiapolitics, a worldwide movement to restore and protect the biosphere; the growth of international "non-place" communities; the changes in technology; the increases in cross-cultural communications; and the explosion in information (Frederick, 1993).

An additional factor that, to a large degree, redefines the organizational environments within which practitioners interact is the increasing internationalization of production and marketing processes by which products are designed in one place, their components are shipped form a number of places, and their marketing strategies are directed from a number of countries simultaneously. Consequently, curricular changes are pivotal, as John Updike (as cited in Carnegie Endowment, 1992) seemed to suggest: ". . . An old world is collapsing and a new world arising; we have better eyes for the collapse than for the rise, for the old one is the world we know" (p. i).

Other definitive factors are the possibility of free trade between Asia and Europe by the year 2025, a plan that was discussed November 1994 during meetings between leaders of the European Union and Asian countries; the possible extension of the North American Free Trade Agreement throughout the Americas, an issue discussed in a December 1994 meeting of leaders of North and South America; and the fall of apartheid in South Africa, which is developing a wellspring of economic growth in Africa's most industrialized country.

To meet these challenges, this chapter outlines, primarily from U.S. perspectives, curricular issues in education for international public relations. The international dimension of public relations practice aside, curricular issues in general often pit educators against practitioners. As Schwartz and Yarbrough (1992) noted from their survey of practitioners, "While public relations programs are offered at more than 200 U.S. universities, there's still ambivalence among practitioners about their quality and curriculum content" (p. 19). There are at least three reasons for such a perception.

First, practitioners argue that faculty members who teach public relations tend to be too theoretical and fail to bring "real-world" experiences to the classroom. However, as German philosopher Kant (1974) argued, a broad-based theory is a guide to action, suggesting the inherent practical and real-world characteristic of theories. The reality, however, is that both practitioners and educators tend not to apply theories to the teaching or practice of public relations, as Botan (1989) explained:

> . . . public relations practitioners, and even scholars, have generally limited themselves to questions of how-to-do-it and how-to-do-it-better. With a few notable exceptions, public relations has not systematically addressed the development of theory or the relationship of practice to research and theory building. (p. 100)

Second, educators bemoan the atheoretical nature of public relations education, which is usually handled as if it were an art or craft bereft of an applied scientific framework.

The third reason, which balances the two preceding reasons, is based on the question: To what extent is public relations education meeting marketplace demands? All these reasons reflect some of the disagreement between practitioners and educators on a blueprint for public relations education.

These issues were so critical that the Board of Trustees of the Institute for Public Relations Research and Education requested that two widely known public relations educators—Donald K. Wright, APR; and Judy VanSlyke Turk, APR—examine the unpleasant issues in public relations education (Wright & Turk, 1990). Their report noted:

> Some of the practitioner criticism probably is justified. There are some university-based public relations programs that are truly terrible. There are some places where the public relations faculty never have published refereed scholarship, and there are institutions who have hired incompetents to teach public relations. (p. 12)

This view is telling, primarily because, at least a decade before the report was published, the very same foundation that sponsored the study had published at least two extensive reports on the same subject. One report, titled "A Design for Public Relations Education," recommended curricula for undergraduate, master's and doctoral programs in public relations (Foundation for Public Relations Research and Education, 1975). A second report, published 10 years later, focused on graduate-level offerings ("National Commission on Graduate Study in Public Relations, 1985). Yet a third report, in recognition of the importance of international education even at the undergraduate level, required that undergraduate students acquire formal knowledge about a world that had grown increasingly complex and interdependent (Commission on Undergraduate Public Relations Education, 1987).

The 1975 report recommended that, at the master's level, curricula address the comparative study of mass media practices in the United States and other nations. The latter alluded to that same direction by recommending a "Public Relations Specialty Option" at the master's level. Even so, only a handful of colleges or universities have free-standing courses in international public relations to which are committed adequate resources for teaching and research in that area.

OTHER CURRICULAR ISSUES IN U.S. HIGHER EDUCATION

Study after study has identified a litany of other issues in U.S. public relations education. Such studies have reported that the teaching of public relations has not included the role of women and racial minorities in the history and the development of the discipline (Creedon, 1989; Kern-Foxworth, 1989, 1990, 1991). Another has observed a gender gap in college programs in public relations (Hunt & Thompson, 1988) and also that, even though women account for 70% of undergraduate public relations majors, few women are involved in public relations instruction at U.S. universities and colleges (Lance, 1986).

A number of studies have observed that a majority of public-relations practitioners are women (e.g., Dozier, 1988; Hon, Grunig, & Dozier, 1992). At the college level, females account for more than twice the enrollment of men in public relations, a trend expected to continue (Peterson, 1988). Despite this, Lance (1986) noted that women were hardly involved in public relations education.

Another problem is that public relations is perceived as a "velvet ghetto," a term that describes the hiring of women primarily to fulfill affirmative-action requirements.

Still other studies have pointed to the inadequacy of current public relations curricula in meeting student, practitioner and academic needs (Brody, 1985a, 1985b, 1991).

Widespread developments in society and improvements in technology suggest new curricula and strategies to deal with new challenges in public relations (Grunig, 1985; Sharpe, 1985, 1992). Further, Ogan and Brownlee (1986) and Paraschos (1980) have called for education in international journalism. And, interestingly, the International Division of the Association for Education in Journalism and Mass Communication (AEJMC) has indicated interest in how international topics are treated in journalism textbooks and in college curricula. Even with such stated interest in internationalizing communication curricula, in a recent survey of practitioners' ratings of curriculum content for undergraduate public relations education, international business trends were rated least frequently in the "quite important" or "very important" category in terms of course emphasis (Schwartz & Yarbrough, 1992).

MAJORING IN PUBLIC RELATIONS

Among U.S. baccalaureate programs in communication, the public relations program is growing most rapidly. Since 1923, when Edward L. Bernays taught the first college-level course in public relations at New York University, there has been phenomenal growth in offerings. In 1945, for example, Lee (1947) reported that 21 colleges offered courses in public relations. In 1947, that number had increased to at least 30.

According to *PR Reporter,* by 1977, 130 schools offered a major in public relations, and 162 other schools offered at least one public relations course by that year (as cited in Baxter, 1981). Today, almost every U.S. university that offers a degree program in journalism or in the broader field of mass communication offers a public relations major or minor.

The precise number of schools offering graduate programs in public relations is not known. But, since 1947, when the first master's program in the field was established at Boston University, the number of institutions offering graduate-level programs in the discipline has risen. That number was 51 by 1981 (Hesse, 1984). Today, a number of schools that offer graduate programs in public relations package them within a standard journalism degree, with a smattering of public relations courses that, for the most part, are the same as those offered at the undergraduate level (Sharpe, 1985).

As the public relations practice matures, a legitimate concern arises regarding curriculum and the education of the men and women entering the practice. Consequently, efforts are being made to address those concerns.

In 1973, for example, the public relations division of the Association for Education in Journalism (AEJ, now AEJMC) established a commission to examine the public relations curriculum and to make recommendations on how it could be improved. The Commission's co-chairmen were the late J. Carroll Bateman, a former president of the Public Relations Society of America (PRSA), and Scott Cutlip, a former dean of the School of Journalism and Mass Communication at the University of Georgia. Its report, titled "A Design for Public Relations Education," was adopted by AEJ in August 1975 and approved in November 1975 by the National Board of PRSA.

Another committee, the Commission on Graduate Study in Public Relations, was established in August 1982 by the Public Relations Division of AEJMC to evaluate the public relations curriculum at the graduate level and to design a model graduate curriculum. The commission completed its work in August 1983. The resulting report, which projected perceived needs of students and public relations practitioners, recommended, among other things, that students working toward graduate degrees in public relations complete—at the minimum—30 semester hours in courses such as research methods, communication theory, public relations management, programming and production (National Commission on Graduate Study in Public Relations, 1985). These courses are similar to those required for a master's degree in public relations at Salzburg University, Austria (see Signitzer, 1987).

For some colleges and universities, curricular concerns have gone beyond merely meeting accreditation requirements of the Accrediting Council of AEJMC. There is now an additional interest in meeting certification requirements of PRSA. Brigham Young University was the first university in the United States to have its public relations program certified. These certification programs are testimonials to educators' willingness to have their curricula, among other things, reviewed independently by their peers. Such curricula are designed to equip students with the knowledge and skills for the increasingly changing currents of international competition. That is why we believe any curriculum that excludes international public relations courses is ineffective in addressing student and practitioner needs, particularly in the next century.

JUSTIFYING COURSES IN INTERNATIONAL PUBLIC RELATIONS

An analysis of events, trends and developments in 1989 indicated that "a combination of shocks and surprises thrust the PR function onto the global scene" (*Public Relations News,* 1990a). The PR Exchange International, a worldwide network of 38 public relations firms, forecasts that one major trend within public relations in the last decade of this century is "localized globalization," which requires an understanding of international marketing by small businesses (*Public Relations News,* 1990b).

Among public relations firms, the growing use of international network affiliates like the Pinnacle Group, the International Public Relations Group of Companies, and the Worldcom Group, all of which localize communications and marketing programs, requires "that U.S. transnational marketers recognize the importance of local nationalism, customs, languages and press relations techniques before embarking on an overseas public relations campaign" (Strenski, 1985, p. 29).

The views of economists, academicians, chief executive officers (CEOs), and public relations practitioners on the climate of uncertainties in the 1990s indicates that public relations would advance worldwide at a pace that would have seemed impossible only a few short years ago (*Public Relations News,* 1990c).

In the January 1990 issue of *Public Relations Journal,* 15 CEOs and top public relations practitioners expressed their views on "What's Ahead in the 1990s" for public relations. Four of them clearly identified international public relations as one such possible trend.

The need for courses in international public relations is further justified by the increasing representation of countries by U.S. public relations firms, and by the increasing evidence of the effects of such representation on client images (Albritton & Manheim, 1983, 1985; Manheim & Albritton, 1984). Between 1967 and 1970, for example, U.S. firms represented the Federal Military Government of Nigeria and secessionist Biafra in their efforts to win international understanding and support for their activities in the 30-month Nigerian civil war (see Davis, 1977). In 1978, 50 countries were represented by U.S. public relations firms, largely for tourism, trade, investments, industrial development, and image building. That number doubled by 1984 (Lobsenz, 1984).

These developments require ongoing, in-depth training of professionals who represent a variety of countries and firms abroad. Such training should be sufficiently broad to equip practitioners with knowledge not only of the geography but also of the gaiapolitical factors (that is, the coalescence of movements directed at protecting the biosphere) and of socioeconomic and cultural milieus of major world regions.

It is also important that practitioners demonstrate in-depth awareness of the politics of ethnicity and religion, and of the cultural dichotomies of the major countries with which U.S. public relations firms do business. However, the U.S. public relations industry, still largely provincial, has adapted to neither the increasingly globalization of the industry itself nor of communications (Farinelli, 1990).

Responses from a random sample of 123 executives in U.S. firms provide at least three reasons for this failure (Tung & Miller, 1990). First, more than 93% of the executives did not consider "international experience or perspective" as a criterion for promotion or recruitment into the ranks of senior management. Second, about 10% of respondents in companies that provided training programs to groom their candidates for top management positions thought that such programs emphasized the international perspective. Third, among seven factors, no respondent identified "increase international market share" as a criterion for determining the size of an incentive package to retain personnel at the senior management level.

Yet, globalization of the U.S. economy challenges business and educational institutions to develop new skills, knowledge and insights. Business leaders need to know more about other cultures and value systems, other political and legal structures, and the philosophical and practical dimensions of other national economic systems. Formal education, including course work in international business, international relations, foreign language and area studies, can help students learn about other cultures (Tung & Miller, 1990). Singer (1987, p. 35) satirized the inadequacy of the foreign-language skills of U.S. nationals:

What do you call a person who can speak two languages?
Bilingual.
How about three?
Trilingual.
How about one language?
American.

Many Western companies such as the Toronto-based telecommunications giant, Northern Telecomm, now send their staff people on overseas tours to prepare them for global business challenges. Others organize one- or two-week courses in public relations practices and customs abroad for their corporate communications staffs. Others have their staffs take college courses on international business practices. Even though such programs help prepare participants to deal with language and communication challenges, there is evidence that their effectiveness is limited (Wilcox, Ault, & Agee, 1992). As David Potts, a public relations counselor in Sydney, Australia, said, "Some overseas corporations . . . make the mistake of assuming that public relations styles and campaigns which have worked overseas, particularly in the U.S.A., will work [domestically]. They don't always" (as cited in Wilcox, Ault, & Agee, 1992, p. 419). Offering college-level courses in international public relations is one of the best avenues for preparing public relations staffs for global business challenges.

Another rationale for an international public relations course is the accelerating pace of societal and technological change today. These changes call for adaptations in academic curricula and professional development programs. The increasing interdependence of nations today also calls for new public relations curricula aimed at educating staffs to understand and meet increasing international social, economic and political complexities and challenges. On this point, Brody (1985a) noted that

> All these societal and technological changes are creating expanded knowledge and skill requirements for entry-level public relations practitioners. These conditions increasingly bring into question the relative applicability of contemporary undergraduate curricula and professional development programs to the practice needs of both students and potential employers. (p. 28)

Brody (1985a, p. 28) asked: "How should undergraduate public relations curriculum be constituted? What skills or bodies of knowledge should the practitioner assimilate before beginning practice?" Part of the answer to both these questions lies in designing public relations curricula that include international courses at both the undergraduate and graduate levels. The public relations practice cannot advance unless new ideas are tested and implemented.

The need for international courses in public relations education becomes clear in light of U.S. students' inadequate knowledge of world affairs as shown in several studies. A U.S. Presidential Commission, for example, found a dangerously inadequate understanding of world affairs among U.S. college students (American Council on Education, 1985). The obvious culprit is U.S. education, which Reischauer (1973, p. 4) noted "is not moving rapidly enough in the right direction to produce the knowledge about the outside world and the attitudes toward other peoples that may be essential for human survival within a generation or two." Consequently, "a sizable percentage [of U.S. college student population] doesn't seem to know the difference between Nigeria and Nicaragua, doesn't know that Mexico is to the south of the United States and Canada to the north. . . ." (Brownlee, 1988, p. 17). This problem can be addressed by exposing students to courses with international foci, thus raising their knowledge of world markets (Steilen, 1988) and guarding against the tendency to be too myopic in college (Staples, 1988). Lim (1993) reiterated this argument:

> we need major orientation in thinking about what we call the "internationalization of education." To prepare for the challenge of the future, our universities and colleges need more than a knowledge about other nations and cultures. We should be willing to change our values accordingly, and transform institutional structures that have governed our life for a long time. We should not simply follow or respond to the trend but should take future-creative action in search of the new normative direction. (p. 571)

The need for international courses in public relations is demonstrated further by the growing global recognition of public relations degree programs and education, a phenomenon that Cantor (1985) predicted more than a decade ago.

One of the countries that has now recognized the importance of a degree program in public relations is the United Kingdom. On October 2, 1989, the

Dorset Institute, a vocational college and one of about 30 polytechnic schools in England, became the first college in Great Britain and Northern Ireland to offer an undergraduate program in public relations ("U.K. Tests First," 1989). In Brazil, entry into public relations requires a university degree in public relations and a professional license (Sharpe, 1992). And one is required to pass a written examination before practicing public relations in the Netherlands.

In addition, there is a growing global recognition of a need to expand courses within the public relations sequence to include more specialized topics, a point emphasized by University of Miami president, Edward T. Foote II. He said, "The need is great for broad-educated professionals in the expanding fields of communication" (as cited in Lehrman, 1985, p. 19).

This concern was reiterated by Sharpe (1985): "Professionals and educators alike must realize that, at the undergraduate level of education, the emphasis must remain on the acquisition of . . . [a] broad range of course-work that enables an individual to function effectively in society" (p. 29). The specialized courses include public relations writing, media publicity, public relations management, business communication, public relations principles and design-and-publications methods. Regrettably, most curricula do not include semester-long, regularly taught courses in international public relations.

Certain changes in the global economy also underscore the thesis of this chapter. One may observe, for example, that changes in the product and financial markets over the past 25 years have led to increases in cross-border investments, external financial markets, openness of most economies to international influences, the emergence of the newly industrialized nations, particularly those of the Pacific Rim, and, for the U.S. manufacturing sector, an increasing awareness of export possibilities (Aggarwal, 1987; Borrus, Zellner, & Holstein, 1990; Ernst, 1990). Other trends suggest global possibilities for U.S. companies: Companies that do business abroad expect their outside revenues to grow from 22% to more than 25% in sales during the next 5 years, about 40% of such companies expect their non-U.S. production to grow by at least 25% during the same period, and about 60% expect to acquire foreign firms (Steingraber, 1990). In each of 3 years prior to 1990, for example, the Coca-Cola Company and General Motors Corporation made more profits overseas than they made in the United States (Farinelli, 1990).

These trends have, in turn, contributed to the growth of global public relations. Specifically, public relations agencies have discovered and moved into overseas markets, encouraging the development of an international perspective on their activities; the trend toward globalization of the media has created a broader audience reach; and the practice has experienced increased sophistication and growth overseas (Booth, 1986; Crespy, 1986).

Further, corporate management now assigns top-level responsibilities to practitioners because of management's greater understanding of their potential for contributing to organizational well-being and social responsibilities. Additionally, the far-reaching changes in the global economy, the increasing urgency of global environmental issues, and the increasing trend toward market forces as a method for democratizing national economies suggest that public relations can play a crucial role in the adjustment of businesses to new realities.

Beyond the business organization per se, public relations practitioners have been known to help modify the behavior of people and active groups by stimulating the flow of knowledge worldwide, by fostering mutual understanding through dialogue and consensus, and by helping people understand one another better (Modoux, 1989). How, then, can future practitioners be prepared in college for these continuing challenges? The Carnegie Endowment for International Peace National Commission (1992) provided an answer:

> Our ranks are filled with experts better trained to deal with the past than the future. We must reorient university curricula and develop new cadres of professionals—not only for government but for business and finance, science and technology, culture and communications. (p. 87)

In regard to technology, differences in techniques used in fact-finding (an activity that precedes public relations action) can be shaped by differences in societies' technological cultures. Although the information superhighway is a near-reality in the developed countries, fledgling countries like Peru and the Republic of Benin, where more than 70 percent of the population does not even have telephones, still struggle with even basic communications by mail.

Burson-Marsteller, as the public relations agency for A. H. Robins, marketers of the Dalkon Shield, found that communication by both direct mail and mass communication posed several problems in Africa and Latin America during its worldwide notification program (Kendall, 1992).

Thus, effective organizational practices call for specific business strategies and communications programs appropriate to a society's culture.

A recent review of the coverage of international content indicates that authors of college-level public relations textbooks have not yet realized the growing importance of international public relations and, thus, deal only marginally with it (Anonymous, 1990).

On the basis of all these factors we suggest that new curricula equip beginning college graduate practitioners with the skills and knowledge for conducting effective global public relations. This emphasis on the undergraduate-level curriculum is based on the notion that entry-level public relations practitioners increasingly are graduates of public relations programs.

SCOPE OF COURSES

Because public relations, in its ideal form, is a social scientific activity, it is influenced by a coalescence of environmental factors, a number of which are listed at the beginning of this chapter. In Turkey, for example, practitioners' efforts to nurture organizational change is constrained by the absolute control that has been the prerogative of generations of historical rulers (Sharpe, 1992).

The importance of understanding our total environment is emphasized by Simöes's (1992) analysis of public relations as a political function in Latin America. "Whoever possesses information," wrote Simöes (1992), "automatically has control over the social, cultural, economic, and political transactions, inherent [in] the life of the organizations (p. 195).

Sriramesh (1992) linked the public relations practice to India's cultural idiosyncrasies. He reported the emergence of a domineering coalition that controls most of an organization's processes and manipulates the organization's environment rather than cooperate with it. Similarly, Al-Enad (1990) described public relations in the Third World as driven by a living rule of public be damned, as geared toward propaganda, and as exploited by government and private institutions both to react to and to rigger positive changes in society.

For Australia, geography is the overarching factor in the public relations practice: Isolation from world population centers has nurtured modern communications and public relations industries (Thomson, 1989).

These disparate environmental influences on the practice cannot be ignored in public relations pedagogy. In light of these influences and in light of the growing importance of international competition and the profound implications of public relations' role for organizations' competitive advantage in the international marketplace, the following goals are suggested for international public relations courses.

These courses should introduce students to the history and development of public relations in other cultures; acquaint students with the practice and function of public relations abroad, emphasizing differences between U.S. and non-U.S. practices; and describe the internal and external dynamics of multinational corporations as well as the problems and difficulties of U.S. corporate public relations abroad, particularly in those countries where major U.S. corporations do business.

In addition, these courses should introduce comparative legal, political and ethical dimensions of public relations practice at home and abroad. They should describe the history, organization, practice and professional operations of the media—a major public relations agenda item—abroad (with special attention to press clubs, press councils, press codes, etc.).[1]

Another goal of these courses is to analyze the public relations aspects of major international political, diplomatic, cultural and socioeconomic developments with special emphasis on superpower relations and regional bilateral cooperation.

---

[1] On the need for public relations practitioners to have knowledge of the media in other countries, Carr (1989) said, "With more U.S. companies than ever now doing business with the Japanese, chances are increasing that you'll soon need to work with the Japanese media" (p. 27).

Finally, these courses should describe the various international organizations, associations, and agencies that provide resources for public relations practitioners, particularly those regularly involved in the global dimension of their activities. Such organizations may include Amnesty International, the International Association for Medical Assistance to Travelers, the International Organization of Journalists and other media contacts abroad (see Caruba, 1984).

Graduates of AEJMC-accredited programs, now fewer than those of communication programs that are not governed by the AEJMC Accreditation board, are required to have a minimum of 90 semester credit hours outside of journalism and mass communication. A survey of public relations programs in the United Stats indicates that public relation offerings have moved toward communication departments and away from journalism departments (Neff, 1992). No fewer than 65 of those hours should be in liberal arts and sciences. Because of such requirements, such programs could, at the minimum, encourage their students to take an international course as an elective. At the graduate level, such a course may well be taken as a "Public Relations Specialty Option."

On the other hand, major aspects of such an international course could be integrated into existing courses by dropping less important aspects of the latter courses. A number of MBA programs include the international aspects of public relations in their courses. Whatever their academic homes, such courses are needed to understand the broad function of public relations.

An attempt to incorporate international issues into the public relations curriculum of a Midwestern university was made in the fall of 1986, when the second author taught a new, semester-long course titled "International Public Relations," which was well received by the students.

CONCLUSION

Recent global developments point to a crucial need for expanded U.S. public relations curricula. Some of these developments are the pervasiveness of technologies for use in public relations, particularly the increasing capabilities of satellite communication; the increasingly transnational nature of business; the restructuring of the European Economic Community in 1991; the fast-changing political structure, particularly in Eastern Europe.

Are public relations practitioners and students up to the challenge? Bourke (1990), chairman and chief executive officer of Reynolds Metals Company, answered that question: "For the public relations professional, this means having a global outlook and the imagination to look beyond national borders for communications programs that help achieve business goals" (p. 40).

Students—tomorrow's practitioners—need be equipped with a broad knowledge of the world. For public relations students, this requires study of the history, development, and public relations practices, not just in the United States, but in other societies as well. A number of U.S. programs are revamping and improving their offerings with the intent of addressing just these challenges. However, they would do well to better prepare public relations students for the complex and rapidly changing international business and governmental environments by offering courses in international public relations in their programs.

REFERENCES

Aggarwal, R. (1987, July–August). The strategic challenge of the evolving global economy. *Business Horizons, 30,* 38–44.

Albritton, R. B., & Manheim, J. B. (1983). News of Rhodesia: The impact of a public relations campaign. *Journalism Quarterly, 60*(4), 622–628.

Albritton, R. B., & Manheim, J. B. (1985). Public relations efforts for the Third World: Images in the news. *Journal of Communication, 35*(1), 43–58.

Al-Enad, A. H. (1990). Public relations' roles in developing countries. *Public Relations Quarterly, 35*(1), 24–26.

American Council on Education. (1985). *Higher education panel reports, general education requirements in the humanities.* Washington, DC: Author.

Anonymous. (1990). *How college textbooks deal with the international aspect of public relations: A descriptive analysis.* Unpublished manuscript.

Baxter, B. (1981). 24 former PRSA heads praise role of PR education. *Journalism Educator, 36*(2), 23–24.

Booth, A. L. (1986). Going global. *Public Relations Journal, 42*(2), 22–27.

Borrus, A., Zellner, W., & Holstein, W. J. (199, May 14). The stateless corporation: Forget multinationals—today's giants are really leaping boundaries. *Business Week, 3159,* 98–106.

Botan, C. H. (1989). Theory development in public relations. In C. H. Botan & Vincent Hazleton, Jr. (Eds.), *Public relations theory* (pp. 99–110). Hillsdale, NJ: Lawrence Erlbaum Associates.

Bourke, W. O. (1990). What's ahead 1990s: Reassessing the public relations role. *Public Relations Journal, 46*(1), 40.

Brody, E. W. (1985a). Hard thinking on education. *Public Relations Journal, 41*(4), 28.

Brody, E. W. (1985b). What ought to be taught students of public relations? *Public Relations Quarterly, 30*(1), 6–9.

Brody, E. W. (1991). How and where should public relations be taught? *Public Relations Quarterly, 36*(2), 45–47.

Brownlee, B. J. (1988). Main street America asks students to give international perspective. *Journalism Educator, 43*(3), 17–20.

Cantor, B. (1985). Forecast '85: The year in public relations. *Public Relations Journal, 41*(2), 24.

Carnegie Endowment for International Peace National Commission (1992). *Changing our ways— America and the New World.* Washington, DC: Author.

Carr, S. (1989). Workshop: How to deal with the Japanese media. *Public Relations Journal, 45*(1), 27–28.

Caruba, A. (1984). Pinpointing international media contacts. *Public Relations Journal, 40*(8), 23–24.

Commission on Undergraduate Public Relations Education. (1987). *The design for undergraduate public relations education.* New York: Public Relations Society of America.

Creedon, P. (1989). Public relations history misses 'her story.' *Journalism Educator, 44*(3), 26–30.

Crespy, C. T. (1986). Global marketing is the new public relations challenge. *Public Relations Quarterly, 31*(2), 5–8.

Davis, M. (1977). *Interpreters for Nigeria: The Third World and International Public Relations.* Urbana, IL: University of Illinois Press.

Dozier, D. M. (1988). Breaking public relations' glass ceiling. *Public Relations Review, 14*(3), 6–14.

Ernst, M. (1990, January–February). U.S. exports in the 1990s. *Business Horizons, 33*(1), 44–49.
Farinelli, J. L. (1990). Needed: A new U.S. perspective on global public relations. *Public Relations Journal, 46*(11), 18–19, 42.
Foundation for Public Relations Research and Education. (1975). *A Design for Public Relations Education.* New York: Author.
Fowler, E. M. (1983, September 7). Careers: Global public relations. *The New York Times,* p. D20.
Frederick, H. H. (1993). *Global communication & international relations.* Belmont, CA: Wadsworth.
Grunig, J. E. (1985). Hard thinking on education. *Public Relations Journal, 41*(4), 30.
Hesse, M. B. (1984). Blueprint for graduate study: From idealism to reality. *Public Relations Journal, 40*(3), 22–24.
Hon, L. C., Grunig, L. A., & Dozier, D. M. (1992). Women in public relations: Problems and opportunities. In J. E. Grunig (Ed.), *Excellence in public relations and communication management* (pp. 419–438). Hillsdale, NJ: Lawrence Erlbaum Associates.
Hunt, T., & Thompson, D. W. (1988). Bridging the gender gap in PR courses. *Journalism Educator, 43*(1), 49–51.
Kant, I. (1974). *On the old saw: That may be right in theory but it won't work in practice* (E. B. Ashton, Trans.) Philadelphia: University of Pennsylvania Press. (Original work published 1793)
Kendall, R. (1992). *Public relations campaign strategies.* New York: Harper Collins.
Kern-Foxworth, M. (1989). Public relations books fail to show women in context. *Journalism Educator, 44*(3), 31–36.
Kern-Foxworth, M. (1990). Ethnic inclusiveness in public relations textbooks and reference books. *The Howard Journal of Communications, 2*(2), 226–237.
Kern-Foxworth, M. (1991). African-American achievements in public relations. *Public Relations Journal, 47*(2), 18–19.
Lance, E. P. (1986). Survey finds that few women are teaching in PR programs. *Journalism Educator, 40*(4), 7–8, 48.
Lee, A. M. (1947). Trends in public relations training. *Public Opinion Quarterly, 11*(1), 83–91.
Lehrman, C. K. (1985). Educational pulse taking. *Public Relations Journal, 41*(4), 16–19.
Lim, G-C. (1993). Reforming education toward the global century. *Environment and Planning B: Planning and Design, 20,* 567–576.
Lobsenz, A. (1984). Representing a foreign government. *Public Relations Journal, 40*(8), 21–22.
Manheim, J. B., & Albritton, R. B. (1984). Changing national images: International public relations and media agenda setting. *The American Political Science Review, 78*(3), 641–657.
Modoux, A. (1989). The growing role of public relations in a changing world. *International Public Relations Review, 12*(3), 4–9.
National Commission on Graduate Study in Public Relations. (1985). *Advancing public relations education: Recommended curriculum for graduate public relations education.* New York: Foundation for Public Relations Research and Education, Inc.
Neff, B. D. (1992). The emerging theoretical perspective in pr: An opportunity for communication departments. In C. H. Botan & V. Hazleton, Jr. (Eds.), *Public relations theory* (pp. 159–172). Hillsdale, NJ: Lawrence Erlbaum Associates.
Ogan, C. L., & Brownlee, B. (1986). *From parochialism to globalism: International perspectives on journalism education.* Columbia, SC: International Division of the Association for Education in Journalism and Mass Communication.
Paraschos, M. (1980). International media course: It's also for small schools. *Journalism Educator, 35*(3), 59–60.
Peterson, J. V. (1988). Journalism and mass comm enrollment leveled off in '87. *Journalism Educator, 43*(1), 4–10.
Public Relations News. (1990a, January 22). *46,* 1.
Public Relations News. (1990b, May 28). *46,* 1.

Public Relations News. (1990c, January 29). *46,* 1.
Reischauer, E. O. (1973). *Toward the 21st century: Education for a changing world.* New York: Knopf.
Schwartz, D. F., & Yarbrough, J. P. (1992). Does public relations education make the grade? *Public Relations Journal, 48*(9), 18–19, 21, 24–25.
Sharpe, M. L. (1985). Hard thinking on education. *Public Relations Journal, 41*(4), 29.
Sharpe, M. L. (1992). The impact of social and cultural conditioning on global public relations. *Public Relations Review, 18*(2), 103–107.
Signitzer, B. (1987). Salzburg begins PR sequence, addresses mid-1980s changes. *Journalism Educator, 42*(1), 18–19.
Simöes, R. P. (1992). Public relations as a political function: A Latin American view. *Public Relations Review, 18*(2), 189–200.
Singer, J. H. (1987). How to work with foreign clients. *Public Relations Review, 43*(10), 35–37.
Sriramesh, K. (1992). Societal culture and public relations: Ethnographic evidence from India. *Public Relations Review, 18*(2), 201–211.
Staples, W. A. (1988, July 18). Avoiding "academic myopia" for 21st century. *Marketing News, 22*(15), 1–2.
Steilen, C. F. (1988, July 18). Educators must raise U.S.'s knowledge of world markets. *Marketing News, 22*(15), 2.
Steingraber, F. G. (1990, January–February). Managing in the 1990s. *Business Horizons, 33*(1), 50–61.
Strenski, J. B. (1985). International networking tailors communications programs across the globe. *Public Relations Quarterly, 30*(1), 28–29.
Thomson, M. (1989). Dealing with isolation—public relations in Australia. In B. Cantor & C. Burger (Eds.), *Experts in action: Inside public relations* (pp. 455–469). New York: Longman.
Tung, R. L., & Miller, E. L. (1990). Managing in the twenty-first century: The need for global orientation. *Management International Review, 30*(1), 5–18.
U.K. tests first undergraduate PR program. (1989). *Public Relations Journal, 45*(11), 8.
Wilcox, D. L., Ault, P. H., & Agee, W. K. (1992). *Public relations: Strategies and tactics.* New York: Harper Collins.
Wright, D. K., & Turk, J. V. (1990). *Public relations education: The unpleasant realities.* New York: Institute for Public Relations Research and Education.

22
Public Relations Education in the United States: Can It Broaden International Students' Horizons?

Hugh M. Culbertson
Ohio University

Ni Chen
University of Toledo

This volume provides ample evidence that public relations is a "hot" vocation around the world. It is changing and growing as people, organizations, and nations realize that they must cooperate, or, at least avoid open, violent combat, in an ever-more complex, contentious, interdependent world.

For better or worse, hundreds of young people are flocking to the United States for training in the field. American programs of study and internships in public relations have multiplied recently. And current as well as would-be practitioners from abroad seem to assume, perhaps often without much evidence, that they can learn useful things by studying in the land that separates Canada from Mexico.

What do these people study—or at least, have a chance to study? What educational philosophies guide their host academic departments and universities?

Few, if any, scholars have tried systematically to answer these questions. Here we report a survey of schools and departments at 33 American universities offering master's programs with at least two graduate-level courses that have the phrase "public relations" in their titles.

RESEARCH QUESTIONS AND HYPOTHESES

The research was guided by six questions. The fifth of these generated five hypotheses.

Research Question 1

In the study of cross-cultural communication, do international students who focus on public relations at American universities and colleges look primarily at the United States plus their home nations and regions? Do they focus only on their native lands? Or do they study a broad range of cultures around the world?

In our own teaching and advising, we have observed the first of these patterns quite often. Many international students at our universities seem bent on learning about the United States. They often write papers analyzing media and other institutions back home in light of western principles. Their goal, obviously, is to find a new and stimulating perspective for use in their homelands.

Although perhaps useful, this approach apparently strikes some students as unduly narrow. Recently, the senior author of this chapter worked with at least one Chinese graduate student who minored in Thai language and culture. A potential student from the Orient has sought to learn about business and finance in Peru where the firm for which she worked had a joint venture. A German student has studied China intensively. And so on.

Clearly regional and world-wide cooperation involves cooperative effort among more than two countries. Witness the growing role of the North American Free Trade Association, the European Economic Community, the Southeast Asia Treaty Organization, the Organization of African Unity, the Organization of American States, and other regional economic as well as political bodies. Also, transnational corporations operate all over the world, often with more resources and power than many governments possess.

In chapter 2 of this volume, Verčič, Grunig, and Grunig present generic principles designed to enhance and define public relations all over the world. However, they note that constraints and conditions shaping the application of these principles vary greatly from country to country and region to region. It follows that a focus on one's home country and host country would hardly prepare one for truly international practice.

Also, recent theorizing by Hofstede (1980) and others base analysis of one culture very largely on comparison of it with many others around the world.

Taken as a whole, these developments point to a need for breadth in cross-cultural study, for analysis of many nations and regions rather than primarily of one's own country and host nation.

Research Question 2

To what degree is international public relations taught as a distinct area of study in the United States? Is it covered as a primary focus in one or a few courses? As a secondary topic in several courses? Or almost not at all?

In this volume, several authors have made a compelling case that theory developed in one nation or region cannot simply be exported to another. (See especially Wakefield, chap. 1; Verčič et al., chap. 2; Wilson, chap. 3; Kruckeberg, chap. 4; Van Leuven, chap. 5; Chen, chap. 7; and Pratt & Ogbondah, chap. 21.) Local conditions create unique barriers to excellent public relations. And different cultures and economies require different approaches in practicing it.

However, there is little systematic theory or research on how national and regional public relations professions might vary. Absent such substance, international public relations courses in the United States seem apt to be few and far between, with case studies and occasional lectures studying public relations in Japan, Nigeria, Peru, Chad, and so forth, largely with Western-based concepts.

We make an assumption here. Occasional international examples scattered across several courses might tend to have little analytical or comparative depth. As Pratt and Ogbondah (chapter 21, this volume) argue, a solid public relations program at the graduate level must offer at least one course focusing on international public relations.

Research Question 3

How many international students complete internships and postgraduate "practical training" experiences during or soon after their academic work? How many of these experiences occur outside U.S. borders? And how many such efforts involve some sort of international or cross-cultural focus?

Commissions on public relations education have stressed the importance of hands-on experience (Commission on Public Relations Education, 1975; National Commission on Graduate Study in Public Relations, 1985). Grunig (1985) has described this as an essential component in the field's maturation. And the Public Relations Society of America has invested much time and effort in its PRIDE-internship program.

Many graduate students from other countries have a special need for practical experience, as they come from undergraduate programs in language, humanities, and social science. Such curricula often lack the practical component found in American undergraduate study.

However, several barriers seem apt to prevent large numbers of international students from gaining internship experience. Many American firms hire only people with intimate knowledge of U.S. institutions, language, and culture. Some students cannot afford to complete the many internships which offer little or no pay. Also, the prospect of prolonged separation from families doubtless discourages some from remaining in the States as interns.

Research Question 4

Do programs completed by international students in the United States focus heavily on theory? On practical, skill-oriented training and experience? Or is there a reasonable balance between the two?

Until quite recently, it appears, a high percentage of American academic programs focused primarily on training of writers and publicists (Grunig & Hunt, 1984; chapter 2). Communication was largely one-way; from client or employer to identified publics. And few practitioners had training in the theory of public relations.

Recent evidence suggests, however, that communication managers now play an essential role in guiding and shaping the field's development (Lauzen & Dozier, 1994). Management skills are required for issues management and environmental scanning, activities needed to insure all-important two-way communication. Consequently, Grunig (1985) and Culbertson, Jeffers, Stone, & Terrell (1993, pp. 3–9) have viewed theoretical development and application as essential to the field's maturation.

At the same time, many factors have made it difficult for universities to offer balanced programs blending theory with practice. In particular, professorial salaries are low when compared with those earned by executive-level practitioners (Culbertson, 1985; Lance, 1986). This often means that a would-be educator with substantial experience in the field has to leave a fairly lucrative position, complete 3–5 years of graduate study with subsistence wages, and enter a new career field (teaching) with an entry-level salary!

Another factor is the publish-or-perish pressure that surely discourages some academics from working in the field during leaves or breaks in the academic calendar. Applied research can help bridge this gap, yielding theoretically relevant papers and articles which satisfy promotion-and-tenure committees. However, such committees sometimes appear to take a rather dim view of applied study.

Finally, quite a few practitioners seem doubtful about academic careers partly because they value their independence as entrepreneurs. They say they enjoy doing research, but only for its own sake and usefulness. They chafe at the idea of having to complete X articles and Y papers within, say, a 6-year period leading to tenure (Culbertson, 1985; Lance, 1986).

Unfortunately, several barriers often make it difficult for professors around the world to move back and forth between workplace and academy. Emphasis on classic and liberal-arts studies has sometimes left little room for applied public relations research ("U. K. tests," 1989). Also, reverence for professors in places like China and India make it seem inappropriate for them to "dirty their hands" as working practitioners (Sriramesh, 1992).

These factors make it especially important for young practitioners and educators from abroad to gain balanced training in host countries, including the United States.

We now move to two questions with a broader curricular focus.

Research Question 5

Do graduate programs offering multiple courses on public relations tend to follow patterns long associated with journalism education? Or do these programs feature primarily courses espoused in departments and schools of communication (especially speech, interpersonal, and organizational communication)?

Historically, public relations has been taught primarily in departments and schools of journalism. The focus supposedly has been on mass rather than on interpersonal communication, on relations with external rather than with internal publics, and on skill training rather than on theory building. Recently, however, several observers have urged growing emphasis on interpersonal communication with specialized and internal publics, and on theory (Brody, 1985; Grunig, 1985; Lehrman, 1985; Newsom, 1984).

Critics such as Brody (1985) have argued that journalism schools lack the flexibility needed to accommodate these changes. These units supposedly have long focused on skill training related to news reporting and editing, leaving few resources for public relations teaching and research despite growing enrollment in public relations sequences.

Further, the Association for Education in Journalism and Mass Communication —the field's primary accrediting body—requires that students take about three fourths of their credits outside of the "professional field." This makes it difficult to add new professionally related courses (Hesse, 1984).

If journalism education continues to dominate public relations education, certain hypotheses should hold with respect to courses taken:

Hypothesis 1. International graduate students take media-oriented skill courses (journalistic writing, layout and design, publicity writing and methods) more often, on the average, than they take an interpersonally oriented skill course (public speaking).

Hypothesis 2. International graduate students take general communication-theory courses (which presumably include at least a component of mass-communication theory) more often than courses in rhetorical theory (which stem largely from an interpersonal tradition).

Hypothesis 3. International graduate students take courses in overall public relations principles (principles, management, and theory) more often than in interpersonal or organizational principles (organizational communication and persuasion theory).

Even casual perusal of *Journalism Quarterly,* the *Newspaper Research Journal* and other mass-communication journals suggests a strong emphasis on words rather than pictures and graphics. That, in turn, implies another hypothesis which should hold if journalism-education practice and theory shape the nature of current public relations instruction.

Hypothesis 4. International graduate students take courses in journalistic writing more often than those in layout and design.

Furthermore, American mass-communication research appears to have focused quite heavily on quantitative methods from its early days. A recent edition of one oft-used text in mass-communication theory (Severin & Tankard, 1988) devotes 17 chapters to specific theoretical perspectives. Only 3 of these 17 chapters deal with clearly qualitative work (in language study, propaganda, and social responsibility of the press). Only recently, it appears, have qualitative studies moved quite high on the mass-communication research agenda in the United States.

On the other hand, communication studies outside of mass communication have focused quite heavily on critical theory, interpretation, discourse, signs and language, dramatism, and other topics generally regarded as qualitative in focus and origin. A recent text on general communication theory lists 9 broad topics, at least 6 of which hinge largely on qualitative research (Littlejohn, 1992).

If public relations studies follow a mass-communication model, then, the following should hold:

Hypothesis 5. International graduate students take courses in quantitative research methodology more often than in qualitative methods.

Recently, quite a few departments of speech, interpersonal communication, and speech communication have begun offering public relations courses and sequences. This trend has gained impetus with the formation of public relations interest groups in the International Communication Association and the Speech Communication Association.

Are these departments moving to lead public relations education in directions markedly different from those established within schools of journalism? That question suggests a sixth and final research question:

Research Question 6

Do international graduate students in departments of communication (including speech and interpersonal communication) differ from those in journalism units as to courses taken more frequently?

At first glance, we might expect students in communication units to take persuasion, organizational communication, public speaking, and rhetoric relatively often. Journalism students, on the other hand, might tend to take courses in journalistic writing, publicity writing and methods, layout and design, and general communication theory.

However, such differences might be small if journalism units and communication units take each other into account when advising students and planning curricula. After all, as noted earlier, AEJMC accreditation requirements are now designed to encourage heavy curricular emphasis on a variety of courses outside journalism per se.

METHODS

Sampling

Counting and defining U.S. graduate programs in public relations have long been challenges.

Apparently, in looking only at programs that formally label degrees as being in public relations, Sharpe (1985) noted a decade ago that just four schools offered a master's in the field. He commented that standard journalism degree programs often provided just one or two public relations courses, frequently the same as those offered for undergrads.

Obviously using a more liberal definition, Hesse (1984) reported that, by 1981, 51 institutions were providing graduate programs in public relations.

We felt it necessary to steer a middle course. Surely some schools offer substantial concentrations in the field without formally attaching the public relations label to their degrees. Thus, we enclosed a cover letter with each questionnaire defining a graduate-level public relations emphasis as existing *"where a university offers at least two graduate-level courses with the phrase public relations in the title."* We asked respondents to fill out the questionnaire if this held, and to return it as "not applicable" otherwise. While arbitrary, this rule required a fairly substantial commitment to teaching public relations rather than bootlegging it under a different guise.

In drawing our sample, we proceeded in three steps.

First, we examined all academic units listed in the most recent directory of the Association for Education in Journalism and Mass Communication (1993). Included here were all schools or departments described by the directory as having both a public relations sequence and a master's program. Where we knew a professor at a given school to be actively involved in teaching public relations, we included that person on our mailing list. Lacking such knowledge, we included public relations sequence heads for certain universities listed in the directory. And, absent that information, we mailed to a listed department or school chair.

Second, we scoured the 1993 membership list of the Public Relations Interest Group, International Communication Association. We included people from schools and departments not listed in the AEJMC directory.

Third, we listed additional programs from a 1990 directory compiled by Kendall, Terhune, and Hesse (1991) which had not been included in the AEJMC and ICA lists.

This procedure yielded 111 universities and colleges—83 in the AEJMC directory, 14 additional units from the ICA-PRIG membership list, and 14 from Kendall et al.

We mailed a questionnaire, with a cover letter and a self-addressed, stamped envelope, to each listed professor in late October 1993. A second wave of questionnaires then went out in early December.

In all, 71 people returned questionnaires, yielding a response rate of 63%. Of these 71, 33 (46.5%) filled out usable questionnaires and reported that their units met our criteria. One would-be respondent declined to answer on the grounds that her unit did not track its students thoroughly enough to permit valid answers. Others marked "not applicable" on their questionnaires.

Of course, some nonresponding units may offer substantial concentrations in public relations. However, a spot check by telephone along with the authors' general knowledge of programs in the field suggested that we missed relatively few units with fairly large, well-established programs.

Measurement

We began with the assumption that many academic units track and describe their students imprecisely if at all. Thus, we asked for general estimates, rather than specific figures, where possible.

At the outset, respondents estimated the total number of students at their institutions who concentrated on public relations at the bachelor's, master's, and doctoral levels. Next, similar estimates were requested for students from nations other than the United States. And finally, professors estimated overall numbers of students at each level from each of seven regions (Latin America, Asia, Africa, the Middle East, East or Central Europe, Western Europe, and Australia plus the Pacific islands). An "other region" category was also included.

Regions were exhaustive given the "other" category. However, overall international-student counts at the bachelor's level substantially exceeded counts summed across regions. This suggested a lack of precise, accurate tracking.

At the master's and doctoral levels, regional counts equalled total figures almost exactly. Perhaps not surprisingly, schools and departments appeared to track graduate students more carefully than undergraduates. And, fortunately, our primary focus was on the study of master's programs.

In attempting to gauge frequency of course completion, we asked respondents to base estimates on courses taken, at the current or at earlier levels of study, by all graduate students from abroad who majored in, or concentrated on, public relations. Response options and numerical values assigned were 5 for all students taking a given course, 4 for most, 3 for some, 2 for few, and 1 for none. Of 33 respondents, about 27 provided estimates for any given course. Other responses were coded as missing values.

To identify course clusters, we performed a factor analysis on responses. Principal-components analysis was followed by varimax rotation, yielding eight factors with eigenvalues of at least one. Although the number of cases was small, the solution was very "clean," lending credence to the factors. Seven of the eight factors seemed interpretable, as each had at least two courses with a clear primary loading on it. All primary factor loadings counted were at least .66, with most being at .79 and above. And only one secondary loading for a given course was above .30.

Clusters of courses, with primary loadings on each given factor, were as follows: *communication technician*—layout and design (.91), journalistic writing (.85), and publicity writing and techniques (.78); *public relations principles and management*—principles (.84), management (.79), and theory (.78); *interpersonal communication*—persuasion theory (.85) and organizational communication (.66); *communication research and theory*—communication theory (.87) and quantitative research methods (.78); *rhetoric*—rhetoric (.84) and technical writing (.79); *business*—management (.89) and marketing (.80); *economics and fund raising*—economics (.86) and fund raising (.81).

We summed scores on individual courses to create factor scores. Then, to make factor scores comparable, we divided each factor mean by the number of items tapping that factor. Resulting scores were in the range of 1 to 5.

Courses that did not load clearly on a given factor were analyzed separately. These included accounting, public speaking, public relations cases, qualitative research methods, and communication law.

Data on frequency of course completion were defined as interval in light of the heavy emphasis on two- and three-item indexes. Mean scores computed across institutions were not weighted as to number of students enrolled. In analyzing data from several other questions, such weighting did occur.

Wording of key questions is indicated in the results section.

RESULTS

Sample Description

Overall, 33 units reported current public relations enrollment at 4,493 undergraduates, 568 master's students, and 34 at the doctoral level. Using the conservative estimates of enrollees from each region, international-student enrollment totaled 214 bachelor's, 167 master's, and 7 doctoral.

International students accounted for 33% of all master's people but only 11% of all undergraduates, based on global estimates not specific to regions. We presume that international students often go abroad at the master's level after studying English as undergraduates. Also, many folks from abroad require financial aid which tends to be available primarily at the master's and doctoral levels.

Regional estimates were viewed with some skepticism because of discrepancies noted earlier. However, Asians clearly dominated, accounting for 49% of all estimated undergraduates, 61% of the master's people, and 71% (5/7) at the doctoral level. In the only other substantial regional grouping, Hispanics accounted for 27% of all undergraduate enrollees.

In all, the responding academic units included 16 schools or departments of journalism, 13 communication units, 3 departments of public relations and advertising, and 1 unidentified unit. The journalism schools and departments included 5 with the title "journalism and mass communication." These 5 did not differ substantially from other journalism units on any variable studied, so all schools and departments with the term journalism in the title were lumped together in the analysis.

Research Questions and Hypotheses

Research question 1 asked whether students had an opportunity to focus primarily on one nation or region, or to focus on a broad range of regions, in their overall international studies.

Responses were weighted by number of international students enrolled at a given institution. In all, six of the 17 universities reported that a plurality of their PR students who wished to work in countries other than the U.S. *concentrated largely on the study of one nation or region in which they planned to work.* About one sixth (17.5%) of all international students covered in the survey attended these universities.

Eleven universities, accounting for 50% of the international enrollees, encouraged *study of a broad range of regions and cultures, but with a primary focus on one nation or region in which a student planned to work.*

Ten institutions, with about one third (32.6%) of all international public relations students, *leaned toward studying a broad range of regions and cultures without concentrating on any one region.*

On the whole, then, most international public relations students in the United States had at least an opportunity to study a broad range of cultures as recommended earlier. However, only about half of the students analyzed were at institutions which, as a matter of policy, combined in-depth study of one nation or region with cultural breadth. Thus, lack of depth with respect to any one location may sometimes be a problem.

Research question 2 asked whether students study international public relations at all. Also, where they do, is such material the focus of one or a few courses? Or are international cases, problems, and content covered in courses which focus primarily on domestic practice?

Results indicated that only 6 academic units reported offering courses that dealt specifically with international public relations. Slightly less than one sixth (15%) of all international students covered were located at these institutions.

Slightly over two fifths (42%) of all students matriculated at 12 schools which offered international content within courses primarily devoted to other things.

A similar number (43%) of students were at 14 institutions which offered little or no content on international practice.

On the whole, then, international public relations does not appear to be a popular, well-developed focus of study at American universities. This is not too surprising given the thin base in research and theory noted earlier. However, the large number of schools (nearly half of all studied) with little or no international content still seems rather alarming.

Lack of resources during tight budgetary times may be a factor here. However, open-ended comments about philosophy of education revealed a "when in Rome, do as the Romans" philosophy in some quarters. One professor commented that basic skills and theories are largely the same world-wide. Another contended that American public relations sets the pace, so students from elsewhere should follow it. And a third placed the onus of adapting American principles on international students, saying they were welcome to adapt what they learn back home if they so desire.

Research question 3 inquired about the number and locations of internships and follow-up practical training completed by international students.

An estimated 52.5% of all students covered had completed or lined up internships of some kind when the survey was completed. Of these, only a few (3%) did, or appeared destined to, intern abroad.

On the plus side, just over two thirds (70%) worked for organizations in the United States that targeted publics from other countries. Yet, over one fourth (27%) had positions that did not involve working or communication with people outside the United States.

In sum, almost half of all international students had neither an internship nor prospects for internships. In part, this may reflect a tendency to view interning as an undergraduate experience. Considering all students, domestic and foreign, 70% of the responding institutions estimated that over half of their undergraduates completed internships. But 72% of the professors questioned felt 50% or fewer of their graduate students held such positions.

On the plus side, most international students who did intern held positions with some cross-cultural relevance. Perhaps these findings reflect reluctance of purely domestic organizations in the United States to hire foreigners. After all, such students appear likely to have a competitive edge over Americans primarily when applying for cross-cultural positions.

In a related area, respondents estimated that about 53% of their international students planned to return home right after graduation. Another 23% were expected to obtain practical experience in the United States for about 1 or 2 years. About one sixth (17%) were presumed anxious to work in the States as long as they could after graduation, suggesting some aversion to returning home. And 7% were undecided.

Overall, then, a brain drain may exist where students come to the United States. However, it appears to be a trickle, not a large flow.

Research question 4 deals with emphasis on theoretical versus practical content. Overall, in the 27 institutions responding on this question, slightly less than half (46%) of all students covered studied in 14 schools or departments which, as a matter of policy, placed roughly equal emphasis on theory and practice. About one third (32.5%) matriculated at nine institutions which emphasized theory more than practice. Roughly one fifth (21.5%) attended nine schools which professed to be primarily practical.

In estimating emphasis on theory versus practice, respondents had five options. These were: emphasizes theory almost to the exclusion of teaching practical skills; emphasizes theory more than practical skills, but with substantial attention to skills; emphasizes theory and practical skills about equally; emphasizes practical skills more than theory, but with substantial attention to theory; and emphasizes practical skills almost to the exclusion of teaching theory.

Encouragingly, most schools professed to strive for some balance. Only one institution (3% of all) stressed only the practical, and only three (9%) claimed to stress only theory.

As noted later, schools of journalism appeared to emphasize theory at least as much as did communication units. Taken as a whole, then, our data do not suggest journalism education as experienced by international PR students focuses unduly on purely skill-oriented, practical concerns. Blanchard and Christ (1993, pp. 66–78), among others, have suggested that such units are under pressure from media managers to focus on skill training.

One issue may be of some concern, however. One-half of the smaller schools based on international enrollment (with two or fewer students from abroad in public relations), but only one sixth of the larger units, place more emphasis on practice than on theory. Apparently, then, primarily larger units manage to develop stronger theoretical programs.

Research question 5 asked whether America PR education, as experienced by international students, follows a model set in schools and departments of journalism. Table 22.1 gives a resounding yes here, supporting all five hypotheses based on this proposition.

As specified under hypothesis 1, which dealt with skill-oriented courses, the frequency-of-course-completion ratings (on a scale from $1 =$ no one takes a course to $5 =$ all take it) was higher for the communication-technician index (3.81) than for the rhetoric factor, rhetoric + technical writing, (2.27). Means for journalistic writing (4.04) and publicity writing and techniques (4.00) exceed that for public speaking (2.44).

Moving to hypothesis 2, in the theoretical realm, the mean rating for communication-theory courses (4.38) exceeds that for rhetoric courses (2.08) as specified. Also, scores on the communication-theory-and-research factor (4.54, averaging theory and research methods) exceed the rhetoric factor (2.29, encompassing rhetoric and technical writing).

Hypothesis 3 focused on basic principles courses. As predicted, the mean score for public relations principles (4.54) exceeded that for organizational communication (3.50). Also, the public relations principles-and-management mean of 4.56 (encompassing principles + management + theory) outscores interper-

TABLE 22.1
Mean Frequency-of-Enrollment Scores for Selected Courses Relating to Journalism and Interpersonal Communication

Journalism	Interpersonal Communication	t	p
Communication technician[a] 3.81	Rhetoric[b] (factor) 2.27	6.93	.001
Journalistic writing 4.04	Public Speaking 2.44	5.43	.001
Publicity writing & methods 4.00	Public Speaking 2.44	5.51	.001
Communication theory 4.38	Rhetoric (course) 2.08	9.36	.001
Communication theory & research[b] 4.54	Rhetoric[b] (factor) 2.27	9.06	.001
Public relations principles & management 4.56	Interpersonal communication[b] 3.56	5.09	.001
Public relations principles 4.54	Organizational communication 3.50	6.43	.001
Journalistic writing 4.04	Layout & design 3.48	2.43	.022
Quantitative research methods 4.67	Qualitative research methods 4.07	2.94	.01

[a]Factor scores were computed by summing across three course ratings and dividing by 3.
[b]Factor scores were computed by summing across two course ratings and dividing by 2.
Note. Matched-sample t-tests were performed in each case, with degrees of freedom ranging from 23 to 26.

sonal communication (organizational communication + persuasion theory), which has a mean of 3.56.

Hypothesis 4 predicted that, following the general perspective of journalism schools, international graduate students took journalistic writing more often than layout and design. The mean of 4.04 for writing exceeds the 3.48 for layout and design. Thus the hypothesis is confirmed.

Hypothesis 5 asserted that, again in line with tradition, students took quantitative research methods more often than qualitative methods. As predicted, the quantitative mean (4.67) exceeds the qualitative (4.07).

Without exception, then, the data suggest public relations education, as experienced by international students in the United States, follows a model established within journalism schools quite closely.

Research question 6 asked whether American schools and departments of communication were adhering to a substantially different model as reflected by the courses taken by their international students.

Table 22.2 presents data here on individual courses. Surprisingly, the answer appears to be a resounding no! In no instance did majors in communication differ substantially, or significantly in a statistical sense, from those in journalism.

To be sure, the number of institutions is small. However, in only four cases did means for individual courses differ by amounts that might warrant extensive comment even if larger numbers were to enhance statistical power. Communication majors did take a bit more organizational communication, public speaking, and accounting, whereas journalism students focused more heavily on journalistic writing. Yet, these differences failed to approach statistical significance. And,

TABLE 22.2
Mean Frequency-of Enrollment Scores for 21 Courses in Journalism and communication Schools and Departments

Course	Communication		Journalism	
Marketing	2.87	(1.13)	3.13	(0.92)
Management	2.85	(1.25)	3.20	(1.21)
Accounting	2.00	(1.41)	1.47	(0.52)
Public speaking	2.71	(1.60)	2.27	(1.10)
Organizational communication	4.00	(0.82)	3.33	(0.98)
Persuasion theory	3.57	(1.27)	3.47	(1.12)
Rhetoric	2.00	(1.29)	2.07	(0.80)
Technical writing	2.57	(1.72)	2.33	(0.98)
Layout and Design	3.75	(1.28)	3.53	(1.30)
Journalistic writing	3.75	(1.39)	4.33	(0.90)
Publicity writing and methods	3.87	(1.36)	4.07	(0.96)
Public relations cases	3.87	(0.83)	4.06	(1.10)
Public relations principles	4.75	(0.46)	4.40	(0.83)
Public relations management	4.38	(0.92)	4.47	(1.12)
Qualitative research methods	4.13	(1.13)	4.13	(0.99)
Quantitative research methods	4.50	(0.76)	4.87	(0.35)
Public relations theory	4.62	(0.74)	4.57	(1.09)
Communication law	3.75	(1.28)	3.80	(1.01)
Communication theory	4.38	(0.92)	4.53	(0.91)
Fund raising	2.12	(1.13)	2.40	(0.99)
Economics	2.62	(0.92)	2.67	(1.17)

Note. Independent-sample t-tests revealed no difference between means on a given course which was significant at $p = .05$. Number of institutions ranged from 8 to 12 for Communication, 14 to 15 for Journalism, with missing values removed.

Scores are on a 5-point scale with 5 = all international students take (or have taken) a given course, 4 = most have, 3 = some have, 2 = few have, and 1 = none have.

Numbers in parentheses are subgroup standard deviations.

even if they had, one might expect four such differences by chance from a total of 21 course comparisons.

Why are communication units not "breaking away" from the mold established by schools of journalism? Perhaps a lack of resources and of staff plays a role, as do pressures to seek AEJMC accreditation.

Recently, the Public Relations Society of American has begun to certify public relations sequences. Future research should explore whether PRSA-certified units follow a clearly different educational pattern.

Some Additional Findings

Journalism and communication units did not differ demonstrably as to curricular areas emphasized. However, they did tend to place students in different occupational realms somewhat in line with their presumed philosophies. This follows from estimated percentages of "international students graduating in the past 2 years or so" who then took positions in each of 6 job sectors.

Specifically, 23% of all international communication-unit grads, but only 11% of their journalism counterparts, took jobs in corporate public relations. Communication graduates also led by 15% to 7% for trade-and-professional-association jobs, and by 18% to 7% for non-profit. These differences make sense because corporations, as well as associations and non-profit groups, emphasize internal communication with members and employees. Interpersonal-communication units have placed some emphasis on internal communication as reflected, for example, by the focus on communication audits within the organizational-communication division of the International Communication Association.

More than one third (36.5%) of journalism-school graduates wound up working in government, compared with just 9% among communication alums. Journalism-school people also had a 15% to 7% edge among agency employees and 17% to 3% in educational institutions. Cutlip, Center & Broom (1994, p. 69) note that universities, in particular, tend to hire many editorial and press-relations people. Also, Hess (1984, pp. 38–53) suggested that in federal government, at least, many public information offices exist primarily to serve the media.

Communication programs also appear to focus a bit more heavily on cross-cultural study of public relations than do journalism units. About 31% of the communication departments, but only 12% of those in journalism, offered one or a few specific courses focusing largely on international public relations. As noted earlier, depth seems apt to be greater in such focused courses than where international concerns receive only passing notice in several offerings.

It should be noted that small n's preclude statistical significance in the individual comparisons just noted. However, taken as a whole, they form a pattern which suggests that each type of academic unit—journalism or communication—fills a fairly clear academic niche.

One final area warrants attention. Do skill courses in mass communication come at the expense of those in the inter-personal and organizational realms? And do skill courses generally come at the expense of a broad liberal education?

Sharpe (1985), Brody (1985), and others seem to say yes. In times of reduced educational spending increased offerings in one area may come at the expense of others.

On the other hand, Blanchard and Christ (1993, pp. 60–78) urge a "new professionalism" which integrates practice with theory. These authors argued that today's communicator must learn to write, edit, speak, and design visual messages in ways which draw on the humanities and social sciences. Only people with such broad training can hope to define and help solve problems in a changing world.

Our data seem to give devotees of Blanchard and Christ (1993) some reason for optimism. In the larger and better American programs, public relations students from abroad appear to get both skill training and a substantial dose of theory. They need not choose between the two.

Specifically, number of journalistic "comm-tech" courses (journalistic writing, publicity writing and methods, and layout and design) taken correlates positively with courses completed in several other areas. Scores on the *communication-technician* index correlate with depth of *international-PR* coverage ($r = .48, p < .01$). Also, high comm-tech scores go along with curricular emphasis on *interpersonal communication* (organizational communication + persuasion theory) ($r = .43, p = .017$), *economics and fundraising* ($r = .32, p = .05$), *rhetoric* (rhetoric + technical writing) ($r = .40, p = .02$), and *public speaking* ($r = .38, p = .029$).

In sum, the oft-criticized 25–75 rule imposed by AEJMC accreditation to preclude overemphasis on professional or skill courses, appears to have had some impact. In line with that rule's intent, international students with solid journalism-skill education appear to take a broad range of communication courses overall.

SUMMARY AND CONCLUSIONS

This survey focused on 33 American universities which offer at least two courses in public relations. The basic goal was to characterize programs of study completed by international students seeking degrees there.

Overall, curricula for these students followed a model often associated with schools of journalism. Heavy emphasis was given to overall communication theory as well as to writing, editing, and layout skills.

Somewhat surprisingly, the 13 communication units did not differ substantially from the 15 schools and departments of journalism studied as to frequency with which international graduate students took particular courses. Communication units did not appear to be blazing new curricular trails, though they did emphasize international public relations study somewhat more than their journalism counterparts.

Most students were enrolled at institutions which placed considerable emphasis on broad international study. However, only about half studied at universities which sought, as a matter of basic policy, to combine depth in study of a particular nation or region with breadth of cross-cultural analysis. Such a combination seems very desirable in light of current academic and social-political-economic trends around the world.

About half of all international graduate students were taking, or planned to take, internships relating to public relations. Many barriers make it difficult for these people to intern. On the plus side, however, most internships appeared to involve some cross-cultural communication.

Overall, programs surveyed appear to offer a reasonable balance between theoretical and practical training. In all, just about 12% of all programs focused on theory or practice almost to the exclusion of the other alternative. And, encouragingly, the number of communication-technician courses taken correlated *positively, not negatively,* with enrollment in several types of theoretical work.

Where do we go from here? This volume suggests many avenues for future development as Western (and other) universities seek to serve current and would-be public relations practitioners from abroad. As editors of this volume, we have been greatly impressed with the extent and variety of related efforts pursued by contributors and other educators.

Also, we recently completed a 1994 lecture tour in mainland China with noted practitioner Isobel Parke, senior counsel in the American firm of Jackson, Jackson and Wagner. Lengthy discussions with many new practitioner and educator friends in that great country lead us to make the following suggestions.

American educators should travel abroad. Also, before getting on the plane, we should talk as much as possible with our own students from the countries we plan to visit. All too often, we fail to apply two-way symmetric notions fully in our teaching. What's more, our students have contacts which can help us learn and serve abroad. And, particularly in the Orient, contacts are very important. In fact, one student commented that, in China, they are almost everything!!

When traveling or working abroad, American scholars and students should listen more than they talk. In China, we heard much talk about former Premier Deng Xioaping's "opening to the West." While there, however, we became convinced that western practitioners can learn a great deal from Chinese culture—from Confucius to Chairman Mao to Deng—which applies to Western public relations practice. We returned to the United States with a firm resolve to help develop an "opening to the East."

In working with international students, we must recognize that their needs differ when it comes to studying theory versus practice. In China, both practitioners and educators often told us, "We have a good handle on theory. What we need is practice." Few practitioners there have much background in media relations; their focus has been at the interpersonal level for a variety of reasons. However, they see a need to communicate via the media with western partners, investors, and customers.

By contrast, in Britain and Sweden, media relations is alive and well as an area of concentration. And in Japan, young people tend to equate public relations with advertising (Cooper-Chen & Kaneshige, chapter 12, this volume). In serving international students, educators must attend to individual needs. The idea that all students can simply learn a western model and adapt it as they wish simply won't wash.

In serving international and domestic students, educators must strive for true integration of theory with practice. Simply requiring that students take X credits in sociology, history, political science, and other fields doesn't guarantee success here. Professors in these departments often criticize communication scholars for being trade-schoolish and narrowly specialized. However, publish-or-perish pressure and other factors have often led these critics to be overly narrow in their own right (Blanchard & Christ, 1993, pp. 5–8). One can only learn so much, perhaps, from a lifetime of studying the earnings of peasants in 18th-century Poland!!

REFERENCES

Blanchard, R. O., & Christ, W. G. (1993). *Media education and the liberal arts: A blueprint for the new professionalism*. Hillsdale, NJ: Lawrence Erlbaum Associates.

Brody, E. W. (1985, Spring). What ought to be taught students of public relations? *Public Relations Quarterly, 30*(1), 6–9.

Commission on Public Relations Education. (1975). *A design for public relations education*. New York: Foundation for Public Relations Research and Education.

Culbertson, H. M. (1985, Spring). Female and minority practitioners see teaching as a good career path—but not a bed of roses. *Public Relations Quarterly, 30*(1), 12–16.

Culbertson, H. M., Jeffers, D. W., Stone, D. B., & Terrell, M. (1993). *Social, political and economic contexts in public relations: Theory and cases*. Hillsdale, NJ: Lawrence Erlbaum Associates.

Cutlip, S. M., Center, A. H., & Broom, G. M. (1994). *Effective public relations*. Englewood Cliffs, NJ: Prentice-Hall.

Grunig, J. E. (1985, April). Hard thinking on education. *Public Relations Journal*, p. 30.

Grunig, J. E., & Hunt, T. (1984). *Managing public relations*. New York: Holt, Rinehart & Winston.

Hess, S. (1984). *The government/press connection: Press officers and their offices*. Washington, D.C.: The Brookings Institution.

Hesse, M. B. (1984, March). Blueprint for graduate study: From idealism to reality. *Public Relations Journal*, pp. 22–24.

Hofstede, G. (1980). *Culture's consequences: International differences in work-related values*. Beverly Hills, CA: Sage.

Journalism & Mass Communication Directory (1993). Columbia, SC: Association for Education in Journalism & Mass Communication.

Kendall, R., Terhune, J., & Hesse, M. B. (1991). *Where to study public relations: A student's guide to academic programs.* New York: The Public Relations Society of America.

Lance, E. P. (1986, Winter). Survey finds that few women are teaching in PR programs. *Journalism Educator, 40*(4), 7–9.

Lauzen, M. M., & Dozier, D. M. (1994). Issues management mediation between environmental complexity and management of the public relations function. *Journal of Public Relations Research, 6,* 163–184.

Lehrman, C. K. (1985, April). Educational pulse taking. *Public Relations Journal,* pp. 16–19.

Littlejohn, S. W. (1992). *Theories of human communication.* Belmont, CA: Wadsworth.

National Commission on Graduate Study in Public Relations. (1985). *Advancing public relations education: Recommended curriculum for graduate public relations education.* New York: Foundation for Public Relations Research and Education.

Newsom, D. A. (1984, March). Realities, questions and challenges for public relations education. *Public Relations Journal,* pp. 15–16.

Severin, W. J. with Tankard, J. W., Jr. (1988). *Communication theories: Origins, methods, uses.* New York: Longman.

Sharpe, M. L. (1985, April). Hard thinking on education. *Public Relations Journal,* p. 29.

Sriramesh, K. (1992). Societal culture and public relations: Ethnographic evidence from India. *Public Relations Review, 18,* 202–212.

U. K. tests first undergraduate PR program. (1989, November). *Public Relations Journal,* p. 8.

About the Authors

Desiree Akel, who has a Costa Rican heritage, is a graduate student in the School of Journalism and Mass Communication at Florida International University. She has supervised the Spanish-language research staff working at FIU's Institute for Public Opinion Research.

Ali Alanazi is assistant professor at King Saud University in Riyadh. He is teaching public relations and serves as a consultant for civil defense in Saudi Arabia. He received his PhD at Ohio University in 1992.

Günter Bentele is professor of public relations at the University of Leipzig, Germany. He is author or co-author of more than 20 books, including *Theories of Public Communication: Problems, Positions, Perspectives* (in German) and *PR Education in Germany: History, State of the Art, and Perspectives* (in German). He has lectured in Austria, Switzerland, Poland, the Ukraine, and the United States. He received his PhD at the Free University of Berlin in 1984 and his Habilitation (second PhD) at the same university in 1989.

Anne Cooper-Chen is professor of journalism and director of the Center for InternationalJournalism at Ohio University. She is author of *Games in the Global Village: A 50-Nation Study of Entertainment Television* and *Mass Communication in Japan*. She conducted research on public relations as a Fulbright Scholar in Japan, 1992–93. She received her PhD from the University of North Carolina in 1984.

Ni Chen is assistant professor of communication at the University of Toledo. She has studied public relations extensively in the People's Republic of China and served as a visiting lecturer there. She earned her PhD in mass communication-journalism at Ohio University in 1992.

Hugh M. Culbertson is professor emeritus of journalism at Ohio University. He is co-author of *Fundamentals of News Reporting* (Kendall-Hunt) and *Social, Political and Economic Contexts in Public Relations: Theory and Cases*. Professor Culbertson was named Educator of the Year in 1990 by the Public Relations Society of America. He has served as visiting lecturer in the People's Republic of China, the Philippines, Germany, and South Korea. He received his PhD at Michigan State University in 1966.

Daradireck Ekachai is assistant professor of speech communication at Southern Illinois University-Carbondale. She has taught public relations in Thailand for four years. She received her PhD at Southern Illinois-Carbondale in 1991.

Hernando González is associate professor of journalism and mass communication at Florida International University. He has worked for UNICEF, the U.S. Agency for International Development, and other organizations on public-information campaigns in various Third World countries. His recent research has focused on alternative media in Cuba and international public affairs. Gonzalez received his PhD at Stanford University.

ABOUT THE AUTHORS

James E. Grunig is professor of journalism at the University of Maryland. He is editor and co-author of *Excellence in Public Relations and Communication Management*. Also, he is senior author of *Managing Public Relations*. He was founding co-editor of *Public Relations Research Annual* (now the *Public Relations Research Journal*). Professor Grunig was named Educator of the Year in 1989 by the Public Relations Society of America. He has studied and lectured about public relations throughout the world since earning his PhD at the University of Wisconsin in 1968.

Larissa A. Grunig is associate professor of journalism at the University of Maryland. Co-author of *Excellence in Public Relations and Communication Management,* she was founding co-editor of the *Public Relations Research Annual* (now the *Public Relations Research Journal*). She has lectured on public relations in many nations after receiving her PhD at the University of Maryland in 1985.

Vincent Hazleton is professor of speech communication at Radford University. He is co-editor and co-author of *Public Relations Theory*. Professor Hazleton has taught courses in international public relations at Salzburg College, Austria in 1988, 1991, and 1995. He was a visiting professor at the University of Salzburg in 1991 and has lectured at several universities in Germany. He received his PhD at the University of Oklahoma in 1977.

Juan F. Jamias is professor emeritus in the Institute for Development Communication, University of the Philippines at Los Banos. He has edited or written several books, including *Readings in Development Communication* and *Writing for Development*. He has served as a communication specialist and consultant in Singapore, as public-affairs coordinator of the University of the Philippines at Los Banos, and as a visiting professor in Malaysia. He has also lectured on development communication in the United States and several other countries. He received his PhD at Michigan State University in 1964.

Mizuo Kaneshige is dean, Chubu University Women's College, Kasugai, Aichi, Japan. He is author of *How to Create a College* and has previously worked for an advertising and public relations firm in Tokyo. He is a graduate of Nihon University.

Ali Kanso is assistant professor of journalism and mass communication at Kansas State University. He has conducted research on public relations in Finland, Sweden, and Lebanon. He earned his PhD at Ohio University in 1986.

Rosechongporn Komolsevin is assistant professor of communication arts and chair of the doctoral program in communication at Bangkok University. She received her PhD from Ohio University in 1992.

Dean A. Kruckeberg is professor of communication studies and coordinator of the public relations degree program at the University of Northern Iowa. Co-author of *Public Relations and Community: A Reconstructed Theory* (Praeger), he has lectured in many nations and served as a visiting professor in the United Arab Emirates. He earned a PhD at the University of Iowa in 1985.

Mauritz S. Mortensen is attached to the Center for Disaster Psychiatry of the Norwegian Armed Forces. A Norwegian journalist specializing in public opinion, mass communication, and military sociology, he has worked as radio officer in the Merchant Navy and on whaling vessels. He has also served as a reporter with Associated Press and as head information editor at the Research Council for Science and the Humanities, and with the Norwegian Navy. He earned a master of arts degree in mass communication from the University of Wisconsin in 1977, and a master of arts in social science at the University of Oslo in 1971.

ABOUT THE AUTHORS

Mariechel J. Navarro is coordinator of the extension communication program of the National Institute of Molecular Biology and Biotechnology (BIOTECH) at the University of the Philippines at Los Banos (UPLB). She supervises the Institute's public relations and technology-transfer functions and leads research and extension projects and bioinformatics. She has headed the communication departments of four other Philippine national institutes, organizing their public relations and publication programs. Dr. Navarro has also lectured in the Philippines, the United Kingdom, Australia, and Thailand. She earned her PhD at UPLB in 1992.

Douglas Ann Newsom is professor and former chair in the Department of Journalism at Texas Christian University. A past president of the Association for Education in Journalism and Mass Communication, she is co-author of four books, including *This is PR: The Realities of Public Relations* and *Media Writing: Preparing Information for the Mass Media*. Professor Newsom was named Educator of the Year in 1982 by the Public Relations Society of America. A former Fulbright lecturer in India, she has held public relations workshops in Singapore, South Africa, Bulgaria, Hungary, Romania, and Poland. She earned her PhD at the University of Texas at Austin in 1978.

Christ W. Ogbandah is associate professor of journalism at the University of Northern Iowa. He has taught public relations, international communication, news writing and reporting, newspaper editing and design, communication theory, and mass communication research methods in the United States and Nigeria. Ogbondah was a producer and news editor at television stations in Ibadan and Port Harcourt, Nigeria. He recently published the book *Military Regimes and the Press in Nigeria, 1966–1993: Human-Rights and National Development*.

Grazyna-Maria Peter teaches public relations at the University of Leipzig, Germany and works as a free-lance public relations consultant at the Leipzig fair. Among her publications is *The Coverage of European Issues in Newspapers: The New German Countries and East Europe*. She has lectured in Poland and the Ukraine. She received her PhD at the University of Leipzig in 1974.

Cornelius B. Pratt is professor in the College of Communication Arts and Sciences at Michigan State University. Co-author of *International Afro Mass Media: A Reference Guide*, he earned his PhD at the University of Minnesota in 1981.

Melvin L. Sharpe is professor of journalism and coordinator of the undergraduate major and minor, as well as of graduate degree programs, in public relations at Ball State University. He is co-author of *Practical Public Relations* and of *Ilmu Hubungan Masyarakat Praktis,* a later edition printed in Indonesian in the Bahasa Indonesian language. Sharpe served as education editor for *International Public Relations Review,* the journal of the International Public Relations Association. He has also spoken at world and international educator and professional congresses in The Netherlands, France, Spain, Canada, Brazil, Uruguay, Chile, and Nigeria. He has served as a visiting lecturer in Brazil and Chile. He received an Ed. D. at the University of Florida in 1973.

Roberto Porto Simoes is professor in the public relations graduate program at the Pontifical Catholic University of Rio Grande do Sul, Brazil. He is author of *Relacoes Publicas: Funcao Politica* and has been recognized by the Inter-American Confederation of Public Relations as an Outstanding Educator. Simoes has been a visiting lecturer at world, international, and national congresses in Spain, Chile, Argentina, Uruguay, Bolivia, Colombia, Cuba, Curacao, Paraguay, Puerto Rico, and Peru. He received his PhD from the Pontifical Catholic University of Rio Grande do Sul in Brazil in 1993.

ABOUT THE AUTHORS

K. Sriramesh is assistant professor of communication at Purdue University. Two co-authored book chapters, "Societal Culture and Public Relations," and "Corporate Culture and Public Relations" are representative of his areas of interest. He has practiced and studied public relations in India extensively. He received his PhD at the University of Maryland in 1992.

Ramon R. Tuazon is vice president and associate director for research and development consultancy of the Asian Institute of Journalism and Communication in Manila. He is also a professorial lecturer in the Institute and at De La Salle University. He is consultant of UNICEF and program coordinator for social mobilization of Philippine education for all programs. He has designed and implemented various local and ASEAN development programs and projects of the United Nations Food and Agricultural Organization (FAO), UNESCO, and other instituions. Mr. Tuazon obtained his master in media management degree from the Asian Institute of Journalism and Communication.

Judy VanSlyke Turk is professor and dean in the College of Journalism and Mass Communication at the University of South Carolina. She is a past president of the Association for Education in Journalism and Mass Communication and co-author of *This is PR: The Realities of Public Relations,* now in its sixth edition. The Public Relations Society of America named her its Public Relations Educator of the Year in 1992. She has lectured and provided curriculum-development assistance in several nations, focusing on Eastern Europe and the Newly Independent States in recent years. She received her PhD from Syracuse University in 1985.

James Van Leuven is professor and chair of the department of journalism at Colorado State University. He writes in the areas of public relations theory and communication management. Professor Van Leuven's overseas teaching assignments have been in Australia and Singapore along with consulting work in Malaysia and Indonesia. He earned his PhD from Washington State University in 1977.

Dejan Verčič is director of the Pristop Communication Group, Ljubljana, Slovenia, the only full-service public relations firm in Slovenia. Within the Pristop Group, Verčič is director of the PR Institute, the research branch of the firm. Verčič holds an M.S. degree in communication science from the University of Ljubljana and is currently a doctoral student in the organizational psychology program at the London School of Economics.

Robert I. Wakefield has organized and coordinated public relations resources in more than 12 countries since 1991 as director of international communication for Nu Skin International. He has done research on how multinational organizations can structure public relations to achieve effective results. A 1990 master's graduate of Brigham Young University, he is now completing a PhD in public relations at the University of Maryland.

Laurie J. Wilson is associate professor of communication at Brigham Young University. She is author of *Strategic Program Planning for Effective Public Relations Campaigns* and co-author of *The Passing of Modernity: Communication and the Transformation of Society.* Professor Wilson's research has focused heavily on international communication, and she recently led an international studies program in Moscow, Prague, and Munich. She received her PhD at The American University in 1988.

Author Index

Italic face denotes reference pages.

A

Abir, M., 244, *255*
Adler, N. J., 20, 22, 23, 24, *28*
Adnan, H., 209, *222*
Adnan, J., 95, *105*
Agee, W., 18, *30,* 69, *80,* 216, *222,* 247, *256,* 387, *395*
Aggarwal, R., 389, *393*
Ake, C., 94, *104*
Albritton, R. B., 20, 25, *29,* 386, *393, 394*
Al-Dakoki, I., 240, *255*
Al-Enad, A. H., 93, 101, *104,* 126, *152,* 208, 210, *221,* 249, 250, *255,* 373, *376,* 391, *393*
Al-Hazmi, W., 250, *255*
Al-Odadi, M., 241, *255*
Alsheekley, A. A., 240, *256*
Al-Tohami, M., 240, *255*
American Council on Education, 388, *393*
Amine, L., 302, *313*
An, G., 123, *152*
Anderson, G., 18, *28,* 32, *63,* 216, *221*
Anderson, J. A., 71, *79*
Anderson, P., 48, 49, *63*
Anderson, R., 162, 164, *168,* 246, 251, *256*
Apiratanakul, W., 159, *169*
Appadurai, A., 20, 21, 23, *28*
Arab News, 244, *255*
Araby, O., 239, 250, 254, *255*
Arendt, H., 43, *63*
Armstrong, H. C., 243, 244, *255*
Arnauld, A., 40, *63*

Arpan, J., 302, *314*
Arun, M., 210, 212, *221*
Asawadorndecha, K., 159, *169*
Athos, A. G., 177, *190*
Ault, P., 18, *30,* 69, *80,* 216, *222,* 247, *256,* 387, *395*
Austin, N., 72, 73, 74, *80*

B

Bagdikian, B., 20, 26, *28*
Bahl, S., 110, 114, 116, *117*
Bailey, H. M., 280, 281, *297*
Barbhaya, M., 112, *117*
Barnlund, D. C., 50, *63*
Barry, T., 257, *271*
Bartlett, C. A., 20, 24, *28*
Basche, J. R., Jr., 84, 85, *91*
Bashirruddin, S., 115, *117*
Baxter, B., 384, *393*
Becher, M., 358, *363*
Bellack, D. W., 81, *91,* 370, *376*
Bellah, R., 48, *63*
Bentele, G., 358, *363*
Bernays, E. L., 43, *63*
Beschluss des Ministerrates der DDR ueber die Grundsdtze zur Gewaehrleistung von Sicherheit und Ordnung, 355, *363*
Bharadwaj, S., 303, *315*
Bhimani, R., 101, *105,* 111, 115, 116, *117*
Black, G., 258, *271*
Black, S., 133, *152*
Blanchard, R. O., 408, 412, 414, *414*
Boeckelmann, F., 358, 359, *363*

421

Bohannan, P., 180, *189*
Bohn, E., 310, *314*
Booth, A. L., 18, *28*, 389, *393*
Borrus, A., 389, *393*
Botan, C., 17, 18, *28*, 99, *105*, 209, *221*, 310, *313*, 382, *393*
Bourke, W. O., 392, *393*
Bovet, S. F., 1, 23, *28*, 107, 109, 110, *117*
Boyd, D., 243, *255*
Boza, M. A., 257, 271, *271*
Braid, F. R., 199, 204, *205*
Brinkerhoff, D. W., 20, 25, *28*, 32, 33, *63*
Brody, E. W., 384, 388, *393*, 401, 412, *414*
Broom, G. M., 69, 70, 71, *79*, 124, 125, 131, 134, 135, 139, 140, 149, *152*, *153*, 162, 163, 164, 166, *168*, 175, *189*, 239, 246, 251, *255*, 411, *414*
Brosnahan, T., 258, 267, *272*
Brownlee, B. J., 384, 388, *393*, *394*
Buchholz, R. A., 70, *79*
Buffington, J., 177, *190*

C

Cantor, B., 388, *393*
Carey, J. W., 376, *376*
Carnegie Endowment for International Peace National Commission, 382, 390, *393*
Carr, S., 391, *393*
Carrell, B., 109, *117*
Cartwright, D., 42, *64*
Caruba, A., 392, *393*
Castaneda, J. G., 259, *271*
Cateora, P. R., 312, *313*
Cavusgil, T., 302, *313*
Center, A. H., 69, 70, 71, *79*, 125, *153*, 411, *414*
Chaffee, S. H., 9, *13*
Chaiwatanarat, C., 157, *168*
Chancharatwatana, W., 159, 160, *168*
Chantarasiri, S., 160, *168*

Chen, N., 102, *105*, 122, 123, 133, 138, 147, *152*, 246, *255*
Cheng, J. Y. S., 126, *152*
Christ, W. G., 408, 412, 414, *414*
Christians, C. J., 87, 89, 90, *91*
Chung, D., 303, *315*
Clark, P., 258, *272*
Cobbey, R. E., 129, *152*
Collier, M. J., 51, *63*
Comision de la Comunidad Europea y el Instituto Costarricense de Turismo, 259, *271*
Commission on Public Relations Education, 399, *414*
Commission on Undergraduate Public Relations Education, 383, *393*
Committee on PR Education, 133, *152*
Conant, J., 227, *236*
Condon, J. C., 48, *63*
Coombs, T. W., 325, *338*
Cooper, T. W., 89, *91*
Corteza-Tinsay, E., 191, 194, *205*
Cousino, K. R., 70, *80*
Creedon, P. J., 20, 27, *28*, 71, *79*, 383, *393*
Crespy, C., 312, *313*, 389, *393*
Crow, J. A., 275, 276, 279, 280, 281, *297*
Crozier, M., 47, *63*
Culbertson, H. M., 4, *13*, 88, *91*, 102, *105*, 122, 123, 125, 133, 135, 137, 138, 140, 147, 148, 150, *152*, 251, *256*, 259, *271*, 400, *414*
Cutlip, S. M., 69, 70, 71, *79*, 125, *153*, 411, *414*

D

Darenblum, J., 260, *271*
Davidson, B., 94, *105*
Davies, J. C., 327, 331, *339*
Davis, M., 386, *393*
de Bono, E., 45, *63*
de Fleur, M. L., 25, *29*
De George, G., 259, *272*
De la Cruz, R. R., 191, 193, *205*

Dechacheep, S., 158, 160, *168*
Delano, B., 290, *297*
Dennis, E., 235, *237*
Dentsu PR Center, 224, 228, 229, 231, 232, 233, 234, *236*
Derks, S., 248, 249, 250, *256*
Dilenschneider, R. L., 84, *91,* 186, *189*
Doktor, R., 22, *28*
Donaldson, T., 85, 87, *91*
Donato, E., 258, *272*
Donnelly, J., Jr., 85, 86, 87, 88, 89, *91,* 303, *313*
Douglas, S., 301, 302, *313*
Dowling, G., 303, *313*
Dozier, D. M., 4, *13,* 34, 36, *63,* 124, 131, 134, 135, 139, 140, 149, *152,* 162, 164, 166, *168, 169,* 175, 184, *189,* 224, 237 239, 246, 251, 255, 279, 281, *297,* 383, *393, 394,* 400, *415*
Drucker, P. F., 44, 45, *63*
Duncan, T., 303, *314*
Dunn, S., 303, *313*
Dzinic, F., 45, 63

E

Edralin, M. J., Jr., 193, 194, *205*
Ehling, W. P., 34, 36, 41, 42, 43, *63,* 323, *339*
Ekachai, D., 159, *169*
Eldersveld, S., 42, *64*
Elfstrom, G., 82, 83, 84, 88, 89, *91*
Elinder, E., 302, *313*
Ellingsworth, H. W., 20, 22, 23, *28*
Epley, J., 17, 21, 25, *28,* 216, *221*
Ernst, M., 389, *394*

F

Fakhri, S. J., 240, *256*
Farinelli, J. L., 18, *28,* 386, 389, *394*
Fatt, A. C., 302, *313*
Featherstone, M., 20, 21, 23, *28*
Ferreira, M. E. S., 291, 292, 293, *297*
Fischer, D. H., 274, *297*

Fitzpatrick, K., 310, 311, *313*
Folb, E. A., 52, *63*
Foundación Neotropica, 271, *271*
Foundation for Public Relations Research and Education, 383, *394*
Fowler, E. M., 381, *394*
Frederick, H. H., 381, *394*
Freeman, R. E., 24, *28*
Frith, K., 303, *313*
Fry, S., 311, *313*
Fu, M., 302, *314*

G

Garbarino, M. S., 178, *189*
Geertz, C., 19, *28*
Ghiselli, E. E., 175, 176, *189*
Ghoshal, S., 20, 24, *28*
Glubb, J. B., 241, *256*
González, H., 268, *271*
Gopalakrishna, P., 303, *315*
Gordon, G. A., 81, *91*
Gordon, J. A., 368, 374, *376*
Gozo, D. A., 196, *205*
Graham, J. L., 20, 23, *28,* 303, *313*
Gross, B. W., 359, 360, 361, *363*
Gross, K., 367, *376*
Gruban, B., 35, *63*
Grunig, J. E., 1, 4, 5, *13,* 18, 19, 20, 22, 24, 25, 26, 27, *28, 29, 30,* 33, 34, 36, 41, 42, 46, 50, *63, 64,* 71, 79, 101, 102, *105,* 124, 125, 128, 133, 134, 135, 149, *153,* 156, 161, 162, 166, 167, *169,* 174, 175, 177, 186, *189, 190,* 246, *256,* 267, *271,* 321, 327, 338, *339,* 343, 344, *347,* 356, *363,* 384, *394,* 399, 400, 401, *414*
Grunig, L. A., 18, 21, 22, 24, 25, 26, *29, 30,* 34, 36, 41, *63,* 101, *105,* 124, 134, 135, *153,* 167, *169,* 216, *221,* 327, 338, *339,* 383, *394*
Gudykunst, W., 224, 225, *237*
Guendell, L., 258, *272*
Gurr, T., 327, *339*

H

Habermas, J., 21, *29*
Hainsworth, B. E., 70, *80*
Haire, M., 175, 176, *189*
Halbach, H., 353, *363*
Hall, E. T., 22, *29,* 47, 50, *64*
Halladay, S., 325, 338
Haller, M., 359, *363*
Hammonds, L., 48, *64*
Hampden-Turner, C., 23, 25, *29,* 67, 68, 72, 74, 75, 76, *80*
Han, Z., 123, *153*
Hardt, H., 375, 376, *376*
Harron, R., 248, 250, *256*
Hasegawa, K., 303, *314*
Hasenauer, G., 325, *338*
Hatch, E., 87, *91*
Hauss, D., 17, *29*
Hazleton, V., 368, 370, 371, 374, *376*
Heath, R. L., 70, *80*
Heller, F., 24, *29*
Hellweg, S. A., 41, *64*
Helming, A., 302, *314*
Hennessy, B., 20, 21, *29*
Henriquez, H., 258, *272*
Hess, R., 401, *414*
Hesse, M. B., 384, *394,* 403, *414, 415*
Hickson, D. J., 175, *189*
Hiebert, R. E., 20, 25, 26, *29,* 100, 102, *105,* 214, 221, 239, *256*
Hill, S., 162, 164, *168,* 246, 251, *256*
Hill & Knowlton, 210, *221*
Hinings, C. R., 175, *189*
Hirsch, P., 176, *190*
Hitchon, J., 303, *314*
Hoffman, E., 343, *347*
Hofstede, G., 6, 11, *13,* 20, 22, 24, *29,* 36, 47, 48, 49, 50, *64,* 177, 180, 181, *190,* 235, *237,* 398, *414*
Holden, D., 242, 244, *256*
Holstein, W. J., 389, *393*
Holzweissig, G., 352, *363*
Hon, L. C., 383, *394*
Hong, J., 303, *314*
Howarth, D., 242, 244, *256*
Howkins, J., 126, *153*
Hui, C. H., 48, *64*
Hunt, T., 4, *13,* 41, 42, *64,* 71, *79,* 124, 125, 134, 135, 149, *153,* 156, 161, 162, 166, *169,* 174, 175, 186, *189,* 246, *256,* 267, *271,* 356, *363,* 383, *394,* 399, *414*
Hunter, J. D., 55, *64*
Hussein, S., 248, 250, *256*
Hyman, M., 303, *315*

I

Ingle, M. D., 20, 25, *28,* 32, 33, *63*
Ingrami, L., 43, *64*
Instituto Costarricense de Acueductos y Alcantarillados, 258, 265, *271*
Instituto Costarricense de Turismo, 258, 271, *272*
Ivanov, V., 45, *64*

J

Jackson, J. O., 368, *368*
Jacobs, L., 304, *314*
Jamieson, I. M., 177, *190*
Janis, I. L., 126, 128, *152*
Javidi, A., 48, *64*
Javidi, M., 48, *64*
Jeffers, D. W., 259, *271,* 400, *414*
Jefkins, F., 210, *221*
Jelinek, M., 176, *190*
Jia, G., 121, 128, *153*
Johannson, L., 81, *92*
Johns, R., 242, 244, *256*
Johnson, W. W., 275, *297*
Josephs, R., 17, *29,* 216, *221*
Journalism and Mass Communication Directory, 403, *414*

K

Kahn, R. l., 24, *29*
Kakar, S., 180, 181, *190*
Kalupa, F., 48, *64*
Kamins, M., 303, *313*

Kanseewan, S., 159, *169*
Kanso, A., 302, 303, 306, *314*
Kant, I., 382, *394*
Kaplan, D., 178, 179, *190*
Karl Marx University, 351, *363*
Katz, D., 24, *29,* 42, *64*
Kaul, J. M., 171, 173, *190*
Keller, N., 258, 267, *272*
Kendall, R., 390, *394,* 403, *415*
Keown, C., 304, *314*
Kern-Foxworth, M., 383, *394*
Kinzer, H., 310, *314*
Klein, A., 350, *363*
Klinpongsa, P., 157, *169*
Kluckhohn, C., 178, *190*
Kluckhohn, F., 47, *64*
Kneale, M., 40, *64*
Kneale, W., 40, *64*
Kotler, P., 302, *314*
Krauss, C., 258, *272*
Kroeber, A. L., 178, *190*
Kruckeberg, D., 71, *80,* 311, *314,* 368, 370, 371, 373, 374, 375, *376*
Kultgen, J. H., 83, *92*
Kunczik, M., 18, 26, *29*
Kuo, E. C. Y., 214, *222*
Kurzweil, R., 45, *64*

L

LaFeber, W., 258, 270, *272*
Lance, E. P., 383, *394,* 400, *415*
Langholm, O., 282, *297*
Lasswell, H. D., 326, *339*
Lauzen, M. M., 400, *415*
Lazarsfeld, P. F., 327, *339*
Lear, J., 86, 90, *92*
Lebra, T., 225, *237*
Lee, A. M., 42, *64,* 384, *394*
Lehrman, C. K., 389, *394,* 401, *415*
Lenin, W. I., 354, *363*
Lerk-Klang, P., 159, *169*
Lerner, D., 327, *339*
Lesly, P., 20, 21, *29*
Levitt, T., 302, *314*
Lieberman, D. A., 49, *64*

Liebold, R., 355, *364*
Lim, G-C., 388, *394*
Lindloff, T. R., 71, *80*
Lines, V., 218, *222*
Littlejohn, S. W., 402, *415*
Liu, Z., 149, *153*
Lobsenz, A., 386, *394*
Lopez-Wendling, M., 202, *205*
Lowe, V., 210, 211, *221, 222*
Lowery, S. A., 25, *29*
Lu, Z., 303, *314*
Lukaszewski, J. E., 75, 77, *80*
Luz, J. M., 192, *205*

M

Madsen, R., 48, *63*
Malasri, W., 159, 160, *169*
Mallinson, B., 368, 372, 373, *376*
Maneechoti, J., 157, *169*
Manheim, J. B., 20, 25, *29,* 386, 393, *394*
Mann, L., 126, *153*
Manners, R. A., 178, 179, *190*
Mansfield, P., 240, *256*
Marquez, F., 303, *314*
Martin, L. J., 25, 26, *29*
Martinez, Z., 24, *29*
Massy, W. F., 34, *64*
Mast, C., 359, *363*
Mata Jimenez, L., 259, *272*
McCarthy, J. E., 299, *314*
McCombs, M. E., 129, *152*
McLuhan, M., 20, 21, *29*
McMillan, C. J., 175, *189*
McPhaul, J., 259, 260, 264, *272*
Melendez Chaverri, C., 258, 270, *272*
Melkote, S. R., 103, *105*
Men, X., 122, *153*
Merkwitschka, F., 351, 355, *364*
Messerly, A., 225, *237*
Meyer, P., 129, *153*
Meyer, T. P., 71, *79*
Meyn, H., 358, *364*
Miller, D. A., 321, *339*
Miller, E. L., 386, 387, *395*

Ministry of Information, 210, *222*
Mizutani, O., 225, *237*
Modoux, A., 390, *394*
Mohamed, R., II, 102, *105*
Mohammed, K., 248, 250, *256*
Moncreiff Arrarte, A., 258, *272*
Montelibano, T. Y., 192, *205*
Morais, B., 95, 105, 209, *222*
Morales, F., 258, *272*
Moriarty, S., 303, *314*
Morrow, L., 94, *105*
Mortensen, M. S., 328, 329, 330, 337, 338, *339*
Muderrisoglu, A., 303, *314*
Mulder, M., 180, *190*

N

Nair, B., 97, *105,* 209, 214, 215, *222*
Naisbitt, J., 21, *29*
Nakane, C., 224, *237*
Narain, L., 171, 174, 185, *190*
Nasatir, A. P., 280, 281, *297*
National Commission on Graduate Study in Public Relations, 383, 385, *394,* 399, *415*
National Public Relations Committee, 155, *169*
National Public Relations Congress of the Philippines, 191, *205*
Neff, B. D., 392, *394*
Negandhi, A. R., 20, 22, 24, *29,* 177, *190*
Nelson, B., 282, *297*
Newsom, D., 109, *117,* 401, *415*
Nicole, P., 40, *63*
Nikkei Weekly, 223, 224, 226, *237*
Nishida, T., 224, 225, *237*
Nolte, L., 240, *256*
NOU, 322, *339*

O

Oblaender, M. H., 361, *364*
Oetomo, D., 303, *313*
Ogan, C. L., 384, *394*

Onkvisit, S., 303, *314*
Orwell, G., 45, *64*
Ouchi, W., 177, *190,* 224, *237*
Ovaitt, F., Jr., 25, *29,* 311, *314,* 373, *376*

P

Pantaleon, V., 194, *205*
Papui, S., 159, 160, *169*
Paraschos, M., 384, *394*
Parsons, T., 47, *64*
Pascale, R. T., 177, *190*
Pavlik, J. V., 19, 27, *29*
Pearson, J., 259, *272*
Pedersen, A., 51, *64*
Pedersen, P., 51, *64*
Peebles, D., 303, *314*
Perez, G., 257, *272*
Perez Iglesia, M., 258, *272*
Perlmutter, H., 301, *314*
Perrault, D. W., Jr., 299, *314*
Peter, G. M., 360, *364*
Peters, T. J., 67, 72, 73, 74, 75, *80*
Peterson, J. V., 383, *394*
Philippine Information Agency, 198, 199, *205*
Photisuvan, T., 159, *169*
Piekos, J. M., 246, *256*
Pimlott, J. A. R., 171, *190*
Pinsdorf, M. K., 17, *29*
Pires, M. A., 26, *29*
Plummer, J., 303, *314*
Poerschke, K., 355, *364*
Politbuero des ZK der SED, 352, *364*
Poobuapuan, O., 157, 158, *169*
Porter, M., 302, *314*
Porter, R. E., 51, 52, *64*
Porter, R. W., 175, 176, *189*
Prajammuang, K., 157, *169*
Pratt, C., 101, 102, *105,* 209, *222*
Programa Centroamericano de Periodismo, 259, *272*
Programa Latinoamericano de Periodismo, 259, *272*
Public Relations News, 385, 386, *395*

AUTHOR INDEX 427

Public Relations Organization of the Philippines, 200, *205*
Public Relations Society of Japan (PRSJ), 226, 227, 235, *237*
Puerer, H., 358, *364*

R

Raabe, J., 358, *364*
Rachowiecki, R., 258, 267, *272*
Ramaprasad, J., 303, *314*
Reagan, J., 162, 164, *168,* 246, 251, *256*
Reddi, C. V. N., 109, 117, *117,* 172, 174, *190*
Redding, S. G., 22, *28*
Reischauer, E. O., 388, *395*
Reitz, J. G., 327, *339*
Repper, F., 19, 24, 26, *29,* 34, 36, *63,* 71, *79*
Revel, J-F., 102, *105*
Rice, M., 303, *314*
Ricks, D., 24, *29,* 302, *314*
Rivera, R., 258, *272*
Rivera Araya, R., 258, *272*
Rivers, W. L., 324, *339*
Robertson, R., 20, 21, *30*
Rodriguez Vega, E., 270, *272*
Rogers, E. M., 9, *13,* 124, 131, 148, *153,* 245, *256*
Rojas Bolanos, M., 258, *272*
Ronnenberger, F., 358, *364*
Rosberg, M-L., 310, 311, *314*
Rose, P. B., 321, *339*
Ruehl, M., 358, *364*
Ruhr, K. H., 355, *365*
Ryans, J., Jr., 303, *313, 314*

S

Samovar, L. A., 51, 52, *64*
Sarathy, R., 308, *315*
Satawedin, L., 159, *169*
Satawedin, P., 159, *169*
Sathe, V., 178, *190*
Satitamorntham, P., 157, *169*
Schein, E. H., 188, *190*
Schjander, N., 333, *340*
Schmelter, R., 355, *364*
Schneider, B. C., 357, 358, 359, *363, 364*
Schoenbach, R., 357, 358, *364*
Schramm, W., 126, *153,* 324, *339*
Schreier, H., 355, *365*
Schulze, K., 360, *364*
Schumacher, J. N., 191, *205*
Schwartz, D. F., 383, 384, *395*
Schwitter, J. P., 175, *189*
Senac, R. P., 291, *297*
Serie, T. L., 75, 77, *80*
Serra e Gurgel, J. B., 290, *297*
Servicios Cablegráficos Combinados, 260, *272*
Severin, W. J., 402, *415*
Sharpe, M. L., 293, 295, *297,* 310, *314,* 384, 389, 391, *395,* 403, 412, *415*
Shaw, J., 303, *314*
Shenoy, S., 177, *190*
Shepherd, G. J., 73, *80*
Shils, E. A., 47, *64*
Shue, H., 82, 85, *92*
Sieny, S., 250, *256*
Signitzer, B., 325, *338,* 358, *364,* 385, *395*
Simoes, R. P., 293, 295, *297,* 391, *395*
Sinclair, J., 26, *30*
Singer, J. H., 387, *395*
Smircich, L., 176, 177, *190*
Smith, G. D., 162, 163, *168,* 246, 251, *255,* 259, *272*
Snowdon, S., 310, *315*
Sorenson, R., 303, *315*
Soto Acosta, W., 259, *272*
Spaemann, R., 86, 89, *92*
Spiers, P., 249, *256*
Spradley, J. P., 182, *190*
Sreberny-Mohammadi, A., 26, *30*
Srichanachaichok, R., 157, 158, 159, 160, *169*
Sriram, V., 303, *315*

Sriramesh, K., 20, 22, *30,* 31, 36, 49, 53, 54, 55, 56, *64,* 101, 102, *105,* 171, 175, 177, *190,* 212, *222,* 373, *376,* 400, *415*
Stanton, E. M., 17, *30*
Staples, W. A., 388, *395*
Starck, K., 71, *80,* 373, 375, *376*
Steilen, C. F., 388, *395*
Steingraber, F. G., 389, *395*
Stoltz, V., 371, *376*
Stone, D. B., 137, 150, *153,* 251, *256,* 257, *271,* 400, *414*
Strauss, G. H., 289, *297*
Strenski, J. B., 386, *395*
Strodtbeck, F., 47, *64*
Stuerzebecher, D., 357, 358, *364*
Sudderuddin, K. I., 217, *222*
Sullivan, W., 48, *63*
Sumner, J., 162, 164, *168,* 246, 251, *256*
Suthiworaset, C., 159, *169*
Swidler, A., 48, *63*
Synodinos, N., 304, *314*
Szymanski, D., 303, *315*

T

Tamme, F., 350, *364*
Tan, J., 216, *222*
Tan, J. C., 214, 215, *222*
Tan, M. L., 216, *222*
Tananchaibutra, B., 156, *170*
Tankard, J. W., Jr., 402, *415*
Tansey, R., 303, *315*
Tantivetchakul, T., 158, *170*
Tasker, G., 271, *272*
Tayeb, M. H., 22, 24, *30,* 36, 47, 48, *64,* 176, 177, 180, 181, *190*
Terhune, J., 403, *415*
Terpstra, V., 308, *315*
Terrell, M., 259, *271,* 400, *414*
Thakur, P., 112, *117*
Thammasat University, 158, *170*
Thanabunlertluck, J., 157, *170*
Thoening, J. C., 47, *63*
Thomazini, M. S., 287, 289, *297*

Thompson, D. W., 383, *394*
Thompson, M., 391, *395*
Tipton, S., 48, *63*
Tiryakian, E. A., 21, *30*
Tolentino, G. N., 199, *205*
Tonnies, F., 71, 72, 75, *80*
Tornquist, K., 332, *340*
Toyne, B., 24, *29*
Trask, G., 48, *65*
Traverse-Healy, T., 25, *30*
Triandis, H. C., 48, *64,* 327, *340*
Trompenaars, A., 23, 25, *29,* 67, 68, 72, 74, 75, 76, *80*
Tsujimura, A., 225, *237*
Tuazon, R. R., 204, *205*
Tung, R. L., 386, 387, *395*
Turk, J. V., 382, *395*
Tyler, E., 178, *190*

U

Ugboahjah, F., 101, *105*
UK Tests First Undergraduate PR Program, 389, *395,* 400, *415*

V

Vaidyanathan, S., 112, *117*
Valverde, J. M., 258, *272*
Van der Muelin, D., 245, *256*
Van Huevel, J., 235, *237*
Van Leuven, J. K., 99, *105,* 207, *222*
Van Wolferen, K., 230, 235, 236, *237*
Varadarajan, R., 303, *315*
Varis, T., 26, *30*
Verčič D., 22, 25, *30,* 35, *63*
Vernon, I., 303, *314*
Villanueva, A. L., Jr., 193, 204, *206*
Virtusio, R. P., 194, 204, *206*
Vogl, F., 17, *30*
Voigt, B., 362, *365*
Vyakarnam, S., 188, *190*

W

Wakefield, R. I., 20, 25, *30*

Walters, L., 310, *315*
Walters, P., 303, *315*
Walters, T., 310, *315*
Wang, X., 139, *153*
Waterman, R. H., 67, 72, 73, 74, 75, *80*
Weichmann, U., 303, *315*
Weick, K. E., 39, *64*
Weitz, B. A., 34, *64*
Wesson, D., 303, *313*
Whillock, R., 310, 311, *313*
White, J., 20, 22, *30,* 31, 33, 34, 36, 48, 49, 50, 53, 54, 55, 56, *63, 64, 65,* 102, *105,* 171, 175, 177, *190,* 224, *237,* 372, 373, *376, 377*
Whitelock, J., 303, *315*
Wilcox, D. L., 18, *30,* 69, *80,* 216, *222,* 247, *256,* 387, *395*
Wilkinson, A., 17, *30*
Williams, B., 86, *92*
Wilson, L. J., 67, 68, 71, 72, 74, *80*
Wind, Y., 301, 302, *313, 315*
Woeltge, H., 355, *365*
Wongsarot, R., 157, *170*
Worakitpokatorn, P., 155, *170*
Wouters, J., 1, 2, *13,* 311, *315*
Wray, H., 227, *237*
Wright, D. K., 382, *395*

Y

Yap, B. T., 214, *222*
Yarbrough, J. P., 382, 384, *395*
Yousef, F., 48, *63*
Yuan, 123, *153*
Yukio, T., 369, *377*
Yum, J. O., 48, 50, *65,* 147, *153*

Z

Zajac, B., 299, *315*
Zalzala, F. S., 240, *256*
Zavrl, F., 35, *63*
Zeledón Cambronero, M., 259, *272*
Zellner, W., 389, *393*
Zeman, Z. A. B., 43, *65*
Zhang, X., 149, *153*
Zhong, H., 303, *314*
Zinkhan, G., 303, *314, 315*
Zorilla, T., 196, *206*
Zwanzig, K., 353, *365*

Subject Index

A

Abdulaziz Ibn Saud, King
  role in Saudi PR, 241-245
Accreditation for public relations, 385, 392, 402, 411
Accountability
  of transnational corporations, 82-85
Acculturation
  third-culture persons and, 23
Activism
  and excellence, 40
  in Costa Rica, 257-258
  in Europe, 370
  in India, 175
  in Latin America, 283
  in Japan, 225
  in Norway
    and whaling, 336
  in Philippines, 203
  in Slovenia, 59-60
  interest groups and, 26
Advertising
  localization in, 299-313
  public relations and, 10, 97
    in German Democratic Republic, 350, 360-363
    in India, 184
    in Japan, 225, 228, 414
    in Malaysia, 215
    in Saudi Arabia, 246
    in Singapore, 215
    in Thailand, 156, 160
  standardization in, 299-313
Africa
  African Public Relations Associations
    Federation of, 95
  Kampala declaration, 95
  national development in, 95
  poverty in, 94
  public relations in, 93-104
Affirmative Action
  in public relations education, 384
Agencies, role of
  changes in
    during development process, 219
  in Egypt, 249
  in Europe
    networks of, 374
  in German Democratic Republic, 360
  in international public relations, 386
  in Japan, 225, 229-231
    advertising, ties to, 230
    Dentsu, role of, 230-231
    native agencies, 230
    publicity focus of, 229
    with western connections, 229-230
  in regional-interdependence stage
  in Malaysia, 216
  in Singapore, 216
  in Saudi Arabia, 246
Arab nations
  Arabian-American Oil Company
    role of in PR, 245
  history of PR in, 239-241
  information dissemination
    central role of, 249
  pictorial bulletins in, 240
  poetry, role of, 240-241
  public relations
    in Saudi Arabia, 239-256
    open market and, 240
    religion and, 241-245
    role in war, 239-241

432 SUBJECT INDEX

tribal relations, 240
Asia
  public relations in, 93-104
Association for Education in Journalism & Mass Communication
  and public relations education, 384-385, 392, 402, 411-412
Association of Public Relations Practitioners
  in Thailand, 158, 163
Asymmetry
  in China, 138, 143, 149
  in Costa Rica, 267-268
  in German Democratic Republic, 356
  in Romania, 345-346
  in Thailand, 155, 158-159, 161-162
  in Third World, 103
  relation to professional PR, 42
Attitude
  importance of emotion in, 330
  importance of knowledge in, 330
  theory of, 327
Audience segmentation (*see* Segmentation of audience)
Authoritarianism
  and public relations, 50
    in India, 181
    in Malaysia, 208
    in Singapore, 208
Authority
  deference to
    in India, 181-182

B

Bank-fraud case (*see* Norway)
Brazil (*see* Latin America)
Brazilian Association of Public Relations, 290
Bribery
  transnational corporations and, 88-89
Britain
  degree PR program in, 389
  public relations in
    and United States, 368-369, 374
    leadership role of, 368-369
    English language, role in, 369
    different from European Union, 372
    government role in, 372
    role in Indian PR, 109

C

Campaigns
  in Costa Rica
    on eco-tourism, 257-258, 267
  in German Democratic Republic
    for Leipzig, 362
    to encourage investment, 362
  in Japan, 232-234
  in Malaysia, 211-212, 217
  in Philippines, 197
  in Saudi Arabia
    management of, 253
  in Singapore, 211-212, 217
Caste
  in India, 113
    decline of, 188
    power distance and, 181, 188-189
Central America (*see* Latin America)
Chile (*see* Latin America)
China
  audience segmentation in, 129, 138
  contexts for PR in
    political, economic, social, and cultural, 122
  decision making in
    freedom of choice and, 126
  dialogue in, 9
  education for PR in, 11, 123-125, 132-133
  and culture, 139
  perceptions of public relations in
    factors affecting, 141-143
  power and autonomy of practitioners in, 135, 137
  and age, 146
  and audience segmentation, 135-137
  and education level, 144
  and management emphasis, 137, 150
  and model orientation, 135-136
  and role orientation, 135-136

SUBJECT INDEX 433

and sector of society, 146
and status within organization, 144
public relations in
  Confucianism and, 122, 147
  Chinese features of, 123
    contrasted with west, 147-148, 150
    cognitive consistency and, 128-129
    development pattern of, 131-133, 148
      stages in, 122-123
    diffusion and evolution of, 121-125
      early adopters, 124
      in key cities, 123-125, 131-134
      late adopters, 124
  growth of, 1, 121
  guanxi and, 122, 147-148, 150
  in government institutions, 126-129, 135, 137-138, 146, 149
  in joint ventures, 126-128, 135, 142, 146, 149
  in manufacturing sector, 142
  in service industries, 127-128, 135, 137-138, 142
  information systems theory and, 128
  research methods
    in study of, 129-131
lady PR practitioners in, 10
media system in
  PR practice and, 126, 148
  role and function of, 126
models of PR in, 149
  one-way communication, 127, 129-130, 134-135, 138, 149
    asymmetric, 139, 143
    in national government, 138
  two-way communication, 125, 129, 130, 134-135
    symmetric
      and management emphasis, 135-136, 150
      and audience segmentation, 140
      and gender, 140
      in local government, 138
relationship building in
  and guest relations, 147-148, 150
roles of practitioners in, 8, 124-125, 149

communication facilitator, 124, 136
  and age, 139
communication manager, 130-131, 134-136, 150
  and age, 139, 141, 144, 146
  and education, 140, 142
  and gender, 139
  and perceptions of PR, 141-142
  and status within organization, 140, 142, 146
  audience definition by, 146
  emphasis on research by, 136
communication technician, 124, 127, 130-131, 134-135, 137-138
  and age, 139-140
  and gender, 139-140, 146
  and government practice, 141
  and perceptions of PR, 141
  and status within organization, 140, 144, 146
expert prescriber, 124, 134-135,
  and emphasis on management function, 135-137
  and autonomy, power, 135-136
  centrality of, 135-137, 150
guest relations
  and education, 139
  and gender, 139, 148
problem-solving process facilitator, 124, 136
status within organization
  age and, 146, 149
  importance of, 146, 149
Class
  in India
    growing role of, 188
Colombia (*see* Latin America)
Colombian Society of Public Relations, 290
Columbus, Christopher
  PR strategy of, 317-319
Comic strips, educational
  in Japan, 232-233
Comparative-management theories, 24-25
  contingency theory and, 24

434 SUBJECT INDEX

open systems and, 24
Collectivism
  as cultural value, 48
  in Japan, 225
Comparative public relations
  definition of, 2
Commission on Undergraduate Public
  Relations Education, 383
Communication
  and journalism courses taken, 133
    relationship to, 12-13, 412
  and public relations education, 132-
    133, 400-402, 408-411
  and universal ethics, 91
  corporate
    in Japan, 228
  importance of, 68
    and career choice, 411
    and cross-cultural study, 411
Communication-facilitator role, 4
  in China, 139
  in Saudi Arabia, 246, 251, 255
  in Thailand, 163-167
Communication infrastructure
  and PR development, 99
Communication-liaison role
  in India, 184
Communication manager
  changing role of
    during development, 220
  definition of, 4
  education for
    emphasis on in Europe, 374-376
  importance of, 38
  need for training of, 39, 400
  prevalence of, 8-9
    and perceptions of PR, 141
    and status within organizations, 146
    in China, 125, 135-136, 139, 150
    in Costa Rica, 264-265
    in India, 184
    in Norway, 325
    in Philippines, 204
    in Romania, 344
    in Saudi Arabia, 246, 251, 254-255
    in Thailand, 163-167

Communication technician
  changing role of
    during development, 220
  graphic-technician facet of
    in Thailand, 164, 166
  importance of, 38
  in China, 127, 130-131
    and government practice, 149
    and perceptions of PR, 141
    and status within organizations, 144
  in Costa Rica, 264-265
  in Romania
    large number of, 344
  in Saudi Arabia, 246, 251, 254-255
  in Thailand, 159
  media-relations facet of
    in Thailand, 164, 166
  prevalence of, 8-9
    in Norway, 325
    in Thailand, 163-167
  role of, 4
Communication technology (see
  Technology)
Communication theories
  approaches to building, 19
  connection with public relations
    lack of, 324, 382
  in European PR education
    emphasis on, 374-376
    pioneering nature of, 375-376
  in Romania
    small PR role of, 344
  integration with practice, 414
  interdisciplinary nature of, 19
  international public relations and, 25-
    26
  normative theory
    nature of, 33-34
  positive theory
    nature of, 33-34
  role in communication management,
    400
  usefulness in PR
    attitude theory, 327
    Lasswellian paradigm, 326-327
    relative deprivation theory, 327

SUBJECT INDEX 435

Communitarianism
  values relating to, 68-69
Community
  and public relations, 71-74
  and universality, 90
  strategic cooperative, 74-78
Community relations
  in Japan, 234
Conflict
  public relations and, 1, 31, 41
Consumer goods
  in India, 109
Contextual variables
  for excellent PR, 40
Contingency theory, 24
Controlled media
  changes in role of
    during development, 219
    in China, 126, 150
  in market-development stage
    in Malaysia, 215
    in Singapore, 215
Convergence theory
  global society and, 21
Cooperation
  in problem solving, 74
Coordination (*see* Integration)
Corporate communication
  corporate identity programs
    in Japan, 228, 231-232
  development of
    in Costa Rica, 268-269
    in Latin America, 284, 290-293
  transnational
    ethics of, 81-91
Corporate culture, 177-178
Costa Rica
  democratic traditions in, 9, 258-260
  development in, 258-260
  ethics of
  political PR in, 261
  foreign affairs of, 258-259
  freedom of expression in, 261-264
  hierarchy in
    implications for PR, 268-269
  journalism

    relationship to PR, 262-264, 266, 269-270
    media relations in, 269-270
    methodology in study of, 259-260
    political campaigns, 260-261
    special events in, 260
    practitioner panel in, 259-260
  private companies
    openness to feedback of, 268-269
  public relations
    credibility of, 269
    education in, 11-12, 266-267
    foreign influence on, 265
    licensure in, 262-264
    models of, 268-269
    history of, 258-260
    partisanship of, 262
    women's role in, 266-267
    roles of practitioners in, 264-265
  tourism
    public relations in, 257-258
Craft public relations
  models and, 41-42
  or profession, 324-325, 382
Credibility
  and relative deprivation theory, 327
  of occupations
    in Norway, 328-329
  of public relations
    in Costa Rica, 269
    in German Democratic Republic, 358
    in Norway, 328-329
    in Romania, 344-345
Crisis management
  in German Democratic Republic, 360
  in Norway, 326, 330-334
  in Japan, 226, 229, 234
  in Saudi Arabia
    training for, 253
  in Slovenia
    two-way symmetric PR and, 60
  rationalist approach to, 69
Culture
  and age, 139-140, 144
  and education, 139, 144

436 SUBJECT INDEX

and organizational theory, 176
corporate, 177-178
definition of, 178
dimensions of, 22, 48-49, 180-182
  power distance, 180-181
domineering character of
  in India, 391
family unit and, 179, 279-281
idealist view of, 178
in China, 122, 146-148, 150
in Europe
  diversity of and PR, 372-374
in India
  and PR evolution, 107-108
  authoritarianism and, 181
  tolerance and, 181
in Japan, 224-225, 235
in Latin America, 273-275, 279-281
  loaning money and, 282
  nepotism and, 280
in Norway
  and views of whaling, 337
in Romania, 343
institutions and, 179
integration of, 99-100
localization in advertising
  related to, 304, 311
management dependency on, 24-25
material aspects of, 373
non-material aspects of, 373
oral and public relations
  in Malaysia, 211
  in Singapore, 211
process of studying, 50-53
public relations and, 6-7, 52-56
realist view of, 178
standardization in advertising
  related to, 304
subsystems of, 178-179
  ideology, 178-179
  personality, 178-179
  social structure, 178-179
  techno-economic, 178-179
values free of, 25
  and Indian public relations, 175-176
values in Philippines, 202-203

values in Saudi Arabia, 242-245
values in Thailand, 161
values specific to, 25, 176-178
varieties of
  and international understanding, 381
Culture theories, 22-24
  acculturation in, 23
  American values and, 23
  communal values and, 23, 224
  definition of, 22, 178
  dimensions of, 22, 48-49, 180
  excellence in public relations and, 22-23
  relative theory in management, 33
Cultural values
  collectivism
    in Japan, 225
  ethical relativism and, 85-90
  gender and, 11
  harmony
    in Japan, 224
  loyalty
    in Japan, 225
  public relations and
    in Philippines, 202-203
  tolerance and, 85-86

D

Decision-making
  factor in management, 73
Dependency on media, 25-26
Deutsche Public Relations
  Gesellschaft, 358-359
Development communication
  convergence with public relations, 5-6, 94-95
Developed world
  public relations in, 93-94
Development
  and culture
    material aspects of, 373
    non-material aspects of, 373
  market-development stage
    in Malaysia, 212-215,
    in Singapore, 216-218

marketing and PR
changing relationship between
during development 220-221
nation-building stage and
in Malaysia, 210-212
in Singapore, 210-212
public relations and, 9-10, 54-55, 101-104
in China, 122-123
in Costa Rica, 270-271
in Malaysia, 209-221
in Philippines, 198, 202-203
in Singapore, 209-221
in Thailand, 156, 159-160
regional-interdependence stage
in Malaysia, 216-218
in Singapore, 216-218
Dialogue
need for in Third World, 103-104
Diffusion of Innovations (*see* Innovation)
Divergence theory
global society and, 21
Diversity
and localization
in advertising, 311-312
and Malaysian PR, 95-96
and Singaporean PR, 98
need for, 39-40
of job experience
in Saudi Arabia, 253
of language in India, 108
within Eastern Europe
Romanian PR and, 343
within Europe
and PR growth, 373
Dominant coalition
of corporate subsidiaries
and localization
of advertising, 312
nature of
in India, 391
public relations' role in, 37
in Costa Rica, 264-265
in Japan
and tenure in firms, 224

in Slovenia, 58

E

East Germany (*see* German Democratic Republic)
Eastern Europe (*see* Europe)
Ecology (*see* Environmentalism)
Economics
and public relations' evolution, 69-72, 390
and Costa Rican public relations, 270-271
and Thai public relations, 161
barriers between nations
reduction of and PR, 371
capital flow and PR
in European Union, 371
culture and, 178-179
Education for public relations
accreditation and, 385, 402, 411-412
adequacy of, 384
changing levels of
in development, 220
communication courses taken
journalism courses and, 412
communication departments and, 12-13, 400-402, 408-411
career niches of, 411
cross-cultural understanding and, 381
elements of unique to U.S., 391
faculty, recruitment of
in India, 116
for foreign students
in United States, 11-12, 397-414
breadth of cultural study in, 397-398, 406, 413
course clusters in, 405, 408-410
depth of cultural study in, 397-398, 406, 413
internships completed by, 399, 406
undergraduate focus of, 406
methodology in study of, 402-405
skill training for, 399, 407-411, 413
theoretical emphasis of, 399, 407-410, 413

438 SUBJECT INDEX

relation to journalism education, 400-402
roles played and, 400
sensitivity to, 413-414
tendency to remain in United States, 407
gaiapolitics and, 381
graduate-level
  distinctiveness of, 384-385
  international courses in, 388
  requirements for, 385
growth of, 384-385
in Brazil, 290-291
in Chile, 290
in China, 11, 133, 149
in Costa Rica, 11-12, 263
in Europe, 11
  breadth of, 375
  management orientation of, 374-376
  theoretical nature of, 374-376
in German Democratic Republic 355, 358, 360, 363
in India, 112, 114-116
in Japan, 225
in Latin America, 287, 289-293
in Malaysia
  during nation-building, 212
in Norway, 321-322
in Philippines, 11, 195
in Romania, 346
in Saudi Arabia, 12, 252
  for public speaking, 253
in Singapore
  during nation-building, 212
in Slovenia, 59
in Thailand, 11, 155, 163
international focus in
  lack of, 384
  in PR textbooks, 390
international PR courses
  goals suggested for, 391
  need for, 12, 385-393, 398-399, 406-407
  successful example of, 392
of clients in India, 112

journalism training and, 12-13, 400-402, 407-411
  communication courses taken and, 412
licensure and, 389
needs in, 11-13, 57, 412
professionalization and, 412
Public Relations Society of India
  role in education, 114
recognition of, 388-389
role in professionalization, 324-325
technology and, 381
theory
  lack of focus on, 382
women
  number involved in, 383-384
Egypt (*see* Arab nations)
Employees as publics
  in India, 173
  in Saudi Arabia, 245
  in Thailand, 157
Entertainment public relations
  in Philippines, 196
Environmental movement, 390
  in Costa Rica, 257-258, 264-265, 267, 271
  in Europe, 370
  in Japan, 234
  in Latin America, 283
Erickson, Lief
  PR strategy of, 317-319
Ethics in public relations
  and exaggeration
    in reporting Soviet submarines, 330-333
  and professionalization, 295
  and excessive secrecy
    in German Democratic Republic, 357
  as focus of international PR courses, 391
  in Costa Rica, 261
    and government control, 262-264
    and hiding bad news, 269
  in Europe
    and European Public Relations

SUBJECT INDEX 439

Confederation, 373
in Japan
  paying journalists, 235
  pressuring journalists, 235-236
in Latin America
  graft and, 279
  journalists
    relationships with PR, 287-288
  loaning money and, 282
  nepotism and, 280
  payments by media, 286
in Philippines
  paying journalists, 203
in Slovenia, 5-8
professional organizations' role in, 324
transnational corporations and, 81-91
truth and, 317, 319
  superficial concern for
    in German Democratic Republic, 356
    in Romania, 345, 347
universality of, 5
Ethnocentric theory
  in management, 33
Ethnographic method, 182
Europe
  agencies in
    networks of in Europe, 374
  education for public relations in, 374-376
    breadth of, 375
    theoretical emphasis of, 375
    pioneering role of, 375
  growth of public relations in, 1, 171
    Britain's role in, 368-369
    cultural differences and, 372-374
    Eastern Europe
      compared with Third World, 373
    English language, role of, 369
    Germany's role in, 368-369
    in European Union, 367, 369-373
    in German Democratic Republic
      (see German Democratic Republic)
    history
      of public relations in, 367-369

organizational structure in, 25
Pan-European PR Practice, 370-372, 374
people orientation in, 74
public relations education in, 11
European Economic Community
(see European Union)
European Union
  capital flow in, 371
  Euro-brands in, 371
  models of PR in, 372
  Nordic countries and, 81
  public relations agencies in
    strains on, 370-371
  public relations in, 367, 369-373
    and economic-barrier removal, 371
    complexity of, 370-371
    cultural differences and, 372-374
    environmentalism and, 370
    ethnic identities in, 370
    government role in, 372
    national identities in, 370
    Pan-European nature of, 369-370
    trade and, 81
    turbulence in, 370-371
  restructuring of
    and public relations, 392
  size of, 370
  worker flow within, 370
European Public Relations Confederation, 373
Evaluation
  in Thailand, 158
Expert-prescriber role, 3-4
  in China, 134-136
  in Saudi Arabia, 246, 251, 255
  prevalence of in Thailand, 163-167

F

Federal Republic of Germany
  public relations in, 357-358
Feminism
  and community, 73
  and cultural values, 49
  and culture in Slovenia, 53

440 SUBJECT INDEX

in Japan, 234-235
Feminization of public relations
  (see Gender)
Finland
  as advertising target, 300-301
  localization in, 10, 299-313
Foreign relations
  public relations and
    in Costa Rica, 258-259
    in Philippines, 197-198, 201-202
Freedom
  role of in ethics, 84

G

Gaiapolitics
  public relations and, 381, 386
Gemeinschaft society
  public relations and, 54
Gender
  and cultural values, 49
  need for diversity in, 39-40
  public relations and, 6, 10-11, 383-384
    in China, 139
    in Costa Rica, 266-267
    in India, 110-111, 117
    in Japan, 234-235
  role models
    for women in India, 111
  role of
    in Saudi Arabia, 254
    in Slovenia, 59
  roles and stereotypes, 10-11, 113-114
Generic principles
  effectiveness of in Slovenia, 56-62
  in public relations, 32-40
German Democratic Republic
  campaign in
    for city of Leipzig, 362
    to encourage investment, 362
  dialogue in, 9
  education for public relations in, 358, 360, 362-363
  enterprise newspapers in, 353
  Federal Republic of Germany
    relations with, 357-358
  Oeffentlichkeitsarbeit in, 350-357
    advertising and, 350
    agitation and, 353
    definition of, 351
    discrepancies in
      practice and theory, 352
    excessive secrecy in, 357
    Marxist-Leninist base of, 354
    propaganda and, 350, 353
    scope of, 350, 353
    teaching of, 354
    theoretical foundations of, 355-356
  press relations in, 359
  public relations in
    advertising and, 360-363
    agencies as sector of, 360
    credibility of, 358
    dialogue-orientation in, 358
    for business sector, 359-360
    for municipal, state sectors, 360-361
    growth of, 375
    Federal Republic of Germany and, 359, 362
    opening of borders and, 360
    professionalization in, 358
    recent growth of, 358
  Socialist Unity Party in, 350-357
  special events in, 359
Germany
  public relations in, 368
  pioneering role of, 368
Gesellschaft Public Relations
  Agenturen, 358
Gesellschaft society
  public relations and, 54-55
Global information flow, 26
Global public relations
  interest in, 17
  nature of, 32
  transnational corporations and, 82, 386-390
Global society theories, 21-22
  convergence vs. dominance in, 21
Globalization (see Standardization)
Government relations (see Lobbying)
Government role in PR

changes in
  during development process, 219
  in China, 123
  in Costa Rica
    licensing of practitioners, 262
  in Romania, 341-343
  in Saudi Arabia, 246-249
Guiding questions for book, 3

H

Harmony
  in Japan, 224-225
  public relations and, 7, 295
  openness and, 7
History of public relations
  in China, 121-123
  in Costa Rica, 258-260
  in Europe, 367-369
  in German Democratic Republic, 349-357
  in India, 173-175
  in international PR courses, 391
  in Japan, 225-227
  in Latin America, 284-289
  in Malaysia, 209-210
  in Norway, 319-323
  in Philippines, 192-194
  in Romania, 341-343
  in Saudi Arabia, 239-246
  in Singapore, 209-210
  in Slovenia, 45-46
  in Thailand, 155-158

I

Ibero-American Public Relations Association, 291
Ideology
  and culture, 178-179
Image building
  effect of PR on, 386
  in India, 184, 189
Implementation
  in management, 73
India
  authoritarian elements in, 181, 391
  caste in, 113-114
  color in, 113
  gender and public relations in, 10-11
  history of public relations in, 172-175
  lady practitioners' progress in, 6, 107-117
  media in, 108-109
  media relations in, 185-186
  methodology of study on, 182-183
  personal influence in, 186-187
  power distance in, 186-189
  public relations in, 171-189
    activities of, 185-186
    history of, 173-175
  religion in, 113
  role models in, 111
Income gaps
  in Third World, 103
Individualism
  as cultural value, 48, 68
  in Slovenia, 53
Information
  explosion of
    public relations and, 381
  importance of in modern PR, 391
Innovation
  diffusion of PR as
    in China, 121-125
  Islam and, 244-245
Institute for Public Relations Research and Education, 382-383
Integrated marketing communication (*see* Marketing)
Integration of public relations, 37-38
  in China, 149
  in Philippines
    government, 199
  in Saudi Arabia
    government, 248
  in Slovenia, 57
Inter-American Federation of Public Relations Associations, 291
Interest groups
  role of, 26
Internal communication

442 SUBJECT INDEX

importance of, 39
International Association of Business Communicators
  excellence study of, 27, 36, 175
International organizations
  as resource for PR education, 392
International public relations
  courses in, 12
  definition of, 2, 18-19
  growth of, 17
International Public Relations Association, 291
International public relations courses (see Education for public relations)
International understanding
  and whaling
    in Norway, 337
  need for, 1
Interpersonal communication
  role of
    in Arab PR, 241-245
    in Chinese PR, 147-148
Investor relations
  in regional-interdependence stage, 217
  in German Democratic Republic, 362
  in Norway
    exaggerated expectations and, 334-335
  in Japan, 232
Iraq
  public relations in, 241
  public relations toward, 239
Islam
  and innovation diffusion, 245
  and Saudi public relations, 241-245
Issues management
  crisis avoidance and, 70
  in development process
    at regional-interdependence stage, 218
  in India, 112
  in Norway, 323
  individualism and, 69, 71
  relationship building and, 74

J

Japan
  activism in, 225
  campaigns in, 232-234
  corporate culture in, 177
  corporate PR in, 231-232
    identity programs, 232
  collectivism in, 225
  comics, educational, in, 232
  crisis communication in, 226, 229, 234
  culture in, 7, 224-225
  Dentsu, role of, 230-231, 233-234, 236
  dominant coalition
    membership in and tenure, 224
  economic growth in, 223, 234
  ethics of PR in, 235-236
  gender and values in, 11, 235
  history of PR in, 225-229
  internationalization in, 227
  investor relations in, 232
  organizational structure in, 24-25
  political public relations in, 236
  public relations
    agencies in, 223, 229-231
    and culture, 7
    education in, 225, 236
    future of, 233-236
      factors affecting, 233-234
    history of, 225-227
    hype in, 17
    women's role in, 234-235
  in municipalities, 232-233
  people orientation in, 74
  press clubs (kisha) in, 223-224
  technology and PR in, 232
  tenure, implications of, 8
Journalism education
  public relations education and, 12-13, 400-402, 408-411
  in Norway, 322
Journalistic skill
  emphasis on, 12-13, 400-402, 408-411

integration with theory, 414
Journalists
  paying of by practitioners
    in Japan, 235
    in Philippines, 203
  paying of corporations
    by media
      in Latin America, 288
  pressuring of
    in Japan, 235-236
  relation to government
    in German Democratic Republic, 356
    in Latin America, 287-288, 293
  relation to PR
    in Costa Rica, 262-264, 270
  sensationalism of
    and public relations, 338
    in Romania, 341-342

K

Kisha
  in Japan, 223-224

L

Language
  diversity in
    and advertising localization, 311-312
    and international PR, 387
    in Japan, 227
    in Latin America, 276-278
    in Malaysia, 211
    in Singapore, 211, 213
    role in India, 108
  English
    role in PR growth, 369
  geographic isolation and
    in Latin America, 276-278
Latin America
  activism in, 283, 289
  Brazil
    boundaries of, 276
    cultural influences on PR, 273-275
    importance of in PR, 290-291
    licensing of practitioners in, 389
    regulation of PR in, 290, 293
    telenovelas in, 286
  Chile
    profession's growth in, 290
  community service in, 281
  corporate role in, 284, 289
  contact with North America, 283
  education for PR in, 287, 289-293
  elites in, 280-284
    resisting land redistribution by, 282
  environmentalism in, 283
  history of
    and PR, 273-289
  immigration patterns
    and PR, 274-275
  journalism development
    public relations and, 284-286, 287-288, 293
  language and PR
    English, influence of, 276-278
    geographic isolation and, 277
    Portuguese, influence of, 276-278
    Spanish, influence of, 276-278
  lobbying in, 283, 289
  marketing & PR in, 292
  military governments
    public relations and, 289
  nationalism in, 289
  native people
    treatment of, 275
  nepotism in, 280
  political public relations in, 292
  protectionism in, 289
  public relations in, 273-297
    compared with North America, 274-275
    democracy and, 282-284
    history of, 284-289
    trade relationships and, 274-276
  regulation of PR
    in Brazil, 290, 293
  viceroy system in, 279-282
    graft and, 279
  Spanish influence on, 275-276, 278-284

community service and, 281, 283-284
elites and, 280
family's role and, 279-281, 283
formality of communication and, 281
graft and, 279
loaning money and, 282
red tape and, 281-282
Lenin, W. I. (*see* German Democratic Republic)
Licensing
of practitioners
in Brazil, 389
in Costa Rica, 262-264
in The Netherlands, 389
Lobbying
in Philippines
to United States, 201-202
in Latin America, 289
in Saudi Arabia
to United States, 247-248
Localization in public relations, 10, 299-313
advantages of, 299
and globalization, 386-390
behavior and beliefs and, 308
beliefs about culture
related to, 304
ethnocentrism and, 301-302
geocentrism and, 301-302
growth in, 310-311
polycentrism and, 301-302
growth in, 310-311
prevalence of
in Finland, 305

M

Majlis, 9, 241-242
Malaysia
changes in PR
during development process, 219-221
development implications in, 7
dialogue in, 9

infrastructure development in, 96
market development in, 212-215, 218-221
nation-building in, 210-212, 218, 221
propaganda in, 96
public relations in, 95-97
definitions of, 293-297
history of, 209-210
regional interdependence in, 216-221
Management
emphasis on
in Europe, 374-376
factors affecting
decision-making, 73
pathfinding, 73
implementation, 73
practitioner loyalty to
in Norway, 333-335
public relations' role in, 37-38
in China, 130-131, 134-136
in international realm, 387, 389
in Norway, 333-335
in Philippines, 195, 204
in Romania, 344
in Slovenia, 57-58
in Thailand, 162, 167
Marginalized groups
representation of
in Philippines, 203
Market-development stage, 212-215, 218-221
in Malaysia, 212-215
in Singapore, 212-215
Market economy
and PR development, 99
Marketing
approaches to international
ethnocentrism, 301-302
geocentrism, 301-302
polycentrism, 301-302
changing role of
during development, 219, 220
integrated marketing communication and, 321, 361
international, importance of, 386-390

SUBJECT INDEX 445

public relations and, 10, 38, 57, 97,
  110, 300-301
  in Costa Rica, 269
  in European Union, 371
  in German Democratic Republic,
    360-363
  in India, 184
  in Latin America, 292
  in Norway, 320, 334, 338
  in Philippines, 196
  in Romania, 344-345
  in Thailand, 156, 169
localization in, 299-313
  advantages & disadvantages of,
    302-303
  prevalence of, 307
  pattern standardization in, 303
  short-term profits in, 338
  standardization in, 299-313
    advantages & disadvantages of,
      302-303, 308
    prevalence of in Finland, 307
Marx, Karl (*see* German Democratic
  Republic)
Masculinity
  and cultural values, 49
  and culture in Slovenia, 53
Media
  changes in role of
    during development, 219
  dependency on, 25-26
  in China
    functions of, 126
    PR practice and, 148
  in European Union
    growth of, 371
  in German Democratic Republic, 356
  in India, 108-109, 173
  in Japan, 223
  in Latin America, 282
  in Malaysia
    in nation-building stage, 211
  in Romania
    sensationalism of, 341-342
  in Saudi Arabia, 243
    importance of, 253

  in Singapore
    in nation-building stage, 212
  in Thailand, 158
  international public relations and,
    26
  relations
    in Costa Rica, 269-270
    in India, 185
  study of
    in international PR courses, 391
    in Scandinavia, 322
  system and public relations, 40, 219,
    243
  treatment of in Slovenia, 60
Methodology
  in study of
    Chinese public relations, 129-131
    Costa Rican public relations, 259-
      260
    foreign students, U.S., 403-405
    Indian public relations, 182-183
    Romanian public relations, 345
    Saudi public relations, 251
    Slovenian public relations, 50-52
    Thai public relations, 162
Miss PR
  Kenning, George, and
    in Norway, 333
  role of, 10
    in China, 139, 148
    in India, 117
Models
  excellence and, 38-39
  for organizing research, 19-21
  of public relations, 4-5, 124-125,
    335
  unique to Europe, 372
Modernization, media and, 26
  Islam and, 244-245
Moral imperialism, 88-91
Multinational organizations
  public relations in, 17
    in Costa Rica, 267
    in India, 173
    in Malaysia, 207-209, 212, 216
    in Singapore, 207-209, 212, 216

446 SUBJECT INDEX

N

Nation building, 210-212, 218-221
  agency role in, 219
  government role in, 210
  implications of, 8
  in Malaysia, 96, 210-212
    media system and, 211
  in Singapore, 98, 210-212
    media system and, 211
National Commission on Graduate Study in Public Relations, 383, 385
National defense case (see Norway)
Normative theory
  nature of, 33-34
North American Free Trade Association
  role of, 82-83
Norway
  banking case in, 333-335
    exaggeration in, 334-335
    excessive loyalty to management in, 334-335
    relative deprivation in, 334-335
  history of, 317-319
  national-defense case in, 329-330
    fear levels in, 330
    role of emotion in, 330
    role of knowledge in, 330
  peacekeeping case in, 337-338
    mutual understanding and, 338
    tribal conflict in, 337-338
    United Nations and, 337
  public relations in, 317-338
    communication managers in, 325
    communication technicians in, 325
    credibility of, 328-329
    crisis management in, 326, 330-334
    education related to, 321-322, 324-325
    history of, 319-323
    marketing and, 320-321
    press relations and, 320
    professionalization of PR in, 324-325
    research on, 322
    strategic planning in, 326
    theories
      disconnected with practice, 326
      useful ones in PR, 326-327
    types of practitioners in, 323
  Soviet-submarine case in
    relative deprivation and, 330-333
  whaling case in, 335-337
    activism and, 336-337
    intercultural understanding and, 338
Norwegian Public Relations Association, 319

O

Olav, Hans
  Norwegian PR pioneer, 319-320
Oral culture and PR
  in Malaysia, 211
  in Singapore, 211
Open-systems management
  international public relations and, 24
Organization
  priority attached to
    in Saudi Arabia, 250
Organizational structure
  culture and, 24
  public relations and
    in Malaysia, 208
    in Singapore, 208

P

Pathfinding
  in management, 73
Peacekeeping case (see Norway)
People
  orientation to, 74
Personal influence
  as PR tool, 186-187
Personal relations
  importance of, 7
Personality
  culture and, 179
Persuasion, importance of
  in Singapore, 98
  in Third World, 100-104

SUBJECT INDEX 447

Philippine Business for Social
  Progress, 192
Philippines
  Aquino, Corazon
    public relations and, 198
  ASEAN
    Filipino PR and, 202, 204
  development implications in, 7
  dialogue in, 9
  education for PR in, 193, 195
  government public relations
    coordination in, 199
    financial support for, 199
    organization of, 198-199
  history of PR in, 192-194
  independence movement
    public relations and, 191
  journalists
    paying of by practitioners, 203
  Marcos government
    public relations by, 197-198
  lobbying by
    to United States, 201-202
  marginalized groups in
    representation of, 203
  objectives of PR in, 193-194
  public relations education in, 11
  San Miguel Corporation
    role in PR evolution, 194
  scope of PR in, 204
  service projects and, 197
  sports public relations, 196
Pictorial messages
  early use of in Assyria, 240
Poetry in public relations
  in Arab world, 240-241
Political consulting
  in Costa Rica, 261
  in Philippines, 194
Political public relations
  in Costa Rica, 260-262
  in German Democratic Republic,
    350-357, 361
  in Japan, 229, 236
  in Latin America, 292
Political system

geopolitics and PR
  in Europe, 373
public relations and, 7-9
  in China, 122
  in German Democratic Republic,
    350-357
  in Philippines, 196
stability in, 99, 103-104
and Thai public relations, 156
Positive theory
  nature of, 33-34
Power distance
  as culture dimension, 48, 180
  in India, 186-189
  in Slovenia, 54
PR Exchange International, 385-386
Practitioner training
  importance of, 5
Press-agent/publicity model, 4, 39
  factors affecting, 69
  in China, 135, 138, 140-143
  in Costa Rica, 267-268
  in German Democratic Republic, 356
  in India, 174, 185-186
  in Japan, 225
  in Norway, 320
  in Philippines, 194
  in Thailand, 156, 158-159, 162
  in Third World, 100-102
Press conferences
  in German Democratic Republic,
    359
  in India, 185-186
Pristop Group
  as laboratory
    for generic principles, 57
  growth of, 62
  nature of, 35
Private firms (*see* corporate communication)
Problem-solving
  cooperative nature of, 74-75
Problem-solving process facilitator
  role, 4
  in Saudi Arabia, 251
  prevalence of in Thailand, 163-167

Professionalization of public relations
  accreditation and, 402, 411
  and ethics, 295
  craft or profession, 324-325, 382
  education's role in, 324-325, 412
  in China, 122, 148-149
  in Costa Rica, 270
    role of government in, 262-264
  in Germany
    supranational character of, 372-374
  in German Democratic Republic, 358
  in India, 111-116, 173
  in Japan, 225, 236
  in Latin America, 282, 289-293
  in Saudi Arabia, 252-254
  in Thailand, 155, 158-160, 153-167
  low level of
    in Norway, 324, 328-329
  in Romania, 346
  uncertain state of in PR, 319
Propaganda
  in German Democratic Republic, 350-357
  in Malaysia, 96
  in Norway, 321
  in Philippines, 197
  in Romania, 344
  in Saudi Arabia, 250
  in Thailand, 156
  in Third World, 391
  nature of, 42-44
  public relations and, 40, 350-357
  power and, 44-45
  vertical communication and, 44-45
Public-information model, 4, 39
  in Arab world, 249
  in Costa Rica, 267-268
  in German Democratic Republic, 356
  in India, 184-185
  in Norway, 320
  in Thailand, 159, 162
  in Third World, 101
Public opinion
  in Soviet-submarine reporting among Norwegians, 332-333
  need for research on, 329
  study of and PR, 326-327
Public relations
  and gaiapolitics, 381
  and journalism, 288-289, 293
  and public opinion, 290
  breadth of
    in regional-interdependence stage, 218
  changes in
    during development process, 219
  credibility and, 293-296
  credibility of
    in German Democratic Republic, 358
    in India, 112-113
    in Norway, 326-329
  cultural specificity of, 373
  definitions of, 293-297, 319
  education for (*see* Education)
  growth in India, 109-110, 171-189
  history of
    in China, 121-123
    in Malaysia, 209-210
    in Norway, 317-323
    in Philippines, 192-194
    in Romania, 341-344
    in Singapore, 209-210
    in Thailand, 155-158
  image-building and, 184
  in Europe
    compared with Third World, 373
  information explosion and, 381
  integrated marketing communication and, 321
  integration of, 38
  marketing and, 38
    in Norway, 320-321
  models of, 4-5, 26, 38-39, 335, 372
  objectives of in Philippines, 193-194
  political consulting
    in Philippines, 194
  professionalization in (*see* Professionalization)
  rationalist approaches in, 70-71
  reputation of
    in India, 112-113
    in Norway, 328-329

SUBJECT INDEX 449

societal level forces and, 98-100
stages of development
  in developing countries
    market-development, 212-215
    nation-building, 210-212
    regional-interdependence, 216-218
technology and, 381
theory
  relationship to practice, 382
women
  number in, 383-384
Public Relations Organization of the Philippines, 192, 199
  history of, 200
  role of, 200
Public Relations Society of America
  and PR education, 385, 411-412
Public Relations Society of India, 109, 111-112, 173
Public Relations Society of Japan, 227-228, 235
Public Relations Society of the Philippines, 192, 193,
Publics
  in marketing, 38
  in public relations, 38
  in socialist countries, 45-46
  knowledge of, 68
Public speaking
  in Saudi Arabia
    importance of, 245
    training for, 253

R

Rationalist management
  problems with, 67
  relationship building and, 73
Rationality
  role of in ethics, 84
Regional cooperation
  implications of, 8, 81-82
Regional interdependence
  stage in development, 216-221
Relationships
  bases for, 73

core values and, 75
importance of, 1, 69
in Third World, 100-104
role of in PR, 147, 295
strategic management and, 73, 74
trust and, 73, 74-75
Relative deprivation
  implications of, 7
  reporting Soviet submarines and
    in Norway, 330-333
Relativism, ethical, 85-90
  challenges to, 86-90
  objectivism and, 87
  tolerance and, 85-86
  vulgar, 86
Religion and public relations
  in India, 113
  in Saudi Arabia, 241-245
Requisite variety
  principle of, 39
Research in public relations
  fact-finding in, 390
  in Japan, 236
  in Latin America, 292
    communication technology and, 286
  in Malaysia, 215
  in Singapore, 215
  in Saudi Arabia, 245, 248, 250-251
  in Slovenia, 59
  in Thailand, 156
  types of
    counting PR activities, 325
    hypothesis-testing, 326
    monitoring media coverage, 325
    public-opinion polls, 325
    need for, 329
Roles of PR practitioners, 3-4, 38
  communication facilitator (*see* Communication facilitator)
  communication manager (*see* Communication manager)
  communication technician (*see* Communication technician)
  expert prescriber (*see* Expert prescriber)

in China, 124-125, 127, 134-137
in Saudi Arabia, 154, 246, 250-251
in Thailand, 159-160, 163-167
measurement of, 164-166
personal influence and
  in India, 186-187
Romania
  agencies in, 341-343
    growth of, 343
  asymmetry in, 344-346
  communication managers in
    lack of, 344
  communication technicians in
    dominance of, 344
  credibility
    of public relations in, 344-345
  democratic tradition in
    dialogue in, 9
    lack of, 342-343
  education
    of practitioners in, 346
  history
    of public relations in, 341-343
  management
    PR and, 344
  marketing
    associated with PR, 344-345
  media in, 341
    sensationalism of, 341-342
  methodology in study of PR, 345
  press-agentry in, 345-346
  propaganda
    prevalence of, 344
  publics in
    vague definition of, 344
  slow PR development in, 346
  strategic planning
    small PR role in, 344
  theory
    small role of in PR, 344
  transnational firms
    role of, 342-343
  two-way symmetric model
    ideal status of, 346
    small role of, 344
  unique culture of, 343

S

Saudi Arabia
  Abdulaziz Ibn Saud, King
    role of in PR, 241-245
  Arabian-American Oil Company
    role of in Saudi PR, 245
  centralization
    of PR departments in, 253
  changes in PR, 255
  crisis management in
    training for, 253
  employee relations in, 245
  government PR in, 246-249
  history of PR in, 239-246
  interpersonal communication
    role in PR, 241-242
  Islam
    role of in PR, 241-245
  lobbying in, 247
  majlis in, 9, 241-242
  media and PR in, 243
  methodology in study of, 251
  models of PR
    balanced public relations, 250
    organizational public relations, 250
    responsible public relations, 250
  propaganda in, 249
  prospects for, 252
  public relations departments
    size of, 8-9, 253
  public relations education in, 12, 252-253
    communication expert, 250
    problem solver, 250
    program manager, 250
  roles, PR, 239, 250-251, 254
  technology in, 244-245
  tribal relations in, 243
  truth, importance of, 345, 347
  west, communication to, 247, 249
  western influence in, 245-246
  women practitioners in, 254
Secrecy (*see* Ethics)
Segmentation of audience, 73
  in China, 129, 137-138

SUBJECT INDEX 451

symmetric approach to, 140
in regional-interdependence stage
  in Malaysia, 216-218
  in Singapore, 216-218
in Romania
  lack of, 344
Service projects
  in Malaysia, 211-212
  in Philippines, 197
  in Singapore, 211-212
Singapore
  changes in PR
    during development process, 218-221
  development implications in, 7
  literacy promotion in, 98
  market development in, 212-215, 218-221
  nation building in, 210-212, 218-221
  public relations in, 97-98
    history of, 209-210
Singapore Airlines
  role of in PR, 215
Speak Mandarin campaign, 98, 214
Slovenia
  activism in, 59-60
  crisis communication in, 60
    two-symmetric PR and, 60
  cultural change in, 55
  generic PR principles in, 56-62
  history of, 45-46
  knowledge
    of PR people in, 59
  methodology in study of, 50-52
  public relations in, 40-62
  research in, 59
Social stratification
  public relations and, 6
Socialism
  public relations and, 43-47
Socialist Unity Party (*see* German Democratic Republic)
Societal-level forces
  communication infrastructure, 99
  cultural integration, 99
  linguistic integration, 99

market economy, 99
political stability, 99
Society, nature of
  and public relations' growth, 72
South America (*see* Latin America)
Soviet submarine case (*see* Norway)
Spain (*see* Latin America)
Speak Mandarin
  campaign in Singapore, 98, 214, 217
Special events
  changes in role of
    during development, 219
  in Arab world, 241
  in Costa Rica
    political campaigns, 260
  in nation-building
    in Malaysia, 215
    in Singapore, 215
  in Romania, 345
  in Saudi Arabia
    training for, 253
Sports public relations
  in Philippines, 196
Standardization
  behavior and beliefs, 308-310
  beliefs about culture
    related to, 304
  ethnocentrism and, 301
  geocentrism and, 301
  in public relations, 10, 299-313, 387
    advantages of, 299
  localized PR and, 386
  obstacles to, 308
  polycentrism and, 302
  prevalence of
    in Finland, 305
Status in society
  public relations and, 6
Stereotyping
  of Arab world, 249
Strategic cooperative communities, 76-78
  attributes of, 76-78
  auditing of, 78

452 SUBJECT INDEX

collective need and, 77
during regional-interdependence stage
  in Malaysia, 216
  in Singapore, 216
Strategic planning
  changing role of
    during development, 219
  importance of, 37
  individualistic approach to, 68, 71
  in India, 185
  in Norway, 326
  in Romania
    small PR role in, 344
  in Philippines, 193, 195, 204
  in Thailand, 156, 158, 160
  issues management and, 70
  lack of in Third World, 101
  public relations and, 10, 37
  rationalist approach to, 73
  steps in, 327
Structural violence
  transnational corporations and, 83
Structured flexibility
  theory in management, 33
Sweden
  reporting of Soviet submarines in, 330-333
Symmetry
  and excellence in public relations, 38
  authoritarian governments and, 9
  in China, 135-136, 138
    and audience needs, 143
    audience segmentation and, 140
    management roles and, 150
  in Costa Rica, 267-268
  in India, 113
  in internal communication, 39
  in Philippines, 195
  in Romania, 346
  in Slovenian public relations, 57
  in Third World, 100-101, 103
  models and, 41-42, 45
  need for education and, 39

T

Technology
  and Islam, 244-245
  changes in
    and public relations, 387
  changing role of
    during development, 219
  communication
    in European Union, 371
    in India, 109
    in Japan, 232
    in Latin America, 285
      radio, 285
      television, 285
        and perceptions of U. S. 285-286
    in Saudi Arabia, 249
  culture and, 179
  in regional-interdependence stage
    in Malaysia, 217
    in Singapore, 217
  public relations and, 381
  satellite television
    growth of
      in European Union, 371
    localization and, 306
    standardization and, 306
Telenovelas, 286
Television (see Technology)
Thailand
  asymmetry in, 158
  communication facilitators in, 163-167
  communication liaison in, 163-167
  development implications in, 7, 157, 159-160
  dialogue in, 9
  expert prescribers in, 163-167
  graphic technicians in, 165-167
  history of public relations in, 155-158
  lady practitioners in, 10
  media relations in, 165-167
  playfulness in, 7
  management role of, 162-167
  methodology of study on, 162
  press agentry in, 159, 162-167

public information model in, 159, 162-167
public relations
 and advertising in, 162
 and marketing in, 162
 cultural context and, 161
public relations education in, 11
roles played in, 8, 159-161
systematic planning in, 158
two-way symmetric public relations in, 162-163
taboos and public relations in, 7, 161
values and, 161
Theoretical bases for book, 3-6
Theory (*see* Communication theory)
Third world
 public relations in, 93-94
 and Eastern Europe, 373
Transnational corporations
 accountability of, 82-85
 and public relations
  in India, 109
  in Latin America, 284, 289
 ethics of, 81-91
 evils of, 83
 localization by, 299-313
  increase in, 310-311
  and decentralization, 312
 marketing approaches of
  ethnocentrism, 301-302
  geocentrism, 301-302
  polycentrism, 301-302
 standardization by, 299-313
 strengths of, 83
 subsidiaries of
  localization by, 303-304
  standardization by, 303-304
Trust, building of, 7
 as basis for cooperation, 76
 as basis for relationship building, 74-75
 as cultural dimension, 48
 in Slovenia, 54
Truth (*see* Ethics)
Two-way asymmetric model, 4
 importance of, 39

in Costa Rica, 267-268
in Malaysia, 96-97
in Romania, 345-346
in Saudi Arabia, 242
in Singapore, 97-98
in Thailand, 161-162
need for training and, 38-39
Two-way communication
evolution of
 in Thailand, 156-157, 159, 167
 in Costa Rica, 263
 excellence and, 38
 prevalence of, 9-10
Two-way asymmetric model (*see* Asymmetry)
Two-way symmetric model, 4
 importance of, 5, 327
 in China, 135-136
 in Costa Rica, 267-268
 in Romania
  small role of, 344
 in Thailand, 155, 162
 introduction of in Slovenia, 61
 role of in Third World, 100-101

U

Uncertainty avoidance
 as cultural dimension, 49
 in Slovenia, 53
United Kingdom (*see* Britain)
United States
 agencies
  role of internationally, 386
  role of in Philippines, 197, 201-202
 communicating to
  by Philippines, 201-202
  by Saudi Arabia, 249-250
 education for foreign students
  in United States, 11-12, 397-414
   breadth of cultural study in, 397-398, 406
   communication education and, 400-402, 408-411
   occupational areas of, 411

journalism education and, 400-402, 408-411
depth of culture study in, 397-398, 406
  occupational areas of, 411
  internships taken in, 399, 406
  methodology in study of, 402-405
  skill training for, 399, 407-410
  theoretical emphasis of, 399, 407-410
    integration with practice, 414
  roles played and, 400
educators' sensitivity
  to other cultures, 413-414
ethical standards in, 83-85
European Union PR and, 372
influence on
  British PR, 368-369, 374
  Costa Rican PR, 265, 266
  Costa Rican PR education, 265
  Latin American trade, 276
  Saudi PR, 245
knowledge of international affairs in, 388
lobbying to
  in Philippines, 201-202
  in Saudi Arabia, 247-248
localization
  by U.S. & non-U.S. firms, 310
organizational structure in, 25
perceptions of
  in Latin America, 285-286
public relations
  development in, 171
  inadequacy of for international realm, 387
rationalist management in, 67
standardization
  by U.S. & non-U.S. firms, 310
theory in
  roots in Europe, 375-376
transnational corporations and, 82-83
unique aspects of PR in
  as focus of PR courses, 391
values and culture theory in, 23

Unity
  national development and, 7
Universalism, ethical
  arguments for, 87-90
  bribery and, 88-89
  human dignity and, 86-89
  viability of, 89-90

V

Values and public relations
  in Philippines
    public relations and, 202-203
  relationships and, 75
Viceroy system
  public relations and, 7, 279-281

W

War, Role of PR in
  in Arab world, 239
  in Costa Rica, 258-259
  in Iraq, 240-241
Whaling case (*see* Norway)
Women
  in public relations
    in India, 6, 10-11, 110-111
    number of, 383-384
    (*see* Gender)
World view
  role of in Slovenia, 60-61